LAWS OF BUSINESS

FOR

ALL THE STATES OF THE UNION.

WITH

FORMS AND DIRECTIONS FOR ALL TRANSACTIONS.

BY

THEOPHILUS PARSONS, LL.D.,

PROFESSOR OF LAW IN HARVARD UNIVERSITY, CAMBRIDGE, AND AUTHOR OF TREATISES ON THE LAW OF CONTRACTS, ON MERCANTILE LAW, ON THE LAW OF PARTNERSHIP, ON THE LAWS OF PROMISSORY NOTES AND BILLS OF EXCHANGE, ON THE LAW OF INSURANCE, AND ON THE LAW OF SHIPPING AND ADMIRALTY.

Cincinnati, Ohio.:
NATIONAL PUBLISHING CO.
CHICAGO, ILL.: JONES, JUNKIN & CO.
1869.

CONTENTS.

Forms.

CHAPTER VI.

AGREEMENT AND ASSENT.

Forms.

CHAPTER VII.

CONSIDERATION.

CHAPTER VIII.

BONDS.

Forms.

CHAPTER IX.

ASSIGNMENTS.

Forms.

CHAPTER X.

SALES OF PERSONAL PROPERTY.

Forms.

CHAPTER XI.

STOPPAGE IN TRANSITU.

CHAPTER XII.

GUARANTY.

Forms.

CHAPTER XIII.

THE STATUTE OF FRAUDS.

CHAPTER XIV.

PAYMENT AND TENDER.

CHAPTER XV.

RECEIPTS AND RELEASES.

Forms.

CHAPTER XVI.

NOTES OF HAND AND BILLS OF EXCHANGE, DRAFTS, AND CHECKS.

CHAPTER XVII.

AGENCY.

Forms.

CHAPTER XVIII.

PARTNERSHIP.

CHAPTER XIX.

ARBITRATION.

CHAPTER XX.

THE CARRIAGE OF GOODS AND PASSENGERS.

CHAPTER XXI.

LIMITATIONS.

CHAPTER XXII.

INTEREST AND USURY.

CHAPTER XXIII.

BANKRUPTCY.

CHAPTER XXIV.

THE LAW OF PLACE.

CHAPTER XXV.

THE LAW OF SHIPPING.

CHAPTER XXVI.

MARINE INSURANCE.

CHAPTER XXVIII.

LIFE INSURANCE.

CHAPTER XXIX.

DEEDS CONVEYING LAND.

Forms.

CHAPTER XXX.

MORTGAGES OF LAND.

Forms.

CHAPTER XXXI.

LEASES.

Forms.

CHAPTER XXXII.

MORTGAGES OF GOODS AND CHATTELS, OR PERSONAL PROPERTY.

Forms.

CHAPTER XXXIII.

LAW OF PATENTS.

Forms.

CHAPTER XXXIV.

LAW OF COPYRIGHT.

CHAPTER XXXV.

MEANS PROVIDED FOR THE RECOVERY AND COLLECTION OF DEBTS.

CHAPTER XXXVI.

LIENS OF MECHANICS AND MATERIAL MEN FOR THEIR WAGES AND MATERIALS.

CHAPTER XXXVII.

PENSIONS.

Forms.

CHAPTER XXXVIII.

THE DISPOSAL OF PROPERTY BY WILL.

CHAPTER XXXIX.

EXECUTORS AND ADMINISTRATORS.

Forms.

CHAPTER XL.

GUARDIANS.

CHAPTER XLI.

STAMP ACT.

NOTE.

My first chapter will state the purpose for which I have made this book, and the use I hope it will perform.

I first attempted to make such a book, compiling it from the law-books I had already made for the profession; and, adding a few Forms, published it in 1857 as "The Laws of Business for Business-Men, in all the States of the Union." I became satisfied that this book was open to three important objections. One, that it contained very much of argument, and the consideration of minute questions, which were out of place in a book intended not for the profession, but for the community. Another objection was, that very many more Forms were necessary to make the book as useful as it might be. The third objection was, that as that book was entirely compiled from my other books, and contained no topic not embraced in them, it did not cover all the ground that the public had a right to expect that a book of this kind would occupy.

I proposed, from time to time, to make a new edition of this work, and, indeed, made a beginning of this; but I became satisfied that this would not suffice, and that nothing would suffice but A NEW BOOK. This I have now made, and offer it to the community.

I have retained in this book a part of the title, and so much of the text, of the former work as I thought would be useful; rewriting it with such changes as might make it more easily understood, and more useful. I have added many chapters on new topics; and I have multiplied the Forms tenfold. Of these Forms some are entirely new, composed by me for this book; others are selected with great care, from the widest collection I could make of Forms sanctioned by use in various parts of the country. In these I have made changes and additions, with directions for use. Some of these Forms will be found brief and simple; others of them, especially those in relation to real estate, are full and minute. No one but a lawyer knows how necessary it is to use the technical, customary, and established language of Forms, every phrase of which has been through repeated litigation, and has thus acquired a certain meaning. Much in such Forms will seem, to those ignorant of law, to be wordy and with much repetition; but, if the Forms are made apparently more simple by omissions and abbreviations, they *may* be good, and they *may not:* and whether they are or not cannot be known except by litigation. And he must be a bold lawyer who would undertake to prefer Forms of his own make to those which the Courts and common use have sanctioned. This I have not done, because the very object of this book is to enable persons who use it to conduct their business-affairs with ease, safety, and certainty.

I think such a book possible, and I venture to hope that I have made such a book. I know only that whatever labor and care could do to make the book useful and safe has been done. I have not made my law-books with the efforts which each required, and then cast off this book for more general use, lightly; for in nothing that I have published have I labored more strenuously to make my work satisfy the just requirements of those to whom it is offered.

THEOPHILUS PARSONS.

THE LAWS OF BUSINESS.

CHAPTER I.

THE PURPOSE AND USE OF THIS BOOK.

THE title of this work indicates, to some extent, its purpose and character; but, as they are in certain respects peculiar, it is thought that some remarks respecting them may make the volume more useful.

Twenty years ago, after more than twenty-five years of practice at the bar, I accepted the office of Dane Professor in the Law School of Harvard University. I have employed whatever leisure the duties of that office have left me, in preparing a series of text-books on Commercial Law. I have published many volumes; and the manner in which they have been received by my brethren, calls for my most grateful acknowledgments. One of those works was entitled "The Elements of Mercantile Law," and was intended as a general epitome of all Commercial Law. I began it mainly for the use of lawyers, but at the same time hoping that it might be so written as to be useful to others who were not lawyers. Before I had made much progress in it, the hope that *one book* could answer these two purposes faded away; and I finally made that work exclusively for lawyers. But the circumstance that many persons who were not lawyers, and did not intend to be, have bought my works, — the remarks that have reached me in relation to them, and particularly in reference to that above mentioned, from such persons, — and many other kindred facts, — have given additional strength to a belief that has led me to prepare this volume, for wide and general use.

That belief is, that there is a strong and growing disposition, among the men of business of this country, to understand the laws of business. This disposition, and the actual diffusion of this knowledge, have both greatly increased of late years, and I believe could not have been arrested; for this progress is one element of advancing and improving civilization; and I think it cannot now be prevented.

The institutions and characteristics of this country have their bearing upon this question. We have no sovereign but the law; or rather the people is the sovereign, and the law is their only utterance. It is a sense of this that has here transferred, in some degree at least, the loyalty which in the kingdoms of the Old World attaches to a person, to the law itself, using this word in its most comprehensive sense. This is a good thing; not because the law is always wise and good, but because it will more probably become wise and good, if the whole community recognize it as entitled to obedience, and *therefore* entitled to their constant, earnest, and vigorous endeavors to cure its defects, and bring it into harmony with those principles of truth and justice of which it should be the expression. This great duty rests upon us with the stronger obligation because of our greater intelligence and activity of mind, or more general education and wider extent of common knowledge; all which are none the less facts, although they are sometimes used as mere food for vanity, or as topics for adulation. And all these things together seem to lead to the conclusion, that here and now proper efforts should be made to supply all of the community who ask for it, — with accurate and practical information concerning those laws which are of the most immediate concern to them.

So far as concerns the whole people, their wish, if expressed in the simplest terms, would undoubtedly be, to know the laws which must regulate their conduct and determine their rights. This wish admits of but one question; it is, How far is this thing practicable? for so far as it is, its propriety and expediency can hardly be denied or doubted. Indeed, they who would most strenuously oppose any effort to teach the people the law, would do so only on the ground that it is impossible to give to the public any knowledge of this kind which would be wide enough and accurate enough for use. They would think that the very endeavor to learn the law, by persons the main business of whose lives must be of a very different kind, would lead only to a superficial and erroneous view of the subject; and this, under the name of knowledge, is only the most dangerous ignorance.

We should, however, remember, that the people generally, here and elsewhere, must necessarily know a certain amount of law, for without this they cannot live safely in society. For example, men in business must know something of the most general laws of business; as how to conduct their sales, how to make notes, how to collect them, and the like; and all men must know so much of ordinary law as protects and defines their common and universal rights. Moreover, it will probably be admitted that important mistakes, leading to much loss and difficulty, are every day made, because many do not know those general principles or rules of law which some do know, and which every man in business might know. The question, therefore, can only be, how much of law it is possible and desirable for men in business to learn; and what is their best way of learning it.

Here let me remark, that few persons, who have not had occasion to study and to teach Commercial Law as a whole, are aware of that unity and harmony of its principles, which make it indeed a *system* of laws; or of the prevailing simplicity and reasonableness of its rules. An eminent English lawyer has said, that it was astonishing within how small a space all the *principles* of commercial law may be compacted. It is equally true, that the laws of business are generally free from mere technicality and obscurity; and the reason is, that they are for the most part, and substantially, nothing more than the actual practice of the business community, expressed in rules and maxims, and invested with the authority of law.

The knowledge which a trader acquires of the laws of trade need not, at all events, be superficial; for a knowledge of principles, and an intelligent appreciation of them, however limited it may be, should not be regarded as superficial. And these limits need not be narrow. The extent of this knowledge, and its accuracy, thoroughness, and utility, must obviously depend upon the books from which it is acquired, and upon the manner of using those books.

Considerations of this kind led me to the belief, that it was *possible* to make a book, which should place within the apprehension of every intelligent trader, and of every young man who proposes to engage in any department of business (and this now means almost every man in the community), at the cost of no more time than every one can conveniently give to it, a *useful* knowledge of *all* the elements, or general rules and principles, of the Laws of Business.

In other words, I thought it an undeserved reproach of our Laws of Business, to say that they were not intelligible by all, if stated with simplicity and accuracy ; and an equally undeserved reproach of our Men of Business, to say that they could not comprehend laws, which were made for them, and were intelligible in themselves, and plainly stated. It seemed to me, therefore, that the time had come, in this country, for a book which no one has ever attempted to make anywhere heretofore. This book should contain all the principles of all the branches of the laws which regulate the common transactions of life, stated with all the accuracy that care and labor could insure in any book, and so stated that any man of good capacity, with reasonable effort, might understand all of them ; and might, with the help of the Index, find in the volume a true and intelligible answer to the questions which every day arise ; and might, if he were willing to make a regular study of the whole book in course, become acquainted with the rules, and the reasons of the rules, by which all business may be safely conducted. And this book I have endeavored to make. I have compiled it, mainly from the law-books I have already made for the profession. If they are accurate and trustworthy, this is so ; and I may be permitted to say, that whatever earnest endeavors could do to make those books trustworthy was done ; and that accumulated testimony, which I have no right to disregard, encourages me to hope that I have not labored in this respect in vain.

I have made changes which seemed to be required by the intended adaptation of this book to merchants and not to lawyers. These are, first, the omission of citations and references to reports and authorities ; next, the addition of some elementary rules and principles and definitions, which would not be necessary in a book for lawyers only ; and lastly, the use of common or non-professional language, the general omission of merely technical words, and the full explanation of such words when they are used.

If there are those who are preparing for a life of business, or are now engaged in it, who will study this volume, in course, — dwelling on what seems most important, and examining with care what seems obscure, — I venture to hope that they will find the work so arranged, and the meaning so expressed, that what comes before explains what follows, and every part of it will be intelligible. At the same time, I have labored to make every thing plain *by itself*, as far as that was possible, that it might not disappoint those who, without reading it in course, look into it for an answer to questions as they arise. And for such persons I have endeavored to have the Index of Subjects (at the end of the book) exceedingly full and minute.

I have added a great variety of Forms. Of course no collection of Forms could be made large enough to meet the exact facts of every case that can arise. But it is possible to give accurate Forms *of all sorts;* and any person can select the Form *nearest* to his particular need, and easily make the alterations which the facts of his case require.

CHAPTER II.

BUSINESS LAW IN GENERAL.

ALL law is divided into what is called, in law-books, common law and statute law. We have legislatures, and our fathers had them; and a very large proportion of the laws now binding upon us were made by those legislatures in a formal and regular way. All these are Statutes; and taken altogether, they compose the Statute Law. Beside this, however, there is another very large portion of our law which was not enacted by our legislatures; and it is called the Common Law. In fewer words, all law was regularly enacted, or it was not. If it was, it is statute law; if it was not so enacted, it is common law.

The common law of the several States of this country consists, in the first place, of all the law of England — whether statute or common there — which was in force in that State at the time of our independence, and recognized by our courts, and which has not since been repealed or disused. And next, of all those universal usages, and all those inferences from, or applications of, established law, which courts in this country have recognized as having among us the force of law. For this common law there is no authority excepting the decisions of the courts; and we have no certain means of knowing what is or is not a part of the common law, excepting by looking for it in those decisions. Hence the value and importance of the reported decisions, which are published by official reporters in most of our States.

A very important part of the common law, especially to all men in business, is what is called, by an ancient phrase, the Law-Merchant. By this is meant the law of merchants; or, more accurately, the law of mercantile transactions; and by this again is meant all that branch of the law, and all those principles and rules, which govern mercantile transactions of any kind. This great department of the law derives its force in part from statutory enactments, but in far greater part from the well-established usages of merchants, which have been adopted, sanctioned, and confirmed by the courts. For example, a large proportion of the law of factors and brokers, most of that of shipping and of insurance, and nearly all the peculiar rules applicable to negotiable paper (or promissory notes and bills of exchange payable to order), belong distinctly to the Law-Merchant.

The courts of this country have always acknowledged that a custom of merchants, if it were proved to be so nearly universal and so long established that it must be considered that all merchants know it and make their bargains with reference to it, constitutes a part of the law-merchant. And the law-merchant is itself a part of the common law, and therefore has the whole obligatory force of law. This would not be true, if the custom was one which violated statute law, or the obvious principles of public policy or common honesty. But we may suppose that no custom of this kind would ever be so generally adopted and established as to come before the courts with any claim for recognition as law.

A great deal of the language of every art or science or profession is technical (indeed, *technical* means belonging to some *art*), and is peculiar to it, and may not be understood by those who do not pursue the business to which it belongs. This is as true of law as of every thing else. In this work, however, I have avoided as far as possible mere law-words; and when I have used them have explained them at the time. There are some, however, which cannot be dropped: they express exactly what is meant, and we cannot express it without them, unless by long and awkward sentences. A good instance of this is in those words which end in *er* (or *or*) and in *ee*. As for example, promisor and promisee, vendor and vendee, indorser and indorsee. These terminations are derived from the Norman-French, which was, for a long time, the language of the courts and of the law in England. And it might seem that we had just as good terminations in English, in *er* and *ed*, which mean the same thing. But it is not so. Originally they meant the same thing, but they do not now; for both *er* and *ee* are applied in law to persons, and *ed* to things; so that we want all three terminations. For example, indors*er* means the man who indorses; indors*ee* means the man to whom the indorsement is made; but the note itself we say is indors*ed*. So vend*or* means the man who sells, vend*ee* means the man to whom something is sold, and the thing sold is vend*ed*. And the promis*or* makes the promise, the promis*ee* receives it, and the thing to be done is promis*ed*. We have retained not only this phraseology, but some other words or phrases, of which similar things might be said.

CHAPTER III.

INFANTS, OR MINORS.

SECTION I.

GENERALLY, all persons may bind themselves by contracts. But some are incapacitated. The incapacity may arise from many causes; as from insanity; or from being under guardianship; or from alienage in time of war; or from Infancy; or from Marriage.

All persons are infants, in law, until the age of twenty-one. But in Vermont, Maryland, Ohio, Maine, Missouri, Texas, and perhaps one or two other States, women are considered of full age at eighteen, for some purposes.

The rule of law is, that a person becomes of age at the beginning of the day before his twenty-first birthday. This rule opposes the common notion, and it rests on no very good reason, but on ancient authority and constant repetition. The reason assigned is, that the law takes no notice of parts of a day. The effect of the rule is, that a person born on the 9th of May in the year 1840, becomes of age at the beginning of the 8th of May, 1861, and may sign a note, or do any thing, with the full power of a person of age, on any hour of that day.

The contract of an infant (if not for necessaries) is voidable, but not void. That is, he may disavow it, and so annul it, either before his majority, or within a reasonable time after it. As he may avoid it, so he may ratify and confirm it. He may do this by word only. But mere acknowledgment that the debt exists is not enough. It must be *substantially*, if not *in form*, a new promise. In England, and a few of our States, it is provided by statute, that this confirmation can only be by a new promise in writing, signed by the promisor. This rule seems to be useful, and we think it will be more widely adopted.

It must be a promise by the party, after full age, to pay the debt; or such a recognition of the debt as may fairly be understood by the creditor as expressive of the intention to pay it; for this would be a promise by implication. There are no particular words or phrases which the law requires or favors as a confirmation. No ratification or confirmation can be used in any action which was brought before the ratification was made. It must also be made voluntarily, and with the purpose of assuming a liability from which he knows that the law has discharged him. And if it be a conditional promise, the party who would enforce it must prove the condition to be fulfilled. Thus, if the plaintiff relies on a new promise, and asserts and proves that the defendant said, after full age, "I will pay when I am able," he must also prove that the defendant was able to pay when the action was brought.

If an infant's contract is not avoided, it remains in force. And it may be confirmed without words; and the question sometimes occurs, whether confirmation by mere silence, after a person arrives at full age, prevents him from avoiding his contract made during his infancy. As a general rule, mere silence, or the absence of disaffirmance, is not a confirmation; because it is time to disaffirm the contract when its enforcement is sought.

But if an infant buys property, any unequivocal act of ownership after majority — as selling it, for example — is a confirmation of the purchase. And, generally, a silent continued possession and use of the thing obtained by the contract is evidence of a confirmation; therefore, if an infant buys a horse, and gives his note for it, and after he is of age the seller puts the note in suit, the buyer may return the horse and refuse to pay the note; but if he keeps the horse, this is considered evidence of a confirmation of the note. The evidence of confirmation is much stronger if there be a refusal to re-deliver the thing when it can be re-delivered; and is generally conclusive, when the conduct of the party must either be construed as a confirmation, or, if not so construed must be regarded as fraudulent, or wrongful. Thus, where an infant purchased a potash-kettle, and gave his promissory note for the price, it being agreed by the parties that he might try the kettle, and return it if it did not suit him; and the vendor, after the infant became of age, requested him to return the kettle if he did not intend to keep it; but he retained and used it a month or two afterwards. The court held that this was a sufficient ratification of the contract, and that an action might be sustained on the note.

The great exception to the rule that an infant's contracts are voidable, is when the promise or contract is for necessaries. The rule itself is for the benefit and protection of the infant, and the same reason causes the exception; for it cannot be for the benefit of the infant that he should be unable to purchase food, raiment, and shelter, on a credit, if he has no funds. The same reason, however, enlarges this exception, until it covers not only strict necessaries, or those without which the infant might perish, or would certainly be uncomfortable, but all those things which are certainly appropriate to his person, station, and means.

There is no exact dividing line which could make this definition precise. But it is settled that mercantile contracts, as of partnership, purchase and sale of merchandise, signing notes and bills, are not necessaries, and that all such contracts are voidable by the infant. So, if he gives his note even for necessaries, he is not bound by it; but may defend against it on the ground that it was for more than their true value; and the jury will be instructed to give against him only a verdict for so much as the necessaries were worth.

If he borrows money, to be expended in the purchase of necessaries, and gives his note, the debt, or the note, has been held, at law, voidable by the infant. But our courts would now hold an infant liable for such a debt; and it is well settled that an infant is liable for money paid at his request for necessaries for him; and if he give a note for necessaries with a surety who pays it, the surety may recover against the infant.

If an infant avoid a contract, he can take no benefit from it; thus, if he contracts to sell, and refuses to deliver, he cannot demand the price; or if he contracts to buy, and refuses the price, he cannot demand the thing sold.

An infant is as liable for torts (by torts or tortious acts the law means *wrongs* or offences) as an adult; and therefore, if he fraudulently represented himself as of age, when he was not, and so made a contract which he afterwards sought to avoid, this fraud will not prevent his avoiding the contract, but for the fraud itself he is answerable just as an adult would be. So if he disaffirms a sale, for which he has received the money, he must return the money; because keeping it would be a *wrong*, or a confirmation of the sale. So if after his majority he destroys or puts out of his hands a thing bought while an infant, he cannot now demand his money back, as he might have done on tendering the thing bought; for by his disposal of it he has acted as owner, and confirmed the sale.

In general, if an infant avoids a contract on which he has advanced money, and it appears that he has received from the other party an adequate consideration for the money so advanced, which he cannot or will not restore, he cannot recover back the money which he advanced. But if an infant has engaged to labor for a certain period, and, after some part of the work is performed, rescinds the contract, he can recover for the work he has done, as much as that work was worth.

The contract of an infant is voidable only by him, or by those having a right to act for him, and not by the other party. The election to avoid or confirm belongs to the infant alone; and his having this right does not affect the obligation of the other party. Therefore, one who gives a note to an infant, or makes any other mercantile contract with him, must abide by it, unless the infant annuls it, which he can do if he chooses to.

But if the note were given or the contract made by a fraud on the part of the infant, the injured party has the same right of defending against it on this ground as if the fraudulent party were not an infant. And it is a universal rule of the law, that no contract which is tainted with fraud is valid against an innocent party; therefore, a wilfully false representation of the infant that he has reached his majority would be a fraud, and would enable the party dealing with him to set the contract aside.

A father is bound to supply an infant child with necessaries; and, if he does not, is liable for their value to any person who supplies them. And for these, as we have seen, the child himself is also liable.

Although in most of our States the law does not require that the confirmation or new promise of an adult, of a promise which he may avoid because it was made by him when an infant, must be in writing, it would always and everywhere be better and safer to have this new promise in writing. It should be in substantially this form.

(1.)

I, Henry Thompson, having promised Nathan Green, to (*here describe the promise, whether by a note, or verbally, for goods bought, or the like, briefly, but so that there may be no mistake about it*) and at the time of making that promise I was a minor, within the age of twenty-one years, now, in consideration of said promise, I do hereby confirm and acknowledge the same, and promise a full performance and execution thereof. HENRY THOMPSON.

It would often be easier, if both parties assented, simply to give a new note for the amount due. But it might, in many cases, be better that the new promise should tell the story of the old promise for which it is given.

CHAPTER IV.

APPRENTICES.

The contract of apprenticeship is generally in writing, and is also most frequently by deed, (or writing under seal) and is to be construed and enforced as to all the parties, by the common principles of the law of contracts. Usually, the apprentice, who is himself a minor, and his father or guardian with him, covenant that he shall serve his master faithfully during the term. And the master covenants that he will teach the apprentice his trade; but the instrument is not made invalid by the omission to specify any trade or profession as that to be taught. He also covenants to supply him with all necessaries, and at the end of the term, give him money or clothes. Slight informalities would not make the instrument void. Even if they are of sufficient magnitude to have this effect, the instrument will prescribe and measure the claim of each of the parties against the other, if they have lived under this instrument as master and servant. But the apprentice's consent will not be inferred from his mere signature, but must be expressed.

In case of sickness the master is bound to provide proper medicines and attendance. The master cannot transfer his trust, or his rights over the apprentice. He has no right to employ the apprentice in menial services not connected with the trade or business which he has agreed to teach him. And when he neglects to take due charge of the apprentice, the parent's or guardian's authority will revive.

The sickness of the apprentice, or his inability to learn or to serve, without his fault, does not discharge the master from his covenants, because he takes this liability on himself. Nor will such misconduct as would authorize a master to discharge a common servant, discharge the master of an apprentice from his liability on his contract. But if the apprentice deserts from his service, and contracts a new relation which disables him from returning lawfully to his master, the latter is not bound to receive him again if he offers to return.

Not only a party who seduces an apprentice from his service is liable, but where one employs an apprentice without the knowledge and consent of his master, the employer is liable to the master for the services of the apprentice, although he did not know the fact of the apprenticeship. It may be added that if an action be brought for harboring an apprentice against the will or without the consent of his master, the plaintiff is bound to prove that the defendant had a knowledge of the apprenticeship. But a defendant who did not know the apprenticeship when he hired or received the apprentice, and who being informed thereof continued to retain and harbor him, thereby makes himself liable.

(2.)

A General Indenture of Apprenticeship, as sometimes used in New England.

This Indenture, Made the   day of   by and between A. B. of   and C. D. his son, of the age of   years, of the one part, and E. F. of   of the other part, witnesseth, that the said C. D. by and with the consent of the said A. B. (testified by his signing and sealing these presents) hath bound out himself as an apprentice, to   of

To be taught in the said trade, science or occupation of a   which the said R. J. now uses, and to live with, continue, and serve him as an apprentice from the day of the date hereof (or from the   day of   next coming) unto the full end and term of seven years from thence next ensuing and fully to be complete and ended. During all which said term of seven years, the said A. B. doth covenant and promise to and with the said R. J. that he, the said C. D. shall and will well and faithfully serve and demean himself, and be just and true to him the said R. J. as his master and keep his secrets, and everywhere willingly obey all his lawful commands; that he shall do no hurt or damage to his said master in his goods, estate, or otherwise, nor willingly suffer any to be done by others, and whether prevented or not, shall forthwith give notice thereof to his said master; that he shall not embezzle or waste the goods of his said master, nor lend them without his consent to any person or persons whatsoever; that he shall not traffic, or buy and sell, with his own goods, or the goods of others, during the said term, without his master's leave; that he shall not play at cards, dice, or any other unlawful games, whereby his said master may sustain any loss or damage, without his consent; that he shall not haunt or frequent play-houses, taverns or ale-houses, except it be about his master's business there to be done; and that he shall not at any time, by day or night, depart or absent himself from the service of his said master without his leave; but in all things, as a good and faithful apprentice, shall and will demean and behave himself to his said master, and all his, during the said term. And for and in consideration of the sum of to him in hand paid, &c., the receipt, &c., the said R. J. doth covenant, promise, and agree to teach and instruct his said apprentice, or otherwise cause him to be well and sufficiently taught and instructed, in the said trade of a after the best way and manner that he can; and shall and will also find and allow unto his said apprentice meat, drink, washing, lodging and apparel, both linen and woollen, and all other necessaries in sickness and in health, meet and convenient for such an apprentice, during the term aforesaid; and at the expiration of the said term, shall and will give to his said apprentice (over and above his then clothing) one new suit of apparel, viz. coat, waistcoat and breeches, hat, shoes and stockings, and linen, fit and suitable for such an apprentice.

In Witness Whereof, The said parties have interchangeably set their hands and seals hereunto. Dated the day of in the year of our Lord one thousand eight hundred and

(Signatures.) *(Seals.)*

(Witnesses.)

(3.)

Shorter Indenture of Apprenticeship.

This Indenture Witnesseth, That by and with the consent of hath put himself, and by these presents doth voluntarily, and of his own free will and accord, put himself Apprentice to to learn the art, trade, and mystery of and after the manner of an Apprentice to serve the said for and during, and to the full end and term of next ensuing. During all which time the said Apprentice doth covenant and promise, that he will serve his master faithfully, keep his secrets, and obey his lawful commands; that he will do him no damage himself, nor see it done by others, without giving him notice thereof — that he will not waste his goods, nor lend them unlawfully — that he will not contract matrimony within the said term — that he will not play at cards, dice, or any other unlawful game, whereby his master may be injured — that he will neither buy nor sell, with his own goods or the goods of others, without license from his master — and that he will not absent himself day nor night from his master's service, without his leave — nor haunt ale-houses, taverns or play-houses, but in all things behave himself as a faithful Apprentice ought to do during the said term. And the said master on his part doth covenant and promise, that he will use the utmost of his endeavors to teach, or cause to be taught or instructed, the said Apprentice in the art, trade, or mystery of and will procure and provide for him sufficient meat, drink, clothing, lodging and washing, fitting for an Apprentice, during the said term, and will give him quarters schooling during said term.

And for the true performance of all and singular the covenants and agreements aforesaid, the said parties bind themselves each unto the other, firmly by these presents.

In Witness Whereof, The said parties have interchangeably set their hands and seals hereunto. Dated the day of in the year of our Lord one thousand eight hundred and

Executed and delivered before

(*Witnesses.*) (*Signatures.*) (*Seals.*)

CHAPTER V.

MARRIED WOMEN.

By the original common law of this country, a married woman is wholly incapable of entering into mercantile contracts on her own account. By the fact of marriage, her husband becomes possessed of all her real estate during her life, and if a living child be born of the marriage, he has her real estate during his own life, if he survive her. This life-right in her real estate is called, in law, his *tenancy by the curtesy*.

All the personal property which she has in actual possession becomes by common law, absolutely his, as entirely as if she had made a transfer of it to him. But by property in possession the law means only her goods and chattels; or things which can be handled; and which actually are in her hands, or under her direct and immediate control. If she have notes of hand, money due her, or shares in various stocks, these are not considered as things in possession, but as things in action.

Things in possession are those things which one has now in his hands, and *things in action* (called in law *choses in action*), those which are so called because he who owns them cannot get possession of them without an action, if other persons choose to resist him.

All debts, and evidences of debt, as bonds, notes, and all shares in stocks, whether national or State, or of incorporated companies or other companies, are things in action. But bank-bills are usually regarded as money, and therefore as things in possession. The common law makes a wide difference between these in many respects.

The common law of husband and wife as to *things in action* is this. The husband may, if he pleases, reduce them to his possession, and so make them absolutely his own. In general, he does this by any act which is distinctly an act of ownership; as if he demands and collects the debts due to her, or indorses her notes — which he can do in his own name — and sells them, or has the stock transferred to his own name, or, in general, makes any final and effectual disposition of these *things in action*. Then they have become absolutely his own.

If, however, he does not reduce them to possession, and dies, and she survives him, her whole right and property revive at his death, without any interest whatever in his representatives. And even if he disposes of them by will, this is ineffectual, unless he had reduced them into his possession while he lived.

If, however, he survives her, he will be made, if he wishes it, her administrator, and then can collect all her *things in action*, and hold them or their proceeds as his own. And if she dies, and then he dies before he has collected these *things in action*, administration on his wife's effects will be granted to *his* next of kin, and not to *hers;* and when collected, they will belong to his estate.

On the other hand, the husband is liable, by the common law, with her, for all the debts for which his wife was liable when he married her. This is true whether they were then payable, or did not mature until after the marriage; and whether he received any thing with her or not. If he does not pay them, and dies before the creditor has obtained a judgment against him, his estate is not liable, even if he had a fortune with her, and that fortune goes to his heirs or his creditors, and her creditors get nothing. So it is if the wife dies before the creditor recovers a judgment against the husband, and the husband then retains all her fortune. But her responsibility revives at his death, and she is liable as before marriage, even if she carried him a fortune, and all her fortune went, as above stated, to his representatives. But if she dies, leaving *things in action* not reduced by the husband to possession, and he reduces them to his possession as her administrator, he must apply them to the payment of her debts, and can hold for himself only what is left after such payment.

Such, we have said, is the common law of England and of this country. We have stated it because it is the origin and common foundation of the law everywhere. But it is not just or right; and there are few, perhaps no one of our States in which it remains wholly unqualified by statutory provisions. But these provisions are very various; and in some of the States they change with almost every year.

In nearly all the States a married woman conveys her own real estate and releases dower by joining in a deed with her husband; but she is not generally bound by covenants therein, and, in many, must be separately examined. In most, she has a certain time, after removal of the disability of coverture, to assert her different rights, otherwise barred. Generally, devises or conveyances to husband and wife create a joint-tenancy, unless the terms of the devise or conveyance are expressly otherwise. And, upon the marriage of a woman who is plaintiff or defendant, the suit does not abate, but the husband may be admitted to prosecute or defend with her.

I give here an abstract of the law of husband and wife, as it stands on the Statutes of the several States: —

ALABAMA.

In Alabama, the wife's separate estate is alone liable for her antenuptial debts. Code of Ala. (1852), § 1981. All her property held before, or acquired after, marriage is secured to her separate use. Id. § 1982. The husband is her trustee, but not liable to account for the profits. Id. § 1983. She need not be of full age to release dower. Id. § 1358. The proceeds of a sale of her property are her separate estate, which the husband may use as most beneficial for her. Id. § 1985. He may receive property coming to her. Her estate is liable for necessaries for the family. If a suit therefor is brought against a husband and execution is not satisfied, her separate estate may be sold by order of court. She may dispose of her property by will. Id. §§ 1986–1989. If the husband is unfit to manage her estate (or his estate, or abandons her, or has no property exempt from execution, id. §§ 2003, 2004), she may be vested with the powers of a *feme sole*. Id. §§ 1994, 1995. If he is unfit to manage *his* estate, a trustee may be appointed to manage that. Id.

§§ 1998–2002. Forty acres of land, in value not exceeding $500, and certain personal property, are exempt from execution, and cannot be sold by any member of the family. Id. §§ 2462, 2464. As to the effect of marriage upon wills, see id. §§ 1597, 1598; recording marriage settlements, id. § 1293.

ARKANSAS.

In ARKANSAS, a *feme covert* may be seized in her own right of any property not coming from her husband. Dig. of Ark. Stat. c. 104, § 1. Such property is not liable for the debts of the husband contracted before marriage. R. S. c. 60, § 19. The homestead and a certain amount of personal property is exempt from execution. Id. c. 67, §§ 19, 20; Public Acts of 1852, p. 9. There are provisions for recording marriage-contracts. Dig. of Stat. c. 103. A married woman cannot be executrix or administratrix. Id. c. 4, § 5. There are other provisions for the wife in case of abandonment by husband, id. c. 102, § 8; and as to dower, id. c. 4, §§ 3, 56, 57; c. 59; Hill's Adm'rs *v.* Mitchell, 5 Ark. 608; Menifee's Adm'rs *v.* Menifee, 3 Eng. 9. A married woman cannot make a will unless empowered by a marriage-settlement, or by her husband. Dig. of Stat. c. 170, § 3. The private property of no married woman is exempt from the payment of debts contracted by her husband, previously to the filing of a schedule of such separate property in the office of the recorder of the county where she lives. Dig. of Stats. 1858, ch. 111, § 7.

CALIFORNIA.

In CALIFORNIA, all property owned before marriage, or subsequently acquired by gift, bequest, devise, or descent, by either party, is the separate property of each; but all otherwise acquired by either after marriage is common property. An inventory of the wife's separate property, acknowledged or proved as for a conveyance of land, must be recorded, and this shall be notice of the wife's title, and her property included therein is exempt from seizure on execution for the debts of her husband. He has the management and control of her separate property during marriage, but no alienation can be made, nor lien nor encumbrance created unless she joins in the deed and acknowledges upon a separate examination. But when she sells her separate property for his benefit, or he uses the proceeds with her written consent, it is deemed a gift, and neither she nor those claiming under her can recover. In certain cases a trustee may be appointed to manage her property. The husband has the entire control and management of the common property, with like absolute power of disposition as of his own separate property; and the rents and profits of the separate property of both are deemed common property, unless with respect to the wife, the terms of the bequest, devise, or gift, are otherwise. Dower and curtesy are abolished. Upon the death of either party, one half the common property goes to the survivor, and the other half to the descendants of the deceased, subject to the payment of his or her debts; if there are no descendants, the whole to the survivor, subject to such payment. Upon divorce, the common property is equally divided. The separate property of the wife is alone liable for her antenuptial debts. But the parties may control these provisions by marriage contract, which must be in writing and recorded, or otherwise shall not affect third parties. It may be entered into by a minor, but cannot alter the legal order of descent, nor derogate from the husband's rights over the persons of his wife and children, as head of the family, or the survivor's rights as guardian of the children. Compiled Laws of Cal. 1850–1853, ch. 147, p. 812. When a married woman is party to a suit, her husband is to be joined, except, if the action concerns her separate property, she may sue alone, and if between herself and her husband, she may sue and be sued alone. If both are sued together, she may defend in her own right. Id. ch. 123, §§ 7, 8, p. 520. There is also a homestead law, exempting the homestead to the amount of $5,000, from final process of court; and it cannot be alienated without the wife joins in the conveyance, and acknowledges apart from her husband. Its other provisions are substantially similar to those before referred to. Id. ch. 158, p. 850. The wife's real estate may be conveyed by separate deed, if her husband has been absent one year. Laws of 1855, ch. 17. She may devise by will, with the written consent of her husband (unless this is rendered unnecessary by marriage-contract). Compiled Laws, ch. 24, § 2, p. 140. By complying with certain requirements, she may carry on, in her own name, any business, trade, profession, or act, and the property, &c., invested belongs exclusively to her, and she has all the legal privileges and disabilities of debtor and creditor, and becomes responsible for the maintenance of her children. Her husband is not liable for her debts thus contracted without special written promise; and she shall not originally invest more than $5,000, without taking oath that the amount above that sum did not proceed from him. Id. ch. 178, p. 881. She may cause the life of her husband to be insured for her benefit. Public Laws of 1854, ch. 40.

CONNECTICUT.

In CONNECTICUT, the husband's interest in wife's real estate cannot be taken for his debts, during her life or that of her children. Compiled St. (1854), Tit. 7, c. 1. § 7; so of her wages. Id. § 8. All real estate conveyed to her during marriage, paid for by money earned by her personal service, is hers to her sole use. Compiled St., p. 377. And the proceeds of her real estate are hers, in equity, and not liable for his debts. Public Acts of 1850, c. 31, Comp. St. p. 377. Personal estate coming to the husband in the right of the wife, or through her as the meritorious cause, is held by him as trustee for her use, Comp. St. Tit. 7, c. 1; Public Acts of 1849, c. 20, § 1; excepting so far as he has paid her debts contracted before marriage, Public Acts of 1855, c. 43, § 1; and he may be required to give bonds as such trustee, or be removed and another appointed. Compiled St. Tit. 7, c. 1. There are also provisions as to executors, guardians, &c. Public Acts of 1856, c. 37, §§ 1, 2, 3. Her receipt for money deposited by her in any bank or savings bank is valid. Compiled St. Tit. 7, c. 1. § 9. Policies of insurance on life, for her benefit, if the premium does not exceed $150, or is paid from her private property, are secured to her. Id. p. 378. All personal property coming to her during his abandonment of her, or their separation from his abuse or intemperance, is hers alone; and he thereby loses all control of all her property. Public Acts of 1850, c. 33, § 2. During the abandonment, she may act as a sole trustee, and after it has continued three years, may, with leave of court, execute deeds of her real estate. Public Acts of 1856, c. 36, § 1. Deed of sale of minor married woman's land, by order of Court of Probate, upon joint application, in writing, of herself and husband will be good, as if she were of full age; the proceeds of such being held subject to the direction of the court. General St., ch. 2, Tit. 13, §§ 14, 15, 18. He may receive, she being a minor, her personal estate upon filing an application in the Probate Court where the will was proved and after proof of marriage and signing a bond for the safe keeping of such estate; but no sale by him of his interest in her estate is valid without her consent, or after her death that of the guardian of her heirs, under age, in writing. Id. §§ 21, 28, 29, 30. During abandonment she may transact business in her own name, and sue and be sued as a *feme sole*. Id. § 25. Husband is not liable for wife's debts incurred before marriage, but is liable for debts incurred for support of wife and children, since the vesting in him of her property. Id. §§ 20, 31. She may with her husband (both being of lawful age) by joint deed convey her real estate, and it as well as her personal property, whether hers before or acquired since marriage, and the rents and income thereof, are not liable for his debts either before or after his death. But such property and the proceeds of the sale thereof, shall upon his death be her sole and separate property. Id. p. 483, § 1.

DELAWARE.

In DELAWARE, the widow of one who made his will before marriage, takes the same share as if he died intestate. R. S. c. 84, § 23. Insurance on life for her benefit is secured to her, if the premium do not exceed $150. Id. c. 76, § 3. If her husband abandon her, the court may provide for the support of herself and her children out of his property. Id. c. 48, § 15. She cannot make a power of attorney. Id. c. 83, § 13. Real estate, mortgages, stocks and silver plate belonging to her at marriage, or acquired during coverture, are not subject to his disposition, or liable for his debts, except judgments recovered against him for her liabilities before marriage; but she may not dispose of such property nor create any encumbrance on her real estate, nor dispose of the rents thereof, nor of the interest of her stock and mortgages, without his consent in writing under seal. This provision does not affect him as tenant by curtesy; but with his consent as aforesaid, the proceeds of such sale as above authorized may be invested in her own name as her sole property, subject to the laws governing the principal. Laws of Delaware 1865, ch. 572, § 1, 2, 3.

FLORIDA.

In FLORIDA, the husband or wife administers in preference to others. Thompson, Dig. 2 Div. Tit. 3, ch. 2, § 1, ¶ 5. Their rights, by marriage, under the Spanish law when in force, are preserved. Id. 2 Div. Tit. 3, ch. 1, § 4; 2 Div. Tit. 3, ch. 1, § 2, ¶ 1. The wife retains independent of her husband and not liable for his debts (if inventoried and recorded, but failure to record confers no rights upon *him*, id. 2 Div. Tit. 5, ch. 1, § 2, ¶ 8), all property owned before, or obtained after, marriage. But he has the management of it. She cannot sue him for rent, nor can he sue her for management. Her property alone is liable for her antenuptial debts. And upon her death, he takes the same interest in her property as a child, but if she leaves no child, the whole. Id. 2 Div. Tit. 5, ch. 1, § 2.

"*Every person* of the age of twenty-one years," of sound mind, may make a will. Id. 2 Div. Tit. 3, ch. 1, § 1, ¶ 1.

GEORGIA.

In GEORGIA, marriage-settlements, if not recorded within a specified time, are invalid as to *bonâ fide* purchasers, creditors, or sureties, without actual notice, becoming so before actual recording. Cobb, Digest (1851), p. 180. The husband takes administration, and is sole heir of his deceased intestate wife, id. p. 294; appendix, p. 1129, § 19; Liptrot *v.* Holmes, 1 Kelly, 381; McGinnis *v.* Foster, 4 Geo. 377; Lee *v.* Wheeler, id. 541; and widows of intestate husbands without issue. Cobb. Dig. p. 295. On marriage, since February 22, 1785, the wife's real estate vests in the husband, like personality; real and personal property are put in respect to distribution on the same footing. Id. p. 305; 2 Kent, Com. (8th ed.), 109, n. (*a*); 4 id. 27. There are provisions as to the marriage of an administratrix, id. pp. 327, 331; of a person who has previously made a will, id. p. 347; disabling the husband to sell a certain amount of property, unless the wife, of her own choice, join in the conveyance. Id. pp. 389–391. The wife of an idiot or lunatic is generally entitled to the guardianship. Id. pp. 342, 343. If deserted, her earnings vest in herself. Laws of 1851–2, Tit. 16, art. iv. p. 237. By an act approved February 28, 1856, Laws of 1855–6, Tit. 19, No. 176, p. 229, a husband married thereafter is not liable for his wife's debts, further than the property received through her will satisfy, and such property is not liable for his debts existing at the time of the marriage. A married woman may deposit in any savings institution, any sum not more than $2,000, the earnings of herself or children, as her own separate property, as if she were unmarried. Laws of Georgia 1865–66, Tit. 26, §§ 1, 2. All her property, whether belonging to her at marriage or acquired during coverture, vest in her, and is not liable for any debt, default, or contract of her husband. Id. 1866 Tit. 18, § 1.

ILLINOIS.

In ILLINOIS, there is a homestead law, similar in its purposes to those before mentioned, exempting the homestead to the value of $1,000. Compiled Statues (1856), ch. 57, (44)–(50). When real or personal estate is held for her by trustees, not coupled with an interest in any other person than the married woman for whom it is held, she may on the death of such trustees be appointed in their stead, and may hold and convey in her own name, and the property is not liable for his debts. Laws of Illinois 1857, p. 52.

INDIANA.

In INDIANA, the husband is liable to the extent of the wife's property only for her antenuptial debts, R. S. (1852), Vol. I. ch. 52, § 1, and such liability is not extinguished by her death. Id. § 2. Her Christian name is sufficient in a suit against them jointly. Cox *v.* Runnion, 5 Blackf. 176. Her admissions subsequent to marriage are not admissible in a suit against them jointly for a debt of hers while single. Brown *v.* Lasselle, 6 Blackf. 147; Lasselle *v.* Brown, 8 id. 221. Process need only be served on the husband when subsequent proceedings are against both.

Campbell *v.* Baldwin, 6 id. 364; King *v.* McCampbell, id. 435. The husband is a proper party to a *scire facias* on a judge's transcript of judgment against the wife while single. Campbell *v.* Baldwin, *supra.* The plaintiff must prove marriage, in assumpsit against both on a note of wife before marriage, when non-assumpsit is pleaded. Wallace *v.* Jones, 7 id. 321. They should sue separately in an action for libel upon both. Hart *v.* Crow, id. 351. As to the wife's agency, see Casteel *v.* Casteel, 8 id. 240. Judgment against them jointly for tort of wife must be satisfied first from her lands if she have any. R. S. ch. 52, § 4. Her lands are not liable for her husband's debts, but remain her separate property. Id. § 5; Barnett *v.* Goings, 8 Blackf. 284. Suits relative thereto should be in the name of both; if separated, in her name, in which case the husband is not liable for costs. R. S. ch. 52, § 7. The wife cannot sue or defend by guardian or next friend, unless under twenty-one. Id. Vol. II. Part II. ch. 1, § 8. She may defend in her own right an action relating to her separate property, and in her husband's, if he neglects. Id. § 9. A general and beneficial power may be given to her to convey, without the concurrence of her husband, lands devised to her in fee. Id. Vol. I. ch. 113, § 16. She may make a will, id. Vol. II. ch. 11, § 1; but the will of an unmarried woman is revoked by marriage. Id. § 5. On abandonment by her husband or his confinement in prison, she may be authorized to sell real or personal estate, which has come to him by the marriage, in the State, and undisposed of; and she may claim any personal estate, or money in the hands of third parties to which he is entitled in her right, and payment for the labor of herself and children; and to make contracts under seal, execute deeds, prosecute and defend suits in her own name, and all contracts so made shall bind him on his return; and if on his return he is not joined with her in any such action pending, judgment will be enforced against him as if rendered before their intermarriage. In case of attachment against his property while absent, she exercises all the rights which would have belonged to him. When under twenty-one years of age she prosecutes by her next friend approved of by Court. Laws of Indiana 1857, ch. 45, 46. In case of a wife deserted by husband or children by parents, judge may on application order a sale of personal, and the rents of real estate, (in the State) for the support of the wife or children; and at the next term after such complaint, real estate may be sold and deed executed to the purchaser. Id. ch. 47, § 1, 2, 3.

IOWA.

In Iowa, the personal property of the wife does not vest at once in the husband, but if left under his control, will, in favor of third persons acting in good faith and without knowledge of the real ownership, be presumed to have been transferred to him. But she may avoid such surrender by filing for record a notice stating the amount of such property, and that she has a claim therefor; and if, during her lifetime, he dies or becomes insolvent, she is deemed a preferred creditor to that amount, without interest, but not as to creditors without knowledge, who become such after the property is placed under the husband's control, and before the filing of such notice. The wife must prove the amount of such property; but after five years the notice is presumptive evidence. Property which ordinarily passes only by written evidence of transfer is presumed, without notice, to belong to the wife, unless she received it from the husband. He is not liable upon contracts relative to her separate property or purporting to bind herself alone, nor is her property or income liable for his debts. Family expenses, education of children, &c., are chargeable upon the property of both or either; they may be sued jointly, or the husband separately. When abandoned by her husband, the wife may obtain permission to act as if sole, and to dispose of a portion of his property, and collect debts due him; and the husband, in like case, may obtain similar power over her property. (Provision is also made for the seizure of his property by public officers in the former instance. Code, § 799.) He cannot remove the wife or children from the homestead without their consent. Code of Iowa, §§ 1447–1462. The estate by the curtesy is abolished, and the husband is entitled to the same rights of dower as the wife. Id. § 1421; Laws of 1852, c. 61, § 3. When judgment is against husband and wife, execution may issue against the property of either or both. Code, § 1891. If both are sued jointly, the wife may defend for her own right, or for her husband's right also. Id. § 1687. A married woman may receive gifts or grants from her husband without the intervention of a trustee, id. § 1192; and may convey her interest in real estate, id. § 1207; and may be executrix independently of her husband. Id. § 1304. There is also a homestead exemption law, similar in its general scope and purpose to those before mentioned. Id. §§ 501, 1245–1266, 1395; Laws of 1852, c. 61, § 2.

KANSAS.

In Kansas, all the property held by a married woman at the time of her marriage, and all that comes to her after her marriage, remains her sole and separate property. It is not subject to the disposition of her husband, nor is it liable for his debts. Gen. Statutes, p. 563. While the marriage continues, she may dispose of all her property to the same extent, in the same way, and with like effect as a married man may dispose of his property. G. S., p. 563. She may sue or be sued as if unmarried, and may carry on any trade or perform any labour or service, on her sole and separate account, and her earnings are her sole property. G. S., 563. If married out of the State, and her husband afterwards becomes a resident of the State, she shall enjoy all the rights of property which she may have acquired by the laws of any other State, Territory, or country, or by any marriage contract or settlement. G. S., p. 563. She shall follow and have the settlement of her husband, if he have any in the State; if he has not, she shall retain any settlement she had at the time of marriage. G. S., p. 621. If sued with her husband, she may defend for her own right, and may defend for his right if he neglects to do so. G. S., p. 636. No married man shall bequeath away from his wife more than half his property without her consent; and no married woman shall bequeath away from her husband more than half of her property without his consent; and in both cases the consent must be in writing in the presence of two witnesses. G. S., p. 1113. Dower is abolished.

KENTUCKY.

In KENTUCKY, the husband has no interest in real estate or chattles real of the wife, except the use of them, with power to let out to rent real estate for three years at a time. R. S. of Kentucky, ch. 47, art 2, § 1. Such estate is only liable for her antenuptial debts, and for necessaries for the family, the husband included. Id. Her chattels real, may be conveyed in the same way as land, and the proceeds go to the husband, unless otherwise provided. Id. § 2. He is not liable for her antenuptial debts except to the amount received by her independent of real estate or slaves. Id. § 3. Provision exists for a married woman's acting as *feme sole* in case of abandonment, imprisonment of husband, &c. Id. § 4. The wife of a non-resident husband may act as a *feme sole*. Id. § 8. An alien wife of a citizen husband may inherit property, ch. 15, art. 3, § 3. The deeds of a *feme covert* may be either joint or separate, ch. 24, § 21; and must be separately acknowledged. Id. § 22. For various provisions relating to dower, see ch. 30. Marriage-agreements must be recorded, ch. 24, § 9. The husband's remedy against the wife's tenant is the same after her death as before, ch. 56, art. 2, § 25. She has the general rights of an unmarried woman in regard to stock held for her exclusive use. Id. § 16. Real or personal estate conveyed or devised to her, except as a gift, cannot be aliened without the consent of her husband. Id. § 17. Provision exists for the sale of married woman's property, ch. 86, art. 1, 5, 6. A married woman may dispose of her separate property by will or execute a power, ch. 106, § 4. Wills are revoked by a subsequent marriage, except when made under power of appointment, when the estate would not, in default of such appointment, go to the heirs. Id. § 9. She may deposit in bank and check as if *sole;* but rights of third parties are not affected if bank has notice. Supplement 1866, p. 727. When there is no appearance of fraud on joint application of husband and wife, Court may empower her to use, sell and convey, for her own benefit, any property she may own or acquire; and to trade in her own name as a *feme sole*, and dispose of her property by deed or by will, and in all cases it is free from the debts of her husband and liable for her own. Id. p. 728.

LOUISIANA.

In LOUISIANA, the wife cannot appear in court without the authority of her husband, though she may be a public merchant, or hold her property separate from him. Even then, she cannot alienate, mortgage, or acquire by gratuitous or unencumbered title without his written consent. She may be authorized by the judge of probate upon his refusal, and if separated from bed and board, has no need of the authorization of her husband. If a public merchant, she may without being empowered by him obligate herself in any thing relating to her trade; her husband is also bound, if there is a community of property. She is considered a public merchant, if she carries on a separate trade, but not if she retails only the merchandise of the commerce carried on by him. If the husband is under interdiction, or absent, the judge may authorize her to act as if unmarried. She may make a will without his authority. Civil Code, art. 121–132, 1239, 1467, 1779. But she cannot become an executrix without his consent or the court's. Id. art. 1757. She may act as a mandatary. Id. art. 1780. Neither party can be a witness for or against the other. Id. art. 2260. They may, by marriage-contract, determine the rights of property; but cannot change the legal order of descents (this restriction not affecting donations *inter vivos* or *mortis causa*, or donation by the marriage-contract according to the rules for donations *inter vivos* or *mortis causa*), nor derogate from the husband's rights over the person of his wife and children, or as head of the family, nor with respect to children if he survive the wife, nor from the prohibitory dispensations of the Code. Id. art. 2305–2307, 2316. The property of married persons is divided into "separate" and "common;" and the separate property of the wife into "dotal" and "extra-dotal" or "paraphernal." The "dotal" is that which the wife brings to the husband to assist him in bearing the expenses of the marriage-establishment. Id. art. 2314, 2315, 2317. Full provisions exist as to the settlement, administration, recovery, subject-matter, &c., of dowry and the rights of both parties therein, effect of insolvency of the husband, marital portion, &c., id. art. 2317–2354, 2358, 2359; as to the administration, fruits, &c. of the extra-dotal effects. Id. art. 2360–2368. The wife has a legal mortgage on her husband's immovables (which he may release by giving a special mortgage to the satisfaction of a family meeting, &c., or in accordance with stipulations in the marriage-contract); but it shall not to be lawful to stipulate that no mortgage shall exist, id. art. 2357; R. S. (1856,) p. 242, Tit. Husband and Wife; and a privilege on his immovables for the restitution of her dowry, &c. Id. art. 2355–2357, 2367, 3182, 3187. This is in lieu of dower, id. art. 3219, and is seventh in the order of preference. Id. art. 3221. A partnership, or community, of acquets or gains exists by operation of law in all cases. But the parties may modify or limit it, or agree that it shall not exist; in which case there are provisions, preserving to the wife the administration and enjoyment of her property and the power of alienating it as if paraphernal, with reference to the expenses of the marriage and liability of the husband. Id. art. 2312, 2369, 2370, 2393–2398. This community consists of the profits of all the effects of which the husband has the administration and enjoyment, either of right or in fact; of the produce of the reciprocal industry and labor of both husband and wife; and of the estates which they may acquire during marriage, either by donations made jointly to them both, or by purchase, or in any similar way, even though the purchase be in the name of one and not of both. Debts contracted during marriage enter into this partnership and must be acquitted out of the common fund; but those contracted before marriage, out of individual effects. The husband is the head and master of the community; administers its effects, disposes of the revenue, and may alienate by an unencumbered title, without the wife's consent. Id. art. 2371–2373. There are special provisions as to conveyances and dispositions of the community property and gains; effect of dissolution of marriage; ability of the wife to exonerate herself from debts contracted during marriage by renouncing the partnership; effect of such renunciation; death; survivorship; separation *a mensa et thoro;* separation of property during coverture; rights of creditors, &c., id. art. 2373–2392, 2398–2412; R. S. 1856, p. 242, Tit. Husband and Wife; the absence of one party. Code, art. 65. Either party, by marriage-contract or during marriage, may give to the other all he or she might give to a stranger. R. S. 1856, p. 79, § 17. Property acquired in the State by non-resident married persons, whether the title is in the name of either or in their joint names, is subject to the same provisions as if owned by citizens of the State. R. S. p. 103. If husband or wife die intestate, without ascendants or descendants, his or her share in the community property is held by the survivor in usufruct for life; if the deceased intestate leave issue of the marriage, the survivor holds such issue's inheritance in usufruct till death or second marriage. R. S. pp. 103, 104. A married woman, in certain cases, may be authorized to contract debts and give mortgages; or renounce her rights in favor of third persons; or appoint an agent. R. S. pp. 560, 561, Tit. Woman.

MAINE.

In MAINE, a married woman holds as her separate property whatever she possessed before marriage, and whatever comes to her after marriage, unless purchased by the husband's money or coming from him so as to defraud his creditors, Acts of 1855, ch. 117; Public Acts of 1847, ch. 27, and has all the usual rights of a single woman as to it, Acts of 1848, ch. 73; R. S. ch. 115, §82; Acts of 1855, ch. 120, but cannot convey property received through the husband or his relatives unless he join. Acts of 1856, ch. 250. Her property is alone liable for her debts before marriage. Acts of 1852, ch. 291. Although under twenty-one years, she is of full age. Id. There are provisions as to a married woman being administratrix, or executrix, R. S. ch. 106, § 35; guardian, R. S. ch. 110, § 24; insane, id. ch. 112, § 1; Acts of 1853, ch. 6; whose husband is under guardianship, Acts of 1853, ch. 33; and the homestead, to the value of $500 is not liable for his debts, and goes to his widow and minor children. Acts of 1850, ch. 207. It is believed that the provisions for the wife upon abandonment by the husband (R. S. ch. 87), are superseded by the above provisions. Real estate may be conveyed to a wife by her husband as security for a *bonâ fide* debt, and this may be conveyed by her without his being joined in the deed. Acts and Resolves 1863, ch. 214. Letters of administration may be granted on her estate and all debts contracted for her benefit shall be paid by her executor and allowed him. She may engage in trade on her own account, and any contract made by her is valid and her property is liable to execution for her debts; his property is exempt in any such case unless he were a party to the contract. Id. ch. 77, 148.

MARYLAND.

In MARYLAND, if a married infant unite with her husband in a conveyance to release dower, courts of equity may declare it valid if equitable. Dorsey, Laws of

Md.; Public Acts of 1832, c. 302, § 7. She cannot be executrix or administratrix unless her husband give a bond. Id.; Public Acts of 1798, c 101, Sub. c. 4, § 8. Her choses in action, at her death, become her husband's without his taking out letters of administration. Id. Sub. c. 5, § 8. An alien wife of a citizen husband residing in the United States, has her dower, and may hold lands by purchase and transfer the same as if a citizen. Id.; Public Acts of 1813, c. 100. Any devise or bequest to her is construed to be in bar of her dower, unless otherwise expressed. Id.; Public Acts of 1798, c. 101, Sub. c. 13, §§ 1, 3. Insurance on life is secured to her, if the premium do not exceed $300. Public Acts of 1840, c. 212. Her receipt for money deposited before her marriage in any bank, is valid, if no creditor of the husband has previously attached it. Public Acts of 1853, c. 335. Married woman may make a will with consent of her husband subscribed if she have been examined apart; not to apply to property acquired after the adoption of this code. Code 1860, p. 686. Her property belonging to her at marriage or acquired during coverture is not liable for his debts, but she holds it for her separate use the same as if *sole*. She may convey by joining with her husband. Property passing from him to her after coverture if in fraud of creditors is void. If she die intestate leaving children, he has a life estate in both real and personal property; but if she leave no children his life estate in her real and personal property vests in him absolutely. Code 1860, p. 325, §§ 1, 2 and 7. It is not necessary for her to have a trustee to secure the separate use of her property, but she may make one by joining to a deed with her husband. When there is none she may sue by her next friend. Id. 325, § 14. She has dower in lands held by equitable title of her husband. If he be convicted of bigamy she is at once endowed of one-third of his real estate, with like remedy for its recovery as in other cases, and to one-third of his personal estate as if he had died intestate. He in such case forfeits his title to curtesy, and his claim to any estate personal or mixed which he might have in her right. She, on such conviction forfeits dower, and her share of the personal estate. Id. p. 207, § 11. If leases for a definite term or renewable forever are made to her, the rent of which shall be unpaid for the space of ninety days, she may levy upon the holders of such lease by distress, or bring an action for the recovery of the premises. She may bind herself and assigns by covenants running with the land as if a *feme sole*. Laws of Md. 1867, p. 427, §§ 1, 2. She may release her right of dower in real estate, by joint or separate deed. Id. 327, § 11.

MASSACHUSETTS.

In Massachusetts, provisions exist for the benefit of the wife when deserted by the husband (R. S. ch. 77), to a great extent superseded by the Laws of 1855, ch. 304, *post*. A married woman coming into the State, whose husband never lived with her in the State, has the same rights as a single woman in matters of contract and suit. R. S. ch. 77, § 18; Gregory *v.* Paul, 15 Mass. 31; Abbott *v* Bayley, 6 Pick. 89. Antenuptial contracts in favor of the wife are valid, and she may receive any conveyance (except from her husband), bequest, or devise to her own use, without a trustee, and has all the powers respecting it a trustee would have, and is liable for any contract made or wrong done before marriage. Laws of 1845, ch. 208. A woman married after June 4, 1845, holds, as a single woman might, all property held before marriage or subsequently acquired, except by gift from her husband; but cannot convey real estate (except for a term not exceeding one year), nor shares in a corporation, without the written assent of her husband, or the consent of a judge of the Supreme Court, Court of Common Pleas, or Probate, nor bequeathe away from her husband more than half her personal estate, without his consent in writing, and her property is alone liable for her antenuptial debts. *Any* married woman may dispose by will of her real estate, but cannot thereby deprive her husband of his tenancy by the curtesy; and her real estate and shares in a corporation are not liable for his debts contracted since June 4, 1855. And any married woman may be a sole trader. Laws of 1855, ch. 304. There are also provisions as to guardianship, R. S. ch. 77, 79, and insanity, Laws of 1855, ch. 233; 1856, ch. 99, 169. A homestead to the value of $500, is not liable for the debts of a householder, but after his death is for the benefit of his widow and family, for her life and while any child is a minor, provided it be designated in the deed of purchase as a homestead under this act, or if already purchased, be so declared in a deed acknowledged and recorded, and is safe only from debts contracted after the record, and is not exempt from taxes, debts incurred by purchase, and debts for ground-rent of land upon which it is situated. This exemption shall not defeat any lien or encumbrance existing when the law was passed. A husband cannot convey such homestead without his wife joins in the deed. Laws of 1851, ch. 340. If a man dies testate, leaving a widow, she may at any time within six months after probate of the will, file in the probate office her waiver of the provisions made for her in the will; and shall be thereupon entitled to such portions of his real and personal estate, as she would have been entitled to if her husband had died intestate. But she takes only for life her share of the personal property, over ten thousand dollars. Acts and Res. 1861, ch. 1. Married woman doing business on her own account must file a certificate in Clerk's Court, giving name of husband, nature and place of business; if she neglects her husband may file one; and in case both neglect so to do, then the woman shall not be allowed to claim any property employed in the business, as against her husband's creditors; and he shall be liable on all contracts made in the prosecution of such business. Laws and Res. 1862, ch. 198. By Act of 1863, id. ch. 165, married women are prohibited from entering into co-partnership in business with any person. Policies of insurance made payable to her or to any one in trust for her, whether by her husband or any other person, shall enure to her separate use, and that of her children, independently of her husband, the person assigning, or the creditors of either. But if the premium be paid with an intent to defraud creditors, an amount equal to such premium shall enure to the benefit of the creditors, subject to Statute of Limitations. Id. 1864, ch. 197. Any accumulation of income of an estate held in trust for her, in the hands of trustees, or which has been received by her and invested together with the accumulations thereof, may be disposed of by her during her lifetime, or by will or appointment to take effect after her death, and with her written consent trustees may hold or invest such income on the same trusts as the principal estate is held. She may be a witness when contract was made by her in the absence of her husband. Supplement to Gen. Stats. p. 270. Id. 407.

MICHIGAN.

In MICHIGAN, if a husband abandons his wife, or is in the state prison, she may be authorized, if of age, to act and be liable, in general, as a *feme sole*, in which case her contracts bind both as if their marriage had subsequently taken place. She may join with her guardian to release dower, and any agreement between her and such guardian is binding. The same rules apply to a married woman who comes into the State without her husband. The property acquired by a married woman, before or after coverture, is free from her husband's liabilities, but she cannot sell it without his consent, or authority from court, nor if separated from him can she remove it from his premises without such authority. R. S. c. 85. She may recover land lost by his default, and defend when he neglects. Id. c. 113, § 3, 4. The marriage of an executrix extinguishes her authority. Id. c. 69, § 8. So of an administratrix. Id. c. 70, § 13. A *feme covert* may have a general and beneficial power to dispose, during marriage, of lands conveyed to her. Id. c. 64, § 8. She may devise her property, id. c. 68, § 1; and may have dower though an alien. Id. c. 66, § 21. There is also a homestead exemption law, Laws of 1848, No. 109, p. 124, and a married woman may insure the life of her husband for her benefit and that of her children, but the annual premium must not exceed $300. Laws of 1848, No. 233, p. 350. When divorced from bed and board, she has the same power over her property as a *feme sole*. Compiled Laws p. 965, § 24. When the divorce is not for her fault, or on the imprisonment of her husband for life, she is entitled to her real estate, and a reasonable amount of the personal, which came to him by reason of the marriage. But when it is divorced for her adultery he holds her real estate as long as they both live, and if there be children, he holds it as tenant by curtesy; and her personal estate forever. Id. 956, § 18, 19, 25.

MISSISSIPPI.

In MISSISSIPPI, a *feme covert* may be separately seized of real or personal property by direct bequest, &c., if it does not come from her husband after coverture. Hutchinson, Miss. Code, ch. 34, art. 4, § 3. She thus holds stock, and implements of husbandry necessary for planting. Id. art. 7, § 3. Rents, issues, and profits of her real estate, enure to her sole and separate use. Id. art. 7, § 2. Id. § 4. Suits affecting her separate property may be prosecuted and defended in their joint names. Id. § 5. Covenants in consideration of marriage and marriage settlement, must be acknowledged and recorded, ch. 42, art. 1, §§ 2, 3. She may defend in a suit for her land if the husband neglects. Id. art. 3, § 5. The husband is not liable for the wife's antenuptial debts until her separate property is exhausted, nor for any debt contracted after marriage if at the time she owned separate property, ch. 34, art. 7, § 8. The will of a *feme covert* is void, ch. 49, art. 1, § 14. Wife may convey her real estate by joint deed, and is bound by her covenants in such deed. Revised code p. 317, art. 4. Every description of property of a married woman and the income of such is her own separate property, and is not liable for his debts nor can it be encumbered in any way but by joint deed. Id. 335, art. 23. He is entitled to curtesy in her real estate, and if she leave no children, inherits her personal property. Id. 337, art. 28. She may dissent from his will if her separate property be not equal to what would be her dower and distributive share in her husband's estate. Id. 338, art. 31, 32. Her separate receipt is good; and her bond executed jointly with her husband binds her separate property. Id. 337, art. 30.

MISSOURI.

In MISSOURI, the husband may recover the rent due on the estate of his deceased wife. R. S. c. 98, § 3. A married woman may not be executrix or administratrix, id. c. 3, § 5, and the marriage of a single woman who is an executrix extinguishes her power. Id. § 32. She may not be guardian of a minor's estate, but may be of his person. Id. c. 73, § 13. Marriage-contracts must be recorded, id. c. 114, § 3, and may be made when the female is over eighteen. Laws of 1849, p. 67. A married woman cannot make a will unless by authority of a marriage-settlement or from her husband. R. S. c. 185, § 3. The will of a single woman is revoked by subsequent marriage. Id. § 8. The property of a wife, whether acquired before or after marriage, and the use and profits of it, are not liable for the antenuptial debts of her husband. The husband's property, owned before marriage, or subsequently acquired by descent, gift, grant, or devise, and the use and profits of it, are not liable for her antenuptial debts. The wife's property owned before marriage, and that subsequently acquired by descent, gift, grant, or devise, cannot be taken to pay a liability of the husband as security incurred at *any* time, and is not liable for any fine or costs imposed upon him in a criminal case. Laws of 1849, pp. 67, 68. The wife may insure for her benefit either her husband's life or her own; and no life-insurance effected, whether before or after marriage, by the husband upon his own life, shall be liable for his debts, unless so expressed upon the face of the policy. But a creditor may insure his debtor's life. Laws of 1851, pp. 296, 297. If husband without cause abandon his wife, or lawful children under twelve years of age, he is punished by fine of not less than $50 nor more than $500, or by imprisonment for not less than one month nor more than twelve months. Laws of Missouri 1867, p. 112. If of eighteen years of age and upwards and of sound mind, she may devise by will; provided that her husband's estate by curtesy is not affected thereby. Id. 1865, p. 57. In all cases where husband is plaintiff and wife defendant, and *vice versâ*, she may sue or defend by agent or attorney and likewise in actions, by or against both. Id. p. 87.

NEW HAMPSHIRE.

In NEW HAMPSHIRE, after three months of desertion, or of any other thing which if longer continued will be a cause of divorce, the wife may hold in her several right, and dispose of property acquired by her in any way, and the earnings of the minor children, until the desertion ceases. And the judge of probate in the county where she resides, may order provision for her and her children from any property of the husband in the State. She shall then have the same rights, and her property shall descend, as if single. The wife of an alien or citizen of another State, who has resided in New Hampshire separate from her husband for six months, has the same rights and powers as if her husband were deceased, except that she cannot marry. And there are provisions for the case of a husband becoming a citizen of the State, and for a divorce, and as to minor children; for partition of a wife's real estate, held by her as joint-tenant, and for joining with his guardian in conveying property. Compiled St. (1853), ch. 158. The will of the married woman passes property held in her right, to any devisee except the husband; but shall not affect his tenancy by the curtesy. Laws of 1854, ch. 1522. By antenuptial contract, she may hold any real or personal property in her own right. And any conveyance, devise, or bequest to a married woman to her sole use, or coming to her under a deed of trust (except a direct conveyance from the husband), is valid, and she is an unmarried woman as to such property, and her rights, &c., in or out of court. If she die intestate, such personal property goes to her husband, subject to her debts. He must take administration, and is entitled to the curtesy. Com. St. ch. 158, §§ 12–17. The homestead, to the value of $500, is exempt from attachment and execution, and is in no way liable for the husband's debts, nor subject to distribution or devise, while a widow or a minor child lives thereon. But this right may be waived by deed of husband and wife, and is not valid against a claim on note or mortgage of husband and wife, or for labor less than $100, or a lien by the seller of the estate for its price, or a debt contracted for the erection of the buildings, or for taxes. Com. St. ch. 196.

NEW JERSEY.

In NEW JERSEY, her property, real or personal, acquired before or after marriage, is free from the husband's control or debts. Public Acts of 1852, p. 407. Antenuptial contracts are valid. Id. Any insurance of life for her benefit is secured to her or her children, if the premium does not exceed $100. Public Acts of 1851, p. 34. If her husband dies, she may recover from his estate the personal property belonging to her before marriage. Public Acts of 1851, p. 201. If she dies, her husband may administer, and retain her personal property. R. S. Tit. 10, c. 7, § 15; Adm'rs of Donnington *v.* Adm'rs of Mitchell, 1 Green, Ch. 243. If he abandon or desert her, she may have, by order of court, maintenance from his property; but during this maintenance he is not liable for her debts. R. S. Tit. 33, c. 3,

§ 10. She cannot dispose of real estate by will. R. S. Tit. 10, c. 10, § 3. If the husband dies leaving a family, his household goods to the value of $200, and real estate occupied by him at his death, to the amount of $1,000, are secured to his widow and children; and no waiver of this exemption is valid. Public Acts of 1851, p. 278, § 4; Public Acts of 1852, p. 222, § 1. Nor can such homestead be sold, or encumbered, unless other $1,000 are invested in other buildings for a homestead; and until this investment, the title of the purchaser is not good. Id. § 7. In a joint deed by husband and wife (if she be of full age) her covenants of warranty will bind her in the same manner as if she were unmarried. If her husband be a lunatic or confined in the States prison for crime, she may dispose of her interest in any property, so as not to interfere with his rights in the same property. Laws of N. J., 1857, c. 189, 277. If living apart from her husband, she may by joining his name with hers (though without his consent) bring her suit in any court of record, and he cannot control, release or discontinue such action. In such case she may also, by decree of court, convey any interest in real or personal property, except a gift from her husband, without his concurrence, but cannot affect any right which he may then have in such property. Id. c. 344, 337.

NEW YORK.

In New York, all a married woman's real and personal estate, whether acquired before or after marriage, if not from her husband, may be held by her for her own use, and is not liable for his debts nor subject to his control. R. S. Part II. c. 8, Tit. 1, art. 6, §§ 65–67, 68. Power of disposal may be given her in any conveyance or devise to her, and she may execute them without the husband's concurrence, P. II. c. 1, Tit. 2, art. 3, §§ 93, 100, 103, unless their terms require that. Id. § 123. But she must acknowledge it privately, as she must also in cases of conveyance. Id. § 130. The husband may administer on her estate, and is liable for her debts to the extent of assets received from her property, and is liable for the whole if he does not take out letters. P. II. c. 6, Tit. 2, art. 2, § 29. Antenuptial contracts are valid. P. II. c. 8, Tit. 1, art. 6, § 69. Insurances of life for her benefit, are secured to her if the premium does not exceed $300. Id. § 70. Her receipt is valid for her deposits in any bank. Id. § 73. She may vote by proxy in corporations, of which she is a member, except mutual fire-insurance companies. Id. § 74. She may have the custody of minor children by order of court. Id. Tit. 2. In an action between herself and her husband, she may sue and be sued alone. Id. P. II. c. 4, Tit. 3, § 114. Only her separate estate is liable for her debts before marriage. Public Acts of 1853, c. 576, §§ 1, 2. Insurance effected by married woman on her husband's life in case of her death before him, goes to his or her children for their use as shall be provided by the policy, and to their guardians if under age. Laws of N. Y., 1862, p. 214. She may convey her real or personal estate and her covenants of warranty bind her separate property. She may sue and be sued, and may bring actions in her own name for injuries to her person and character; money received as compensation in such cases is her separate property. No bargain made by her respecting her sole property, or in the carrying on of any trade, will render her husband or his property liable. Nor is he liable for costs of action brought in her name. He cannot apprentice her child or part transfer control of him, without her consent in writing. Judgments may in all cases be enforced against her separate property as if she were *sole*. Id. 1862, c. 172. She may act as an executrix or administratrix or guardian of minor, and her bonds given in these respects bind her as an unmarried woman. Id. vol. 2, 1867, p. 1927. In any action except a criminal one, the husband or wife of any party thereto, or of any person in whose behalf it is brought, are competent witnesses; and are so to prove the fact of marriage in cases of bigamy. Id. 22, 21.

NORTH CAROLINA.

In North Carolina, a marriage settlement or contract is invalid against creditors, if a greater value is secured to the intended wife and children of the marriage than is received with her in marriage, and the estate of the husband free from debt at the time of the marriage. In case of suit, the burden of proof is on the person claiming under such contract. A legacy to the wife in general words and not in trust, or a distributive share of an intestate estate falling to her during coverture (if the estate of the husband and wife is not at the time of the marriage thus sufficient) is taken as a part of the portion received with the wife. Revised Code, ch. 37. Real estate belonging to the wife at the time of the marriage cannot be sold or leased by the husband, except with her consent, ascertained by private examination, and no interest of the husband therein is subject to execution against him. Id. ch. 56, § 1. The proceeds of the wife's land sold by court are secured to her or her representatives. Id. ch. 82, § 7. Provision also exists, by which a married woman may insure the life of her husband for her sole benefit, ch. 56, § 2. Power may be given her by will, deed, &c., to dispose by will of property thereby conveyed, ch. 119, § 3. If she marry under the age of fifteen, unless her father assents to the marriage in writing, her estate is secured to her separate use, ch. 68, § 10.

OHIO.

In Ohio, the interest of the husband in the wife's real estate, her personal property acquired before and after marriage, and her choses in action, unless he has reduced them to possession, cannot be taken for his debts during her life or the life of her heirs. Swan, R. S. (Derby's ed. 1854), ch. 87, tit. 21, (657)–(660). The husband of an insane wife may be authorized to sell his real estate without her joining. Id. ch. 70, (61). The husband must be joined with the wife in all actions to which she is a party, except those concerning her separate property, when she may sue by her next friend; as she may in actions between themselves, except for divorce or alimony, when she sues alone. Id. ch. 87, (28). If sued jointly, she may defend for her own right, and for his, if he neglect to defend. Id. (29). Husband and wife may not testify for or against each other while the relation subsists or afterwards. Id. ch. 87 (314). As to the rights of the wife to children and property when her husbands joins the Shakers, see ch. 105. The husband or wife may insure his life (the annual premium not to exceed $150, otherwise the surplus insurance to go to his representatives) for the benefit of her and her children. Id. ch. 59. A married woman may dispose of her property by will. Id. ch. 122, (1); and the will of a *feme sole* is not revoked by her subsequent marriage. Id. (37). The homestead to the value of $500, is exempt from execution, &c. Id. ch. 87, (647)-(656). A married woman whose property is appropriated for public use is empowered to do any thing necessary for an owner to do, as if she were unmarried. Id. 1859, p. 147. She has full power to contract for repairs and for cultivating her own property in her own name, during coverture, but cannot lease for a longer period than three years, and during her life and the life of any of her heirs, such property cannot be taken by his creditors; but his estate by curtesy remains: and in all actions in regard to her separate estate it only is liable for any judgment rendered. Id. 1866, pp. 47, 48.

PENNSYLVANIA.

In PENNSYLVANIA, the wives of mariners and others at sea may trade as, and have generally, the rights of *femes sole.* Dunlop, Laws of Penn. (3d ed. 1853), pp. 75, 76. The husband administers upon his deceased wife's estate, and she generally upon his. Id. pp. 461, 462. If money is awarded to a married woman upon distribution, or on partition or sale of her real estate, it must be secured to her benefit. Id. pp. 483, 484, 982. She retains all property owned before, or obtained after, marriage, free from the control or debts of her husband. But he is not liable for her antenuptial debts. Her property is liable for her debts and torts, and execution must first be had against it. And she may dispose of it by will. Id. pp. 996, 997; Lancaster Co. Bank *v.* Stauffer, 10 Penn. St. 398; Lefever *v.* Witmer, id. 505; Cummings' Appeal, 11 id. 272; Goodyear *v.* Rumbaugh, 13 id. 480, s. c. Law Journ. July 29, 1850. But (except in case of property held in trust for her separate use by virtue of the terms of a deed or will) her power to bequeath is restricted so that her surviving husband may elect to take such interest in her property as she, surviving, could elect to take in his; or else his estate by the curtesy. Laws of 1855, No. 456, p. 430. She may sue alone for her money, or perhaps with her husband, Goodyear *v.* Rumbaugh, *supra,* and with her husband for her estate, a recovery to be for her benefit, Dunlop, p. 1099; or maintain trespass for injury to her property, though he dissents, and he cannot sue therefor alone. Goodyear *v.* Rumbaugh, *supra.* Marriage does not, even with her consent, dissolve her testamentary guardianship. Cummings' Appeal, *supra.* His property is first liable for necessaries; for want of it, the wife's. Dunlop, p. 997. He retains his estate by the curtesy, id.; but as to when it is generally liable to his creditors, see id. p. 1093; Lancaster Co. Bank *v.* Stauffer, *supra;* Lefever *v.* Witmer, *supra.* A trustee may be appointed of a married woman's property, and she may declare trusts. Dunlop, p. 1096. There are also provisions by which claims for personal injury to the husband survive to the widow, id. p. 1145; by which married women may loan to their husbands, id., and for insanity of the wife. Id. p. 1170. If the husband does not provide for his wife, or deserts her, she has the rights of a *feme sole;* and if intestate her property descends as if he had previously died. Laws of 1855, No. 456, p. 430. In such case, or if divorced *a mensa et thoro*, she may maintain an action for slander or libel, and may recover her separate earnings and property; but if her husband is defendant, in the name of her next friend. Laws of 1856, No. 334, p. 315. If of lawful age, and entitled to a legacy, &c., she may execute a refunding bond and other instruments to an executor or administrator. Id. Married women are allowed to be members of a charitable corporation composed of women. Laws of Penn. 1859, p. 78. No judgment obtained against her husband before, or during marriage shall bind or be a lien on her real estate, or his interest as tenant by curtesy. And by joining with him she may convey any lands conveyed to or acquired by her to her separate use, which conveyance will be as valid as if in execution of a power contained in the deed creating such estate. Laws of Penn. 1863, pp. 212, 215. But if such right has been withheld in the deed, will, or other instrument which created the separate estate, she cannot convey. Id. 1867, p. 67.

RHODE ISLAND.

In Rhode Island, there is a provision substantially like that in Massachusetts as to a married woman coming into the State without her husband, and there living without him. Public Laws of R. I., 1841–2, p. 2056. Real estate of a wife, who is a citizen of the United States, and whose husband is an alien, descends to her children. Acts and Resolves, May Session, 1853, p. 16. Any married woman may dispose of her real estate by will, but not to deprive her husband of his tenancy by the curtesy. Acts and Res., January Session, 1856, p. 63. Her deposits in an institution for savings are her own property, id. p. 73; and any insurance for the life of any one for her benefit, if the premium does not exceed $300, is hers, independently of her husband and his creditors. Public Laws, 1846–8, p. 715. Any policy of insurance for her benefit not exceeding the sum of $10,000 is hers independently of her husband, or the person effecting the insurance, or the creditors of either. Public Laws p. 91, § 1. Repealing c. 136, § 20, R. S.

SOUTH CAROLINA.

In South Carolina, having a right to land or any other action, the wife may appoint an attorney to bring suit, either in her own name or joined with her husband. Statutes at Large, Vol. II. p. 587. And the husband can have no control over the suit, without her voluntary consent, given in open court and recorded. Id. Any *feme covert*, being a sole trader, is liable to be sued, as if single, id. p. 593, and may sue and be sued, naming the husband for conformity, id. Vol. III. pp. 620,

794, n. and cases cited. A husband cannot be compelled to make distribution of the personal estate of his wife, but it becomes his, upon administration. Id. Vol. II. p. 529. As to the light in which the contract of marriage is considered, see Statutes at Large, Vol. II. p. 733, n.; and Vol. X. p. 357, n. Marriage-settlements must be recorded, or else, as to creditors, *bonâ fide* purchasers and mortgagees, are deemed void: for the various provisions as to recording, see Statutes at Large, Vol. IV. pp. 656, 657, 767, n.; Vol. V. preface, pp. ii. 203, 204; Vol. VI. pp. 213, 483, 636, 637, appendix.; Vol. VII. p. 234. As to the requirement of a specification or a schedule, of the property covered by a marriage-settlement, manner of executing, and effect of want of, see id. Vol. V. p. 204. The will of a *feme covert* is void. Id. Vol. III. p. 342.

TENNESSEE.

In Tennessee, the wife may manage her own and her husband's property, when he is incapacitated, Public Acts of 1835, ch. 56, § 1; and her property is not liable in such case for his debts. Id. § 2. Property acquired by her, subsequent to an abandonment by him, or separation from him, in consequence of ill usage, is not liable for his debts. If she live with him again it is. Public Acts of 1825, ch. 10. Marriage contracts and settlements must be recorded to be valid against creditors. They are not good where more property is concerned than husband and wife possessed at the time of marriage; but subsequent legacies to her are considered as property received by her. Public Acts of 1785, ch. 12. As to dower and provisions in lieu of, see Laws of 1823, ch. 37, § 4, Laws of 1784, ch. 22, § 8; property exclusive of dower, and exempt from execution, set off to widow, Laws of 1837, ch. 13, §§ 1, 2; other property in widow's hands exempt from execution, Laws of 1833, ch. 80; this provision applies to a married woman whose husband absconds, id. ch. 2; other provisions in relation to widows, Laws of 1844, ch. 211. A *feme covert* may dispose by will of her own estate. Laws of 1852, ch. 180, § 4.

TEXAS.

In Texas, the marriage of a female minor gives her all the right she would have if of age. Hartley, Digest of Texas Laws, art. 2420. All property acquired by either party before marriage or by gift, devise, or descent afterwards, is the separate property of each; but the husband has the management of the whole. Id. art. 2421. Property acquired by either during marriage, in other ways, is common; the husband may dispose of it during coverture; if there are no children, the whole goes to the survivor, otherwise one-half. Id. art. 2422. The parties may be jointly sued for necessaries and for expenses benefiting the wife's separate estate. Id. art. 2423. Execution may be levied on common property, or her separate property at the plaintiff's option. Id. art. 2424. Marriage-agreements must be made before a notary, and may be acknowledged by a minor with the parent's or guardian's consent, id. art. 2411, 2412, and are unalterable after marriage. Id.

art. 2413. A reservation of property therein to be good must be recorded. Id. art. 2414. Husband and wife may sue jointly and separately, for her effects. Id. 2415. The wife may, on failure of the husband to support or educate her and her children, upon application, do it with her separate property. Id. art. 2416. The homestead, not exceeding two hundred acres (or, if in a town or city, a thousand dollars in value), is exempt from execution. Const. of Texas, art. 7, § 22. The husband cannot alienate it without his wife's consent. Id. For other provisions as to homestead, see Hartley, Dig. art. 1154. The wife acts jointly with her husband, when she is appointed executrix or administratrix. Id. art. 1133, 1134. The will of a *feme sole* is revoked by her subsequent marriage. Id. art. 1090, and a nuncupative will does not prevent the wife and children from inheriting. Id. The survivor takes the common property subject to its debts, nor is it necessary for her husband to administer on such property on her death; as he has the same control of it then that he had in her lifetime. In case of his death she has the same control, till she marries; when it will be subject to administration. Paschall's, Dig. art. 4647, 4652. Husband may fill antecedent contracts, and be compelled to give bonds for the proper management of the common property. Id. art. 4650. Her separate property is not chargeable with necessaries procured for him. Id. art. 4641, sec. 4. The common property is liable for all debts contracted during marriage. Id. art. 4646. Either may by will give to the survivor the power to keep his and her separate property together, until each of the several heirs come of age; and to manage and control it subject to law and the provisions of the will. Id. art. 4653.

VERMONT.

In VERMONT, in case of desertion, the Supreme Court may authorize a wife of eighteen years of age, to convey her real estate, and the personal estate which came to her husband through her, if in the State and undisposed of by him; and require any one owing her husband money in her right to pay it to her; and the proceeds, and her own earnings, and those of her minor children shall be held by her for her own use. If the real estate of a wife be taken for public use, the damages are to be secured to her benefit. The wife of a man under guardianship may join with the guardian in making partition, &c. The wife of a man confined in the State prison is as a *feme sole* as to suits for causes arising after his sentence. Married women may devise by will their inheritable real estate. The rents, &c., of all her real estate, and her husband's interest in it, shall be exempt from attachment or execution for his sole debts, nor can he convey them without her. She may insure the life of her husband for her own use, if the premium do not exceed $300. Compiled Statutes (1850), ch. 68. The homestead provision is substantially similar to that of New Hampshire. Id. ch. 65; Acts of 1851, No. 29. The earnings of a married woman and her deposits in Savings bank are not subject to trustee process by her husband. Gen. Stats. pp. 305 and 549. The annual product of her real estate is subject to the payment of necessaries for herself and family, and for work and materials for their benefit. Stocks and bonds given to her by a parent are governed by the same law. Id. 47, § 18. When abandoned by her husband she may maintain an action in her own name as if unmarried. Laws of Vermont, 1866, p. 43. All personal property, and rights of personal acquired during coverture, or by inheritance, or distribution, shall be held to her sole and separate use. 'Id. 1867, p. 29.

VIRGINIA.

In VIRGINIA, the husband of an insane wife may make a deed to bar her right of dower on leave of court; but the same interest in the proceeds shall be secured to her. Code of Virginia, Tit. 36, c. 128, § 11. If the husband die intestate, and without issue by her, she has the personal property which he had from or with her, and which he has not disposed of, if his other personal estate suffices to pay his debts. Id. Tit. 33, c. 123, § 10. She can make no will except of her separate estate, or by a power of appointment. Id. Tit. 33, c. 122, § 3.

WISCONSIN.

In WISCONSIN, the marriage of a *feme sole* executrix or administratrix extinguishes her authority, R. S. c. 67, § 8; c. 68, § 13, and of a female ward terminates the guardianship, c. 80, § 27. The husband holds his deceased wife's lands for life, unless she left by a former husband issue to whom the estate might descend, c. 62, § 30. She may sue upon a rumseller's bond, for injury done to herself or children. Laws of 1850, c. 139, § 4. Provisions exist by which powers may be given to married women, and regulating their execution of them. R. S. c. 58, §§ 8, 15, 40, 44, 57. If husband and wife are impleaded, and the husband neglect to defend the rights of the wife, she, applying before judgment, may defend without him; and if he lose her land by default, she may bring an action of ejectment after his death, c. 3, §§ 3, 4. The real estate of females married before, and the real and personal property of those after, Feb. 21, 1850, remain their separate property. And any married woman may receive, but not from her husband, and hold any property as if unmarried. Laws of 1850, c. 44.

It should be added, that the wife may everywhere even by common law be the agent of the husband, and transact for him his business transactions, making, accepting, or indorsing bills or notes, purchasing goods, rendering bills, collecting money and receipting for it, and in general entering into any contract so as to bind him, if she has his authority to do so. And while they continue to live together, the law considers the wife as clothed with authority by the husband to buy for him and his family all things necessary in kind and quantity for the proper support of his family; and for such purchases made by her, he is liable.

The husband is responsible for necessaries supplied to his wife, if he does not supply them himself. And he continues so liable if he turns her out of his house, or otherwise separates himself from her, without good cause. But he is not so liable if she deserts him (unless on extreme provocation), or if he turns her away for good cause.

If she leaves him because he treats her so ill that she has good right to go from him and his house, this is the same thing as turning her away; and she carries with her his credit for all necessaries supplied to her. But what the misconduct must be to give this right, is uncertain. Some English cases are very severe on this point. In one, a husband brought a prostitute into his house, and confined his wife to her own room under pretence of her insanity. But the court held this to be insufficient. The Supreme Court of New York, in commenting upon this case, said that "the doctrine contained in it cannot be law in a Christian country." In America the law must be, and undoubtedly is, that the wife is not obliged to stay and endure cruelty or indecency.

It may be added, that if a man lives with a woman as his wife, and represents her to be so, he is liable for necessaries supplied to her, and for her contracts, in the same way as if she were his wife; and this even to one who knows that she is not his wife.

The statutes of which we have given an abstract are intended to secure to a married woman all her rights. But in all parts of this country, women about to marry — or their friends for them — often wish to secure to them certain powers and rights, and to limit these in certain ways, or to make sure that their property is in safe and skilful hands. This can only be done by conveying and transferring the property to TRUSTEES; that is, to certain persons to hold the same in trust. This is done by a legal instrument, which is almost always an *Indenture;* by which is meant an instrument under seal between two or more parties. This instrument must set forth precisely, and with legal accuracy, just what the trust is; that is to say, just what the trustees, or the woman, or her husband *may* do, and just what they *must* do. This is one of those instruments which require peculiar care and exactness. We give as models, or forms, two, differing in their terms and purposes. Both were drawn by very skilful lawyers, and with such changes, of omission or addition or alteration, as the circumstances of any case or the wishes of the parties make necessary, will be useful and safe guides in the preparation of such instruments.

(4.)
An Indenture to put in Trust the Property of an Unmarried Woman.

This Indenture of two parts, made and concluded this day of , A.D. eighteen hundred and , by and between of , singlewoman, of the first part, and , and , of , of the second part,

Witnesseth, That the said party of the first part is seized and possessed of certain real and personal estate, to wit, one undivided moiety of the reversion in and of a messuage and land in , bounded as follows:

a mortgage of a lot of land bounded on Street, and described in the deed of to , which is recorded in the Registry of Deeds, lib. , fol. ; a mortgage of a lot of land bounded on Street, and described in the deed of , recorded in the said Registry, lib. , fol. ; a mortgage of two lots of land bounded on Street, and described in the deed of to , recorded in the said Registry, lib. , fol. ; a mortgage of a lot of land bounded on Street, and described in the deed of to recorded in the Registry aforesaid, lib. , fol. ; one hundred shares in the capital stock of the Bank in ; twenty-five shares in the capital stock of the Bank in ; and fifty shares in the capital stock of the Bank of ; also a note of hand signed by the said , for the sum of fifteen thousand dollars; a note of hand signed by the said , for the sum of three thousand dollars; a note of hand signed by and , for the sum of two thousand five hundred dollars; a note of hand signed by , for the sum of six thousand dollars, which notes are severally secured by the lands and tenements, mortgaged as aforesaid; also a note of hand signed by , for the sum of one thousand dollars.

All which real and personal estate the said party of the first part is desirous that the party of the second part should have and hold in trust for certain uses and purposes hereinafter set forth and expressed; and in conformity with said intention, and for the purpose of carrying the same into effect, the said party of the first part, in consideration of the sum of five dollars paid to her by the party of the second part, the receipt of which she doth hereby acknowledge, and for divers other good considerations moving her thereto, hath given, granted, sold, and conveyed, and doth give, grant, bargain, sell, and convey, all the said lands, tenements, and real estate, and doth hereby bargain, sell, transfer, assign, and set over all the aforesaid chattels and personal estate, as the same are above specified and described, unto the said and , and their heirs and assigns. To have and to hold the said granted premises unto the said and , and their heirs and assigns, and to the survivor of them and his heirs and assigns forever to their own use, but in trust nevertheless for the purposes, objects, and intents hereinafter set forth and expressed, and for none other, namely:

First, That the said trustees and their successors in the said trust shall permit the said party of the first part, without any hinderance or interference by them, so long as she shall remain sole and unmarried, and shall see fit so to do, to receive and take in her proper person, or by her agent or attorney, the rents, income, dividends, interest, and profits of the said trust estate, real and personal, without any accountability therefor, to them the said parties of the second part; but if required by her, the said party of the first part, so to do, the said trustees and their successors shall collect and receive the said rents, income, and profits of the trust estate, and shall from time to time pay over the same unto the said party of the first part for her own use.

Secondly, That from and after the solemnization of the marriage of the said party of the first part, whenever that event may take place, the said trustees and their successors shall collect, take, and receive all the rents, income, and profits of the trust estate, real and personal, and shall from time to time pay over the same to the said party of the first part, to and upon her separate order or receipt, made and signed by her, at or about the time of such payments respectively and for her proper use, free from the control or interference of any husband she may have.

Thirdly, That at and after the decease of said party of the first part, the said trustees and their successors shall be seized and possessed of the said trust estate to and for the use of such person or persons as the said party of the first part, by any last will and testament, duly executed, if she die sole and unmarried, or, in case she be at her decease a married woman, by any paper writing signed by her in presence of two or more credible witnesses, shall order, and appoint to take, receive, and hold the same, and in such shares and manner, and upon such terms and conditions, as she shall direct, order, and appoint as aforesaid; and in case the said party of the first part shall omit to make any such will or testamentary appointment, then the said trustees and their successors shall hold the trust estate to the use of such person or persons as by the laws of this Commonwealth would, in case the party of the first part had died seized and possessed of the then existing trust property in her own right, have been entitled to the same as heirs-at-law, or distributees; provided always that in such case the husband of the said party of the first part, if she leave a husband, shall be entitled to his life estate in all the real estate, as if he were tenant by the curtesy in and of the same, and be subject to all the duties incident to a tenant by the curtesy.

Fourthly, That the said trustees and their successors shall keep the said trust estate, real and personal, constantly invested in the most safe and profitable manner in their power, but relying always on their discretion in this behalf, and shall accordingly have power to sell and dispose of any of the said trust estate, and to make and pass all necessary deeds and instruments of conveyance thereof, and to purchase any other estate, real or personal, and the same to sell again, and so from time to time to change the property composing the trust fund and estate; provided always that all real and personal estate which may be purchased by them the said trustees with the trust moneys, or the proceeds of sale of the trust property, shall be conveyed and assigned to them and their successors as trustees as aforesaid, and shall be holden always upon the same trusts, and with the same powers, and for the same purposes, as are set forth and declared in this indenture of and concerning the estate firstly above described and conveyed to the said trustees.

Fifthly, That the said trustees or their successors, in case the said party of the first part shall so order and direct, shall invest the trust money or estate, or such part thereof as they shall be ordered as aforesaid, in the purchase of such house for the habitation and dwelling of the said party of the first part as she may select, and shall lay out and expend such other part of the said trust money and estate as she, the said party, shall order and direct, in the purchase of such furniture, plate, horses, and equipages, as she may choose and select for her own use; and shall permit her, the said party of the first part, with any husband she may have, to occupy and inhabit the said house, and to use and enjoy the said furniture, plate, carriages, and horses without impeachment of waste, and without any accountability to them the said trustees for the reasonable wear and use thereof, or injury by casualty; and the trustees shall keep the said house and furniture insured against fire, and, in case of loss or injury by fire, shall lay out and expend the money which they may receive from the assurers, in the repairing or rebuilding of the said house, if so directed by the said party of the first part, and in the purchase of other and new furniture, plate, horses, and equipages in place of those which have been injured or destroyed by fire, and shall permit the said party of the first part to use and enjoy the same in manner aforesaid. And the said trustees and their successors shall, when required by the said party of the first part so to do, sell and dispose of any house which may have been purchased by them for the personal occupation and habitation of the said party of the first part, and shall in manner aforesaid lay out the proceeds of sale of such house, and such other moneys as she shall direct, in the purchase of such other house as she shall select and direct them to purchase, and shall permit her to occupy the same in manner above set forth and expressed; and they shall also, when directed by the said party of the first part, sell and dispose of any of the furniture and other chattels, so as aforesaid, purchased by them for her use, and shall from time to time lay out and ex pend the proceeds of such sales and such other sums of money as they shall be directed by the said party of the first part to do, in the purchase of such other furniture, plate, horses, and equipages as she shall select for her own use; and shall permit her to use and enjoy the same in manner aforesaid: provided always that in case of any attempt by any person to sell or remove the said furniture or other chattels out of the personal care and custody of the party of the first part, without the consent of the trustees, they shall forthwith take possession thereof, and convert the chattels so attempted to be removed or sold, into money, and shall hold the said money upon the trusts and for the uses set forth in this indenture; and in all the cases in which any order or direction shall be given by the said party of the first part it shall be in writing, and be signed by her in presence of one witness at least.

Sixthly, That in case of the decease of the said trustees, or either of them, others shall be nominated by the party of the first part (if she see fit so to do), to be appointed as trustees in the place of the deceased; and upon such nomination being made and notified to the surviving trustee, he shall forthwith, if such person be suitable, make and execute all such instruments in the law as shall be needful in the opinion of counsel, to associate such person in the said trust, and to transfer and convey to him the same interest in the trust estate, with the same powers over the same, and subject to the same duties, as are vested in and assumed by the parties of the second part in and by this instrument and the laws of the land. And in case either of the said trustees, the parties of the second part, or their successors, shall wish to resign said trust, they shall be at liberty to do so, first giving reasonable notice to the party of the first part, that she may find some suitable person, who shall be acceptable to the remaining trustee, to assume the said trust in place of the trustee resigning; and the same proceedings shall then be had for the introduction and appointment of a new trustee as are above provided in case of the decease of a trustee; and in case of the decease or resignation at any time of any of the persons who may be hereafter appointed trustees, in manner aforesaid, similar proceedings shall be had for supplying the vacancy created by such decease or resignation. And the trust fund, property, and estate shall always be had and held by the persons so appointed from time to time in trust for the uses and purposes set forth in this indenture, and none other. And all nominations made as aforesaid shall be in writing.

Seventhly, That the purchasers of any estate, real or personal, which may be sold and conveyed by the trustees under this indenture, shall not be bound to see to the application of the purchase-money; but the receipt and acquittance of the trustees shall be a full and adequate discharge to such purchasers for such purchase-money.

Eighthly, That all the expenses and incidental charges of the trustees shall be deducted from the income of the trust property, as well as a reasonable allowance to the trustees for their own services.

Ninthly, That the resignation of any trustee shall not be, nor be pleaded as, a bar to the chancery jurisdiction of the courts of the Commonwealth, in case a resort against such trustee to the said court shall be necessary.

Tenthly, That the trustees under this indenture, each for himself and not for each other, shall be responsible for the want of due diligence only in the execution of the said trusts, and for their wilful defaults, and in case of the omission by the party of the first part to nominate a successor to either of the parties of the second part, or to any person appointed instead of them, or either of them who may resign or decease, the surviving or continuing trustee shall have power and authority to execute all the trusts herein specified and declared, in as ample manner as both the said parties of the second part might jointly have done.

In Testimony Whereof, The said and hereto set their hands and seals, the day and year first above written.

(*Signatures.*) (*Seals.*)

Signed, Sealed and Delivered in Presence of
(*Witnesses.*)

MAY 18

Then the within-named acknowledged this instrument to be his free act and deed before me.

(Signed) *Justice of the Peace.*

(5.)

Another Form of Indenture in Trust, for Property of Unmarried Woman.

This Indenture, Made and concluded this day of , in the year of our Lord one thousand eight hundred and , by and between , of in the county of , singlewoman, of the one part, and of said the father of the said , of the other part: Witnesseth,

Whereas the said is seized and possessed in her own right, as tenant in common, of one undivided fifth part of the following-described real estate;

and is also seized and possessed of and in one undivided fifth part of a certain piece of land, situate on Street in said ; with the buildings thereon standing, and privileges and appurtenances thereto belonging; the whole of which were conveyed by to , by deed bearing date the twenty-eighth of , in the year of our Lord one thousand eight hundred , and recorded in the Registry of Deeds for said county, lib. , fol. : also of and in one undivided fifth of one undivided fortieth part of thirty acres of land situate in said ; which was conveyed to , by , by deed bearing date the eighteenth day of , in the year of our Lord eighteen hundred , and recorded with Suffolk Deeds, lib. , fol. . And whereas the said is possessed of the following personal estate: to wit, of eighteen thousand dollars in the capital stock, or shares, of the Bank in said , as appears by a certificate thereof, and is also possessed of the promissory note of said for the sum of fifteen hundred dollars, dated the ninth day of last, and payable by instalments of five hundred dollars in one, two, and three years therefrom; and of another promissory note of said , for five hundred dollars, dated the seventeenth day of last, and payable in one year therefrom; and also of the bond of , and , dated the seventh day of , in the year of our Lord one thousand eight hundred and , conditioned for the payment of five hundred dollars and interest, and of the principal of which there has been paid one hundred and fifty dollars, and all the interest up to the seventh day of last. And whereas she, the said , is desirous of securing the said estate, both real and personal, in the event of her marriage, to her sole use and benefit; and for this purpose it hath been agreed, that all the estate and property aforesaid shall be granted, assigned, and transferred unto the said , and to such other trustee as shall hereafter be appointed according to the provisions hereinafter expressed, to be held in trust by them for the separate and sole use and benefit of her, the said , and her heirs (notwithstanding any such coverture), upon the terms and conditions, for the uses, intents, and purposes, under the limitations, and for and during the time, as hereinafter is expressed.

Now, this indenture witnesseth, that the said , in consideration of the premises, and of the covenants hereinafter contained, and also of one dollar now paid to her by the said , the receipt whereof is hereby acknowledged, hath granted, bargained, sold, and transferred, and by these presents doth grant, bargain, sell, and transfer, unto the said , his heirs and assigns, forever, all the real and personal estate, stocks, notes, and bond, hereinbefore described and specified:

To have and to hold the same to him, the said , his heirs and assigns, forever, to and for the several uses, trusts, and purposes, and subject to the several provisions, limitations, powers, and agreements, hereinafter limited, declared, and expressed; that is to say, to the sole use and behoof of the said and her heirs until the solemnization of any such marriage, and, from and immediately afterwards, to and for the following uses, intents, and purposes: to wit,

That the said estate, both real and personal, stocks, notes, and bond, shall be held, during the natural life of the said , by him, the said , and by such other trustee as shall be appointed for that purpose in the manner hereinafter expressed and provided, to the sole use and separate benefit of her, the said , without being liable to the debts, incumbrances, or control of any husband she may have during the existence and continuance of said trust: that said shall, from time to time, lease and demise said real estate to the best profit and advantage; and, at such time as he shall see fit and think proper, sell and dispose of all or any part of said real estate, upon the most advantageous terms, for the interest of said ; and shall invest the proceeds thereof in the safest and most productive funds; and, upon payment of the capital stocks, notes, or bond aforesaid, invest the same in like manner: that he shall pay all the rents and profits of said real estate while unsold, and the clear interest and income of said funds, and also the clear interest and income of said personal property hereby assigned, and all the net profits arising and accruing therefrom, as well as such portion of the principal as he shall judge necessary for her convenience and support, unto her, the said , or to such person or persons as she shall in writing, without the signature or interference of any husband, appoint, for and during the natural life of her, the said ; that is to say, for and during the term for which said trust shall continue, according to the provisions and limitations hereinafter expressed; and, after the decease of the said , the remaining income and profit unpaid, to the child or children of the said , if she shall leave any; and, upon such decease, grant, convey, and transfer the same estate, both real and personal, and any investments in funds, unto such child or children, his and their heirs and assigns, forever; and also grant and convey, in like manner, any real estate which may be purchased with the proceeds of said property: and, in case the said should die without issue, then to grant, convey, and transfer the same, in like manner, unto the heirs-at-law of her the said .

And the said , for himself, his heirs, executors, and administrators, doth covenant, grant, and agree, to and with the said , her executors and administrators, that in case she, the said , should desire any real estate to be purchased with any part of said capital stock, funds, or interest, of the estate and property hereby conveyed, and it should be deemed advantageous and proper by the said to comply therewith, then he will make a purchase thereof, and take deeds of conveyance of such estate in his own name, and will hold the same subject to the like trusts, limitations, powers, and agreements as are herein limited, declared, and expressed; and will pay over the rents and income thereof as is above provided, unless she, the said , shall choose to occupy and live on the same; and, in such case, no rents shall be exacted or required of any husband of the said . And in case of mental infirmity, or any other incapacity, which shall, in the opinion of the Judge of Probate for the County of for the time being, prevent a suitable execution of the aforesaid trusts by him, the said , he does also covenant as aforesaid to grant, sell, and transfer the aforesaid estate and property, both real and personal, which shall then remain in his possession and under his control, and such other as he may have purchased in pursuance of the trusts aforesaid, unto any trustee who shall be appointed by the said Judge of Probate for the time being (who, on the happening of such infirmity or other incapacity, is hereby authorized to make such appointment); to have and to hold the same to such trustee, subject to the several provisions, limitations, powers, and agreements, and upon the same intent, uses, and trusts, in like manner as held by him, said . And upon the happening of the death of him, the said , he doth further covenant that his heirs or executors or administrators shall and will, as soon as practicable thereafter, make good and sufficient instruments of conveyance to transfer and grant the aforesaid estate, both real and personal, or such parts thereof as shall then remain undisposed of, and such as may be purchased by him, said , in pursuance of the trusts and intent of this indenture, unto such person as shall be appointed the trustee of the said for that purpose by the said Judge of Probate for the time being; who is, in that event, authorized to make the appointment. And the said doth also further covenant as aforesaid, that upon the death of the said , if he shall then be her trustee under the provisions of this indenture, he will grant, transfer, and assign all and singular the estate and property, both real and personal, which he may then hold under the grant and trusts aforesaid, unto the child or children of her, the said , if she shall leave any. But no grant and conveyance, as is above provided, shall be made unto any such trustee until he shall have given bond, with sufficient sureties, to the Judge of Probate for said county for the time being, for the benefit of the said and her heirs, upon condition that he, the said trustee, his heirs, executors, or administrators, shall hold the said estate and property, to be granted and transferred, subject to all the limitations, provisions, powers, and agreements, and for the several uses, purposes, and trusts, in this indenture limited, declared, and expressed; and upon the condition that he shall at all times well and truly observe, fulfil, and perform the same.

And the said trustee so appointed shall thereupon have all the powers, and be bound to perform all the duties, enjoined upon and required by this indenture, of him, the said

In Witness Whereof, The said parties have hereto interchangeably set their hands and seals, the day and year first above written.

(Signatures.) *(Seals.)*

Signed, Sealed and Delivered in Presence of
(Witnesses.)

, *ss.* 30th September, A.D. 18 .

Then personally appeared the above-named and , and severally acknowledged this indenture to be their free act and deed.

(Signature.) *Justice of the Peace.*

CHAPTER VI.

AGREEMENT AND ASSENT.

SECTION I.

THE LEGAL MEANING OF AGREEMENT.

No contract which the law will recognize and enforce exists, until the parties to it have agreed upon the same thing, in the same sense. Thus, in a case where the defendants by letter offered to the plaintiffs a certain quantity of "good" barley, at a certain price. Plaintiffs replied: "We accept your offer, expecting you will give us fine barley and full weight." The jury found that there was a distinction in the trade between the words "good" and "fine," and the court held that there was not a sufficient acceptance to sustain an action for non-delivery of the barley. So where a person sent an order to a merchant for a particular quantity of goods on certain terms of credit, and the merchant sent a less quantity of goods, and at a shorter credit, and the goods were lost by the way, it was held by the court that the merchant must bear the loss; for there was no sale or contract between the parties.

There is an apparent exception to this rule, when, for example, A declares that he was not understood by B, or did not understand B, in a certain transaction, and that there is therefore no bargain between them; and B replies by showing that the language used on both sides was explicit and unequivocal, and constituted a distinct contract. Here, B would prevail. The reason is, that the law presumes that every person means that which he distinctly says. If A had offered to sell B his horse for twenty dollars, and received the money, and then tendered to B his cow, on the ground that he was thinking only of his *cow*, and used the word *horse* by mistake, this would not avoid his obligation, unless he could show that the mistake was known to B; and then the bargain would be fraudulent on B's part. This would be an extreme case; but difficult questions of this sort often arise. If A had agreed to sell, and had actually delivered, a cargo of shingles at "3.25," supposing that he was to receive that price for a "bunch," which contains five hundred, and B supposed that he had bought them at that price for a "thousand," which view should prevail? The answer would be, first, that if there was, honestly and actually, a mutual mistake, there was no contract, and the shingles should be returned. But, secondly, if a jury should be satisfied, from the words used, from the usage prevailing where the bargain was made and known to the parties, or from other circumstances attending the bargain, that B knew that A was expecting that price for a bunch, B would have to pay it; and if they were satisfied that A knew that B supposed himself to be buying the shingles by the thousand, then A could not reclaim the shingles, nor recover more than that price. There was such a case so decided.

In construing a contract, the actual and honest intention of the parties is always regarded as an important guide. But it must be their intention as expressed in the contract.

If the parties, or either of them, show that a bargain was honestly but mistakenly made, which was materially different from that intended to be made, it would be a good ground for declaring that there was no contract.

Mistakes of fact in a contract can be corrected by the courts, but not mistakes of law; no man being permitted to take advantage of a mistake of the law, either to enforce a right, or avoid an obligation; for it would be obviously dangerous and unwise to encourage ignorance of the law, by permitting a party to profit, or to escape, by his ignorance. But the law which one is required at his peril to know, is the law of his own country. Ignorance of the law of a foreign state is ignorance of fact. In this respect the several States of the Union are foreign to each other. Hence, money paid through ignorance or mistake of the law of another State may be recovered back.

Fraud annuls all obligation and all contracts into which it enters, and the law relieves the party defrauded. If both of the parties act fraudulently, neither can take advantage of the fraud of the other; and if one acts fraudulently, he cannot set his own fraud aside for his own benefit. Thus, if one gives a fraudulent bill of sale of property, for the purpose of defrauding his creditors, *he* cannot set that bill aside and annul that sale, although those who are injured by it may.

SECTION II.

WHAT IS AN ASSENT.

The most important application of the rule stated at the beginning of this chapter, is the requirement that an acceptance of a proposition must be a simple and direct affirmative, in order to constitute a contract. For if the party receiving the proposition or offer accepts it on any condition, or with any change of its terms or provisions which is not altogether immaterial, it is no contract until the party making the offer consents to these modifications.

Therefore, if a party offers to buy certain goods at a certain price, and directs how the goods shall be sent to him, and the owner accepts the offer and sends the goods as directed, and they are lost on the way, it is the buyer's loss, because the goods were his by the sale, which was completed when the offer was accepted. But if the owner accepts the offer, and in his acceptance makes any material modification of its terms, and then sends the goods, and they are lost, it is his loss now, because the contract of sale was not completed.

Nor will a voluntary compliance with the conditions and terms of a proposed contract always make it a contract obligatory on the other party, unless there have been an accession to, or an acceptance of, the proposition itself. In general, if A says to B, if you will do this, I will do that; and B instantly does what was proposed to him, this doing so is an acceptance, and A is bound. But if the doing of the thing may be something else than an acceptance of the offer, or if the thing may be done for some other reason than to signify an acceptance or assent, there must be express acceptance also, or there is no bargain.

SECTION III.

OFFERS MADE ON TIME.

It sometimes happens that one party makes another a certain offer, and gives him a certain time in which he may accept it. The law on this subject was once somewhat uncertain, but may now be considered as settled. It is this. If A makes an offer to B, which B at once accepts, there is a bargain. But it is not necessary that the acceptance should follow the offer instantaneously. B may take time to consider, and although A may expressly withdraw his offer at any time before acceptance, yet if he does not do so, B may accept within a reasonable time; and if this is done, A cannot say: "I have changed my mind." What is a reasonable time must depend upon the circumstances of each case. If A when he makes the offer says to B that he may have a certain time wherein to accept it, and is paid by B for thus giving him time, he cannot withdraw the offer; or if he withdraws it, for this breach of his contract, the other party, B, may have his action for damages. If A is not paid for giving the time, A may then withdraw the offer at once, or whenever he pleases, provided B has not previously accepted it. But if B has accepted the offer before the time which was given expired, and before the offer was withdrawn, then A is bound, although he gave the time voluntarily and without consideration. For his offer is to be regarded as a continuing offer during all the time given, unless it be withdrawn. A railroad company asked for the terms of certain land they thought they might wish to buy. The owner said in a letter, they might have it at a certain price, if they took it within thirty days. After some twenty-five days, the railroad company wrote accepting the offer. The owner says, No, I have altered my mind; the land is worth more; and I have a right to withdraw my offer, because you paid me nothing for the time of thirty days allowed you. But the court held that he was bound, because this was an offer continued through the thirty days, unless withdrawn. They said that the writing when made was without consideration, and did not therefore form a contract. It was then but an offer to contract, and the party making the offer most undoubtedly might have withdrawn it at any time before acceptance. But when the offer was accepted, the minds of the parties met, and the contract was complete, and no withdrawal could then be made.

SECTION IV.

A BARGAIN BY CORRESPONDENCE.

WHEN a contract is made by correspondence, the question occurs, At what time, or by what act, is the contract completed? The law as now settled in this country may be stated thus. If A writes to B proposing to him a contract, this is a continued proposition or offer of

A until it reaches B, and for such time afterwards as would give B a reasonable opportunity of accepting it. It may be withdrawn by A at any time before acceptance; but is not withdrawn in law until a notice of withdrawal reaches B. This is the important point. Thus if A, in Boston, writes to B, in New Orleans, offering him a certain price for one hundred bales of cotton; and the next day alters his mind, and writes to B, withdrawing his offer; if the first letter reaches B *before* the second reaches him, although *after* it was written and mailed, B has a right to accept the offer *before* he gets the letter withdrawing it, and by his acceptance he binds A. But if B delays his acceptance until the second letter reaches him, the offer is then effectually withdrawn. It is a sufficient acceptance if B writes to A declaring his acceptance, and puts his letter into the post-office. It seems now quite clear, that as soon as the letter leaves the post-office, or is beyond the reach of the writer, the acceptance is complete. That is, on the 5th of May, A in Boston writes to B, in New Orleans, offering to buy certain goods there at a certain price. On the 8th of May, A writes that he has altered his mind and cannot give so much, and mails the letter. On the 14th of May, B in New Orleans receives the first letter, and the next day, the 15th, answers it, saying that he accepts the offer and mails his letter. On the 17th, he receives the second letter of A withdrawing the offer. Nevertheless the bargain is complete and the goods are sold. But if B had kept his letter of acceptance by him until he had received A's letter of withdrawal, he could not then have put his letter into the mail and bound A by his acceptance.

The party making the offer by letter is not bound to use the same means for withdrawing it which he uses for making it; because any withdrawal, however made, terminates the offer, if only it reaches the other party before his acceptance. Thus, if A in the case just supposed, a week after he has sent his offer by letter, telegraphs a withdrawal to B, and this withdrawal reaches him before he accepts the offer, this withdrawal would be effectual. So if he sent his offer by letter to England, in a sailing ship, and a fortnight after sent a revocation in a steamer, or by telegraph, if this last arrives before the first arrived and was accepted, it would be an effectual revocation.

SECTION V.

WHAT EVIDENCE MAY BE RECEIVED IN REFERENCE TO A WRITTEN CONTRACT.

If an agreement upon which a party relies be oral only, it must be proved by evidence. But if the contract be reduced to writing, it proves itself; and now no evidence whatever is receivable for the purpose of varying the contract or affecting its obligations. The reasons are obvious. The law prefers written to oral evidence, from its greater precision and certainty, and because it is less open to fraud. And where parties have closed a negotiation and reduced the result to writing, it is presumed that they have written all they intended to agree to, and therefore, that what is omitted was finally rejected by them.

But some evidence may always be necessary, and therefore admissible; as, evidence of the identity of the parties to the contract, or of the things which form its subject-matter. Quite often, neither the court nor the jury can know what person, or what thing, or what land, a contract relates to, unless the parties agree in stating this, or evidence shows it. The rule on this subject is, that, while no evidence is receivable to *contradict* or *vary* a written contract, evidence may be received to explain its meaning, and show what the contract is in fact.

There are some obvious inferences from this rule. The first is, that, as evidence is admissible only to explain the contract, if the contract needs no explanation, that is, if it be by itself perfectly explicit and unambiguous, evidence is inadmissible, because it is wholly unnecessary unless it is offered to vary the meaning and force of the contract, and that is not permitted. Another, following from this, is, that if the evidence purports, under the name of explanation, to give to the contract a meaning which its words do not fairly bear, this is not permitted, because such evidence would in fact make a new contract.

A frequent use of oral evidence is to explain, by means of persons experienced in the particular subject of the contract, the meaning of technical or peculiar words and phrases; and such witnesses are called Experts, and are very freely admitted.

It may be remarked, too, that a written receipt for money is not within the general rule as to written contracts, being always open, not only to explanation, but even to contradiction, by extrinsic evidence. And this is true of the *receipt part* of any instrument. If a written instrument not only recites or acknowledges the receiving of money or goods, but contains also a contract or grant, such instrument, as to the contract or grant, is no more to be affected by any evidence than if it contained no receipt; but as to the receipt itself, it may be varied or contradicted in the same manner as if the instrument contained nothing else. Thus, if a deed recites that it was made in "consideration of ten thousand dollars, the receipt whereof is hereby acknowledged," the grantor may sue for the money, or any part of it, and prove that the amount was not paid; for this affects only the *receipt part* of the deed. But he cannot say that the grant of the land was void because he never had his money, nor that any agreement the deed contained was void for such a reason; because, if he proved that the money was not paid for the purpose of thus annulling his grant or agreement, he would be offering evidence to affect the *other part* of the deed; and that he cannot do.

A legal inference from a written promise can no more be rebutted by evidence than if it were written. Thus, if A, by his note, promises to pay B a sum of money in sixty days, he cannot when called upon resist the claim by proving that B, when the note was made, agreed to wait ninety days; and if A promise in writing to pay money, and no time is set, this is by force of law a promise to pay on demand, and evidence is not receivable to show that a distant period was agreed upon.

Generally speaking, all written instruments are construed and interpreted by the law according to the simple, customary, and natural meaning of the words used.

It should be added, that when a contract is so obscure or uncertain that it must be set wholly aside, and regarded as no contract whatever, it can have no force or effect upon the rights or obligations of the parties, but all of these are the same as if they had not made the contract.

SECTION VI.

CUSTOM, OR USAGE.

A CUSTOM, or usage, which may be regarded as appropriate to a contract, has often great weight in reference to it. This it may have, first, as to the construction or meaning of its words; and next, as to the intention or understanding of the parties.

The ground and reason for this influence of a custom is this. If it exist so widely and uniformly among such persons as make the contract, and for so long a time, that every one of them must be considered as knowing it, and acting with reference to it, then it ought to have the same force as if both parties expressly adopted it; because each party has a right to think that the other acted upon it.

Sometimes this is carried very far. In one English case, a man had agreed to leave in a certain rabbit warren *ten thousand rabbits;* and the other party was permitted to prove that, by the usage of that trade, a thousand meant one hundred dozen, or *twelve hundred.* In an American case, a man agreed to pay a carpenter twelve shillings a day for every man employed by him about a certain building; the carpenter was permitted to prove that, by the usage of that trade, "a day" meant ten hours' work; and as his men had worked twelve and a half, he was permitted to charge fifteen shillings, or for one and one-fourth days' work, for every day so spent.

In these cases the custom affected the meaning of the words. But it also has the effect of words; as if a merchant employed a broker to sell his ship, and nothing was said about terms, and the broker did something about it, and the ship was sold, if the broker could prove a universal and well-established custom of that place, that for doing what he did under the employment he was entitled to full commissions, he would have them, as much as if they were expressly promised.

Any custom will be regarded by the court, which comes within the *reason* of the rule that makes a custom a part of the contract. It comes within the reason only when it is *so far* established, and *so well* known to the parties, that it must be supposed that their contract was made with reference to it. For this purpose, the custom must be established and not casual, uniform and not varying, general and not personal, and known to all the parties. But the degree in which these characteristics must belong to the custom will depend in each case upon its peculiar circumstances. Let us suppose a contract for the making of an article which has not been made until within a dozen years, and only by a dozen persons. Words are used in this contract of which the meaning is to be ascertained; and it is proved that these words have been used and understood in reference to this article, always, by all who have ever made it, in one way. Then this custom will be permitted to explain and interpret the words of the parties. But if the article had been made a hundred years or more, in many countries and by multitudes of persons, the evidence of this use of these words by a dozen persons in a dozen years would not be sufficient to give to this practice the force of *custom.*

Other facts must be considered; as, how far the meaning sought to be put on the words by custom varies from their common meaning in the dictionary, or from general use; and whether other makers of the article use these words in various senses, or use other words to express the alleged meaning. Because the *main question* is always this: Can it be said that both parties *must* have used, or *ought* to have used, these words in this sense, and that each party had good reason to believe that the other party so used them? Thus, when the brief but violent "Morus multicaulis" (or mulberry) speculation prevailed, a few years ago, a man made a contract to sell and deliver a certain number of the trees "a foot high;" and the buyer was permitted to prove that, by the usage and custom of all who dealt in that article, the length was measured to the top of the ripe wood only, rejecting the green and immature top; and the "foot high" was to be so understood.

No custom, however, can be proved or permitted to influence the construction of a contract, or vary the rights of the parties, if the custom itself be illegal. For this would be to permit, or even oblige, parties to break the law, because others had broken it.

Nor would the courts sanction a custom which was in itself unreasonable and oppressive. There was a vessel cast ashore on the coast of Virginia, and the master sold the cargo on the spot; and on trial the jury found that he was authorized to do so by the usage there; but the Supreme Court of Massachusetts, where the ship and cargo were insured, said that the usage was unreasonable, and they would not allow it. The Supreme Court of Pennsylvania in one case refused to allow a usage, as unreasonable, by which plasterers charged half the size of the windows at the price per square yard agreed on for the plastering of a house.

Lastly, no custom, however universal, or old, or known (unless it has actually become law), has any force whatever, if the parties see fit to exclude and refuse it by the words of their contract, or provide that the thing which the custom affects shall be done in a way different from the custom. For a custom can never be set up against either the express agreement or the clear intentions of the parties.

I will now give forms for various agreements or contracts: —

FORMS OF CONTRACTS OR AGREEMENTS.

Every agreement should be written, and signed by both parties, and witnessed, where this can be done; although the law absolutely requires witnesses in very few cases, and in none of mere contract. It is prudent, however, to have them, for it is a rule of law, that things which cannot be proved and things which do not exist are the same in the law.

Every thing agreed upon should be written out distinctly, and care should be taken to say all that is meant, and just what is meant, and nothing else; for it is a rule of law, that no *oral* testimony shall control a *written agreement*, unless fraud can be proved. Against fraud nothing stands.

(6.)

1.—*A General Agreement, sufficient for many purposes.*

MUTUAL AGREEMENT OF TWO.

A. B. of (*place of residence, and business or profession*), and C. D. of (*as before*), have agreed together, at (*place*), on (*the day should always be named*), and do hereby promise and agree to and with each other, as follows: A. B., in consideration of the promises hereinafter made by C. D. (*if there are any such promises*), and of (*here state any other consideration which A. B. has*), promises and agrees to and with C. D., that (*here set forth, as above directed, the whole of what A. B. undertakes to do*).

And C. D. in consideration (*set forth consideration and promise as before*).

Witness our hands, to two copies of this agreement interchangeably.

A. B.
C. D.

Signed and Interchanged in Presence of

E. F.
G. H.

(7.)

A General Agreement, as used in the Western States.

Articles of Agreement, Made this day of in the year of our Lord one thousand eight hundred and sixty between party of the first part and party of the second part,

Witnesseth, That the said party of the first part hereby covenants and agrees, that if the party of the second part shall first make the payments and perform the covenants hereinafter mentioned on part to be made and performed, the said party of the first part will

And the said party of the second part hereby covenants and agrees to pay to said party of the first part the sum of dollars, in the manner following: dollars cash in hand paid, the receipt whereof is hereby acknowledged, and the balance

with interest at the rate of per centum per annum, payable annually. And in case of the failure of the said party of the second part to make either of the payments, or perform any of the covenants on part hereby made and entered into, this contract shall, at the option of the party of the first part, be forfeited and determined, and the party of the second part shall forfeit all payments made by on this contract, and such payments shall be retained by the said party of the first part in full satisfaction and in liquidation of all damages by sustained, and shall have the right to

It is mutually agreed that all the covenants and agreements herein contained shall extend to and be obligatory upon the heirs, executors, administrators and assigns of the respective parties.

In Witness Whereof, The parties to these presents have hereunto set their hands and seals, the day and year first above written.

(*Signatures.*) (*Seals.*)

Signed, Sealed and Delivered in presence of

(8.)

General Contract for Mechanics' Work.

Contract made this day of A.D. 18 by and between of of the first part, and of of the second part,

Witnesseth, That the party of the first part, for the consideration hereinafter mentioned, covenants and agrees with the party of the second part to perform in a faithful and workmanlike manner the following specified work, viz.:

And in addition to the above to become responsible for all materials delivered and receipted for, the work to be commenced and to be completed and delivered free from all mechanic or other liens, on or before the day of And the party of the second part covenants and agrees with the party of the first part, in consideration of the faithful performance of the above specified work, to pay to the party of the first part the sum of dollars, as follows:

And it is further mutually agreed by and between both parties, that in case of disagreement in reference to the performance of said work, all questions of disagreement shall be referred to and the award of said referees, or a majority of them, shall be binding and final on all parties.

In Witness Whereof, We hereunto set our hands and seals on the day and year first above written.

(*Signatures.*) (*Seals.*)

Executed in Presence of

(9.)

An Agreement for Purchase and Sale of Land, in Use in the Middle States.

Agreement, Made and concluded the day of A.D. 18 by and between of the State of of the first part, and of the State of of the second part,

Whereas, The party of the second part hath agreed to purchase from the party of the first part, either on his own account or for whom it may concern, certain land in Township, County, and State of

And it is agreed that the party of the second part shall have the right to divide and subdivide said land in such manner, and appropriate to his own use so much thereof, as he may see fit, giving and paying to the party of the first part the sum of dollars, on or before the day of A.D. 18 , and reserving to his own use any amount for which the whole or any be sold over the said dollars.

And these Articles further Witness, That the party of the first part, for and in consideration of the premises and the sum of lawful money, to him paid by the party of the second part, at and before the execution hereof, doth covenant, promise, grant and agree, with the party of the second part, his heirs and assigns, upon sale of said lands being made by the party of the first part, to sufficiently grant, convey and assure said lands, with the appurtenances, to the said party of the second part, or such person or persons as he may direct; and in default of the said party of the second part paying the amount hereinbefore specified at the time mentioned, then these articles are to be deemed and considered cancelled to all intents and purposes, the same as though they never had been made.

In Witness Whereof, The parties hereto have hereunto set their hands and seals the day and year first aforesaid.

(*Signatures.*) (*Seals.*)

Sealed and Delivered in Presence of

(10.)

An Agreement for Sale of Land, in Use in the Western States.

Articles of Agreement, Made this day of in the year one thousand eight hundred and sixty between

of the first part, and of the second part,

Witnesseth, That the party of the first part, at the request of the party of the second part, and in consideration of the money to be paid, and the covenants as herein expressed to be performed by the party of the second part (the prompt performance of which payments and covenants being a condition precedent, and time being of the essence of said condition), hereby agree to sell to the said party of the second part, all certain lot and parcel of land, situate in County of and State of , known and designated as follows, viz.:

with the privileges and appurtenances thereto belonging.

And the said party of the second part, in consideration of the premises, hereby agrees to pay the party of the first part, his or their executors, administrators or assigns, in days, the sum of dollars

as follows, viz.:

with interest at the rate of per cent per annum from to

be paid semi-annually in each year, on the whole sum from time to time remaining unpaid. And also that he will well and faithfully, in due season, pay, or cause to be paid, all ordinary taxes assessed for revenue purposes upon said premises, or any part thereof, subsequent to the year 18 . And also all other assessments which now are, or may be hereafter, charged or assessed upon or against said premises, or any part thereof. But in case the said party of the second part fail to pay any or all such taxes or assessments upon said premises or appurtenances, or any part thereof, whenever and as soon as the same shall become due and payable; and the party of the first part shall pay from time to time, or at any time, any or all such taxes or assessments, or cause the same to be paid; the amount of any and all such payments so made by the party of the first part, with interest thereon from the date of payment, shall immediately thereupon become an additional consideration, and payment thereof shall be made by the party of the second part hereto, for the premises herein agreed to be conveyed.

And the said party of the first part further covenants and agrees with the said party of the second part, that upon the faithful performance by said party of the second part of undertaking in his behalf, and of the payment of principal and interest of the sum above mentioned, in the manner specified, he the said party of the first part, shall and will, without delay, well and faithfully execute, acknowledge, and deliver in person, or by attorney duly authorized, to the party of the second part, heirs or assigns, a deed of conveyance of all the right, title and interest of the party of the first part, of, in and to the above described premises, with the appurtenances, with full covenants of warranty, also of waiver and release of all rights of the said party of the first part, resulting from the laws of this State pertaining to the exemption of homesteads.

And it is Mutually Covenanted and Agreed, by and between the parties hereto, that in case default shall be made in the payments of principal or interest at the time or any of the times above specified, for the payment thereof, and for days thereafter, this agreement, and all the preceding provisions hereof, shall be null and void, and no longer binding, at the option of said party of the first part, representatives or assigns; and all the payments which shall then have been made thereon, or in pursuance hereof, absolutely and forever forfeited to the said party of the first part; or at the election of the said party of the first part, representatives and assigns, the covenants and liability of said party of the second part shall continue and remain obligatory upon the said party of the second part, and may be enforced, and the said consideration-money, and every part thereof, with the annual interest as above specified, be collected by proper proceedings in law or equity, from the said party of the second part, heirs, executors, administrators or assigns.

And it is Further Mutually Covenanted and Agreed, by and between the parties hereto, that in case of default in the payment stipulated to be made by the said party of the second part, or any part thereof, and the election of the party of the first part, representatives or assigns, to consider the foregoing contract of sale at an end, and prior payments forfeited, the said party of the second part, heirs, representatives or assigns, who may have possession, or the right of possession, of said premises at the time of such default, or at any time thereafter, shall be considered, and are hereby agreed and declared to be, in law and equity, the tenant or tenants at will of said party of the first part, representatives and assigns, on a rent equal to an interest of ten per cent per annum on the whole sum of the purchase-money above specified, payable quarter-yearly in advance from the day of such default in payment of principal or interest. And after such default in payment, and election to consider the above contract of sale as void, the said party of the first part, representatives and assigns, shall and may have and exercise all the powers, rights and remedies provided by law or equity to collect such rent, or to remove such tenant or tenants, the same as if the relation of landlord and tenant, hereby declared, were created by an original absolute lease, for that purpose, on a special rent, payable quarterly on a tenure at will. And that in such case the said tenant or tenants shall and will pay, or cause to be paid, all taxes, assessments, ordinary and extraordinary, which may be laid or assessed on such premises or any part thereof, during the continuance of such tenancy; and will not permit or suffer any waste or damage to said premises or the appurtenances, but will keep and deliver up, on the termination of such tenancy, the said premises and appurtenances, in as good order and repair (ordinary wear and decay, and unavoidable injury by the elements, excepted) as they were in at the commencement of said tenancy.

In Witness Whereof, The party of the first part and the party of the second part, in own proper person, have hereunto respectively set their hands and seals on the day and year first above written.

(Signatures.) *(Seals.)*

Signed, Sealed, and Delivered in Presence of

(11.)

An Agreement for Warranty Deed Used in the Western States.

Articles of Agreement, Made this day of in the year of our Lord one thousand eight hundred and sixty between party of the first part, and party of the second part,

Witnesseth: That said party of the first part hereby covenants and agrees, that if the party of the second part shall first make the payment and perform the covenants hereinafter mentioned on part to be made and performed: the said party of the first part will convey and assure to the party of the second part, in fee simple, clear of all incumbrances whatever, by a good and sufficient warranty deed, the following lot, piece or parcel of ground, viz.:

And the said party of the second part hereby covenants and agrees to pay to said party of the first part the sum of dollars, in the manner following: dollars, cash in hand paid, the receipt whereof is hereby acknowledged, and the balance

with interest at the rate of per centum per annum, payable annually, on the whole sum remaining from time to time unpaid, and to pay all taxes, assessments or impositions that may be legally levied or imposed upon said land, subsequent to the year 18 . And in case of the failure of the said party of the second part to make either of the payments, or perform any of the covenants on part hereby made and entered into, this contract shall, at the option of the party of the first part, be forfeited and determined, and the party of the second part shall forfeit all payments made by on this contract, and such payments shall be retained by the said party of the first part in full satisfaction and in liquidation of all damages by sustained, and shall have the right to re-enter and take possession of the premises aforesaid.

It is mutually agreed that all the covenants and agreements herein contained shall extend to and be obligatory upon the heirs, executors, administrators and assigns of the respective parties.

In Witness Whereof, The parties to these presents have hereunto set their hands and seals the day and year first above written.

(Signatures.) *(Seals.)*

Signed, Sealed and Delivered in Presence of

(12.)

A Contract to convey Real Estate, in Use in the Middle States.

This Article of Agreement, Made and entered into the day of one thousand eight hundred and between of the first part, and of the second part,

Witnesseth, as follows: The said party of the first part hereby agrees to sell unto the said party of the second part all that parcel of land situated, bounded and described as follows. That is to say

for the sum of

to be paid by the said party of the second part, in manner and at the times hereinafter mentioned and covenanted, on the part of the said party of the second part: And the said party of the first part further agrees, that on the day of on receiving from the said party of the second part the sum of

the said party of the first part shall and will, at at own proper cost and expense, execute and deliver to the said party of the second part, or to assigns, a proper deed of conveyance, duly acknowledged, for the conveying and assuring to them the fee simple of the said premises, free from all incumbrances,

which deed of conveyance shall contain a general warranty, and the usual full covenants.

And the said party of the second part hereby agrees to purchase of the said party of the first part the premises above mentioned, at and for the price and sum above mentioned, and to pay to the said party of the first part the purchase-money therefor, in manner and at the times following, to wit:

And it is further agreed by and between the parties to these presents, that the said party of the first part shall have and retain the possession of said premises, and be entitled to the rents and profits thereof
until the day of when full possession of the same shall be delivered to the said party of the second part, by the said party of the first part:

And it is understood and agreed, that the stipulations aforesaid are to apply to and bind the heirs, executors, administrators and assigns of the respective parties.

And it is further hereby agreed, that in case the said party of the first part shall fail or refuse to execute and deliver a proper deed of conveyance in manner and at the time and place above specified for that purpose, provided the party of the second part shall be ready to fulfil and perform the covenants then to be fulfilled on part; or in case the said party of the second part shall fail or refuse to pay the said sum of

at the time and place as above agreed upon, provided the party of the first part shall be ready to deliver such deed of conveyance, as aforesaid; then the party so failing shall and will pay to the other party, or assigns, the sum of dollars, which sum is hereby declared fixed and agreed upon, as the liquidated amount of damages to be paid by the party so failing as aforesaid, for non-performance.

(*Signatures.*) (*Seals.*)

Signed, Sealed and Delivered in Presence of

(13.)

An Agreement for the Purchase of an Estate, in Use in New England.

Articles of Agreement, Had, made, concluded, and agreed upon this day of A.D. between of of the one part, and of of the other part. First, the said (*seller*) in consideration of the sum of, to him paid by the said (*buyer*) at or before the sealing and delivery of these presents, and of the further sum of to be paid as hereinafter is mentioned, doth hereby for himself, his heirs, executors, and administrators, and every of them, covenant, promise, and agree, to and with the said his heirs, executors, and administrators, and every of them, by these presents, that he the said his heirs and assigns (and all and every other person and persons whatsoever, claiming or to claim any right, title, or interest under him, or any other person or persons whatsoever, of, in, or to the lands and premises hereinafter mentioned) shall and will, at the proper costs and charges of the said his heirs and assigns (except fees to counsel), on or before the day of next ensuing, by such conveyances, assurances, ways and means in the law, as he the said his heirs and assigns, or his or their counsel, shall reasonably devise, advise, or require, well and sufficiently grant, sell, release, convey, and assure to the said and his heirs, or to whom he or they shall appoint or direct, all that situate now in the tenure or occupation of or his assigns, with covenants to be therein contained, that the said premises, at the time of such conveyance, are free from all incumbrances and demands whatsoever (except) and all other usual and reasonable covenants. In consideration whereof, the said for himself, his heirs, executors, administrators, and assigns, doth hereby covenant, promise, and agree, to and with the said his heirs, executors, and administrators, by these presents, that he the said his heirs, executors, or administrators, or some of them, shall and will, well and truly, pay, or cause to be paid, unto the said his heirs, executors, or administrators, the aforesaid sum of at the time of executing the said conveyances. And for the true performance of all and every the covenants and agreements aforesaid, each of the said parties to these presents doth hereby bind himself, his heirs, executors, and administrators to the other of them, his heirs, executors, administrators, and assigns in the penal sum of

In Witness Whereof, The said parties to these presents have hereunto set their hands and seals the day and year first above written.

(Signatures.) *(Seals.)*

Signed, Sealed and Delivered in Presence of

An agreement for the sale of lands should always state the covenants, whether of general or special warranty, which it is intended that the contemplated conveyance shall contain.

COVENANTS, PROVISOS, AND AGREEMENTS, WHICH MAY BE INSERTED IN THE PRECEDING FORM.

1. Covenant that the vendor, before the purchase is completed, shall not commit waste, or grant any new leases.

And also that the said (*the seller*) shall not nor will, in the mean time, cut down any timber or trees, or commit any waste or spoil whatsoever, in or upon the premises, or any part thereof, nor shall or will grant any new leases of the premises, or any part thereof, without the privity or consent of the said (*the buyer*) or his heirs or assigns.

2. Another covenant for the payment of the purchase-money.

And the said (*the buyer*) doth hereby covenant and agree to and with the said (*the seller*) his heirs, executors, and administrators, that upon sealing and executing such conveyance and assurance of the said unto him and them as aforesaid, according to the true intent of these presents, he the said his heirs, executors, or administrators, shall and will pay, or cause to be paid, unto the said his heirs, executors, or administrators, the said sum of in full for the purchase of the said premises. (*Or there may be an agreement to retain part of the purchase-money to pay off an incumbrance, as follows:*

And it is agreed between the said parties that the said shall or may retain out of the said purchase-money the sum of for the purpose of paying off the sum of secured by a mortgage on the said premises, given by the said to bearing date when the said sum shall become due by virtue of the said mortgage.

3. This agreement may be inserted.

And it is agreed, that if the counsel of the said shall not approve of the title of the said to the said premises, this agreement shall be void.

4. This proviso may be inserted.

Provided always, and it is hereby mutually covenanted and agreed, by and between the parties to these presents, for themselves and their respective heirs, in manner as follows, viz. That in case the counsel of the said (*the buyer*) shall not approve of the title of him the said (*the seller*) to the said or in case (*the buyer*) on his view thereof (he not having ever viewed the same) will not proceed in the purchase thereof, and shall and do, within one month next after the date hereof, give notice, in writing, to the said (or to of) that he will not purchase the said then and in either of the cases, these presents shall be absolutely void; and that then he the said (*the seller*) his heirs, executors, or administrators, shall and will, within six months now next ensuing, well and truly, repay or cause to be repaid unto the said (*the buyer*) his heirs, executors, administrators, or assigns, the said sum of so by him now paid as aforesaid, together with legal interest for the same, from henceforth to be computed until payment thereof.

5. A provision in articles of purchase, in case of the delay or default of either party.

that if by reason of any delay, neglect or default, by or on the part of the said (*the purchaser*) or his heirs, or his or their counsel or agents, the said conveyances of the said estates and premises shall not be ready and tendered to the said (*the vendor*) or his heirs, to be executed, on or before the said day of then and in such case, the said his shall and will pay and allow to the said his interest for the said sum of at the rate of to be computed from the day of until the said (*the principal sum*) shall be paid as aforesaid; but if, by reason of any delay, neglect or default, by or on the part of the said or any claiming under him, such conveyances as aforesaid shall not be executed on or before the said day of then and in such case, no such interest as aforesaid shall be paid or allowed during the time of such delay of the said

6. An agreement that if a good title, &c., cannot be made on, &c., the premises shall stand as security for the money paid down, &c.

It is hereby further agreed and declared by and between all the said parties to these presents, and particularly the said (*the vendors*) do hereby agree and declare, that in case they cannot make out a good title to, and execute and perfect such conveyances and assurances of the premises as aforesaid, on or before the day of now next ensuing, then the said and every part thereof, shall remain and be a security to the said (*the purchaser*) for securing to him, his the repayment of the said sum of now by him paid as aforesaid, at or upon the said day of now next ensuing, together with interest for the same after the rate of from henceforth in the mean time and until payment thereof, which interest in such case they the said (*the purchasers*) do hereby for themselves, severally and respectively, and for their several and respective heirs, promise and agree to pay accordingly, and then, also, in such case all such rents, as he the said (*the purchaser*) shall have received, by or out of the premises as aforesaid, shall be deemed and allowed by him in part of payment of the same (*the principal purchase-money*) and interest.

7. That if the other parties do not perform their covenants, the purchaser shall not be obliged to perform his.

And it is mutually agreed and declared to be the true intent and meaning of these presents, that if it shall happen that any of them the said their heirs, shall neglect to perform his or their parts of the covenants and agreements herein contained, that then, and in any such case, the said his heirs, executors, and administrators, or any of them, shall not be hereby obliged to perform his and their covenants herein contained, or any of them, but shall, if he shall think fit, be absolutely discharged from the same.

(14.)

Agreement for the Sale of an Estate by Private Contract.

Articles of Agreement, Made this day of between of and of

The said agrees to sell the said all that with the appurtenances, for the sum of and will, on or before the day of next, on the receipt of the said sum of at the charges of the said execute a proper conveyance thereof, with a covenant of general warranty and against incumbrances, to the said and his heirs and assigns.

And the said agrees, that, on the execution of such conveyance, he will pay the said sum of to the said or his assigns.

And it is further agreed, that the conveyance shall be prepared by and at the expense of the said to the approbation of the respective counsel of the said and and that all taxes and outgoings in respect of the premises in the mean time shall be paid by the said . And it is agreed, that the said shall receive the rents and profits of the premises, from next, to his proper use. And it is agreed, that if the said conveyance shall not be executed, and the purchase-money paid on or before the day of then the said shall pay interest for the same from the same day, unto the said after the rate of *per cent per annum.*

In Witness Whereof,

(*Signatures.*) (*Seals.*)

(15.)

An Agreement to be signed by an Auctioneer, after a Sale by Auction.

I Hereby Acknowledge, That has been this day declared the highest bidder and purchaser of (*describe the real estate*) at the sum of ; and that he has paid into my hands the sum of as a deposit, and in part payment of the purchase-money; and I hereby agree that the vendor shall in all respects fulfil the conditions of sale.*

Witness my hand,

(*Signatures.*) (*Seals.*)

(16.)

An Agreement to be signed by the Purchaser, after a Sale by Auction.

I Hereby Acknowledge, That I have this day purchased by public auction all that (*describe the estate*) for the sum of ; and have paid into the hands of the sum of as a deposit and in part payment of the said purchase-money; and I hereby agree to pay the remaining sum of unto (*the vendor*) at on or before the day of ; and in all other respects, on my part, to fulfil the annexed conditions of sale.

Witness my hand this day of

(*Signatures.*) (*Seals.*)

* It would be well to have the conditions of sale annexed, and refer to them by saying *hereunto annexed.*

(17.)

An Agreement to make an Assignment of a Lease.

Whereas, (*the lessor*) hath by his deed indented, dated, , demised unto the said (*the lessee*) all that to have and to hold to him the said his (*reciting the lease*) as by the said deed indented more fully appears: Now the said for and in consideration of dollars doth hereby for himself, (*his heirs, &c.*) covenant, that he the said before the day of shall and will, at the costs and charges of (*the assignee*), his (*heirs, &c.*) by deed indented, assure, assign, and grant over to the said his (*his heirs, &c.*) the said (*the premises*) and all his estate, right, title, and demand therein: To have and to hold to the said (*the assignee*) his (*heirs, &c.*) during the residue of the said term of years, then to come, of, in, and to the same, by virtue of the said recited indenture, and under the rents, covenants, and agreements therein specified.

(*Signatures.*) (*Seals.*)

(18.)

An Agreement for making a Quantity of Manufactured Articles.

Articles of Agreement between (*the buyer*) of the one part, and of the other part.

The said (*the manufacturer*) for the consideration hereinafter mentioned doth covenant that he will, at his own charge, make for the said (*describe the articles to be made*) of the same quality of materials and goodness, as, and in all other respects according to a pattern agreed between the said parties, , and deliver the same to the said at within months from the date hereof. And the said in consideration thereof, doth covenant to pay to the said at the rate of after months from the delivery of the said as aforesaid. And it is agreed, that if any of the said shall not be made agreeable to the said pattern, and for that reason shall be rejected by the said he the said shall take back such as shall so be refused, and deliver the said the like quantity of the goodness and make, according to the pattern aforesaid.

In Witness

(*Signatures.*) (*Seals.*)

(19.)

Agreement between a Trader and a Book-keeper.

Articles of Agreement between (*the trader*) of and (*the book-keeper*) of . The said agrees that he will, during the term of years from the date hereof, dwell with the said and faithfully keep the books of accounts of the said , and diligently serve the said in such other business as the said shall direct, and shall therein perform the reasonable directions of the said without disclosing the same, or any of his correspondence, or the secrets of his employment or business to any person whatsoever; and shall not correspond with any person corresponding with the said , nor use any traffic or dealing for himself, or any other person, without the consent of the said in writing. And the said further covenants, that he will, during the said term, keep true and perfect accounts for the said , and will not embezzle, waste or destroy any of the goods, moneys, or effects of the said or any of his correspondents; and also that he the said will, from time to time, during the said term, upon request, make and give unto the said his a just and perfect account in writing of all money, which he the said shall receive and pay out, and of all goods and commodities, which he shall, at any time during the said term, receive in or deliver out upon the account of the said , or any of his correspondents, or by the order of the said . And also, that he the said his will pay to the said , his all such sums of money as shall be due upon the foot of every such account. And also that he the said will not deliver forth upon credit any of the goods, merchandise or moneys, of the said or any of his correspondents, to any person or persons whatsoever, without the express consent of the said

And the said (*the trader*) for himself (*and his heirs, &c.*) covenants that he will pay to the said (*the book-keeper*) in consideration of the said services, the yearly sum of in equal payments on the days following, viz., on and will, during the said term, provide for the said sufficient and suitable meat, drink, washing and lodging.

In Witness

(*Signatures.*) (*Seals.*)

(20.)

Agreement for Damages in laying out or altering Road.

Whereas, A road was laid out on the day of A.D. 186 , by and Commissioners of Highways of the Town of in the County of and State of on the application of the requisite number of legal voters residing within three miles of said road, as follows: commencing

which road passes through the land of being known and described as follows, viz.:

Now, therefore, it is hereby agreed between the said Commissioners and the said that the damages sustained by the said by reason of the laying out and opening said road upon his land, hereinbefore described, be liquidated and agreed upon at dollars.

In Witness Whereof, The said Commissioners and the said have hereunto subscribed their names this day of A.D. 186 .

(*Signatures.*) *Commissioners of Highways.*

(21.)

An Agreement between a Person who is Retiring from the Active Part of a Business, and another who is to conduct the same for their Mutual Benefit.

Articles of Agreement Made, entered into, and concluded upon, this day of A.D. , between of of the one part, and of of the other part: Whereas the said hath conducted and managed for some time past the trade or business of the said , and in consideration of the attention and assiduity of the said thereunto, the said is willing to continue the said in the management thereof under the covenants, restrictions, and agreements hereinafter contained; and in consequence thereof, an inventory and appraisement hath been made and taken of the stock, and entered in two receipt-books, one of which is to remain in the custody of each of them, the said parties to these presents, and is subscribed by both of them, and the value of the said stock in the whole, appears to the amount of the sum of : Now these presents witness, that for and in consideration of the covenants and agreements hereinafter contained on the part of the said to be performed, the said for himself, his executors, and administrators, doth hereby covenant, promise, and agree, to and with the said , that it shall and may be lawful to and for the said from time to time, during the term of eleven years, to be computed from the day of the date of these presents, if they the said and shall jointly so long live, to trade with the said stock, and to manage and improve the same, in such manner as to the said under the direction of the said , shall seem meet, upon trust nevertheless, and to the intent and purpose that the said shall and do, by and out of the money which shall arise by sale of any part or parts of the said stock, buy such goods as shall be requisite to keep up and continue the present quality and value thereof, and by and out of the profits which shall arise from the trade and dealing, in the first place yearly and every year, pay the whole rent of the said house and shop, and pay and discharge all taxes which now are, or shall hereafter be, assessed or imposed on him the said or the said on account of the said house and trade, and in the next place to pay to him the said or his assigns, yearly and every year during the said term of eleven years, if they the said and shall so long live, one clear annuity or yearly sum of by equal half-yearly payments, on the day of and the day of without any deduction or abatement whatsoever, and subject thereto, to retain the residue and overplus of the profits which shall arise from his trade and dealing, to and for his own sole use and benefit, as a recompense and satisfaction for his care and trouble in the sale and management of the said stock. And the said in consideration of the premises, and of the covenant and agreement hereinbefore on the part of the said contained, doth for himself, his executors, and administrators, covenant, declare, and agree, that he the said shall and will from time to time, and at all times, for and during the said term of eleven years, if they the said and shall so long jointly live, diligently apply himself to the care and management of the said stock, trade, and business, according to his best skill, abilities, and discretion, and apply and dispose of the money which shall arise from the sale thereof, and all the profits of his trade and dealings, to answer and discharge the trusts hereby reposed in him, in such manner as hereinbefore is directed, declared, or expressed. And also shall and will write true and perfect entries, in proper books of accounts, of all such goods as shall be sold, and of all moneys which shall be paid and received by him, and permit the same, from time to time, to be inspected by him the said or such other person or persons as he shall appoint. And further, that he the said shall not nor will, at any time during the continuance of the said term of eleven years, buy or sell, or in any wise trade or deal in his own name, but in the name only of him the said upon the trusts aforesaid; nor do any act whatsoever, whereby the said stock, or any part thereof, may be attached, or taken in execution. And also that at Christmas next, and so at every succeeding Christmas during the said term of eleven years, or oftener, if thereto required by the said , he the said shall and will take a full account in writing of the said stock, then remaining in the said trade, and of the profits thereof, and deliver the same to the said in order to manifest to him a true state thereof, and of his proceedings in the trade by him carried on therewith. And at the expiration, or other sooner determination, of the said term of eleven years, he the said , his executors or administrators, shall and will deliver up to him the said , his executors or administrators, the stock then remaining for his or their own use and benefit, to the value of the sum of losses by bad debts, decay of goods, and other inevitable casualties excepted.

Witness our hands and seals, this day of in the year 18 .

(*Signatures.*) (*Seals.*)

In Presence of

(22.)

A Brief Building Contract.

Contract for building made this day of one thousand eight hundred and by and between of in the County of and of in the County of Builder .

The said covenant and agrees to and with the said to make, erect, build, and finish, in a good substantial and workmanlike manner, upon situate said to be built agreeable to the draught, plans, explanations or specifications, furnished or to be furnished to said by of good and substantial materials; and to be finished complete on or before the day of And said covenant and agrees to pay to said for the same dollars, as follows:

Security against mechanics, or other lien, is to be furnished by said prior to payment by said

And for the performance of all and every the articles and agreements above mentioned, the said and do hereby bind themselves, their heirs, executors and administrators, each to the other, in the penal sum of dollars, firmly by these presents.

In Witness Whereof, We, the said and have hereunto set our hands the day and year first above written.

(*Signatures.*) (*Seals.*)

Executed and Delivered in Presence of

Contracts for building are among those most frequently made, and also among those which require the utmost care. A specification stating and describing all the things which the parties desire and intend to have done should always accompany the contract; and it is very difficult for persons not accustomed to the work to remember and specify, and properly describe, all the things they propose to have in the building; and all these things should be accurately and precisely stated in the specification. From omissions or errors of this kind, cases and questions are constantly arising. To assist those who have to prepare for themselves or others a contract of this sort, I have given, first, a brief and simple form; I now give a very full and minute form, prepared by a skilful lawyer, and in wide use; and then a full and minute specification for building a block of houses, prepared by a very eminent architect.

(23.)

A Full and Minute Building Contract.

An Agreement, of two parts, made this day of in the year one thousand eight hundred and sixty- by and between part of the first part and

part of the second part.

The said part of the first part, in consideration of the sum of money to be paid by the said part of the second part, as hereinafter mentioned, and the covenants and agreements hereinafter recited, to be kept and performed by the said part of the second part, do for sel and **Covenant, Promise,** and **Agree,** to and with the said part of the second part, that the said part of the first part, shall and will, in a good and workmanlike manner, and according to the best of art and ability, do and perform the following work, and provide materials for the same, that is to say:

The whole of said work is to be performed, and all the said materials furnished, in conformity with the plans and specifications of the same, as made by the ARCHITECT hereby appointed by said part of the second part, which plans and specifications bear even date herewith, and are signed by the parties hereto, and under the superintendence and direction of hereby appointed SUPERINTENDENT and AGENT of the said part of the second part, which plans and specifications are to be considered as forming a part of this agreement, as if herein fully written and drawn.

The said part of the first part further agree that the work aforesaid shall be commenced and be constantly prosecuted, and the materials aforesaid promptly furnished and that all said work shall be completed on or before the day of in the year one thousand eight hundred and sixty- and, furthermore, that no charge of any kind shall be made by the said part of the first part to the said part of the second part, beyond the sum of dollars, unless the said part of the second part, and the said Superintendents, shall alter the aforesaid plans and specifications, in which case the value of such alterations shall be added to the amount to be paid under this contract, or deducted therefrom, as the case may require: it being expressly understood that no extra work of any kind shall be performed, or extra materials furnished, by the said part of the first part, unless first authorized by the said part of the second part, and the said Superintendents, in writing; and that the said part of the second part, and the said Superintendents may, from time to time, make any alterations of, to, and in the said plans and specifications, upon the terms aforesaid.

The said part of the first part, for sel and legal representatives, further promise and agree that insurance shall be effected upon the building as soon as the roof is put on and covered; the amount of said insurance to be for such sum as the said part of the second part, and the said Superintendents shall direct, to be further increased, from time to time, at the direction of the said party of the second part, and the said Superintendents; the policy to be in the name and for the benefit of said part of the second part, or legal representatives, and to be made payable, in case of loss, to for whom it may concern: — each party to this agreement hereby agreeing to pay one-half the cost of such insurance.

The said part of the second part, for sel and legal representatives, in consideration of the materials being provided and the labor done as herein required, and all other of the stipulations, requirements, matters and things herein set forth, being kept and performed by said part of the first part, **Covenant, Promise,** and **Agree,** to and with the said part of the first part: that will well and truly pay, or cause to be paid, unto the said part of the first part, or legal representatives, the sum of dollars, in the manner following: —

It is agreed by and between the parties to this agreement, as follows: —

1st. That for each and every day's delay in the performance and completion of this agreement, or of any extra work under it, after the said day of in the year one thousand eight hundred and , there shall be allowed and paid by said part of the first part, to said part of the second part, or representatives, damages for such delay, if the same shall arise from any act or default on the part of the said part of the first part

2d. That the said part of the first part, or representatives, shall not be delayed in the constant progress of the work under this agreement, or any of the extra work under the same or connected therewith, by said party of the second part, or by his Superintendents or any other contractor employed by the said part of the second part, upon or about the premises; and for each and every day, if any, shall be so delayed, additional day to be allowed to complete the work aforesaid, from and after the day hereinbefore appointed for its entire completion, unless upon the contingency provided for below in the 5th article.

3d. That each and every person employed, by sub-contract or "piece work," by the said part of the first part, in the providing materials or performing labor or works in the fulfilment or execution of this agreement, shall be, in the opinion of the said Superintendents, a suitable, competent, and satisfactory person.

4th. That the said part of the first part shall and will engage and provide, at own cost and expense, during the progress of the works under, and until the completion and fulfilment of this agreement, a thoroughly competent "Foreman of the Works," whose duty it shall be to attend to the general supervision of all matters hereby undertaken by said part of the first part, and also to the correct and exact making, preparing, laying-out, and locating of all patterns, moulds, models, and measurements in, to, for, and upon the works hereby agreed upon, from and in conformity with the said plans and specifications, and according to the direction of said Architects.

5th. That if at any time during the progress of the work the said Superintendents shall find that said work is not carried forward with sufficient rapidity and thoroughness, or that the materials furnished, foreman of the works, sub-contractors or workmen employed by the part of the first part, are unsatisfactory, and insufficient for the completion of the work within the time and in the manner stipulated in the plans and specifications aforesaid, shall give notice of such insufficiency and defects in progress, materials, foreman, sub-contractors, or workmen, to the party of the first part; and if within three days thereinafter such insufficiency and defects are not remedied in a manner satisfactory to —the party of the second part, through the agency of said Superintendents, or otherwise, may enter upon the work, and suspend or discharge said party of the first part, and all employed under him, and carry on and complete the work, by "days' work," or otherwise, as may elect, providing and substituting proper and sufficient materials and workmen; and the expense thereof shall be chargeable to the said party of the first part, and be deducted from any sum which may be due to him on a final settlement; and the opinion of said Superintendents shall be final, and their certificate in writing conclusive evidence between the parties hereto, on all questions and issues arising on or out of this fifth article of this Agreement, subject to the final decision of the referees hereinafter named.

6th. That the said part of the first part shall be solely responsible for any injury or damage sustained by any and all person or persons, or property, during or subsequent to the progress and completion of the works hereby agreed upon, from or by any act or default of the said part of the first part; and shall be responsible over the party of the second part for all costs and damages which said party of the second part may legally incur by reason of such injury or damage; and that the said part of the first part shall give all usual, requisite, and suitable notices to all parties whose estates or premises, being adjoining those upon which the works hereby agreed upon are to be done, may or shall be any way interested in or affected by the performance of said works.

7th. That the said part of the first part shall, from time to time, during the progress of the said works, apply to the said Architects for all needful explanations of the true intent and meaning of the said plans and specifications; and that "working-plans" shall, at the expense of the said part of the second part, be from time to time, and whenever requisite, furnished by the said Architects to the said part of the first part, upon reasonable notice being given to the said Architects that the same are requisite and needful; and further, that the said part of the first part will not and shall not, in the execution, performance, and fulfilment of this agreement, in any way deviate from the entire and exact compliance with, adherence to, and fulfilment of the said plans, "working-plans," and specifications, by reason of any practical difficulty which, in opinion, may or shall arise or occur; unless some such deviation shall, in the opinion and by the certificate of the said Architects, become absolutely necessary and unavoidable, in which case said part of the first part to make such deviation as they may be directed by said Architects.

And Whereas it is the intention of the parties hereto, that the said part of the first part shall bear and pay all the expenses necessary for and incident to the carrying into full and entire execution and completion all the works contemplated in this agreement, it is further understood and agreed by and between the parties to this agreement, that in case any lien or liens for labor or materials shall exist upon the property or estate of the said part of the second part, at the time or times when by the foregoing terms or provisions of this agreement a payment is to be made by the said part of the second part to the said part of the first part, such payment, or such part thereof as shall be equal to not less than double the amount for which such lien or liens shall or can exist, shall not be payable at the said stipulated time or times, notwithstanding any thing to the contrary in this agreement contained; and that the said part of the second part may and shall be well assured that no such liens do or can attach or exist before shall be liable to make either of the said payments.

It is expressly understood by the part of the first part, that all the works described or referred to in the annexed specifications are to be executed by the said part of the first part, whether or not the said works are illustrated by the aforesaid plans and working-drawings; and that said part of the first part to execute all works shown by the aforesaid plans and working-drawings, whether or not said works are described or referred to in the said specifications.

If any apparent discrepancy shall be found to exist between the plans, working-drawings, and the specifications, the decision as to the fair construction of said discrepancy, and of the true intent and meaning of the plans, working-drawings, and specifications, shall be made by the Architects hereinbefore named; and said part of the first part shall provide and execute the said works in accordance with said decision, — with the right of a final decision by the referees hereinafter named, — as a part of the original works undertaken by said part of the first part

And Further Know all Men, That the parties hereto of the first part and of the second part severally, respectively, and mutually, hereby agree to submit, and hereby do submit, each, all, and every demand between them hereinafter arising, if any, concerning the value of any changes of, or omissions in, or additions to, the aforementioned plans or specifications, or concerning the manner of performing or completing the work, or the time or amount of any payment to be made under this agreement, or the quantity or quality of the labor or materials, or both, to be done, furnished, or provided under this agreement, or any other cause or

matter touching the work, the materials, or the damages contemplated, set forth, or referred to, in or by this agreement, or concerning the construction of this agreement, to the determination of
the award of whom, or the award of a majority of whom
being made and reported within year from the time hereinbefore fixed upon for the final completion of this agreement to the Superior Court for the County of the judgment thereof shall be final; and if either of the parties shall neglect to appear before the Arbitrator , after due notice given of the time and place appointed for hearing the parties, the Arbitrator may proceed in absence.

In Witness Whereof, The parties aforesaid have interchangeably set their hands and seals, the day and year first above written, to this and other instrument of like tenor and date.

(*Signatures.*) (*Seals.*)

Executed and Delivered in Presence of

STATE OR COMMONWEALTH OF
COUNTY OF A.D., 18 .

Then the above-named personally appeared and acknowledged the above instrument, by them signed, to be their free act.

Before me,

Justice of the Peace.

(24.)

Specification to be annexed to the Building Contract.

Specifications of Materials to be provided and labor to be performed in the erection, and completion ready for occupancy (excepting plumbing and other water-works, painting, glazing, and piling) a block of houses for to be located on an estate recently purchased by him of on the easterly side of Street in within about 116 feet of the north-east corner of Street and Street. Said houses are to be constructed agreeably to plans prepared by , *Architect*, and under the direction of , acting for and on behalf of said as superintendent of said building.

Description. — The block is to occupy and cover the full width from north to south of said estate, with its north and south ends located on the true boundaries of the estate (measuring about 117 feet in length, and just $45\frac{8}{12}$ feet in width). Said block is to be of four finished stories in height, besides a finished story within the intended French roof proposed to cover the whole structure. A cellar is to be constructed beneath the entire area of the building, and an area in the rear of the same; the latter to be of the form and dimensions indicated upon the drawings referred to. The clear heights of all the stories when finished are to be as follows, to wit: first, second, and third stories each 10 feet; and the French-roof story 9 feet. The cellar is to be 8 feet high in clear of the plastered ceiling and concrete flooring. The top of the flooring of the first story is to be located 3 feet 4 inches above the intended grade of the court-yard designed to be located in front or to the west of the block, as indicated particularly upon the profile drawing of the estate from east to west, forming one of the drawings before referred to; it being fully understood that the contractor for said block is to fill in, grade, and enclose with bank stone-walls, the north and south ends of the front or west yard of said estate, and the north, south, and east (or rear) yard walls of the said block, which walls are to be of the sectional form indicated by drawing of the same, forming one of the sets of drawings referred to.

Memo. — The front or west yard of the block will reach in width to the rear or east wall of a second block of tenement-houses designed to be erected by said Parker upon the front or westerly portion of said estate, but forming no part of the works to be estimated for under the specifications or plans.

Works. — The contractor for the block is at his own proper cost and expense to perform all labor of every kind requisite for its full completion, including all labor necessary for exterior grading, bank-walling, sewerage, flagging and paving, enclosing walls and fences, and for all other matters by these specifications required, and by the plans shown. Said works are to be of the best quality, and are to be performed by first-class workmen only, with the full right reserved to the said superintendent to discharge from the employ of the contractor for said block any workmen not of satisfactory capacity to him. Said works are further to be performed in such manner as to warrant and insure on the part of the contractor the most reliable and thorough construction, warranted in all cases to stand without start or flaw, and, in the case of all wood-work, warranted free from shrinkage, and so to remain. Said works are further to be so done as to progress at such rates of progress as are hereinafter stipulated, not, however, inconsistent with the quality of work required as aforesaid.

Materials. — All materials of every kind requisite for the full and entire completion of the block, together with its exterior adjuncts hereinbefore and hereinafter named, are to be provided at the sole cost of the contractors. Said materials are to be of the several kinds and quality hereinafter recited and described, but when not fully set forth in these plans and specifications, then the kinds to be used are in all cases to be the very best marketable qualities. All materials proposed to be used by them (the contractors) are at all times to be subject to inspection for approval or rejection by said superintendent; and the said superintendent shall be duly notified, and have the full opportunity in case he so elects to examine and inspect all materials before any of the same are delivered at the site of the building; and all materials he shall elect to reject shall be promptly replaced by such other stock as shall be satisfactory to the said superintendent, with the right on the part of the contractor to appeal from the decision of said superintendent to the referees named over the signatures of the owner of the property and the contractor for the block, in the agreement to be by them executed as a part of these presents. All materials designed for the building shall at all times be suitably housed, covered, and protected, including all walls daily on leaving the works. No window-frame or other exterior wood-finish shall be left unprimed more than one day after the same is worked or set. Any work or material damaged in any way during the erection of the building shall be promptly replaced on demand of the superintendent. The premises are not to be considered accessible from Gloucester Place for the passage of men or materials, unless the written consent of the owners of the fee of said place is first obtained. The care and protection of the street (Washington) by day and night is not to be charged upon the contractors for said block; and, for this reason, all the materials of every kind designed to be used therein, must be landed fairly in the rear or to the west of the contemplated second or front block, with the right of passage, however, through the centre opening in said second or front block, for materials, and men engaged in the construction of said rear block.

Basement and Yard Drainage. — (See detailed plans of drains, cesspools, and aqueducts.) Three main drains of 16 inches clear diameter are to start from the three rear-yard cesspools, at proper levels of being wholly below basement-story flooring. These drains are to pass directly into and under the front yard of the block, after passing and connecting with three cesspools to be located on the basement-story centre passageway under same, and in the said yard. They are to enter a single drain of two feet clear diameter; which drain the contractor for this block is to build through and under the archway of the contemplated front block of buildings, at proper levels, and with sure pitch, to connect with the Washington-street sewer in front of said Parker estate; which said connection is to be fully and legally made with said city sewer. But the cost of right to enter, including right to run plumbing works therein, will be arranged for and paid by said Parker. In addition to the three drains through the block aforesaid, there are to be branch-drains from the soil pipes of all water-closets, of 12 inches clear diameter each; and these drains are all to enter the principal drains aforesaid to the west or outside of the three cellar cesspools before referred to; and all other waste-pipes of sinks are to enter said drains to the east or inside of these basement-story cesspools. Eight aqueducts are to be laid from the shoes of the eight roof-conductors, and five others from the bottom of the five stone staircases outside of the basement. Three aqueducts may be square, but are to be fully six inches clear each way and are to be covered with 1½ inch slate stones (not brick); and said aqueducts are to have full fall, workmanlike and endurable connections, with the other drains, all of which connections shall be in such localities as to make sure that no "soil" odor can "blow up" through the aqueducts into conductors or into areas at the foot of the several basement steps aforesaid.

Memo. — The paving of the yards and that of the centre passageways inside of basement story is to pitch toward the several cesspools properly and regularly on inclines.

Memo. — Every wall and pier and wooden partition of basement story is to be lime-whitewashed (three heavy coats by an experienced expert). Proper aqueducts in brick are to be laid for Cochituate mains and metres, and for gas ditto ditto so far as the same may be required by superintendent to insure workmanlike construction for "entering" these matters from such points in the front yard of the block as the water and gas company bring same.

The two north and south boundaries of the front yard and three boundaries of the rear yard, excepting across the rear end of Gloucester Place, are to be fully enclosed with 12 inch brick walls resting on the copings of the several bank-walls, above which level (taken to be the front-yard level of the block), said walls are to be ten feet high. Said walls are to have in connection therewith buttresses of 8 by 16 inches each, from inside face of each wall; and the walls and the buttresses are to be capped with granite coping of 2 inches more width than the buttresses and walls, 4 inches thickness at the edges, and 9 inches in centre, and to be straight and well tooled, and cramped on under side, each piece to the other — all which cramps are to pass down into the walls and buttresses. Said coping is to be wholly set in cement, and the whole of the joints flushed with same material. All yard paving is to be wholly in cement, and grouted and bedded in same manner as cellar paving aforesaid.

First Story. Brickwork. — The four exterior walls of this story are each to be 12 inches thick, and the two main, cross, party, subdivision-walls to be of corresponding thickness with the outside walls. The two main corridor walls and those around stairways (three stairways) in this story are to be each 8 inches thick the entire length of the building, reaching fully in all cases to the top of flooring-planks of the second story. The twelve stacks of chimneys indicated on plans of this story are to be built in connection with and made part of the several walls, as shown. Said chimneys are to be commenced as floor-levels of the basement story, upon stone-platform foundations to be made part of the other wall foundations, and built throughout said story with two piers of 20 by 20 inches each, to be covered with a semicircular arch tied with an iron beam bar, and the whole levelled up solid to first floor, with a flue in each chimney of 8 by 12 inches clear, square, and true, and plastered honorably over every square inch of inside surface, thick and heavy. No hearths or open fire-places are intended in chimneys. Water-closet flues, and the single flue of each room in which a chimney exists, is to be fitted with a 7 inch cast iron funnel-piece and stopper of heavy and durable make; but no ventilating-flue is to be provided separate from the single smoke-flue of each apartment. All the said brickwork of the first story is to be laid in lime-mortar of first quality, Eastern stock, using sharp sea-sand only for same. All chimneys to have 8 inch backs and 4 inch withes.

Second and Third Stories. — The exterior walls are all to be continued 12 inches thick, and the chimneys built up in connection therewith in the same manner as before described for first story, with an additional flue of the second and third stories. The two interior, cross, division-walls will be carried through both these stories, but need be only eight inches thick. The two enclosing walls of each of the two end stair-flights in both these stories are to be continued of brick, and of 8 inch thick each. The several window and door openings in all the walls of the three stories above the basement story are to be formed with reliable, arched heads on wooden lintels, and the exterior wall-windows to have full and square returns for window-frames. All frames are to be fitted in solid, and plastered in connection with brickwork. None of the walls are to be recessed beneath the windows. Every floor-plank is to be accurately levelled up, and the brickwork filled solid around it, and the roof-planks also at bottom. The fourth or French-roof story will have the four exterior walls built to top of plates of frame of roof, say 2½ feet above its flooring; and besides this the brickwork of the said four walls is to be continued up entirely to the roof-boarding under the gutter-flashing. The several corner quoins of the front side of the four corner pilasters of the side and the dentil course over the third-story windows of this side are all to be formed of brick; and all of them are to be made outside of the faces of the wall, thereby increasing in thickness as much more than 12 inches as the several matters project.

All chimneys are to be topped out, of one uniform height and one pattern; and this pattern is to be precisely like the detailed drawing to be given.

Memo. — The enclosing walls of the two end staircases are to be carried to roof-boarding of 8 inches thickness each.

Memo. — The 9 nine cesspools hereinbefore referred to are to be 36 inches square in clear of walls; which walls shall be 8 inches thick, with an 8 inch bottom to same, and a four inch cut-off wall on iron bars, across the same. The whole inside to be rendered in hydraulic cement; and the curb and iron-trap strainer aforesaid to be set complete. The whole of the drains and aqueducts are to be most thoroughly rendered in hydraulic cement. The aqueducts may have 4 inch walls; but all the remaining drains shall have 8 inch walls, and shall be Gothic shaped at bottom; and the stone covering of said drains shall not be less than 2 inches thick, with full and square joints: the whole set in hydraulic cement. The walls of the drains shall be laid wholly in hydraulic cement. The contractor shall use all reasonable care that the grounds on which the drains, aqueducts and cesspools to be built, is properly prepared to prevent settlement or start of said works; and, if the superintendent elects on account of the instability of the soil to substitute drain-pipe or plank drains for the brick ones hereinbefore stipulated, the contractor is to make the changes as directed; and all such difference of cost (more or less) as the superintendent elects to be just, shall be accepted by said contractor, and settlement made accordingly. Turn arches over all openings between cellar-piers, and level up to floors. The bricks to be supplied by the contractor are to be as follows, in quality: those for backing exterior walls, and for all interior walls and chimneys, may be of the Boston Brick Co.'s most costly cull; those for the drains and paving and other underground shall be Pilastow's Eastern or Charlestown clay brick, hand-made; the outside courses of the two end-walls and of the rear wall and of the chimney-tops shall be of same hand-made, even-colored, darkened, hard brick of uniform size, straight and true, and jointed-laid; the outside courses of the front wall shall be of a quality of face-brick as good and as fair a quality of Danvers face-brick, to be laid plumb-bond, and properly jointed off. All bricks shall be wet immediately previous to laying same. The contractor assumes all cost of supplying himself with Cochituate for use. The exterior cornices, brackets beneath, and small band mouldings beneath brackets, are all to be of wood, to be constructed and put up by carpenter; but the mason is to build in all brackets, and assist carpenter to space off and lay out same.

Slating. — The two upright sides of the roof are to be covered with 16 inch slates, Welsh; the whole to be of first quality, and agreeable to a sample which the superintendent will select, and submit to bidders before estimating. Said slates are to be put on with 2½ inch lap (full), and to be truly bonded, to break joints in centres to be put on with the heaviest quality of composition (not galvanized) nails. The chimney-tops; sides, tops, and sills of luthern windows; angle-corners of roof; top of upper wood-finish of roof; skylights; scuttle; scuttle over centre staircase, or near it; as also all other required places, — are to be flashed with 10 oz. zinc and 4 lb. lead where the superintendent calls for the same; and the contractor for the slating is to be held responsible that furnishes and applies flashing-stock amply sufficient to insure an extra, first-class, tight, and permanent job, with every piece of stock cut and fitted and secured of such sizes and shapes as the superintendent, if he elects so to do, may direct.

Memo. — The slates of the front side of roof to have semicircular ends.

Gutters and Conductors. — The front and rear walls of the block, including the four heads or returns on the two ends of the block, are to be fitted with 20 oz., best-quality sheet-copper to be of cima recta pattern, and made exactly in accordance with a full-size drawing to be given. This gutter is to be seated on to wood coving or casing of main cornice; and there is to be a back flashing from the inner edge of said gutter, on its top, of same quality and 16 oz. weight of copper, passing up beneath slating 8 inches, and passing under sills of each luthern window, and up to inside face to its top, and there turned on and secured with all suitable bends and heads of copper on each side of the lutherns, as well as over their entire top-surface or roof. The skylight-hatches, and that of the scuttle in flat of main roof, must be covered with 16 oz. copper also, and the whole made everywhere tight and secure and workmanlike. There are to be eight conductors of cold and rolled copper, of 16 oz. to the foot, put up, and firmly secured to the outside faces of the four exterior walls. Said conductors are to be connected with the gutters above by massive goose-necks most substantially soldered and secured, and of proper diameter; and the fifteen feet of said conductor, together with the shoes and underground lengths necessary for reaching and fully entering the aqueduct of brick, are to be made of the heaviest pattern of cast-iron, to be strongly connected with the four exterior walls, as to resist the most possible abuse that *boys* can bring to bear on the said pipes.

Plastering. — The walls, ceilings, and partitions of each of the four finished stories of the building, throughout every apartment, passageway, stairway, corridor, and hall, and including all closets and water-closets, are to be lathed on wood furring for five nailings, with sound, dry, pine-laths, free from sap and other defects, and secured with heavy 3d penny nails. The laths to be universally a full quarter of an inch apart. The ceilings of the cellar to be lathed for plastering throughout. Each floor of the four finished stories is to be plastered between upper and under with a heavy coat, $\frac{3}{4}$ inch thick, of lime and hair mortar. All other plastering is to be done two coats, — one of lime and hair mortar, and the second a skim coat of lime and sand putty. All other plastering is to be done two coats, — one of lime and hair mortar, and the second a skim coat of lime and sand putty; forming the first quality of two-coat work, as usually understood in best houses, as the walls are not to be papered. The ceilings and walls both are to be finished of entire uniform shade of plastering, without staging-streaks, or break-offs in any place. No cornices or centre-pieces are required. The contractor shall do the usual and fair amount of patching after carpenters have finished, without charge to owner of the building. The risk of the plastering being touched by frost, if work of building is delayed, rests with the plasterer wholly.

Miscellaneous. — Mason. In both parlor and kitchen of each tenement, there is to be a red slate-stone mantel, to be supported by two iron bronzed brackets of some neat pattern, the whole to be selected and approved by the superintendent. The mason is to include the paving of the whole area of the yard in front of the block up to the rear line of the contemplated front block of houses; and said paving is to be done in cement, like that hereinbefore required.

Carpentry. — The carpenter is to be equally responsible with the mason that all parts of the building are correctly laid out, from the several plans by the architect; and he is, in consultation with the superintendent and mason, to arrange all details and portions of construction in ample season for them all to be applied correctly to the buildings. He is also at his own cost to prepare all centres, not only for windows and openings, but also for drains. He is also to make all necessary poles and rods as guides for laying out all works. He is to make skeleton frames, and set the same, for all openings in walls. He is to cover all freestone and granite projections, including doorways, and water-table of underpinning. He is to safely shore all floors, under all such points as the superintendent directs, while the skeleton of the structure is in progress. He is to make one set of patterns from the full-size drawings of all freestone, moulded, and arch work. His works are to embrace all branches of trades hereinbefore stipulated under the head of work and labor and materials, it being understood that in connection with the contractor for the masonry, the buildings are to be left in a completed state, ready for occupancy, excepting only metal-works of the plumbing. No furnaces, fireplaces, grates, stoves, or heating-apparatus of any kind, being intended to be required of the contractors, saving only chimneys, funnel pieces, and stoppers.

No papering is to be required of contractors; and no gas piping or fixtures is to be embraced in the estimates of contractors. Such of the water-closet ventilators as are required of wood are to be constructed and topped out, and otherwise fully put up and completed, precisely as superintendent says.

Framing. — To provide the first marketable quality of Eastern spruce stock, and frame, put on, and otherwise fully complete, the floors of the first, second, third, and fourth stories, with planks of 2 by 12 inches, to be placed as indicated by flooring-plans; spanning in all cases from the front and rear exterior walls on to the corridor-walls, which run through the centre of the length of the entire building. Each floor is to contain headers and trimmers of 4 by 12 inches wherever indicated by the plans, excepting those for enclosing staircases, which are, in all the floors, to be 6 by 12 inches. The planks in all the floors over the centre corridor may be 2 by 9 inches only. The first floor will contain girders of 7 by 10 inches, to be located in the position indicated by the flooring-plan of that story. These girders are to be of the soundest white pine, of last year's growth, and last year's delivery in Boston, and not in water for the last six months at least. These girders are to be worked square and true, and are to rest on the exterior walls and interior piers. Each flooring is to have four full rows of diagonal bridging of inch-board pieces 3 inches in width and 1 inch thick, to be accurately cut in, and nailed with twelvepennies. The whole of the flooring-planks are to rest just one full half-brick in length of bearing on walls, and four inches full on the corridor walls and partitions; and the same of the headers and trimmers in each floor. All headers and trimmers are to be mortised and tenoned and oak-pinned, and those of the stairways are to have wrought-iron stirrup-straps of 2 by $\frac{3}{8}$ inch iron. The upper and under edges of every flooring-plank is to be worked by a plane to a regular crown of $\frac{3}{4}$ of an inch in their length. There shall be twelve wrought-iron ties attached to the trimmers of each floor in the position the superintendent shall say; and all these ties are to go to, and be "upset" in, the exterior walls to within 4 inches of the outer face of each wall. Each tie to be $3\frac{1}{2}$ feet long, of $\frac{7}{8}$ inch round iron, in addition to the length required for "upsetting" the two ends.

The roof to be framed with its two upright, angular sides of plank 3 by 9 inches, to be placed only 18 inches apart on centres. Said planks are to be footed, and securely spiked to wall-plates of 3 by 10 inches; which plates are to be bedded on and bolted to the exterior walls by bolts being built in for the height of 5 feet in said walls once in every 15 feet length thereof. The tops of the aforesaid rafters are to be headed into a border-stick, which is to extend the entire length of the two sides of the block, and is to measure 5 by 9 inches; being properly framed (not merely spiked) on to the rafters. This border-piece and the heads of the two main corridor-partitions are to form supports for the two ends of the planks designed to form the top or flat portion of the roof. Said planks are to be fully 3 by 12 inches, to be placed only 8 inches apart on centres, and bridged precisely like the floors aforesaid by with one row only on each side of the corridor-partitions. The roof-stock is all to be as dry and as perfect as that for the floors aforesaid; and the upper edges on outer edges of all the planks are to be worked true with plane, and those in the flat to be crowned regular 1 inch in their length. Every part of the framing of floors and roof is to be so mortised, tenoned, spiked, nailed, stayed, and otherwise finished and secured, as to make, not only a first-class, workmanlike job, but one to be warranted free from start or tremble, and permanently so to remain. On each side of each luthern window, there is to be a stud of 3 by 6 inches, with a head-piece of same size at top of window; and these six studs are designed to go perpendicularly down to the top of the roof-story flooring, just down the exterior walls, and there to foot on a plank which is to run the whole length of the building; which plank, as well as the side-studs and head-piece, are all to be firmly spiked and secured.

Furring and Partitions. — The brick walls, ceilings, and stairway throughout the four finished stories, are to be furred with 3 by 1 inch dry spruce furrings, set to give five nailings to a lath. They are to be put on the walls with twelvepenny nails, and on the ceilings with tenpennies. Grounds $\frac{3}{4}$ of an inch thick are to be put up for all finish, and $\frac{3}{4}$ inch beads for the angles of the walls and stairways.

The partitions, except those which are brick, are to be framed with sound, seasoned spruce lumber; the studs to be 2 by 4 inches; door studs and girths, and window studs and girths, 3 by 4 inches; plates 3 by 4; and sills 2 by 4 inches: all to be thoroughly bridged with cross bridging, and to be braced over the doors and windows.

All of the above work is to be done in the most thorough manner, and, when ready for the plastering, is to be plumb, square, and straight.

Memo. — The caps and sills of every partition in every story are to be seasoned Southern pine, properly fitted and secured.

Tinning. — The dormer-window roofs, and the upper portion or flat of the main roof, are to be covered with best quality of charcoal-leaded, of first quality MF brand roofing-tin; to be laid, lapped, soldered, and secured in the most thorough manner, and warranted a first-class and permanently-tight job throughout.

Rough Boarding. — The roofs are to be boarded, and the under-floors to be laid with sound, seasoned white-pine boards, matched and mill-planed; laid close, and thoroughly nailed; and those to the slated portion of the roof are to be covered with the best quality of tarred sheathing-paper.

Outside Finish. — The dormer-windows, cornices, brackets, and small band-mouldings beneath them, are to be wrought of thoroughly-seasoned, clear, white-pine stock, in the forms shown by the drawings; and they are to be thoroughly secured to the brickwork where they come in contact with it.

The doorway is to be framed with 2 by 4 inch studs, and 2 by 6 inch rafters, and is to be boarded with matched and mill-planed pine covering-boards, and covered with tin, like the roof. It is to have a rebated plank door-jamb, 4 inch outside and inside casings, and a white-pine door with four plain panels. The door is to be 2 inches thick, hung with stout, loose butt-hinges, and fitted with a good lock, inside bolts, and neat and durable trimmings.

Windows. — All the windows inside and out, excepting those in the cellar, are to have box-frames with 2 inch sills and yokes, and 1 inch inside, outside, and back casings; and staff-beads of white pine for those in the brick walls; but no back casings or staff-beads for those in the wooden partitions. They are to have 1 inch pulley-stiles, $\frac{5}{8}$ inch inside, and $\frac{3}{8}$ inch parting beads of hard pine.

Each of the above windows is to be fitted with two $1\frac{3}{4}$ inch white-pine sashes, moulded and coped. The lower sashes in the inside of partition-windows are to be firmly secured to the frames; the upper sashes in the said windows, and both sashes in each of the other windows, are to be hung with best flax sash-lines, steel axle-pulleys, and round iron counter-weights, and fitted with bronze sash-fastenings, to cost $7 per dozen. They are to have pockets neatly cut into the pulley-stiles, and secured by brass screws. Each window is to be cased as shown by the drawings, and finished with moulded stools and moulded architraves, as therein represented. The upper sash of each and every window in all the halls and staircases is invariably to be hung and fastened.

The cellar-windows are to have white-pine rebated plank frames, and a single sash each. The sashes to be hung with stout iron hinges, and fitted with neat and durable buttons and catches.

The skylight frames are to be of thoroughly-seasoned, clear, white-pine stock, rebated for the sashes, put together with white lead, and finished off in a neat and durable manner.

Doors. — All the doors are to be made of thoroughly-seasoned, clear, white-pine stock; the outside doors to both front and rear being 2 inches thick, the principal doors in the rooms and entries $1\frac{3}{4}$, and the closet doors $1\frac{1}{2}$ inches thick. The outside doors are to be made in the forms shown on the drawings; are to be hung with three sets of 5 inch, ornamental, bronzed, loose, butt-hinges, and fitted with locks, bolts, and trimmings, to be selected by the superintendent, and to cost for such locks, bolts, and trimmings, the sum of $6 exclusive of the cost of putting on. The basement doors are to have locks, trimmings, bolts, and loose butt-hinges, to cost $5 to each door. The doors to the entries, rooms, and closets, are to have four moulded panels to each, and are to be of the sizes marked on the plans. All are to be hung with stout, iron, loose butt-hinges. Those for the storerooms, pantries between the different rooms, and the entry doors, are to have locks and trimmings to cost $5 to each door, on the average. The doors to the bedrooms, closets and to the water-closets, are to have mortised spring-latches with knobs, &c., to correspond to those to the other doors; and each water-closet is to be fitted with an inside brass bolt, neat and durable. The doors to the coal-bins are to be made of matched and mill-planed white-pine stock, battened; are to be hung with stout strap-hinges; and each is to be fitted with a

The fly-doors of the vestibule are to be $1\frac{1}{2}$ inches thick, with plain panels. They are to be hung with loose butts, double-action springs of a satisfactory quality, brass bolts to the top and bottom of one half, and a lock to the other half. This door, or the outside door, at the option of the superintendent, is to have a lever night-lock of good quality, with fifty (50) keys.

The inside doors are to be finished with hard-pine thresholds, 2 inch rebated and beaded frames of white pine, and architraves to correspond with the window-finish in the various parts of the building.

The outside doors are to be hung to 3 inch plank frames, properly dogged to the thresholds; and jambs finished inside like the inside door, and outside with staff-moulding.

Blinds. — Each window (excepting those in the basement and French roof) on the exterior of the building is to have a pair of $1\frac{1}{4}$ inch mortised slat-blinds, made with rebated and beaded stiles, and three rails to each. They are to be hung with the best quality of blind-hinges, and fitted with satisfactory fastenings.

Stairs. — The stairs are to be framed with deep spruce-plank stringers and landings and winders, as shown on the drawings. They are to have white-pine string and gallery finish, hard-pine risers, treads, and balusters. The balusters to be round, and $1\frac{1}{8}$ inches in diameter. The posts are to be 10 inches square, and the newels 5 inches. They are to be moulded and capped, and the post panelled as per drawings. The rail is to be $3\frac{1}{2}$ inches in width, and of a satisfactory pattern. The posts, rails, and newels are to be of thoroughly-seasoned black walnut; and the rails are to be not less than 3 feet high. The stairs to the cellar are to be framed with plank stringers, and to be finished with planed pine-plank risers, and hard-pine treads, and plank hand-rails and supporters.

Dado and Inside Finish. — The walls of the entries throughout the four finished stories, and of the kitchens and water-closets throughout the building, are to be dadoed to the height of $3\frac{1}{2}$ feet above the floor with narrow matched and beaded white-pine sheathing finished with a moulded capping of the form of the stool nosing.

The walls of the parlors and bedrooms are to have moulded bases 10 inches high, and $1\frac{1}{4}$ inches thick. The other walls are to have levelled bases 8 inches high, and $\frac{7}{8}$ of an inch thick.

The water-closets are to be finished off with black-walnut stock, the covers and seats being hung to raise, and all woodwork being put up with brass screws. Ventilating boxes or flues of brick are to be made for the water-closets where indicated by the drawings, carried out through the roof, and finished in a neat and durable manner.

All the inside woodwork not otherwise specified is to be wrought of thoroughly-seasoned, clear, white-pine stock, free from shakes and sap, and put in in the best and most workmanlike manner.

Closets. — Each pantry and china-closet is to be fitted with a case of four drawers made in a neat and substantial manner. One set of drawers in each tenement to have strong tumbler-locks, and each drawer to have two drawer-pulls.

These closets are to have shelves and cupboards as directed, and each is to have cleats of cast-iron (single) hooks.

The bedroom closets are to have cleats of double cast-iron clothes-hooks placed 6 inches apart on three walls of each, and are to be shelved round over the clothes-hooks. The cupboards above mentioned are to have brass thumb-slides, strong tumbler-locks and drawer-pulls.

Floors. — The floors to the halls and corridors are to be laid with thoroughly-seasoned, clear, hard-pine stock, not exceeding 5 inches in width, laid close, and thoroughly nailed and smoothed. All the other floors in the four finished stories are to be laid with thoroughly-seasoned, kiln-dried, spruce floorings, selected for clearness and soundness. They are not to exceed 6 inches in width, and are to be laid close, thoroughly nailed and smoothed, and put down as soon as taken from the dry-house.

Sinks. — Each kitchen is to have soapstone set in a pine-plank frame. The sinks are to be 3 feet long, and 1 foot high, and 18 inches wide inside, and are to be finished beneath in a neat and durable manner, with cupboards. They are to be backed up with pine, and fitted to receive the plumbing. Each sink is to have a composition cesspool.

Coal-Bins. — There are to be coal-bins finished off in the cellars, one for each tenement. Each bin is to be fitted inside the door with two separate compartments capable of holding 1 ton of coal to each compartment, and with another to take 2 barrels of kindlings. The exterior woodwork is to be of pine, mill-planed, and the interior partitions of spruce; these latter being fitted with sliding gates, and boxings around them to keep the coal from the floor. All the above work is to be done in the most thorough and workmanlike manner.

Bells. — The outside door to each tenement is to be fitted with a bell leading to the kitchen. It is to have a handle to correspond with the door-knobs. Each tenement is to have a bell to the porter's room, fitted with a bronze slide. All the above are to be gong-bells with tubed wires, and put in the most perfect manner.

CHAPTER VII.

CONSIDERATION.

SECTION I.

THE NEED OF A CONSIDERATION.

It is an ancient and well-established rule of the common law prevailing in this country, that no promise can be enforced at law, unless it rests upon a *consideration;* by which word is meant a cause or reason for the promise. If it do not, it is called *a naked bargain*, and the promisor, even if he admits his promise, is under no legal obligation to perform a promise that he made without a *consideration.*

There are two exceptions to this rule. One is when the promise is made by a sealed instrument, or deed; (every written instrument which is sealed is a deed.) Here the law is said to imply a consideration; the meaning of which is that it does not require that any consideration should be proved. The seal itself is said to be a consideration, or to import a consideration.

The second exception relates to negotiable paper; and is an instance in which the law-merchant has materially qualified the common law. We shall speak more fully of this exception when we treat of negotiable paper.

The word "consideration," as it is used in this rule, has a peculiar and technical meaning. It denotes some *substantial* cause for the promise. This cause must be one of two things; either a benefit to the promisor, or else an injury or loss to the promisee sustained by him at the instance and request of the promisor. Thus, if A promises B to pay him a thousand dollars in three months, and even promises this in writing, the promise is worthless in law, if A makes it as a merely voluntary promise, without a consideration. But if B, or anybody for him, gives to A to-day a thousand dollars in goods or money, and this was the ground and cause of the promise, then it is enforceable. And if A got nothing for his promise, but B, at the request of A, gave the same goods or money to C, this would be an equally good consideration, and the promise to pay B would be equally valid in law.

This requirement of a consideration sometimes operates harshly and unjustly, and permits promisors to break their word under circumstances calling strongly for its fulfilment. Courts have been led, perhaps, by this, to say that the consideration is sufficient if it be a substantial one, although it be not an adequate one. This is the unquestionable rule now, and it is sometimes carried very far. In one case an American court refused to inquire into the *adequacy* of the consideration, — or whether it was *equal* to the promise *made* upon it, — and said, if there was the *smallest spark* of consideration it was enough, if the contract was fairly made with a full understanding of all the material facts. Still, there must be some consideration.

SECTION II.

WHAT IS A SUFFICIENT CONSIDERATION.

THE law detests litigation; at least courts say so; and therefore they consider any thing a sufficient consideration which arrests and suspends or terminates litigation. Thus the compromise, or forbearance, or mutual reference to arbitration, or any similar settlement, of a suit, or of a claim, is a good consideration for a promise founded upon it. And it is no defence to a suit on this promise, to show that the claim or suit thus disposed of would probably have been found to have no foundation or substance. If there be an honest claim, which he who advances it believes to be well grounded, and which within a rational possibility may be so, this is enough; the court will not go on and try the validity of the claim or of the suit in order to test the validity of a promise which rests upon its settlement; for the very purpose for which it favors this settlement is the avoidance of all necessity of investigating the claim by litigation. But for reasons of public policy, no promise can be enforced of which the consideration was the discontinuance of criminal proceedings; or any conduct by which public interests are harmed, as, for example, the procurement of the passage of a law by corrupt means.

If any work or service is rendered to one, or for one, and he requested the same, it is a good consideration for a promise of payment; and if he makes no promise, the law will imply the promise, that is, will suppose that he has made it, and will not permit him to deny it. The rule is the same as to payment for goods, or property of any kind, delivered to any one at his request.

No person can make another his debtor against that other's will, by a voluntary offer of work, or service, or money, or goods. But if that other accept what is thus offered, and retain the benefit of it, the law will, generally, imply or presume that it was offered at the request of that other party, and will also imply his promise to pay for it, and will enforce the promise; unless it is apparent, or is shown, that it was offered and received as a mere gift.

A promise is a good consideration for a promise; and it is one which frequently occurs in fact.

If A says to B, "If you will deliver goods to C, I will pay for them," although there is no obligation upon B to deliver the goods, if he does deliver them, he furnishes a consideration for the agreement, and may enforce it against A.

An agreement by two or more parties to refer disputes or claims between them to arbitration, is not binding upon any of the parties unless all have entered into it.

The principle, that a promise is a good consideration for a promise, has been sometimes applied to subscription-papers; all who sign them being held on the ground that the promise of each is a good consideration for the promises of the rest. The law on the subject of these subscription-papers, and of all voluntary promises of contribution, is substantially this: no such promises are binding, unless something is paid for them, or unless some party for whose benefit they are made, — and this party may be one or more of the subscribers, — at the request, express or implied, of the promisors, and on the faith of the subscriptions, incurs actual expense or loss, or enters into valid contracts with other parties which will occasion expense, or loss. As the objection to these promises or the doubt about them, comes from the want of consideration, it may be cured by a seal to each name, or by one seal which all the parties consider the seal of each.

It is to be regretted that the law does not regard a merely moral consideration as a sufficient legal consideration ; but so it is. Thus, it has been held in this country, that a note given by a father to a party who had given needful medicines, food, and shelter to his sick son, who was of full age, was void in law, because there was no legal consideration. And the same doctrine was applied where a son made a similar promise for food and support to his aged father. If, in either case, the promise had been made *before* the food or other articles were supplied, or even a request made *before* the supply, then the supply of the food and support would have been a good consideration. But they had all been supplied before any request or promise, and nothing was left but the moral obligation of a father to compensate one who had supported his son, or of a son to support his father ; and this the law does not deem sufficient to make even an express promise enforceable at law.

SECTION III.

AN ILLEGAL CONSIDERATION.

If the whole of a consideration, or if any part of the consideration of an entire and indivisible promise, be illegal, the promise founded upon it is void. Thus, where a note was given in part for the compounding of penalties and suppressing of criminal prosecutions, it was held to be wholly void and uncollectable. And where a part of the consideration of a note was spirituous liquors, sold by the payee in violation of a Statute, such note was held to be wholly void. But if the consideration consists of separable parts, and the promise consists of corresponding separable parts, which can be apportioned and applied, part to part, then each illegality will affect only the promise resting on it; for in fact there are many considerations and many promises.

If the consideration be entire and wholly legal, and the promise consists of separable parts, one legal and the other illegal, the promisee can enforce that part which is legal.

SECTION IV.

AN IMPOSSIBLE CONSIDERATION.

No contract or promise can be enforced by him who knew that the performance of it was wholly impossible; and therefore a consideration which is obviously and certainly impossible is not sufficient in law to sustain a promise. But if one makes a promise, he cannot always defend himself when sued for non-performance by showing that performance was impossible; for it may be his own fault, or his personal misfortune, that he cannot perform it. He had no right to make such a promise, and must answer in damages; or if he had a right to make it in the expectation of performance, and this has become impossible subsequently, — as by loss of property, for example, — this is his misfortune, and no answer to a suit on the promise. There are, however, obviously, promises or contracts, which, from their very nature, must be construed as if the promisor had said, "I will do so and so, if I can." For example, if A promises to work for B one year, at $20 a month, and at the end of six months is wholly disabled by sickness, he is not liable to an action by B for breach of his contract; and he can recover his pay for the time that he has spent in B's service. A mere want of money, which makes a pecuniary impossibility, is not regarded by the law as a legal impossibility.

SECTION V.

FAILURE OF CONSIDERATION.

If a promise be made upon a consideration which is apparently valuable and sufficient, but which turns out to be nothing; or if the consideration was originally good, but becomes wholly valueless before part performance on either side, there is an end of the contract, and the promise cannot be enforced. And if money were paid on such a consideration, it can be recovered back. But only the sum paid can be so recovered, without any increase or addition as compensation for the plaintiff's loss and disappointment, unless there were fraud or oppression.

If the failure of consideration be partial only, leaving a substantial, though far less valuable, consideration behind, this may still be a sufficient foundation for the promise, if that be entire. The promisor may then be sued on the promise; but he will then be entitled, by deduction, set-off, or in some other proper way, to due allowance or indemnity for whatever loss he may sustain as to the other parts of the bargain, or as to the whole transaction, from the partial failure of the consideration. Thus, if he promised so much money for work done in such a way, or as the price of a thing to be made and sold to him, if no work is done, or the thing is not made or sold, there is an end of the promise, because the consideration has failed. But if the work was done, but not as it should have been, or the thing made and sold, but not what it should have been, and the promisor accepted the work or the thing, he may now show that the consideration for his promise has partially failed, and may have a proportionate reduction in his promise, or in the amount he must pay. And if the promise be itself separable into parts, and a distinct part or proportion of the consideration failed, to which part some distinct part or proportion of the promise could be applied, that part of the promise cannot be enforced, although the residue of the promise may be.

If A agrees with B to work for him one year, or any stated time, for so much a month, or so much for the whole time, and, after working a part of the time, leaves B without good cause, it is the ancient and still prevailing rule, that A can recover nothing in any form or way. It has, however, been held in New Hampshire, that A can still recover whatever his services are worth, B having the right to set off or deduct the amount of any damage he may have sustained from A's breach of the contract. This view seems just and reasonable, although it has not been supported by adjudication in other States. If A agrees to sell to B five hundred barrels of flour at a certain price, and, after delivering one-half, refuses to deliver any more, B can certainly return that half, and pay A nothing. But if B chooses to retain that half, or if he has so disposed of or lost it that he cannot return it, he must pay what it is worth, deducting all that he loses by the breach of the contract. And this case we think analogous to that of a broken contract of service; but B's liability to pay, even in the case supposed as to goods, has been denied by some courts.

A difficulty sometimes arises where A, at the request of B, undertakes to do something for B, for which he is to be paid a certain price; and in doing it he departs materially from the directions of B and from his own undertaking. What are now the rights of the parties? This question arises most frequently in building-contracts, in which there is usually some departure from the original undertaking. The general rules are these. If B assent to the alteration, it is the same thing as if it were a part of the original contract. He may assent expressly, by word or in writing; or constructively, by seeing the work, and approving it as it goes on, or being silent; for silence under such circumstances would generally be equivalent to an approval. But if the change be one which B had a right, either from the nature of the change, or the appearance of it, or A's language respecting it, to suppose would add nothing to the cost, then no promise to pay an increased price would be inferred from either an express or tacit approval. Generally, as we have seen, if A does or makes what B did not order or request, B can refuse to accept it, and, if he refuses, will not then be held to pay for it. But if he accepts it, he must pay for it. This consequence results, however, only from a voluntary acceptance. For if A choose, without any request from B, to add something to B's house, or make some alteration in it, which being done cannot be undone or taken away without detriment to the house, B may hold it, and yet not be liable to pay for it; and A has no right to take it away, unless he can do so without inflicting any injury whatever on B. This rule would apply whether the addition or alteration were larger or smaller.

It is sometimes provided in building-contracts that B shall pay for no alteration or addition, unless previously ordered by him in writing. But if there be such provision, B would be liable for any alteration or addition he ordered in any way, or voluntarily accepted after it was made, when he could have rejected it.

So it is sometimes agreed that any additions or alterations shall be paid for at the same rate as the work contracted for. The law would imply this agreement if the parties did not make it expressly.

CHAPTER VIII.

BONDS.

A BARGAIN where both parties make promises, and come under obligations, each to the other, may be made without seal, and would then be called an Agreement. If made under seal, it would generally be in the form of, and bear the name of, an Indenture. If a promise by one only, is made in writing, without a seal, it is a simple promise; but if it be made with a seal, then it would generally be in the form of, and bear the name of, a BOND.

The essentials of a bond are only that one party should acknowledge himself "held, bound, and obliged" unto another party, to pay to him a sum of money; and neither of the words "held," or "bound," or "obliged," are strictly necessary, although usual and proper: other words of the same meaning will have the same effect. In such a bond, the party bound is called the *obligor*, and the party to whom he is bound is called the *obligee.* The sum for which the obligor is bound is called the penal sum, or the *penalty.* Such a bond is simply an obligation to pay so much money. But a bond is not often given only for this purpose. It is usually intended to be, in fact, an obligation to do something else, *on the penalty* of paying so much money if it be not done. This something else may be any thing whatever which the obligor may contract to do. All this is contained in an addition, which is written on the same paper immediately after the bond itself; that is, after the words of obligation. And this is called the "Condition" of the bond. It begins with saying, This bond is on the condition following; and then recites the things which the obligor has undertaken to do; and then adds, that if all these things are fully done and performed, then the bond shall be void and of no effect, and otherwise shall remain in full force.

The meaning and effect of all this is, that if the obligor fails, in any respect, to do what the condition recites, then he is bound to pay the money he acknowledges himself, in the bond, bound to pay. But now the law comes in to mitigate the severity of this contract. And whatever be the sum which the obligor acknowledges himself, in the bond, bound to pay, he is held by the courts to pay to the obligee only that amount which will be a complete indemnification to him for the damage he has sustained by the failure of the obligor to do what the condition recites.

For example; suppose A B makes a bond to C D, acknowledging himself bound to C D in the sum of ten thousand dollars. The condition recites that one E F has been hired by C D as his clerk, and that A B guarantees the good conduct of E F; and if E F does all his duty honestly and faithfully, then the bond is void, and otherwise remains in full force. Then suppose E F to cheat C D out of some money. A B is sued on the bond; C D cannot recover from him, in any event, *more* than the ten thousand dollars; and he will in fact recover from him only so much of this as will make good to C D all the loss he has sustained by E F's misconduct. As the obligee can recover from the obligor only actual compensation for what he loses, it is usual, in practice, to make the penal sum in the bond large enough to cover all the loss that can happen.

There need be no "consideration," alleged or asserted in the bond, or proved, because, in the language of the law, the seal is (or implies) a consideration.

The following forms are those of bonds frequently given; and it will be easy to frame from some one of them any bond that is wanted for other purposes.

(25.)

A Simple Bond, without Condition.

Know all Men by these Presents, That I (*the obligor*) am held and firmly bound unto (*the obligee*) in the sum of lawful money of the United States of America, to be paid to the said or his certain attorney, or assigns: to which payment well and truly to be made, I bind myself, my heirs, executors and administrators, firmly by these presents. Sealed with my seal Dated the day of in the year of our Lord one thousand eight hundred and .

In Testimony Whereof, I have set my hand and seal to this instrument, on the day of , in the year of our Lord eighteen hundred and .

(*Witnesses.*) (*Signature.*) (*Seal.*)

Executed and Delivered in Presence of

(26.)

Bond for Payment of Money, with a Condition to that Effect, with Power of Attorney to confess Judgment annexed.

Know all Men by these Presents, That held and firmly bound unto in the sum of lawful money of the United States of America, to be paid to the said or his certain attorney, executors, administrators or assigns: to which payment well and truly to be made, heirs, executors and administrators, firmly by these presents. Sealed with seal Dated the day of , in the year of our Lord one thousand eight hundred and .

The Condition of this Obligation is such, That if the above bounden heirs, executors, administrators, or any of them, shall and do well and truly pay, or cause to be paid, unto the above-named certain attorney, executors, administrators or assigns, the just sum of dollars,

without any fraud or further delay, then the above obligation to be void, or else to be and remain in full force and virtue.

(*Signature.*) (*Seal.*)

Sealed and Delivered in the Presence of

To , Esq., Attorney of the Court of Common Pleas, at in the County of , in the State of , or to any other Attorney of the said Court, or of any other Court, there or elsewhere.

Whereas, (*the obligor*) in and by a certain obligation bearing even date herewith, do stand bound unto (*the obligee*) in the sum of lawful money of the United States of America, conditioned for the payment of

These are to desire and authorize you, or any of you, to appear for heirs, executors or administrators, in the said court or elsewhere, in an action of debt, there or elsewhere brought, or to be brought, against me, or my heirs, executors or administrators, at the suit of the said (*the obligee*) executors, administrators or assigns, on the said obligation, as of any term or time past, present, or any other subsequent term or time there or elsewhere to be held, and confess judgment thereupon against me, or my heirs, executors or administrators, for the sum of . lawful money of the United States of America, debt, besides costs of suit, in such manner as to you shall seem meet: and for your, or any of your so doing, this shall be your sufficient warrant. And I do hereby for myself, and for my heirs, executors and administrators, remise, release, and forever quit claim unto the said (*the obligee*) or his certain attorney, executors, administrators and assigns, all and all manner of error and errors, misprisions, misentries, defects and imperfections whatever, in the entering of the said judgment, or any process or proceedings thereon or thereto, or anywise touching or concerning the same.

In Witness Whereof, have hereunto set hand and seal , the day of , in the year of our Lord one thousand eight hundred and .

(*Signature.*) (*Seal.*)

Sealed and Delivered in the Presence of

(27.)

Bond for Conveyance of a Parcel of Land.

Know all Men by these Presents, That we, as principals, and as sureties, are holden and stand firmly bound unto in the sum of dollars, to the payment of which to the said or executors, administrators, or assigns, we hereby jointly and severally bind ourselves, our heirs, executors, and administrators.

The Condition of this obligation is such that whereas the said obligors have agreed to sell and convey unto the said obligee a certain parcel of real estate situated and bounded as follows, namely:

The same to be conveyed by a good and sufficient (*warranty or other*) deed of the said obligors, conveying a good and clear title to the same, free from all incumbrances .

And whereas, for such deed and conveyance it is agreed that the said obligee shall pay the sum of dollars, of which dollars are to be paid in cash upon the delivery of said deed, and the remainder by the note of the said obligee, bearing interest at per cent per annum, payable semi-annually, and secured by a mortgage in the usual form upon the said premises, such note to be (*describe the note*)

Now, therefore, if the said obligors shall upon tender by the said obligee of the aforesaid cash, note , and mortgage at any time within from this date, deliver unto the said obligee a good and sufficient deed as aforesaid, then this obligation shall be void, otherwise it shall be and remain in full force and virtue.

In Witness Whereof, We hereunto set our hands and seals this day of A.D., 18 .

Signed and Sealed in Presence of

(28.)

Bond for a Deed of Land, with Acknowledgment before Notary Public.

Know all Men by these Presents, That of the County of and State of held and firmly bound to of in the sum of dollars, to be paid to said his executors, administrators or assigns, to the payment whereof bind sel heirs, executors and administrators, firmly by these presents, sealed with seal, and dated the day of A.D., 186 .

The Condition of this Obligation is, That if the said upon payment of dollars, and interest, by said within years from this date, agreeably to note of even date herewith, shall convey to said and heirs forever, a certain tract of land, situated in the County of and State of to wit:

by a deed in common form duly executed and acknowledged, and in the mean time shall permit said to occupy and improve said premises for own use, then this obligation shall be void, otherwise to remain in full force and effect.

In Testimony Whereof, have hereunto set hand and seal , the day and year first above written.

(Signature.) *(Seal.)*

STATE OF
COUNTY OF } ss.

Be it Remembered, That on this day of eighteen hundred and , before me, the undersigned, Notary Public in and for said County and State, duly commissioned and qualified, came who to be the same person whose name subscribed to the foregoing instrument of writing, as party thereto, and acknowledged the same to be act and deed for the purpose therein mentioned.

In Testimony Whereof, I have hereunto set my hand and affixed my official seal, at my office, in the City of , the day and year last aforesaid.

Notary Public.

(29.)

Bond in another Form, for Conveyance of Land, with Acknowledgment.

Know all Men by these Presents, That of in the County of and State of held and firmly bound unto of in the County of and State of in the penal sum of dollars, for the payment of which sum, well and truly to be made to heirs, executors and administrators, I bind myself, my heirs, executors and administrators, firmly by these presents.

Sealed with my seal and dated this day of A.D. 18

The Condition of the above Obligation is such, That whereas the said this day has given the said promissory note of even date herewith

Now, if, on payment of the said note being made on or before the time shall become due, and all taxes on the land hereinafter described having been paid by the said and no right of pre-emption having been established or claimed on the said land, or any part thereof, the said or his legal representatives, shall, whenever thereunto afterwards requested, execute and deliver to the said or legal representatives, a good and sufficient deed, conveying to the *(here describe the land)* free and clear of all incumbrance then this obligation to be null and void, otherwise of full force and effect, it being distinctly understood and agreed by and between the parties hereto that the time of payment herein above fixed material and of the essence of this contract, and that in case of failure therein, the intervention of equity is forever barred.

(Signatures.) *(Seals.)*

Signed, Sealed and Delivered in Presence of

STATE OF
COUNTY OF } ss.

I, in and for the said county, in the State aforesaid, do hereby certify that personally known to me as the same person whose name subscribed to the above bond for deed, appeared before me this day, in person, and acknowledged that he signed, sealed and deliverd the said bond as free and voluntary act, and for the use and purpose therein set forth.

Given under my hand and seal, this, day of A.D. 18 .

Notary Public.

(30.)

Bond to Corporation for Payment of Money due for Contribution to Capital Stock, with Power of Attorney to confess Judgment.

Know all Men by these Presents, That held and firmly bound unto *(name of the corporation)* in the sum of lawful money of the United States of America, to be paid to aforesaid, their certain attorney, successors or assigns. To which payment well and truly to be made, firmly by these presents. Sealed with seal . Dated the day of in the year of our Lord one thousand eight hundred and

The Condition of this Obligation is such, That if the above bounden heirs, executors and administrators, or any of them, shall and do well and truly pay, or cause to be paid unto the above-named their certain attorney, successors or assigns, the just sum of such as abovesaid, at any time within years from the date hereof, together with lawful interest for the same, in like money, payable monthly, on the of each and every month hereafter, and shall also well and truly pay, or cause to be paid unto aforesaid, their successors or assigns, the sum of dollars, on the said of each and every month hereafter, as and for the monthly contribution on share of the capital stock of aforesaid, now owned by the said without any fraud or further delay; provided, however, and it is hereby expressly agreed, that if at any time default shall be made in the payment of the said principal money when due, or of the said interest, or the monthly contribution on said stock, for the space of after any payment thereof shall fall due, then and in such case, the whole principal debt aforesaid shall, at the option of aforesaid, their successors and assigns, immediately thereupon become due, payable and recoverable, and payment of said principal sum and all interest thereon, as well as any contribution on said share of stock, then due, may be enforced and recovered at once, any thing hereinbefore contained to the contrary thereof notwithstanding. And the said for heirs, executors, administrators and assigns, hereby expressly waive and relinquish unto aforesaid, their successors and assigns, all benefit that may accrue to by virtue of any and every law, made or to be made, to exempt the premises described in the indenture of mortgage herewith given, or of any other premises whatever, from levy and sale under execution, or any part of the proceeds arising from the sale thereof, from the payment of the moneys hereby secured, or any part thereof, then the above obligation to be void, or else to be and remain in full force and virtue.

(*Signatures.*) (*Seals.*)

Executed and Delivered in Presence of

To Esquire, Attorney of the Court of Common Pleas at in the County of in the State of or to any other Attorney, or to the Prothonotary of the said Court, or of any other Court, there or elsewhere.

Whereas, in and by a certain obligation, bearing even date herewith, do stand bound unto in the sum of lawful money of the United States of America, conditioned for the payment of the just sum of such as abovesaid, at any time within years from the date thereof, together with lawful interest for the same in like money, payable monthly, on the of each and every month thereafter, and should also well and truly pay or cause to be paid unto aforesaid, their successors or assigns, the sum of dollars, on the of each and every month thereafter, as and for the monthly contribution on share of the capital stock of aforesaid, now owned by the said without any fraud or further delay; provided, however, and it is thereby expressly agreed, that if at any time default should be made in the payment of the said principal money when due, or of the said interest, or the monthly contribution on said stock, for the space of after any payment thereof should fall due, then and in such case the whole principal debt aforesaid should at the option of aforesaid, their successors and assigns, immediately thereupon become due, payable and recoverable, and payment of said principal sum, and all interest thereon, as well as any contribution on said share of stock then due, might be enforced and recovered at once, any thing thereinbefore contained to the contrary thereof notwithstanding. And the said heirs, executors, administrators and assigns, thereby expressly waive and relinquish unto aforesaid, their successors and assigns, all benefit that might acrue to by virtue of any and every law, made or to be made, to exempt the premises described in the indenture of mortgage therewith given, or of any other premises whatever, from levy and sale under execution, or any part of the proceeds arising from the sale thereof, from the payment of the moneys thereby secured, or any part thereof. These are to desire and authorize you, or any of you, to appear for heirs, executors, or administrators, in the said court or elsewhere, in an action of debt, there or elsewhere brought or to be brought, against heirs, executors, or administrators, at the suit of aforesaid, their successors or assigns, on the said obligation, as of any term or time past, present, or any other subsequent term or time, there or elsewhere to be held, and confess or enter judgment thereupon against heirs, executors, or administrators, for the sum of lawful money of the United States of America, debt, besides costs of suit, in such manner as to you shall seem meet; and for your or any of your so doing this shall be your sufficient warrant. And heirs, executors and administrators, remise, release, and forever quit claim, unto aforesaid, their certain attorney, successors and assigns, all and all manner of error and errors, misprisions, misentries, defects and imperfections whatever, in the entering of the said judgment, or any process or proceedings thereon or thereto, or anywise touching or concerning the same.

In Witness Whereof, have hereunto set hand and seal the day of in the year of our Lord one thousand eight hundred and

(*Signatures.*) (*Seals.*)

Sealed and Delivered in Presence of

CHAPTER IX.

ASSIGNMENTS.

THE word "assign" usually occurs in almost all forms of transfer and conveyance; but there are certain instruments to which the name of "Assignment" is more particularly given. They are instruments by which other instruments or debts or obligations, as bonds, judgments, wages, and the like, are transferred. Sometimes they are written on the backs of, or elsewhere on the same paper with, the instruments to be transferred by the assignment. Some of these, as assignments of deeds of grant and conveyance, of mortgages, of leases, will be given in the chapters which treat of those topics. Here are given such forms as will enable one to make an assignment for any of the purposes for which assignments are usually made.

(31.)

Brief Form of an Assignment to be indorsed on a Note, or any Similar Promise or Agreement.

I Hereby, for value received, assign and transfer the within written (*or the above written*) , together with all my interest in and all my rights under the same, to (*name of the assignee*).

(*Signature.*)

(32.)

A General Assignment, with Power of Attorney.

Know all Men by these Presents, That I for value received, have sold, and by these presents do grant, assign and convey unto (*name of the assignee and description of the things assigned*)

To Have and to Hold the same unto the said executors, administrators and assigns forever, to and for the use of hereby constituting and appointing my true and lawful attorney irrevocable in my name, place and stead, for the purposes aforesaid, to ask, demand, sue for, attach, levy, recover and receive all such sum and sums of money which now are, or may hereafter become due, owing and payable for, or on account of all or any of the accounts, dues, debts, and demands above assigned giving and granting unto the said attorney, full power and authority to do and perform all and every act and thing whatsoever requisite and necessary, as fully, to all intents and purposes, as might or could do, if personally present, with full power of substitution and revocation, hereby ratifying and confirming all that the said attorney or substitute shall lawfully do or cause to be done by virtue hereof.

In Witness Whereof, I have hereunto set my hand and seal the day of , one thousand eight hundred and

(*Signature.*) (*Seal.*)

Executed and Delivered in the Presence of

(33.)

Assignment of a Bond.

Know all Men by these Presents, That in the hereunto annexed obligation named, for and in consideration of the sum of lawful money of the United States of America, unto well and truly paid by at the time of the execution hereof, the receipt whereof hereby acknowledge, have assigned, transferred and set over, and by these presents, do assign, transfer and set over unto the said (*assignee*) his executors, administrators and assigns, to and for his and their only proper use and behoof, the said hereunto annexed obligation, which is given and executed by to bearing date the day of Anno Domini, 18 , to secure the payment of the sum of with lawful interest therein expressed, and all moneys, both principal and interest, thereon due and payable, or hereafter to grow due and payable, with the warrant of attorney to the said obligation annexed: together with all rights, remedies, incidents and appurtenances, whatsoever thereunto belonging, or in any wise appertaining, and all right, title and interest therein.

In Witness Whereof, the said have hereunto set hand and seal , this day of Anno Domini, one thousand eight hundred and

Sealed and Delivered in the Presence of us,

(34.)

Assignment of a Bond, with Power of Attorney, and a Covenant.

Know all Men by these Presents, That of the first part, for and in consideration of the sum of lawful money of the United States of America, to in hand paid by of the second part, at or before the ensealing and delivery of these presents, the receipt whereof is hereby acknowledged, ha bargained, sold and assigned, and by these presents do bargain, sell and assign, unto the said party of the second part, executors, administrators, and assigns, a certain written bond or obligation and conditions thereof, bearing date the day of one thousand eight hundred and executed by

and all sum and sums of money due, and to grow due thereon: and the said party of the first part do covenant with the said party of the second part, that there is now due on the said bond or obligation, according to the conditions thereof, for principal and interest, the sum of and do hereby authorize the said party of the second part, in name to ask, demand, sue for, recover, receive, and enjoy, the money due and that may grow due thereon, as aforesaid.

In Witness Whereof, have hereunto set hand and seal the day of one thousand eight hundred and

Sealed and Delivered in the Presence of

(35.)

Assignment of a Judgment, in the Form of an Indenture.

This Indenture, Made the day of one thousand eight hundred and between (*assignor*) of the first part, and (*assignee*) of the second part.

Whereas, The said part of the first part one thousand eight hundred and recovered by judgment in the (*name of court*) against one the sum of

Now this Indenture Witnesseth, That the said part of the first part, in consideration of to duly paid, ha sold, and by these presents do assign, transfer, and set over unto the said part of the second part, and assigns, the said judgment, and all sum and sums of money that may be had or obtained by means thereof, or on any proceedings to be had thereupon. And the said part of the first part, do hereby constitute and appoint the said part of the second part, and assigns, true and lawful attorney, irrevocable, with power of substitution and revocation for the use, and at the proper costs and charges of the said part of the second part, to ask, demand and receive, and to sue out executions, and take all lawful ways for the recovery of the money due or to become due on the said judgment: and on payment to acknowledge satisfaction, or discharge the same. And attorneys one or more under for the purpose aforesaid, to make and substitute, and at pleasure to revoke; hereby ratifying and confirming all that said attorney or substitute shall lawfully do in the premises. And the said part of the first part do covenant, that there is now due on the said judgment the sum of and that will not collect or receive the same, or any part thereof, nor release or discharge the said judgment, but will own and allow all lawful proceedings therein, the said part of the second part saving the said part of first part, harmless of and from any costs in the premises.

In Testimony Whereof, The part of the first part, ha hereunto set hand and seal the day and year first above written.

(*Seals.*)

Sealed and Delivered in the Presence of

(**36.**)

Assignment of Wages, with Power of Attorney.

Know all Men by these Presents, That I of in the County of in consideration of to me paid by of the receipt whereof I do hereby acknowledge, do hereby assign and transfer to said all claims and demands which I now have, and all which, at any time between the date hereof and the day of next, I may and shall have against for all sums of money due, and for all sums of money and demand which, at any time between the date hereof and the said day of next, may and shall become due to me, for services as to have and to hold the same to the said his executors, administrators and assigns forever.

And I, do hereby constitute and appoint the said and his assigns to be my attorney irrevocable in the premises, to do and perform all acts, matters, and things touching the premises, in the like manner to all intents and purposes as I could if personally present.

In Witness Whereof, I have set my hand and seal, this day of 18 .

(*Seal.*)

Signed, Sealed and Delivered in Presence of

CHAPTER X.

SALES OF PERSONAL PROPERTY.

SECTION I.

WHAT CONSTITUTES A SALE.

It is important to distinguish carefully between a sale and an agreement for a future sale. This distinction is sometimes overlooked; and hence the phrase "an executory contract of sale," that is, a contract of sale which is to be executed hereafter, has come into use; but it is not quite accurate to speak of this as if it were a sale. Every actual sale is an executed contract, although payment or delivery may remain to be made. There may be an executory contract *for* sale, or a bargain that a future sale shall be made; but such a bargain is not a present sale; nor does it confer upon either party the rights or the obligations which grow out of the contract of sale.

A sale of goods is the exchange thereof for money. More precisely, it is the transfer of the property in goods from a seller to a buyer, for a price paid, or to be paid, in money. It differs from an exchange, in law; for that is the transfer of chattels for other chattels; while a sale is the transfer of chattels for money, which is the representative of all value.

Here we must pause to speak of the *legal* meaning of the word "property." It is seldom or never used in the law as it is in common conversation, to mean the things themselves which are bought, or sold, or owned. Because in law it means the *ownership* of the things, and not the things themselves.

If a bargain transfers the property in (which means the ownership of) the thing to another person for a price, it is a sale; and if it does not transfer the property, it is not a sale; and, on the other hand, if it be not a sale, it does not transfer the property. As soon as a thing is *sold*, the buyer *owns* it, wherever it may be. And to constitute a sale at common law, all that is necessary is the agreement of competent parties that the property in (or ownership of) the subject-matter shall then pass from the seller to the buyer for a fixed price.

The sale is made when the agreement is made. The completion of the sale does not depend upon the delivery of the goods by the seller, nor upon the payment of the price by the buyer. By the mutual assent of the parties to the terms of the sale, the buyer acquires at once the property and all the rights and liabilities of property; so that, in case of any loss or depreciation of the articles purchased, the buyer will be the sufferer; and he will be the gainer by any increase in their value.

It is, however, a presumption of the law, that the sale is to be immediately followed by payment and delivery, unless otherwise agreed upon by the parties. If therefore nothing appears but a proposal and an acceptance, and the vendee departs without paying or tendering the price, the vendor may elect to consider it no sale, and may, therefore, if the buyer comes at a later period and offers the price and demands the goods, refuse to let him have them. But a credit may be agreed on expressly, and the seller will be bound by it; and so he will be if the credit is inferred or implied from usage or from the circumstances of the case. And if there be a delivery and acceptance of the goods, or a receipt by the seller of earnest, or of part payment, the legal inference is that both parties agree to hold themselves mutually bound by the bargain. Then the buyer has either the credit agreed upon, or such credit as from custom or the nature or circumstances of the case is reasonable. But neither delivery, nor earnest, nor part payment, is essential to the completion of a contract of sale. They only prevent the seller from rescinding the contract of sale without the consent of the purchaser. Their effect upon sales under the provisions of the Statute of Frauds will be considered in the chapter on that subject. It may also be said that no one can be made to buy of another without his own assent. Thus, if A sends an order to B for goods, and C sends the goods, he cannot sue for the price, if A repudiates the sale, although C had bought B's business.

The seller (if no delivery with credit for the price is agreed on) has a right to retain possession of the property sold until the price is paid. This right is called a *lien*, which means the right of retaining possession of property until some charge upon it, or some claim on account of it, is satisfied. It rests therefore on possession. Hence the seller (and every other person who has a lien) loses it by voluntarily parting with the possession, or by a delivery of the goods. And it is a delivery for this pupose, if he delivers a part without any purpose of severing that part from the remainder; or if he make a symbolical delivery which vests this right and power of possession in the buyer, as by the delivery of the key of a warehouse in which they are locked up.

If the seller delivers the goods to the buyer, as he thereby loses his lien, he cannot afterwards, by virtue of this lien, retake the goods and hold them. But if the delivery was made with an express agreement that non-payment of the price should revest the property in the seller, this agreement may be valid, and the seller can reclaim the goods from the buyer if the price be not paid.

If the buyer neglect or refuse to take the goods and pay the price within a reasonable time, the seller may resell them on notice to the buyer, and look to him for the deficiency by way of damages for the breach of the contract. The seller, in making such resale, acts as agent or trustee for the buyer; and his proceedings will be regulated and governed by the rules usually applicable to persons acting in those capacities; and the principal one of these is, that he will be held to due care and diligence, and to perfect good faith.

Certain consequences flow from the rules and principles already stated, which should be noticed. Thus, if the party to whom the offer of sale is made, accepts the offer, but still refuses or neglects to pay the price, and there are no circumstances indicating a credit, or otherwise justifying the refusal or neglect, the seller may, as we have said, disregard the acceptance of his offer, and consider the contract as never made, or as rescinded. It would, however, be proper and prudent on the part of the seller expressly to demand payment of the price before he treated the sale as null; and a refusal or neglect would then give him at once a right to hold and treat the goods as his own. So, too, if the seller unreasonably neglected or refused to deliver the goods sold, and especially if he refused to deliver them, the buyer thereby acquires the right to consider that no sale was made, or that it has been avoided (or annulled). But neither party is bound to exercise the right thus acquired by the refusal or neglect of the other, but may consider the sale as complete; and the seller may sue the buyer for non-payment, or the buyer may sue the seller for non-delivery.

If the seller has merely the right of possession, as if he hired the goods; or if he has the possession only, as if he stole them, or found them; he cannot sell them and give good title to the buyer against the owner; and the owner may therefore recover them even from an honest purchaser who was wholly ignorant of the defect in the title of him from whom he bought them. This follows from the rule above stated, that only he who has in himself a right of property can sell a chattel, because the sale must transfer the right of property from the seller to the buyer. The only exception to the above rule is where money, or negotiable paper transferable by delivery (which is considered as money), is sold or paid away. In either case, he who takes it in good faith, and for value, from a thief or finder, holds it by good title. But if the owner once sold the thing, although he was deceived and induced to part with his property through fraud, he cannot reclaim it from one who in good faith buys it from the fraudulent party.

If any thing remains to be done by the seller, to or in relation to the goods sold, for their ascertainment, identification, or completion, the property in the goods does not pass until that thing is done; and there is as yet no completed sale. Therefore, if there be a bargain for the sale of specific goods, but there remains something material which the seller is to do to them, and they are casually burnt or stolen, the loss is the seller's, because the property (or ownership,) had not yet passed to the buyer.

So, if the goods are a part of a large quantity, they remain the seller's until selected and separated; and even after that, until recognized and accepted by the buyer, unless it is plain from words or circumstances that the selection and separation by the buyer are intended to be conclusive upon both parties.

If repairing or measuring or counting must be done by the seller, before the goods are fitted for delivery or the price can be determined or their quantity ascertained, they remain, until this be done, the seller's. And where part is measured and delivered this part passes to the vendee, but the portion not so set apart does not. But if the seller delivers them and the buyer accepts them, and any of these acts remain to be done, these acts will not be considered as belonging to the contract of sale, for that will be regarded as completed, and the ownership of the goods will have passed to the buyer; and these acts will be taken only to refer to the adjustment of the final settlement as to the price.

Thus, a purchaser offers a nursery-man a dollar apiece for two hundred out of a row of two thousand trees, which are all alike, and the offer is accepted. This is no sale, because any two hundred may be delivered, and therefore the property or ownership of any specific two hundred does not pass. But if the purchaser or seller had said, the first two hundred in the row, or the last, or every third tree, or otherwise indicated the specific trees, there would have been a sale, and by the sale those specific trees would have become at once the trees of the buyer. The seller would dig up and deliver them as the buyer's trees, and if they were burned up by accident an hour after the sale, and before digging, the buyer would lose the trees. If not specified, however, even if they were paid for, they remain the property of the nurseryman, because, instead of an actual sale, there is only a bargain that he will select two hundred from the lot, and take up and deliver them. And if they are destroyed before delivery, this is the loss of the nurseryman.

Moreover, it is to be noticed that a contract for a future sale, to take place either at a future point of time, or when a certain event happens, does not, when that time arrives, or on the happening of the event, become of itself a sale, transferring the property. The party to whom the sale was to be made does not then acquire the property, and cannot by tendering the price acquire a right to possession; but he may tender the price, or whatever else would be the fulfilment of his obligation, and then sue the owner for his breach of contract, if he will not deliver the goods. But the property in the goods remains in the original owner.

For the same reason that the property in the goods must pass by a sale, there can be no actual sale of any chattel or goods which have no existence at the time. It may, as we have seen, be a good contract for a future sale, but it is not a present sale. Thus, in contracts for the sale of articles yet to be manufactured, the subject of the contract not being in existence when the parties enter into their engagement, no property passes until the chattel is in a finished state, and has been specifically appropriated to the person giving the order, and approved and accepted by him.

As there can be no sale unless of a specific thing, so there is no sale but for a price which is certain, or which is capable of being made certain by a distinct reference to a certain standard.

SECTION II.

DELIVERY AND ITS INCIDENTS.

WHEN a sale is effected, the buyer has an immediate right to the possession of the goods, as soon as he pays or tenders the price; or at once, without payment, if the sale be on credit. And the seller is bound to deliver the goods.

What is a sufficient delivery is sometimes a question of difficulty. In general, it is sufficient, if the goods are placed in the buyer's hands or his actual possession, or if that is done which is the equivalent of this transfer of possession. Some modes and instances of delivery we have already seen. We add, that if the goods are landed on a wharf alongside of the ship which brings them, with notice to the buyer, or knowledge on his part, this may be a sufficient delivery, if usage, or the obvious nature of the case, make it equivalent to actually giving possession. And usage is of the utmost importance in determining questions of this kind.

In general, the rule may be said to be, that that is a sufficient delivery which puts the goods within the actual reach or power of the buyer, with immediate notice to him, so that there is nothing to prevent him from taking actual possession.

When, from the nature or situation of the goods, an actual delivery is difficult or impossible, as in case of a quantity of timber floating in a boom, slight acts, as touching the timber, or even going near it and pointing it out, are sufficient to constitute a delivery, if they sufficiently indicate the transfer of possession. So if the property which is the subject of the sale is at sea, the indorsement and delivery of the bill of lading, or other instrument of title, is sufficient to constitute a delivery, and by such indorsement and delivery of the bill of lading the property in the goods immediately vests in the buyer; and he can transfer this to one who buys of him, by his own indorsement and delivery of the bill of lading. Where goods at sea are sold, the seller should send or deliver the bill of lading to the buyer within a reasonable time, that he may have the means of offering the goods in the market. And it has been held that a refusal of the bill of lading authorized the buyer to rescind the sale.

Until delivery, the seller is bound to keep the goods with ordinary care, and is liable for any loss or injury arising from the want of such care or of good faith. But if he exercises ordinary care and diligence in keeping the commodity, he is not liable for any loss or depreciation of it, unless this arises from some defect which he has warranted not to exist. Thus, in a case in New York, A sold to B a certain quantity of beef, B paying the purchase-money in full; and it was agreed between them that the beef should remain in the custody of A until it should be sent to another place. Some time after, B received a part, which proved to be bad, and the whole was found, on inspection, to be unmerchantable. The court held that, as the beef was good at the time of its sale, the vendee (or buyer) must bear the loss of its subsequent deterioration.

If the buyer lives at a distance from the seller, the seller must send the goods in the manner indicated by the buyer. If no directions are given, he must send them in such a way as usage, or in the absence of usage, as reasonable care would require. And generally all customary and proper precautions should be taken to prevent loss or injury in the transit. If these are taken, the goods are sent at the risk of the buyer, and the seller is not responsible for any loss. But he is responsible for any loss or injury happening through the want of such care or precaution. And if he sends them by his own servant, or carries them himself, they are in his custody, and, generally, at his risk, until delivery. But if the buyer distinctly indicates the way or means by which he wishes that the goods should be sent to him, as by such a carrier, or such a line, if the seller complies with his directions, and exercises ordinary care over the goods until they are delivered to the person or line so pointed out, his responsibility ends with this delivery, in the same manner as it would if he delivered the goods into the hands of the owner.

This question of delivery has a very great importance in another point of view; and that is, as it bears upon the honesty, and therefore the validity, of the transaction. As the owner of goods ought to have them in his possession, and as a transfer of possession usually does, and always should, accompany a sale, the want of this transfer is an indication, more or less strong, that the sale is not a real one, but a mere cover. The prevailing rule may be stated thus. Delivery is not essential to a sale at common law; but if there is no delivery, and a third party, without knowledge of the previous sale, purchases the same thing from the seller, he gains an equally valid title with the first buyer; and if he completes this title by acquiring possession of the thing before the other, he can hold it against the other. So, also, unless delivery or possession accompany the transfer of the right of property, the things sold are subject to attachment by the creditors of the seller. And if the sale be completed, and nevertheless no change of possession takes place, and there is no certain and adequate cause or justification of the want or delay of this change of possession, the transaction will be regarded as fraudulent and void in favor of a third party, who, either by purchase or by attachment, acquires the property in good faith, and without a knowledge of the former sale. This fact, that the thing sold remained in the possession of the seller, might be explained, and if shown to be perfectly consistent with honesty, and to have occurred for good reasons, and especially if the delay in taking possession was brief, the title of the first buyer would be respected.

If goods are sold in a shop or store, separated, and weighed or numbered if that be necessary, and put into a parcel, or otherwise made ready for delivery to the buyer, in his presence, and he request the seller to keep the goods for a time for him, this is so far a delivery as to vest the property in the goods in the buyer, and the seller becomes the *bailee* of the buyer. And if the goods are lost while thus in the keeping of the seller, without his fault, it is the loss of the buyer. (In law the word *bail* means "to deliver." Thus a "bailor" is one who delivers a thing to another; the "bailee" is the party to whom it is delivered; and "bailment" is the delivery. The "bail" of a party who is arrested, is he or they to whom the arrested person is delivered or given up, on their agreement that he shall be forthcoming when required by law.)

In a contract of sale there is sometimes a clause providing that a mistake in description, or a deficiency in quality or quantity, shall not avoid the sale, but only give the buyer a right to deduction or compensation. But if the mistake or defect be great and substantial, and affects materially the availability of the thing for the purpose for which it was bought, the sale is nevertheless void, for the thing sold is not that which was to have been sold.

If the buyer knowingly receives goods so deficient or so different from what they should have been that he might have refused them, he will be held to have waived the objection, and to be liable for the whole price; unless he can show a good reason for not returning them, as in the case of materials innocently used before discovery of the defects, or the like. Thus, where a man bought a chandelier warranted sufficient to light a certain room, and kept it six months, the court did not permit him to return it and refuse payment, although it was not what it had been warranted to be. Sometimes two or three months, or even less, is held too long a keeping to permit a subsequent return. But though the buyer cannot return the thing, yet, when the price is demanded, he may set off whatever damages he has sustained by the seller's breach of contract, and the seller can recover only the value to the buyer of the goods sold, even if that be nothing. But a long delay or silence may imply a waiver of even this right on the part of the buyer.

One who orders many things at one time, and by one bargain, may, generally, refuse to receive a part without the rest; but if he accepts any part, he severs that part from the rest, and rebuts (or removes) the presumption that it was an entire contract; the buyer will then be held as having given a separate order for each thing, or part, and as therefore bound to receive such parts as are tendered, unless some distinct reason for refusal attaches to them. If many several things are bought at one auction, but by different bids, and especially if the name of the buyer be marked against each, there is a separate sale to him of each one, and it is independent of the others; so that he must take and pay for any one or more, although the others are not what they should be, or cannot be had. If, however, it could be shown by the nature of the case, or by evidence, that the things were so connected that one was bought entirely for the sake of the other, he would not be obliged to take the one unless he could have the other. This rule applies also when the things sold are lots of land. Indeed, the general rule may be stated thus. The question whether it is one contract, so that the buyer shall not be bound to receive any part unless the whole be tendered to him, will be determined by ascertaining from all the facts whether the parts so belong together that it may reasonably be supposed that none would have been purchased if the whole had not been purchased, or if any part could not have been purchased.

The buyer may have, by the terms of the bargain, the right of redelivery. For sales are sometimes made upon the agreement that the purchaser may return the goods within a fixed, or within a reasonable time. He may have this right without any condition, and then has only to exercise it at his discretion. But he may have the right to return the thing bought, only if it turns out to have, or not to have, certain qualities; or only upon the happening of a certain event. In such case the burden of proof is on him to show that the circumstances exist which are necessary to give him this right. In either case the property vests in the buyer at once, as in ordinary sales; but subject to the right of return given him by the agreement. If he does not exercise his right within the agreed time, or within a reasonable time if none be agreed upon, the right is wholly lost, the sale becomes absolute, and the price of the goods may be recovered in an action for goods sold and delivered. And if during the time the buyer so misuse the property as to materially impair its value, he cannot tender it back, but is liable for the price.

SECTION III.

CONTRACTS VOID FOR ILLEGALITY OR FRAUD.

As the law will not compel or require any one to do that which it forbids him to do, no contract can be enforced at law which is tainted with illegality. It may, however, be necessary to consider whether the contract be entire or separable into parts, and whether it is wholly or partially illegal. If the whole consideration, or any part of the consideration, be illegal, the promise founded upon it is void, whether the promise is legal or not. But if the consideration is legal, and the promise is in part legal and in part illegal, it is valid for the legal part and may be enforced for that part. Thus, if a master of a vessel agreed to smuggle goods, and in consideration of his doing so the owner promised to pay him one-fourth of his profits, and also to advance twenty dollars a month to his family during a certain time, the master could enforce no part of this promise, and recover no damages for any breach of it, because the consideration is illegal. But if, for one thousand dollars paid, the receiver agreed to sell and deliver a quantity of merchandise, and also to assist the buyer in some contemplated fraud, he would be bound to sell and deliver the goods, because the consideration was legal, and this part of the promise was legal, but not to assist in the fraud, because this part of the promise is illegal. I mean to say, that if a whole promise, or any part of a promise that cannot be severed into substantial and independent parts, is illegal, the whole promise is void. But if the consideration is legal, and the promise is legal in part and illegal in part, and that part of the promise which is legal can be severed from that part which is illegal, and then be a substantial promise having a value of its own, this legal part can be enforced. For further remarks upon this subject, however, I refer to the previous chapter on Consideration.

Formerly, an agreement to sell at a future day goods which the promisor had not at the time, and had not contracted to buy, and had no notice or expectation of receiving by consignment, was considered open to the objection that it was merely a wager, and therefore void. But later cases have admitted it to be a valid contract.

We have already said, in a preceding chapter, that fraud vitiates and avoids every contract and every transaction. Hence, a wilfully false representation by which a sale is effected; or a purchase of goods with the design of not paying for them; or hindering others from bidding at auction by wrongful means; or selling at auction, and providing by-bidders to run the thing up fraudulently; or selling "with all faults," and then purposely concealing and disguising them, as when a man advertised a ship for sale at auction "with all faults," but purposely put her in a situation where an important fault could not be easily detected; or any similar act, will avoid a sale. No title or right passes by such sale to the fraudulent party; but the innocent party, whether buyer or seller, may waive the fraud, and insist that the fraudulent party shall not take advantage of his own fraud to avoid the sale.

A buyer who is imposed upon by a fraud, and therefore has a right to annul the sale, must exercise this right as soon as may be after discovering the fraud. He does not lose the right necessarily by every delay, but certainly does by any considerable and unexcused delay.

A seller may rescind and annul a sale if he were induced to make it by fraud. But he may waive the right and sue for the price. If, however, the fraudulent buyer gets the goods on a credit, and the seller sues for the price before the credit expires, this suit is a confirmation of the whole sale, including the credit; or rather it is an entire waiver of his right to annul the sale, and the suit cannot be maintained until the credit has wholly expired.

If a party who has been defrauded by any contract brings an action to enforce it, this is a waiver of his right to rescind, and a confirmation of the contract. Or if, with knowledge of the fraud, he offers to perform the contract on conditions which he had no right to exact, this has been held so effectual a waiver of the fraud that he cannot set it up in defence, if sued on the contract.

SECTION IV.

SALES WITH WARRANTY.

A SALE may be with warranty; and this may be general, or particular and limited. A general warranty does not extend to defects which are known to the purchaser; or which are open to inspection and observation, unless the purchaser is at the time unable to discover them readily, and relies rather upon the knowledge and warranty of the seller. A warranty may also be either express or implied. It is *not* implied by the law generally merely from a full, or, as it is called, a sound price. The rule of law, *caveat emptor* (*let the buyer take care*), prevents this. But this rule never applies to cases of fraud. As a general rule however, mere silence on the part of the seller is not fraud; but the usage of the trade will be considered, and if that require a declaration of certain defects whenever they exist, the absence of such declaration is a warranty against such defects. Mere declarations of opinion are not a warranty. Thus, in England, an action was brought on a warranty that certain goods were fit for the China market. The plaintiff produced a letter from the defendant, saying that he had goods fit for the China market, which he offered to sell cheap. But the court held that such a letter was not a warranty, but merely an invitation to trade, it not having any specific reference to the goods actually bought by the plaintiff.

If these declarations are intended to deceive, and have that effect, they may avoid the sale for fraud. And affirmations of quantity or quality, which are made pending the negotiations for sale, with a view to procure a sale, and have that effect, will be regarded as a warranty; thus, in New York, it was held that a representation made by a vendor, upon a sale of flour in barrels, that it was in quality superfine or extra-superfine, and worth a shilling a barrel more than common, coupled with the assurance to the buyer's agent, that he might rely upon such representation, was a warranty of the quality of the flour. So in England, where upon the sale of a horse the vendor said to the vendee, "You may depend upon it, the horse is perfectly quiet and free from vice;" this was held to amount to an express warranty that he was quiet and free from vice.

Goods sold by sample are warranted by such sale to conform to the sample; but there is no warranty that the sample is what it appears to be. Thus, in England, there was a sale of five bags of hops, with express warranty that the bulk answered the samples by which they were sold. The sale was in January; at that time the samples fairly answered to the commodity sold, and no defect was at that time perceptible to the buyer. In July following, every bag was found to have become unmerchantable and spoiled, by heating, caused probably by the hops having been fraudulently watered by the grower, or some other person, before they were purchased by the defendant. The seller knew nothing of this fact at the time of sale, and the samples were as much damped as the rest; and it was then impossible to detect it. It was held by the court that there was here no implied warranty that the bulk of the commodity was merchantable at the time of sale, although a merchantable price was given.

A breach of warranty does not always authorize the buyer to return the article sold, unless there be an agreement to that effect, or fraud; but only to sue on the warranty, and recover damages for the breach of it. But if one orders a thing for a special purpose known to the seller, he may certainly return it if it be unfit for that purpose, if he does so as soon as he ascertains its unfitness.

The seller of goods actually in his possession as owner is held to warrant his own title by the fact of the sale. But if the property be not in the possession of the vendor, and there be no assertion of ownership by him, no implied warranty of title arises.

If a thing is ordered for a special purpose, and is supplied, there is an implied warranty that it is fit for that purpose. In one case, the defendant was a dealer in ropes, and represented himself to be a manufacturer of the article. The buyer, a wine-merchant, applied to him for a crane-rope. The seller's foreman went to the buyer's premises, in order to ascertain the dimensions and kind of rope required. He examined the crane and the old rope, and took the necessary admeasurements, and was told that the new rope was wanted for the purpose of raising pipes of wine out of the cellar, and letting them down into the street; when he informed the buyer that a rope must be made on purpose. The seller did not make the rope himself, but sent the order to his manufacturer, who employed a third person to make it. It was held that, as between the parties to the sale, there was an implied warranty that the rope was a fit and proper one for the purpose for which it was ordered. And the seller was held responsible, not only for the rope, which broke, but for a pipe of wine which was thereby lost.

This principle must not be applied to those cases where an ascertained article is purchased, although it be intended for a special purpose. For if the thing itself is specifically selected and purchased, the purchaser takes upon himself the risk of its effecting its purpose. This is illustrated in an English case thus: "If a man says to another, 'Sell me a horse fit to carry me,' and the other sells a horse which he knows to be unfit to ride, he will be liable for the consequences; but if a man says, 'Sell me that gray horse to ride,' and the other sells it, knowing that the buyer will not be able to ride it, that would not make him liable." If he said, "Sell me that gray horse *if* he is fit to ride," and the seller sold it knowing he was not fit, he would be liable.

It has been much discussed whether a bill of sale, describing the article sold, amounts to a warranty that the article conforms to the description. It seems now to be well settled that it does. In a recent Massachusetts case, there was a bill of sale as follows: "H. & Co. bought of T. W. & Co. *two cases of indigo*, $272." The article sold was not indigo, but principally Prussian blue. No fraud was imputed to the seller, and the article was so prepared as to deceive experienced and skilful dealers in indigo. The naked question was presented, whether the bill of sale constituted a warranty that the article sold was *indigo.* And the court held that it did. Here the warranty implied by the bill of sale was as to the *kind of goods.* In another case the bill was, "Sold E. T. H. 2,000 gallons *prime quality winter oil.*" The thing sold was oil, and winter oil; but not *prime quality.* And the court held that the bill of sale amounted to a warranty that it was of *that quality.* In an English case, a vessel was advertised for sale as "copper fastened;" and this was held to be a warranty that she was so fastened according to the usual understanding of merchants.

One who sells provisions is always considered in law as warranting that they are good and wholesome.

(37.)

Bill of Sale of Personal Property.

Know all Men by these Presents, That I (*name of the seller*) in the county of for and in consideration of the sum of to in hand well and truly paid, at or before signing, sealing, and delivery of these presents, by (*name of the buyer*) the receipt whereof I the said do hereby acknowledge, have granted, bargained, and sold, and by these presents do grant, bargain, and sell unto the said

To Have and to Hold the said granted and bargained unto the said heirs, executors, administrators, and assigns, to only proper use, benefit, and behoof forever, and the said does vouch himself to be the true and lawful owner of the goods and effects hereby sold, and to have in himself full power, good right, and lawful authority to dispose of the said in manner as aforesaid, and I do, for myself, my heirs, executors, and administrators, hereby covenant and agree to warrant and defend the said (*the goods sold*) unto the said heirs, executors, and administrators, and assigns, against the lawful claims and demands of all persons whomsoever:

In Witness Whereof, the said have hereunto set hand and seal this day of in the year of our Lord one thousand eight hundred and sixty-

Executed and Delivered in Presence of

(38.)

Bill of Sale of Personal Property, with a Condition to make it a Mortgage, with Power of Sale.

Know all Men by these Presents, That in consideration of paid by the receipt whereof is hereby acknowledged, do hereby grant, sell, transfer, and deliver unto the said the following goods and chattels, namely: —

To Have and to Hold all and singular the said goods and chattels to the said and executors, administrators, and assigns, to their own use and behoof forever.

And hereby covenant with the grantee that the lawful owner of the said goods and chattels; that they are free from all incumbrances, that have good right to sell the same as aforesaid; and that will warrant and defend the same against the lawful claims and demands of all persons.

Provided Nevertheless that if the grantor , or executors, administrators, or assigns, shall pay unto the grantee , or executors, administrators, or assigns the sum of in from this date, with interest semi-annually at the rate of per cent per annum, and until such payment shall not waste or destroy the same, nor suffer them or any part thereof to be attached on mesne process; and shall not, except with the consent in writing of the grantee or representatives, attempt to sell or to remove from the same or any part thereof, — then this deed, as also note of even date herewith, signed by the said whereby promise to pay to the grantee or order the said sum and interest at the times aforesaid, shall be void.

But upon any Default in the performance of the foregoing condition, the grantee , or executors, administrators, or assigns, may sell the said goods and chattels by public auction, first giving days' notice in writing of the time and place of sale to the grantor or representatives. And out of the money arising from such sale the grantee , or representatives shall be entitled to retain all sums then secured by this mortgage, whether then or thereafter payable, including all costs, charges, and expenses incurred or sustained by them in relation to the said property, or to discharge any claims or liens of third persons affecting the same, rendering the surplus, if any, to the grantor or executors, administrators, or assigns.

And it is Agreed that the grantee , or executors, administrators, or assigns, or any person or persons in their behalf, may purchase at any sale made as aforesaid; and that, until default in the performance of the condition of this deed, the grantor and executors, administrators, and assigns, may retain possession of the above-mortgaged property and may use and enjoy the same.

In Witness Whereof, the said hereunto set hand and seal and affix and cancel the stamp required by law, this day of in the year one thousand eight hundred and

Signed, Sealed and Delivered in Presence of

SECTION V.

THE SALE OF ONE'S BUSINESS.

SUCH sales are not unfrequent in this country; and the seller always agrees and promises that he will not pursue that trade, business, or occupation again. There are numerous cases, both in English law-books and in our own, which have arisen from bargains of this kind. The law seems now to be settled, that such a contract is wholly void and inoperative, *provided* the seller agrees to give up his business and never resume it again, *at any time or anywhere ;* that is, without any limitation of space or time; because it is against the public interest that a man should be permitted to cast himself out from his business or trade for the rest of his life. But the contract is good, if for a fair consideration the seller agrees not to resume or carry on that business within a certain time, or within certain limits. What these limits must be is not certain. The courts say they must be "reasonable," and made in good faith. A contract not to carry on a business in a certain town would undoubtedly be good. So, we should say, would be a bargain not to do so within a certain State. In one case in Massachusetts, a contract not to use certain machines in any of the United States except *two* (which were Massachusetts and Rhode Island) was held valid, all of the States but two being considered as a sufficiently defined or limited place; but this was unusual. The courts generally would sanction such a bargain, if it were limited to only a part of the United States; as to all New England, for example.

In such a contract, it would be better for the parties to agree upon the amount which the seller should pay by way of damages, if he violated his bargain, because it might be very difficult to prove specific damages; and such a bargain, if it were reasonable, would be enforced by law.

Such damages, agreed on beforehand, are called *liquidated damages.* In all cases where damages are demanded, and are not agreed on, they are called *unliquidated damages*, and it is the duty of the jury to determine, from the evidence before them, what damages the injured party has suffered, and what amount would indemnify him.

CHAPTER XI.

STOPPAGE IN TRANSITU.

HERE is an instance where a Latin phrase has become English, by general adoption and use. *In transitu* means "in the transit," and the English phrase may just as well be used; but the Latin one is used much oftener. What the whole phrase *Stoppage in transitu* means, is this. A seller, who has sent goods to a buyer at a distance, and after sending them learns that the buyer is insolvent, may stop the goods at any time before they reach the buyer. His right to do this is called the right of *Stoppage in transitu*.

If the goods are sent to pay a precedent and existing debt, they are not subject to this right.

The right exists only upon actual insolvency; but this need not be formal insolvency, or bankruptcy at law; an actual inability to pay one's debts in the usual way being enough. If the seller, in good faith, stops the goods, in a belief of the buyer's insolvency, the buyer may at once defeat this stoppage, and reclaim the goods, by payment of the price. So he may, by a tender of adequate security, if the sale be on credit.

The stoppage must be effected by the seller, and evidenced by some act; but it is not necessary that he should take actual possession of the goods. If he gives a distinct notice to the party in possession, whether carrier, warehouseman, middleman, or whoever else, before the goods reach the buyer, this is enough. But a notice of stoppage *in transitu*, to be effectual, must be given either to the person who has the immediate custody of the goods; or if to the principal whose servant has the custody, then at such a time, and under such circumstances, as that he may, by the exercise of reasonable diligence, communicate it to his servant in time to prevent the delivery to the consignee.

Goods can be stopped only while *in transitu;* and they are in transitu only until they come into the possession of the buyer. But this possession need not be actual, a constructive possession by the buyer being sufficient to prevent this stoppage; as if the goods are placed on the wharf of the buyer, or on a neighboring wharf with notice to him; or in a warehouse with delivery of the key to him, or of an order on the warehouse-man.

But the entry of the goods at the custom-house, without payment of duties, does not terminate the transit. If the buyer has demanded and marked them at the place where they had arrived on the termination of the voyage or journey, personally or by his agent; or if the carrier still holds the goods, but only as the agent of the buyer; in all these cases the transit is ended. But if the carrier holds them by a lien for his charges against the buyer, the seller may pay these charges and discharge the lien, and then stop the goods *in transitu.*

If the buyer has, in good faith and for value, sold the goods, "to arrive," before he has received them, and indorsed and delivered the bill of lading, this second purchaser holds the goods free from the first seller's right to stop them. But if the goods and bill are transferred only as security for a debt due from the first purchaser to the transferee, the original seller may stop the goods, and hold them subject to this security, and need pay only the specific advances made on their credit, or on that very bill of lading, and not a general indebtedness of the first purchaser to the second.

A seller who stops the goods *in transitu* does not rescind the sale, but holds the goods as the *property* of the buyer; and they may be redeemed by the buyer or his representatives, by paying the price for which they are a security; and if not redeemed, they become the seller's, only in the same way as a pledge might become his; that is, he may sell them at a proper time, and in a proper manner, and with due notice, so that the buyer may protect his interests. And if the seller then fails to obtain from them the full price due, he has a claim for the balance upon the buyer. If he gets more than the amount due to him, he must pay over the balance to the buyer or his assignees.

An honest buyer, apprehending bankruptcy, might wish to return the goods to their original owner; and this he could undoubtedly do, if they have not become distinctly his property, and the seller his creditor for the price. But if they have, the buyer has no more right to benefit this creditor by such an appropriation of these goods, than any other creditor by giving him any other goods.

CHAPTER XII.

GUARANTY.

A GUARANTOR is one who is bound to another for the fulfilment of a promise, or of an engagement, made by a third party. This kind of contract is very common. Generally, it is not negotiable; that is, not transferable so as to be enforced by the transferee as if it had been given to him by the guarantor. No special form or words are necessary to the contract of guaranty; and if the word "guarantee" be used, and the whole instrument contains all the characteristics of a note of hand, payable to order or bearer, then it is negotiable. Thus, in a case in New York, the instrument was as follows: "For and in consideration of thirty-one dollars and fifty cents received of B. F. Spencer, I hereby guarantee the payment and collection of the within note to him or *bearer*. Auburn, Sept. 25, 1837. (Signed) Thomas Burns." And it was held negotiable. What *negotiable* means will be more fully explained in the chapter on Notes of Hand and Bills of Exchange.

The guaranty may be enforced, although the original debt cannot; as, for example, the guaranty of the promise of a wife or an infant; and sometimes the guaranty of a debt is requested, and given, for the very reason that the debt is not enforceable at law. But, generally, the liability of the principal measures and limits the liability of the guarantor. And if the creditor agree that the principal debt shall be reduced or lessened in a certain proportion, the obligation of the guarantor is reduced by law in an equal proportion.

A contract of guaranty is construed somewhat strictly. Thus, a guaranty of the notes of one, does not extend to notes which he gives jointly with another.

A guarantor who pays the debt of the principal may demand from his creditor the securities he holds, although not an assignment of the debt itself, or of the note or bond which declares the debt, for that is paid and discharged. And sometimes the creditor will not be permitted to resort to the guarantor, until he has collected as much as he can from these securities.

Unless the guaranty is by a sealed instrument, there must be a consideration to support it. If the original debt or obligation rest upon a good consideration, this will support the promise of guaranty, if this promise was made at the same time with or prior to the original debt. But if that debt or obligation be first incurred and completed, before the guaranty is given, there must be a new consideration for the promise to guarantee that debt, or the guaranty is void. But the consideration need not pass from him who receives the guaranty to him who gives it. Any benefit to him for whom the guaranty is given, or any injury to him who receives it, is a sufficient consideration if the guaranty be given because of it.

A guaranty is not binding unless it is accepted, and unless the guarantor has knowledge of this. But the law presumes this acceptance in general, when the giving of the guaranty and any action on the faith of it, by the party to whom it is given, are simultaneous. In New York, wherever the guaranty is absolute, notice of its acceptance is unnecessary, unless expressly or impliedly required by the offer of guaranty. But, generally, an offer to guarantee a future operation, especially if by letter, does not bind the offerer, unless he has such notice of the acceptance of his offer as would give him a reasonable opportunity of making himself safe.

If the liability of the principal be materially varied by the act of the party guaranteed, without the consent of the guarantor, the guarantor is discharged. Many interesting cases have arisen, which involve this question. Thus, where a bond was given conditioned for the faithful performance of the duties of the office of deputy collector of direct taxes for eight certain townships, and the instrument of appointment, referred to in the bond, was afterwards altered, so as to extend to another township, without the consent of the surety, the Supreme Court of the United States held that the surety was discharged from his responsiblity for moneys collected by his principal after the alteration. Again, in an English case, the facts were, that, in a bond by sureties for the careful attention to business and the faithful discharge of the duties of an agent of a bank, it was provided "that he should have no other business of any kind, nor be connected in any shape with any trade, manufacture, or mercantile copartnery, nor be agent of any individual or copartnery in any manner or way whatsoever, nor be security for any individual or copartnery in any manner or way whatsoever." The bank subsequently, without the knowledge of the sureties, increased the salary of the agent, he undertaking to bear one-fourth part of all losses which might be incurred by his discounts. It was held that this was such an alteration of the contract, and of the liability of the agent, that the sureties were discharged, notwithstanding that the loss arose, not from discounts, but from improper conduct of the agent.

The guarantor is also discharged if the liability or obligation be renewed or extended by law. As if a bank, incorporated for twenty years, be renewed for ten more, and the officers and business of the bank go on without change; the original sureties of the cashier are not held beyond the first term. So a guaranty to a partnership is extinguished by a change among the members, although neither the name nor the business of the firm be changed. But a guaranty, by express terms, may be made to continue over most changes of this kind.

A specific guaranty, for one transaction which is not yet exhausted, is not revocable. If it be a continuing or a general guaranty, it is revocable, unless an express agreement, founded on a consideration, makes it otherwise.

A creditor may give his debtor some accommodation or indulgence, without thereby discharging his guarantor. It would seem just, however, that he should not be permitted to give him any indulgence which would materially prejudice the guarantor. Generally, a guarantor may always pay a debt, and so acquire at once the right of proceeding against the party whose debt he has paid. On this ground, it has been held, that where a surety requested the creditor to proceed against the principal debtor, and the creditor refused to do this, and afterwards the debtor became insolvent and the surety was without indemnity, still, the surety (or guarantor) was not discharged, because he might have paid the debt, and then sued the party whose debt he paid. In New York, it seems to be the law, that, if the surety requests the creditor to proceed against the principal debtor, and he refuses, and the principal debtor afterwards becomes insolvent, the surety will be discharged. If, by gross negligence, the creditor has lost his debt, and has deprived the surety of security or indemnity, the surety must be discharged, unless he was equally negligent. If a creditor gives time to his debtor, by a binding agreement which will prevent a suit in the mean time, this undoubtedly discharges the guarantor (unless the surety consents to the delay) because it deprives him of his power of acquiring a right of proceeding against the debtor, by paying the debt; for the debtor cannot during that time be sued.

If there be a failure on the part of the principal, and the guarantor is looked to, he should have reasonable notice of this. And, generally, any notice would be reasonable which would be sufficient in fact to prevent his suffering from the delay. And if there be no notice, and the guarantor has been unharmed thereby, he is not discharged.

If a guaranty purport to be official, that is, if it be made by one who claims to hold a certain office, and to give the promise of guaranty only as such officer, and not personally, the general rule is, that he is not liable personally, provided he actually held that office and had a right to give the guaranty officially. But he would still be held personally, if the promise made, or the relations of the parties indicated that credit was given personally to the parties promising, and not merely to them in their official capacity; or if he had no right to give the promise in his official capacity.

A guaranty was given for the price of a cargo of iron; and the buyer bargained with the seller to pay him more than the fair price, the excess to go towards an old debt. The guaranty was held to be altogether void, because fraudulent; and could not be enforced even for the fair price.

FORMS OF GUARANTY.

(39.)

Guaranty to be indorsed on a Note.

For value received I guarantee the due payment of the within written note.

(*Date.*) (*Signature.*)

(40.)

Guaranty of a Note on Separate Paper.

For value received I guarantee the due payment of a promissory note, dated whereby promises to pay to , dollars, in months.

(*Date.*) (*Signature.*)

(41.)

Guaranty in Another Way.

For value received I guarantee that the within (*note or bill, or that such a note or bill, describing it*) will be collected and paid if demanded in due course of law.

(*Date.*) (*Signature.*)

(42.)

Letter of Guaranty.

Sir, — If you will sell to Mr. of the goods he wishes to buy (*or the goods may be described*) to the amount of (*this may be omitted if the guaranty is intended to be of any amount*), within year (*or days or months, or the time may be omitted if it is not intended to limit it*) from the date hereof, I, for value received, hereby promise and guarantee that the price thereof shall be duly paid. (*This letter should also state on what terms the goods should be sold, as to credit, delivery, &c., unless it is intended to leave all this to the buyer and seller.*)

(*Date.*) (*Signature.*)

When goods or stocks or other securities are given as collateral security for borrowed money or any other debt, an instrument is sometimes given, the intention of which is to guarantee that the collaterals should be and remain sufficient to secure the indebtedness. It may be in one of the following forms, as the bargain requires. These are sometimes called "margin guaranties."

(43.)

Guaranty with Collaterals authorizing Sale.

Whereas, I (*or we*) have deposited with as collateral security for payment at maturity of the following (*here describe the debt guaranteed*)

Now this Witnesseth, That in the event of the non-payment at maturity of any or all of these hereby authorize or assigns, to sell the above (*the collaterals*) at public or private sale, or at the brokers' board, without notice to and apply proceeds to payment of said and all necessary expenses, holding responsible for any deficiency.

In Witness Whereof, have hereunto set hand and seal , this day of one thousand eight hundred and

(*Signature.*)

(*Witness.*)

(44.)

Guaranty with Collaterals, promising Additional Security or authorizing Sale.

Having Borrowed this Day of (*the sum borrowed*) on the following collaterals (*here describe the collaterals*).

I Hereby Agree, in case the market-price of the said stock should fall at any time during the continuance of the loan to an amount insufficient to cover the sum loaned, with per cent margin added thereto, that in such event I will, on demand, deposit additional security to be approved by him, which shall be sufficient to keep the collaterals thus deposited, equal to a sum per cent above said loan, and so as often as said collaterals shall diminish; and that, in default thereof, the said shall have power to sell at public or private sale, without notice, all, or any of the said securities (as well as any others he may hold), to pay the amount of the said loan, with all interest and charges thereon, and for so doing, I fully release him of all claims, actions, and causes thereof.

CHAPTER XIII.

THE STATUTE OF FRAUDS.

SECTION I.

ITS PURPOSE AND GENERAL PROVISIONS.

The Statute of Frauds, so called, was passed in the 29th year of Charles II. (1677) for the purpose of preventing frauds and perjuries, by requiring in many cases written evidence of a contract. In nearly all our States a similar statute has been enacted. But no two of the statutes of the different States agree exactly in all their provisions. They do, however, agree substantially; and we shall give in this chapter the prevailing and nearly universal rules for the construction and application of this statute. It is often of very great importance in commercial transactions. Those provisions which especially relate to business law are contained in the fourth and seventeenth sections.

By the fourth section, it is enacted that "no action shall be brought whereby to charge any executor or administrator, upon any special promise, to answer damages out of his own estate; or whereby to charge the defendant, upon any special promise, to answer for the debt, default, or miscarriages of another person; or to charge any person upon any agreement made upon consideration of marriage; or any contract for sale of lands, tenements, or hereditaments, or any interest in or concerning them; or upon any agreement that is not to be performed within the space of one year from the making thereof; unless the agreement, upon which such action shall be brought, or some memorandum or note thereof, shall be in writing, and signed by the party to be charged therewith, or some other person thereunto by him lawfully authorized."

By the seventeenth section, it is enacted that "no contract for the sale of any goods, wares, and merchandises, for the price of

£10 sterling, or upwards, shall be allowed to be good, except the buyer shall accept part of the goods so sold, and actually receive the same, or give something in earnest to bind the bargain, or in part of payment, or that some note or memorandum in writing of the said bargain be made and signed by the parties to be charged by such contract, or their agents thereunto lawfully authorized."

The second and fifth clauses of the fourth section, and the whole of the seventeenth, relate to our present subject. The second clause prevents an *oral* guaranty from being enforced at law ; but if money be paid on one, it cannot be recovered back.

SECTION II.

A PROMISE TO PAY THE DEBT OF ANOTHER.

It is very often difficult to say whether the promise of one to pay for goods delivered to another is an *original* promise, as to pay for one's own goods, and then it need not be in writing, or a promise to pay the debt or guaranty the promise of him to whom the goods are delivered, and then it must be in writing. If it be a promise to pay the debt of another, it is said to be a *collateral* promise, and not an *original* promise. The question may always be said to be: *To whom did the seller give, and was authorized to give, credit?* This question the jury will decide, upon consideration of all the facts, under the direction of the court. If a seller sues one to whom he did not deliver the goods, on the ground that this other promised to pay for them, then the question is, Did this other promise to pay for them as for his own goods? for then the promise need not be in writing. Or did he promise to pay for them as for the goods of the party receiving them? and then it is a promise to pay the debt of another, and must be in writing. If, on examination of the books of the seller, it appears that he charged the goods to the party who received them, it will be difficult, if not impossible, for the seller to maintain that he sold them to the other party. But if he charged them to this other, such an entry would be good evidence, and, if confirmed by circumstances, strong evidence that this party was the purchaser. But it cannot be conclusive; for the party not receiving the goods may always prove, if he can, that he was not the buyer, and that he promised only as surety for the party who was the buyer; and, consequently, that his promise cannot be enforced if not in writing. And, in general, in determining this question, the court will always look to the actual character of the transaction, and the intention of the parties.

The courts, both in England and in America, have often endeavored to illustrate this question. Thus, in an early English case, the court said: "If two come to a shop, and one buys, and the other, to gain him credit, promises the seller, 'If he does not pay you, I will,' this is a *collateral* undertaking, and void, without writing, by the Statute of Frauds. But if he says, 'Let him have the goods, I will be your paymaster,' this is an undertaking as for himself, and he shall be intended to be the very buyer, and the other to act but as his servant." So, in a case in Maryland, the court said: "If B gives credit to C for goods sold and delivered to him, on the promise of A to 'see him paid,' or 'to pay him for them if C should not,' in that case it is the immediate debt of C, for which an action will lie against him, and the promise of A is a collateral undertaking to pay that debt [and must be in writing], he being only liable as a surety. But where the party undertaken for is under no liability himself, the promise is an original undertaking of the party promising, and binding upon him without being in writing. Thus, if B furnishes goods to C, on the express promise of A to pay for them, as if A says to him, 'Let C have goods to such an amount, and I will pay you,' and the credit is given to A, in that case C being under no liability, there is nothing to which the promise of A can be collateral; but A being the immediate debtor, it is his original undertaking, and not a promise to answer for the debt of another;" and therefore need not be in writing.

Whenever the main purpose and object of the promisor is not to answer for another, but to subserve some purpose of his own, his promise is not within the statute, although it may be in form a promise to pay the debt of another, and although the performance of it may incidentally have the effect of extinguishing the liability of another. If an old debt is extinguished by a new promise, this promise is considered as an original one and not within the requirement of the statute.

If there be an oral promise to pay the debt of another, and also to do some other thing, this last can be enforced at law, if this other thing, and so much of the promise as relates to it, can be severed from the debt of the other and the promise relating to that debt; for although *that* promise must be in writing, the other may be oral.

SECTION III.

AN AGREEMENT NOT TO BE PERFORMED WITHIN A YEAR.

UNDER the fifth clause in the fourth section, it is held that an agreement which *may* be performed within the year is not affected by the statute, as the words, "that is not to be performed within one year," do not apply to an agreement which, when made, was, and by the parties was understood to be, fairly capable of complete execution within a year, without the intervention of extraordinary circumstances, — although in point of fact its execution was extended much beyond the year. So where one agreed orally, for one guinea, to give another a number of guineas on the day of his marriage, it was held that this promise was not within the statute, that is, not one which the statute required to be in writing, because he might be married within a year, and the promisor was therefore bound by it. So where one agreed orally never to go into the staging business in a certain place, as this contract could last only while the promisor lived, and he might die within a year, he was held to be bound by it.

SECTION IV.

THE FORM AND SUBJECT-MATTER OF THE AGREEMENT.

THE "agreement" must be in writing; but generally, in this country, the writing need not contain or express the consideration, which may be proved otherwise. Nor need it be all on one piece of paper. For it is sufficient if on several pieces, as in several letters, which, however, relate to one and the same business, and may fairly be read together as the statement of one transaction. But it must appear from the papers that they are so connected.

The "signature" may be in any part of the paper, — the beginning, middle, or end, except in those of our States in which the statute has the word "subscribed" instead of "signed;" in which case it should be in the usual place at the bottom. If the name and the agreement be *printed*, it is sufficient; hence, a printed shop-bill, with the name of the seller, as usual, at the beginning, if delivered to the buyer, is generally sufficient to charge the seller in an action for refusing to deliver the goods.

Shares in railroad companies, in manufacturing companies, and, generally, in all corporations and joint-stock companies, are "goods, wares, or merchandises," within the meaning of the statute, in this country, and an agreement for their purchase and sale must therefore be in writing.

It may be further remarked, that the operation of the statute has been always limited to such contracts as have not been executed in any substantial part, and therefore remain wholly executory. For if they have been executed substantially in good part, they are binding, although only oral.

In Massachusetts, the Statute of Frauds also provides (3d section) that no action shall be brought to charge any person upon, or by reason of, any representation or assurance made concerning the character, conduct, credit, ability, trade, or dealings of any other person, unless it be made in writing, and signed by the party to be charged. And there are provisions substantially similar to this in the statutes of Maine and Vermont.

Instead of the "£10" in the seventeenth section of the English Statute, the sum mentioned in the Statutes of Frauds of the different States, is, generally, from thirty to fifty dollars.

CHAPTER XIV.

PAYMENT AND TENDER.

SECTION I.

HOW PAYMENT MAY BE MADE.

THE obligations which arise out of most mercantile contracts are to be satisfied by payment of money. The parties may always agree to any specific manner of payment, and then that becomes obligatory on the creditor as well as the debtor. As, by deducting the amount to be paid from a debt due to the debtor either from the creditor or from any one else. Or the amount may be made, by agreement, payable by a bill or note. If the debt is to be paid by a bill, it must be such a bill as is agreed upon, and this must be tendered by the debtor. But the word "bill" does not necessarily mean an "approved bill;" and if this phrase be itself used, it means only a bill to which there is no reasonable objection; that is, one which ought to be approved.

In the absence of any especial agreement, the only payment known to the law is by cash, which the debtor must pay when it is due, or tender to the creditor.

The tender should, properly, be in cash, or in bills made a legal tender by law, and must be so if that is required; but a tender in good and current bank-bills is sufficient, unless it be objected to because they are not money.

Generally, if the tender be refused for any express and specific reason, the creditor cannot afterwards take advantage of any *informality*, to which he did not object at the time of the tender.

The tender may be of a larger sum than is due. But a tender of a larger sum, if made with a requirement of change or of the balance, is not good. Nor must it be accompanied with a demand or condition that any instrument or document shall be delivered; nor that the sum tendered shall be received as all that is due; nor that a receipt in full shall be given. But a simple receipt for so much money paid may be demanded. We have already seen that, if a receipt be given, it is only strong evidence of payment, but not conclusive. And even if it be "in full of all demands," it is still open to explanation or denial by evidence.

A lawful tender, and payment of the money into court, is a good defence to an action for the debt. But the creditor may break down this defence by proving, that, subsequently to the tender, he demanded the money of the debtor, and the debtor refused to give it.

If the buyer or debtor give, and the seller or creditor receive, a negotiable note or bill for the sum due, this is not anywhere absolute and conclusive payment. In Maine and in Massachusetts the law presumes that such note or bill is payment of the debt, unless a contrary intention is shown. In nearly all the States of this Union but those two, and in the Supreme Court of the United States, it is not payment, unless the intention of the parties that it should be so is shown. In New York, it has been held that the debtor's own promissory note is not payment, even if it be intended or expressly agreed that it should be. If a creditor, who receives from his debtor any bill or note, negotiates or sells it for value to a third party, without making himself liable, the bill or note was payment, although it be dishonored, because it has been good to the debtor, and he has received the avails of it; and if the law did not hold that the bill had paid the debt, he could sue the original debt, and then he would have the value of the bill, or payment, twice. Not so, however, if he negotiates it in such a way that he is himself liable upon it; for if he pays it, he loses what he sold it for, unless he can recover his debt from his debtor.

SECTION II.

APPROPRIATION OF PAYMENT.

If one who owes several debts to his creditor makes to him a general payment, it may be an important question to which of those debts this payment shall be appropriated; for some of them may be secured, and others not, or some of them may carry interest, and others not, or some of them be barred by the Statute of Limitations, and others not.

There is no doubt that the payor may appropriate his payment, at the time of the payment, at his own pleasure. And if he does not exercise this right, the receiver may, at the time of payment, make the appropriation. But if neither party does this *at that time*, and at a future period the question comes up as to which party may then make the appropriation, or rather, how the law will then appropriate the payment, it is then the better and prevailing rule, that, if the court can ascertain, either from the words used, or from the circumstances of the case, or from any usage, what was the intention and understanding of the parties at the time of the payment, that intention will be carried into effect. And if this cannot be ascertained, then the court will direct such appropriation of the payment as will best protect the rights and interests of both parties, and do justice between them. And one reason for this conclusion would be, that the law would presume that this was the original intention of the parties. A very general rule, which would indeed be always adopted in the absence of especial reason to the contrary, is, to apply the payment first to the oldest debt, until that is satisfied, and then go on applying the payment to the other debts in the order of their age.

If A owes a debt to B, on B's own account, and another debt to B as trustee for somebody, and A pays B a sum of money without appropriating it, B cannot apply it all to the debt due him on his own account; but must divide it between that debt and the debt due to him as trustee, in proportion to their respective amounts. Because it is his duty as trustee to take as good care of the debts due to him for another, as of those due to him on his own account.

We have spoken of a "bill or note;" and notes are sometimes called bills; so bank-notes are often called bank-bills. But the legal meaning of "bill" is always a *draft* or *order* on somebody to pay money. A note is a *promise* to pay. See chapter on Notes and Bills.

CHAPTER XV.

RECEIPTS AND RELEASES.

A RECEIPT is only an acknowledgment that a sum of money has been paid. It may be in one word, as when, under a bill of parcels, the seller writes the word "paid," and signs it. More commonly the words are, "Received Payment." Formerly it was usual to add the words "Errors Excepted." Then it grew customary to write the initial letters "E. E." instead of the words; but all this is unnecessary. If there be an error in the receipt, or in the paper receipted, the law permits the party injured by it to explain and correct the error, although there be no express reservation or exception of errors.

Receipts are of all degrees of fulness, from the single word "paid," to those which relate the particulars for which the receipt is given, and the manner in which the money was paid, or the thing delivered. I give the following forms: —

(45.)

(*Date.*) This day I have received from . . . . dollars.

(*Signature.*)

(46.)

(*Date.*) This day I have received from . . . . dollars, on account of

(*Signature.*)

(47.)

(*Date.*) This day the following (*papers*, or other articles, enumerating and describing them) were delivered to me by , (*add, on account of, or in execution of, the promise or bargain, describing it; and, if they are delivered for any particular purpose, describe that*), and I hereby acknowledge the receipt of them.

(*Signature.*)

Every receipt is open to evidence, not only to explain it, but to contradict it. Herein releases differ from receipts. A release gives up some right or claim which the releasor had against the releasee. It is in the nature of a contract, and therefore cannot be controlled or contradicted by evidence, unless on the ground of fraud. But if its words are ambiguous, or may have either of two or more meanings, evidence is receivable to determine the meaning.

Like every other contract, it requires a consideration, and is of no force without one. But here comes in the rule of law as to a seal. The general rule is, as has been stated before, a seal implies, or is the same as, the assertion of a consideration; and therefore it is always customary to put a seal to a release. But a release, even with a seal, if it can be shown to have been given without any consideration whatever, can be set aside. It is always best to state in the release itself that it was given for a consideration, and what the consideration is. A release properly drawn, and duly signed and sealed, is a complete defence to an action grounded on any of the debts or claims released.

The following forms are for releases of various kinds: —

(48.)

A General Release.

Know all Men by these Presents, That I, (*the name of the releaser*) of   for and in consideration of the sum of   , to me paid by   of   , have remised, released, and forever discharged, and by these presents do, for me, my heirs, executors, and administrators, remise, release, and forever discharge the said   his heirs, executors, and administrators, of and from all and all manner of action and actions, cause and causes of action, suits, debts, dues, sum and sums of money, accounts, reckonings, bonds, bills, specialties, covenants, contracts, controversies, agreements, promises, variances, damages, judgments, extents, executions, claims, and demands whatsoever, in law and in equity, which against the said   I ever had, now have, or which I, my executors or administrators hereafter can, shall, or may have, for, upon, or by reason of, any matter, cause, or thing whatsoever, from the beginning of the world to the day of the date of these presents.

In Witness Whereof, &c.

(49.)

A Mutual General Release by Indenture.

This Indenture, Made between of and of , witnesseth, that the said doth, by these presents remise, release and forever quit claim, unto the said , all and all manner of actions, (*as before;*) and this indenture further witnesseth, that the said by these presents, doth remise, release, and forever quit claim, unto the said all and all manner of actions, (*as before*).

In Witness Whereof, &c.

(50.)

A Release from Creditors to a Debtor, under a Composition.

To all Persons to whom these Presents may come, we who have hereunto set our hands and seals, creditors of of , send greeting. Whereas the said is indebted to us his said creditors, in several sums of money, which he is not able fully to satisfy and discharge; we therefore have agreed, and do hereby agree, to accept of the sum of in full payment and satisfaction of all the debts, owing to us respectively at the date hereof, by and from the said , which is paid by or for the said (*the name of the debtor*) to (*the names of the persons to whom the money is to be paid for the creditors releasing*) * *and assignees by virtue of a commission, of bankrupt awarded against the said* , for the use of, and to the intent that the same may be shared and divided amongst us his said creditors, *seeking relief under the said commission*, in proportion and according to the debts to us severally due and owing: Now therefore know ye, that for the consideration aforesaid, each of us, the said creditors who have hereunto set our hands and seals, for him and herself, his and her heirs, executors, and copartners, doth by these presents, remise, release, and forever discharge the said his heirs, executors, and administrators, of and from our said several debts, and all and all manner of action and actions which against the said , each and every of us the said creditors now hath, or which each and every of our heirs, executors, or administrators respectively, hereafter may, can, or ought to have, claim, or demand, for, upon, or by reason of, the said several and respective debts to us severally due and owing, or for or by reason of any other matter, cause, or thing whatsoever from the beginning of the world.

In Witness Whereof, &c.

* The words *following* in *Italic* may be omitted according to circumstances.

(51.)

A Release of all Legacies.

Know all Men by these Presents, That I of widow, have remised, released, and forever quit claimed, and by these presents do for me unto of , gentleman, executor of the last will and testament of late of , deceased, and to the heirs, executors, and administrators of the said , all legacies, gifts, bequests, sum and sums of money and demands whatsoever, bequeathed and given unto me the said , in and by the last will and testament of , deceased, and all and all manner of actions and suits, sum and sums of money, debts, duties, reckonings, accounts, and demands whatsoever, which I the said ever had, now have, or that I, my executors or administrators, can or may, at any time or times hereafter, have, challenge, or demand against the said his executors, administrators, or assigns, for or by reason of any matter, cause, or thing whatsoever, from the beginning of the world until the day of the date hereof.

In Witness Whereof, &c.

(52.)

A Release of a Bond, it being Lost.

To all to whom these Presents may come, (*name of releaser*) sendeth greeting. Whereas by his bond or obligation, bearing date (*recite the bond*), as by the said bond or obligation, and the condition thereof may appear: And whereas the sum of mentioned in the said bond, with all the interest for the same, is paid and satisfied unto me the said , in full discharge for the said bond or obligation: And whereas the said bond or obligation is lost, or at present mislaid, so that it cannot be found to be delivered up to the said , to be cancelled: Now know ye, that I the said for the consideration aforesaid, have remised, released, and quit claimed, and by these presents do, for me, my executors and administrators, remise unto the said his heirs, executors, and administrators, as well the said recited bond or obligation, as all such sums of money as therein are mentioned to be due and payable, unto me the said my executors, administrators, or assigns; and also all actions, suits, cause and causes of action, accounts, debts, reckonings, sums of money, judgments, executions, and demands whatsoever, which I, the said ever had, now have, or that I, my executors, administrators, or assigns, or any of us, can or may have, for or against the said his executors or administrators, for, or by reason of, the said recited bond or obligation, or any other matter, cause, or thing whatsoever, concerning the same, from the beginning of the world to the day of the date hereof.

In Witness Whereof, I the said have hereunto set my hand and seal this day of

(Signatures.) *(Seals.)*

In Presence of

(The following covenant may be inserted before "In witness.")

And I, the said for me, my executors, , do covenant , to and with the said , his , that if I the said , my executors, , or any of us, at any time hereafter, do find or can obtain the said recited bond or obligation, then I, the said , my executors , or some of us, shall and will, within two months next after the said obligation shall be found as aforesaid, deliver, or cause to be delivered, the said bond or obligation, unto the said his .

(53.)

A Release of a Judgment.

This Indenture, Made the day of in the year one thousand eight hundred and between of the second part,

Whereas, Judgment was rendered on the day of in the year one thousand eight hundred and in an action in the between plaintiff and defendant in favor of the said against the said for the sum of as appears by the

Now this Indenture Witnesseth, That the said part of the first part in consideration of the sum of to duly paid at the time of the sealing and delivery of these presents, the receipt whereof is hereby acknowledged, ha granted, released, discharged and set over, and by these presents do grant, release, discharge and set over, unto the said part of the second part, the following described premises, to wit:

Together with the hereditaments and appurtenances thereto belonging; and all the right, title and interest of the said part of the first part, of, in and to the same, to the intent that the lands hereby conveyed may be released and discharged from the said above-mentioned judgment, and from all lien or incumbrance that has attached to the same, by reason of the recovery of the said judgment, as free and clear in all respects as though said judgment had not been rendered. To have and to hold, the lands and premises hereby released and conveyed, to the said part of the second part heirs and assigns, to their only proper use, benefit and behoof forever, free, clear and discharged of and from all lien and claim, under and by virtue of the judgment aforesaid.

In Witness Whereof, The said part of the first part ha hereunto set hand and seal the day and year first above written.

(*Signatures.*) (*Seals.*)

In Presence of

(54.)

A Release of a Condition.

Know all Men by these Presents, That I, of , for divers good considerations me hereunto moving, have remised, released, and quit claimed, and by these presents, for me, my executors, administrators, and assigns, do unto of , his heirs, executors, administrators, and assigns, as well one proviso or condition and all and every the sum and sums of money, specified in the same proviso or condition, contained or comprised in one pair of indentures of bearing date , made between me the said , of the one part, and the said of the other part, and also all and all manner of actions and suits, cause and causes of actions and suits, for or concerning the said proviso or condition.

In Witness Whereof, I the said have hereunto set my hand and seal this day of

(*Signature.*) (*Seal.*)

In Presence of

(55.)

A Release of a Covenant contained in an Indenture of Lease.

To all Persons to whom these Presents may come, (*name of releaser*) sendeth greeting. Whereas in and by an indenture of lease, bearing date made between , of the one part, and the said of the other part, there is contained a covenant in these words following, viz. (*recite the covenant verbatim, as therein contained*) whereunto relation being had, it doth at large appear: Now know ye, that I, the said , for divers good causes and considerations, me hereunto moving, have remised, released, and quit claimed and by these presents for me do unto the said , his the said covenant, grant, clause, agreement, and article, before rehearsed or recited, and all and every other matter, thing, and things specified, declared, and contained in the same covenant, clause, and agreement, and all the benefit, profit, advantage, and commodity, that by any manner of means, may or might arise, grow, come, or happen to me the said , for or by reason of the same covenant, clause, article, or agreement, or any word, sentence, matter, thing, or things therein contained, so that the said his executors and assigns, and every of them, from henceforth forever, shall be fully acquitted, released, and discharged against me the said my executors, and administrators, and every of us, of, from, and for the said covenant, grant, clause, article, and agreement before rehearsed or recited, and of, from, and for, every thing and things, touching the same (but this present release shall not in anywise extend to any other covenant, clause, or article in the said indenture contained).

In Witness Whereof, I the said have hereunto set my hand and seal this day of

In Presence of (*Signature.*) (*Seal.*)

(56.)

A Release in Extinguishment of a Power.

To all Persons to whom these Presents may come, Now know ye, that I, the said , pursuant to the said agreement, and for divers good causes and considerations me hereunto moving, have released, extinguished, and discharged, and by these presents do fully and absolutely release, extinguish, and discharge, the said recited power for raising the said sum of as aforesaid, and all the lands therein comprised, or subject thereto, so that I, the said shall not, nor will, at any time or times hereafter, raise the same, or any part thereof, or hereafter charge the said lands with the payment thereof, or any part thereof.

In Witness Whereof, I the said have hereunto set my hand and seal this day of

In Presence of (*Signature.*) (*Seal.*)

(57.)

A Release from a Lessor to a Lessee (upon his surrendering his Lease) from the Covenants therein.

To all Persons to whom these Presents may come, (*name of releaser*) sends greeting: Whereas the said by his indenture of lease, bearing date , did demise unto a messuage in at a certain rent, for a certain term of years, of which about years are yet to come and undetermined, in which said lease are contained covenants for repairing the said premises, and other covenants, on the part of the said to be performed: And whereas, by agreement between the said and the said hath delivered up the said recited lease, and surrendered the same, and all his interest and term in and to the said house and premises: Now therefore know ye, that the said , in consideration tnereof, doth hereby, for himself, his heirs, executors and administrators, remise, release, and forever discharge the said his executors and administrators, of and from all and every the covenants and agreements, in the said recited lease contained, by and on the part and behalf of the said his to be done and performed, and from all actions, suits, costs, charges, payments, damages, claims, and demands whatsoever, in law and equity, for or concerning the same in any manner of wise.

In Witness Whereof, I the said have hereunto set my hand and seal this day of

(*Signature.*) (*Seal.*)

In Presence of

(58.)

A General Release of Dower.

To all to whom these Presents shall come, (*name of releaser*) send greeting: Know ye, that the said the party of the first part to these presents, for and in consideration of the sum of lawful money of the United States, to her in hand paid at or before the ensealing and delivery of these presents, by of the second part, the receipt whereof is hereby acknowledged, hath granted, remised, released, and forever quit claimed, and by these presents doth grant, remise, release, and forever quit claim, unto the said party of the second part, heirs and assigns forever, all the dower and thirds, right and title of dower and thirds, and all other right, title, interest, property, claim and demand whatsoever, in law and equity, of her, the said party of the first part, of, in, and to (*here describe the estate the dower in which is released*)

so that she, the said party of the first part, her heirs, executors, administrators or assigns, nor any other person or persons, for her, them, or any of them, shall not have, claim, challenge, or demand, or pretend to have, claim, challenge, or demand, any dower or thirds, or any other right, title, claim or demand whatsoever, of, in or to the same, or any part or parcel thereof, in whosoever hands, seisin, or possession the same may or can be, and thereof and therefrom shall be utterly barred and excluded forever by these presents.

In Witness Whereof, The said party of the first part to these presents hath hereunto set her hand and seal, the day of in the year of our Lord one thousand eight hundred and

Signature.) (*Seal.*)

In Presence of

(59.)

A Release of Dower to the Heir

Know all Men by these Presents, That I relict of late , as well for and in consideration of to me paid, at or before , by my son , the receipt whereof I do hereby acknowledge, and for the love and affection which I have to my said son, have granted, remised, released and forever quit claimed, and by these presents do unto the said his heirs and assigns forever, all the dower and thirds, right and title of dower and thirds, and all other right, title, interest, property claim, and demand whatsoever, in law and in equity, of me the said of, in, and to (*a description of the parcel of land in which dower is released*) so that neither I, the said my heirs, executors, or administrators, nor any other person or persons for me, them, or any of them, shall have, claim, challenge, or demand, or pretend to have any dower or thirds, or any other right, title, claim, or demand, of, in, or to the said premises, but thereof and therefrom, shall be utterly debarred and excluded, forever, by these presents.

In Witness Whereof, The said party of the first part to these presents hath hereunto set her hand and seal, the day of in the year of our Lord one thousand eight hundred and

(*Signature.*) (*Seal.*)

In Presence of

(60.)

A Release of Dower in Consideration of an Annuity given by Will.

To all Persons to whom these Presents may come, (*name of releaser*) widow, relict and residuary legatee of late of , deceased, sendeth greeting. Whereas the said , in and by his last will and testament, duly signed, sealed, published, and declared in my presence and with my approbation, bearing date , did settle and secure unto and upon me the said , an annuity of to be paid unto me half yearly, by equal payments, in lieu and full satisfaction of the dower or thirds at common law, which I might otherwise have, claim, or be entitled unto, out of all and every the lands, tenements, and hereditaments whatsoever, of my said late husband, deceased, or of, in, to, or out of the reversion or remainder, rents, issues, and profits thereof: Now know ye, that I the said for and in consideration of the said annuity so secured to me as aforesaid, and in pursuance and part performance of the said last will and testament of my said late husband, do hereby declare myself fully satisfied and contented therewith, and do hereby remise, release, and forever quit claim unto of , and of , trustees, appointed in and by the said last will and testament of my said late husband (in their actual possession and seisin now being) their executors , all and all manner of dower in and to the said premises, but thereof and therefrom, shall be utterly debarred and excluded, forever, by these presents.

In Witness Whereof, The said party of the first part to these presents hath hereunto set her hand and seal, the day of in the year of our Lord one thousand eight hundred and

(*Signature.*) (*Seal.*)

In Presence of

(61.)

A Release of Dower where the Husband of the Widow joins in the Deed. MSS.

Know all Men by these Presents, That (*name of husband*) of and (*name of wife*) his wife, in her right, in consideration of paid them by of , the receipt whereof they hereby acknowledge, have granted, remised, released, and forever quit claimed, and by these presents do unto the said his heirs and assigns forever, all the right which the said hath to dower or thirds, of and in (*here describe the estate*) whereof her late husband (*name of former husband*) late died seized, situate, , which she claims as of the endowment of the said deceased, and all the right, title, interest, and claim whatsoever, which the said and have, or either of them hath, or by law might have, of, in, and to the same : To have and to hold the same to the said and his heirs and assigns forever; and the said and for themselves, their heirs, executors, and administrators, do hereby covenant with the said and his heirs and assigns, that he and they shall henceforth forever, have and quietly enjoy the released premises, without any claim or demand had or made, or to be had or made by them, or any persons, claiming, or who may claim the same or any part thereof, by, from, or under them or their heirs.

In Witness Whereof, The said party of the first part to these presents hath hereunto set her hand and seal, the day of in the year of our Lord one thousand eight hundred and

(*Signature.*) (*Seal.*)

In Presence of

(62.)

A Release of a Trust.

To all to whom these Presents may come, (*name of releaser*) sendeth greeting. Whereas, by indenture bearing date , made between (*here recite the deed*) in which said indenture the said doth hereby declare, that his name was only used in trust, for the benefit and behoof of of : Now know ye, that I, the said , in discharge of the trust reposed in me, at the request of the said , have remised, released, and surrendered, assigned, and set over, and by these presents, for me, my executors and administrators, do freely and absolutely remise unto the said his executors , all the estate, right, title, interest, use, benefit, privilege, and demand whatsoever, which I the said have, or may have or claim, of, or to the said premises, or of and in any sum of money, or other matter or thing whatsoever, in the said indenture contained, mentioned, and expressed, so that neither I the said my executors or administrators, or any of us, at any time hereafter, shall or will ask, claim, challenge, or demand any interest or other thing, in any manner whatsoever, by reason or means of the said indenture, or any covenant therein contained, but thereof and therefrom, and from all actions, suits, and demands, which I, my executors, administrators, or assigns, may have concerning the same, shall be utterly excluded and forever debarred, by these presents.

In Witness Whereof, The said party of the first part to these presents hath hereunto set her hand and seal, the day of in the year of our Lord one thousand eight hundred and

In Presence of (*Signature.*) (*Seal.*)

(63.)

A Release of Right to Lands.

Know all Men by these Presents, That I (*name of releaser*) of , in consideration of to me paid by (*name of releasee*) the receipt , have remised, released, and forever quit claimed, and by these presents do unto the said and his heirs, all the estate, right, title, interest, use, trust, claim, and demand whatsoever, both at law and in equity, which I, the said have, of, in, to, or out of, all and singular the following described parcel of land (*here describe the land*) so that neither I the said , my heirs or assigns, or any other person or persons in trust for me or them, or in my or their name or names, or in the name, right, or stead of any of them, shall or will, can or may, by any ways or means whatsoever, hereafter have, claim, challenge, or demand, any right, title, or interest, property, claim, and demand, of, in, to, or out of the same , or any of them, or any part thereof, but that I the said , my heirs and assigns, and every of them, from all estate, right, title, interest, property, claim, and demand, of, in, to, or out of the said , or any of them, or any part thereof, are, is, and shall be, by these presents forever excluded and debarred.

In Witness Whereof, The said party of the first part to these presents hath hereunto set her hand and seal, the day of in the year of our Lord one thousand eight hundred and

In Presence of (*Signature.*) (*Seal.*)

(64.)

A Release between two Traders on Settling Accounts.

Whereas sundry accounts, current and otherwise, and divers dealings in trade have been subsisting for a long time past, between of trader, and of trader, which said accounts and dealings, the said and have balanced and adjusted, whereby it appears that nothing remains due from the one to the other; and whereas, therefore, to prevent any future disputes, concerning the said accounts and dealings, and to confirm the said adjustment, the said and have mutually agreed to give reciprocal releases to each other. Now know all men by these presents, that the said (*one of the parties*) (for the considerations abovesaid, and to prevent all future disputes) for himself, his executors, and administrators, doth remise, release, and forever quit claim unto the said (*the other party*) his all and all manner of action and actions, cause and causes of action, suits, debts, dues, sum and sums of money, accounts, reckonings, bonds, specialties, covenants, contracts, controversies, agreements, promises, variances, damages, extents, executions, claims and demands whatsoever, both at law and in equity, which against the said his the said now hath or ever had, on account of their said mutual dealings, or for or by reason of any other cause, matter, or thing whatsoever, from the beginning of the world to the day of the date of these presents.

And the said (*the other party*) (for the considerations abovesaid, and to prevent all future disputes) for himself, his executors, and administrators, doth remise, release, and forever quit claim unto the said (*the other party*), his all and all manner of action and actions, cause and causes of action, suits, debts, dues, sum and sums of money, accounts, reckonings, bonds, specialties, covenants, contracts, controversies, agreements, promises, variances, damages, extents, executions, claims and demands whatsoever, both at law and in equity, which against the said his the said now hath or ever had, on account of their said mutual dealings, or for or by reason of any other cause, matter, or thing whatsoever, from the beginning of the world to the day of the date of these presents.

In Witness Whereof, We have hereunto set our hands and seals, this day of in the year

(*Signatures.*) (*Seals.*)

In Presence of

CHAPTER XVI.

NOTES OF HAND AND BILLS OF EXCHANGE, DRAFTS, AND CHECKS.

SECTION I.

THE PURPOSE OF, AND THE PARTIES TO, SUCH PAPERS.

THESE instruments are usually negotiable. By *negotiable* paper is meant evidence of debt which may be transferred by indorsement or delivery, so that the transferee or holder may sue the same in his own name, and as if it had been made to him originally; or, in other words, it means paper, that is, bills of exchange or promissory notes, or drafts, or checks payable to the order of a payee, or to bearer.

The rules of law on the subject of negotiable paper are more exact and technical than those of any other department of Mercantile Law. They reach, on many points, an extreme nicety, which makes it difficult to express them intelligibly to persons who do not already possess some familiarity with the subject. All difficulty of this kind could have been easily avoided by me, by omitting any notice of these nice points. But it was thought better to mention them, one and all, for these are the things an intelligent man of business should know; and although the rules stated, especially those in reference to presentment, demand, notice, and some other subjects, may seem to be intricate and difficult, they require, it is believed, only careful consideration to be fully understood.

Where and when bills of exchange were invented is not certainly known. They were not used by any ancient nations, but have been employed and recognized by most commercial nations for some centuries. A still more recent invention is the promissory negotiable note, which, in this country, for inland and domestic purposes, has taken the place of the bill of exchange very generally. Besides these two, bills of lading, and some other documents, have a kind of negotiability, but it is quite imperfect. The utility of bills and notes in commerce arises from the fact that they represent money, which is the representative of the market value of every thing; and many of the peculiar rules respecting negotiable paper are derived from this representation, and intended to make it adequate and effectual.

A negotiable bill of exchange is a written order whereby A orders B to pay to C *or his order*, or *to bearer*, a sum of money, absolutely and at a certain time.

(65.)

Common Form of a Bill of Exchange.

New York, January 5, 1869.

Value received, please pay to C *or order,* *dollars, in* *days* (or months) *after sight* (it may be after date), *on account of*

(Signed) *A*

To B

A is the Drawer, B the Drawee, and C the Payee. If the bill is presented to B, and he agrees to obey the order, he "accepts" the bill, and this he does in a mercantile way by writing the word "Accepted" across the face of the bill, and also writing his name below this word; then the drawee becomes the Acceptor. If C, the payee, chooses to transfer the paper and all his rights under it to some other person, he may do this by writing his name on (usually across) the back; this is called Indorsement, and C then becomes an Indorser. The person to whom C thus transfers the bill is an Indorsee. The indorsee may again transfer the bill by writing his name below that of the former Indorser, and the Indorsee then becomes the second Indorser; and this process may go on indefinitely. If the added names cover all the back of the note, a piece may be wafered on to receive more. In France, this added piece is called "*allonge*," and this word is used in some law-books, but not by our merchants.

(66.)

Common Form of a Promissory Note.

New York, January 5, 1869.

Value received I promise to pay B *or order,*
dollars, in *days* (or months, or on demand) *from date.**

(Signature.)

It is quite important to have a clear idea of the difference between the parties to a note, and the parties to a bill of exchange. If A makes a note to B, then A promises to pay, and is the promisor, and B is the promisee, or payee. But if it be payable to B or order, B may write his name across the back, that is, may indorse it, and is an indorser. And if he directs, over his signature on the back, that the note be paid to any person in particular, such payee is now an indorsee. But when a bill is drawn, nobody promises, in words, to pay it. A orders B to pay to C. If B, when requested, says he will not do as ordered, the law supposes A, the drawer, to have promised that he would pay if B did not. If B "accepts," the law now supposes that B promises C to pay the bill to him. Now B, being the acceptor, is held by the law just as a maker of a note is, because he is supposed to have promised in the same way. A, the drawer, is held just as the first indorser of a note is held, because he is supposed to have promised to pay if B did not. If the bill was negotiable, that is, payable to C, or his order, then C may indorse the bill, and although his name is the only one on the back of the bill, he is treated in law only as second indorser, because the drawer is bound in the same way as a first indorser. And if D then puts his name below C's, he is treated as third indorser, and so on. For the rights, obligations, and duties of all these parties, see the subsequent sections.

We repeat, that a negotiable promissory note is a written promise to pay to a certain person or his order, or to bearer, at a certain time, a certain sum of money; and he who signs this is called the Maker or the Promisor; the other party is the Promisee or Payee. The

* *It is best* to write the words, "from date," although they are often omitted, and the law construes the note as if they were written.

payee of such a note has the same power of indorsement as the payee of a bill of exchange. If the note be not payable "to order," nor to "bearer," it is then not negotiable; these words "or order" or "to bearer" being the words which make it negotiable. The maker of a negotiable note holds, as has been said, the same position as the acceptor of a bill, the drawer the same as the first indorser of a note; that is, a party holding a note and seeking payment of it looks first to the maker, and then to the indorser; one holding a bill looks first to the drawee or acceptor, and, on his failure, to the drawer.

Neither indorsement, nor acceptance, nor making, is complete until delivery and reception of the bill, or note, or acceptance; and a defendant may show that there was no legal delivery of the paper.

The law of negotiable paper first defines a bill or note, and determines what instruments come under these names, and then describes and ascertains the duties and obligations of all the parties we have named above. We shall follow this order.

SECTION II.

WHAT IS ESSENTIAL TO A NEGOTIABLE NOTE OR BILL.

A WRITTEN order or promise may be perfectly valid as a written contract or promise, but, although made "to order," will not be *negotiable*, unless certain requisites of the law-merchant are complied with.

The difference between a note that is negotiable and one that is not, is very important in many respects. One of these is as to the operation of the trustee process, or foreign attachment, or garnishee process, as it is sometimes called. If A owes B a hundred dollars, C, a creditor of B, may *trustee* A (to use the common phrase), and A must then pay to C what he owes to B. And this is so, even if A have given his note to B for the hundred dollars, if the note be *not negotiable*, that is, not to B or order. But if the note be negotiable, A cannot be trusteed. The reason is, that if he is obliged to pay the money to C, and B should indorse the note to D for value, and D take it honestly, A must pay the note to D, and so would have to pay it twice. But if the note is not negotiable, B cannot indorse it, and A is safe in paying the money over.

1. The Promise must be absolute and definite. — The promise of the note, and the order of the bill, must be absolute. Words expressive of intention only do not make a promissory note, and a mere request without an order does not make a bill of exchange. But no one word, and no set of words, are absolutely necessary; for if from all the language the distinct promise or positive order can be inferred, that is sufficient.

The time of payment is usually written in a bill or note; if not, it is payable on demand. The time of payment must not depend on a contingency. In fact, any contingency apparent on the face of the instrument prevents it from being a negotiable note; and the happening of the contingency does not cure it. And the payment promised or ordered must be of a definite sum of money.

A negotiable bill of exchange or promissory note must be payable in money only, and not in goods or merchandise, or property of any kind, or by the performance of any act. If payable in "current funds," or "good bank-notes," or "current bank-notes," this should not be sufficient on general principles, and according to many authorities; some courts, however, construe this as meaning notes convertible on demand into money, and therefore as the same thing as money, and call the note negotiable.

A bill or note may be written upon any paper or proper substitute for it, in any language, in ink or pencil. A name may be signed or indorsed by a mark; and, though usually written at the bottom, it may be sufficient if written in the body of the note; as, "I, A B, promise," &c.; unless it can be shown that the note was incomplete, and was intended to be finished by signature. If not dated, it will be considered as dated when it was made; but a written date is *prima facie* evidence (this means evidence which may be overcome by opposite and better evidence, but until so overcome is sufficient) of the time of making. The amount is usually written in figures at the corner or bottom. If the sum is written at length in the body, and also in figures at the corner, the written words control the figures, and evidence is not admissible to show that the figures were right and the words inaccurate. But in an American case, a promissory note, expressed to be for "thee hundred dollars," and in figures in the margin, $300, was held to be a good note for three hundred dollars, if the maker when he signed it intended "three" when he wrote "thee;" and whether such was his intention was a question for the jury. And the omission of such a word as "dollars," or "pounds," or "sterling," may be supplied, if the meaning of the instrument is quite clear.

It has been just said that any contingency apparent on the face of the instrument prevents it from being a *negotiable* note. Hence it is not safe to write in the body of the note, or in connection with the promise, any condition or contingency. But, if what is so written in no way affects the promise itself, the note may still be negotiable.

Thus, in some parts of this country, persons who sell a machine, or other thing, on a credit, sometimes take a promissory note payable to the seller *or order*, and containing an additional clause, providing, that, until the note is paid, the property in the thing sold (or the ownership of it) shall be and remain in the seller. Such notes are often made in the following form: —

(67.)

Form of a Note given for a Chattel sold, with a Condition preserving the Ownership of the Seller.

$ *(Place and date)* 18

On the day of 18 the subscriber whose P. O. is , County of and State of , promise to pay , or order dollars at the First National Bank in with interest at per cent per annum until paid. And it is further agreed that the title to the *(reaper)* for which this note is given shall remain in said *(the seller)* until this note is fully paid; and, if not paid when due, I will pay all expenses incurred in collecting.

Value received

(Witness.) *(Signature.)*

On the back of this note is sometimes the following statement: —

Statement made for the Purpose of obtaining Credit.

I own acres of land in my own name in the Town of County of and State of which is worth at a fair valuation, $

It is not incumbered by mortgage or otherwise, except the amount of $ and the title is perfect in me in all respects. I have stock and personal property to the amount of $ over and above my debts and liabilities.

The above property being worth over and above my debts, liabilities and exemptions at least FIVE TIMES the amount of the within note.

The question has arisen whether such a note is negotiable. Suppose the seller of the chattel, who is payee of the note sells the note and indorses it for value to an innocent indorsee; then the buyer finds that he was cheated, and puts in this defence of fraud when he is sued on the note by the indorser. He can make this defence if this note be *not negotiable;* but he cannot make it if it be *negotiable.* I should say it was negotiable; and that the only effect of the condition or provision annexed to the promise, was, that it operated much as a mortgage of the thing, by the buyer, back to the seller, to secure the payment.

2. The Payee must be designated. — The payee should be distinctly named, unless the bill or note be made payable to bearer. If it can be gathered from the instrument, by a reasonable or necessary construction, who is the payee, that is enough. The note may be made payable to the promisor or his order; that is, a man may say, I promise to pay to my own order; and such note is nothing until the promisor not only signs it, but indorses it.

A note indorsed in blank is always transferable by delivery, just as if it were made payable to bearer; because any holder may write over the indorsement an order to pay to himself. Indorsements are either *indorsements in blank*, by which is meant the name of the indorser and nothing more, or *indorsements in full*, which are so called when over the name of the *indorser* is written, " pay to A B." (By A B we mean the name of the person to whom the note or bill is indorsed.) These two kinds of indorsements are fully explained subsequently in section VI. of this chapter. A note to the order of the promisor himself, and indorsed by him in blank, is therefore much the same thing as a note to bearer. But it is quite commonly used in our mercantile cities, because the holder can always pass it away without indorsing if he chooses, or can put his name on it as second indorser if he likes to. If the indorsee be named, and the note get into the possession of a wrong person of the same name, this person neither has nor can give a title to it. If the name be spelt wrong, evidence of intention is receivable. If a father and son have the same name, and either of them has possession of the note and indorses it, this would be evidence of his rightful ownership.

If neither payable to bearer, nor to the maker's or drawer's order, nor to any other person, it would be an incomplete and invalid instrument.

A note to a fictitious payee, with the same name indorsed by the maker, would undoubtedly be held to be the maker's own note, either payable to bearer, or to himself or order, by another name, and so indorsed. If a blank be left in a bill for the payee's name, a *bonâ fide* holder may fill it with his own, the issuing of the bill in blank being an authority to a *bonâ fide* holder to insert the name. And if the name of the payee be not the name of a person, as if it be the name of a ship, the instrument is payable to bearer. A note payable to different persons in the alternative, that is, to one or the other of them, is not a good promissory note. A bill or note "to the order of" any person is the same as if to him "or his order," and may be sued by him without indorsement.

3. Of Ambiguous and Irregular Instruments. — The law in relation to protest and damages makes it sometimes important to distinguish between a promissory note and a bill of exchange, because, by law, a foreign bill of exchange, if unpaid, should be protested, but not a promissory note; but it is a common practice to protest promissory notes when they are not paid. The rule in general is, that, if an instrument be so ambiguous in its terms that it cannot be certainly pronounced one of these to the exclusion of the other, the holder may elect and treat it as either. As if written, "Value received, in three months from date, pay the order of H. L. $500. (Signed) A. B.;" and an address or memorandum at the bottom, "At Messrs. E. F. & Co."

4. Of Bank-Notes. — Bank-notes or bank-bills are promissory notes of a bank, payable to bearer; and, like all notes to bearer, the property in them passes by delivery. They are intended to be used as money; and, while a finder, or one who steals them, has no title himself against the owner, still, if he passes them away to a *bonâ fide* holder, that is, a holder for value without notice or knowledge, such owner holds them against the original owner. And if the bank pays them in good faith on regular presentment, the owner has no claim. They pass by a will bequeathing money. They are a good tender, unless objected to at the time because not money. Forged bills, given in payment, are a mere nullity. Bills of a bank which has failed, but of which the failure is unknown to both parties, are now, generally, put on the footing of forged or void bills. But if the receiver of them, by holding them, and by a delay of returning or giving them up, injures the payer and impairs his opportunity or means of idemnity, the receiver must then lose them.

5. Of Checks on Banks. — A check on a bank is undoubtedly a bill of exchange; but usage and the nature of the case have introduced some important qualifications of the general law of bills in its application to checks. A check requires no acceptance, because a bank, after a customary or reasonable time has elapsed since deposit, and while still in possession of funds, is bound to pay the checks of the depositors. The drawer of a check is not a surety, as is the drawer of a bill, but a principal debtor, like the maker of a note. Nor can a drawer complain of any delay whatever in the presentment; for it is an absolute appropriation, as between the drawer and the holder, to the holder of so much money in the banker's hands; there it may lie at the holder's pleasure. But delay is at the holder's risk; for if the bank fails after he could have got his money on the check, the loss is his. If the bank before he presents his check pay out all the money of the drawer on other checks, he may then look to the drawer.

If one who holds a check as payee, or otherwise, transfers it to another, he has a right to insist that the check shall be presented in the course of the banking hours of that day, or at farthest the next; that is, he is not responsible for the failure of the bank to pay, unless it is so presented, provided it would then have been paid. And if the party receiving the check live elsewhere than where the bank is, it seems that he should send it for collection the next day; and if to an agent, the agent should present it, at latest, in the course of the day after he receives it. If the check be drawn when the drawer neither has funds in the bank, nor has made any arrangement by which he has a right to draw the check, the drawing it is a fraud, and the holder may bring his action at once against the drawer, without presentment or notice.

Checks are seldom accepted. But they are often marked by the bank as good; and this binds the bank as an acceptor.

Checks are usually payable to bearer, but may be and often are drawn payable to a payee or his order; for this guards against loss or theft, because the check will not be paid unless the payee writes his name on it; and it gives to the drawer, when the check is paid and returned by the bank to him, what is the same as the receipt of the payee. Generally, a check is not payment until it is cashed; then it is payment if the money was paid to the creditor, or the check had passed through his hands. A bank cannot maintain a claim for money lent and advanced, merely by showing the defendant's check paid by them, because the general presumption is, that the bank paid the check because it was drawn by a depositor against funds.

While the death of a drawer countermands his check, if the bank pay it before notice of the death reaches them, they are discharged. This would seem to be almost a necessary inference from the general purpose of banks of deposit, and the use which merchants make of them.

If a bank pay a forged check, it is so far its own loss, that the bank cannot charge the money to the depositor whose name was forged. But the bank could recover the money back from one who presented a forged check, and was paid, provided the payee, if innocent, loses no opportunity of indemnity in the mean time, and can be put in as good a position as if the bank had refused to pay it. But if somebody must lose, the bank should, because it is the duty of the bank to know the writing of its own depositors. If it pay a check of which the amount has been falsely and fraudulently increased, it can charge the drawer only with the original amount. But if the drawer himself causes or facilitates the forgery, as by so carelessly writing it, or leaving it in such hands, that the forgery or alteration is easy, so that it may be called his fault, and the bank is innocent, then the loss falls on the drawer. If many persons, not partners, join in a deposit, they must join in a check; but if one or more abscond, a court of equity will permit the remainder to draw the money.

6. Of Accommodation Paper. — An accommodation bill or note is one for which the acceptor or maker has received no consideration, but has lent his name and credit to accommodate the drawer, payee, or holder. Of course he is bound to all other parties, precisely as if there were a good consideration; for, otherwise, it would not be an effectual loan of credit. But he is not bound to the party whom he thus accommodates; on the contrary, that party is bound to take up the paper, or to provide the accommodation acceptor, or maker, or indorser, with funds for doing it, or to indemnify him for taking it up. And if, before the bill or note is due, the party accommodated provides the party lending his credit with the necessary funds, he cannot recall them; and if he becomes bankrupt, they remain the property of the accommodation acceptor, or maker, who, if sued on the bill or note, can charge the party accommodated with the expense of defending the suit, even if the defence were unsuccessful, if he had any reasonable ground of defence, because the defence was for the benefit of the party accommodated; inasmuch as he must repay the accommodation party if he pays the bill or note.

7. Of Foreign and Inland Bills. — Bills of exchange may be foreign bills, or inland bills. Foreign bills are those which are drawn or payable in a foreign country; and for this purpose, each of our States is *foreign* to the others. Inland bills are drawn and payable at home. Every bill is, on its face, an inland bill, unless it purports to be a foreign bill. If foreign on its face, evidence is admissible to show that it was drawn at home. If a bill be drawn and accepted here, but afterwards actually signed by the drawer abroad, it is a foreign bill. If a foreign bill be not accepted, or be not paid at maturity, it should at once be protested by a notary-public. Inland bills are generally, and promissory notes frequently, protested; but this is not generally required by the law. The holder of a foreign bill, after protest for non-payment, or for non-acceptance, may sue the drawer and indorser, and recover the face of the bill, and, in addition thereto, his damages, which damages on protest are generally adjusted in this country by various statutes, — which give greater damages as the distance is greater; and an established usage would supply the place of statutes if they were wanting.

8. **Of the Law of Place.** — The different States of the Union, are, as to questions arising under Mercantile Law, *foreign countries as to each other*. Important questions sometimes arise in the case of foreign bills (as well as in some other cases), dependent upon what is called the Law of Place, the Latin phrase for which, *Lex Loci*, is often used. In general, every contract is to be governed by the law of the place where it is made. Thus, if a bill is drawn in France, and there indorsed in a way which is sufficient here, but insufficient there, the indorsement would here be held void. But if a contract entered into in one place is to be performed in another, as in the case of a note dated, or a bill drawn, in one State, but payable in another, the prevailing rule is, that the law of the place where the note is payable construes and governs the contract. Therefore, if a bill be drawn in England, payable in France, the protest and notice of dishonor must be regulated by the law of France. But one who makes such a note may elect, for many purposes, which law shall govern it. Thus, if he makes it in New York, and it is payable in Boston, he may promise to pay the legal interest of New York, and will be bound to this payment in Boston, although the legal interest in Boston is less; but if there be no such express promise, the interest payable will be that of the place where the note is payable.

While the law of the place of the contract interprets and construes it as a debt, the law of the place where it is put in suit — which is called the Law of the Forum, or Court — determines all questions as to remedy; that is, all questions which relate to the legal means of recovering the debt. Thus, in general, the statutes of limitation of the place of the court are applied. But if a cause of action relating to any special subject-matter which has a definite location, as a parcel of land has, be barred by a statute of limitations where the subject-matter is situated, it is barred everywhere. A promisor, not subject to arrest in the country where the note is made, may be arrested under the laws of the country where the note is sued.

It will always be presumed, in the absence of testimony, that the law of a foreign country is the same with that of the country in which the suit is brought. If a difference in this respect is a ground of defence, or of action, it must be proved by evidence.

SECTION III.

THE CONSIDERATION OF NEGOTIABLE PAPER.

1. Exception to the Common Law Rule, in the Case of Negotiable Paper. — By the common law of England and of this country, as we have seen, no promise can be enforced, unless made for a consideration, or unless it be sealed. But bills and notes payable to order, that is, negotiable, are, to a certain extent, an exception to this rule. Thus, an indorsee cannot be defeated by the promisor showing that he received no consideration for his promise; because the promisor made an instrument for circulation as money; and it would be fraudulent to give to paper the credit of his name, and then refuse to honor it. But as between the maker and the payee, or between indorser and indorsee, and, in general, between any two *immediate* parties, the defendant may rely on the want of consideration; that is, if an indorsee sues the maker, and the maker says he had no consideration for the note, this is no defence; but if the indorsee sues his indorser, and the indorser shows that the indorsee paid him nothing, this would be a good defence; and so it would be if the payee sued the maker. So, if a distant indorsee has notice or knowledge, when he buys a note, that it was made without consideration, he cannot recover on it against the maker, unless it was an accommodation note, or was intended as a gift.

Thus, if A, supposing a balance due from him to B, gives B his negotiable note for the amount, and afterwards discovers that the balance is the other way, B cannot recover of A; nor can any third or more distant indorsee who knows these facts before buying the note. But if A gives B his note wholly without consideration, for the purpose of lending him his credit, or for the purpose of making him a gift to the amount of the note, and C buys the note with a full knowledge of the facts, he will nevertheless hold A, although B could not. If the note was bought honestly for a fair price, the buyer should recover its whole amount. Every promissory note *imports* a consideration; that is, none, in the first place, need be proved; but when want of consideration is relied on in defence, and evidence is given on one side and the other, the burden of proof is on the plaintiff to satisfy the jury that consideration was given.

If an indorser, sued by an indorsee, shows that the note was originally made in fraud, he may require the holder to prove that he paid consideration; but if this be proved, he must pay the whole of the note, unless he was himself defrauded by the holder. And if an accommodation note be discounted in violation of the agreement of the party accommodated, the holder can still recover, provided he received the note in good faith, and for valuable consideration.

2. Of "Value Received." — "Value received" is usually written, and therefore should be; but is not necessary. If not written, it will be presumed by the law, or may be supplied by the plaintiff's proof. If expressed, it may be denied by the defendant, and disproved. And if a special consideration be stated in the note, the defendant may prove that there was no consideration, or that the consideration was different. If "value received" be written in a note, it means received by the maker from the payee; if the note be payable to the bearer, it means received by the maker from the holder. In a bill, "value received" means that the value was received from the payee by the drawer. But if the bill be payable to the drawer's own order, then it means received by the acceptor from the drawer.

3. What the Consideration may be. — A valuable consideration may be either any gain or advantage to the promisor, or any loss or injury sustained by the promisee at the promisor's request. A previous debt, or a fluctuating balance, or a debt due from a third person, might be a valuable consideration. So is a *moral* consideration, if founded upon a previous legal consideration; as, where one promises to pay a debt barred by the statute of limitations, or by infancy. But a *merely* moral consideration, as one founded upon natural love and affection, or the relation of parent and child, is no legal consideration.

No consideration is sufficient in law if it be *illegal* in its nature; and it may be illegal because, first, it violates some positive law, as, for example, the Sunday law, or the law against usury. Secondly, because it violates religion or morality, as an agreement for future illicit cohabitation, or to let lodgings for purposes of prostitution, or an indecent wager; for any bill or note founded upon either of these would be void. Thirdly, if distinctly opposed to public policy; as an agreement in restraint of trade, or injurious to the revenue, or in restraint of marriage, or for procurement of marriage, or suppressing evidence, or withdrawing a prosecution for felony or public misdemeanor.

SECTION IV.

THE RIGHTS AND DUTIES OF THE MAKER.

THE maker of a note or the acceptor of a bill is bound to pay the same at its maturity, and at any time thereafter, unless the action be barred by the statute of limitations, or he has some other defence under the general law of contracts. As between himself and the payee of the note or bill, he may make any defences which he could make on any debt arising from simple contract; as want or failure of consideration; payment, in whole or in part; set-off; accord and satisfaction; or the like. The peculiar characteristics of negotiable paper do not begin to operate, so to speak, until the paper has passed into the hands of third parties. Then, the party liable on the note or bill can make none of these defences, unless the time or manner in which it came into the possession of the holder lays him open to these defences. But the law on this subject may better be presented in our next section.

SECTION V.

THE RIGHTS AND DUTIES OF THE HOLDER OF NEGOTIABLE PAPER.

1. What a Holder may do with a Bill or Note. — An indorsee has a right of action against all whose names are on the bill when he received it. And if one delivers a bill or note which he ought to indorse and does not, the holder has an action against him for not indorsing, or may proceed in a court of equity to compel him to indorse. If a bill comes back to a previous indorser, he may strike out the intermediate indorsements and sue in his own name, as indorsee; but he has, in general, no remedy against the intermediate parties, because, if he made them pay as indorsers to him, they would make him pay as indorser to them. If, however, the circumstances are such that *they*, if compelled to pay, would have no right against him as an indorser to them, as, for example, if he indorsed it "without recourse," then he may have a claim against them.

The holder of a bill indorsed and deposited with him for collection, or only as a trustee, can use it only in conformity with the trust. And if the indorsement express that it is to be collected for the indorser's use, or use any equivalent language, this is notice to any one who discounts it; and the party discounting the paper against this notice will be obliged to deliver the note, or pay its contents if collected, to the indorser. Thus, Mr. Sigourney, a merchant in Boston, remitted to Williams, a London banker, for collection, a bill of exchange indorsed by him, and over his name was written, "Pay to Williams or order for my use." Williams had the bill discounted for his own benefit by his bankers, and failed; and the English court held that the indorsement showed that the bill did not belong to Williams, and that the discounters had no right to discount it for him; and they were obliged to pay the amount of it to Sigourney.

2. Of a Transfer after Dishonor of Negotiable Paper. — So long as a note remains due, everybody has a right to believe that it has not been paid, and will be paid at maturity, and may purchase it in that belief. But as soon as it is overdue, the date shows it, and every person must know that it is either paid, and so extinguished, or that it has not been paid, and therefore is dishonored, and that there may be good reasons why it was not paid, or good defences against it. He therefore now takes it at his own peril; and therefore a holder who took the note after it became due is open to many of the defences which the promisor could have made against the party from whom the holder took it; because, having notice that the bill or note is dishonored, he ought to have ascertained whether any, and, if so, what defence could be set up.

So, too, if an indorsee takes the note or bill *before* it is due, but with notice or knowledge of fraud or other good defence which could be made against his indorser if he sued it, it is a general rule that the same defence may be made against him.

A promissory note payable on demand is considered as intended to be a continuing security, and therefore as not overdue, unless very old indeed, without some evidence of demand of payment and refusal. But it is not so with a check; for this should be presented without unreasonable delay.

3. Of Presentment for Acceptance. — It is most important to the holder of negotiable paper to know distinctly what his duties are in relation to presentment for acceptance or payment, and notice to others interested in case of non-acceptance or non-payment.

It is always prudent for the holder of a bill to present it for acceptance without delay; for if it be accepted, he has new security; if not, the former parties are immediately liable; and it is but just to the drawer to give him as early an opportunity as may be to withdraw his funds or obtain indemnity from a debtor who will not honor his bills. And if a bill is payable at sight, or at a certain period after sight, there is not only no right of action against anybody until presentment, but, if this be delayed beyond a reasonable time, the holder loses his remedy against all previous parties. And although the question of reasonable time is generally one only of law, yet, in this connection, it is treated as so far a question of fact, that it is submitted to the jury. There is no certain rule determining what is reasonable time in this respect. If a bill of exchange be payable on demand, it is not like a promissory note, but must be presented within a reasonable time, or the drawer will be discharged. A holder may put a bill payable after sight into circulation, without presenting it himself; and in that case, if a subsequent holder presents it, a longer delay in presentment would be allowed than if the first holder had kept it in his own possession.

The presentment should be made during business hours; but in this country they extend through the day and until evening, excepting in the case of banks. Any distinct usage established where the presentment is made would probably be received in evidence, and permitted to affect the question.

Ill health, or other actual impediment without fault, may excuse delay on the part of the holder; but the request of the drawer to the drawee not to accept does not excuse non-presentment for acceptance.

Presentment for acceptance should be made to the drawee himself, or to his agent authorized to accept. And when it is presented, the drawee may have a reasonable time to consider whether he will accept, during which time the holder is justified in leaving the bill with him. And this time would be as much as twenty-four hours, unless the mail goes out before. And if the holder gives more than twenty-four hours for this purpose, or the mail goes out before, he should inform the previous parties of it. If the drawee has changed his residence, the holder should use due diligence to find him; and what constitutes due or reasonable diligence is a question of fact for a jury. And if he be dead, the holder should ascertain who is his personal representative, if he has one, and present the bill to him. If the bill be drawn upon the drawee at a particular place, it is regarded as dishonored if the drawee has absconded, so that the bill cannot be presented for acceptance at that place.

4. Of Presentment for Demand of Payment.—The next question relates to the duty of demanding payment; and here the law is much the same in respect both to notes and to bills.

The universal rule of the law-merchant is, that the indorsers of negotiable paper are supposed to agree to pay it *only* if the maker or previous indorsers do not, and *provided* due measures are taken by the holder to get it paid by those who ought, in the first place, to pay it. Every holder of negotiable paper can hold it as long as he likes, and not lose his claim against the *maker* of a note, or the *acceptor* of a bill, unless he holds it more than six years, and the Statute of Limitations bars his claim. The reason is, that the maker or acceptor promises *directly*, and not merely to pay if another does not. But every indorser of a note or bill, and every drawer of a bill, only promises to pay if a maker or acceptor or some previous indorser does not. If there is a bill of exchange with six indorsers, the last promises in law to pay it only if the acceptor, the drawer, and the five previous indorsers do not pay. He has therefore a right that a demand according to law should be made against every one of these persons, and that their refusal to pay should be notified to him, forthwith, so that he may secure himself if he can. And the law-merchant is very rigorous and precise in defining what demand should be made by the holder, and when and how demand should be made on every *prior* party, in order to hold any *subsequent* party; and also as to what notice of the demand and refusal of the *prior* party should be given to any *subsequent* party to whom the holder looks for payment.

A demand is sufficient if made at the usual residence or place of business of the payer, either of himself, or of an agent authorized to pay; and this authority may be inferred from the habit of paying, especially if the agent be a child, a wife, or a servant. The demand should not be made in the street, although a demand then would probably be held good, unless objected to at the time because made there. When a demand is made, the bill or note should be exhibited; and if lost, a copy should be exhibited, although this is not absolutely necessary. And when the payer calls on the holder, and declares to him that he shall not pay, and desires him to give notice to the indorsers, this constitutes a demand and refusal, provided this declaration be made at the maturity of the paper; but not if it was made before maturity, because the payer may change his intention.

Bankruptcy or insolvency of the payer is no excuse for non-demand; although the shutting up of a bank may be regarded as a refusal to all their creditors to pay their notes. Absconding of the payer is generally a sufficient excuse; but if the payer has shut up his house, the holder must nevertheless inquire after him, and find him, if he can by proper efforts. Even in case of absconding, it is always better to go through the formality of making a demand at the payer's last residence or place of business; and this is held necessary in Massachusetts. If the payer be dead, demand should be made at his house, unless he have personal representatives, and in that case, of them. And if the holder die, presentment should be made by his personal representatives; that is, by his executor or administrator.

If the drawer has no effects in the hands of the drawee, and has no arrangement or understanding which gives him a right to draw, non-presentation for payment is not a defence which he can make if sued on the bill.

Impossibility of presenting a bill for payment, without the fault of the holder, as the actual loss of a bill, or the like, will excuse some delay in making a demand for payment; but not more than the circumstances require. And the mere mistake of the holder as to the time, place, person or manner, is no excuse, because he has no right to make mistakes to the injury of other people.

In this country, all negotiable paper payable at a time certain is entitled to grace, which here means three days' delay of payment, unless it be expressly stated and agreed that there shall be no grace; and a presentment for payment before the last day of grace is premature, the note not being due until then. If the last day of grace falls on a Sunday, or on a legal holiday, the note is due on the Saturday, or other day before the holiday. But if there be no grace, and the note falls due on a Sunday, or other holiday, it is not payable until the next day.

Generally, if a bill or note be payable in or after a certain number of days from date, sight, or demand, in counting these days, the day of date, sight, or demand is excluded, and the day on which it falls due included. And the law would supply the word "*from*," &c., if the word were not used. Thus, a note dated January 1, and payable in "twenty days" would be held payable in twenty days (and three days' grace) *after* the day of the date; that is on the 24th. If a note is made payable in one or more months, this means calendar months, whether shorter or longer. If made on the 13th of December, and payable in two months, it is payable on the 13th of February and grace, that is, on the 16th. But if so many days are named, they must be counted, whether they are more or less than a month. Thus, if the above note were payable in sixty days, it would be due on the 11th and grace, or on the 14th of February. If dated 13th January, and payable in sixty days, it would be due on the 14th of March, with grace, or on the 17th.

Although payment must be demanded promptly, that is, on the day on which it is due, it need not be done instantly; a holder has all the business-part of the day in which the bill or note falls due to make his demand in.

Bills and notes payable on demand should be presented for payment within a reasonable time. If said to be "on interest," this strengthens the indication that they were intended to remain for a time unpaid and undemanded. But to hold indorsers, they should still be presented within whatever time circumstances may make a reasonable time; and this is such a time as the interests and safety of all concerned may require; and it may be a few days, or even one or two weeks. A bill or note in which no time of payment is expressed is held to be payable on demand. And evidence to prove it otherwise is inadmissible.

The holder of a check should present it at once; for the drawer has a right to expect that he will; it should, therefore, be presented, or forwarded for presentment, in the course of the day following that in which it was received, or, upon failure of the bank, the holder will lose the remedy he would otherwise have had against the person from whom he receives it. If the drawer of the check had no funds, he is liable always.

Every demand of payment should be made at the proper place, which is either the place of residence or of business of the payer, and within the proper hours of business. If made at a bank after hours of business, if the officers are there, and refuse payment for want of funds, the demand is sufficient.

A note payable at a particular place should be demanded at that place; and a bill drawn payable at a particular place should be demanded there, in order to charge the drawer of a bill, and the indorsers of a bill or note. But in this country an action may be maintained against the maker or acceptor without such demand; but the defendant may discharge himself of damages and costs beyond the amount of the paper, by showing that he was ready at that place with funds. If a note is payable at any of several different places, presentment at any one of them will be sufficient. If a bill which is drawn payable generally, be accepted payable at a particular place, the holder may and should so far regard this as non-acceptance, that he should protest and give notice. But if this limited acceptance is assented to and received, it must be complied with by the holder, and the bill must be presented for payment at that place, or the drawer and indorsers are discharged.

If payable at a banker's, or at the house or counting-room of any person, and such banker or person becomes the owner at maturity, this is demand enough; and if there are no funds deposited with him for the payment, this is refusal enough. If any house be designated, a presentment to any person there, or at the door if the house be shut up, is enough.

If this direction be not in the body of the note, but added at the close, or elsewhere, as a memorandum, it is not part of the contract, and should not be attended to.

If the payer has changed his residence, he should be sought for with due diligence; and, if he has absconded, it is better to make the demand at his last place of residence or business.

Where a bill or note is not presented for payment, or not presented at the time, or to the person, or in the place, or in the way, required by law, all parties but the acceptor or maker are discharged, for the reasons before stated.

5. Of Protest and Notice. — If a bill of exchange be not accepted when properly presented for that purpose, or if a bill or note, when properly presented for payment, be not paid, the holder has a further duty to perform to all who are responsible for payment. In case of non-payment of a *foreign* bill, there should be a regular protest by a public notary; but this is not strictly necessary in the case of an inland bill, or a promissory note, whether foreign or inland. But in practice, all bills if not accepted, and all bills and notes if unpaid, are protested. By a *foreign* bill is meant a bill drawn in one State or country, and payable in another. But notice of non-payment should be given to all antecedent parties, equally, and in the same way, in the case of both bills and notes.

The demand and protest must be made according to the laws of the place where the bill is payable. It should be made by a notary-public, who should present the bill himself; but, if there be no notary-public in that place or within reasonable reach, it may be made by any respectable inhabitant in the presence of witnesses.

The protest should be noted on the day of demand and refusal; and may be filled up afterwards, even so late as at the trial.

The loss of a bill is not a sufficient excuse for not protesting it. But a subsequent promise to pay by a drawer or indorser is held to imply, or be equal to, a previous protest and notice to him.

The notarial seal is, of itself, evidence of the dishonor of a foreign bill, but not of an inland bill. And no collateral statement in the certificate is evidence of the fact therein stated; thus the statement by a notary, that the drawee refused to accept or pay because he had no funds of the drawer, is no evidence of the absence of such funds.

Notice must be given even to one who has knowledge. No particular form is necessary; it may be in writing, or oral; all that is absolutely essential is, that it should designate the note or bill with sufficient distinctness, and state that it has been dishonored; and also that the party notified is looked to for payment; but it has been held that the notice to the party bound to pay, when given by the immediate holder of the bill, sufficiently implies that he is looked to. Notice of protest for non-payment is sufficient notice to indorsers of demand and refusal. How distinctly the note or bill should be described cannot be precisely defined. It is enough if there be no such looseness, ambiguity, or misdescription as might mislead a man of ordinary intelligence; and if the intention was to describe the true note, and the party notified was not actually misled, this would always be enough. The notice need not state for whom payment is demanded, nor where the note is lying; and even a misstatement in this respect may not be material if it do not actually mislead.

No copy of the protest need be sent to indorsers; but information of the protest should be given.

If the letter be properly put into the post-office, any miscarriage of the mail does not affect the party giving notice. The address should be sufficiently specific. Only the surname, — as "Mr. Ames," — especially if sent to a large city, would not, in general, be enough. If a letter, however generally directed, can be shown to have reached the right person at the right time, it is sufficient. The postmarks are strong evidence that the letter was mailed at the very time these marks indicate; but this evidence may be rebutted, that is contradicted.

A notice not only may, but should, be sent by the public post. It may, however, be sent by a private messenger; but is not sufficient if it do not arrive until after the time at which it would have arrived by mail. It may be sent to the town where the party resides, or to another town, or to a more distant post-office, if it is clear that he may thereby receive the notice earlier. And if the notice is sent to what the sender deems, after due diligence, the nearest post-office, this is enough. If the parties live in the same town, notice should not be sent by mail.

The notice should be sent either to the place of business, or to the residence, of the party notified. But if one directs a notice to be sent to himself elsewhere than at home, it may be so sent, and bind not only him, but prior parties, although time is lost by so sending it.

The notice of non-payment should be sent within reasonable time; and in respect to negotiable paper, the law-merchant defines this within very narrow limits. If the parties live in the same town, notice must be given or sent so that the party to whom it is sent may receive the notice in the course of the day next after that in which the party sending has knowledge of the fact. If the parties live in different places, the notice must be sent as soon as by the first practicable mail of the next day, or the next mail, if there be none on the next day.

Each party receiving notice has a day, or until the next post after the day in which he receives it, before he is obliged to send the notice forward. Thus, if there be six indorsers, and the note is due on the 10th of May, in New York, and is then demanded and unpaid, the holder may send it by any mail which leaves New York on the 11th of May, to the last indorser, wherever he lives; and that indorser may send it to the indorser immediately before him, by any mail on the day after he receives it; and so may each of the parties receiving notice; and all the parties to whom notice is sent in this way will be held. So, too, a banker, with whom the paper is deposited for collection, is considered a holder, and entitled to a day to give notice to the depositor, who then has a day for his notice to antecedent parties. The different branches of one establishment have been held distinct holders for this purpose, and each to be entitled to a day. It should be sent by the first safe opportunity.

Neither Sunday nor any legal holiday is to be computed in reckoning the time within which notice must be given.

There is no presumption of notice; and the plaintiff must prove that it was given, and was sufficient. Thus, proving that it was given in "two or three days" is insufficient, if *two* would have been right, but *three* not.

Notice should be given only by a party to the instrument, who is liable upon it, and not by a stranger; and it has been held that notice could not be given by a first indorser, who, not having been notified, was not himself liable. A notice by any party liable will operate to the benefit of all antecedent or subsequent parties; that is, will hold them all to the original holder of the note, if the original holder gave notice properly to the party nearest to him. The notice may be given by any authorized agent of a party who could himself give notice.

Notice must be given to every antecedent party who is to be held. And we have seen that this may be given by a holder to the first party liable, and by him to the next, &c. But the holder may always give notice to all antecedent parties; and it is always prudent, and in this country, usual, to do so. For the holder loses all remedy against all those who are discharged by the failure of any one receiving notice to transmit it properly. But if a holder undertakes to notify *all* the antecedent parties, he must notify all as soon as he was obliged to notify the party nearest to him; that is, the day after the dishonor of the note. We mean by this, that every party has a *day;* so that, if there be six indorsers, if the first indorser is notified on the seventh day from the dishonor, it is enough, *if* the holder took his day to notify the sixth indorser, and that indorser his day to notify the fifth, and so on. But the holder has nobody's day but his own; and if he undertakes to notify all the parties, he must notify them all on the first day after the non-payment.

Notice may be given personally to a party, or to his agent authorized to receive notice, or left in writing at his home or place of business. If the party to be notified is dead, notice should be given to his personal representatives. A notice addressed to the "legal representative of," &c., and sent to the town in which the deceased party resided at his death, has been held sufficient. But a notice addressed to the party himself, when known to be dead, or to "the estate of," &c., would not be of itself sufficient, but might become so with evidence that the administrator or executor actually received the notice.

If two or more parties are jointly liable on a bill as partners, notice to one is enough; but, if the indorsers are not partners, notice should be given to each.

One transferring by delivery, without indorsement, a note or bill payable to bearer, is not generally entitled to notice of non-payment, because, generally, he is not liable to pay such paper; but if the circumstances of the case are such as to make him liable, then he must have notice, but is entitled not to the exact notice of an indorser, but only to such reasonable notice as is due to a guarantor. If, for instance, the paper was transferred as security, or even in payment of a pre-existing debt, this debt revives if the bill or note be dishonored; and therefore there must be notice given of the dishonor.

In general, a guarantor of a bill or note, or debt, is not entitled to such strict and exact notice as an indorser is entitled to, but only to such notice as shall save him from actual injury; and he cannot make the want of notice his defence, unless he can show that the notice was unreasonably withheld or delayed, and that he has actually sustained injury from such delay or want of notice. If an indorser give also a bond, or his own note, to pay the debt, he is not discharged from his bond or note by want of notice.

In general, all parties to negotiable paper, who are entitled to notice, are discharged by want of notice. The law presumes them to be injured, and does not put them to proof.

The right to notice may be waived by any agreement to that effect prior to the maturity of the paper. It is quite common for an indorser to write, "I waive notice," or, "I waive demand," or some words to this effect. It should, however, be remembered, that these rights are independent, and one does not imply the other. A waiver of notice of non-payment does not imply a waiver of demand; therefore, if an indorser writes on the note, "I waive notice," still he will be discharged if there be not a due *demand* on the maker. And it has been held that a waiver of protest is a waiver of *demand*, but not of *notice*. So if a drawer countermands his order, the bill should still be presented, but notice of dishonor need not be given to the drawer. Or, if a drawer has no funds, and nothing equivalent to funds, in the drawee's hands, and would have no remedy against the drawee or any one else, as the drawer cannot be prejudiced by want of notice, it is not necessary to give him notice. But the indorser must still be notified; and a drawer for the accommodation of the acceptor is entitled to notice, because he might have a claim upon the acceptor.

Actual ignorance of a party's residence justifies the delay necessary to find it out, and no more; and after it is discovered, the notifier has the usual time.

Death, or severe illness, of the notifier or his agent, is an excuse for delay; but the death, bankruptcy, or insolvency of the drawee of a bill is no excuse.

As the right to notice may be waived before maturity, so the want of notice may be cured afterwards by an express promise to pay; and an acknowledgment of liability, or a payment in part, is evidence, but not conclusive evidence, of notice; the jury *may* draw this conclusion from part payment, but are not *bound* to, even if the evidence be not rebutted. If the promise be conditional, and the condition be not complied with, the promise has been held to be still evidence of protest. Nor is it sufficient to avoid such promise, that it was made in ignorance of the law; but it is void if made in ignorance of the *fact* of non-notice.

SECTION VI.

THE RIGHTS AND DUTIES OF THE INDORSER.

ONLY a note or bill payable to a payee or order is, strictly speaking, subject to indorsement. Those who write their names on the back of any note or bill are indorsers in one sense, and are sometimes called so; but are not meant in the law-merchant by the word "indorsers."

The payee of a negotiable bill or note — whether he be also maker or not — may indorse it, and afterwards any person, or any number of persons, may indorse it. The maker promises to pay to the payee or his order; and the indorsement is an order on the maker to pay the indorsee, and the maker's promise is then to pay the note to him. But if the original promise was to the payee or order, this "or order," which is the negotiable element, passes over to the indorsee, though not written in the indorsement, and the indorsee may indorse, and so may his indorsee, indefinitely.

Each indorser, by his indorsement, does two things: first, he orders the antecedent parties to pay to his indorsee; and next, he engages with his indorsee, that, if they do not pay, he will.

If the words "to order," or "to bearer," are omitted accidentally, and by mistake, they may be afterwards inserted without injury to the bill or note; and whether a bill or note is negotiable or not, is a question of law.

By the law-merchant, bills and notes which are payable to order can be effectually and fully transferred only by indorsement. This indorsement may be *in blank*, or *in full*. The writing of the name of a payee, — either the original payee or an indorsee, — with nothing more, is an indorsement in blank; and a blank indorsement makes the bill or note transferable by delivery, in like manner as if it had been originally payable to bearer. After a note has been indorsed by a payee, any person may write his name on the note under that of the payee, and be held as indorser, — because any subsequent holder may write over the name of the first indorser a direction to pay the note to the next signer, and this makes the next signer an indorsee, and so gives him a right to indorse; and he or any holder may write over his name an order to pay the holder, or anybody else. If the indorsement consist not only of the name, but of an order above the name to pay the note to some specified person, then it is an indorsement in full, and the note can be paid to no one else unless that person indorses it; nor can the property in it be fully transferred, except by his indorsement; and his indorsee may again indorse it in blank or in full. If the indorsement is, Pay to A B *only*, or in equivalent words, A B is indorsee, but cannot indorse it over.

Any holder for value of a bill or note indorsed in blank, whether he be the first indorsee or one to whom it has come through many hands, may write over any name indorsed an order to pay the contents to himself; and this makes it a special indorsement, or an indorsement in full. This is often done for security; that is, to guard against the loss of the note by accident or theft. For the rule of law is, that negotiable paper transferable by delivery (whether payable to bearer or indorsed in blank) is, like money, the property of whoever receives it in good faith. The same rule has been extended in England to exchequer bills; to public bonds payable to bearer; and to East India bonds; and we think it would extend here to our railroad and other corporation bonds, and, perhaps, to all such instruments as are payable to bearer, whether sealed or not, and whatever they may be called. If one has such an instrument, and it is stolen, and the thief passes it for consideration to a *bonâ fide* holder, this holder acquires a legal right to it, because the property and possession go together. But if the bill or note be *specially* indorsed, no person can acquire any property in it, except by the indorsement of the special indorsee.

It may be well to remark here, that the finder of negotiable paper, as of all other property, ought to make reasonable endeavors to discover the owner, and is entitled to use the thing found as his own only when he has made such endeavors unsuccessfully. If he conceals the fact of finding, and appropriates the thing to his own use, he is liable to the charge of larceny or theft.

The written transfer of negotiable paper is called an indorsement, because it is almost always written on the back of the note; but it has its full legal effect if written on the face.

Joint payees of a bill or note, who are not partners, must all join in an indorsement.

An indorser may always prevent his own responsibility by writing "without recourse," or other equivalent words, over his indorsement; and any bargain between the indorser and indorsee, written or oral, that the indorser shall not be sued, is available by him against that indorsee; but he cannot make this defence against subsequent indorsees who had no notice of the bargain before they took the note.

Every indorsement and acceptance admits conclusively the genuineness of the signature of every party who has put his name upon the bill previously in fact, and who is also previous in order. By this is meant, that if an indorser — say a third indorser — is sued, he cannot defend himself by saying that the names of the maker and first and second indorsers, or either of them, were forged, because by indorsing it himself he gives his indorsee a right to believe that the previous signatures were genuine. And an acceptor cannot say that his drawer's name is forged; but he may say that an indorsement which was on the bill when he accepted it was forged, because an indorsement of a bill comes properly and in *order of law* after acceptance.

If a holder strike out an indorsement by mistake, he may restore it; if on purpose, the indorser is permanently discharged.

A holder may bring his action against any prior indorser, either by making title through all the subsequent indorsements, or by filling any blank indorsement specially to himself, and suing accordingly; but then he invalidates all the indorsements which are subsequent to that which he has made special to himself.

One may make a note or bill payable to his own order, and indorse it in blank; and this is now very common in our commercial cities, because the holder of such a bill or note can transfer it by delivery, and it needs not his indorsement to make it negotiable further. A note to the maker's own order, if not indorsed by him, is, strictly speaking, of no force against him. But there is some disposition in the courts to say that a holder of such note may sue the maker as if the note were to bearer.

A transfer by delivery, without indorsement, of a bill or note payable to bearer, or indorsed in blank, does not generally make the transferrer responsible to the transferree for the payment of the instrument. Nor has the transferree a right to fall back, in case of non-payment, upon the transferrer for the original consideration of the transfer, if the bill were transferred in good faith, in exchange for money or goods; for such transfer would be held to be a sale of the bill or note, and the purchaser takes it with all risk.

An indorsement may be made on the paper before the bill or note is drawn; and such indorsement, says Lord Mansfield, "is a letter of credit for an indefinite sum, and it will not lie in the indorser's mouth to say that the indorsements were not regular." The same rule applies to an acceptance on blank paper. So an indorsement may be made after or before acceptance, though strictly proper only after.

A bill or note once paid at or after maturity, ceases to be negotiable, in reference to all who had been discharged by the payment. If issued again, it is like a new note without their names. If a bill or note is paid before it is due, it is valid in the hands of a subsequent *bonâ fide* indorsee, and must be paid to him.

A portion of a negotiable bill or note cannot be transferred, so as to give the transferree a right of action for that portion in his own name. But if the bill or note be partly paid, it may be indorsed over for the balance.

After the death of a holder of a bill or note, his executor or administrator may transfer it by his indorsement. The husband who acquires a right to a bill or a note which was given to the wife either before or after marriage, may indorse it.

If the rule that the same party cannot be plaintiff and defendant, prevents the action, as where A, B, & Co. hold the note of A, C, & Co., so that if a suit were brought A would be one of the plaintiffs and one of the defendants also, which cannot be, A, B, & Co. may indorse the note to D, who may then sue A, C, & Co.

SECTION VII.

THE RIGHTS AND DUTIES OF THE ACCEPTOR.

Acceptance applies to bills, and not to notes. It is an engagement of the person on whom the bill is drawn to pay it according to its tenor. The usual way of entering into this agreement, or of accepting, is by the drawee's writing his name across the face of the bill, and writing over it the word "accepted." But any other word of equivalent meaning may be used, and it may be written elsewhere, and it need not be signed, or the drawee's name alone on the bill may be enough. A written promise to accept a future bill, if it distinctly define and describe that very bill, has been held in this country as the equivalent of an acceptance, if the bill was taken on the credit of such promise.

A banker is liable to his depositor without acceptance of his checks, if he refuses to pay checks drawn against funds in his hands.

If a bill is accepted by a part only of those jointly responsible, or joint drawees, it may be treated by the holder as dishonored; but if not so treated, the parties accepting will be bound.

An acceptance may be made after maturity, and will be treated as an acceptance to pay on demand.

The acceptance may be cancelled by the holder; and if this cancelling be voluntary and intended, it is complete and effectual; but if made by mistake, by him or other parties, and this mistake can be shown, the acceptor is not discharged. And if the cancelling be by a third party, it is for the jury to say whether the holder authorized or assented to it.

If a qualified acceptance be offered, the holder may receive or refuse it. If he refuses it, he may treat the bill as dishonored; if he receives it, he should notify antecedent parties, and obtain their consent; without which they are not liable. But if he protests the bill as dishonored, for this reason, he cannot hold the acceptor upon his qualified acceptance.

A bill drawn on one incompetent to contract, as from infancy, marriage, or lunacy, may be treated by the holder as dishonored.

14

A bill can be accepted only by the drawee, — in person or by his authorized agent, — or by *some one who accepts for honor.*

SECTION VIII.

ACCEPTANCE OR PAYMENT FOR HONOR.

If a bill be protested for non-acceptance or for non-payment, any person may accept it, or pay it *for the honor* either of the drawer or of any indorser. This he usually does by going with the bill before the notary-public who protested the bill, and there declaring that he accepts or pays the bill *for honor;* and he should designate for whose honor he accepts or pays it, at the time, before the notary-public, and it should be noted by him.

A general acceptance *supra protest* (which is the phrase used both by merchants and in law, meaning *upon* or *after protest*) for honor, is taken to be for honor of the drawer. The drawee himself, refusing to accept it generally, may thus accept for the honor of the drawer or an indorser. And after a bill is accepted for honor of one party, it may be accepted by another person for honor of another party. And an acceptance for honor may be made at the intervention and request of the drawee.

No holder is obliged to receive an acceptance for honor: he may refuse it wholly. If he receive it, he should, at the maturity of the bill, present it for payment to the drawee, who may have been supplied with funds in the mean time. If not paid, the bill should be protested for non-payment, and then presented for payment to the acceptor for honor.

The undertaking of the acceptor for honor is collateral only; being an engagement to pay if the drawee does not. It can only be made for some party who will certainly be liable if the bill be not paid; because, by an acceptance or by a payment, properly made, for honor, *supra protest,* such acceptor or payer acquires an absolute claim against the party for whom he accepts, or pays, and against all parties to the bill antecedent to him, for all his lawful costs, payments, and damages, by reason of such acceptance or payment.

This is an entire exception to the rule that no person can make himself the creditor of another without the request or consent of that other; but it is an exception established by the law-merchant.

The reason why bills of exchange are sometimes accepted or paid *for honor* is to save the party for whose honor this is done, from the very heavy damages of a protested bill.

In many of our States it is a common practice to give a promissory note, and include in it *a confession of judgment*, for the amount. A suit may then be brought on the note as soon as it is due and unpaid, and a judgment taken out at once without the delay of a trial; and execution may issue on the judgment. Sometimes by the same note the promisor waives or renounces the benefit or protection of all exemption laws; and then the execution may be satisfied from any of his property that the sheriff can find.

(68.)

Form of a Judgment Note with Waiver.

$ 18

(*Time.*) after date, for value received, promise to pay or bearer, dollars, with interest, and without defalcation or stay of execution. And do hereby confess judgment for the above sum, with interest and costs of suit, a release of all errors, and waiver of all rights to inquisition and appeal, and to the benefit of all laws exempting real or personal property from levy and sale.

(*Signature.*)

Sometimes, in addition to the above, the same note has below it a power of attorney, authorizing the attorney whose name is put into the blank left for that purpose to appear in court for the promisor, and confess judgment. Sometimes the power is given to an attorney whom the parties agree upon, and then no other attorney can confess the judgment. It is, however, far more usual, and better, to insert the name of an attorney, and add, as in the following form, "or any attorney of any court of record."

(69.)

Judgment Note with Waiver, and Power of Attorney.

$ 186

after date the subscriber , of County of State of promise to pay to the **National Bank of** or order dollars, at their office, value received, with interest, at per cent per annum after due.

Due

Know all Men by these Presents, That the subscriber justly indebted to the **National Bank of** upon a certain promissory note, bearing even date herewith, for the sum of dollars, with interest, at the rate of per cent per annum, after due, and due day after date.

Now, Therefore, In consideration of the premises do hereby make, constitute, and appoint or any attorney of any court of record, to be true and lawful attorney, irrevocably for and in name , place, and stead, to appear in any court of record, in term time or in vacation, in any of the States or Territories of the United States, at any time after the said note becomes due, to waive the service of process, and confess a judgment in favor of the said **National Bank of** or their assigns or assignees, upon the said note for the above sum and interest thereon, to the day of the entry of the said judgment, together with costs, and twenty dollars, attorney's fees, and also to file a cognovit for the amount thereof, with an agreement therein, that no writ of error or appeal shall be prosecuted upon the judgment entered by virtue hereof, nor any bill in equity filed to interfere in any manner with the operation of said judgment, and to release all errors that may intervene in the entering-up of said judgment, or issuing the execution thereon; and also to waive all benefit of advantage to which may be entitled by virtue of any homestead or other exemption law, now, or hereafter in force, in this or any other State or Territory where judgment may be entered by virtue hereof. Hereby ratifying and confirming all that said attorney may do by virtue hereof.

Witness hand and seal this day of A. D. 186

(*Signature.*) (*Seal.*)

In Presence of

Sometimes the note is followed on the same paper by a power to confess judgment, and a waiver of all right of exemption; both the power and the waiver extending beyond the above-written note, and covering other notes and bonds and other evidence of debt.

(70.)

Judgment Note with fuller Waiver, and Power of Attorney.

$ 18

for value received, premise to pay to the order of the sum of dollars, with interest, in (*time*)

(*Signature.*)

Know all Men by these Presents, That whereas, the subscriber now justly indebted to upon a certain promissory note, bearing even date herewith, for the sum of dollars, and cents, made payable to the order of the said and due , and may from time to time hereafter become further or otherwise justly indebted to the said upon bonds, promissory notes, due bills, and other written evidences of debt, made, or to be made, indorsed or accepted by and held or owned by the said assignee or assignees hereof.

Now, Therefore, in consideration of the premises, and of the sum of one dollar to paid by the said the receipt whereof is hereby acknowledged do hereby make, constitute, and appoint or any attorney of any court of record, to be true and lawful attorney, irrevocable, for and in name , place , and stead, to appear in and before any court of record, either in term time or in vacation, in any of the States or Territories of the United States, at any time after the of said note, or of any such bond, promissory note, due bill, or other written evidence of debt, so already made or to be made, indorsed or accepted by as aforesaid, respectively, to waive service of process, and confess a judgment in favor of the said executors, administrators, assignee, or assignees, or the legal holder or holders of said note or of any one or more of such bonds, promissory notes, due bills, or other written evidences of debt, as aforesaid, for so much money as shall by the same appear to be due or owing thereon, with interest thereon according to the tenor and effect thereof respectively, together with costs; also, for dollars attorney's fees, to be added to the amount due or owing on entering up judgment; also, to file a cognovit for the amount that may be so due or owing, including attorney's fees as aforesaid, with an agreement therein that no writ of error or appeal shall be prosecuted upon the judgment entered up by virtue hereof, nor any bill in equity filed to restrain or in any manner interfere with the operation of said judgment, or any execution issued or to be issued thereon, and to release all errors that may intervene in the entering-up of any such judgment or issuing any execution thereon, and to consent, stipulate, and agree, that any execution issued or to be issued upon such judgment, may be immediately levied upon, and satisfied out of any personal property which may have or own, and to waive and relinquish all right to have personal property last taken and levied upon to satisfy such execution, and also to consent that execution may issue upon any such judgment immediately. Hereby ratifying and confirming all that said attorney may do by virtue hereof.

And, in consideration of the premises, do hereby stipulate, covenant, and agree with the said executors, administrators, and with the assignee, assignees, or the legal holder or holders of said note, or of any one or more of such bonds, promissory notes, due bills, or other written evidences of debt as aforesaid, that any execution so issued or to be issued as aforesaid, may first be levied upon and satisfied out of any personal property which may have or own, hereby expressly waiving all right to have personal property last taken and levied upon to satisfy such execution.

Witness hand and seal this day of A. D. 18

In Presence of (*Signature.*) (*Seal.*)

CHAPTER XVII.

AGENCY.

SECTION I.

AGENCY IN GENERAL.

THE relation of principal and agent implies that the principal acts by and through the agent, so that the acts in fact of the agent are the acts in law of the principal; and only when one is authorized by another to act for him in this way, and to this extent, is he an agent. One who is disqualified from contracting on his own account may act as the agent of another; thus infants, married women, and aliens may act as agents for others.

A principal is responsible for the acts of his agent, not only when he has actually given full authority to the agent thus to represent and act for him, but when he has, by his words, or his acts, or both, caused or permitted the person with whom the agent deals to believe him to be clothed with this authority. And a man may be thus held as a principal, either because he has in some way authorized *all* persons to believe that he has constituted some other man his agent, or because he has authorized only the party dealing with the supposed agent to so believe. For all responsibility rests upon two grounds, which are commonly united, but either of which alone is sufficient: one, the giving of actual authority; the other, such appearing to give authority as justifies those who deal with the supposed agent in believing that this authority was given him.

A general agent is one authorized to represent his principal in all his business, or in all his business of a particular kind. A particular agent is one authorized to do only a specific thing or a few specified things. It is not always easy to discriminate between these; but it is often important, by reason of the rule that the authority of a *general* agent is measured by the usual scope and character of the business he is empowered to transact. By appointing him to do that business, the principal is considered as saying to the world that his agent has all the authority necessary to the doing of it in the usual way. And if the agent transcends his actual authority, but does not go beyond the natural and usual scope of the business, the principal is bound, unless the party with whom the general agent dealt knew that the agent exceeded his authority. For if an agent does only what is natural and usual in transacting business for his principal, and yet goes beyond the limits prescribed by him, it is obvious that the principal must have put particular and unusual limitations to his authority; and these cannot affect the rights of a third party who deals with the agent in ignorance of these limitations. But, on the other hand, the rule is, that, if an agent who is specially authorized to do a specific thing exceeds his authority, the principal is not bound, because the party dealing with such agent must inquire for himself, and at his own peril, into the extent and limits of the authority given to the agent. Here, however, as before, if the party dealing with the agent, and inquiring, as he should, into his authority, has sufficient evidence of this authority furnished to him by the principal, and, in his dealings with the agent, acts within the limits of the authority thus proved, he cannot be affected by any reservations and limitations made secretly by the principal, and wholly unknown to the person dealing with the agent.

SECTION II.

HOW AUTHORITY MAY BE GIVEN TO AN AGENT.

It may be given under seal, or in writing without seal, or orally. If given by a written instrument, this instrument is called a Power of Attorney, of which we shall give various forms at the close of this chapter. An oral appointment authorizes the agent to make a written contract, but not to execute instruments under seal. But an instrument under seal, signed and sealed in the principal's presence, and by his request and authority, will be regarded as the principal's deed, made by himself. One employed by another to act for him in the usual trade or business of the agent, as auctioneer, broker, or the like, acquires thereby authority to do all that is necessary or usual in that business. And if a person puts his goods into the custody of another whose ordinary and usual business it is to sell such goods, he authorizes the whole world to believe that this person has them for sale; and any person buying them honestly, in this belief, would hold them.

Therefore, if fraudulent by-bidding be procured or permitted by the auctioneer, even without the knowledge of the owner of the goods, the owner is answerable for this fraud of his agent, and the buyer has a right to refuse to take the goods. So neither party is bound until the agreement of sale is completed. Therefore the actioneer may withdraw any article, and a bidder may withdraw any bid, until the article is "knocked down," but not afterwards; for then the sale is completed, and the property in (or ownership of) the article passes to the buyer.

If one is repeatedly employed to do certain things, — as a wife or a son to sign bills or receipts; or a domestic servant to make purchases; or a merchant or broker to sign policies, and the like, — in all these cases, one dealing with the person thus usually employed is justified in believing him authorized to do those things with the assent and approbation of his employer, and in the same way in which he has done them, but not in any other way. Thus, if a servant is usually employed to buy, but always for cash, this implies no authority to buy on credit.

An agency may be confirmed and established, and in fact created, by a subsequent adoption and ratification; and a ratification relates back to the original transaction; and a corporation is bound by the ratification of an agent's acts, in the same manner as an individual would be. But no ratification is effectual to bind the principal, unless made by the principal with a knowledge of all the material facts. And there can be ratification only where the act is done by one purporting to be an agent, or by an assumed authority. Generally, one who receives and holds a beneficial result of the act of another as his agent, is not permitted to deny such agency; and in some cases this is extended even to acts of such agent under seal.

Thus, if an agent sell under seal property of a supposed principal, an individual or a corporation, and receive payment, and hand this over to the principal, if the principal could show that the agent had no authority, he might avoid the sale, and recover the property; but he could not do this and also hold the money paid for it. And if one, knowing that another has acted as his agent, does not disavow the authority as soon as he conveniently can, but lies by and permits a person to go on and deal with the supposed agent, or to lose an opportunity of indemnifying himself, this is an adoption and confirmation of the acts of the agent. Nor can a supposed principal adopt a part for his own benefit, and repudiate the rest of the supposed agency; he must adopt the whole or none.

If an agent makes a sale, and his principal ratifies the sale, he thereby ratifies the agent's representations made at the time of the sale and in relation to it, and is bound by them.

The whole subject of mercantile agency is influenced and governed by mercantile usage. Thus, as to the difference between factors and brokers, the law adopts a distinction usual among merchants, although it may not always be regarded by them. A factor is a mercantile agent for sales and purchases, who has possession of the goods; a broker is such agent, but without possession of the goods. Hence, a factor may act for his principal, and yet in his own name, because the actual owner, by delivering to him the goods, gives to him the appearance of an owner; but a broker must act only in the name of his principal.

A purchaser of goods from a factor may set off against the price a debt due from the factor, unless he buys the goods knowing that they are another's; not so, if the purchaser buy from a broker. Again, a factor has a lien on the goods for his claims against his principal; but a broker generally has not.

One may be a factor as to all rights and duties, who is called a *broker;* as an exchange-broker, who has notes for sale on discount, certificates of stock, &c., delivered into his possession; and such broker, being actually a factor, would have a lien on the policies of insurance or other documents held by him, for his commissions and charges about those documents.

A cashier of a bank, or other official person, may be an agent for those whose officer he is, or for others who employ him. He has, without special gift, all the authority necessary or usual to the transaction of his business. But he cannot bind his employers by any unusual or illegal contract made with their customers. The same law, and the same qualifications, apply to the case of officers of railroad companies, or other corporations. Their acts bind their employers or companies, so far as they have authorized those acts, or have justified those who dealt with the officers in believing that the officers possessed such authority; but no further.

Nor would the acts or permissions of such officer have any validity if they violate his official duties, and are certainly and obviously beyond his power, even if sanctioned by his directors; as if the cashier of a bank permitted overdrawing, or the like. And all parties who deal with such agent in such a transaction would be unable to hold the principal; for the law would consider them as knowing that the officer could have no right to do such things.

Therefore, the general agent of a corporation, clothed with a certain power by the charter or the lawful acts of the corporation, may use that power for an authorized, or even a prohibited purpose, in his dealings with an innocent third party, and render the corporation liable for his acts, if they be really within the power given him, or seem to be within it by the fault or act of the corporation; but not otherwise. Thus, a treasurer of a corporation has no power to release a claim which belongs to the corporation.

SECTION III.

EXTENT AND DURATION OF AUTHORITY.

A GENERAL authority may continue to bind a principal after its actual revocation, if the agency were known, and the revocation be wholly unknown to the party dealing with the agent, without that party's fault.

An authority to sell implies an authority to sell on credit, if that be usual; otherwise not; and if an agent sells on credit without any authority, or by exceeding his authority, the principal may claim his goods from the purchaser, or hold the agent responsible for their price. Neither an auctioneer, nor a broker employed to sell, has any right to sell on credit, unless this authority is given him expressly, or by some known and established usage. And the agent is generally responsible if he mixes the goods of his principal with his own, in such a manner as to confuse them together, or takes a note payable to himself, unless this be authorized by the usage of the trade.

If the agent (or factor) takes a note payable to himself, and be comes bankrupt, such note belongs to his principal, and not to the agent's assignees.

A power to sell gives a power to warrant, where there is a distinct usage of making such sales with warranty, and the want of authority to warrant is unknown to the purchaser, without his fault; and not otherwise. Thus, it has been held that an authority to sell a horse implies an authority to sell with warranty, because horses are usually sold with warranty. A general authority to sell goods carries with it an authority to sell by sample. General authority to transact business, or even to receive and discharge debts, does not enable an agent to accept or indorse bills or notes, so as to charge his principal. Indeed, special authorities to indorse are construed strictly. But this authority may be implied from the previous usage of the agent, recognized and sanctioned by the principal. Where a confidential clerk was accustomed to draw bills for his employer, and this employer had authorized him in one instance to indorse, and on two other occasions had received money obtained by his indorsement of his employer's name, the court held that a jury might consider the clerk authorized generally to indorse for his employer. An agent to receive cash has no authority to take bills or notes, except bank-notes.

If an agent sells, and makes a material representation which he believes to be true, and the principal knows it to be false, and does not correct it, this is the fraud of the principal, and avoids the sale.

If an agency be justly implied from general employment, it may continue so far as to bind the principal after his withdrawal of the authority, if that withdrawal be not made known, in such way as is usual or proper, to all who deal with the agent as such.

Revocation, generally, is always in the power and at the will of the principal. His death operates of itself a revocation. But the death of an agent does not revoke the authority of a sub-agent appointed by the agent under an authority given him by the principal. If the power be coupled with an interest, — as where one gives a person power to sell goods and apply the money for his own benefit, or the like, — or if it is given for a valuable consideration, and the continuance of the power is requisite to make the interest available, then it cannot be revoked at the pleasure of the principal. Marriage of a woman revokes a revocable authority given by her while single.

If an agent to whom commercial paper is given for collection be negligent or mistaken about it, and so in fault towards his principal, the measure of his responsibility is the damage actually sustained by his principal.

If a bank receive notes or bills for collection, although charging no commission, the possible use of the money is consideration enough to make them liable as agents having compensation; that is, liable for any want of due and legal diligence and care. But if the bank exercise proper skill and care in the choice of a collecting agent, or of a notary, or other person or officer, to do what may be necessary in relation to the paper committed to them, the bank is not liable for *his* want of care or skill.

In general, an exigency, or even necessity, which would make an extension of the power of an agent very useful to his employer, will not give that extension. A master of a ship, however, may sell it, in case of necessity, or pledge it by bottomry, to raise money. But this is a peculiar effect of the law-merchant, to be considered more fully in the chapter on the Law of Shipping; and no such general rule applies to ordinary agencies.

SECTION IV.

THE EXECUTION OF AUTHORITY.

GENERALLY, an authority must be conformed to with great strictness and accuracy; otherwise, the principal will not be bound, although the agent may be bound personally. But the old strictness is now abated considerably; and, whatever be the form or manner of the signature of a simple contract, it will be held to bind the principal, if that were the certain and obvious intent. In the case of sealed instruments, the ancient severity is more strictly maintained.

That the authority must be conformed to with strict accuracy, in all matters of substance, is quite certain; but the whole instrument will be considered, in order to ascertain the intention of the parties and the extent of authority. A power given to two cannot be executed by one; but some exception to the rule as to joint power exists in the case of public agencies, and also in many commercial transactions. Thus, either of two factors — whether partners or not — may sell goods consigned to both. And where there are joint agents, whether partners or not, notice to one is notice to both.

In commercial matters, usage, or the reason of the thing, may sometimes seem to add to an authority; so far, at least, as is requisite for the full discharge of the duty committed to the agent in the best and most complete manner. Thus, it is held that an agent to get a bill discounted may indorse it in the name of his principal, unless he is expressly forbidden to indorse. So a broker, employed to procure insurance, may adjust a loss under the same; but he cannot give up any advantages, rights, or securities of the assured, by compromise or otherwise, without special authority.

SECTION V.

LIABILITY OF AN AGENT.

Generally, an agent makes himself liable by his express agreement, or by transcending his authority, or by a material departure from it, or by concealing his character as agent, or by such conduct as renders his principal irresponsible, or by his own bad faith. If he describes himself as agent for some unnamed principal, he is not liable, unless he is proved to be the real principal. If an agent execute an instrument the language of which would hold him personally, he cannot exonerate himself by showing that in fact he signed it as agent, and that this was known to the other party. Because this would be to vary the terms of a written contract by evi dence, which is not permitted, as we have before stated.

A party with whom an agent deals as agent cannot hold him personally, on the ground that he transcended or departed from his authority, if that party knew at the time that the agent did so. If he exceeds his authority, he is liable on the whole contract, although a part of it is within his authority. One who, having no authority, acts as agent, is personally responsible. But if an agent transcends his authority through an ignorance of its limits, which is actual and honest, and is not imputable to his own neglect of the means of knowledge, he would not be held, unless an innocent party dealing with him as agent would otherwise suffer loss.

SECTION VI.

RIGHTS OF ACTION GROWING OUT OF AGENCY.

If an agent intrusted with goods sell the same without authority, the principal may affirm the sale, and sue the buyer for the price, or he may disaffirm the sale, and recover the goods from the buyer.

In case of a simple contract, that is, a contract not under seal, an undisclosed principal may show that the nominal party was actually his agent, and thus make himself actually a party to the contract, and sue upon it; but if the other party has previously in good faith settled with the supposed agent, or paid him any thing, in cash or by charge, or in account, this other party must not lose by the coming forward of the principal. So, too, an undisclosed principal, when discovered, may be made liable on such contract; but would be protected, if his accounts or relations with his agent had been in the mean time changed in good faith, so as to make it detrimental to him to be held liable. If one sells to an agent, knowing him to be an agent, and knowing who is his principal, and elects to charge the goods to the agent alone, he cannot afterwards transfer the charge to the principal.

Notice to an agent, before the transaction goes so far as to render the notice useless, is notice to the principal. And knowledge obtained by an agent in the course of the transaction itself is the same thing as knowledge of the principal. Notice to an officer or member of a corporation is notice to that corporation, if the officer or member, by appointment, or by usage, had authority to receive it for the corporation; but notice to any member is not necessarily notice to a corporation.

SECTION VII.

HOW A PRINCIPAL IS AFFECTED BY THE ACTS OF HIS AGENT.

If an agent makes a fraudulent representation, a principal would be liable for resulting injury, although personally ignorant and innocent of the wrong; nor can he take any benefit therefrom. A principal cannot, of course, restrict his liability by calling himself an agent, although this is sometimes attempted.

Payment to an agent of money due to the principal binds the principal only when it is made to the agent in the regular course of business. Payment to a sub-agent appointed by the agent, but whose appointment is not authorized by the principal, binds the agent, and renders him liable to the principal for any loss of the money in the sub-agent's hands. Where a legacy was left to a tradesman, and the executors paid it to a shopman who was in the habit of receiving daily payments, this was held not a sufficient payment to discharge the executors. And, generally, a shopman authorized to receive money at the counter, or any person authorized to receive money at any particular place or in any particular way, is not thereby authorized to receive it in any other place or in any other way. Nor is the principal bound, if the agent be authorized to receive the money, but, instead of actually receiving it, discharge a debt due from him to the payer, and then give a receipt as for money paid to his principal, unless it can be shown that he has special authority to receive payment in this way, or that such payment is justified by known usage.

In general, although a principal may be responsible for the deliberate fraud of his agent in the execution of his employment, he is not responsible for his *criminal* acts, unless he expressly commanded them. There is, however, a class of cases in which the principal has intrusted property to his agent, and the agent has used it illegally; and this act of the agent is evidence, which, if unexplained and unanswered, suffices to render the principal liable criminally, without proof of his direct participation in the act itself. The smuggling of goods, the issue of libellous publications, and the sale of intoxicating liquors, by agents, belong to this class.

SECTION VIII.

MUTUAL RIGHTS AND DUTIES OF PRINCIPAL AND AGENT.

An agent cannot depart from his instructions without making himself liable to his principal for the consequences. In determining the purport or extent of his instructions, custom and usage in like cases will often have great influence; because, on the one hand, the agent is entitled to all the advantages which a known and established usage would give him; and, on the other, the principal has a right to expect that his agent will conduct himself according to such usage. But usage is never permitted to prevail over express instructions. A principal who accepts the benefit of an act done by his agent beyond or aside from his instructions, discharges the agent from responsibility therefor. And any unnecessary delay in renouncing the transaction, or any endeavor to wait and make a profit out of it, is an acceptance of the act. But if the agent has bought goods for his principal without authority, the latter may renounce the purchase, and, nevertheless, hold the goods as security for his money, if that has been advanced on them.

In general, every agent is entitled to indemnity from his principal, when acting in obedience to his lawful orders, or when he, in conformity with his instructions, does an act which is not wrong in itself, and which he is induced by his principal to suppose right at that time.

An attorney or agent cannot appoint a sub-attorney or agent, unless authorized to do so expressly, or by a certain usage, or by the obvious reason and necessity of the case. Thus, a consignee or factor for the sale of merchandise may employ a broker to sell, when this is the usual course of business. A sub-agent, appointed without such authority, is only the agent of the agent, and not the agent of the principal; unless his appointment is in some way authorized or confirmed and ratified by the principal.

An agent is bound to use, in the affairs of his principal, all that care and skill which a reasonable man would use in his own. And he is also bound to the utmost good faith. Where, however, an agent acts gratuitously, without an agreement for compensation, or any legal right to compensation growing out of his services, he will not be held responsible for other than gross negligence. A strictly gratuitous agent will be held responsible for property intrusted to him, if it be lost or injured by his gross negligence.

For any breach of duty, an agent is responsible for the whole injury thereby sustained by his principal; and, generally, a verdict against the principal for misconduct of the agent measures the claim of the principal over against the agent. The loss must be capable of being made certain and definite; and then the agent is responsible, if it could not have happened but for his misconduct, although not immediately caused by it. Thus, where an insurance-broker was directed to effect insurance on goods "from Gibraltar to Dublin," and caused the policy to be made, "beginning from the lading of the goods on board," and they were laden on board at Malaga, and went thence to Gibraltar, and sailed for Dublin, and were lost on the voyage, so that the policy did not cover them because they were not laden at Gibraltar, this was held to be gross negligence on his part, and he was held responsible for the value of the goods.

If any agent embezzles his employer's property, it is quite clear that the employer may reclaim it whenever and wherever he can distinctly trace and identify it. But if it be blended indistinguishably with the agent's own goods, and the agent die or become insolvent, the principal can claim only as a common creditor, as against other creditors; but as against the factor or agent himself, the whole belongs in law to the principal; because the factor or agent had no right thus to mix up the property of another with his own, and if he chooses to do so, he must lose all of his own property that cannot be separated from that which is not his own.

An agent employed to sell property cannot buy it himself; nor, if employed to buy, can he buy of himself; unless expressly authorized to do so. Nor can a trustee purchase the property he holds in trust for another. But the other party may ratify and confirm such sale or purchase by his agent; and he will do this by accepting the proceeds and delaying any objection for a long time after the wrongful act is made known to him. And if a trustee or agent to sell property buys it, not in his own name, but through somebody else, the sale is void.

Among the obvious duties of all agents is that of keeping an exact account of their doings, and particularly of all pecuniary transactions. After a reasonable time has elapsed, the court will presume that such an account was rendered, accepted, and settled. Otherwise, every agent might always remain liable to be called upon for such account. Moreover, he is liable not only for the balances in his hands, but for interest; or even, where there has been a long delay to his own profit, he might be liable for compound interest, on the same ground on which it has been charged in similar cases against executors, trustees, and guardians. No interest whatever would be charged, if such were the intention of the parties, or the effect of the bargain between them; and this intention may be inferred either from direct or circumstantial evidence, — as the nature of the transaction, or the fact that the principal knew that the money lay useless in the agent's hands, and made no objection or claim.

The general rule is, that a principal may revoke his agency, and an agent may throw up the agency, at pleasure. But neither would be permitted to exercise this power in an unfair and injurious manner which circumstances do not require or justify, without being responsible to the other party for any damages caused by his wrongful act.

Insanity revokes authority, especially if legally ascertained. But if the principal, when sane, gave an authority to his agent, and a third party acts with the agent in the belief of his authority, but after the insanity of the principal has revoked it, the insanity not being known to this third party, this revocation will not be permitted to take effect to the injury of this third party.

SECTION IX.

FACTORS AND BROKERS.

ALL agents who sell goods for their principals, and guarantee the price, are said in Europe to act under a *del credere commission.* In this country, this phrase is seldom used, nor is such guaranty usually given, except by commission-merchants. And where such guaranty is given, the factor is so far a surety, that his employers must first have recourse to the principal debtor. Still his promise is not "a promise to pay the debt of another," within the Statute of Frauds. Nor does he guarantee the safe arrival of the money received by him in payment of the goods, and transmitted to his employer, but he must use proper caution in sending it. And if it is agreed that he shall guarantee the remittance, and charge a commission for so doing, he is liable, although he does not charge the commission. If he takes a note from the purchaser, this note is his employer's; and if he takes depreciated or bad paper, he must make it good.

A broker or factor is bound to the care and skill properly belonging to the business which he undertakes, and is responsible for the want of it.

A factor intrusted with goods may pledge them for advances to his principal, or for advances to himself to the extent of his lien for charges and commissions. And his power to pledge them, which grows out of the law-merchant, has been much enlarged by statute in many of our States.

The mere wishes or intimations of his employer, if sufficiently distinct, have the force of instructions. Thus, in New York, a principal wrote to his factor, stating that he thought there was a short supply of the goods he had consigned, and giving facts on which his opinion was founded, and concluded, "I have thought it best for you to take my pork out of the market for the present, as thirty days will make an important change in the value of the article." This was considered by the court to be a distinct instruction, binding upon the factor; and he was therefore held liable for the loss caused by selling the pork within the thirty days.

All instructions the agent or factor must obey; but may still, as we have already stated, depart from their letter, if in good faith, and for the certain benefit of his employer, in an unforeseen exigency. Having possession of the goods, he may insure them; but is not bound to do so, nor even to advise insurance, unless requested, or unless a distinct usage makes this his duty. He has much discretion as to the time, terms, and manner of a sale, but must use this discretion in good faith. For a sale which is precipitated by him without reason and injuriously is void, as unauthorized. If he send goods to his principal without order, or contrary to his duty, the principal may return them, or, acting in good faith and for the benefit of the factor, may sell them as the factor's goods.

Although a factor charges no guaranty commission, he is liable to his principal for his own default; so he is if he sells on credit, and, when it expires, takes a note to himself: but if he takes at the time of the sale a negotiable note from a party in fair credit, and the note is afterward dishonored, this is the loss of his employer, unless the factor has guaranteed it.

If he sells the goods of many owners to one purchaser, taking a note for the whole to himself, and gets it discounted for his own use or accommodation, he is then liable without any guaranty for the payment of that note. So he is if he gets discounted for his own use a note taken wholly for his principal's goods. But he may discount the note to reimburse himself for advances, without making himself liable. If he sends his own note for the price to his employer, he must pay it.

As a factor has possession of the goods, he may use his own name in all his transactions, even in suits at law; but a broker can buy, sell, receipt, &c., only in the name of his employer. So, a factor has a lien on the goods in his hands for his advances, his expenses, and his commissions, and for the balance of his general account. And the factor may sell from time to time enough to cover his advances, unless there be something in his employment or in his instructions from which it may be inferred that he had agreed not to do so. But a broker, having no possession, has no lien. The broker may act for both parties, and often does so. But, from the nature of his employment, a factor should act only for the party employing him.

A broker has no authority to receive payment for the goods he sells, unless that authority be given him, expressly or by usage. Nor will payment to a factor discharge a debtor who has received notice from the principal not to make such payment.

Generally, neither factor nor broker can claim their commissions until their whole service be performed, and in good faith, and with proper skill, care, and industry; and their negligence may be given in evidence either to lessen their compensation or commissions, or to bar them altogether. But if the service begins, and is interrupted wholly without their fault, they may claim a proportionate compensation. If either bargains to give his whole time to his employer, he will not be permitted to derive any compensation for services rendered to other persons. Nor can either have any valid claim against any one for illegal services, or those which violate morality or public policy.

A principal cannot revoke an authority given to a factor, after advances made by the factor, without repaying or securing the factor.

The distinction between a *foreign* and a *domestic* factor is quite important, as they have quite different rights, duties, and powers, by the law-merchant generally. A domestic factor is one who is employed and acts in the same country with his principal. A foreign factor is one employed by a principal who lives in a different country; and a foreign factor is as to third parties — for most purposes and under most circumstances — a principal. Thus, they cannot sue the principal, because they are supposed to contract with the factor alone, and on his credit, although the principal may sue them; and a foreign factor is personally liable, although he fully disclose his agency, and his principal is known.

The following forms of powers of attorney are those most frequently required; and from them, by suitable alterations, powers of attorney may be framed for any purpose.

(71.)

Power of Attorney.

Know all Men by these Presents, That I (*the name of the principal or party appointing*) of (*residence*) have constituted, ordained, and made, and in my stead and place put, and by these presents do constitute, ordain, and make, and in my stead and place put (*name of attorney*) to be my true, sufficient, and lawful attorney for me and in my name and stead to (*here set forth the purposes for which the power is given*)

Giving and hereby granting unto him, the said attorney, full power and authority in and about the premises; and to use all due means, course, and process in law, for the full, effectual, and complete execution of the business afore described; and in my name to make and execute due acquittance and discharge; and for the premises to appear, and the person of me the constituent to represent before any governor, judges, justices, officers, and ministers of the law whatsoever, in any court or courts of judicature, and there on my behalf, to answer, defend, and reply unto all actions, causes, matters, and things whatsoever relating to the premises. Also to submit any matter in dispute, respecting the premises, to arbitration or otherwise; with full power to make and substitute, for the purposes aforesaid, one or more attorneys, under him, my said attorney, and the same again at pleasure to revoke. And generally to say, do, act, transact, determine, accomplish, and finish all matters and things whatsoever relating to the premises, as fully, amply and effectually, to all intents and purposes, as I the said constituent, if present, ought or might personally, although the matter should require more special authority than is herein comprised, I the said constituent ratifying, allowing, and holding firm and valid all whatsoever my said attorney or his substitutes shall lawfully do, or cause to be done, in and about the premises, by virtue of these presents.

In Witness Whereof, I have hereunto set my hand and seal, this day of in the year of our Lord eighteen hundred and sixty-

(Signature.) *(Seal.)*

Signed, Sealed and Delivered in Presence of us

Sometimes a power of attorney is given without any power of substitution. This may be by inadvertence, or because it was not intended that the attorney should substitute anybody in his place. Afterwards, it is desired to give him this power to substitute others. And this may be done by a separate instrument, as follows: —

(72.)

Power of Substitution.

Know all Men by these Presents, That I, by virtue of the power and authority to me given, in and by the letter of attorney of *(the principal)* which is hereunto annexed *(or described without being annexed)*, do make, substitute and appoint *(name of substitute)* as well for me as the true and lawful attorney and substitute of the said constituent named in the said letter of attorney, to do, execute, and perform all and every thing requisite and necessary to be done, as fully, to all intents and purposes, as the said constituent or I myself could do if personally present; hereby ratifying and confirming all that the said attorney and substitute hereby made shall do in the premises by virtue hereof and of the said letter of attorney.

In Witness Whereof, I have hereunto set my hand and seal the day of in the year of our Lord one thousand eight hundred and

(Signature.) *(Seal.)*

Executed and Delivered in the Presence of

(73.)

Power of Attorney in a Shorter Form.

Know all Men by these Presents, That I *(name of principal)* have made, constituted and appointed, and by these presents do make, constitute and appoint *(name of attorney)* my true and lawful attorney for me and in my name, place, and stead to

(here describe the thing to be done)

giving and granting unto my said attorney full power and authority to do and perform all and every act and thing whatsoever requisite and necessary to be done in and about the premises, as fully to all intents and purposes, as I might or could do if personally present, with full power of substitution and revocation, hereby ratifying and confirming all that my said attorney or his substitute shall lawfully do or cause to be done by virtue hereof.

In Witness Whereof, I have hereunto set my hand and seal the day of in the year one thousand eight hundred and

(*Signature.*) (*Seal.*)

Executed and Delivered in the Presence of

(74.)

Full Power of Attorney to demand and recover Debts.

Know all Men by these Presents, That I (*name of principal*) have constituted, ordained and made, and in my stead and place put, and by these presents do constitute, ordain, and make, and in my stead and place put (*name of attorney*) to be my true, sufficient and lawful attorney for me and in my name and stead, and to my use, to ask, demand, levy, require, recover and receive of and from all and every person or persons whomsoever the same shall or may concern, all and singular sum and sums of money, debts, goods, wares, merchandise, effects and things, whatsoever and wheresoever they shall and may be found due, owing, payable, belonging and coming unto me the constituent, by any ways and means whatsoever.

Giving and hereby Granting unto my said attorney full and whole strength, power and authority in and about the premises; and to take and use all due means, course and process in the law, for the obtaining and recovering the same; and of recoveries and receipts thereof, and in my name to make, seal and execute due acquittance and discharge; and for the premises to appear, and the person of me the constituent to represent before any governor, judges, justices, officers and ministers of the law whatsoever, in any court or courts of judicature, and there, on my behalf, to answer, defend and reply unto all actions, causes, matters and things whatsoever, relating to the premises. Also to submit any matter in dispute to arbitration or otherwise, with full power to make and substitute one or more attorneys and my said attorney, and the same again at pleasure to revoke. And generally to say, do, act, transact, determine, accomplish and finish all matters and things whatsoever, relating to the premises, as fully, amply, and effectually, to all intents and purposes, as I the said constituent if present, ought or might personally, although the matter should require more special authority than is herein comprised, I the said constituent ratifying, allowing and holding firm and valid, all and whatsoever my said attorneyor his substitutes shall lawfully do, or cause to be done, in and about the premises, by virtue of these presents.

In Witness Whereof, I have hereunto set my hand and seal, this day of in the year of our Lord one thousand eight hundred and

(*Signature.*) (*Seal.*)

Signed, Sealed and Delivered in Presence of us,

(75.)

Power of Attorney to sell and deliver Chattels.

Know all Men by these Presents, That I the undersigned, for value received, do hereby irrevocably constitute and appoint to be my true and lawful attorney, for me and in my name and behalf, to sell, transfer and deliver, unto or any other person or persons (*here describe the things to be sold*)

And further, one or more persons under him to substitute with like power.

In Witness Whereof, I have hereunto set my hand and seal this day of 18 .

(*Witnesses.*) (*Signature.*) (*Seal.*)

(76.)

Power of Attorney given by Seller to Buyer.

Know all Men by these Presents, That I for value received, have bargained, sold, assigned and transferred, and by these presents, do bargain, sell, assign and transfer, unto (*name of the buyer*) the following articles, namely, (*describe the articles*) and I do hereby constitute and appoint the said (*the buyer*) my true and lawful attorney irrevocable, for me and in my name and stead, but to my use, to sell, assign, transfer and set over all or any part of the said (*the goods*) and for that purpose to make and execute all necessary acts of assignment and transfer, and one or more persons to substitute with like full power, hereby ratifying and confirming all that my said attorney or his substitute or substitutes, shall lawfully do by virtue hereof.

In Witness Whereof, I have hereunto set my hand and seal the day of one thousand eight hundred and

(*Signature.*) (*Seal.*)

Signed, Sealed and Delivered in Presence of

(77.)

Power of Attorney to sell Shares of Stock, with Appointment by Attorney of Substitute.

Know all Men by these Presents, That, for value received, I (*name of the principal*) of do hereby make, constitute, and appoint irrevocably, my true and lawful attorney (with power of substitution), for and in my name and on my behalf, to sell, assign, and transfer unto (*name of buyer*) share now standing in my name in the capital or joint stock of the And my said attorney is hereby fully empowered to make and pass all necessary acts for the said assignment and transfer.

Witness my hand and seal, 186

(*Signature.*) (*Seal.*)

Signed, Sealed and Delivered in the Presence of

For value received, I appoint, irrevocably, (*name of the substitute*) as my substitute, with all the powers above given to me.

Witness my hand and seal, 186

(*Signature.*) (*Seal.*)

Signed, Sealed and Delivered in the Presence of

(78.)

Power of Attorney to subscribe for Stock.

Know all Men by these Presents, That I the undersigned, do hereby irrevocably constitute and appoint to be my true and lawful attorney, for me and in my name and behalf, to subscribe for shares in the capital stock of the And further, one or more persons under him to substitute with like power.

In Witness Whereof, I have hereunto set my hand and seal this day of 18

Witnesses present, (*Seal.*)

(79.)

Proxy, or Power of Attorney to vote.

Know all Men by these Presents, That I (*name of the principal*) of do hereby appoint to be my substitute and proxy for me and in my name and behalf to vote at any election of directors or other officers, and at any meeting of the stockholders of said company as fully as I might or could were I personally present.

In Witness Whereof, I have hereunto set my hand and seal this day of 18

Witnesses present, *(Signature.)*

(80.)

Proxy, revoking all Previous Proxies.

Know all Men by these Presents, That I the undersigned, stockholder in the (*name of the company*) do hereby appoint my true and lawful attorney, with power of substitution, for me and in my name, to vote at the meeting of the stockholders in said company, to be held at or at any adjournment thereof, with all the powers I should possess if personally present, hereby revoking all previous proxies.

18

Witness. *(Signature.)*

(81.)

Proxy, with Affidavit of Ownership, in Use in New York.

Know all Men by these Presents, That I, do hereby constitute and appoint my attorney and agent for me and in my name, place, and stead, to vote as my proxy at any election of directors of the according to the number of votes I should be entitled to vote if then personally present.

In Witness Whereof, I have hereto set my hand and seal, this day of one thousand eight hundred and

(Signature.) *(Seal.)*

Signed, Sealed and Delivered in Presence of

I do swear (*or affirm*) that the shares on which my attorney and agent in the above proxy is authorized to vote, do not belong, and are not hypothecated, to the said company, and that they are not hypothecated or pledged to any other corporation or person whatever; that such shares have not been transferred to me for the purpose of enabling me to vote thereon at the ensuing election, and that I have not contracted to sell or transfer them upon any condition, agreement, or understanding, in relation to my manner of voting at the said election.

Sworn to this *day of* 18 *, before me,*

(Signature.)

(82.)

Power to receive Dividend.

Know all Men by these Presents, That I of do authorize, constitute, and appoint to receive from the (*name of the company*) the dividend now due to me on all stock standing to my name on the books of the said company, and receipt for the same: hereby ratifying and confirming all that may lawfully be done in the premises by virtue hereof.

Witness my hand and seal this day of 18

(*Signature.*) (*Seal.*)

Signed, Sealed and Delivered in the Presence of

CHAPTER XVIII.

PARTNERSHIP.

SECTION I.

WHAT A PARTNERSHIP IS.

When two or more persons combine their property, labor, or skill, for the transaction of business for their common profit, they enter into partnership. Sometimes the word "firm" is used as synonymous with partnership; sometimes, however, it means only the copartnership-name.

A single joint transaction, out of which, considered by itself, neither profit nor loss arises, will not create a partnership. If a joint purchase be made, and each party then takes his distinct and several share of the goods, this is no partnership.

Any persons competent to transact business on their own account may enter into partnership for that purpose, and no others.

SECTION II.

HOW A PARTNERSHIP MAY BE FORMED.

No especial form or manner is necessary. It may be by oral agreement, or by a written agreement, which may have a seal or not. But the liability and authority of the partners begin with the *actual* formation of the partnership, and do not wait for the execution of any articles. In general, if there be an agreement to enter into business, or into some particular transaction, together, and share the profits and losses, this constitutes a partnership, which is just as extensive as the business proposed to be done, and not more so. The parties may agree to share the profits in what proportion they choose; but in the absence of any agreement, the law presumes equal shares.

They may agree as to any way of dividing the losses, or even that one or more partners alone shall sustain them all, without loss to the rest. And this agreement is valid as between themselves; but it will not protect those partners who were to sustain no loss from responsibility to third parties, unless the third parties knew of this agreement between the partners, and gave credit accordingly. If A, B, & C, being partners, agree that A should not lose any thing by their business, and a person knowing this bargain dealt with the firm on the credit of B & C, he could not call on A. But an agreement exempting partners from loss generally, or from loss beyond the amount invested, will only operate between the partners, unless it can be shown that the third party not only knew the agreement, but contracted with the firm on the basis of this agreement. And, generally, stipulations in articles of copartnership limiting the power of a partner, are not binding on third parties who are ignorant of them. Each partner is absolutely responsible to every creditor of the copartnership for the whole amount of the debt. And, if thereby obliged to suffer loss, his only remedy is against the other partners.

Although partners may agree and provide as they will in their articles, a long neglect of these provisions will be regarded as a mutual waiver of them.

Persons may be liable as partners to third parties or strangers, who are not partners as between themselves. Whether they are partners as to each other would generally be determined by the intention of the parties, as drawn from their contract, — whether oral or written, — under the ordinary rules of evidence and construction. But whether one is liable as a partner to one who deals with the firm must depend in part upon his intention, but more upon his acts; for if by them he justifies those who deal with the firm in thinking him a partner in that business, he must bear the responsibility; as if he declare that he has a joint interest in the property, or conducts the business of the firm as a partner, accepting bills, or suffers his name to be used upon cards, or in advertisements, or on signs, or in any similar manner. The declarations or acts of one person cannot, however, make another person liable as partner, without co-operation or consent, by word or act, on his part. The rule is this: that one who thus holds himself out as a partner, when he really is not one, is responsible to a creditor who on these grounds believed him to be a partner; but not to one who knew nothing of the facts, or who, knowing them, knew also that this person was not a partner.

A *secret* partner is one who is actually a partner by participation of profit, but is not avowed or known to be such; and a *dormant* partner is one who takes no share in the conduct or control of the business of the firm. Both of these are liable to creditors (even if the creditors did not know them to be members of the firm), on the ground of their interest and participation in the profits, which constitute, with the property of the firm, the funds to which creditors may look for payment. A *nominal* partner is one who holds himself out to the world as such, but is not so in fact. He is liable to creditors of the firm, on the ground that he justifies them in trusting the firm on his credit, and, indeed, invites them to do so, by declaring himself to be a partner.

The principal test of membership in a mercantile firm is said to be the participation in the profits. Thus, if one lend money to be used in a business, for which he is to receive a share in the profits, this would make him a partner; and if he is to receive lawful interest, and, in addition thereto, a share of the profits, this would generally make him liable as a partner to a creditor of the firm.

Sometimes a clerk or salesman, or a person otherwise employed for the firm, receives a share of the profits, instead of wages. Formerly it was held, that if such person received any certain share, say "one-tenth part of the net annual profits," this made him liable as a partner; but if he received "a salary equal in amount to one-tenth of the net profits," this did not make him a partner. Now, the courts would look more at the actual intention of the parties, and their actual ownership of an interest in the funds of the partnership, and not be governed by the mere phraseology used. If in fact he works for wages, although these wages are measured by the profits, he is no partner, and therefore not liable for the debts, as every partner is.

Hence, factors and brokers for a commission on the profits, masters of vessels who engage for a share of the profits, or seamen employed in whale-ships, are none of them partners.

A partnership usually has but one business name; but there does not seem to be any legal objection to the use of two names, especially for distinct business transactions; as A B & Co. for general business, and the name of A C & Co. for the purpose of making or indorsing negotiable paper.

SECTION III.

HOW A PARTNERSHIP MAY BE DISSOLVED.

If the articles between the partners do not contain an agreement that the partnership shall continue for a specified time, it may be dissolved at the pleasure of either partner. But no partner can exercise this power wantonly and injuriously to the other partners, without making himself responsible for the damage he thus causes. If there be a provision that the partnership shall continue a certain time, this is binding.

If either partner were to undertake to assign his interest, for the purpose of withdrawing from the firm, against the will of the partners, without good reason, and in fraud of his express agreement, a court of equity would interfere and prevent him. For the assignment of a partner's interest, or of his share of the profits, operates at once a dissolution of the partnership.

Such assignment may transfer to the assignee the whole interest of the assignor, but cannot give him a right to become a member of the firm. There seems to be an exception to this rule where the partnership is very numerous, and the manner of holding shares, by scrip or otherwise, indicates the original intention of making the shares transferable. Such a partnership is in effect a joint-stock company; which form of association is not usual here, because incorporation is better, and is easily obtained.

Death of a general or even of a special partner operates a dissolution; and the personal representatives of the deceased do not take his place, unless there be in the articles an express provision that they shall. And such provisions are construed as giving the heirs or personal representatives the right of electing whether to become partners or not. If either party is unable to do his duty to the partnership, as by reason of insanity, or a long imprisonment; or if he be guilty of material wrong-doing to the firm; a court of equity will decree a dissolution. And if the original agreement were tainted with fraud, the court will declare it void, from its beginning.

Whenever a court of equity decrees a dissolution of the partnership, it will also decree that an account be taken between the partners, if requested by either partner. And if necessary to do justice, it will decree a sale of the effects and a distribution of the proceeds, after a consideration of all the facts of the case and the whole condition of the firm. Such a decree will be made if a partner die or become bankrupt.

If the whole interest of a copartner is levied upon and sold on execution, this makes a dissolution, and the purchaser becomes, — like every other assignee of a partner, — not a partner, but only a tenant in common (that is, a joint owner) with the other partners; but if the levy and sale are only of a part, which may be severed from the rest, this may not operate a dissolution except as to that part.

If one partner retires, this operates in law a dissolution, and the remaining partners constitute in law a new firm, although in fact the old firm frequently continues and goes on with its business, with or without new members, as if it were the same firm.

The partner retiring should withdraw his name from the firm, and give notice, by the usual public advertisement, of his retirement, and also, by personal notice, by letter or otherwise, to all who usually do business with the firm; and after such notice he is not responsible, even if his name be retained in the firm by the other partners, if this is done without his consent. Nor is he responsible to any one who has in any way actual knowledge of his retirement.

A dormant or secret partner is not liable for a debt contracted after his retirement, although he give no notice; because his liability does not rest upon his giving his credit to the firm, but upon his being actually a partner.

SECTION IV.

THE PROPERTY OF THE PARTNERSHIP.

A PARTNERSHIP may hold real estate as well as personal estate, and a partnership may be formed to trade in land, or to cultivate land. But the rules of law in respect to real estate, as in relation to title, conveyance, dower, inheritance, and the like, make some difference. As far, however, as is compatible with these rules, it seems to be agreed that the real estate of the partnership is treated as if it were personal property, if it have been purchased with the partnership funds and for partnership purposes.

There is some difficulty in explaining this matter to those who are not acquainted with the peculiar law of real estate. Thus, no sale of land is valid except by deed, recorded: and only one who is thus a grantee under seal by record has a *legal* title. But a court of equity acknowledges and protects an *equitable* title in those who really possess all the interest in the land; as partners do who have paid for it, though it stands in the name of one partner only. But a court of equity cannot disregard the laws of conveyance and record, and therefore says that this partner is the only *legal owner*, but that he owns the land as *trustee* for the firm. And then they compel him to sell it, or otherwise dispose of it, as the interests of the firm or of their creditors require.

So land thus purchased does not go to the heirs of the partner or partners in whose name it may stand, but is first subject to the debts of the firm, and then to the balance which may be due to either partner on winding up their affairs. But when these debts and claims are adjusted, any surplus of the real estate will then descend as real estate, and not as personal estate.

Improvements made with partnership funds on the real estate of a partner will be regarded as partnership property.

The widow has her dower only after the above-mentioned debts and claims are adjusted. And while the legal title is protected, as it must be for the purpose of conveyance and other similar purposes, the person holding this legal title will be held as a trustee for the partnership, if the partnership be entitled to the beneficiary interest.

But a purchaser of partnership real property, without notice or knowledge, from a partner holding the same by a legal title, is protected against the other partners. If, however, the purchaser has such knowledge, the conveyance may be avoided as fraudulent, or he may be held as trustee, the land being in his hands chargeable with the debts and claims of the partnership.

SECTION V.

THE AUTHORITY OF EACH PARTNER, AND THE JOINT LIABILITY OF THE PARTNERSHIP.

This authority is very great, because the law-merchant makes each partner an agent of the whole partnership, with full power to bind all its members and all its property, in transactions which fall within the usual business of the firm; as loans, borrowing, sales, even of the whole stock, pledges, mortgages, or assignments; and this last extends even to an honest and prudent assignment of the whole stock and personal property to trustees to pay partnership debts. It extends to the making or indorsing negotiable paper; and to transactions out of the usual business of the firm, if they arose from and were fairly connected with that business.

Nor is any party dealing with a partner affected by his want of good faith towards the partnership, unless he colluded with the partner, and participated in his want of good faith, by fraud or gross negligence. But a holder of a note or bill signed or indorsed by a partner without authority has no claim against the partnership, if he knew or should have known the want of authority.

A partner cannot, in general, bind the firm by a guaranty, a letter of credit, or a submission to arbitration, without authority, because these things do not belong generally and properly to commercial business. But any thing so done by a partner may be adopted and ratified by the partnership, and then it has the same force as if originally authorized. And this ratification may be formal and express, or consist only of acts which distinctly imply it; such as assenting to and acting with reference to it; and especially receiving and holding the beneficial results of it; as, for example, taking and holding money paid for it.

By the earlier and more stringent rules of law, a partner could not bind his copartners by an instrument under seal, unless he was himself authorized under seal; and their subsequent acknowledgment of his authority did not cure the defect. Now, however, a partner may bind his firm by an instrument under seal, if it be in the name and for the use of the firm, and in the transaction of their usual business, provided the other copartners assent thereto before execution, or adopt and ratify the same afterwards; and they may assent or ratify by word as well as by seal; or provided he could have made the same conveyance, or done the same act effectually, without a deed. And a deed executed by one partner in the presence and with the assent of the other partners will bind them.

A partnership has no seal at law, and can have none: only a person or a corporation can have a seal. Instruments are sometimes executed, "A B & Co.," and a seal is affixed to the name. This is, strictly speaking, no seal at all; and if the instrument needs a seal to make it valid, as if it were a deed of land, it would, at law, be wholly void. But the courts in some of our States are somewhat lax on this subject, and might construe it as the seal of each one of the partners to give the instrument validity.

A majority of the members cannot conclusively bind the minority, unless in reference to the internal concerns of the firm; as, for example, the salary or appointment of a clerk, the hiring or fitting-up of a counting-room, the manner of keeping accounts, and the like. But one member may, so far as he is concerned, arrest a negotiation which was only begun, and prevent a bargain which would be binding on him, by giving notice to the third party of his dissent and refusal in season to enable him to decline the bargain without detriment.

Partners must act *as such*, to bind each other. Thus, if a partner makes a note, and signs it with his own name and his partner's name, as a joint and several note, it does not bind his partner, for he had no authority to make such a note.

If the name of one partner be also the name of the firm, — for John Smith and Henry Robinson may do business as partners under the name of "John Smith," — this name is not necessarily the name of the firm when used in a note or contract; and if the partner whose name is used carries on mercantile business for himself, it will not be supposed to be used as the name of the firm, without sufficient proof.

Persons may give a joint order for goods without becoming jointly liable, if it appear otherwise that credit was given to them severally. Nor will one have either the authority or the obligation of a partner cast upon him by an agreement of the firm to be governed by his advice. Nor shall one be charged as partner with others, unless he has incurred the liability by his own voluntary act.

The reception of a new member constitutes, in law, a new firm; but the new firm may recognize the old debts, as by express agreement, or paying interest, or other evidence of adoption, and then the new firm is jointly liable for the old debt. But there must be some fact from which the assent of the new member to this adoption of the old debt may be inferred, for his liability is not to be presumed.

A notice in legal proceedings, abandonment to insurers by one who was insured for himself and others, a notice to quit of one of joint lessors or lessees who are partners in trade, notice to one partner of the dishonor of a note or bill bearing the name of the firm, a release to one partner, or by one partner, — will bind all the partners, and render them jointly liable. But a service of legal process should be made upon each partner personally.

If money be lent to a partner for partnership purposes, it creates a partnership debt; but not if lent expressly on the individual credit of the person borrowing; and not if the borrowing partner receives it to enable him to pay his contribution to the capital of the firm. Though the money be not used for the firm, if it was borrowed by one partner on the credit of the firm, in a manner and under circumstances justifying the lender in trusting to that credit, it creates a partnership debt. And if a partner uses funds in his hands as trustee, for partnership purposes, the firm are certainly jointly bound, if it was done with their knowledge. And if it was done without their knowledge, and the partners are distinctly and directly benefited by the transaction, they will be deemed to have authorized it.

If in any case a person, knowing the existence of the firm, gave credit to a single partner only, then he can look only to that partner, and not to the firm, although the money was applied to, and used for, partnership purposes. But if the partner held himself out as borrowing for the firm, and the lender without any want of due care gave credit to the firm, and the transaction was a fair business transaction on the part of the lender, the firm will be liable, although the money is fraudulently appropriated by the partner to his own use.

In the absence of evidence showing to whom the credit was given, the fact that money lent to one partner was applied to the use of the firm will make the firm liable for the payment; but not if the partner employed it as his contribution to increase the capital of the firm.

If the purchaser of goods or the borrower of money have a dormant and secret partner, and the goods were bought or the money borrowed for partnership purposes, the seller or lender may look to both partners for payment, unless the seller or lender, knowing all the partners, gave credit to one only.

The firm is liable only to one who deals with a partner in good faith. Thus, if one receives negotiable paper bearing the name of a firm, knowing that it is not in the business of the firm, and is given for no consideration received by the firm, he cannot hold the firm. And if a creditor of one partner receive for his separate debt a partnership security, this would be a fraud, unless the partner had, or was supposed by the creditor to have, the authority of the rest.

If he supposed the partner had this authority, he cannot hold the partnership if the partner had not the authority, unless the partnership had caused him to believe it. And if the partnership security be transferred for two considerations, one of which is private and fraudulent, and the other is joint and honest, the partnership is bound for so much of it as is not tainted with fraud, and only for that.

The partnership may be liable for injury caused by the criminal or wrongful acts of a partner, if these were done in the transaction of partnership business, and if it was the partnership which gave to the wrong-doer the means and opportunity of doing the wrong. But an illegal contract will not bind the copartners, for the parties entering into it must be presumed to know its illegality; and the law enforces no bargain that is contrary to law.

The acknowledgment of one who had been a partner, after the dissolution of the partnership, may take the debt out of the statute of limitations as to him, but not so as to restore the liability of all the partners without their assent.

SECTION VI.

REMEDIES OF PARTNERS AGAINST EACH OTHER.

It is seldom that a partner can have a claim against another partner, *as such*, which can be examined and adjusted without an investigation into the accounts of the partnership, and, perhaps, a settlement of them. Courts of law have ordinarily no adequate means of doing this; and therefore it is generally true that no partner can sue a copartner at law for any claim growing out of partnership transactions and involving partnership interests. But the objection to a suit at law between partners goes no further than the reason of it; and, therefore, one may sue his copartner upon his agreement to do any act which is not so far a partnership matter as to involve the partnership accounts.

If the accounts are finally adjusted, either partner may sue for a balance; and so it would be if the accounts generally remained open, but a specific part of them were severed from the rest, and a balance found on that. The rule is generally laid down, that an action cannot be sustained by a partner against a partner for a balance, unless there is an express promise to pay it. But such promise would be inferred in all cases in which an account had been taken, and a balance admitted to be due.

In general, any action at law between partners can be maintained, only when a rendering of judgment in this action will completely terminate all partnership matters, so that no further cause of action can grow out of them.

What a court of law cannot do as to actions between partners a court of equity can; and, generally, a court of equity has a full jurisdiction over all disputes and claims between partners, and may do whatever is necessary to settle them in conformity with justice.

A partner may sue his copartner for money advanced before the partnership was formed, although the loan was made to promote the partnership. And for work done for the firm before he became a member of it, he may sue those who were members when he did the work. And he may sue a copartner on his note or bill, although the consideration was on partnership account; but, in general, no action at law can be maintained for work and labor performed, or money expended for the partnership.

A partner who pays more than his proportion of a debt of the partnership cannot demand specific contribution from his copartners, but must charge his payment to the firm. The reason is, that they may have claims against him on other accounts, and they must be all settled together to strike the balance.

If one of a firm be a member also of another firm, the one firm cannot sue the other; for the same person cannot be plaintiff and defendant of record. A cannot sue A; and therefore A, B, & C cannot sue C, D, & E. In all these cases an adequate remedy may be found in a court of equity.

If a firm have a negotiable note which it cannot sue, because one of its own firm is liable upon it and must be made defendant, it can indorse the note over, and the indorsee may sue it in his own name, as we have before stated.

The partners are entitled to perfect good faith from each copartner; and a court of equity will interfere to enforce this. No partner will be permitted to treat privately, and for his own benefit alone, for a renewal of a lease, or to transfer to himself any benefit or interest properly belonging to the firm. And so careful is a court of equity in this respect, that it will not permit a copartner, by his private contract or arrangement, to subject himself to a bias or interest which might be injurious to the firm, and conflict with his duty to them, but will declare void any contract of this kind.

SECTION VII.

RIGHTS OF THE FIRM AGAINST THIRD PARTIES.

If a partner sells the goods of the firm in his own name, the firm may sue for the price. But the rights of one who deals in good faith with a copartner, as with him alone, are so far regarded, that he may set off any claim, or make use of any other defences against the suit of the firm, which he could have made had the person with whom he dealt sued alone.

Therefore, if A honestly bought goods of a firm from a partner whom he supposed to be sole owner of them, and paid him the price, the firm cannot recover this price from the buyer, although the seller sold the goods fraudulently, and cheated the firm out of the money, but must charge the price to the selling partner.

A guaranty to a copartner, if for the use and benefit of the firm, gives to them a right of action.

A new firm, created by some change in the membership of an old firm, is entitled to the benefit of a guaranty given to the old firm, even if sealed, provided it shall distinctly appear that the instrument was intended to have that effect, and extend to the new firm.

SECTION VIII.

RIGHTS OF CREDITORS IN RESPECT TO FUNDS.

THE property of a partnership is bound to pay the partnership debts; and, therefore, a creditor of one copartner has no claim to the partnership funds until the partnership debts are paid. If there be then a surplus, he may have that copartner's interest therein, in payment of his private debt.

If a private creditor attaches partnership property, or in any way seeks to appropriate it to his private debt, the partnership debts being unpaid, he cannot hold it, either at law or in equity. Such attachment or appropriation is wholly subject to the paramount claims of the partnership creditors, and is wholly defeated by the insolvency of the partnership, although the partnership creditors have not brought any actions for their debts.

Hence, if a creditor of A attaches his interest in the property of A, B, & Co., and a creditor of A, B, & Co. attaches the same property, the first attachment is postponed to the second; that is, it has no effect until the debt of the second creditor is fully satisfied, and then it is good for the surplus of property. If, however, one partner is dormant and unknown, the creditor of the other attaching the stock is not postponed to the creditor who discovers the dormant partner and sues him with the other; unless the first attaching creditor's claim has no reference to the partnership business, and that of the second attaching creditor has such reference.

The partnership creditors are restrained from appropriating the private property of the copartners until the claims of their private creditors are satisfied in courts of equity. And some recent adjudications indicate that the rule will become established at law.

I think the law ought to be, and that it is now tending to become, this. A partnership is a kind of body by itself, somewhat like a corporation. It has its own funds, and its own debts. The individual members may also have each his own funds and his own debts.

The funds of the partnership should first be applied to the debts of the partnership; and, if there be any surplus, the members have it, and their creditors get it. So the private funds of each member should first be applied exclusively to the payment of that person's private debts; and, when they are wholly paid, the surplus should go to the partnership creditors, because each partner is responsible for the partnership debts. This rule prevails on the continent of Europe very generally.

It is now quite certain that the levy of a private creditor of one copartner upon partnership property can give him only what that copartner has; that is, not a separate personal possession of any part or share of the stock or property, but an undivided right or interest in the whole, subject to the payment of debts and the settlement of accounts; including also the right to demand an account.

As to how such levy and sale of the interest of one copartner shall be made by the sheriff, there is much diversity both of practice and of authority. Upon principle, we think the sheriff can neither seize, nor transfer by sale, either the whole stock or any specific portion of it. He should, we think, without any *actual seizure*, sell all the interest of the defendant partner in the stock and property of the partnership; much in the same way in which he would sell his right to redeem a mortgage, or any other incorporeal right, subject to attachment. The purchaser would then have a right to demand an account and settlement, and a transfer to himself of any balance or property to which the copartner whom he sued would have been entitled.

Where the trustee process, or process of foreign attachment, is in use, the better way would be for the sheriff to return a general attachment of all the interest of the debtor in the partnership property, and summon the other partners as the trustees of the debtor.

It must be stated, however, that the rules of law in regard to the liability of partnership property for the private debts of partners, and as to how any such liability may be enforced, are, at present, somewhat obscure and uncertain.

SECTION IX.

THE EFFECTS OF DISSOLUTION.

If the dissolution is caused by the death of any partner, the whole property goes to the surviving partners. They hold it, however, not as their own, but only for the purpose of settlement; and therefore they have, in relation to it, all the power which is necessary for that purpose, and no more. If they carry on the business with the partnership funds, they do so at their own risk; and the representatives of the deceased may require their share of the capital, and choose between calling on them, in addition, for interest, or for a share of the profits.

The survivors are not partners, but tenants in common (joint owners) with the representatives of the deceased of the stock or property in possession; and have all necessary rights to settle the affairs of the concern and pay its debts. After a dissolution, however caused, one who had been a partner has no authority to make new contracts in the name of the firm, as to make or indorse notes or bills with the name of the firm, even if he be expressly authorized to settle the affairs of the firm. There must be a distinct authority to sign for the others who were formerly partners. A parol authority will be sufficient, even if the general terms of the partnership had been reduced to writing.

It is common, where a partnership is dissolved by mutual consent, to provide that some one of the partners shall settle up the affairs of the concern, collect and pay debts, and the like. But this will not prevent any person from paying to any partner a debt due to the firm; and, if such payment be made in good faith, the release or discharge of the partner is effectual.

If all the debts were assigned and transferred to any person, as his property, any debtor who had notice of this would be bound to make payment to this person alone; and, if he paid anybody else, he would be obliged to pay the money over again.

It is frequently provided, that one partner shall take all the property and pay all the debts; but this agreement, though valid between the partners, has no effect upon the rights of third parties against the other partners; for they have a valid claim against all the partners, of which they cannot be divested without their consent.

This consent of the creditor may be inferred, but not from slight evidence; thus, not from receiving the single partner's note as a collateral security, nor from receiving interest from him on the joint debt, nor from a mere change in the head of the account, charging the single partner and not the firm. Still, as the creditor certainly can assent to this arrangement, and accept the indebtedness of one partner instead of that of the firm, so it must be equally clear that such assent and intention will bind him, if distinctly proved by circumstances.

SECTION X.

LIMITED PARTNERSHIPS.

THESE have been introduced into some of our States, by statutes, which differ somewhat in their provisions. Generally, they require, first, one or more *general* partners, whose names shall be known; secondly, *special* partners, who do not appear as members, nor possess the powers or discharge the duties of actual partners; thirdly, the sum to be contributed by the special partners shall be actually paid in; lastly, all these arrangements, with such other information as may be needed for the security of the public, must be verified under oath, signatures of all the parties, and acknowledgment before a magistrate, and correctly published. When these requisites are complied with, the special partners may lose all they have put in, but cannot be held to any further responsibility. But any neglect of them, or any material mistake in regard to them, even on the part of the printer of the advertisement, wholly destroys their effect; and then the special partner is liable for the whole debt, precisely like a general partner.

In a New-York case, the amount contributed by the special partner was, by mistake of the printer, stated at $5,000, instead of $2,000, and it was held that the associates were liable as general partners, although the plaintiff did not show that he was actually misled by the error. In another New-York case, it was held that an assignment of the partnership property, providing for the payment of a debt due to the special partner, ratably with the other creditors of the firm, or before all the other creditors are satisfied in full for their debts, is void as against the creditors; but it would be valid as against the assignor and those creditors who think proper to affirm it.

(83.)

Articles of Copartnership between two Tradesmen.

Articles of Agreement, Had, made, concluded, and agreed upon, this day of A.D. between of trader, and of trader.

First of all, the said and have agreed, and by these presents do agree, to become copartners together in the art or trade of and all things thereto belonging, and also, in buying, selling, vending, and retailing all sorts of wares, goods, and commodities belonging to the said trade of which said copartnership, it is agreed, shall continue from for and during, and unto the full end and term of years, from thence next ensuing, and fully to be complete and ended. And to that end and purpose he the said hath the day of date of these presents, delivered in as stock, the sum of and he the said the sum of to be used, laid out, and employed, in common trade between them, for the management of the said trade of to their utmost benefit and advantage. And it is hereby agreed between the said parties, and the said copartners, each for himself respectively, and for his own particular part, and for his executors and administrators, that each doth covenant, promise, and agree, to and with the other of them, his executors and administrators, by these presents, in manner and form following (that is to say) that they the said copartners shall not nor will, at any time hereafter, use, exercise, or follow the trade of aforesaid, or any other trade whatsoever during the said term, to their private benefit and advantage; but shall and will, from time to time, and at all times, during the said term (if they shall so long live), do their and each of their best and utmost endeavors, in and by all means possible, to the utmost of their skill and power, for their joint interest, profit, benefit, and advantage, and truly employ, buy, sell, and merchandise, with the stock aforesaid, and the increase thereof in the trade of aforesaid, without any sinister intentions or fraudulent endeavors whatsoever. And also that they the said copartners shall and will, from time to time, and at all times hereafter, during the said term, pay, bear, and discharge, equally between them, the rent of the shop, which they the said copartners shall rent or hire, for the joint exercising or managing of the trade

aforesaid. And that all such gain, profit, and increase, as shall come, grow, or arise, for or by reason of the said trade, or joint business as aforesaid, shall be from time to time, during the said term, equally and proportionably divided between them the said copartners, share and share alike. And also that all such losses as shall happen in the said joint trade, by bad debts, ill commodities, or otherwise without fraud or covin, shall be paid and borne equally and proportionably between them. And further, it is agreed by and between the said copartners, that there shall be had and kept from time to time, and at all times during the said term and joint business and copartnership together as aforesaid, perfect, just, and true books of accounts, wherein each of the said copartners shall duly enter and set down, as well all money by him received, paid, expended and laid out, in and about the management of the said trade, as also all wares, goods, commodities, and merchandises, by them or either of them bought and sold by reason or means or upon account of the said copartnership, and all other matters and things whatsoever, to the said joint trade, and the management thereof, in any wise belonging or appertaining, which said books shall be used in common between the said copartners, so that either of them may have free access thereto without any interruption of the other. And also that they the said copartners, once in three months, or oftener if need shall require, upon the reasonable request of one of them, shall make, yield, and render, each to the other, or to the executors or administrators of the other, a true, just, and perfect account of all profits and increase, by them or either of them made, and of all losses by them or either of them sustained, and also of all payments, receipts, and disbursements whatsoever, by them or either of them made or received, and of all other things by them or either of them acted, done, or suffered in the said copartnership and joint business as aforesaid; and the same account being so made, shall and will clear, adjust, pay, and deliver, each unto the other, at the time of making such account, their equal shares of the profits so made as aforesaid; and at the end of the said term of   or other sooner determination of these presents (be it by the death of one of the said partners or otherwise), they the said copartners, each to the other, or in case of the death of either of them, the surviving party to the executors or administrators of the party deceased, shall and will make a true, just, and final account of all things as aforesaid, and divide the profits aforesaid, and in all things well and truly adjust the same, and that also upon the making of such final account, all and every the stock and stocks, as well as the gains and increase thereof, which shall appear to be remaining, whether consisting of money, wares, debts,
shall be equally parted and divided between them the said copartners, their executors, or administrators, share and share alike.

In Witness Whereof, &c.

(*Signatures.*)

Various Covenants and Clauses which may be introduced in Articles of Copartnership according to circumstances.

Not to trust any one whom the Copartner shall forbid.

And that neither of the said parties shall sell or credit any goods or merchandise belonging to the said joint trade, to any person or persons, after notice in writing from the other of the said parties, that such person or persons are not to be credited or trusted.

Not to release any Debt without Consent, &c.

And that neither of the said parties shall, without the consent of the other, release or compound any debt or demand, due or coming to them on account of their said copartnership, except for so much as shall actually be received, and brought into the stock or cash account of the said partnership.

Not to be bound, or indorse Bills, &c., for any one without Consent, &c.

And that neither of the said parties shall, during this copartnership, without the consent of the other, enter into any deed, covenant, bond, or judgment, or become bound as bail or surety, or give any note, or accept or indorse any bill of exchange for himself and partner, without the consent of the other first had and obtained, with or for any person whatsoever.

Neither Party to assign his Interest, &c.

And it is agreed between the said parties, that neither of the said parties shall, without the consent of the other, obtained in writing, sell or assign his share or interest in the said joint trade, to any person or persons whatsoever.

Principal Clerk to be Receiver of Moneys, &c.

That the principal clerk for the time being shall be the general receiver of all the money belonging to the said joint trade, and shall thereout pay all demands ordered by the said parties, and shall from time to time pay the surplus cash to such banker as the said partners shall nominate.

Parties to draw quarterly, &c.

That it shall be lawful for each of them to take out of the cash of the joint stock the sum of quarterly, to his own use, the same to be charged on account, and neither of them shall take any further sum for his own separate use, without the consent of the other in writing; and any such further sum, taken with such consent, shall draw interest after the rate of per cent, and shall be payable together with the interest due, within days after notice in writing given by the other of the said parties.

(84.)

Shorter Form of Articles of Copartnership.

Articles of Agreement, Made the day of one thousand eight hundred and between (*the names and residence of the two parties*) as follows: The said parties above named have agreed to become copartners in business, and by these presents do agree to be copartners together under and by the name or firm of in the buying, selling, and vending all sorts of goods, wares, and merchandise to the said business belonging, and to occupy the their copartnership to commence on the day of and to continue and to that end and purpose the said (*here state the contributions of each of the parties*) to be used and employed in common between them for the support and management of the said business, to their mutual benefit and advantage. And it is agreed by and between the parties to these presents, that at all times during the continuance of their copartnership, they and each of them will give their attendance, and do their and each of their best endeavors, and to the utmost of their skill and power exert themselves for their joint interest, profit, benefit, and advantage, and truly employ, buy, sell, and merchandise with their joint stock, and the increase thereof, in the business aforesaid. And also that they shall and will at all times during the said copartnership bear, pay, and discharge equally between them, all rents and other expenses that may be required for the support and management of the said business; and that all gains, profit, and increase that shall come, grow, or arise from or by means of their said business, shall be divided between them (*state whether equally, or in what proportions*) and all loss that shall happen to their said joint business, by ill commodities, bad debts, or otherwise, shall be borne and paid between them.

And it is agreed by and between the said parties, that there shall be had and kept at all times during the continuance of their copartnership, perfect, just, and true books of account, wherein each of the said copartners shall enter and set down, as well all money by them or either of them received, paid, laid out, and expended in and about the said business, as also all goods, wares, commodities, and merchandise, by them or either of them, bought or sold by reason or on account of the said business, and all other matters and things whatsoever to the said business and the management thereof in any wise belonging; which said books shall be used in common between the said copartners, so that either of them may have access thereto, without any interruption or hindrance of the other. And also the said co-partners, once in or oftener if necessary, shall make, yield, and render, each to the other, a true, just, and perfect inventory and account of all profits and increase by them, or either of them, made, and of all losses by them, or either of them, sustained; and also all payments, receipts, disbursements, and all other things by them made, received, disbursed, acted, done, or suffered in this said copartnership and business, and the same account so made shall and will clear, adjust, pay, and deliver, each to the other, at the time, their just share of the profits so made as aforesaid.

And the said parties hereby mutually covenant and agree to and with each other, that, during the continuance of the said copartnership, neither of them shall nor will indorse any note, or otherwise become surety for any person or persons whomsoever, without the consent of the other of the said copartners. And at the end, or other sooner determination of their copartnership, the said copartners, each to the other, shall and will make a true, just, and final account of all things relating to their said business, and in all things truly adjust the same; and all and every the stock and stocks, as well as the gains and increase thereof, which shall appear to be remaining, either in money, goods, wares, fixtures, debts, or otherwise, shall be divided between them.

In Witness Whereof,

(*Signatures.*)

(85.)

Certificate of a Limited Partnership, with Acknowledgment and Oath.

This is to Certify, That the undersigned have, pursuant to the provisions of the Statutes of the State of formed a limited partnership, under the name or firm of that the general nature of the business to be transacted is (*describe the business*) and that the general *partner* and is the special *partner* and that the said (*the special partner*) hath contributed the sum of dollars, as capital towards the common stock, and that the said partnership is to commence on the day of and is to terminate on the day of 18

Dated this day of one thousand eight hundred and

(*Signatures.*)

County of ss. On the day of one thousand eight hundred and before me came

to be the individuals described in, and who executed the above certificate, and they severally acknowledged that they executed the same.

County of ss.

the general *partner* named in the above certificate, being duly sworn, doth depose, and say, that the *sum* specified in the said certificate to have been contributed by the special *partner* to the common stock has been actually and in good faith paid in cash.

Sworn this *day of* 18 *before me,*

In some of the States, the oath should be made by the general partner; and it would always be safe for all the partners, general and special, to take the oath, and be included in the certificate.

CHAPTER XIX.

ARBITRATION.

SECTION I.

OF THE SUBMISSION AND AWARD.

[By the Submission (or reference) is meant the submission of the question or questions to arbitrators.]

THE law favors arbitration in many respects as a peaceable and inexpensive mode of settling difficulties. Parties may agree to refer a question by an oral agreement, or by a written agreement. The form is not essential. But it is always best to reduce the agreement to writing, and to express it carefully. But parties may, in many of our States, go before a magistrate and agree to refer in the manner pointed out by the statute. In all of them a case may be taken out of court and submitted to referees under an order of court.

The first essential of an award, without which it has no force whatever, is, that it be conformable to the terms of the submission. The authority given to the arbitrators should not be exceeded; and the precise question submitted to them, and neither more nor less, should be answered. Neither can the award affect strangers (or those who are not parties to it); and, if one part of it is that a stranger shall do some act, it is not only of no force as to the stranger, but of no force as to the parties if this unauthorized part of the award cannot be taken away without affecting the rest of the award.

Nor can it require that one of the parties should make a payment, or do any similar act, to a stranger. But if the stranger is mentioned in an award only as agent of one of the parties, which he actually is, or as trustee, or as in any way paying for, or receiving for, one of the parties, this does not invalidate the award. And in favor of awards, it has been said that this will be supposed, where the contrary is not indicated.

If the award embrace matters not included in the submission, it is fatal. If, however, the portion of the award which exceeds the submission can be separated from the rest without affecting the merits of the award, it may be rejected, and the rest will stand; otherwise the whole is void. If the submission specify the particulars to which it refers, or if, after general words, it make specific exceptions, its words must be strictly followed.

If these words are very general, they will be construed liberally, but yet without extending them beyond their fair meaning. On the other hand, all questions submitted must be decided, unless the submission provides otherwise; and either party may object to an award, that it omits the decision of some question submitted; but the objection is invalid if it be shown that the party objecting himself withheld that question from the arbitrators. Nor is it necessary that the award embrace all the topics which might be considered within the terms of a general submission. It is enough if it pass upon those questions brought before the arbitrators, and they are so far distinct and independent that the omission of others leaves no uncertainty in the award. If the award does not embrace all of the matters within the submission which where brought to the notice of the arbitrators, it is altogether void.

In the next place, an award must be *certain;* that is, it must be so expressed that no reasonable doubt can be entertained as to the meaning of the arbitrators, the effect of the award, or the rights and duties of the parties under it. For the very purpose of the submission, and the end for which the law favors arbitration, is the final settlement of all questions and disputes; and this is inconsistent with uncertainty.

In the next place, the award must be *possible;* for an award requiring that to be done which cannot be done is senseless and useless. But the impossibility which vitiates an award is one which belongs to the nature of the thing, and not to the accidental disability of the party at the time. Thus, if he be ordered to pay money on a day that is past, this is void; so if he be required to give up a deed which he neither has nor may expect to have; but if he be directed to pay money, the award is good, although he has no money, for it creates a valid debt against him. Nor can a party avoid an award on the ground of an impossibility created by himself, after the award, or indeed beforehand, if he created it for the purpose of evading an expected award.

This impossibility may be actual, or it may be that created by law; for an award which requires that a party should do what the law forbids him to do is void, either in the whole, or else for so much as is thus against the law, if that illegal part can be severed from the rest.

An award must be *reasonable;* if it be of things in themselves of no value or advantage to the parties, or out of all proportion to the justice and requirements of the case, or if it undertake to determine for the parties what they should determine for themselves, as that the parties should intermarry, it is void.

Lastly, the award must be *final* and *conclusive.* This necessity springs also from the very purpose for which the law favors arbitration, namely, the settlement and closing of disputes. It is not a valid objection to an award, that it is upon a condition, if the condition be clear and certain, consistent with the rest of the award, in itself reasonable, and such that there could be no doubt whether it were performed or not, or what were the rights or obligations dependent upon it.

An award may be open to any or all of these objections in part, without being necessarily void in the whole. So much of it as is thus faulty is void; but if this can be severed distinctly from the residue, leaving a substantial, definite, and unobjectionable award behind, this may be done, and the award then will take effect. It is therefore void in the whole because bad in part, only where this part cannot be severed from the residue; or where, if it be severed and amended, leaving the residue in force, one of the parties will be held to an obligation imposed upon him, but deprived of the advantage or recompense which it was intended that he should have. Generally, in the construction of awards, they are favored and enforced, wherever this can properly be done.

If the submission be in the most general terms, and the award equally so, covering " all demands and questions " between the parties, either party may still show that a particular demand either did not exist, or was not known to exist, when the submission was entered into, or that it was not brought before the notice of the arbitrators, or considered by them; and then the award will not be permitted to affect this demand.

If, by an award, money is to be paid in satisfaction of a debt, this implies an award of a release on the other side, and makes this release a condition to the payment.

There is no especial form of an award necessary in this country. If the submission requires that it should be sealed, it must be so. And if the submission was made under a statute, or under a rule of court, the requirements of the statute or the rule should be followed. But even here mere formal inaccuracies would seldom be permitted to vitiate the reward.

If the submission contains other directions or conditions, as that it should be delivered to the parties in writing, or to each of the parties, such directions must be substantially followed. Thus, in the latter case, it has been held that it is not enough that a copy be delivered to one of the parties on each side, but each individual party must have one.

It may happen, where an award is offered in defence, or as the ground of an action, that it is open to no objection whatever for any thing which it contains or which it omits; and yet it may be set aside for impropriety or irregularity in the conduct of the arbitrators, or in the proceedings before them. Awards are thus set aside if " procured by corruption or undue means." This rule rests, indeed, on the common principle, that fraud vitiates and avoids every transaction.

So, too, it may well be set aside if it be apparent on its face that the arbitrator has made a material mistake of fact or of law. It must, however, be rather a strong case in which the court would receive evidence of a mere mistake, either in fact or in law, which did not appear in the award, and was not supposed to spring from or indicate corruption.

Another instance of irregularity is the omission to examine witnesses; or an examination of them when the parties were not present, and their absence was for good cause; or a concealment by either of the parties of material circumstances; for this would be fraud. So if the arbitrators, in case of disagreement, were authorized to choose an umpire, but drew lots which of them should choose him. But it has been held enough that each arbitrator named an umpire, and lots were drawn to decide which of these two should be taken, because it might be considered that both of these men were agreed upon. And if an umpire be appointed by lot, or otherwise irregularly, if the parties agree to the appointment, and confirm it expressly, or impliedly by attending before him, with a full knowledge of the manner of the appointment, this covers the irregularity.

SECTION II.

THE REVOCATION OF A SUBMISSION TO ARBITRATORS.

It is an ancient and well-established rule, that either party may revoke his submission at any time before the award is made; and by this revocation render the submission wholly ineffectual, and of course take from the arbitrators all power of making a binding award. And, generally, this power exists until the award is made.

In this country, our courts have always excepted from this rule submissions made by order or rule of court; for a kind of jurisdiction is held to attach to the arbitrators, and the submission is quite irrevocable, except for such causes as make it necessarily inoperative.

There is a strong reason why a submission by order of court, or before a magistrate, should be preferred where it can be had, from the fact above stated, that the law permits any party who finds an award is going against him to revoke his submission or reference when he will, before the award is made; provided the award was only by agreement out of court, or not before a magistrate. In some of our

States, the statutes authorizing and regulating arbitration provide for the revocation of the submission.

It should be stated, however, that, as an agreement to submit is a valid contract, the promise of each party being the consideration for the promise of the other, a revocation of the agreement or of the submission is a breach of the contract, and the other party has his damages. And damages would generally include all the expenses the plaintiff has incurred about the submission, and all that he has lost by the revocation, in any way.

If either party exercise this power of revocation, he must give notice in some way, directly or indirectly, to the other party; and until such notice, the revocation is inoperative.

Bankruptcy or insolvency of either or both parties does not necessarily operate as a revocation, unless the terms of the agreement to refer, or the provisions of the insolvent law, required it. But the assignees acquire whatever power of revocation the bankrupt or insolvent possessed, and, generally, at least, no further power.

The death of either party before the award is made vacates the submission, if made out of court, unless that provides in terms for the continuance and procedure of the arbitration, if such an event occur. But a submission under a rule of court is not revoked or annulled even by the death of a party. So the death or refusal or inability of an arbitrator to act would annul a submission out of court, unless provided for in the agreement; but not one under a rule of court, unless for especial reasons, satisfactory to the court, which would make an appointment of a substitute, if it saw fit to continue the reference.

It may be well to add, that, after an award is fully made, neither of the parties without the consent of the other, nor either nor all of the arbitrators without the consent of all the parties, have any further control over it.

If the submission provides for any method of delivering the award, this should be followed. If not, it is common for the referees to deliver the award to the prevailing party or his attorney, on payment by him of the fees of arbitration. Then the prevailing party looks to the losing party, for the whole, or a part, or none of the costs, as the award may determine.

The award should be sealed, and addressed to all the parties ; and it should not be opened except in presence of all the parties, or of their attorneys, or with the consent of those absent indorsed on the award. If the submission is under a rule of court, it should be returned to court by the arbitrators, or the counsel receiving it, sealed, and opened only in court, or before the clerk, or with the written consent of parties.

The submission, or agreement to refer, may be made by exchange of Bonds, each party executing and delivering a Bond to the other party.

This would be a formal proceeding. But, as has been already said, no especial form is necessary; and often a very simple one, like that below, would suffice.

(86.)

Simple Agreement to Refer.

Know all Men, That we, of and of do hereby promise and agree, to and with each other, to submit, and do hereby submit, all questions and claims between us (*or any specific question or claim, describing it*) to the arbitrament and determination of (*here name the arbitrators*) whose decision and award shall be final, binding, and conclusive on us; (*add if there are more arbitrators than one, and it is intended that they may choose an umpire*) and, in case of disagreement between the said arbitrators, they may choose an umpire, whose award shall be final and conclusive; (*or add, if there be more than two arbitrators*) and, in case of disagreement, the decision and award of a majority of said arbitrators shall be final and conclusive.*

In Witness Whereof,

(*Signatures.*)

(87.)

Arbitration Bond. One or more Arbitrators.

Know all Men by these Presents, That I, (*one of the parties*) am held and firmly bound unto (*the other party*) in the sum of dollars, lawful money of the United States of America, to be paid to the said (*the other party*) executors, administrators, or assigns; for which payment, well and truly to be made, I hereby bind myself, my heirs, executors, and administrators, firmly by these presents.

Sealed with my seal Dated the day of one thousand eight hundred and

The Condition of the above Obligation is such, That if the above bounden shall well and truly submit to the decision of (*the referee*) named, selected, and chosen *arbitrator* as well by and on the part and behalf of, the said as of the said between whom a controversy exists, to hear all the proofs and allegations of the parties of and concerning

(*here set forth the claims or questions referred*)

and all matters relating thereto, and that the award of the said arbitrator be made in writing, subscribed by him (or them) and attested by a subscribing witness, ready to be delivered to the said parties on or before the day of next. But before proceeding to take any testimony therein, the arbitrator shall be sworn, "faithfully and fairly to hear and examine the matters in controversy between the parties to these presents, and to make a just award according to the best of his (or their) understanding." And the said parties to these presents do hereby agree, that judgment in the case (in question) shall be rendered upon the award which may be made pursuant to this submission, to the end that all matters in controversy in that behalf, between them, shall be finally concluded. Then the above obligation to be void, otherwise to remain in full force and virtue.

(*Signature.*) (*Seal.*)

Sealed and Delivered in Presence of

[To make the contract complete, the other party should execute and deliver a counterpart to this Bond.]

(88.)

Award of Arbitrators.

To all to whom these Presents shall Come, We (*names of the arbitrators*) to whom was submitted as *arbitrators* the matters in controversy existing between as by the condition of their respective bonds of submission, executed by the said parties respectively, each unto the other, and bearing date the day of one thousand eight hundred and more fully appears.

Now, therefore, know ye, That we the *arbitrators* mentioned in the said bonds having been first duly sworn according to law, and having heard the proofs and allegations of the parties, and examined the matters in controversy by them submitted, do make this award in writing; that is to say, the said (*here follows the award*)

In Witness Whereof, have hereunto subscribed these presents, this day of one thousand eight hundred and

(*Signatures.*)

In the Presence of

CHAPTER XX.

THE CARRIAGE OF GOODS AND PASSENGERS.

SECTION I.

A PRIVATE CARRIER.

ONE who carries goods for another is either a private carrier or a common carrier.

A private carrier is one who carries for others once, or sometimes, but who does not pursue the business of carrying as his usual and professed occupation. The contract between him and the owner of the goods which he carries is one of service, and is governed by the ordinary rules of law. Each party is bound to perform his share of the contract. Such a carrier must receive, care for, carry, and deliver the goods, in such wise as he bargains to do.

If he carries the goods for hire, whether actually paid or due, he is bound to use ordinary diligence and care; by which the law means such care as a man of ordinary capacity would take of his own property under similar circumstances. If any loss or injury occur to the goods while in his charge, from the want of such care or diligence on his part, he is responsible. But if the loss be chargeable as much to the fault of the owner as of the carrier, he is not liable. The owner must show the want of care or diligence on the part of the private carrier, to make him liable; but slight evidence tending that way would suffice to throw upon him the burden of accounting satisfactorily for the loss. And if there is such negligence on the part of the carrier, or of a servant for whom he is responsible, the carrier is liable, although the loss be caused primarily by a defect in the thing carried.

If he carries the goods without any compensation, paid or promised, he is, in the language of the law, a gratuitous bailee, or mandatary: he is now bound only to slight care; which is such care as every person, not insane or fatuous, would take of his own property. For the want of this care, which would be gross negligence, he is responsible, but not for ordinary negligence.

We sum up what may be said of the private carrier in the remark, that the general rules which regulate contracts and mutual obligations apply to the duties and the rights of a *private carrier*, with little or no qualification. But it is otherwise with a *common carrier*.

SECTION II.

THE COMMON CARRIER.

THE law in relation to the rights, the duties, and the responsibilities of a common carrier is quite peculiar. The reasons for it are discernible, but it rests mainly upon established usage and custom. And, as these usages have changed considerably in modern times, this law has undergone important modifications.

He is a *common carrier* "who undertakes, for hire, to transport the goods of such as choose to employ him from some known and definite place or places to other known and definite place or places." He is one who undertakes the carriage of goods *as a business;* and it is mainly this which distinguishes him from the private carrier.

The rights and responsibilities of the common carrier may be briefly stated thus: He is bound to take the goods of all who offer, if he be a carrier of goods, and the persons of all who offer, if he be a carrier of passengers; and to take due care and make due transport and delivery of them. He has a lien on the goods which he carries, and on the baggage of passengers, for his compensation. He is liable for all loss or injury to the goods under his charge, although wholly free from negligence, unless the loss happens from the act of God, or from the public enemy. These three rules will be considered in the next section.

The important thing to be remembered is, that a *private carrier* is not liable for injury to persons, or loss of or injury to goods, without fault or negligence on his part; but a *common carrier* is liable, without any fault or negligence on his part.

Truckmen or draymen, porters, and others who undertake the carriage of goods for all applicants from one city or town to another, or from one part of a city to another, are chargeable as common carriers. So, proprietors of stage-coaches are chargeable as common carriers of passengers, and of the baggage of passengers; or the baggage of others, if they so advertise themselves. So are hackney-coachmen within their accustomed range.

If drivers of stages, or omnibuses, commonly carry and receive pay for goods or parcels which are not the baggage of passengers, and are held out or advertised, or generally known, as so carrying them, they are common carriers of goods, and the proprietors are liable for the loss of such parcels, although neither they nor the drivers were in fault. But if there is no such habit or usage, and the driver receives such a parcel to be carried somewhere, and is paid for it, the driver carries it as a private carrier, and not as a common carrier, and is chargeable only for negligence or fault. And if the line of carriages is established for passengers, and the driver does not account for what is paid him for occasional parcels, but takes it as his own perquisite, the proprietors are not answerable even for the driver's fault or negligence, unless circumstances in some way bring the fault home to them.

In this country, in recent times, the business of carrying goods and passengers is almost monopolized by what are called expressmen, by railroads, or by lines of steam-packets along our coasts, or upon our navigable streams or lakes. All these are undoubtedly common carriers; and although their peculiar method of carrying on this business is new, and will require from us especial consideration in another chapter, there can be no doubt of their being, to all intents and purposes, common carriers.

Ordinary sailing-vessels are sometimes said to be common carriers. We should be disposed to restrict this term, however, to regular packets; or, at most, to call by this name general freighting ships. It is not, however, necessary to consider this question, as waterborne goods are now almost always carried under bills of lading, which determine the relations and respective rights of the parties; and these we shall consider in our chapter on the Law of Shipping.

The boatmen on our rivers and canals are common carriers; and ferrymen are common carriers of passengers by their office, and may become common carriers of goods by taking up that business. A steamboat usually employed as a carrier may do something else, as tow a vessel out of a harbor, or the like ; and the character of common carrier does not attach to this especial employment, and carry with it its severe liabilities. Therefore, for a loss occurring to a ship in her charge while so employed, the owner of the steamer is not liable without negligence on his part, or on the part of those whom he employs.

The same person may be a common carrier, and also hold other offices or relations. He may be a warehouseman, a wharfinger, or a forwarding merchant. The peculiar liabilities of the common carrier do not attach to either of these offices or employments. Thus, a warehouseman is liable for loss of the goods which he takes for storage, only in case of his own negligence : he is not, as a com-com carrier is said to be, an insurer of the goods. The question then arises, when the liability of such a person is that of a warehouseman, and when it is that of a carrier.

If a carrier receives goods to be stored until he can carry them, — a canal-boatman, for example, — or if, at the end of the journey, he stores them for a time for the safety of the goods or the conveinence of the owner, while thus stored he is liable only as warehouseman. But if he puts them into his store or office only for a short time, and for his own convenience, either at the beginning or end of the transit (or journey), they are in his hands as carrier.

Where these relations seem to unite and mingle in one person, it may be said to be the general rule, that, wherever the deposit, in whatever place or building, is secondary and subordinate to the carriage of the goods, which is therefore the chief thing, the party taking the goods is a carrier ; and otherwise a depositary only of some kind. If, therefore, goods are delivered to a carrier, or at his depot or receiving-room, with directions not to carry them until further orders, he is only a depositary, and not a carrier, until those orders are received ; but when they are received, he becomes a carrier ; and if the goods are afterwards lost or injured before their removal, he is liable as a common carrier without negligence or fault on his part.

SECTION III.

THE OBLIGATION OF THE COMMON CARRIER TO RECEIVE AND CARRY GOODS OR PASSENGERS.

He cannot refuse to receive and carry goods offered, without good cause ; for, by his openly announcing himself in any way as engaged in this business, he makes an offer to the public which becomes a kind of contract as to any one who accepts it. He may demand his compensation, however ; and, if it be refused, he may refuse to carry the goods ; nor is he bound to carry them if security be offered to him, but not the money. But if the freight-money be not demanded, the owner of the goods, if he is able, ready, and willing to pay it, has all his rights although he does not make a formal tender of the money. A carrier may refuse if his means of carriage are already fully employed. But, in a case where a railway company, being common carriers, had issued excursion-tickets for a journey, it was held that they were not excused from carrying passengers according to their contract, upon the ground that there was no room for them in their conveyance ; and that, in order to avail themselves of this answer, they should make their contract conditional upon there being room. If the common carrier cannot carry the goods without danger to them, or to himself or other goods ; or without extraordinary inconvenience ; or if they are not such goods as it is his regular business to carry ; he is excused for not carrying them. He is always entitled to his *usual* charge ; but not to extraordinary compensation, unless for extraordinary service.

The common carrier of goods is bound to receive them in a suitable way, and at suitable times and places. If he has an office or station, he must have proper persons there, and proper means of security. During the transit, and at all stopping-places, due care must be taken of all goods ; and that means the kind and measure of care appropriate for goods of that description. If he have notice, by writing on the article or otherwise, of the need of peculiar care, — as, " Glass, with great care," or " This side uppermost," or " To be kept dry," — he is bound to comply with such directions, supposing them not to impose unnecessary care or labor.

If he carry passengers, he must receive all who offer, unless he has some special and sufficient reason for refusing.

In a case tried before the Supreme Judicial Court of Massachusetts, it was held, that if an innkeeper, who has frequently entered a railroad depot and annoyed passengers by soliciting them to go to his inn, receives notice from the superintendent of the depot that he must do so no more, and he nevertheless repeatedly enters the depot for the same purpose, and afterwards obtains a ticket for a passage in the cars, with an actual intention of entering the cars as a passenger, and goes into the depot on his way to the cars, and the superintendent, believing that he has entered the depot to solicit passengers, orders him to go out, and he does not exhibit his ticket, nor give notice of his real intention, but presses forward towards the cars, and the superintendent and his assistants therefore forcibly remove him from the depot, using no more force than is necessary for that purpose, such removal is justifiable, and not an indictable assault and battery.

A common carrier is bound to carry his passengers over the whole route, and at a proper speed, or supply proper means of transport; to demand only a reasonable or usual compensation; to notify his passengers of any peculiar dangers; to treat all alike, unless there be actual and sufficient reason for the distinction, as in the filthy appearance, dangerous condition, or misconduct of a passenger; and to behave to all with civility and decorum.

He must also have proper carriages, and keep them in good condition, and not overload them; and suitable horses and drivers; stop at the usual places, with proper intervals for rest or food; take the proper route; and drive at proper speed; and leave the passengers at the usual stopping-places, or wherever he agrees to. In none of these things can he depart from what is usual and proper at his own pleasure. And if by any breach of these duties a passenger is injured, the carrier is responsible. So if he puts his passengers in peril, and one of them be hurt by an effort to escape, as in jumping off, it is no defence for the carrier to show that he would have been safe if he had remained.

In one case, it was held that a common carrier who had received a pickpocket as a passenger on board his vessel, and taken his fare, could not put him on shore so long as he was not guilty of any impropriety. But this may be doubted. The common carrier must certainly employ competent and well-behaved persons for all duties; and for failure in any of the particulars of his duties and obligations, he is responsible not only to the extent of any damage caused thereby, but also, in many cases, for pain and injury to the feelings. He is also bound to deliver to each passenger all his baggage at the end of his journey; and is held liable if he delivers it to a wrong party on a forged order, and without personal default.

Lastly, he must make due delivery of the goods at the proper time, in the proper way, and at the proper place, and to the proper person; and this person should be some one who was authorized by the owner or sender to receive the goods.

If a party authorized to receive the goods refuse, or is unable, to do so, the carrier must keep them for the owner, and with due care; but now under the liability of a warehouseman, and not of a carrier: that is, he is now liable only for fault of some kind.

So the carrier must keep the goods for the owner, if he has good reason to believe that the consignee is dishonest, and will defraud the owner of his property. As to the time when goods should be delivered, it must be within the proper hours for business, when they can be suitably stored; or if the goods are delivered to the sender himself, or at his house, then at some suitable and convenient hour.

There must be no unnecessary delay, and the goods must be delivered as soon after a detention as may be with due diligence.

As to the way and the place at which the goods should be delivered, much must depend upon the nature of the goods, and much also upon the usage in regard to them, if such usage exists.

The goods should be so left, and with such notice, as to secure the early, convenient, and safe reception of them by the person entitled to have them. Something also must depend, on this point, on the mode of conveyance. A man may carry a parcel into the house, and deliver it to the owner or his servant; a wagon or cart can go to the gate, or into the yard, and there deliver what it carries. A vessel can go to one wharf or another; and is bound to go to that which is reasonably convenient to the consignee, or to one that was agreed upon; but a vessel is not always bound to comply with requirements of the consignee as to the very wharf the goods should be left at, but may leave the goods at any safe, convenient, and accessible wharf at which such goods are usually left.

Where the goods are not delivered to the owner personally, or to his agent, immediate notice should be given to the owner. The carrier is generally obliged to give notice of the delivery of goods, and if the owner has in any way designated how the goods may be delivered to himself, he is bound to obey this direction. The notice must be prompt and distinct. And if the goods are delivered at an unsuitable or unauthorized place, no notice will make this a good delivery.

Railroads terminate at their station, and although goods might be sent by wagons to the house or store of consignees, this is not usually done, as it is considered that the railroad carrier has finished his transit at his own terminus. Usually, the consignee of goods sent by railroad has notice from the consignor when to expect them; and this is so common, that it is seldom necessary, in fact, for the agents of the railroad to give notice to the consignee. But this should be given where it is necessary; and should be given as promptly, directly, and specifically as may be necessary for the purpose of the notice.

A railroad company may be compared to owners of ships in this respect, that neither can take the cars or the ships farther than the station or the wharf, and therefore may deliver the goods there. But a carrier by water is bound to give notice that the goods are on the wharf, and is not exonerated as carrier until he gives such notice; whereas, a railroad company is not bound to give notice.

It may happen that some third party may claim the goods under a title adverse to that of the consignor or consignee. If the carrier refuse to deliver them to this third party, and it turns out that the claimant had a legal right to demand them, the carrier would be liable in damages to him. But the carrier may and should demand full and clear evidence of the claimant's title; and if the evidence be not satisfactory, he may demand security and indemnity. If the evidence or the indemnity be withheld, he certainly should not be held answerable for any thing beyond that amount which the goods themselves would satisfy, for he is in no fault. If he delivers the goods to such claimant, proof that the claimant had good title is an adequate defence against any suit by the consignor or consignee for non-delivery.

SECTION IV.

THE LIEN OF THE COMMON CARRIER.

THE legal meaning of this word, as we have said before, when we have had occasion to use the word in preceding chapters, is the right of holding or detaining property until some charge against it, or some claim upon the owner on account of it, is satisfied.

The common carrier has this right against all the goods he carries, for his compensation. While he holds them for this purpose, he is not liable for loss or injury to them as a common carrier; that is, not unless the injury happen from his own fault.

He may not only hold the goods for his compensation, but may recover this out of them, by any of the usual means in which a lien upon personal chattels is made productive. That is, he holds them just as if they were pledged to him by the owner as a security for the debt. Therefore, if the debt be not paid in a reasonable time after it is due and demanded, the carrier may have a decree of a court of equity for their sale; or may sell them himself at auction, retaining his pay from the proceeds, and paying over the remainder. But to make this course justifiable and safe, the carrier must wait a reasonable time, and give full notice of his intention, so that the owner may have a convenient opportunity to redeem the goods; and there must be proper advertisement of the sale, and every usual precaution taken to insure a favorable sale; and the carrier must not himself buy the goods, and must act in all respects with entire honesty.

SECTION V.

THE LIABILITY OF THE COMMON CARRIER.

THIS is perfectly well established as a rule of law, although it is very exceptional and peculiar. It is sometimes said to arise from the public carrier being a kind of public officer. But the true reason is the confidence which is necessarily reposed in him, the power he has over the goods intrusted to him, the ease with which he may defraud the owner of them, and yet make it appear that he was not in fault, and the difficulty which the owner might have in making out proof of his default. This reason it is important to remember, because it helps us to construe and apply the rules of law on this subject. Thus, the rule is that the common carrier is liable for any loss or injury to goods under his charge, unless it be caused by the act of God, or by the public enemy. The rule is intended to hold the common carrier responsible wherever it was *possible* that he caused the loss, either by negligence or design.

Hence, the act of God means some act in which neither the carrier himself, nor any other man, had any direct and immediate agency. If, for example, a house in which the goods are at night is struck by lightning, or blown over by a tempest, or washed away by inundation, the carrier is not liable. This is an act of God, although man's agency interferes in causing the loss; for without that agency, the goods would not have been there. But no man could have directly caused the loss. On the other hand, if the building was set on fire by an incendiary at midnight, and the rapid spread of the flames made it absolutely impossible to rescue the goods, this might be an inevitable accident if the carrier were wholly innocent, but it would also be possible that the incendiary was in collusion with the carrier for the purpose of concealing his theft; and therefore the carrier would be liable for such a loss, however innocent.

As a general rule, the common carrier is always liable for loss by fire, unless it be caused by lightning, an accidental fire not being considered an act of God, or a peril of the sea; and this rule has been applied to steamboats and other vessels. So, it may be true that after the lightning, the tempest, or inundation, the carrier was negligent, and so lost the goods which might have been saved by proper efforts, or that he took the opportunity to steal them. If this could be shown, the carrier would, of course, be liable; but the law will not suppose this without proof, if the first and main cause were such that the carrier *could not* have been guilty in respect to it. So, a common carrier would be liable for a loss caused by a robbery, however sudden, unexpected, and irresistible, or by a theft, however wise and full his precautions, and however subtle and ingenious the theft, although either of these might seem to be unavoidable by any means of safety which it would be at all reasonable to require.

The general principles of agency extend to common carriers, and make them liable for the acts of their agents, done while in the discharge of the agency or employment. So, the knowledge of his agent is the knowledge of the carrier, if the agent be authorized expressly, or by the nature of his employment, to receive this notice or knowledge. But an agent for a common carrier may act for himself, — as a stage-coachman in carrying parcels, for which he is paid personally and does not account with his employer, — and then the employer, as we have said, is not liable, unless the owner of the goods believed the stage-coachman carried the goods for his employer, and was justified by the facts and apparent circumstances in so believing.

A carrier may be liable beyond his own route. It is very common for carriers, who share between them the parts of a long route, to unite in the business and the profits, and then all are liable for a loss on any part of the route.

If they are not so united in fact, but say they are so, or say what indicates that they are so, they justify a sender in supposing they are united, and then they are equally liable.

If a carrier takes goods to carry only as far as he goes, and then engages to send them forward by another carrier, he is liable as carrier to the end of his own route ; he is liable also if he neglects to send the goods on ; but he is not liable for what may happen to them afterwards.

SECTION VI.

THE CARRIER OF PASSENGERS.

THE carriers of passengers are under a more limited liability than the carriers of goods. This is now well settled. The reason is, that they have not the same control over passengers as over goods ; cannot fasten them down, and use other means of securing them. But while the liability of the carrier of passengers is thus mitigated, it is still stringent and extreme. No proof of care will excuse the carrier if he loses goods committed to him. But proof of *the utmost care* will excuse him for injury done to passengers; for the carrier of passengers is liable for injury to them, unless he can show that he took all possible care, — giving always a reasonable construction to this phrase; and in the case of railroad companies there is authority for using the words in almost their literal meaning; that is, for holding them liable for all injury to passengers which could have been *possibly* avoided.

SECTION VII.

A NOTICE BY THE CARRIER, RESPECTING HIS LIABILITY.

THE common carrier has a right to make a special agreement with the senders of goods, which shall materially modify, or even wholly prevent, his liability for accidental loss or injury to the goods.

The question is, What constitutes such a bargain? A mere notice that the carrier is not responsible, or his refusal to be responsible, although brought home to the knowledge of the other party, does not necessarily constitute an agreement. The reason is this. The sender has a right to insist upon sending his goods, and the passenger has a right to insist upon going himself with customary baggage, leaving the carrier to his legal responsibility; and the carrier is bound to take them on these terms. If, therefore, the sender or the passenger, after receiving such notice, only sends or goes in silence, and without expressing any assent, especially if the notice be given at such time, or under such circumstances, as would make it inconvenient for the sender not to send, or for the passenger not to go, then the law will not presume from his sending or going an assent to the carrier's terms.

But the assent may be expressed by words, or made manifest by acts; and it is in each case a question of evidence for the jury, whether there was such an agreement.

But a notice by the carrier, which only limits and defines his liability to a reasonable extent, without taking it away, as one which states what kind of goods he will carry, and what he will not; or to what amount only he will be liable for passengers' baggage, without special notice; or what information he will require, if certain articles, as jewels or gold, are carried; or what increased rates must be paid for such things, — any notice of this kind, if in itself reasonable and just, will bind the party receiving it.

No party will be affected by any notice, — neither the carrier, nor a sender of goods, nor a passenger, — unless a knowledge of it can be brought home to him. In a case in Pennsylvania, where the notice was in the English language, and the passenger was a German, who did not understand English, it was held that the carrier must prove that the passenger had actual knowledge of the limitation in the notice.

But the knowledge may be brought home to him by indirect evidence. As by showing that it was stated on a receipt given to him, or on a ticket sold him, or in a newspaper which he read, or even that it was a matter of usage, and generally known. This question is one of fact, which the jury will determine upon all the evidence, under the direction of the court. And if the notice is ambiguous, they will be directed to give it the meaning which is against the carrier, because it was his business to make it plain and certain.

Any fraud towards the carrier, as a fraudulent disregard of a notice, or an effort to cast on him a responsibility he is not obliged to assume, or to make his liability seem to be greater than it really is, will extinguish the liability of the carrier so far as it is affected by such a fraud.

If a carrier gives notice which he is authorized to give, the party receiving it is bound by it, and the carrier is under no obligation to make a special inquiry or investigation to see that the notice is complied with, but may assume that this is done.

It should, however, be remarked that such notice affects the liability of the common carrier only so far as it is peculiar to him; that is, his liability for a loss which occurs without his agency or fault; for he is just as liable as he would be without any notice, for a loss or injury caused by his own negligence or default.

Perhaps a common carrier might make a valid bargain which would protect him against every thing but his own wilful or fraudulent misconduct. But no bargain could be made to protect him against this.

SECTION VIII.

THE CARRIER'S LIABILITY FOR GOODS CARRIED BY PASSENGERS.

A CARRIER of goods knows what goods, or rather what parcels and packages, he receives and is responsible for. A carrier of passengers is responsible for the goods they carry with them as baggage; what that is, the carrier does not always know; and he is responsible only to the extent of what might be fairly and naturally carried as baggage. This must always be a question of fact, to be settled as such by the jury, upon all the evidence, and under the direction of the court. But there can be no precise and definite standard. A traveller on a long journey needs more money and more baggage than on a short one; one going to some places and for some purposes needs more than one going to other places or for other purposes.

Thus in New York it was decided that *baggage* does not properly include money in a trunk, or any articles usually carried about the person. And in another New York case, it was held that, where the baggage of a passenger consists of an ordinary travelling-trunk, in which there is a large sum of money, such money is not considered as included under the term *baggage*, so as to render the carrier responsible for it. But generally a passenger may carry as baggage, money not exceeding an amount ordinarily carried for travelling-expenses. So in Massachusetts it was held that common carriers are responsible for money *bonâ fide* included in the baggage of a passenger, for travelling-expenses and personal use, to an amount not exceeding what a prudent person would deem proper and necessary for the purpose.

In Pennsylvania, carriers have been held responsible for ladies' trunks containing apparel and jewels. And in Illinois, a common carrier of passengers has been held liable for the loss of a pocket-pistol, and a pair of duelling-pistols, contained in the carpet-bag of a passenger, which was stolen out of the possession of the carrier. But in Tennessee, it has been held that "a silver watch, worth about thirty-five dollars, also medicines, handcuffs, locks, &c., worth about twenty dollars," were not included in the term baggage, and that the carrier was not responsible for their loss. In Ohio, it has been held that a gold watch, of the value of ninety-five dollars, was a part of the traveller's baggage, and his trunk a proper place to carry it in. In another New-York case, it has been held that the owners of steamboats were liable as common carriers for the baggage of passengers; but, to subject them to damages for loss thereof, it must be strictly baggage; that is, such articles of necessity and personal convenience as are usually carried by travellers. And it was accordingly held, in that case, that the carrier was not liable for the loss of a trunk containing valuable merchandise and nothing else, although it did not appear that the plaintiff had any other trunk with him. But in a case in Pennsylvania, where the plaintiff was a carpenter moving to the State of Ohio, and his trunk contained carpenters' tools to the value of fifty-five dollars, which the jury found to be the reasonable tools of a carpenter, it was held that he was entitled to recover for them as baggage.

There is some diversity, and perhaps some uncertainty, in the application of the rule; but the rule itself is well settled, and a reasonable construction and application of it must always be made; and, for this purpose, the passenger himself, and all the circumstances of the case, must be considered.

The purpose of the rule is to prevent the carrier from becoming liable by the fraud of the passenger, or by conduct which would have the effect of fraud; for this would be the case if a passenger should carry merchandise by way of baggage, and thus make the carrier of passengers a carrier of goods without knowing it and without being paid for it.

Generally, a common carrier of passengers, by stage, packet, steamer, or cars, carries the moderate and reasonable baggage of a passenger, without being paid specifically for it. But the law considers a payment for this so far included in the payment of the fare, as to form a sufficient ground for the carrier's liability to the extent above stated.

The carrier is only liable for the goods or baggage delivered to him and placed under his care. Hence, if a sender of goods send his own servant with them, and intrust them to him and not to the carrier, the carrier is not responsible. So, if a passenger keeps his baggage, or any part of it, on his person, or in his own hands, or within his own sight and immediate control, instead of delivering it to the carrier or his servants, the carrier is not liable, *as carrier*, for any loss or injury which may happen to it; that is, not without actual default in the matter. Thus, in an action brought in New York to charge a railroad company, as common carriers, for the loss of an overcoat belonging to a passenger, it appeared that the coat was not delivered to the defendants, but that the passenger, having placed it on the seat of the car in which he sat, forgot to take it with him when he left, and it was afterwards stolen; and it was held that the defendants were not liable. But if the baggage of a passenger is *delivered* to a common carrier, or his servant, he is liable for it in the same way, and to the same extent, as he is for goods which he carries.

In this country the rules of evidence permit the traveller to maintain his action against the carrier by proving, by his own testimony, the contents of a lost trunk or box, and their value. And the testimony of the wife of the owner is similarly admissible. But it is always limited to such things — in quantity, quality, kind, and value — as might reasonably be supposed to be carried in such a trunk or valise. The rule, with this limitation, seems reasonable and safe, and is quite generally adopted. In Massachusetts it was distinctly denied by the Supreme Court, but was afterwards established by statute.

The common carrier of goods or of passengers is liable to third parties for any injury done to them by the negligence or default of the carrier, or of his servants. And it would seem that he is liable even for the wilful wrong-doing of his servants, if it was committed while in his employ, and in the management of the conveyance under his control, although the wrong was done in direct opposition to his express commands. So he is for injury to property by the wayside, caused by his fault. But the negligence of the party suffering the injury, if it was material and contributed to the injury, is a good defence for the carrier; unless malice on the carrier's part can be shown.

Where the party injured is in fault, the common carrier has still been held liable, if that fault was made possible and injurious through the fault of the carrier. If passengers are carried gratuitously, that is, without pay, the common carrier is still liable for injury caused by his negligence.

Whether a railroad company is responsible for fire set to buildings or property along the road, without negligence on its part, has been much considered in this country. In some of our States they are made so liable by statute provision. And this fact, together with the general principles of liability for injury done, would seem to lead to the conclusion that they are not liable, unless in fault, or unless made so by statute.

(89.)

.... ***Steam Packet Company.***

Marks and Numbers.

Received from

the following articles, being marked and numbered as in the margin, in apparent good order, the contents and value unknown,

to be transported from to on one of the company's steamers, and to be delivered on their wharf in , in like good order and condition, the dangers of the sea, of fire on board or on wharf, collision, and all other accidents excepted.

DATED AT , 186 *For the company.*

The following form will show the terms and conditions on which our express-companies carry their freight. This paper, given and received, constitutes a contract.

(90.)

Duplicate.

.... *Express Company.*

Fast Freight Line.

18

Received from

the following packages, in apparent good order, contents and value unknown:

.... EXPRESS COMPANY.

Advanced Charges, $

RATES.

		Marked and numbered as in the margin, to
D'ble 1st Class	cts. per 100 lbs.	be forwarded by railroad and delivered at
		upon payment of freight therefor,
1st Class	cents per 100 lbs.	as noted in the margin, subject to the condi-
		tions and rules on the back hereof and those
2d Class	cents per 100 lbs.	of the several railroads over which the prop-
		erty is transported, which constitute a part of
3d Class	cents per 100 lbs.	this contract.
4th Class	cents per 100 lbs.	*Agent.*

AS PER CLASSIFICATION ON BACK.

On the back of this receipt is a minute and very full classification of all articles likely to be offered for transportation, followed by the

Conditions and Rules.

The destination, name of the consignee, and weight of all articles of freight, must be plainly and distinctly marked, or no responsibility will be taken for their miscarriage or loss; and when designed to be forwarded, after transportation on the route, a written order must be given, with the particular line of conveyance marked on the goods, if any such be preferred or desired.

The companies will not hold themselves liable for the safe carriage or custody of any articles of freight, unless receipted for by an authorized agent; and no agent of the line is authorized to receive, or agree to transport, any freight, which is not thus receipted for.

No responsibility will be admitted, under any circumstances, to a greater amount upon any single article of freight than $200, unless upon notice given of such amount, and a special agreement therefor. Specie, drafts, bank-bills, and other articles of great intrinsic or representative value, will only be taken upon a representation of their value, and by a special agreement assented to by the superintendent of the receiving road.

The companies will not hold themselves liable at all for injuries to any articles of freight during the course of transportation, arising from the weather, or accidental delays, or natural tendency to decay. Nor will their guaranty of special despatch cover cases of unavoidable or extraordinary casualties or storms, or delays occasioned by low water and ice; and may be stored at the risk and expense of the owner. Nor will they hold themselves liable, as COMMON CARRIERS, for such articles, after their arrival at their place of destination at the company's warehouses or depots.

Carriages and sleighs, eggs, furniture, looking-glasses, glass and crockery ware, machinery, mineral acids, piano-fortes, stoves and castings, sweet-potatoes, wrought marble, all liquids put up in glass or earthen ware, fruit, and live animals, will only be taken at the owner's risk of fracture or injury during the course of transportation, loading and unloading, unless specially agreed to the contrary.

Gunpowder, friction matches, and like combustibles, will not be received on any terms; and all persons procuring the reception of such freight by fraud or concealment, will be held responsible for any damage which may arise from it while in the custody of the company.

It is further stipulated and agreed, that goods shipped to points west of shall be subject to a change in classification and corresponding change of rates beyond those points.

Cases or packages of boots and shoes, and of other articles liable to peculation or fraudulent abstraction, must be strapped with iron or wood, or otherwise securely protected, or the companies will not be liable for diminution of the original contents, and the companies will hold the freighter, in all cases, to bear the loss arising from improper packing.

It is also agreed between the parties that the said companies, and the railroads and steamboats with which they connect, shall not be held accountable for any deficiency in packages if receipted for to them in good order.

All articles of freight arriving at their places of destination must be taken away within twenty-fours hours after being unladen from the cars, — each company reserving the right of charging storage on the same, or placing the same in store at the risk and expense of the owner, if they see fit, after lapse of that time.

CHAPTER XXI.

LIMITATIONS.

SECTION I.

THE STATUTE OF LIMITATIONS.

ALL of our States have what is called a Statute of Limitations. It is not exactly the same everywhere; but generally it enacts that all actions of account, and all which can be brought for indebtedness or damages, and all actions of debt grounded upon any lending, or contract without seal, and all actions for arrearages of rent, shall be commenced and sued within six years next after the cause of such actions or suit arises, and not after. In few words, all claims which do not rest on a seal or a judgment must be sued within six years from the time when they arise.

In some States, a statute provides, in substance, that, if a debt or promise be once barred by the Statute of Limitations, no acknowledgment of the debt or new promise shall renew the debt, and take away the effect of the statute, unless the new promise is in writing, and is signed by the party who makes the promise. But this statute expressly permits a part-payment either of principal or interest of the old debt to have the same effect as a new promise. And this statute also provides, that if there be joint contractors or debtors, and a plaintiff is barred by the statute against both, but the bar of the statute is removed as to one by a new promise or otherwise, the plaintiff may have judgment against this one, but not against the other.

Such statutes have been passed in Maine, Massachusetts, Vermont, New York, Indiana, Michigan, Arkansas, and California.

SECTION II.

CONSTRUCTION OF THE STATUTE.

FOR the law of limitation there is a twofold foundation: in the first place, the actual probability that a debt which has not been claimed for a long time was paid, and that this is the reason of the silence of the creditor. But, besides this reason, there is the inexpediency and injustice of permitting a stale and neglected claim or debt, even if it has not been paid, to be set up and enforced after a long silence and acquiescence.

Before inquiring into the rules of law which now apply to the case of an acknowledgment or new promise, it should be remarked that a prescription, or limitation, of common law, much more ancient than the statutes above quoted, is still in full force. This is the presumption of payment after twenty years, which is applicable to all debts; not only the simple contracts to which the Statutes of Limitation refer, that is, contracts which are merely oral, or which if written have no seal, but to specialties, or contracts or debts under seal or by judgment of court. Of these it will not be necessary to speak here, excepting to remark, that in a few of our States the Statute of Limitation excepts a promissory note which is signed in the presence of an attesting witness, and is put in suit by the original payee, or his executor or administrator; such a note in those States, as in Maine and Massachusetts, may be sued any time within twenty years after it is due. Bank-bills and other evidences of debt issued by banks, are everywhere excepted from the operation of the statute.

SECTION III.

THE NEW PROMISE.

WHAT is the new promise which suffices to take a case out of the statute? A mere acknowledgment, which does not contain, by any reasonable implication or construction, a new promise, is not sufficient, and still less so if it expressly excludes a new promise. In the leading American case upon this point, before the Supreme Court of the United States, it was proved, in answer to the plea of the Statute of Limitations, that the defendant, one of the partners of a firm then dissolved, said to the plaintiff, "I know we are owing you;" "I am getting old, and I wish to have the business settled:" it was held that these expressions were insufficient to revive the debt. So, in New Hampshire, in an action on a promissory note, the defendant, on being asked to pay the note, said "he guessed the note was outlawed, but that would make no difference, he was willing to pay his honest debts, always." As he did not state in direct terms that he was willing to pay the note, this was held not sufficient to revive the debt. A new promise is not now implied by the law itself, from a mere acknowledgment.

The new promise need not define the amount of the debt. That can be done by other evidence, if only the existence of the debt and the purpose of paying it are acknowledged. Still, the new promise must be of the specific debt, or must distinctly include it; for if wholly general and undefined, it is not enough. A testator who provides for the payment of his debts generally, does not thereby make a new promise as to any one of them.

If the new promise is conditional, the party relying upon it must be prepared to show that the condition has been fulfilled. Thus, if the new promise be to pay "when I am able," the promisee must prove not only the promise, but that the promisor is able to pay the debt.

As the acknowledgment should be voluntary, it follows that one made under process of law, as by a bankrupt, or by answers to interrogatories which could not be avoided, should never have the effect of a new promise.

SECTION IV.

PART-PAYMENT.

A PART-PAYMENT of a debt is such a recognition of it as implies a new promise; even if it was made in goods or chattels, if they were offered as payment, and agreed to be received as payment, or by negotiable promissory note or bill. Thus, in a case where one was sued for money due for a quantity of hay, and pleaded that it had been due more than six years, which was a good defence, the plaintiff proved in reply that defendant had given him within six years a gallon of gin as part-payment for his debt; and it was held that this took the case out of the Statute of Limitations, and the plaintiff recovered. But a payment has this effect only when the payment is made as of a part of a debt. If it is made in settlement of the whole, of course it is no promise of more. And a bare payment, without words or acts to indicate its character, would not be construed as carrying with it an acknowledgment that more was due and would be paid.

If a debtor owes several debts, and pays a sum of money, he has the right of appropriating that money to one debt or another as he pleases. If he pays it without indicating his own appropriation, the general rule is, that the creditor who receives the money may appropriate it as he will. There is, however, this exception. If there be two or more debts, some of which are barred by the statute, and others are not barred by it, the creditor cannot appropriate the payment to a debt that is barred, for the purpose of taking it out of the statute by such part-payment.

SECTION V.

SOME STATUTORY EXCEPTIONS.

THE original English statute, which ours is taken from, also provides, that if a creditor, at the time when the cause of action accrues, is a minor, or a married woman, or not of sound mind, or imprisoned, or beyond the seas, the six years do not begin to run; and he may bring his action at any time within six years after such disability ceases to exist. And also, if any person against whom there shall be a cause of action, shall, when such cause accrues be beyond the seas (which means out of the country, and here, out of the State), the action may be brought at any time within six years after his return. Similar exceptions and disabilities are usually contained in our own statutes.

The effect of these is, that the disability must exist when the debt accrued; and then, so long as the disability continues to exist, the statute does not take effect. But it is a general rule, that, if the six years begin to run, they go on without any interruption or suspension from any subsequent disability. Thus, if a creditor be of sound mind, or a debtor be at home, when the debt accrues, and one month afterwards the creditor becomes insane, or the debtor leaves the country, nevertheless the six years go on, and after the end of that time no action can be commenced for the debt. Or if the disability exists when the debt accrues, and some months afterwards ceases, so that the six years begin to run when it ceases, and afterwards the disability comes again, it does not interrupt the six years.

If, when a debt is due, the debtor is out of the State, the six years do not begin to run. If afterwards he returns to the State, they then begin to run; and, having begun, they continue to run, although he goes out of the State again, and returns no more.

In this country, a rational construction has been given to the disability of being out of the State, and its removal; and it is not understood to be terminated merely by a return of the debtor for a few days, if during those days he was not within reach. If, however, the creditor knew that he had returned, or might have known it by the exercise of reasonable care and diligence, soon enough to have profited by it, this removal of the disability brings the statute into operation, although the return was for a short time only.

SECTION VI.

WHEN THE PERIOD OF LIMITATION BEGINS.

It is sometimes a question from what point of time the six years are to be counted. And the general rule is, that they begin when the action might have been commenced. If a credit is given, this period does not begin until the credit has expired. If a note on time be given, the six years do not begin until the time has expired, including the additional three days of grace; if a bill of exchange be given, payable at sight, then the six years begin after presentment and demand; but if a note be payable on demand, or money is payable on demand, then the limitation begins at once, because there may be an action at once. If there can be no action until a previous demand, the limitation begins as soon as the demand is made. If money be payable on the happening of any event, then the limitation begins after that event has happened. If several successive credits are given, as if a note is given which is to be renewed; or if a credit is given, and then a note is to be given; or if the credit is longer or shorter, at the purchaser's option, as if it be agreed that a note shall be given at two or four months, — then the six years begin when the whole credit or the longer credit has expired.

SECTION VII.

THE STATUTE DOES NOT AFFECT COLLATERAL SECURITY.

It is important to remember that the Statute of Limitations does not avoid or cancel the debt, but only provides that "no action shall be maintained upon it" after a given time. Therefore, it does not follow that no right can be sustained by the debt, although the debt cannot be sued. Thus, if one who holds a common note of hand, on which there is a mortgage or pledge of real or of personal property, without valid excuse neglects to sue the note for more than six years, he can never bring an action upon that note; but the pledge or mortgage is as valid and effectual as it was before; and, as far as it goes, his debt is secure; and for the purpose of realizing this security, by foreclosing a mortgage, for example, he may have whatever process is necessary, although he cannot sue the note itself. And the debtor cannot redeem the property pledged or mortgaged except by payment of the debt.

CHAPTER XXII.

INTEREST AND USURY.

SECTION I.

WHAT INTEREST IS, AND WHEN IT IS DUE.

INTEREST means a payment of money for the use of money. In most civilized countries the law regulates this; that is, it declares how much money may be paid or received for the use of money; and this is called legal interest; and if more is paid or agreed to be paid than is thus allowed, it is called usurious interest. By interest is commonly meant legal interest; and by usury, usurious interest.

Interest may be due, and may be demanded by a creditor, on either of two grounds. One, a bargain to that effect; the other, by way of damages for withholding money that is due. Indeed, it may be considered as now the settled rule, that wherever money is withheld which is certainly due, the debtor is to be regarded as having promised legal interest for the delay. And upon this implication, as on most others, the usage of trade, and the customary course of dealings between the parties, would have great influence.

Thus, in New York, it was held, that, where it was known to one party that it was the uniform custom of the other to charge interest upon articles sold or manufactured by him after a certain time, the latter was allowed to charge interest accordingly.

In general, we may say that interest is allowed by law as follows: on a debt due by judgment of court, it is allowed from the rendition of judgment; and on an account that has been liquidated, or settled, from the day of the liquidation; for goods sold, from the time of the sale, if there be no credit, and if there be, then from the day when the credit expires; for rent, from the time that it is due, and this even if the rent is payable otherwise than in money, but is not so paid; for money paid for another or lent to another, from the payment or loan.

Interest is not generally recoverable upon claims for unliquidated damages, nor in actions founded on tort. By *unliquidated damages* is meant damages not agreed on, and of an uncertain amount, and which the jury must determine. By *torts* is meant wrongs, or injuries inflicted. But although interest cannot be given under that name, in actions of this sort, juries are sometimes at liberty to consider it in estimating the damages.

It sometimes happens that money is due, but not now payable; and then the interest does not begin until the money is payable. As if a note be on demand, the money is always due, but it is not payable until demand; and therefore is not on interest until demand. But a note payable at a certain time, or after a certain period, carries interest from that time, whether it be demanded or not.

The laws which regulate interest and prohibit usury are very various, and are not perhaps precisely the same in any two of our States. Formerly, usury was looked upon as so great an offence, that the whole debt was forfeited thereby. The law now, however, is — generally, at least — much more lenient. The theory that money is like any merchandise, worth what it will bring and no more, and that its value should be left to fix itself in a free market, is certainly gaining ground. In many States there are frequent efforts so to change the statutes of usury that parties may make any bargain for the use of money which suits them; but when they make no bargain, the law shall say what is legal interest. And, generally, the forfeiture is now much less than the whole debt.

At the close of this chapter will be found a statement of the usury laws of the States.

There is no especial form or expression necessary to make a bargain usurious. It is enough for this purpose if there be a substantial payment, or promise of payment, of more than the law allows, either for the use of money lent, or for the forbearance of money due and payable. One thing, however, is certain: there must be a usurious intention, or there is no usury. That is, if one miscalculates, and so receives a promise for more than legal interest, the error may be corrected, the excess waived, and the whole legal interest claimed. But if one makes a bargain for more than legal interest, believing that he has a right to make such a bargain, or that the law gives him all that he claims, this is a mistake of law, and does not save the party from the effect of usury.

It may be well to remark, that the law makes a very wide distinction between a *mistake of fact* and a *mistake of law*. Generally, it will not permit a party to be hurt by a mistake of fact; but it seldom suffers any one to excuse himself by a mistake of law, because it holds that everybody should know the law, and because it would be dangerous to permit ignorance of the law to operate for any one's benefit.

The question has been much discussed, whether the use of the common tables which are calculated on the supposition that a year consists of 360 days, is usurious. In New York, it has been held that it is; but in Massachusetts, and some other States, it is held that the use of such tables does not render the transaction usurious. We think this latter the better opinion.

If a debtor requests time, and promises to pay for the forbearance legal interest, and as much more as the creditor shall be obliged to pay for the same money, this is not a usurious contract. And, even if usurious interest be actually taken, this, although strong evidence of an original usurious bargain and intent, is not conclusive, but may be rebutted by adequate proof or explanation.

When a statute provides that a usurious contract is wholly void, such a contract cannot become good afterwards; and therefore a note which is usurious, if it be therefore void by law in its inception, is not valid in the hands of an innocent indorsee. But it is otherwise where the statute does not declare the contract void on account of the usury. If a note, or any securities for a usurious bargain, be delivered up by the creditor and cancelled, and the debtor thereupon promises to pay the original debt and lawful interest, this promise is valid.

New securities for old ones which are tainted with usury are equally void with the old ones, or subject to the same defence. Not so, however, if the usurious part of the original securities be expunged, and not included in the new; or if the new ones are given to third parties, who were wholly innocent of the original usurious transaction. And if a debtor suffers his usurious debt to be sued, and a judgment recovered against him for the whole amount, it is then too late for him to take any advantage of the usury.

So, if land or goods be mortgaged to secure a usurious debt, and afterwards conveyed to an innocent party, subject to such mortgage, the latter cannot set up the defence of usury, and thereby defeat an action tc enforce the mortgage.

Usurers resort to many devices to conceal their usury ; and sometimes it is very difficult for the law to reach and punish this offence. A common method is for the lender of money to sell some chattel, or a parcel of goods, at a high price, the borrower paying this price in part as a premium for the loan. In England, it would seem from the reports to be quite common for one who discounts a note to do this nominally at legal rates, but to furnish a part of the amount in goods at a very high valuation. In all cases of this kind, or rather in all cases where questions of this kind arise, the court endeavors to ascertain the real character of the transaction. Such a transaction is always suspicious, for the obvious reason that one who wants to borrow money is not very likely to desire at the same time to buy goods at a high price. But the jury decide all questions of this kind ; and it is their duty to judge of the actual intention of the parties from all the evidence offered. If that intention is substantially that one should loan his money to another, who shall therefor, in any manner whatever, pay to the lender more than legal interest, it is a case of usury. " Where the real truth is a loan of money," said Lord Mansfield, " the wit of man cannot find a shift to take it out of the statute." If this great judge meant only that, whenever legal evidence shows the transaction to be a usurious loan, the law pays no respect whatever to any pretence or disguise, this is certainly true. But the wit of man does undoubtedly devise many " shifts," which the law cannot detect. There seems to be a general rule in these cases in reference to the burden of proof; the borrower must first show that he took the goods on compulsion ; and then it is for the lender to prove that no more than their actual value was received or charged for them.

If one should borrow stock at a valuation much above the market rate, and agree to pay interest on this value for the use of the stock to sell or pledge, this would be usurious.

One may lend his stock, and may, without usury, give the borrower the option to replace the stock, or to pay for it at even a high value, with interest. But, if he reserves this option to himself, the bargain is usurious, because it gives the lender the right to claim more than legal interest. So, the lender may reserve either the dividends or the interest, if he elects at the time of the loan ; but he cannot reserve the right of electing at a future time, when he shall know what the dividends are.

A contract may seem to be two, and yet be but one, if the seeming two are but parts of a whole. Thus, if A borrows one thousand dollars, and gives a note promising to pay legal interest for it, and then gives another note for (or otherwise promises to pay) a further sum, in fact for no consideration but the loan, this is all one transaction, and it constitutes a usurious contract.

But if there be a loan on legal terms, with no promise or obligation on the part of the borrower to pay any more, this might not be invalidated by a mere understanding that the borrower should, when the money was paid by him, make a present to the lender for the accommodation. And if, after a payment has been made, which discharged all legal obligation, the payer voluntarily adds a gift, this would not be usurious. But in every such case the question for a jury is, What was this additional transfer of money, in fact ; was it a voluntary gift, or was it the payment of a debt ? If an honest gift, it was not usurious ; if a payment, it was usurious.

A foreign contract, valid and lawful where made, may be enforced in a State in which such a contract, if made there, would be usurious. But if usurious where it was made, and, by reason of that usury, wholly void in that State, if it is put in suit in another State where the penalty for usury is less, it cannot be enforced under this mitigated penalty; but it is wholly void there also.

SECTION II.

A CHARGE FOR RISK OR FOR SERVICE.

It is undoubtedly lawful for a lender to charge an extra price for the risk he incurs, provided that risk be perfectly distinct and different from the merely personal risk of the debtor's being unable to pay. If any thing is paid for this last risk, it is certainly usury.

So, one may charge for services rendered, for brokerage, or for rate of exchange, and may even cause a domestic loan or discount to be actually converted into a foreign one, so as to charge the exchange; and this would not be usurious. But here, as before, and indeed throughout the law of usury, it is necessary to remember that the actual intention, and not the apparent purpose or form of the transaction, must determine its character. So, if one lends money to be used in business, and lends it upon such terms that he becomes a partner in fact with those who use it, taking his share of the profits, and becoming liable for the losses, this is not usurious.

So, if one enters into a partnership, and provides money for its business, and the other party is to bear all the losses, and also to pay the capitalist more than legal interest as his share of the profits, this is not usurious, because there is no loan, if there be in fact a partnership; for then there is a very important risk, as he becomes liable for all the debts of the partnership.

The banks always get more than legal interest by their way of discounting notes and deducting the whole interest from the amount they give. This is perfectly obvious if we take an extreme case; as if a bank discounted a note of a thousand dollars at fifteen years, in Massachusetts, the bank would discount the interest of all the fifteen years; the borrower would receive one hundred dollars, and at the end of fifteen years he would pay back one thousand dollars, which is equivalent to paying nine hundred dollars for the use of one hundred for fifteen years, whereas the legal interest would be but ninety dollars. But this method is now established by usage and sanctioned by law. It should, however, be confined to discounts of negotiable paper, not having a very long time to run. For the rule is founded upon usage, and the usage goes no further.

SECTION III.

THE SALE OF NOTES.

THERE are, perhaps, no questions in relation to interest and usury of more importance than those which arise from the sale of notes or other securities. In the first place, there is no doubt whatever that the owner of a note has as good a right to sell it for the most he can get, as he has to sell any goods or wares which he owns. There is here no question of usury, because there is no loan of money, nor forbearance of debt. But, on the other hand, it is quite as certain that if any person makes his own note, and sells that for what he can get, this, while in appearance the sale of a note, is in fact the giving of a note for money. It is a loan and a borrowing, and nothing else. And if the apparent sale be for such a price that the seller pays more than legal interest, or, in other words, if the note bear interest and is sold for less than its face, or is not on interest, and more than interest is discounted, it is a usurious transaction. Supposing these two rules to be settled, the question in each case is, under which of them does that case come, or to which of them does it draw nearest.

We are not aware of any general principle so likely to be of use in determining these questions as this: if the seller of a note acquired it by purchase, or if it is his for money advanced or lent by him to its full amount, he may sell it for what he can get; but if he be the maker of the note, or the agent of the maker, and receives for the note less than would be paid him if only a lawful discount were made, it is a usurious loan. In other words, the first holder of a note (and the maker of a note is not and cannot be its first holder) must pay to the maker the face of the note, or its full amount. And after paying this, he may sell it, and any subsequent purchaser may sell it, as merchandise. The same rule must apply to corporations, and all other bodies or persons who issue their notes or bonds on interest. If sold by brokers for them, for less than the full amount, it is usurious. Nor can such notes come into the market free from the taint and the defence of usury, unless the first party who holds them pays for them their full value.

But then comes another question. If a note be offered for sale, and be sold for less than its face, and the purchaser supposes himself to buy it from an actual holder and not from the maker, can the maker interpose the defence that it was actually usurious, on the ground that the seller was only his agent? I should say that he could not; that there can be no usury unless this is intended; and that the guilty intention of one party cannot affect another party who was innocent.

I should say, also, that one who, having no interest in a note, indorses or guarantees it for a certain premium, will be liable for its face; he does not now add his credit to the value of his property and sell both together, as where he indorses a note which he holds himself, but sells his credit alone. This transaction I should not think usurious. And if it was open to no other defence, as fraud, for example, and was in fact what it purported to be, and not a mere cover for a usurious loan, we know no good reason why such indorser or guarantor should not be held liable to the full amount of his promise.

SECTION IV.

COMPOUND INTEREST.

Compound interest is sometimes said to be usurious; but it is not so; and even those cases which speak of it as "savoring of usury" may be thought to go too far, unless every hard bargain for money is usurious. As the authorities now stand, however, a contract or promise to pay money with compound interest cannot, generally, be enforced. On the other hand, it is neither wholly void, nor attended with any penalty, as it would be if usurious; but is valid for the principal and simple interest only.

Nevertheless, compound interest is sometimes recognized as due by courts of law, as well as of equity; and sometimes, too, by its own name. Thus, if a trustee be proved to have had the money of the party for whom he is trustee (who is called in law his *cestui que trust*) for a long time, without accounting for it, he may be charged with the whole amount, reckoned at compound interest, so as to cover his unlawful profits. If compound interest has accrued under a bargain for it, and been actually paid, it cannot be recovered back, as money usuriously paid may be. And if accounts are agreed to be settled by annual rests, which is in fact compound interest, or are actually settled so in good faith, the law sanctions this. Sometimes, in cases of disputed accounts, the courts direct this method of settlement.

Where money due on interest has been paid by sundry instalments, the mode of adjusting the amount which has the best authority, and the prevailing usage in its favor, seems to be this: Compute the interest due on the principal sum to the time when a payment, either alone or in conjunction with preceding payments, shall equal or exceed the interest due on the principal. Deduct this sum, and upon the balance cast interest as before, until a payment or payments equal the interest due; then deduct again, and so on.

Abstracts of the Usury Laws of the States.

These laws are stated from the latest information; but are constantly undergoing change, and are likely to be so, until abolished, as they now are in some States.

Alabama. Legal interest, eight per cent. More cannot be recovered.

Arkansas. Legal interest, six per cent. Parties may agree by written contract for ten per cent. More cannot be recovered.

California. Legal rate of interest, when no bargain, seven per cent. Parties may agree on any rate of interest in writing. A judgment draws only seven per cent.

Connecticut. Six per cent legal interest. Usurious contracts void. Penalty for receiving more than six per cent. Person so receiving shall forfeit value so taken; *half* to the prosecutor, *half* to the State Treasury. Contracts to pay taxes and insurance on sums loaned in addition to the legal interest are *valid.*

Delaware. Legal rate, six per cent. Penalty for taking more, — forfeiture of the money lent; half to the prosecutor, half to the State.

Florida. Legal interest, six per cent. If more than eight per cent is agreed for or taken, the whole amount of interest is forfeited.

Georgia. Legal interest, seven per cent. More than legal interest cannot be recovered.

Illinois. Legal interest, six per cent. Parties may agree upon ten per cent. If more is agreed on or is taken, only the principal can be recovered.

Indiana. Legal interest, six per cent. It may be taken in advance. If more be promised, only the legal interest can be recovered.

Iowa. Six per cent. legal. Ten per cent. permitted if contract in writing. If a contract be made for greater interest, one-fourth of the sum contracted for is forfeited.

Kansas. Legal interest, seven per cent. Parties may stipulate for any rate not exceeding twelve per cent. Usurious payments held to be made on account of principal.

Kentucky. Legal interest, six per cent. Extra interest forfeited.

Louisiana. *Conventional* interest shall in no case exceed eight per cent under penalty of forfeiture of entire interest. Legal interest, eight per cent. Usurious interest may be recovered back, but must be sued for within twelve months.

Maine. Legal interest, six per cent; but not to apply to letting cattle, or other similar contracts in practice among farmers; or to maritime contracts, as bottomry or insurance; and not to course of exchange in practice among merchants. Excessive interest not recoverable, and, if paid, may be recovered back.

Maryland. Legal interest, six per cent. Excess forfeited.

Massachusetts. In absence of agreement, legal interest to be six per cent. Any rate of interest or discount may be made by agreement; but, if greater than six per cent, it must be in writing.

Michigan. Legal rate, seven per cent. Parties may agree upon any rate not exceeding ten per cent. If more interest is taken, contract void.

Minnesota. Legal rate seven per cent. Parties may agree for more, but agreement not valid for any excess over twelve per cent.

Mississippi. Legal interest, six per cent. Parties may agree for ten per cent. If more is taken or agreed for, the excess is forfeited.

Missouri. Legal rate, six per cent; but parties may agree in writing for any rate not to exceed ten per cent. Parties may contract in writing for the payment of interest upon interest; but the interest shall not be compounded oftener than once a year.

Nebraska. Legal interest, ten per cent. Parties may agree on any rate not exceeding fifteen per cent. On proof of illegal interest, plaintiff shall recover only principal.

Nevada. Legal interest ten per cent, unless agreement for more. But parties may agree for any rate.

New Jersey. Legal rate, seven per cent.

New Hampshire. Legal interest, six per cent. A person receiving more forfeits threefold the amount; but contracts are not invalidated by securing or taking more. If excess be paid, it may be recovered back.

New York. Legal rate, seven per cent. A contract for more than legal interest is wholly void. If more than legal interest is paid, it may be recovered back within a year by payer, or within the next three years by the overseers of the poor.

North Carolina. Interest, six per cent. For usury the taker forfeits double the sum lent.

Ohio. Legal interest, six per cent. More cannot be recovered.

Oregon. Legal interest, ten per cent. Parties may agree for twelve per cent. Usurious excess works a forfeiture of the principal and interest.

Pennsylvania. Legal interest, six per cent. Excess cannot be recovered.

Rhode Island. Legal interest, six per cent, unless otherwise specified.

South Carolina. Interest, seven per cent. More than legal interest cannot be recovered unless otherwise specified.

Tennessee. Legal interest, six per cent. More cannot be recovered.

Texas. Legal interest, eight per cent. Parties may agree in writing for twelve per cent. If more than this agreed for, no interest can be recovered.

Vermont. More than six per cent prohibited; and a person paying more may recover excess; but this is not to extend to the usage of farmers.

Virginia. Legal rate, six per cent. All contracts for a greater rate void. Excess, if paid, may be recovered back

West Virginia. Same as Virginia; but a new code is under consideration, which will probably make a change in the law of usury.

Wisconsin. Legal interest, seven per cent; but parties may agree upon a rate not exceeding ten per cent. Parties paying greater interest may recover three times the excess.

CHAPTER XVIII.

BANKRUPTCY.

The Constitution of the United States authorizes Congress to establish "uniform laws on the subject of bankruptcies throughout the United States." In 1800, a Bankrupt Law was passed, limited to five years; but it was repealed before it had been in operation three years. In 1841, another Bankrupt Law was passed, and was repealed eighteen months afterwards. In March, 1867, another

Bankrupt Law was passed: it is entitled "An Act to establish a Uniform System of Bankruptcy throughout the United States." This act is in force now. It is so well adjusted, and provides so carefully that fraud shall be prevented and justice done in all cases, and seems to be so generally useful and acceptable, that I think it will probably be permanent, and, without being repealed, will be amended from time to time as new exigencies arise, and as experience shows the need of new or different provisions. It contains forty-eight sections; and I will now give an abstract of all the sections, excepting those of the greatest and most frequent practical importance, and these I give in full.

SECTION 1. Makes the several District Courts of the United States Courts of Bankruptcy, with full jurisdiction over all cases which come before them, and arose within their districts.

SECT. 2. The several Circuit Courts of the United States shall have a general superintendence and jurisdiction of all cases and questions arising under this act.

SECT. 3. Concerns the appointment of registers in bankruptcy, the manner of the appointment, and who they may be.

SECT. 4. Describes the powers and duties of registers, and their fees.

SECT. 5. Provides for the proceedings before the registers, the removal of registers by the judge of the District Court, and the filling of the vacancy.

SECT. 6. That the register or the parties concerned may take the opinion of the judge of the District Court in cases or upon questions where that is desired.

SECT. 7. Provides for the attendance of parties and witnesses when and where summoned, and for the punishment of perjury.

SECTS. 8, 9, and 10. Relate to appeals from the District Court to the Circuit Court, and from the Circuit Court to the Supreme Court if the matter in dispute exceeds $2,000. And gives the Supreme Court power to provide rules, orders, and forms for practice under this act.

SECT. 11. States how a person wishing to be made a bankrupt may proceed, and what he must not do. This section I give in full.

Voluntary Bankruptcy.—Commencement of Proceedings.

SECT. 11. *And be it further enacted,* That if any person residing within the jurisdiction of the United States, owing debts provable under this act exceeding the amount of three hundred dollars, shall apply by petition, addressed to the judge of the judicial district in which such debtor has resided or carried on business for the six months next immediately preceding the time of filing such petition, or for the longest period during such six months, setting forth his place of residence, his inability to pay all his debts in full, his willingness to surrender all his estate and effects for the benefit of his creditors, and his desire to obtain the benefit of this act, and shall annex to his petition a schedule, verified by oath before the court, or before a register in bankruptcy, or before one of the commissioners of the circuit court of the United States, containing a full and true statement of all his debts, and, as far as possible, to whom due, with the place of residence of each creditor, if known to the debtor, and, if not known, the fact to be so stated, and the sum due to each creditor, also the nature of each debt or demand, whether founded on written security, obligation, contract, or otherwise, and also the true cause and consideration of such indebtedness in each case, and the place where such indebtedness accrued, and a statement of any existing mortgage, pledge, lien, judgment, or collateral or other security given for the payment of the same; and shall also annex to his petition an accurate inventory, verified in like manner, of all his estate, both real and personal, assignable under this act, describing the same, and stating where it is situated, and whether there are any, and, if so, what incumbrances thereon, the filing of such petition shall be an act of bankruptcy, and such petitioner shall be adjudged a bankrupt; *Provided* that all citizens of the United States, petitioning to be declared bankrupt, shall, in filing such petition, and before any proceedings thereon, take and subscribe an oath of allegiance and fidelity to the United States, which oath shall be filed and recorded with the proceedings in bankruptcy. And the judge of the district courts, or, if there be no opposing party, any register of said court, to be designated by the judge, shall forthwith, if he be satisfied that the debts due from the petitioner exceed three hundred dollars, issue a warrant, to be signed by such judge or register, directed to the marshal of said district, authorizing him forthwith, as messenger, to publish notices in such newspapers as the warrant specifies; to serve written or printed notice, by mail or personally, on all creditors upon the schedule filed with the debtor's petition, or whose names may be given to him, in addition, by the debtor, and to give such personal or other notice to any persons concerned as the warrant specifies, which notice shall state:

First, That a warrant in bankruptcy has been issued against the estate of the debtor.

Second, That the payment of any debts and the delivery of any property belonging to such debtor to him or for his use, and the transfer of any property by him, are forbidden by law.

Third, That a meeting of the creditors of the debtor, giving the names, residences, and amounts, so far as known, to prove their debts and choose one or more assignees of his estate, will be held at a court of bankruptcy, to be holden at a time and place designated in the warrant, not less than ten nor more than ninety days after the issuing of the same.

SECT. 12. Provides for the meetings of creditors, called under the preceding section.

SECTS. 13 and 14. Provide for the election or appointment, the duties, authority, and conduct of the assignee; determine what property shall be exempted, and what property must be transferred to the assignee. These sections I give in full.

Assignments and Assignees.

SECT. 13. *And be it further enacted,* That the creditors shall, at the first meeting held after due notice from the messenger, in presence of a register designated by the court, choose one or more assignees of the estate of the debtor; the choice to be made of the greater part in value and in number of the creditors who have proved their debts. If no choice is made by the creditors at said meeting, the judge, or, if there be no opposing interest, the register, shall appoint one or more assignees. If an assignee, so chosen or appointed, fails within five days to express in writing his acceptance of the trust, the judge or register may fill the vacancy. All elections or appointments of assignees shall be subject to the approval of the judge; and when in his judgment it is for any cause needful or expedient, he may appoint additional assignees, or order a new election. The judge at any time may, and, upon the request in writing of any creditor who has proved his claim, shall require the assignee to give good and sufficient bond to the United States, with a condition for the faithful performance and discharge of his duties; the bond shall be approved by the judge or register by his indorsement thereon, shall be filed with the record of the case, and inure to the benefit of all creditors proving their claims, and may be prosecuted in the name and for the benefit of any injured party. If the assignee fails to give the bond within such time as the judge orders, not exceeding ten days after notice to him of such order, the judge shall remove him, and appoint another in his place.

SECT. 14. *And be it further enacted,* That as soon as said assignee is appointed and qualified, the judge, or, where there is no opposing interest, the register, shall, by an instrument under his hand, assign and convey to the assignee all the estate, real and personal, of the bankrupt, with all his deeds, books, and papers relating thereto, and such assignment shall relate back to the commencement of said proceedings in bankruptcy, and thereupon, by operation of law, the title to all such property and estate, both real and personal, shall vest in said assignee, although the same is then attached on mesne process as the property of the debtor, and shall dissolve any such attachment made within four months next preceding the commencement of said proceedings: *Provided, however*, That there shall be excepted from the operation of the provisions of this section the necessary household and kitchen furniture, and such other articles and necessaries of such bankrupt as the said assignee shall designate and set apart, having reference in the amount to the family, condition, and circumstances of the bankrupt, but altogether not to exceed in value, in any case, the sum of five hundred dollars; and also the wearing apparel of such bankrupt, and that of his wife and children, and the uniform, arms, and equipments of any person who is or has been a soldier in the militia or in the service of the United States, and such other property as now is, or hereafter shall be, exempted from attachment or seizure, or levy on execution by the laws of the United States, and such other property not included in the foregoing exceptions as is exempted from levy and sale upon execution or other process, or order of any court, by the laws of the State in which the bankrupt has his domicile at the time of the commencement of the proceedings in bankruptcy, to an amount not exceeding that allowed by such State exemption laws in force in the year eighteen hundred and sixty-four. *Provided*, That the foregoing exception shall operate as a limitation upon the conveyance of the property of the bankrupt to his assignees, and in no case shall the property hereby excepted pass to the assignees, or the title of the bankrupt thereto be impaired or affected by any of the provisions of this act; and the determination of the assignee in the matter shall, on exception taken, be subject to the final decision of the said court: *And provided further*, That no mortgage of any vessel or of any other goods or chattels, made as security for any debt or debts, in good faith and for present considerations, and otherwise valid, and duly recorded, pursuant to any statute of the United States, or of any State, shall be invalidated or affected hereby; and all the property conveyed by the bankrupt in fraud of his creditors; all rights in equity, choses in action, patents, and patent rights and copyrights; all debts due him, or any person for his use, and all liens and securities therefor; and all his rights of action for property or estate, real or personal, and for any cause of action which the bankrupt had against any person arising from contract or from the unlawful taking or detention or of injury to the property of the bankrupt; and all his rights of redeeming such property or estate, with the like right, title, power, and authority to sell, manage, dispose of, sue for, and recover or defend the same, as the bankrupt might or could have had if no assignment had been made, shall, in virtue of the adjudication of bankruptcy and the appointment of his assignee, be at once vested in such assignee; and he may sue for and recover the said estate, debts, and effects, and may prosecute and defend all suits at law or in equity, pending at the time of the adjudication of bankruptcy, in which such bankrupt is a party in his own name, in the same manner and with the like effect as they might have been presented or defended by such bankrupt; and a copy, duly certified by the clerk of the court under the seal thereof, of the assignment made by the judge or register, as the case may be, to him as assignee, shall be conclusive evidence of his title as such assignee to take, hold, sue for, and recover the property of the bankrupt, as hereinbefore mentioned; but no property held by the bankrupt in trust shall pass by such assignment. No person shall be entitled to maintain an action against an assignee in bankruptcy for any thing done by him as such assignee, without previously giving him twenty days' notice of such action, specifying the cause thereof, to the end that such assignee may have an opportunity of tendering amends, should he see fit to do so. No person shall be entitled, as against the assignee, to withhold from him possession of any books of account of the bankrupt, or claim any lien thereon; and no suit in which the assignee is a party shall be abated by his death or removal from office, but the same may be prosecuted and defended by his successors, or by the surviving or remaining assignee, as the case may be. The assignee shall have authority, under the order and direction of the court, to redeem or discharge any mortgage or conditional contract, or pledge or deposit, or lien upon any property, real or personal, whenever payable, and to tender due performance of the condition thereof, or to sell the same subject to such mortgage, lien, or other incumbrances. The debtor shall also, at the request of the assignee, and at the expense of the estate, make and execute any instruments, deeds, and writings which may be proper, to enable the assignee to possess himself fully of all the assets of the bankrupt. The assignee shall immediately give notice of his appointment by publication, at least once a week for three successive weeks, in such newspapers as shall, for that purpose, be designated by the court, due regard being had to their general circulation in the district or in that portion of the district in which the bankrupt and his creditors shall reside, and shall, within six months, cause the assignment to him to be recorded in every registry of deeds or other office within the United States where a conveyance of any lands owned by the bankrupt ought by law to be recorded; and the record of such assignment, or a duly certified copy thereof, shall be evidence thereof in all courts.

SECT. 15. Gives some further direction to the assignee, as to demanding, receiving, and selling the property.

SECT. 16. Gives directions in relation to suits by the assignee to recover debts or other effects assigned to him.

SECT. 17. Gives directions as to the settlement by the assignee of the estate of the bankrupt; and gives him power to submit disputed demands against debtors to the estate, to arbitration, or to compound and settle them.

SECT. 18. Provides for death, resignation, or removal of the assignee, and filling the vacancy; and states the general duties of assignees.

SECT. 19. Relates to the debts of the bankrupt payable at the time of bankruptcy; and also his debts payable at a future time. This section I give in full.

SECT. 19. *And be it further enacted*, That all debts due and payable from the bankrupt at the time of the adjudication of bankruptcy, and all debts then existing but not payable until a future day, a rebate of interest being made when no interest is payable by the terms of contract, may be proved against the estate of the bankrupt. All demands against the bankrupt for or on account of any goods or chattels wrongfully taken, converted, or withheld by him, may be proved and allowed as debts to the amount of the value of the property so taken or withheld, with interest. If the bankrupt shall be bound as drawer, indorser, surety, bail, or guarantor upon any bill, bond, note, or any other specialty or contract, or for any debt of another person, and his liability shall not have become absolute until after the adjudication of bankruptcy, the creditor may prove the same after such liability shall have become fixed, and before the final dividend shall have been declared. In all cases of contingent debts and contingent liabilities contracted by the bankrupt, and not herein otherwise provided for, the creditor may make claim therefor, and have his claim allowed, with the right to share in the dividends, if the contingency shall happen before the order for the final dividend; or he may at any time apply to the court to have the present value of the debt or liability ascertained and liquidated, which shall then be done in such manner as the court shall order, and he shall be allowed to prove for the amount so ascertained. Any person liable as bail, surety, guarantor, or otherwise for the bankrupt, who shall have paid the debt or any part thereof in discharge of the whole, shall be entitled to prove such debt, or to stand in the place of the creditor if he shall have proved the same, although such payments shall have been made after the proceedings in bankruptcy were commenced. And any person so liable for the bankrupt, and who has not paid the whole of said debt, but is still liable for the same or any part thereof, may, if the creditor shall fail or omit to prove such debt, prove the same either in the name of the creditor or otherwise, as may be provided by the rules, and subject to such regulations and limitations as may be established by such rules. Where the bankrupt is liable to pay rent, or other debt falling due at fixed and stated periods, the creditor may prove for a proportionate part therof up to the time of the bankruptcy, as if the same grew due from day to day, and not at such fixed and stated periods. If any bankrupt shall be liable for unliquidated damages arising out of any contract or promise, or on account of any goods or chattels wrongfully taken, converted or withheld, the court may cause such damages to be assessed in such mode as it may deem best, and the sum so assessed may be proved against the estate. No debts other than those above specified shall be proved or allowed against the estate.

SECT. 20. Relates to mutual debts and set-offs; that the balance shall be struck.

SECT. 21. Prohibits a creditor who proves his debt from bringing any action against the bankrupt.

SECT. 22. Provides for proof of debts of the creditors of the bankrupts, whether individuals or corporations. It must be by oath or solemn affirmation, and other and further evidence if it be required. This proof may be made before a commissioner, and sent by him to the assignee. Debts or claims not duly and sufficiently proved are to be rejected.

SECT. 23. Provides for proof of debts before assignee is chosen; declares no creditor who has received any preference or advantage from the bankrupt shall receive any dividend unless he surrenders the preference or advantage, of whatever kind it may be, to the assignee.

SECT. 24. Provides for appeal from District Court to Circuit Court from a decision rejecting his claim.

SECT. 25. Court may order perishable property, or property to which right is disputed, to be sold.

SECT. 26. Relates to the attendance of bankrupts, and the examination of them, and their duties and rights. This section I give in full.

SECT. 26. *And be it further enacted*, That the court may, on the application of the assignee in bankruptcy, or of any creditor, or without any application, at all times require the bankrupt, upon reasonable notice, to attend and submit to an examination on oath, upon all matters relating to the disposal or condition of his property, to his trade and dealings with others, and his accounts concerning the same, to all debts due to or claimed from him, and to all other matters concerning his property and estate and the due settlement thereof according to law, which examination shall be in writing, and shall be signed by the bankrupt and be filed with the other proceedings; and the court may, in like manner, require the attendance of any other person as a witness, and if such person shall fail to attend, on being summoned thereto, the court may compel his attendance by warrant directed to the marshal, commanding him to arrest such person, and bring him forthwith before the court, or before a register in bankruptcy, for examination as such witness. If the bankrupt is imprisoned, absent, or disabled from attendance, the court may order him to be produced by the jailer, or any officer in whose custody he may be, or may direct the examination to be had, taken, and certified, at such time and place and in such manner as the court may deem proper, and with like effect as if such examination had been in court. The bankrupt shall at all times, until his discharge, be subject to the order of the court, and shall, at the expense of the estate, execute all proper writings and instruments, and do and perform all acts required by the court touching the assigned property or estate, and to enable the assignee to demand, recover, and receive all the property and estate assigned, wherever situated; and for neglect or refusal to obey any order of the court, such bankrupt may be committed and punished as for a contempt of court. If the bankrupt is without the district, and unable to return and personally attend at any of the times, or do any of the acts which may be specified or required pursuant to this section, and if it appears that such absence was not caused by wilful default, and if, as soon as may be after the removal of such impediment, he offers to attend and submit to the order of the court in all respects, he shall be permitted so to do, with like effect as if he had not been in default. He shall also be at liberty, from time to time, upon oath, to amend and correct his schedule of creditors and property, so that the same shall conform to the facts. For good cause shown, *the wife of* any bankrupt may be required to *attend* before the court, to the end that she may be examined as a witness; and if such wife do not attend at the time and place specified in the order, the bankrupt shall not be entitled to a discharge unless he shall prove to the satisfaction of the court that he was unable to procure the attendance of his wife. No bankrupt shall be liable to arrest during the pendency of the proceedings in bankruptcy in any civil action, unless the same is founded on some debt or claim from which his discharge or bankruptcy would not release him.

SECT. 27. Relates to the distribution of the bankrupt's estate. This section I give in full.

The Distribution of the Bankrupt's Estate.

SECT. 27. *And be it further enacted,* That all creditors whose debts are duly proved and allowed shall be entitled to share in the bankrupt's property and estate pro rata, without any priority or preference whatever, except that wages due from him to any operative, or clerk, or house-servant, to an amount not exceeding fifty dollars, for labor performed within six months next preceding the adjudication of bankruptcy, shall be entitled to priority, and shall be first paid in full: *Provided,* That any debt proved by any person liable as bail, surety, guarantor, or otherwise, for the bankrupt, shall not be paid to the person so proving the same until satisfactory evidence shall be produced of the payment of such debt by such person so liable, and the share to which such debt would be entitled may be paid into court, or otherwise held for the benefit of the party entitled thereto, as the court may direct. At the expiration of three months from the date of the adjudication of bankruptcy in any case, or as much earlier as the court may direct, the court, upon the request of the assignee, shall call a general meeting of the creditors, of which due notice shall be given, and the assignee shall then report, and exhibit to the court and to the creditors just and true accounts of all his receipts and payments, verified by his oath, and he shall produce and file vouchers for all payments for which vouchers shall be required by any rule of the court; he shall also submit the schedule of the bankrupt's creditors and property as amended, duly verified by the bankrupt, and a statement of the whole estate of the bankrupt as then ascertained, of the property recovered and of the property outstanding, specifying the cause of its being outstanding, also what debts or claims are yet undetermined, and stating what sum remains in his hands. At such meeting the majority in value of the creditors present shall determine whether any and what part of the net proceeds of the estate, after deducting and retaining a sum sufficient to provide for all undetermined claims, which, by reason of the distant residence of the creditor, or for other sufficient reason, have not been proved, and for other expenses and contingencies, shall be divided among the creditors; but unless at least one-half in value of the creditors shall attend such meeting, either in person or by attorney, it shall be the duty of the assignee so to determine. In case a dividend is ordered the register shall, within ten days after such meeting, prepare a list of creditors entitled to dividend, and shall calculate and set opposite to the name of each creditor who has proved his claim the dividend to which he is entitled out of the net proceeds of the estate set apart for dividend, and shall forward by mail to every creditor a statement of the dividend to which he is entitled, and such creditor shall be paid by the assignee in such manner as the court may direct.

SECT. 28. Relates to subsequent meetings of the creditors, dividends, compensation of assignee, and order of dividend and payment from bankrupt's estate. This section I give in full.

SECT. 28. *And be it further enacted*, That the like proceedings shall be had at the expiration of the next three months, or earlier, if practicable, and a third meeting of creditors shall then be called by the court, and a final dividend then declared, unless any action at law or suit in equity be pending, or unless some other estate or effects of the debtor afterwards come to the hands of the assignee, in which case the assignee shall, as soon as may be, convert such estate or effects into money, and within two months after the same shall be so converted, the same shall be divided in manner aforesaid. Further dividends shall be made in like manner as often as occasion requires; and after the third meeting of creditors, no further meeting shall be called, unless ordered by the court. If at any time there shall be in the hands of the assignee any outstanding debts or other property, due or belonging to the estate, which cannot be collected and received by the assignee without unreasonable or inconvenient delay or expense, the assignee may, under the direction of the court, sell and assign such debts or other property in such manner as the court shall order. No dividend already declared shall be disturbed by reason of debts being subsequently proved; but the creditors proving such debts shall be entitled to a dividend equal to those already received by the other creditors before any further payment is made to the latter. Preparatory to the final dividend, the assignee shall submit his account to the court, and file the same, and give notice to the creditors of such filing, and shall also give notice that he will apply for a settlement of his account, and for a discharge from all liability as assignee, at a time to be specified in such notice; and at such time the court shall audit and pass the accounts of the assignee, and such assignee shall, if required by the court, be examined as to the truth of such account, and, if found correct, he shall thereby be discharged from all liability as assignee to any creditor of the bankrupt. The court shall thereupon order a dividend of the estate and effects, or of such part thereof as it sees fit, among such of the creditors as have proved their claims, in proportion to the respective amount of their said debts. In addition to all expenses necessarily incurred by him in the execution of his trust, in any case, the assignee shall be entitled to an allowance for his services in such case, on all moneys received and paid out by him therein, for any sum not exceeding one thousand dollars, five per centum thereon; for any larger sum, not exceeding five thousand dollars, two and a half per centum on the excess over one thousand dollars; and for any larger sum, one per centum on the excess over five thousand dollars; and if, at any time, there shall not be in his hands a sufficient amount of money to defray the necessary expenses required for the further execution of his trust, he shall not be obliged to proceed therein until the necessary funds are advanced or satisfactorily secured to him. If, by accident, mistake or other cause, without fault of the assignee, either or both of the said second and third meetings should not be held within the times limited, the court may, upon motion of an interested party, order such meetings, with like effect as to the validity of the proceedings as if the meeting had been duly held. In the order for a dividend, under this section, the following claims shall be entitled to priority or preference, and to be first paid in full in the following order: —

First, The fees, costs, and expenses of suits, and the several proceedings in bankruptcy under this act, and for the custody of property, as herein provided.

Second, All debts due to the United States, and all taxes and assessments under the laws thereof.

Third, All debts due to the State in which the proceedings in bankruptcy are pending, and all taxes and assessments made under the laws of such State.

Fourth, Wages due to any operative, clerk, or house-servant, to an amount not exceeding fifty dollars, for labor performed within six months next preceding the first publication of the notice of proceedings in bankruptcy.

Fifth, All debts due to any persons who, by the laws of the United States, are or may be entitled to a priority or preference, in like manner as if this act had not been passed: *Always provided,* That nothing contained in this act shall interfere with the assessment and collection of taxes by the authority of the United States or any State.

SECTS. 29, 30, 31, 32, 33, and 34. Relate to the discharge of the bankrupt, and its effect. These sections I give in full.

The Bankrupt's Discharge, and its Effect.

SECT. 29. *And, be it further enacted,* That at any time after the expiration of six months from the adjudication of bankruptcy, or if no debts have been proved against the bankrupt, or if no assets have come to the hands of the assignee, at any time after the expiration of sixty days, and within one year from the adjudication of bankruptcy, the bankrupt may apply to the court for a discharge from his debts, and the court shall thereupon order notice to be given by mail to all creditors who have proved their debts, and *by publication* at least once a week in such newspapers as the court shall designate, due regard being had to the general circulation of the same in the district, or in that portion of the district in which the bankrupt and his creditors shall reside, to appear on a day appointed for that purpose, and show cause why a discharge should not be granted to the bankrupt. No discharge shall be granted, or, if granted, be valid, if the bankrupt has wilfully sworn falsely in his affidavit annexed to his petition, schedule, or inventory, or upon any examination in the course of the proceedings in bankruptcy, in relation to any material fact concerning his estate or his debts, or to any other material fact: or if he has concealed any part of his estate or effects, or any books or writings relating thereto, or if he has been guilty of any fraud or negligence in the care, custody, or delivery to the assignee of the property belonging to him at the time of the presentation of his petition and inventory, excepting such property as he is permitted to retain under the provisions of this act, or if he has caused, permitted, or suffered any loss, waste, or destruction thereof; or if, within four months before the commencement of such proceedings, he has procured his lands, goods, money, or chattels to be attached, sequestered, or seized on execution; or if, since the passage of this act, he has destroyed, mutilated, altered, or falsified any of his books, documents, papers, writings, or securities, or has made or been privy to the making of any false or fraudulent entry in any book of account or other document, with intent to defraud his creditors; or has removed or caused to be removed any part of his property from the district, with intent to defraud his creditors; or if he has given any fraudulent preference contrary to the provisions of this act, or made any fraudulent payment, gift, transfer, conveyance, or assignment of any part of his property, or has lost any part thereof in gaming, or has admitted a false or fictitious debt against his estate; or if, having knowledge that any person has proved such false or fictitious debt, he has not disclosed the same to his assignee within one month after such knowledge; or if, being a merchant or tradesman, he has not, subsequently to the passage of this act, kept proper books of account; or if he, or any person in his behalf, has procured the assent of any creditor to the discharge, or influenced the action of any creditor at any stage of the proceedings, by any pecuniary consideration or obligation; or if he has, in contemplation of becoming bankrupt, made any pledge, payment, transfer, assignment, or conveyance of any part of his property, directly or indirectly, absolutely or conditionally, for the purpose of preferring any creditor or person having a claim against him, or who is or may be under liability for him, or for the purpose of preventing the property from coming into the hands of the assignee, or of being distributed under this act in satisfaction of his debts; or if he has been convicted of any misdemeanor under this act, or has been guilty of any fraud whatever contrary to the true intent of this act; and before any discharge is granted, the bankrupt shall take and subscribe an oath to the effect that he has not done, suffered, or been privy to any act, matter, or thing specified in this act as a ground for withholding such discharge, or as invalidating such discharge if granted.

SECT. 30. *And be it further enacted*, That no person who shall have been discharged under this act, and shall afterwards become bankrupt, *on his own application*, shall be again entitled to a discharge whose estate is insufficient to pay seventy per centum of the debts proved against it, unless the assent in writing of three-fourths in value of his creditors who have proved their claims is filed at or before the time of application for discharge; but a bankrupt who shall prove to the satisfaction of the court that he has paid all the debts owing by him at the time of any previous bankruptcy, or who has been voluntarily released therefrom by his creditors, shall be entitled to a discharge in the same manner and with the same effect as if he had not previously been bankrupt.

SECT. 31. *And it is further enacted*, That any creditor opposing the discharge of any bankrupt may *file* a specification in writing of the grounds of his opposition, *and the court may, in its discretion, order any question of fact so presented to be tried at a stated session of the district court.*

SECT. 32. *And be it further enacted*, That if it shall appear to the court that the bankrupt has in all things conformed to his duty under this act, and that he is entitled, under the provisions thereof, to receive a discharge, the court shall grant him a discharge from all his debts except as hereinafter provided, and shall give him a certificate thereof under the seal of the court, in substance as follows:

District Court of the United States. District of   Whereas
has been duly adjudged a bankrupt under the act of Congress establishing a uniform system of bankruptcy throughout the United States, and appears to have conformed to all the requirements of law in that behalf, it is therefore ordered by the court that said   be forever discharged from all debts and claims which by said act are made provable against his estate, and which existed on the
day of   , on which day the petition for adjudication was filed by (or against) him; excepting such debts, if any, as are by said act excepted from the operation of a discharge in bankruptcy. Given under my hand and the seal of the Court at
                    in the said district, this   day of   , A.D.

(*Seal.*)   , *Judge.*

SECT. 33. *And be it further enacted*, That no debt created by the fraud or embezzlement of the bankrupt, or by his defalcation as a public officer, or while acting in any fiduciary character, shall be discharged under this act; but the debt may be proved, and the dividend thereon shall be a payment on account of said debt; and no discharge granted under this act shall release, discharge, or affect any person liable for the same debt for or with the bankrupt, either as partner, joint contractor, indorser, surety, or otherwise. [And in all proceedings in bankruptcy commenced after one year from the time this act shall go into operation, no discharge shall be granted to a debtor whose assets do not pay fifty per centum of the claims against his estate, unless the assent in writing of a majority in number and value of his creditors who have proved their claims is filed in the case at or before the time of application for discharge.]

SECT. 34. *And be it further enacted*, That a discharge duly granted under this act shall, with the exceptions aforesaid, release the bankrupt from all debts, claims, liabilities, and demands which were or might have been proved against his estate in bankruptcy, and may be pleaded, by a simple averment that on the day of its date such discharge was granted to him, setting the same forth in hæc verba, as a full and complete bar to all suits brought on any such debts, claims, liabilities, or demands, and the certificate shall be conclusive evidence in favor of such bankrupt of the fact and the regularity of such discharge: *Always provided*, That any creditor or creditors of said bankrupt, whose debt was proved or provable against the estate in bankruptcy, who shall see fit to contest the validity of said discharge on the ground that it was fraudulently obtained, may, at any time within [two years] after the date thereof, apply to the court which granted it to set aside and annul the same. Said application shall be in writing, shall specify which, in particular, of the several acts mentioned in section twenty-nine it is intended to give evidence of against the bankrupt, setting forth the grounds of avoidance, and no evidence shall be admitted as to any other of the said acts; but said application shall be subject to amendment at the discretion of the court. The court shall cause reasonable notice of said application to be given to said bankrupt, and order him to appear and answer the same, within such time as to the court shall seem fit and proper. If, upon the hearing of said parties, the court shall find that the fraudulent acts, or any of them, set forth as aforesaid by said creditor or creditors against the bankrupt, are proved, and that said creditor or creditors had no knowledge of the same until after the granting of said discharge, judgment shall be given in favor of said creditor or creditors, and the discharge of said bankrupt shall be set aside and annulled. But if said court shall find that said fraudulent acts, and all of them, set forth as aforesaid, are not proved, or that they were known to said creditor or creditors before the granting of said discharge, then judgment shall be rendered in favor of the bankrupt, and the validity of his discharge shall not be affected by said proceedings.

SECT. 35. Relates to fraudulent conveyances or transfers by the bankrupt, declares them to be void, and defines what are such conveyances or transfers. This section I give in full.

Preferences and Fraudulent Conveyances Declared Void.

SECT. 35. *And be it further enacted*, That if any person, being insolvent, or in contemplation of insolvency, within four months before the filing of the petition by or against him, with a view to give a preference to any creditor or person having a claim against him, or who is under any liability for him, procures any part of his property to be attached, sequestered, or seized on execution, or makes any payment, pledge, assignment, transfer, or conveyance of any part of his property, either directly or indirectly, absolutely or conditionally, the person receiving such payment, pledge, assignment, transfer, or conveyance, or to be benefited thereby, or by such attachment, having reasonable cause to believe such person is insolvent, and that such attachment, payment, pledge, assignment, or conveyance is made in fraud of the provisions of this act, the same shall be void, and the assignee may recover the property, or the value of it, from the person so receiving it, or so to be benefited; and if any person being insolvent, or in contemplation of insolvency or bankruptcy, within six months before the filing of the petition by or against him, makes any payment, sale, assignment, transfer, conveyance, or other disposition of any part of his property to any person who then has reasonable cause to believe him to be insolvent, or to be acting in contemplation of insolvency, and that such payment, sale, assignment, transfer, or other conveyance, is made with a view to prevent his property from coming to his assignee in bankruptcy, or to prevent the same from being distributed under this act, or to defeat the object of, or in any way impair, hinder, impede, or delay the operation and effect of, or to evade any of the provisions of this act, the sale, assignment, transfer, or conveyance shall be void, and the assignee may recover the property, or the value thereof, as assets of the bankrupt. And if such sale, assignment, transfer, or conveyance is not made in the usual and ordinary course of business of the debtor, the fact shall be prima facie evidence of fraud. Any contract, covenant, or security made or given by a bankrupt or other person with, or in trust for, any creditor, for securing the payment of any money as a consideration for or with intent to induce the creditor to forbear opposing the application for discharge of the bankrupt, shall be void; and if any creditor shall obtain any sum of money or other goods, chattels, or security from any person as an inducement for forbearing to oppose, or consenting to such application for discharge, every creditor so offending shall forfeit all right to any share or dividend in the estate of the bankrupt, and shall also forfeit double the value or amount of such money, goods, chattels, or security so obtained, to be recovered by the assignee for the benefit of the estate.

SECTS. 36 and 37. Relate to the bankruptcy of partnerships or corporations, and apply to them the provisions of this act.

SECT. 38. Provides that the filing of the petition for bankruptcy shall be taken as the beginning of the proceedings, and also for the taking of testimony by depositions.

SECT. 39. Relates to what is called Involuntary Bankruptcy, or bankruptcy on the petition of a creditor. This section I give in full.

Involuntary Bankruptcy.

SECT. 39. *And be it further enacted*, That any person residing and owing debts as aforesaid, who, after the passage of this act, shall depart from the State, district, or Territory, of which he is an inhabitant, with intent to defraud his creditors, or, being absent, shall, with such intent, remain absent; or shall conceal himself to avoid the service of legal process in any action for the recovery of a debt or demand provable under this act; or shall conceal and remove any of his property to avoid its being attached, taken, or sequestered on legal process; or shall make any assignment, gift, sale, conveyance, or transfer of his estate, property, rights, or credits, either within the United States or elsewhere, with intent to delay, defraud, or hinder his creditors; or who has been arrested and held in custody under or by virtue of mesne process of execution, issued out of any court of any State, district, or Territory, within which such debtor resides or has property, founded upon a demand in its nature provable against a bankrupt's estate under this act, and for a sum exceeding one hundred dollars, and such process is remaining in force and not discharged by payment, or in any other manner provided by the law of such State, district, or Territory applicable thereto, for a period of seven days; or has been actually imprisoned for more than seven days in a civil action, founded on contract, for the sum of one hundred dollars or upwards; or who, being bankrupt or insolvent, or in contemplation of bankruptcy or insolvency, shall make any payment, gift, grant, sale, conveyance, or transfer of money, or other property, estate, rights, or credits, or give any warrant to confess judgment, or procure or suffer his property to be taken on legal process, with intent to give a preference to one or more of his creditors, or to any person or persons who are or may be liable for him as indorsers, bail, sureties, or otherwise, or with the intent, by such disposition of his property, to defeat or delay the operation of this act; or who, being a banker, merchant, or trader, has fraudulently stopped or suspended and not resumed payment of his commercial paper, within a period of fourteen days, shall be deemed to have committed an act of bankruptcy, and, subject to the conditions hereinafter prescribed, shall be adjudged a bankrupt, on the petition of one or more of his creditors, the aggregate of whose debts provable under this act amount to at least two hundred and fifty dollars, provided such petition is brought within six months after the act of bankruptcy shall have been committed. And if such person shall be adjudged a bankrupt, the assignee may recover back the money or other property so paid, conveyed, sold, assigned, or transferred contrary to this act, provided the person receiving such payment or conveyance had reasonable cause to believe that a fraud on this act was intended, or that the debtor was insolvent, and such creditor shall not be allowed to prove his debt in bankruptcy.

SECTS. 40, 41, 42. Regulate the proceedings under such a petition.

SECT. 43. Relates to the superseding of the proceedings in bankruptcy, by placing the property in the hands of trustees, if three-fourths in value of the creditors desire it. This section I give in full.

Of Superseding the Bankrupt Proceedings by Arrangement.

SECT. 43. *And be it further enacted,* That if at the first meeting of creditors, or at any meeting of creditors to be specially called for that purpose, and of which previous notice shall have been given for such length of time and in such manner as the court may direct, three-fourths in value of the creditors whose claims have been proved shall determine and resolve that it is for the interest of the general body of the creditors that the estate of the bankrupt should be wound up and settled, and distribution made among the creditors by trustees, under the inspection and direction of a committee of the creditors, it shall be lawful for the creditors to certify and report such resolution to the court, and to nominate one or more trustees to take and hold and distribute the estate, under the direction of such committee. If it shall appear to the court, after hearing the bankrupt and such creditors as may desire to be heard, that the resolution was duly passed and that the interests of the creditors will be promoted thereby, it shall confirm the same; and upon the execution and filing, by or on behalf of three-fourths in value of all the creditors whose claims have been proved, of a consent that the estate of the bankrupt be wound up and settled by said trustees, according to the terms of such resolution, the bankrupt, or his assignee in bankruptcy, if appointed, as the case may be, shall, under the direction of the court, and under oath, convey, transfer, and deliver all the property and estate of the bankrupt to the said trustee or trustees, who shall, upon such conveyance and transfer, have and hold the same in the same manner, and with the same powers and rights, in all respects, as the bankrupt would have had or held the same if no proceedings in bankruptcy had been taken; or as the assignee in bankruptcy would have done had such resolution not been passed; and such consent and the proceedings thereunder shall be as binding in all respects on any creditor whose debt is provable, who has not signed the same, as if he had signed it, and on any creditor whose debt, if provable, is not proved, as if he had proved it; and the court, by order, shall direct all acts and things needful to be done to carry into effect such resolution of the creditors; and the said trustees shall proceed to wind up and settle the estate under the direction and inspection of such committee of the creditors, for the equal benefit of all such creditors, and the winding up and settlement of any estate under the provisions of this section shall be deemed to be proceedings in bankruptcy under this act; and the said trustees shall have all the rights and powers of assignees in bankruptcy. The court, on the application of such trustees, shall have power to summon and examine, on oath or otherwise, the bankrupt, and any creditor, and any person indebted to the estate, or known or suspected of having any of the estate in his possession, or any other person whose examination may be material or necessary to aid the trustees in the execution of their trust, and to compel the attendance of such persons and the production of books and papers in the same manner as in other proceedings in bankruptcy under this act; and the bankrupt shall have the like right to apply for and obtain a discharge after the passage of such resolution and the appointment of such trustees as if such resolution had not been passed, and as if all the proceedings had continued in the manner provided in the preceding sections of this act. If the resolution shall not be duly reported, or the consent of the creditors shall not be duly filed, or if, upon its filing, the court shall not think fit to approve thereof, the bankruptcy shall proceed as though no resolution had been passed, and the court may make all necessary orders for resuming the proceedings. And the period of time which shall have elapsed between the date of the resolution and the date of the order for resuming the proceedings shall not be reckoned in calculating periods of time prescribed by this act.

SECT. 44. Provides that debtors, who, after the commencement of proceedings in bankruptcy (which means the filing of the petition), fraudulently conceal any property, or hinder the assignee from getting hold of it, or spend any part of it in gaming, or, within three months next before the petition, dispose of any property otherwise than by honest transactions in his trade, which property was bought on credit and is unpaid for, shall be punished by imprisonment not exceeding three years.

SECT. 45. Provides that defaulting officers shall be punished by a fine not less than three hundred nor more than five hundred dollars, and imprisonment not more than three years.

SECT. 46. Provides that forgery or counterfeiting of any court seal, any court paper, or the tendering for use of any document so forged or counterfeited, shall be punished by a fine not less than five hundred nor more than five thousand dollars, and imprisonment not exceeding five years.

SECT. 47. Relates to fees and costs of proceedings.

SECT. 48. Gives the meaning and definition of sundry words used in the act.

SECT. 49. Gives jurisdiction in cases of bankruptcy to the Supreme Court of the District of Columbia and of the several Territories, when the bankrupt resides therein.

SECT. 50. Declares that the act goes into force when approved, but no petition can be filed before 1st of June, 1867. On July 25, 1868, a short amendatory act was passed, as follows: —

Amendatory Act of 1868.

A BILL IN AMENDMENT TO AN ACT ENTITLED "AN ACT TO ESTABLISH A UNIFORM SYSTEM OF BANKRUPTCY THROUGHOUT THE UNITED STATES," APPROVED MARCH 2, 1867.

Be it enacted, &c., That the provisions of the second clause of the 33d section of said act shall not apply to cases of proceedings in bankruptcy commenced prior to the first day of January, 1869, and the time, during which the operation of the provisions of said clause is postponed, shall be extended until the said first day of January, 1869, and said clause is so amended as to read as follows: —

In all proceedings in bankruptcy commenced after the first day of January, 1869, no discharge shall be granted to a debtor whose assets shall not be equal to fifty per centum of the claims proved against his estate, upon which he shall be liable as the principal debtor, unless the assent in writing of a majority in number and value of his creditors to whom he shall have become liable as principal debtor, and who shall have proved their claims, be filed in the case at or before the time of the hearing of the application for discharge.

SECT. 2. *And be it further enacted*, That said act be further amended as follows: The phrase "presented or defended," in the 14th section of said act, shall read "prosecuted or defended." The phrase "nor resident debtors," in line 5, section 22, of the act as printed in the statute at large, shall read "non-resident creditors;" that the word "or," in the next to the last line of the 39th section of the act, shall read "and;" that the phrase "section 13," in the 42d section, shall read "section 11;" and the phrase "or spends any part thereof in gaming," in the 44th section of said act, shall read "or shall spend any part thereof in gaming;" and that the words "with the senior register or," and the phrase "to be delivered to the register," in the 47th section of said act, be stricken out.

SECT. 3. *And be it further enacted*, That the register in bankruptcy shall have power to administer oaths in all cases and in relation to all matters in which oaths may be administered by commissioners of the circuit courts of the United States, and such commissioners may take proof of debts in bankruptcy in all cases, subject to the revision of such proofs by the register and by the court, according to the provisions of said act.

Approved July 25, 1868.

The various forms required are not given here, because they have been issued on the authority of the Supreme Court of the United States, and are uniform throughout the States, and are supplied by the Registers of bankruptcy to every applicant; and to one of them every person desiring to become a bankrupt, and every person desiring to bring another person into bankruptcy, must apply.

In the District Court of the United States for the Southern District of New York, the Hon. Judge Blatchford has established certain rules for practice under the Bankrupt Law. Resting on his high authority, and the usage of the principal centre of business in the country, these rules will doubtless be regarded everywhere; and the practice in all the States will be in substantial conformity with them. These rules are as follows: —

Rules in Bankruptcy.

Rule 1. — In voluntary bankruptcy, where the petition states that the debtor, whether an individual, a copartnership, a corporation, or a joint-stock company, has resided or carried on business for the six months next immediately preceding the time of filing the petition, or for the longest period during such six months, in the city and county of New York, the petitions shall be referred, in rotation, by Form No. 4, to the several registers, appointed in the six Congressional districts therein, commencing with the fourth, and ending with the ninth, in the order of the times of filing such petitions; and where in any other county, the petition shall be referred, by Form No. 4, to the register appointed in the Congressional district in which such county is embraced. A petition may be otherwise referred for special reasons, or in cases not herein provided for. In involuntary bankruptcy, the register will be designated with reference to the special circumstances of each case.

The order, Form No. 4, designating the register to act upon the petition, in voluntary bankruptcy, shall, in the case of a register in any district in the city and county of New York, specify as the place where the register shall act upon the matters arising under the case, and the warrant, Form No. 59, in involuntary bankruptcy, shall, in a like case, specify as the place where the meeting of the creditors will be held, the office of the register as designated by him, by a writing filed with the clerk. In the case of a register in any district other than one in the city and county of New York, the order, Form No. 4, in voluntary bankruptcy, shall specify as the place where the register shall act upon the matters arising under the case, an office of the register as designated by him in like manner, in the county in which is the place of residence of the petitioner, or the place of business of the copartnership, corporation, or joint-stock company, as set forth in the petition, having due regard always to the proximity and convenience of such office to such place of residence or place of business; and, in a like case, in the warrant, Form No. 59, in involuntary bankruptcy, the place will be designated with reference to the special circumstances of the case.

The day named in the order, Form No. 4, for the attendance of the bankrupt before the register, in voluntary bankruptcy, and the day named in the warrant, Form No. 59, for the meeting of creditors, in involuntary bankruptcy, will be fixed with reference to the convenient and speedy progress of the case.

Every register in a district other than the city and county of New York shall, by a writing filed with the clerk, designate the days on which he will attend at a place or places within each county in his district.

Every register may, in any case referred to him, fix the times when he will act upon the several matters arising under such case, other than the attendance of the bankrupt, as fixed by the order, Form No. 4, and the meeting of creditors as fixed by the warrant, Form No. 59; but the register shall not, without leave of the court, be at liberty to change the place specified in the order, Form No. 4, or to act upon the matters arising under a case in involuntary bankruptcy at any other place than the one specified in the warrant, Form No. 59, as the place for the meeting of creditors.

Rule 2. — The adjudication of bankruptcy, Form No. 58, shall contain a provision that the case be referred to one of the registers, naming him, to take such proceedings thereon as are required by the act.

Rule 3. — Whenever a petition is referred to a register in a voluntary case, and whenever, in an involuntary case, an order is made on an adjudication of bankruptcy, referring the case to a register, the clerk at the time he sends or delivers to the register a copy of the order of reference, shall pay to him the sum of fifteen dollars out of the fifty dollars deposited with the clerk, under Section 47 of the act, the same to be applied to the payment of such fees of the register as are chargeable to the petitioner making the deposit. Whenever by a return made to the court, under oath, by the register, of the fees so chargeable for services rendered by him, it shall appear that the aggregate amount of such fees exceeds the aggregate payments made thereon to the register out of the fifty dollars, the clerk shall, if requested by the register, make further payments to him thereon to the amount of such fees, until the fifty dollars shall all of it be paid out, and thereafter the fees of the register which are chargeable to such petitioner shall be paid or secured in like manner with the other fees provided for by Rule 29, of the "General Orders in Bankruptcy."

The foregoing provisions of this rule shall not apply to a case of voluntary bankruptcy, where under Rule 30 of the "General Orders in Bankruptcy," the judge shall direct that the fees and costs in the case shall not exceed the sum required by the act to be deposited with the clerk; but, in every such case, such of the disbursements paid out by the register and marshal for the purposes specified in Rule 12 of the "General Orders in Bankruptcy," and returned by them under oath, under said Rule 12, as are chargeable to the petitioning debtor, shall be refunded to them severally by the clerk out of such sum; and the clerk, marshal, and register shall perform the duties required of them by such petitioning debtor without first requiring payment or security for their fees, subject to the application by the court to such fees, of so much of such sum as shall remain after refunding such disbursements.

Ordered, That Rule 3 of the Rules, Orders, and Regulations, in Bankruptcy, prescribed by this court, June 22, 1867, be amended by striking out the word "fifteen," and inserting the word "twenty-five," and by striking out the words "under oath," where they first occur in said rule.

Passed July 1, A.D. 1867.

Rule 4. — The register shall, under Rule 7 of the "General Orders in Bankruptcy," examine the duplicate copy of the petition and schedules specified in Form No. 4, and such duplicate copy shall either be a copy of such filed original, certified by the clerk under the seal of the court, or else a duplicate original, signed and verified in like manner with the original petition and schedules filed with the clerk, and shown by evidence satisfactory to the register to be such duplicate original; and the certificate of the register, required by said Rule 7, as to the correctness in form of the petition and schedules, shall be made in writing, and be signed by him, on the duplicate copy which he so examines; and he shall not issue any warrant under Form No. 6, until he shall have so made a certificate, after such examination, that the petition and schedules are correct in form. No such certificate shall be made unless the whole eleven of the sheets composing schedules A and B, in Form No. 1, form part of the schedules to the petition.

Rule 5. — The warrant issued under Section 11 or Section 42 of the act, according to Form No. 6 or Form No. 59, shall specify two, if there be two, and if not, then one of the newspapers named in Rule 21, published in the county stated in the petition as the one in which the debtor, whether an individual, a copartnership, a corporation, or a joint-stock company, has resided or carried on business for the six months next immediately preceding the time of filing the petition, or for the longest period during such six months, the selection of such newspapers to be made by the petitioner, or his attorney, or, in default thereof, by the register to whom the petition or case is referred; but in the city and county of New York, one of them shall be a morning paper, and one an evening paper. The notices to be published in pursuance of the warrant shall be published twice in each newspaper selected.

The warrant shall designate the creditors on whom personal service is to be made, and notice shall be served by mail upon all creditors other than those so designated. No creditor resident out of this district shall be designated for personal service.

Whenever a debtor shall furnish, at his own expense, to the marshal, printed copies of the notices required to be served by the warrant, no fee shall be allowed to the marshal for copying into the notices the names and places of residences of the creditors, and the amounts of their debts.

The warrant, Form No. 6, shall be regarded as process under Rule 2 of the "General Orders in Bankruptcy," and such warrant shall, before it is issued to the marshal, in addition to being signed by the clerk, and sealed with the seal of the court, be signed by the judge or the register at the foot thereof, in the following form, with the date: "Issued by me, 18 , *District Judge* [or *Register in Bankruptcy*."]

Whenever the order Form No. 10 is used by a register, the conclusion of said Form may be varied so that the order may be attested or signed by the register alone.

Ordered, That Rule 5 of said Rules, Orders, and Regulations, be amended by striking out the words "by the petitioner or his attorney, or in default thereof;" and also by striking out the words "but in the city and county of New York, one of them shall be a morning paper, and one an evening paper."

Passed July 1, A.D. 1867.

Rule 6. — All proofs of debt which shall be made and verified prior to the election or appointment of an assignee shall be delivered or sent to the register to whom the case is referred. If the register entertains doubts of the validity of any claim, or of the right of a creditor to prove it, and is of opinion that such validity or right ought to be investigated by the assignee, he may postpone the proof of the claim until the assignee is chosen.

Rule 7. — In case no choice of an assignee is made by the creditors at their first meeting, or in case an assignee, chosen by the creditors, fails within five days to express in writing his acceptance of the trust, or in case of a vacancy in the office of an assignee, caused by his removal, resignation, death, or other cause, John Sedgwick, Esquire, of the city of New York, counsellor at law, will be appointed assignee where the judge is required by the act to appoint the assignee, and also where the assignee is appointable by the register, subject to the approval of the judge. In special cases, vacancies in the office of assignee will be filled by an election by the creditors.

Ordered, That Rule 7 of said Rules, Orders, and Regulations, be amended by striking out the words "also where the assignee is appointable by the register subject to the approval of the judge," and inserting instead the following: "where the said John Sedgwick shall be appointed by any register, such appointment is hereby approved by the judge;" and also by striking out the last sentence, and inserting instead the following: "In special cases, vacancies in the office of assignee will be filled by an election by the creditors, or by the appointment of an assignee other than the one above named."

Passed July 1, A.D. 1867.

Rule 8. — Under Rule 9 of the "General Orders in Bankruptcy," an assignee shall notify the register of his acceptance or rejection of the trust, and the register shall immediately, on receiving such notice, report it to the clerk of the court.

Rule 9. — Every assignee shall, immediately on receiving an assignment of an estate in bankruptcy, send or deliver such assignment to the clerk of the court, who shall make a true copy of it, and certify such copy under his hand and the seal of the court; and such certified copy shall then be placed by him on file, and the original assignment shall be returned to the assignee.

Rule 10. — Notice of the appointment of an assignee shall be given by publication once a week for three successive weeks in two of the newspapers named in Rule 21, at least one of which shall be a newspaper published in the city and county of New York; such newspapers to be selected by the assignee with due regard to the requirements of Section 14 of the act.

Ordered, That Rule 10 of said Rules, Orders, and Regulations, be amended by striking out the word "assignee," where it last occurs, and inserting instead the word "register."

Passed July 1, A.D. 1867.

Rule 11. — Notices of sale by an assignee under Rule 21 of the "General Orders in Bankruptcy," shall be advertised in two, if there be two, and if not, then in one of the newspapers named in Rule 21, published in the county where the sale is to take place, the selection of such newspapers to be made by the assignee; but in the city and county of New York, one of them shall be a morning paper, and one an evening paper.

Ordered, That Rule 11 of said Rules, Orders, and Regulations, be amended by striking out the words "assignee; but in the city and county of New York, one of them shall be a morning paper, and one an evening paper," and inserting instead the word "register."

Passed July 1, A.D. 1867.

Rule 12. — The notice to creditors of dividends or meetings required by the 17th, 27th, and 28th Sections of the act, shall be such as is provided for by the order contained in Form No. 28; and the assignee shall select one newspaper, in which the notice shall be published, from among the newspapers specified in Rule 21.

Ordered, That Rule 12 of said Rules, Orders, and Regulations, be amended by striking out the word "assignee," and inserting instead the word "register."

Passed July 1, A.D. 1867.

Rule 13. — The list of debts provided for by Section 23 of the act shall be made and certified by the register to whom the petition or case is referred, and he shall place thereon all debts which are duly proved.

Rule 14. — The assignee shall, under Section 27 of the act, produce and file vouchers for all payments made by him, except as to items in regard to which the court shall, for reasonable cause, dispense with vouchers.

Rule 15. — The notice by the assignee, under Section 28 of the act, of the filing of his account, and of his application for a settlement and discharge, shall be given by him by sending written or printed notices by mail, prepaid, of such filing, and of the time of such application, to all known creditors of the bankrupt.

Rule 16. — All questions for trial or hearing, under Sections 31 and 34 of the act, shall be tried or heard at a stated session of the court, on four days' notice of trial or hearing, to be served by either party upon the other party, and upon the clerk; and a calendar of the same shall be made.

Rule 16 of this Court in Bankruptcy is hereby amended so as to read as follows: —

All questions for trial or hearing under Sections 31 and 34 of the act, and all questions under Section 41 of the act, which are not ordered to be tried by a jury, shall be brought on upon testimony taken before a register, a commissioner, or a referee, and shall be tried or heard by the court, and will be so tried or heard on any Saturday in term, at a stated session of the court, on four days' notice of trial or hearing, to be served by either party upon the other party, and upon the clerk, and a separate calendar of the same shall be made by the clerk for every Saturday in the term, on which the cases shall be arranged in the order in which the same are numbered, according to General Order No. 1.

Passed Feb. 21, A.D. 1868.

Rule 17. — The application, under Section 34 of the act, to set aside and annul a discharge, shall be verified by the oath or affirmation of the applicant, and the answer of the bankrupt to the application shall answer specifically the allegations of the application, and shall be verified in like manner.

Rule 18. — The demand in writing for a trial by jury, under Section 41 of the act, shall be signed by the debtor or his attorney.

Rule 19. — All issues, questions, points, and matters stated in writing, under Rule 11 of the "General Orders in Bankruptcy," or under the 4th Section or the 6th Section of the act, or according to Form No. 50, and adjourned into court for decision, or stated in a special case for the opinion of the court, shall be certified to the judge by the register by a certificate, which shall also state briefly the opinion of the register on the issue, question, point or matter, and shall be delivered or sent to the clerk; and no oral or written argument shall be allowed on any such issue or question, unless by special leave of the court.

Rule 20. — In pursuance of Rule 28 of the "General Orders in Bankruptcy," the following National Banks in this district are designated as those in which all moneys received by assignees or paid into court in the course of any proceedings in bankruptcy shall be deposited, namely: —

The list of banks is here omitted, as is the list of newspapers in the next rule; as they must necessarily be different in the different States.

All moneys received by the clerk of the court on account of any bankrupt estate, or paid into court in the course of any proceedings in bankruptcy (except the sums deposited with the clerk under Section 47 of the act), shall be deposited in said bank in the city and county of New York; and all sums received by an assignee on account of any estate of which he is assignee shall be deposited in such one of said banks as he shall select by a writing to be signed by him, and filed with the clerk. The check, or warrant, for drawing moneys deposited by the clerk, shall be signed by the clerk, and countersigned by the judge. The check, or warrant, for drawing moneys deposited by an assignee, shall be signed by him, and countersigned by the register designated to act in the case of the estate on account of which such moneys were deposited.

Rule 21. — The following newspapers are designated as those in which all publications required by the act, or the "General Orders in Bankruptcy," or these rules, may be made, namely: — (*the names of the newspapers are here omitted.*)

The marshal and the clerk, and every register or assignee, when required to publish any notice or advertisement, shall preserve and return to the court a copy, cut from each newspaper in which it is published, of each notice and advertisement as published, with a certificate as to the particulars of the publishing, showing that the required publication has been made.

Rule 22. — In case of the absence of the judge at the time and place noticed or appointed for any hearing or proceeding before him in bankruptcy, or if the matter then fails to be called or acted on, the same shall be deemed continued, without other order, to the next sitting of the court thereafter, at which time the like proceedings may be had thereupon as if first noticed or appointed for such day.

Rule 23. — If the marshal shall, under Rule 13 of the "General Orders in Bankruptcy," appoint special deputies to act as messengers, he shall, as far as possible, designate one or more of such special deputies to be attached to the office of each register, for the purpose of causing the notices to be published and served which are specified in the warrants issued in the cases referred to such register.

Rule 24. — All notices served or sent by mail by the marshal, the clerk, or an assignee, shall be so written or printed and folded, that the direction, postage-stamp, and post-mark shall be upon the notice itself, and not upon an envelope or other separate piece of paper.

Rule 25. — Special cases not comprehended within the foregoing Rules, or the "General Orders in Bankruptcy," or the Forms, shall be submitted to the judge.

CHAPTER XXIV.

THE LAW OF PLACE.

SECTION I.

WHAT IS MEANT BY THE LAW OF PLACE.

If either of the parties to a contract is not at home, or if both are not at the same home, when they enter into the contract, or if it is to be executed abroad, or if it comes into litigation before a foreign tribunal, then the rights and the obligations of the parties may be affected either by the law of the place of the contract, or by the law of the domicil or home of a party, or by the law of the place where the thing is situated to which the contract refers, or by the law of the tribunal before which the case is litigated. All of these are commonly included in the Latin phrase *lex loci*, or, as the phrase is translated, the Law of Place.

It is obvious that this law must be of great importance wherever citizens of distinct nations have much commercial intercourse with each other. In this country it has an especial and very great importance, from the circumstance that, while the citizens of the whole country have at least as much business connection with each other as those of any other nation, our country is composed of thirty-six separate and independent sovereignties, which are, for most commercial purposes, regarded by the law as foreign to each other.

SECTION II.

THE GENERAL PRINCIPLES OF THE LAW OF PLACE.

The general principles upon which the law of place depends are four. First, every sovereignty can bind, by its laws, all persons and all things within the limits of the State. Second, no law has any force or authority of its own, beyond those limits. Third, by the comity or courtesy of nations, — aided in our case, as to the several States, by the peculiar and close relation between the States, and for some purposes by a constitutional provision, — the laws of foreign States have a qualified force and influence.

The fourth rule is perhaps that of the most frequent application. It is, that a contract which is not valid where it is made is valid nowhere else; and one which is valid where it is made is valid everywhere. Thus a contract made in Massachusetts, and there void because usurious, was sued in New Hampshire and held to be void there, although the law of New Hampshire would not have avoided it if it had been made there. But courts do not take notice of foreign revenue laws, and will enforce foreign contracts made in violation of them. If contracts are made only orally, where by law they should be in writing, they cannot be enforced elsewhere where writing is not required; but if made orally where writing is not required, they can be enforced in other countries where such contracts should be in writing. The rule, that a contract which is valid where it is made is valid everywhere, is applicable to contracts of marriage.

As contracts relate either to movables or immovables, or, to use the phraseology of our own law, to personal property or to real property, the following distinction is taken. If the contract refers to personal property (which never has a fixed place, and is therefore called, in some systems of law, movable property), the place of the contract governs by its law the construction and effect of the contract. But if the contract refers to real property, it is construed and applied by the law of the place where that real property is situated, without reference, so far as the title is concerned, to the law of the place of the contract. Hence, the title to land can only be given or received as the law of the place where the land is situated requires and determines. And it has been said that the same rule may properly apply to all other local stock or funds, although of a personal nature, or so made by the local law, such as bank stock, insurance stock, manufacturing stock, railroad shares, and other incorporeal property, owing its existence to, or regulated by, peculiar local laws; and therefore no effectual transfer can be made of such property, except in the manner prescribed by the local regulations.

As to the capacity of a person to enter into contracts, it is undoubtedly the general rule, that this is determined by the law of his domicil; and whatever that permits him to do he may do anywhere.

SECTION III.

THE PLACE OF THE CONTRACT.

A CONTRACT is made *when* both parties agree to it, and not before. It is therefore made *where* both parties agree to it, if this is one place. But if the contract be made by letter, or by separate signatures to an instrument, the contract is then made where that signature is put to it, or that letter is written, which in fact completes the contract. But this rule is subject to a very important qualification, when the contract is made in one place, and is to be performed in another place; for then, in general, the law of this last place must determine the force and effect of the contract, for the obvious and strong reason, that parties who agreed that a certain thing should be done in a certain place intended that a thing should be done there, which was lawful there, and therefore bargained with reference to the laws of the place, not in which they stood, but in which they were to act. This principle has been applied to an antenuptial contract, and it was held, that when parties marry in reference to the laws of another country as their intended domicil, the law of the intended domicil governs the construction of their marriage-contract as to the rights of personal property.

But, for many commercial transactions, both of these rules seem to be in force; or rather to be blended in such a way as to give the parties an option as to what shall be the place of the contract, and what the rule of law which shall apply to it. Thus, a note written in New York, and expressly payable in New York, is, to all intents and purposes, a New-York note; and if more than seven per cent interest was promised, it would be usurious, whatever was the domicil of the parties. If made in New York, and no place of payment is expressed, it is payable and may be demanded anywhere, but would still be a New-York note. But if made in New York, but expressly payable in Boston (where any amount of interest may be agreed for), and promised to pay ten per cent interest, when payment of the note was demanded in Boston, the promise of interest would be held valid. So, if the note were made in New York, payable in Boston, and promising to pay ten per cent interest, it would not be usurious.

In other words, if a note is made in one place, but is payable in another, the parties have their option to make it bear the interest which is lawful in either place.

If the contract be entered into for money, and is made in one place but is payable at another place on a day certain, and no interest be stipulated, and payment be delayed, interest by way of damages shall be allowed, according to the law of the place of payment, where the money may be supposed to have been required by the creditor for use, and where he might be supposed to have borrowed money to supply the deficiency thus occurring, and to have paid the rate of interest of that country. If a note made in New York and payable in Massachusetts were demanded in Massachusetts and unpaid, and afterwards put in suit in Massachusetts, and personal service made on the promisor there, I should say that any interest which it bore should be recovered, provided it were lawful in Massachusetts. And indeed, generally, that such a note, being made in good faith, might always bear any interest lawful where it was payable. But a note made in a State where the law permitted only a low interest, and intended in fact to be paid in that State, but written payable in some State permitting higher interest, merely to get this higher interest, could not by this trick escape the usury laws of the State where it was made, and get the higher interest.

SECTION IV.

DOMICIL.

It is sometimes very important to determine where a person has his domicil, or Home. In general, it is his residence; or that country in which he permanently resides. He may change it by a change of place *both* in fact and in intent, but not by either alone. Thus, a citizen of New York, going to London and remaining there a long time, but without the intention of relinquishing his home in New York, does not lose that home. And, if he stays in New York, his *intention* to live and remain abroad does not affect his domicil until he goes in fact.

He may have his legal domicil in one place, and yet spend a very large part of his time in another. But he cannot have more than one domicil. His words or declarations are not the only evidence of his intent; and they are much stronger evidence when against his interest, than when they are in his favor. Thus, one goes from Boston to England. If he goes intending not merely to travel, but to change his residence permanently, and not to return to this country unless as a visitor, he changes his domicil from the day that he leaves this country. Let us suppose, however, that he is still regarded by the assessors as residing in Boston, although travelling abroad, and is heavily taxed accordingly. If he can prove that he has abandoned his original home, he escapes from the tax which he must otherwise pay. Now, his declarations that he has no longer a home here, and that his residence is permanently fixed in England, and the like, would be very far from conclusive in his favor, and could indeed be hardly received as evidence at all, unless they were confirmed by facts and circumstances. But if it could be shown that he had constantly asserted that he was still an American, that he had no other permanent residence, no home but that which he had temporarily left as a traveller, such declarations would be almost conclusive against him. In general, such a question would be determined by all the words and acts, the arrangement of property at home, the length and the character of the residence abroad, and all the acts and circumstances which would indicate the actual intention and understanding of the party.

Two cases have occurred in the city of Boston, which illustrate this question. In one, a citizen of Boston, who had been at school in the city of Edinburgh when a boy, and formed a predilection for that place as a residence, and had expressed a determination to reside there if he ever should have the means of so doing, removed with his family to that city, in 1836, declaring, at the time of his departure, that he intended to reside abroad, and that, if he should return to the United States, he should not live in Boston. He resided in Edinburgh and vicinity, as a housekeeper, taking a lease of an estate for a term of years, and endeavored to engage an American to enter his family for two years, as instructor of his children. Before he left Boston, he made a contract for the sale of his mansion-house and furniture there, but shortly afterward procured said contract to be annulled (assigning as his reason therefor, that, in case of his death in Europe, his wife might wish to return to Boston), and let his house and furniture to a tenant. Held, that he had changed his domicil, and was not liable to taxation as an inhabitant of Boston in 1837. In the other case, a native inhabitant of Boston, intending to reside in France, with his family, departed for that country in June, 1836, and was followed by his family about three months afterwards. His dwelling-house and furniture were leased for a year, and he hired a house for a year in Paris. At the time of his departure he intended to return and resume his residence in Boston, but had not fixed on any time for his return. He returned in about sixteen months, and his family in about nine months afterwards. Held, that he continued to be an inhabitant of Boston, and that he was rightly taxed there, during his absence, for his person and personal property. This last case was distinguished from the former, by the different intent of the parties upon their departure from home.

It is a general rule, that, if one has a domicil, he retains it until he acquires another. Thus, if a seaman, without family or property, sails from the place of his nativity, which may be considered his domicil of origin, although he may return only at long intervals, or even be absent for many years, yet, if he does not, by some actual residence or other means, acquire a domicil elsewhere, he retains his domicil of origin.

It seems to be agreed that one may dwell for a considerable time, and even regularly during a large part of the year, in one place, or even in one State, and yet have his domicil in another.

A woman marrying takes her husband's domicil, and changes it with him. A minor child has the domicil of his father, or of his mother if she survive his father; and the surviving parent, with whom a child lives, by changing his or her own domicil in good faith, changes that of the child. And even a guardian has the same power.

CHAPTER XXV.

THE LAW OF SHIPPING.

SECTION I.

THE OWNERSHIP AND TRANSFER OF SHIPS.

The Law of Shipping may be considered under three divisions. First, as to ownership and transfer of ships. Second, as to the employment of ships as carriers of goods, or of passengers, or both. Third, as to the navigation of ships. I begin with the first topic.

Ships are personal property; or, in other words, a ship is a chattel; and yet its ownership and transfer are regulated in this country by rules quite analogous to those which apply to real property.

The Constitution of the United States gives to Congress the power to enact laws for the regulation of commerce. In execution of this power, acts were passed in 1792, and immediately after, which followed substantially the Registry and Navigation Laws of England, some of which had been in force about a century and a half. The English laws were intended to secure English commerce to English men and English ships; and it was supposed that the commercial prosperity of England was in a great measure due to them.

To secure the evidence of the American character of a vessel, the statute of 1792 provides for an exact system of registration in the custom-house. There is no *requirement* of registratior.. The law does not say that a ship shall or must be registered, but that certain ships or vessels may be; and, if they are registered, they shall have certain privileges. And the disadvantage of being without registry operates as effectually to make registration universal, as a positive requirement with a heavy penalty could do.

The ships which may be registered are those already registered, 31 December, 1792, under the act of September, 1789; those built within the United States, and owned wholly by citizens thereof; and those captured and condemned as prizes, or adjudged forfeited by violation of law, if at the time of registry they are owned wholly by citizens of this country. No ship can be registered, if an owner or part-owner usually reside abroad, although he is a citizen, unless he is a consul of the United States, or agent for, and a partner in, a mercantile house established and doing business here; nor if the master be not a citizen of the United States; nor if the owner or part-owner be a naturalized citizen, and reside in the country whence he came more than a year, or in any foreign country more than two years, unless he be consul or public agent of the United States. But a ship which has lost the benefits of registry by the non-residence of an owner, in such a case may be registered anew if she become the property of a resident citizen, by *bonâ fide* purchase; nor can a ship be registered which has been, at any time, the property of an alien, unless she becomes the property of the original owner or his representative.

Sometimes Congress, by special acts, permits the registration, as an American ship, of a vessel which has become, by purchase, American property. If a registered American ship be sold or transferred, in whole or in part, to an alien, the certificate of registry must be delivered up, or the vessel is forfeited; but if, in case of a sale in part, it can be shown that any owner of a part not so sold was ignorant of the sale, his share shall not be subject to such forfeiture. As soon as a registered vessel arrives from a foreign port, her documents must be deposited with the collector of the port of arrival, and the owner, or, if he does not reside within the district, the master, must make oath that the register contains the names of all persons who are at that time owners of the ship, and at the same time report any transfer of the ship, or of any part, that has been made within his knowledge since the registry; and also declare that no foreigner has any interest in the ship. If a register be issued fraudulently, or with the knowledge of the owners, for a ship not entitled to one, the register is not only void, but the ship is forfeited. If a new register is issued, the old one must be given up; but where there is a sale by process of law, and the former owners withhold the register, the Secretary of the Treasury may authorize the collector to issue a new one. If a ship be transferred while at sea, or abroad, the old register must be given up, and all the requirements of law, as to registry, &c., must be complied with, within three days after her arrival at the home port.

Important exclusive privileges have been granted to registered vessels of the United States. By the statute of 1817, it is provided, that no merchandise shall be brought from any foreign country to this, except in American vessels, or in vessels belonging to that country of which the merchandise is the growth. Also, that no merchandise shall be carried from port to port in the United States, by any foreign vessel, unless it formed a part of its original cargo.

A ship that is of twenty tons' burden, to be employed in the fisheries, or in the coasting-trade, need not be registered, but must be enrolled and licensed accordingly. If under twenty tons' burden, she need only be licensed. If licensed for the fisheries, she may visit and return from foreign ports, having stated her intention of doing so, and being permitted by the collector. And if registered, she may engage in the coasting-trade or fishery, and if licensed and enrolled, she may become a registered ship, subject to the regulations provided for such cases.

A ship that is neither registered nor licensed and enrolled can sail on no voyage with the privilege or protection of a national character or national papers. If she engages in foreign trade, or the coasting-trade, or fisheries, she is liable to forfeiture; and if she have foreign goods on board, must at all events pay the tonnage-duties leviable on foreign ships. In these days, no ship engaged in honest business, and belonging to a civilized people, is met with on the ocean, without having the regular papers which attest her nationality, unless she has lost them by some accident.

SECTION II.

THE TRANSFER OF PROPERTY IN A SHIP

THE Statute of Registration provides, that, "in every case of sale or transfer, there shall be some instrument in writing, in the nature of a bill of sale, which shall recite at length the said certificate; otherwise the said ship or vessel shall be incapable of being registered anew." It follows, therefore, that a merely oral transfer, although for valuable consideration, and followed by possession, gives the transferee no right to claim a new register setting forth his ownership. But this is all. There is nothing in this statute to prevent the property from passing to and vesting in such transferee. It is, however, unquestionably a principle of the maritime law generally, that property in a ship should pass by a written instrument. And as this principle seems to be adopted by the statute, the courts have sometimes almost denied the validity of a merely parol transfer. The weight of authority and of reason is, however, undoubtedly in favor of the conclusion stated by Judge Story, that "the registry acts have not, in any degree, changed the common law as to the manner of transferring this species of property." It would follow, therefore, that such transfer would be valid, and would pass the property.

In 1850, Congress, however, passed an act, "to provide for recording the conveyances of vessels, and for other purposes." By this statute it was provided "that no bill of sale, mortgage, hypothecation, or conveyance of any vessel or part of any vessel of the United States, shall be valid against any person other than the grantor or mortgagor, his heirs and devisees, and persons having actual notice thereof; unless such bill of sale, mortgage, hypothecation, or conveyance be recorded in the office of the collector of the customs where such vessel is registered or enrolled." Then follows an exception in favor of liens by bottomry, and in subsequent sections are provisions for recording by the collector, and giving certificates, &c.

This statute has no effect, that I perceive, upon oral transfers, excepting that, as they cannot be recorded, their operation is limited to the grantors and those who have actual notice. Where the transfer is by bill of sale, the record of this, under the late statute, is notice to all the world. But in most of our States there are already provisions for the record of mortgages of personal property, and the question arises how these are affected by this statute of the United States. I should say that it controlled and superseded the State statute, so as to make that unnecessary and ineffectual; and therefore a record in the custom-house only would be sufficient, and a record under the State law would affect only those who had actual knowledge of it.

As a ship is a chattel, a transfer of it should be accompanied by a delivery of possession. Actual delivery is sometimes impossible where a ship is at sea; and the statute of 1850 makes the record of the transfer equivalent to change of possession. If there be no record, possession should be taken as soon as possible; and prudence would still require the same course in case of transfer by writing and record.

By the word "ship," and still more by the phrase "ship and her appurtenances," or "apparel," or "furniture," every thing would pass which was distinctly connected with the ship, and is on board of her, and fastened to her if that be usual, and needed for her navigation or for her safety. Kentledge, a valuable kind of permanent ballast, has been held to pass with the ship; so have a rudder and cordage prepared for a vessel, but not yet attached to her, and not quite finished; and so would a boat, anchors, &c., generally. But the answer to the question, What is part of the ship? must always depend somewhat upon the words of the instrument, and upon the circumstances of the case and the intention of the parties.

A sale by the decree of any regular court of admiralty, with due notice to all parties, and with proper precautions to protect the interests of all, and to guard against fraud or precipitancy, would undoubtedly be acknowledged by courts of admiralty of every other nation as transferring the property effectually.

SECTION III.

PART-OWNERS.

Two or more persons may become part-owners of a ship, in either of three ways. They may build it together, or join in purchasing it, or each may purchase his share independently of the others. In either case, their rights and obligations are the same.

If the register, or the instrument of transfer, or other equivalent evidence, do not designate specific and unequal proportions, they will be presumed to own the ship in equal shares.

Part-owners are not necessarily or usually partners. But a ship, or any part of a ship, may constitute a part of the stock or capital of a copartnership; and then it will be governed, in all respects, by the law of partnership.

A part-owner may at any time sell his share to whom he will. But he cannot sell the share of any other part-owner, without his authority. If he dies, his share goes to his representatives, and not to the surviving part-owners.

A majority of the part-owners may, generally, manage and direct the employment of the property at their discretion. But a court of admiralty will interfere and do justice between them, and prevent either of the part-owners from inflicting injury upon the others.

One part-owner may, in the absence of the rest, and without prohibition from them, manage the ship, as for himself and for them. And the contracts he enters into, in relation to the employment or preservation of the ship, bind all the part-owners in favor of an innocent third party.

In general, all the part-owners are liable, each one for the whole amount, for all the repairs of a ship, or for necessaries actually supplied to her, in good faith. If one pays his part of what is due, or even more than his share, and it is agreed between him and the creditor that he shall not be held further, still, if the others do not pay, he must pay, unless there is a better consideration for the promise not to call on him than his merely paying a part of what he was legally bound to pay; for where a man is bound to pay all, his paying a part is no consideration whatever for a promise to him. If he had a discharge under seal, it might protect him at law, but would not in admiralty, unless the circumstances of the case made this just.

If it can be clearly shown, however, that especial credit was given, and intended to be given, to one part-owner personally, to the exclusion of the others, then the others cannot be holden. If the goods were charged to "ship" so and so, or to "ship and owners," this would tend strongly to show that it was intended to supply the goods on the credit of all the owners. If charged to some one owner alone, this would not absolutely prove that credit was intentionally given to him exclusively. But it would raise a presumption to that effect which could be rebutted only by showing that no other owner was known; or by some other evidence which disproved the intention of discharging the other part-owners.

So, if the note, negotiable or otherwise, of one part-owner were taken in payment, if the promisor refused to pay, the others would be liable, unless they could show a distinct bargain by which they were exonerated.

Commonly, the "ship's husband," as the agent of all the owners for the management of the ship has long been called, is one of the part-owners. He may be appointed in writing or otherwise. His duties are, in general, to provide for the complete equipment and repair of the ship, and take care of her while in port; to see that she is furnished with all regular and proper papers; to make proper contracts for freight or passage, and collect the receipts and make the disbursements proper on these accounts. For these things he has all the necessary powers. But he cannot, without special power, insure for the rest, nor buy a cargo for them, nor borrow money, nor give up their lien on the cargo for the freight, nor delegate his authority.

Where he acts within his powers, a ship's husband binds all his principals, that is, all the part-owners. But a third party may deal with him on his personal credit alone; and if the part-owners, believing this, and authorized to believe it by any acts or words of the third party, settle their accounts with the ship's husband accordingly, this third party cannot now establish a claim against them to their detriment. If a ship's husband is not a part-owner, all the part-owners are liable to him, each for the whole amount. If he is a part-owner, each of the others is liable to him for his share of the expense incurred. The "ship's husband" is called in the Statutes of the United States the "managing owner."

SECTION IV.

THE LIABILITY OF MORTGAGEES.

A MORTGAGEE of a ship, who is in possession, is, in general, liable for supplies, repairs, &c., in the same way as an owner. But if he has not taken possession, he is not liable for supplies or repairs merely on the ground that his security is strengthened by whatever preserves or increases the value of the vessel. Nor can he be made liable, except by some act or words of his own, which show that credit was *properly* given to him, or that he has come under a valid engagement to assume this responsibility.

SECTION V.

THE CONTRACT OF BOTTOMRY.

BY this contract, a ship is hypothecated (which means pledged) as security for money borrowed. The form of this contract varies in different places, and, indeed, in the same place. Its essentials are: — First, that the ship itself is bound for the payment of the money. Second, that the money is to be repaid only in case the ship performs a certain voyage, and arrives at its destined termination in safety; or, as it is sometimes provided in modern bottomries, in case that the ship is in safety on a certain day; therefore, if the ship is lost before the termination of the voyage or the expiration of the period, no part of the money is due, or, as is sometimes said, the whole debt is paid by the loss. As the lender thus consents that the repayment of the money shall depend upon the safety of the ship, he has a legal right to charge "marine interest," which means as much more than legal interest as will serve to cover his risk.

The lender may require, and the borrower pay, this marine interest, which may be much more than lawful interest, on a bottomry bond, without usury.

If the interest be not expressed in the contract, it will generally be presumed to be meant and included in the sum named as principal.

If, by the contract, the lender takes more than legal interest, and yet the money is to be paid to him whether the ship be lost or not, this is not a contract of bottomry, and it is subject to all the consequences of usury. But the lender may take security for his debt and marine interest, additional to the ship itself, provided the security is given, like the ship itself, to make the payment certain when it becomes due by the safety of the ship, but is wholly avoided if the ship be lost; for then the lender takes the risk of losing the whole, principal and interest, by the loss of the ship, and may therefore charge more than simple interest.

The most common contracts of bottomry are those entered into by the master in a foreign port, where money is needed and cannot otherwise be obtained. Therefore the security goes with the ship, and the debt may be enforced, as soon as it is payable, against the ship, wherever the ship may be. But in this country, these contracts are frequently made by the owner himself, in the home port. And sometimes they are nothing else than contrivances to get more than legal interest. Thus, if A lends to B $20,000 on B's ship for one year, at fifteen per cent interest, conditioned that, if the ship be lost, the money shall not be paid, and the lender insures the ship for three per cent, he gets twelve per cent interest, which may be much more than the legal interest, and yet incurs no risk. If such a contract were obviously and certainly merely colorable, and only a pretence for getting usurious interest, the courts would probably set it aside; but it might be difficult to show this.

If the money is payable at the end of a certain voyage, and the owner, or his servant the master of the ship, terminate the voyage sooner, — either honestly, from a change in their plan, or dishonestly, by intentional loss or wreck, — the money becomes at once due.

A bottomry bond made abroad would override all other liens or engagements, except the claim for seamen's wages, and the lien of material men for repairs and supplies indispensable to the safety of the vessel. The reason is, that a bottomry bond is supposed to be made from necessity, and to have provided the only means by which the ship could be brought home. For the same reason, a later bond is sustained as against an earlier, and the last against all before it.

The lien of bottomry depends in no degree on possession, for the ship may go all over the world with the bottomry security attached to her; but the lender ought to collect the sum due, and so discharge the bond as soon as he conveniently can; and therefore an unreasonable delay in enforcing it will destroy the lien; and any connivance by the lender at any fraud on the part of the master avoids the bond entirely.

SECTION VI.

THE EMPLOYMENT OF A SHIP BY THE OWNER.

An owner of a ship may employ it in carrying his own goods, or those of another. He may carry the goods of others, while he himself retains the possession and direction of the ship; or he may lease his ship to others, to carry their goods. In the first case, he carries the goods of others *on freight;* in the second, he lets his ship *by charter-party*. We shall consider first the carriage of goods on freight.

He may load his ship as far as he can with his own goods, and then take the goods of others to fill the vacant space; or he may put up his ship as "a general ship," to go from one stated port to another, and to carry the goods of all who offer.

It may be remarked, that the word "freight" is used in different ways; sometimes to designate the goods or cargo that is carried; sometimes to denote the money which the shipper of the goods pays to the owner of the ship, for their transportation. Not unfrequently, when the word is used in this latter sense, the word "money" is added, and the phrase "freight-money" leaves no question as to what is meant. Sometimes a ship-owner who lets the whole burden of his ship to another is said to carry the shipper's goods on freight. But the most common meaning of the word, especially in law proceedings, is the money earned by a ship not chartered, for the transportation of the goods; and in this sense we shall use it.

Nearly the whole law of freight grows out of the ancient and universal principle that the ship and the cargo have reciprocal duties or obligations towards each other, and are reciprocally pledged to each other for the performance of these duties. In other words, not only is the owner of the ship bound to the owner of the cargo, as soon as he receives it, to lade it properly on board, take care of it while on board, carry it in safety (so far as the seaworthiness of the ship is concerned) to its destined port, and there deliver it, all in a proper way, but the ship itself is bound to the discharge of these duties. That is to say, if, by reason of a failure in any of these particulars, the shipper of the goods is damnified, he may look to the ship-owner for indemnity; but he is not obliged to do so, because he may proceed by proper process against the ship itself. This lien, like that of bottomry, is not dependent upon possession, but will be lost by delay, especially if the vessel passes into the hands of a purchaser for value without notice. On the other hand, if the ship discharges all its duties, the owner may look to the shipper for the payment of his freight; but is not obliged to do so, because he may keep his hold upon the goods, and refuse to deliver them until the freight is paid.

The party who sends the goods may or may not be the owner of them. And he may send them either to one who is the owner, for whom the sender bought them, or to one who is only the agent of the owner. In either of these cases, the sender is called the consignor of the goods, and the party to whom they are sent is called the consignee. The sending them is called the consigning or the consignment of them; but it is quite common to hear the goods themselves called the consignment.

The rights and obligations of the ship-owner and the shipper are stated generally in an instrument of which the origin is lost in its antiquity, and which is now in universal use among commercial nations, with little substantial variety of form. It is called the Bill of Lading. It should contain the names of the consignor, of the consignee, of the vessel, of the master, of the place of departure, and of the place of destination; also the price of the freight, with primage and other charges, if any there be, and either in the body of the bill or in the margin, the marks and numbers of the things shipped, with sufficient precision to designate and identify them.

It should be signed by the master of the ship, who, by the strict maritime law, has no authority to sign a bill of lading until the goods are actually on board. There is some relaxation of this rule in practice; but it should be avoided.

Usually one copy is retained by the master, and three copies are given to the shipper; one of them he usually retains, another he sends to the consignee with the goods, and the other he sends to the consignee by some other conveyance.

The delivery of the goods promised in the bill is to the consignee, or his assigns; and the consignee may designate his assigns by writing on the back of the bill, "Deliver the within-named goods to A B," and signing this order; or the consignee may indorse the bill with his name only in blank, and any one who acquires an honest title to the goods and to the bill may write over the signature an order of delivery to himself. The consignee has this power, if such be the usage, even if the word "assigns" be omitted. Such indorsement not only gives the indorsee a right to demand the goods, but makes him the owner of the goods.

As the bill of lading is evidence against the ship-owner as to the reception of the goods, and their quantity and quality, it is common to say "contents unknown," or "said to contain," &c. But without any words of this kind, the bill of lading is not conclusive upon the ship-owner in favor of the shipper, because he may show that its statements were erroneous through fraud or mistake. But the ship-owner, or master, is bound much more strongly by the words of the bill of lading, in favor of a third party, who has bought the goods for value and in good faith, on the credit of the bill of lading. In a case which occurred in New York, the court said, that, as between the shipper of the goods and the owner of the vessel, a bill of lading may be explained or corrected as far as it is a receipt; that is, as to the quantity of the goods shipped, and the like; but as between the owner of the vessel and an assignee of the bill, for a valuable consideration, paid on the strength of the bill of lading, it may not be explained or corrected; because the master, by signing the bill, authorizes the purchaser to believe the goods are what the bill says they are.

The law-merchant gives to the ship, as we have seen, a lien on the goods for the freight. The master cannot demand the freight without a tender of the goods at the proper time, in the proper way, to the proper person, and in a proper condition; but then the consignee is not entitled to the goods without paying freight. The law gives this lien, whether it be expressed or not. But it may be expressly waived. The bill of lading, or other evidence, may show the agreement of the parties that the goods should be delivered first, and the freight not be payable until a certain time afterwards; and such an agreement is in general a waiver of the lien.

Nevertheless, if it seemed that the ship-owner did not intend to give up his security on the goods, a court of admiralty would so construe such an agreement as to give the consignee possession of the goods, for a temporary purpose, as to ascertain their condition, or, possibly, that he might offer them in the market, and by an agreement to sell raise the means of paying the freight; and yet would preserve for the master his security upon the goods for a reasonable time, unless, in the mean time, they should actually become, by sale, the property of a *bonâ fide* purchaser.

The contract of affreightment is entire; therefore no freight is earned unless the whole is earned, by carrying the goods quite to the port of destination. If by wreck, or other cause, the transportation is incomplete, no absolute right of freight grows out of it. We say no absolute right, because a conditional right of freight does exist. To understand this, we must remember, that, as soon as the ship receives the goods, it, on the one hand, comes under the obligation of carrying them to their destination, and on the other, at the same time or on breaking ground and beginning the voyage, acquires the right of so carrying them. Therefore, if a wreck or other interruption intervenes, the ship-owner has the right of transshipping them, and sending them forward in the original ship, or another ship, to the place of their original destination. When they arrive there, he may claim the whole freight originally agreed on;

but if forwarded in the original ship, he can claim no more; for then the extra cost of forwarding the goods is his loss. If the master or owner of the ship forwards them in another ship from necessity, and at an increased cost, the shipper must pay this increased cost.

The ship-owner not only may, but must, send forward the goods, at his own cost, if this can be done by means reasonably within his reach. He is not, however, answerable for any delay thus occurring, or for any damage from this delay. The shipper himself, by his agent, may always reclaim all his goods, at any intermediate port or place, on tendering all his freight; because the master's right of sending them forward is merely to earn his full freight. If, therefore, the goods are damaged and need care, and the master can send them forward at some time within reasonable limits, and insists upon his right to do so, the shipper can obtain possession of his goods only by paying full freight. If, however, the master tenders the goods there to the shipper, and the shipper there receives them, this is held to sever or divide the contract by agreement, and now what is called a freight *pro rata itineris*, or for that part of the voyage which is performed, is due. This is quite a common transaction.

Difficult questions sometimes arise as to what is a reception of the goods by their owner. The rights of the master and of the shipper are apparently opposed to each other, and neither must be pressed too far. The master must not pretend to hold the goods for forwarding, to the detriment of the goods or their value, when he cannot forward them, but merely uses this pretence to compel a payment of full freight. And the shipper must not refuse to receive the goods, when the master can do no more with them, and offers their delivery in good faith.

If freight for a part of the voyage is payable, the question arises by what rule of proportion shall it be measured. One is purely geographical, and was formerly much used; that is, the whole freight would pay for so many miles, and the freight for a part must pay for so many less. Another is purely commercial. The whole freight being a certain sum for the whole distance, what will it cost to bring the goods to the place where they are received, and how much to take them thence to their original destination. Let the original freight be divided into two parts proportional to these, and the first part is the freight for the part of the voyage through which they were carried, or, as it is called, the freight *pro rata*, and is to be paid by the shipper who receives the goods. Neither of these, nor indeed any other fixed and precise rule, is generally adopted in this country. But both courts and merchants seek, by combining the two, to ascertain what proportion of the increase of value expected from the intended transportation has been actually conferred upon the goods by actual partial transportation, and this is to be taken as the freight that is due *pro rata itineris*.

If the bill of lading requires delivery to the consignee or his assigns, "he or they paying freight," — which is usual, — and the master delivers the goods without receiving freight, which the consignee fails to pay, the master or owner cannot in the absence of express contract fall back on the consignor and make him liable, unless he can show that the consignor actually owned the goods, or by his words or acts made himself responsible therefor; in which case the bill of lading, in this respect, is nothing more than an order by a principal upon an agent to pay money due from the principal.

Under the usual bill of lading, the goods are to be delivered to the consignee or his assigns, on the payment of freight. If goods are accepted under this bill of lading, the party receiving them, whether the consignee or his assignee, becomes liable for the freight. If the master delivers goods to any one, saying that he shall look to him for the freight, he may demand the freight of him unless that person had the absolute right to the goods without payment of freight; which must be very seldom the case. If the consignee is not liable for the freight, his indorsement of the bill of lading does not make him so. And if the consignee is liable, and the goods are received by any one only as agent of the consignor, this agent does not thereby become liable.

If freight be paid in advance, and not subsequently earned, it must be repaid, unless it can be shown that the owner took a less sum for ready cash than he would otherwise have had, and for this or some other equivalent reason the money paid was as a final settlement, and was to be retained by the owner at all events.

If a consignee pay more than he should, he may recover it back, if paid through ignorance or mistake of fact; but not if, with full knowledge of all the facts, he was ignorant or mistaken as to the law.

If one sells his ship after a voyage is commenced, he alone can claim the freight of the shipper of goods, although by the contract of sale the seller is to pay it over to the purchaser. A mortgagee of a ship who has not taken possession has not, in general, any right to the freight, unless this is specially agreed. Neither has a lender on a bottomry bond.

No freight, of course, can be earned by an illegal voyage; as the law will not enforce any illegal contract, or sanction any illegal conduct.

The goods are to be delivered, by the bill of lading, in good condition, excepting "the dangers of the seas," and such other risks or perils as may be expressed. If the goods are damaged to any extent by any of these perils, and yet can be and are delivered *in specie* (that is, if the goods are actually delivered although hurt or spoilt, as corn or hides although rotten, flour although wet, fish although spoilt), the freight is payable.

The shipper or consignee cannot abandon the goods for the freight, if they remain *in specie*, although they may be worthless; for damage caused by an excepted risk is his loss, and not the loss of the owner. If they are lost by a risk which the ship-owner does not except in the bill of lading, he is answerable for that loss, and it may be charged in settlement of freight.

If they are lost in substance, though not in form, that is, although the cases or vessels are preserved, as if sugar is washed out of boxes or hogsheads, or wine leaks out of casks, by reason of injury sustained from a peril of the sea, though the master may deliver the hogsheads or boxes or casks, this is not a delivery of the sugar or of the wine, and no freight is due.

If the goods are injured, or actually perish and disappear, from internal defect or decay or change, that is, from causes inherent in the goods themselves, with no fault of the master, freight is due. But if it can be shown that the loss or injury might have been avoided by the use of proper precautionary measures, and that the usual and customary methods for this purpose have been neglected, the master or ship-owners may be held liable for the damage.

If they are lost from the fault of the ship-owner, the master, or crew, the ship-owner must make the loss good; but in this case may have, by way of offset or deduction, his freight, because the shipper is entitled to full indemnification, but not to make a profit out of this loss. If goods are delivered, although damaged and deteriorated from faults for which the owner is responsible, as bad stowage, deviation, negligent navigation, or the like, freight is due; the amount of the damage being first deducted.

The rules in respect to passage-money are quite analogous to those which regulate the payment of freight. Usually, however, the passage-money is paid in advance. But it is not earned except by carrying the passenger, or *pro rata*, by carrying him only a part of the way with his consent. And if paid in advance, and not earned by the fault of the ship or owner, it can be recovered back.

SECTION VII.

CHARTER-PARTIES.

THE owner may let his ship to others; and the written instrument by which this is done is called by an ancient name, a Charter-Party. The form of this instrument varies considerably, because it must express the bargain between the parties, and this of course varies with circumstances and the pleasure of the parties. An agreement to make and receive a charter, though not itself equivalent to a charter, will, if the purposes of the proposed charter are carried into effect, be considered as evidence that such a charter was made and completed.

Generally, only the burden of the ship is let; the owner holding possession of her, finding and paying her master and crew and supplies and repairs, and navigating her as is agreed upon. Sometimes, however, the owner lets his ship as he might let a house; and the hirer takes possession, mans, navigates, supplies, and even repairs her.

In the latter case, bills of lading are not commonly given by the ship-owner to the hirer; but if the hirer takes the goods of other shippers, bills of lading are given by him to them ; but in the former, which we have said is much more common, bills of lading are usually given by the ship-owner to the charterer (or hirer), as they are in the case of a general ship. They are then, however, little more than evidence of the delivery and receipt of the goods, for the charter-party is the controlling contract as to all the terms or provisions which it expresses. The master is not authorized to sign bills promising to carry and deliver the goods for less freight than has been stipulated for. And if he signs such bills, and goods are shipped by the charterer, neither the charterer, nor any person shipping the goods with a knowledge of the charter-party, could defend on account of the bills of lading, against the owner's claims under the charter-party.

There is no particular form required for a charter-party. It should however, designate particularly the ship, the voyage, the master, and the parties; should describe the ship generally, and particularly as to her tonnage or capacity; should designate especially what parts of the ship are let, and what parts, if any, are reserved to the owner, or to the master, to carry goods, or for the purpose of navigation; should describe the voyage, or the period of time for which the ship is hired, with proper particularity; should set forth the lay-days, the demurrage, the obligation upon either party, to man, navigate, supply, and repair the ship, and all other particulars of the bargain, for this is a written instrument of an important character, and cannot be *varied* by any external evidence. Finally, it should state, distinctly and precisely, how much is to be paid for the ship, — whether by ton, and if so, whether by ton of measurement or ton of capacity of carriage, or in one gross sum for the whole burden, — and when the money is payable, and how; that is, in what currency or at what exchange, especially if it be payable abroad. The charter-party usually binds the ship and freight to the performance of the duties of the owner, and the cargo to the duties of the shipper. But the law-merchant would create this mutuality of obligation, if it were not expressed.

If the hirer takes the whole vessel, he may put the goods of other shippers on board (unless prevented by express stipulation); but whether he fills the whole ship or not, he pays for the whole; and what he pays for so much of the ship as is empty is said to be paid for dead freight; and if the master brought back the cargo because it could not be disposed of, the owner of the cargo would pay freight for bringing it back, although the charter-party said nothing about a return cargo. The freight is calculated on the actual capacity of the ship, unless she is agreed to be of a specified tonnage. If either party is deceived or defrauded by any statement in the charter-party, he has, of course, his remedy against the other party.

If a charterer takes the goods of other shippers, payment by one of them to the master or ship-owner is a good defence against the claim of the charterer against him, for so much as the charterer was bound to pay the owner, but no more.

The voyage may be a double one; a voyage out, and then a voyage home; or a voyage to one port, and thence to another. The question sometimes arises, whether any freight is payable if the ship arrives in safety out, and delivers her cargo there, and is lost on her return with the cargo that represents the cargo out. Of course, the parties may make what bargain they please, and the law respects it; but in the absence of an agreement on this point, the courts would generally consider each voyage, at the termination of which goods are delivered, as a voyage by itself, earning its own freight.

As time has become of the utmost importance in commercial transactions, both parties to this contract should be punctual, and cause no unnecessary delay; and for such delay the party injured would have his remedy against the party in fault. The charter-party usually provides for so many "lay-days," and for so much "demurrage." Lay-days, or working-days, are so many days which the charterer is allowed, without paying for them, or paying only a small price, for loading or for unloading the vessel. These lay-days are counted from the arrival of the ship at her dock, wharf, or other place of discharge, and not from her arrival at her port of destination, unless otherwise agreed on by the parties; and the usage of the port is often adverted to, to determine the place and manner of loading. In the absence of any custom or bargain to the contrary, Sundays are computed in the calculation of lay-days at the port of discharge; but if the contract specifies "working lay-days," Sundays and holidays are excluded. If more time than the agreed lay-days is occupied, it must be paid for; and "demurrage" means what is thus paid. Usually, the charterer agrees to pay so much demurrage a day. If he agrees only to pay demurrage, without specifying the sum, or if so many working days are agreed on, and nothing more is said, it would, generally, be considered that the number of lay-days determined what was a reasonable and proper delay, and that for whatsoever was more than this the party in fault must pay a reasonable indemnity.

If time be occupied in the repairs of the ship, which become necessary without the fault of the ship-owner or master, or of the ship itself, that is, if they do not arise from her original unseaworthiness, the charterer pays during this time. The charterer or hirer must not abandon the vessel while he can keep her afloat, and suitably provided for the employment and destination for which she was hired; and the ship-owner must be ready to pay all expenses and damages necessarily incurred for the purpose. But the charterer will not be bound by the charter-party to wait for the repair, unless the vessel can be repaired within a reasonable time.

Many cases have arisen where the ship was delayed by different causes, and the question occurred, which party should pay for the time thus lost. I should say that no delay arising from the elements, as from ice, or tide, or tempest, or from any act of government, or from any real disability of the consignee which could not be imputed to his own act, or to his own wrongful neglect, would give rise to a claim on the charterer for demurrage.

Demurrage seems essentially due only for the fault or voluntary act of the charterer; but if he hires at so much on time, that is, by the day, week, or month, then, if the vessel be delayed by seizure, embargo, or capture, and the impediment is removed, and the ship completes her voyage, the charterer pays for the whole time. If she be condemned, or otherwise lost, this terminates the voyage and the contract.

The contract may be dissolved by the parties, by mutual consent, or against their consent by any circumstance which makes the fulfilment of the contract illegal; as, for example, by a declaration of war, on the part of the country to which the ship belongs, against that to which she was to go. So, either an embargo, or an act of non-intercourse, or a blockade of the port to which the ship was going, may either annul or suspend the contract of charter-party. And we should say they would be held to suspend only, if they were temporary in their terms, and did not require a delay which would be destructive of the purposes of the voyage.

In reference to all these points, it is to be understood, that if the parties know or expect the circumstance when they make their bargain, and provide for it, any bargain they choose to make in relation to it would be enforced, unless it required one or other of the parties to do something prohibited by the law of nations, or the law of the country in which the parties resided, and to whose tribunals they must resort.

SECTION VIII.

GENERAL AVERAGE.

Whichever of the three great mercantile interests — ship, freight, or cargo — is voluntarily lost or damaged for the benefit of the others, if the others receive benefit therefrom, they must contribute ratably to the loss. That is to say, such a loss is *averaged* upon all the interests and property which derive advantage from it. The phrase "general average" is used, because a loss of a part is thus divided among all the other parts, and is sustained by all in equal proportion. This rule is ancient and universal. It would be held to apply to all our inland navigation, whether of river or lake, steam or canvas.

There are three essentials in general average without the concurrence of all of which there can be no claim for a loss. First, the sacrifice must be voluntary; second, it must be necessary; third, it must be successful. Or, in other words, there must be a common danger, a voluntary loss, and a saving of the imperilled property by that loss.

The loss must not only be voluntary, but, what is indeed implied in its being voluntary, it must be for the purpose and with the intention of saving something else. And this intention must be carried into effect; for only the interest or property which is actually saved can be called on to contribute for that which was lost.

The reason of what has been said must be distinctly understood, because the whole law of general average rests upon it. It is simply this: if any man's property be destroyed for the benefit of his neighbors, they who are helped by his loss ought to make up his loss. The law supposes that all who are interested in the ship or the cargo, or any part of either, agree together beforehand, that, if a sacrifice of a part can save the rest, that sacrifice shall be made, without stopping to ask who it is that suffers in the first place; and that afterwards, if the sacrifice be beneficial to any for whom it was made, such persons shall bear their share of it, by contributions to him whose property was purposely destroyed for their good. And their contributions shall be in proportion to the value of the property saved for them by the sacrifice.

Any loss which comes within this reason is an average loss; as ransom paid to a captor or pirate; not so, however, if he take what he will, and leave the ship and the rest; for this there is no contribution. So, cutting away bulwarks or the deck, to get at goods for jettison, is an average loss. As is also the cutting away of the masts and rigging, or throwing overboard a boat to relieve the ship, or the loss of a cable and anchor, or either, by cutting the cable to avoid an impending peril. So is a damage which, though not intended, is the direct effect and consequence of an act which was intended; as, where a mast is purposely cut away, and by reason of it water gets into the hold, and damages a cargo of corn, this damage is as much a general average as the loss of the mast.

But if a ship makes all sail in a violent gale to escape a lee shore, and so saves ship and cargo, but carries away her spars, &c.; or if an armed ship fights a pirate or enemy, or beats him off at great loss; the first is a common sea risk, the second a common war risk, and neither of them is a ground for average contribution.

It is not considered prudent to lade goods on deck, because they are not only more liable to loss there, but hamper the vessel, and perhaps make her top-heavy, and increase the common danger for the whole ship and cargo. Therefore, by the general rule, if goods on deck are *jettisoned* (which old mercantile wor l means cast overboard), they are not to be contributed for. But there are some voyages on which there is a known and established usage to carry goods of a certain kind on deck. This justifies the carrying them there, and then the jettison of them would entitle the owner to contribution.

The repairs of a ship are for the benefit of the ship itself. But if a ship be in a damaged condition, at a port where she cannot be permanently repaired, and receive there a temporary repair, which enables her to proceed to another port where she may have a thorough repair, and thereby the voyage is saved, the cost of all of the first repair which was of no further use than to make the permanent repair possible, is to be contributed for by ship, freight, and cargo, because all these were saved by it.

If a ship put into a port for necessary repair, and receive it, and the voyage is by reason thereof successfully prosecuted, the wages and provisions of the crew, from the time of putting away for the port, the expense of loading and unloading, and every other necessary expense arising from this need of repair, are an average.

As to the expenses, wages, &c., during a capture, or a detention by embargo, the claim for contribution is limited to those expenses which were necessarily and successfully incurred in saving or liberating the property.

The loss or sacrifice must be necessary or justified by a reasonable probability of its necessity and utility. In former times the law guarded with much care against wanton and unnecessary loss by requiring that the master should formally consult his officers and crew, and obtain their consent before making a jettison. But this rule has passed away and the practice is almost unknown; and it has been held that where a consultation is had this merely proves that the jettison was deliberately made, but does not prove the necessity of it.

An "Adjustment of Average" means an account stated, which exhibits accurately all the losses to be contributed for, and all the property or interests bound to contribute, and all the persons entitled to receive contribution, and the amounts they should each receive, and all persons bound to pay contribution, and the amounts they should each pay.

It is the master's duty to have an average adjustment made at the first port of delivery at which he arrives. And an adjustment made there, especially if this be a foreign port, is generally held to be conclusive upon all parties. For the purpose of this rule, our States are foreign to each other; as they are indeed for most purposes under the Law of Admiralty, or the Law of Shipping. And we should state the rule to be that an adjustment, when properly made, according to the law of the port where it is made, is binding everywhere. But a foreign adjustment might doubtless be set aside or corrected, for fraud or gross error.

The master has the right of refusing delivery of the goods, until the contribution due from them on general average is paid to him. That is, he cannot hold the whole cargo, if it belong to different consignees, until the whole average is paid; but he may hold all that belongs to each consignee, until all that is due from that consignee is paid. And the master may retain public property belonging to the United States until the average contribution due upon it has been paid.

As the purpose of average and contribution is to divide the loss proportionably over all the property saved by it, the whole amount which any one loses is not made up to him, but only so much as will make his loss the same percentage as every other party suffers. Thus, if there be four shippers, and each has on board $5,000, and the ship is worth $15,000, and the freight $5,000, and all the goods of one shipper are thrown over, and every thing else saved; now the the whole contributing interest is $40,000, and the loss, which is $5,000, is one-eighth of this contributory interest. The shipper whose goods are jettisoned therefore loses one-eighth of his goods, and the remaining seven-eighths are made up to him, by each owner of property saved giving up one-eighth.

There are usually in every commercial place persons whose business it is to make up Adjustments. As the losses usually consist of many items, some of which are general average, and some rest on the different interests on which they fell, and as the contributory interests must all be enumerated, and the value of each ascertained according to the general principles of law, and then the average struck on all these items, it is obvious that this must be a calculation requiring great care and skill; and as the adjustment affects materially persons who may not be present, nor specially represented, — for all these reasons only those who are known to be competent to the work should be employed to make this adjustment. With us this work is generally done by insurance brokers.

SECTION IX.

SALVAGE.

In the Law of Shipping and the usage of merchants, the word "salvage" has two quite different meanings. If a ship or cargo meets with disaster, and the larger part is destroyed or lost, and a part be saved, that which is saved is called the "salvage." Thus if a ship be wrecked, and sold where she lies because she cannot be got off, her materials, wood and metal, her spars, sails, cordage, boats, and every thing else about her which has any value, constitute the "salvage." And all of this, or the proceeds of it if it be sold by the master, belong to the owner or to the insurer, accordingly as circumstances may indicate; and this question will be considered in the chapter on the Law of Insurance.

Besides this, which is the primary meaning of the word, salvage has quite another signification. By an ancient and universal law, maritime property which has sustained maritime disaster, and is in danger of perishing, may be saved by any person who can save it, whether they are or are not requested to do so by the owner or his agent. And the persons so saving it acquire a right to compensation, and a lien or claim on the property saved for compensation. The persons saving the property are called "salvors;" the amount paid to them is paid for saving the property, or, as it was called, for the "salvage," meaning at first by this word the act of saving it; but the habit of paying so much for "salvage" led to understanding by "salvage" the money paid. Then it was said, the money was paid *as* salvage. This is now the more common use of the word. Thus a party bringing a saved vessel in demands "salvage," and estimates the salvage as so much; and the owners are said to lose so much by salvage, or so much money is charged to salvage, and insurers are said to be liable for salvage, meaning in all these and similar cases the amount paid for saving, or for the act of salvage.

This law is not only applicable to all maritime property, but is confined to that; and is nearly unknown in reference to property saved from destruction on land.

Because this principle is wholly and exclusively maritime, no court but that of Admiralty acknowledges and enforces it. The way in which it is enforced is this. Salvors have a lien on the property saved for their compensation; that is, they have possession of it, and have a right to keep possession of it until their claim be satisfied. For this purpose they bring the ship or goods into the nearest port, and then make their claim of the owner or his agent, if they can find him, and he is within reach. If he cannot be found, or if he refuses what they think proper to demand, they employ counsel who are acquainted with the practice in Admiralty courts, who present to the court in the district where the property is a *libel*, as it is called in Admiralty law, setting forth the facts, and the demand for salvage. Thereupon the court takes possession of the property, and orders notice to the owners, if possible. The owners thereupon appear, and either resist all the demand for salvage, on the ground that no services were performed which entitled the party to salvage, or, admitting the service, they go to trial to determine whether any salvage, and, if so, how much, shall be paid. On this question, evidence and argument are heard, and the court then issues such decree as the case seems to require.

Although services were rendered to the ship or cargo, or both, it does not follow that they were salvage services in the legal sense of the word. For certainly every person who helps another at sea does not thereby acquire a right to take possession of the property in reference to which his assistance was given, and carry it into port. To give this right, the property, whether ship or cargo, must have been, in the proper and rational sense of the term, *saved;* that is, there must have been actual disaster and impending danger of destruction; and from this danger the property must have been rescued by the exertions of the salvors, either alone, or working together with the original crew.

It is to be noticed, however, that neither the master nor officers nor sailors of the ship that is saved can be salvors, or entitled to salvage. The policy of the law-merchant forbids the holding out such a reward for merely doing their duty. It considers that sailors might be induced to let the vessel get into danger, if they could expect a special reward for getting her out of it. They are already bound by law to do all they possibly can do to save the ship and cargo under all circumstances. But courts of Admiralty have sometimes allowed gratuities to seamen for extraordinary exertions and very meritorious conduct. A passenger may be a salvor of the ship he sails in, because he has no especial duty in regard to it.

If the court of Admiralty find it to be a case for salvage, there are no positive and certain rules which determine how much shall be given, or in what proportions, to the different salvors. In every case the court are governed by the circumstances of that case; and even if a ship or cargo be entirely abandoned at sea, or, in maritime phrase, *derelict*, those who find it and take possession of it, and bring it in, take according to their merits, and not one-half, as used to be the rule. More than one-half is very seldom given; but this has been done in a few extraordinary cases.

If the property is not entirely derelict or deserted, and all hope of recovering it by the original crew given up, then less than half is usually given by way of salvage. How much less depends on the circumstances. It may be very little, or nearly half. The court inquire how much time was lost by the salvors, how much labor the saving of the property required, and, most of all, how much exposure the salvors underwent, or how much danger they incurred. For it is an established rule, that in addition to a fair compensation for time, labor, and loss of insurance (for which see the chapter on Insurance), the court will give a further sum by way of reward, and for the purpose of encouraging others to make similar exertions and incur similar perils to save valuable property. And, in this point of view, all necessary exposure and danger are considered as entitled to liberal reward.

If the court have not restored the property to its owners on their giving bonds with sureties to pay the salvage and costs, they order the property sold; and they may do either of these things at any period of the proceedings. At the close, they decree the whole amount of salvage, and also direct particularly its distribution.

A large part, usually about one-fourth, of the whole salvage, is allowed to the owners of the saving ship or ships; another large part to her master, less parts to the officers, in proportion to their rank, and the residue is divided among the crew, with such discrimination between one and another as greater or less exertions or merit require.

The trial is had, and the whole decree and this distribution of the salvage made, by the court alone, without a jury. But the statute of the United States, which gives our courts of Admiralty (which are exclusively United-States courts, no State court having any Admiralty power) jurisdiction in Admiralty over our inland lakes and rivers, provides that disputed facts shall be tried by a jury, in most cases, at the request of either party.

SECTION X.

THE NAVIGATION OF THE SHIP.

1. Of the Powers and Duties of the Master. — The master has the whole care and the supreme command of his vessel, and his duties are co-equal with his authority. He must see to every thing that respects her condition; including her repair, supply, loading, navigation, and unloading. He is principally the agent of the owner; but is, to a certain extent, the agent of the shipper, and of the insurer, and of all who are interested in the property under his charge.

Much of his authority as agent of the owner springs from necessity. He may even sell the ship in a case of extreme necessity; so he may make a bottomry bond which shall pledge her for a debt; so he may charter her for a voyage or a term of time; so he may raise money for repairs, or incur a debt therefor, and make his owners liable. All these, however, he can do only from necessity. If the owner be present, in person or by his agent, or is within easy access, or can be consulted, by telegraph or otherwise, without a loss of time which would be seriously injurious, the master has no power to do any of these things unless specially authorized.

If he does them in the home port, the owner is liable only where, by some act or words, he ratifies or adopts the act of his master. If in a foreign port, even if the owner were there, he may be liable, on his master's contracts of this kind, to those who neither knew nor had the means of knowing that the master's power was superseded or qualified by the presence of the owner. The master being by the law-merchant the *general agent* of the owner of the ship, no one dealing with him can be prejudiced by any private or secret limitations to his authority by the owner.

Beyond the ordinary extent of his power, which is limited to the care and navigation of the ship, he can go, as we have said, only from necessity. But this necessity must be greater to justify some acts than for others. Thus, he can sell the ship only in a case of extreme and urgent necessity; that is, only when it seems in all reason impossible to save her, and a sale is the only way of preserving for the owners or insurers any part of her value. We say "seems;" for if such is the appearance at the time, when all existing circumstances are carefully considered and weighed, the sale is not void, if some accident, or cause which could not be anticipated, as a sudden change in the wind or sea, enables the purchaser to save her easily. Several such cases have occurred.

So, to justify him in pledging her by bottomry, there must be a stringent and sufficient necessity; but it may be far less than is required to authorize a sale. It is enough if the money is really needed for the safety of the ship, and cannot otherwise be raised, or not without great waste.

So, to charter the ship, there must be a sufficient necessity, unless the master has express power to do this. But the necessity for this act may be only a mercantile necessity; or, in other words, a certain and considerable mercantile expediency.

So, to bind the owners to expense for repairs or supplies, there must also be a necessity for them. But here it is sufficient if the repairs or supplies are such as the condition of the vessel, and the safe and comfortable prosecution of the voyage, render proper.

So the master — unlike other agents, who have generally no power of delegation — may substitute another for himself, to discharge all his duties, and possess all his authority, if he is unable to discharge his own duties, because, in that case, the safety of the ship and property calls for this substitution.

Generally, the master has nothing to do with the cargo between the lading and the delivery. But, if the necessity arises, he may sell the cargo, or a part of it, at an intermediate port, if he cannot carry it on or transmit it, and it must perish before he can receive specific orders. So, he may sell it, or a part, or pledge (or hypothecate) it, by means of a *respondentia* bond, in order to raise money for the common benefit. A bond of respondentia is much the same thing as to the cargo that a bottomry bond is as to the ship. Money is borrowed by it, at maritime interest, on maritime risk, the debt to be discharged by a loss of the goods. But it can be made by the master only on even a stronger necessity than that required for bottomry; only when he can raise no money by bills on the owner, nor by a bottomry of the ship, nor by any other use of the property or credit of the owner. Indeed, it seems, that, when goods are sold by the master to repair the vessel, it is to be considered as in the nature of a forced loan, for which the owner of the vessel is liable to the shipper, whether the vessel arrive or not.

The general remark may be made, that a master has no ordinary power, and can hardly derive any extraordinary power even from any necessity, except for those things which are fairly within the scope of his business as master, and during his employment as master. Beyond this, he has no agency or authority that is not expressly given him.

The owner is liable also for the wrong-doings of the master; but with the limitation which belongs generally to the liability of a principal for the torts of his agent, or of a master for the torts of his servant. That is, he is liable for any injury done by the master while acting *as the master of his ship*, but not for the wrongful acts which he may do personally when he is not acting in his capacity of master, although he holds the office at the time. Thus if, through want of skill or care while navigating the ship, he runs another down, the owner is liable for the collision. But the owner is not liable if the master embezzles goods which he takes on board to fill his own privilege, to have himself all the freight and profit.

2. Of Collision. — The general rules in this country in respect to collision are that the party in fault suffers his own loss and compensates the other part for the loss he may sustain. If neither is in fault, the loss rests where it falls. If both parties are in fault, the loss rests where it falls by the rules of the common law, but is equally divided in Admiralty. There are certain rules in regard to sailing, founded on the principle that the ship which can change its course to avoid collision with least inconvenience must do so; and therefore that the ship that has a fair or leading wind shall give way to one on a wind, or go under her stern; and if vessels are approaching each other, both having the wind on the beam, or so far free that either may change its course in either direction, the vessel on the larboard tack must give way, and each pass to the right. The same rule governs vessels sailing on the wind, and approaching each other, when it is doubtful which is to the windward. But if the vessel on the larboard tack is so far to windward, that, if both persist on their course, the other will strike her on the lee side, abaft the beam, or near the stern, in that case the vessel on the starboard tack should give way, as she can do so with greater facility, and less loss of time and distance, than the other. Again, when vessels are crossing each other in opposite directions, and there is the least doubt of their going clear, the vessel on the starboard tack should persevere on her course, while that on the larboard tack should bear up, or keep away before the wind.

It is also held that steam-vessels are regarded in the light of vessels navigating with a fair wind, and are always under obligations to do whatever a sailing-vessel going free or with a fair wind would be required to do under similar circumstances. Their obligation extends still further, because they possess a power to avoid the collision not belonging to sailing-vessels, even if they have a free wind, the master having the steamer under his command, both by changing the helm and by stopping or reversing the engines.

As a general rule, therefore, when meeting a sailing-vessel, whether close-hauled or with the wind free, the latter has a right to keep her course, and it is the duty of the steamer to adopt such precautions as will avoid her.

Vessels in tide-ways, or otherwise in danger of collision, should hang out lights, but there is no positive rule or usage requiring the master, always, in the night-time, to keep a light exhibited on his vessel. In each case, whether common prudence required of the plaintiffs to have a light, and whether the omission of it amounted to negligence, must depend upon the darkness of the night, the number and situation of the vessels in the harbor, and all other circumstances connected with the transaction. This is a question of fact, within the province of the jury. A United-States statute requires lights in the case of certain steamboats, and directs where they shall be placed on the vessel.

All these rules should be observed, and neglect of them would go far to imply a want of care or skill. But none of these rules are in this country so positive as to bind masters or ship-owners in all cases with the force of law.

For any misdeed of the master, for which the owner is liable, this liability is limited in our own country, as well as in many others, to the value of the ship and freight.

SECTION XI.

THE SEAMEN.

THE law makes no important distinction between the officers, or mates, as they are usually called, and the common sailors. Our statutes contain many provisions in behalf of the seamen, and in regulation of their rights and duties, although the contract between them and the ship-owner is in general one of hiring and service. They relate principally to the following points: 1st, the shipping articles; 2d, wages; 3d, provisions and subsistence; 4th, the seaworthiness of the ship; 5th, the care of seamen in sickness; 6th, the bringing them home from abroad; 7th, regulation of punishment.

First. Every master of a vessel bound from a port in the United States to any foreign port, or of any ship or vessel of the burden of fifty tons or upwards, bound from a port in one State to a port in any other State, is required to have shipping articles, which articles every seaman on board must sign, under a penalty of twenty dollars for every person who does not sign, and they must describe accurately the voyage, and the terms on which each seaman ships. Courts will protect seamen against uncertain or catching language, and against unusual and oppressive stipulations. And the shipping articles ought to declare explicitly the ports of the beginning and of the termination of the voyage. If a number of ports are mentioned, they are to be visited only in their geographical and commercial order, and not revisited unless the articles give the master a discretion. Admiralty courts enforce the stipulations if they are fair and legal, or disregard them if they are otherwise, and exercise a liberal equity on this subject; but courts of common law are more strictly bound by the letter of the contract. The articles are generally conclusive as to wages; but accidental errors or omissions may be supplied or corrected by either party, by parol.

Second. Wages are regulated as above stated, and also by limiting the right to demand payment in a foreign port to one-third the amount then due, unless it be otherwise stipulated. Seamen have a lien on the ship and on the freight for their wages, which is enforceable in Admiralty. By the ancient rule, that freight is the mother of wages, any accident or misfortune which makes it impossible for the ship to earn its freight destroys the claim of the sailors for wages. The reason is, to hold out to the seamen the strongest possible inducement to enable the ship to carry the goods and earn the freight.

Third. Provisions of due quality and quantity must be furnished by the owner, and double wages are given to the seamen when on short allowance, unless the necessity be caused by some peril of the sea, or other accident of the voyage. The master may at any time put them on a fair and proper allowance to prevent waste.

Fourth. The owner is bound to provide a seaworthy vessel, and our statutes provide the means of lawfully ascertaining her condition at home or abroad, by a regular survey, on complaint of the mate and a majority of the seamen. But this very seldom occurs in practice. If seamen, after being shipped, refuse to proceed upon their voyage, and are complained of and arrested, the court will inquire into the condition of the vessel, and if the complaint of the seamen is justified, in a greater or less degree, will discharge them, or mitigate or reduce their punishment.

Fifth. As to sickness, our statutes require that every ship of the burden of one hundred and fifty tons or more, navigated by ten persons or more in the whole, and bound on a voyage without the limits of the United States, and also that vessels of seventy-five tons or more, navigated by six or more persons in the whole, bound from the United States to any port in the West Indies, shall have a proper medicine-chest on board. Moreover, twenty cents a month are deducted from the wages of every seaman to make up a fund for the maintenance of marine hospitals, to which every sick seaman may repair without charge. In addition to this the general law-merchant requires every ship-owner or master to provide suitable medicine, medical treatment, and care, for every seaman who becomes sick, wounded, or maimed, in the service of the ship, at home or abroad, at sea or on shore; unless this is caused by the misconduct of the seaman himself. The right to these things extends to the officers of the ship.

Sixth. The right of the seaman to be brought back to his own home is very jealously guarded by our laws. The master should always present his shipping articles to the consul or commercial agent of the United States, at every foreign port which he visits, but is not required by law to do this unless the consul desires it. He must, however, present them to the first boarding officer on his arrival at a home port. And if, upon an arrival at a home port from a foreign voyage, it appears that any of the seamen are missing, the master must account for their absence. If he discharge a seaman abroad with his consent, he must pay to the American consul of the port, or the commercial agent, over and above the wages then due, three months' wages, of which the consul gives two to the seaman, and remits one to the treasury of the United States to form a fund for bringing home seamen from abroad. This obligation does not apply where the seaman is discharged because the voyage is necessarily broken up by a wreck, or similar misfortune. But proper measures must be taken to repair the ship if possible, or to obtain her restoration, if captured. And the seamen may hold on for a reasonable time for this purpose, and if discharged before, may claim the extra wages.

Our consuls and commercial agents may authorize the discharge of a seaman abroad for his gross misconduct, and he then has no claim for the extra wages. On the other hand, if he be treated cruelly, or if the ship be unseaworthy by her own fault, or if the master violate the shipping articles, the consul or commercial agent may direct the discharge of the seaman; and he then has a right to these extra wages, and this even if the seaman had deserted the ship by reason of such cruelty. They may also send our seamen home in American ships, which are bound to bring them for a compensation not to exceed ten dollars each, and the seamen so sent must work and obey as if originally shipped. It is of great importance that the powers and duties of our consuls abroad should be distinctly defined and well known. And Congress has recently enacted an excellent statute on this subject.

If a master discharges a seaman against his consent, and without good cause, in a foreign port, he is liable to a fine of five hundred dollars, or six months' imprisonment. And a seaman may recover full indemnity or compensation for his loss of time, or expenses incurred by reason of such discharge.

Seventh. As to the regulation of punishment, flogging has been abolished and prohibited by law. Flogging means the use of the cat, or a similar instrument, but not necessarily blows of the hand, or a stick or a rope. Desertion, in maritime law, is distinguished from absence without leave, by the intention not to return. This intention is inferred from a refusal to return. If he returns and is received, this is a condonation (or forgiving) of the offence, and is a waiver of the forfeiture. If he desert before the voyage begins, he forfeits the advanced wages, and as much more; but he may be apprehended by a warrant of a justice, and forcibly compelled to go on board, and this is a waiver of the forfeiture. By desertion on the voyage, he forfeits all his wages and all his property on board the ship, and is liable to the owner for all damages sustained in hiring another seaman in his place.

Desertion, under the statute of the United States on this subject, is a continued absence from the ship for more than forty-eight hours, without leave; and there must be an entry in the log-book of the time and circumstance. But any desertion or absence without leave, at a time when the owner has a right to the seaman's service, is an offence by the law-merchant, giving the owner a right to full indemnity.

SECTION XII.

PILOTS.

An act of Congress authorizes the several States to make their own pilotage laws; and questions under these laws are cognizable in the State courts. No one can act as pilot, and claim the compensation allowed by law for the service, unless duly appointed. And he should always have with him his commission, which should always designate the largest vessel he may pilot, or that which draws the most water. If a pilot offers himself to a ship that has no pilot, and that is entering or leaving a harbor and has not already reached certain geographical limits, the ship must pay him pilotage fees, whether his services are accepted or not. As soon as the pilot stands on deck, he has control of the ship. But it remains the master's duty and power, in case of obvious and certain disability, or dangerous ignorance or error, to disobey the pilot, and dispossess him of his authority; but the master should interfere with the pilot only in extreme cases. If a ship neglect to take a pilot when it should and can take one, the owners will be answerable in damages to shippers or others for any loss which may be caused by such neglect or refusal. Pilots are themselves answerable for any damage resulting from their own negligence or default, and have been held strictly to this liability.

SECTION XIII.

MATERIAL MEN.

Maritime law calls by this name all persons employed to repair a ship or furnish her supplies. Such persons, and indeed all who work upon her, have a lien on the ship for their charges. There is, however, this important distinction. Material men, by Admiralty law, have a lien only on foreign ships, and not on domestic ships. But many of our States have by statute given this lien to material men on all ships, without distinction; as in New York, Pennsylvania, Massachusetts, Maine, Illinois, Indiana, Missouri, Alabama, and Michigan; and in Louisiana the same lien exists under the general Spanish law.

It has been held that such a lien extends beyond mere repairs, — certainly to alterations, and perhaps to reconstruction, — but not to original building, unless the statute includes ship-building. A laborer, employed in general work by a shipwright or mechanic, and by him sometimes employed on the vessel, and sometimes elsewhere, gets no lien on the vessel for that part of the labor performed about it. These statute liens take precedence of the claims of all other creditors.

It has been said in previous pages, that our States are foreign to each other for most purposes under the law of Admiralty; and they are so as to the lien of material men. Therefore, in States in which there is no statute on the subject, material men would have a lien for supplies or repairs for a vessel belonging to any other of our States, but not for a vessel belonging to the State in which the supplies were furnished or the repairs were made. See the chapter on Liens.

(91.)

Bill of Sale of Vessel.

To all to whom these Presents shall come, Greeting: Know ye, that (*name of seller*) of the (*town or city and county where he resides*) in the State of owner (*if the seller owns only a part of the vessel, here say what part*) of the (*ship, or what else it is*) or vessel called the of the burden of tons, or thereabouts, for and in consideration of the sum of dollars lawful money of the United States of America, to me (*or us, if more sellers than one*) in hand paid, before the ensealing and delivery of these presents, by (*name of the buyer*) the receipt whereof I (*or we*) do hereby acknowledge, have granted, bargained and sold, and by these presents do grant, bargain and sell, unto the said (*name of the buyer*) and his executors, administrators, and assigns, the whole (*or name the part*) of said or vessel, together with the masts, bowsprit, sails, boats, anchors, cables, tackle, apparel and furniture, and all other necessaries thereunto appertaining and belonging. The certificate of the enrolment of which said or vessel is as follows:

No. . ENROLMENT.

In conformity to an act of Congress of the United States of America, entitled "An Act for enrolling and licensing Ships and Vessels," &c., passed the 18th of February, 1793; and "An Act to regulate the Foreign and Coasting Trade on the Northern, North-eastern and North-western Frontiers of the United States, and for other purposes," passed the 17th of June, 1864, and all the acts of the 7th July, 1838; 29th July, 1850, and 6th May, 1864 (*name of the owner*) having taken or subscribed the oath required by the said acts, and having sworn that he citizen of the United States, and sole owner of the or vessel, called the of whereof is at present Master; and as he ha citizen of the United States, and that the said or vessel was built at in the year 18 , as appears by And having certified that the said vessel has deck mast , and that her length is feet, her breadth feet, her depth feet, her height feet, and that she measures tons and hundredths.

	Tonnage.	$\frac{1}{100}$
Capacity under tonnage deck		
Capacity between decks above tonnage deck		
Capacity of enclosure on upper deck		
Total tonnage		

that she has a figure-head (*describing it*).

And the said having agreed to the description and admeasurement above specified, and sufficient security having been given, in conformity with the terms of the said acts, the said has been duly enrolled at the port of

Given under my hand and seal of office, at the port of this day of in the year one thousand eight hundred and sixty

Collector.

To Have and to Hold the said or vessel, and appurtenances thereunto belonging, to him (*or them*), the said (*name of the buyer*) and his (*or their*) executors, administrators and assigns, to the sole and only proper use, benefit and behoof of him (*or them*), the said (*name of the buyer*) and his (*or their*) executors, administrators and assigns forever; and I (*or we*) the said (*name of the seller*) ha and by these presents do promise, covenant and agree, for myself (*or ourselves*) and my (*or our*) heirs, executors, administrators and assigns, to and with the said (*name of buyer*) and with his (*or their*) heirs, executors, administrators and assigns, to warrant and defend the said or vessel, and all the other before mentioned appurtenances against the lawful claims and demands of all and every person or persons whomsoever, and that I (*or we*) ha good right and authority to sell and dispose of the same in manner aforesaid.

In Testimony Whereof, The said has hereunto set his hand and seal this day of one thousand eight hundred and

(*Signature.*) (*Seal.*)

Sealed and Delivered in the Presence of

STATE OF ,
COUNTY. } ss.

I, a Notary Public in and for the in the County of and State of , do hereby certify, that personally known to me as the same person whose name subscribed to the annexed instrument of writing, appeared before me this day in person, and acknowledged that signed, sealed and delivered the said instrument or writing as free and voluntary act, for the uses and purposes therein set forth.

Given under my hand and notarial seal this day of A.D. 186

Notary Public,

(92.)

Mortgage of a Vessel.

Know all Men by these Presents, That I (*or we, giving the names and residence of all the mortgagors*) am (*or are*)

held and firmly bound unto (*the names and residence of the mortgagees*) in the just and full sum of dollars, lawful money of the United States of America, to be paid to the said or his (*or their*) executors, administrators or assigns: for which payment well and truly to be made, I bind myself, my heirs, executors and administrators firmly by these presents.

Dated at this day of in the year one thousand eight hundred and

Whereas, *(name of the mortgagee)* has this day lent and advanced unto the said *(name of the mortgagor)* the sum of dollars on the body, tackle and appurtenances of the or vessel called the of the burden of tons, or thereabouts; the said *(name of the mortgagor)* being the *(owner)* of the same.

Now the Condition of this Obligation is such, That if the said *(name of the mortgagor)* shall pay or cause to be paid to the said *(name of the mortgagee)* the sum of dollars (the amount loaned), and interest thereon on or before the day of in the year 18

then this obligation to be void; otherwise, to remain in full force and virtue. And in consideration of and as security for said loan as aforesaid, the said *(vessel, or ship, or steamer, as it may be)* is by these presents assigned, pledged, mortgaged, set over and conveyed to the said heirs and assigns; the certificate of the enrolment of which vessel is as follows, viz.:—

(Enrolment as in the previous form of a Bill of Sale of a Vessel.)

It being Mutually Understood and Agreed, That in case the amount of said loan and interest, or any part thereof, according to the terms of these presents, shall remain due and unpaid to said *(name of mortgagee)* after the expiration of the said *(name of mortgagee)* may take possession of said and appurtenances, and sell the same at public auction, in order to satisfy the amount then due, without any proceedings in court or otherwise, for the purpose of authorizing such sale, and thereupon may execute and deliver a sufficient bill of sale to transfer completely to any purchaser or purchasers all title and property in and to the said and appurtenances, to the said *(name of mortgagor)* as *(owner)* thereof, now belonging.

The said *(name of the mortgagee)* thereupon to account to the said *(name of the mortgagor)* for any surplus of such sale, after paying all charges and expenses.

And in case of such sale as aforesaid, the said *(name of the mortgagor)* executors, administrators or assigns, shall, whenever thereto requested, make, execute and deliver to such purchaser or purchasers, another bill of sale of said and appurtenances, in which the enrolment shall be recited as above, for the transferring completely to said purchaser or purchasers all the *(right)*, *(interest)* and *(claim)*, of said executors, administrators or assigns, as *(owner)* of said And in default of the prompt execution and delivery of such other bill of sale to such purchaser or purchasers, by the said when thereto requested, the said is hereby constituted and appointed the legal attorney of the said for the purpose of making, executing and delivering such bill of sale, and the said hereby ratifies and confirms the act of the said as attorney for said purpose.

And it is hereby further Agreed, That insurance shall be made at some office in on the said for the security of the said *(name of the mortgagee)* to an amount not less than the sum loaned as aforesaid, and the said *(name of the mortgagee)* is hereby authorized to procure such insurance, at the expense of the said *(name of the mortgagor)* if not seasonably obtained by him.

(Signature.) *(Seal.)*

Signed, Sealed and Delivered in Presence of
(Witness.)

STATE OF } ss.
COUNTY OF }

On the day of in the year one thousand eight hundred and before me personally came to be the individual described in, and who executed the foregoing instrument, and acknowledged that he executed the same.

(93.)

A Charter-Party.

This Charter-Party, Made and concluded upon in the day of in the year one thousand eight hundred and between *(name of the owner)* owner of the of of the burden of tons or thereabouts, register measurement, now lying in the harbor of of the first part, and *(name of the hirer)* of the second part, witnesseth, that the said part of the first part, for and in consideration of the covenants and agreements hereinafter mentioned, to be kept and performed by the said part of the second part, do covenant and agree on the freighting and chartering of the said vessel unto the said part of the second part, for the voyage from the port of

on the terms following; that is to say, —

First. The said part of the first part do engage that the said vessel in and during the said voyage shall be kept tight, stanch, well-fitted, tackled, and provided with every requisite, and with men and provisions necessary for such a voyage.

Second. The said part of the first part do further engage that the whole of said vessel (with the exception of the cabin, the deck, and the necessary room for the accommodation of the crew, and of the sails, cables, and provisions) shall be at the sole use and disposal of the said part of the second part during the voyage aforesaid; and that no goods or merchandise whatever shall be laden on board, otherwise than from the said part of the second part, or agent, without consent, on pain of forfeiture of the amount of freight agreed upon for the same.

Third. The said part of the first part do further engage to take and receive on board the said vessel, during the aforesaid voyage, all such lawful goods and merchandise as the said part of the second part, or agents, may think proper to ship.

And the said part of the second part, for and in consideration of the covenants and agreements to be kept and performed by the said part of the first part, do covenant and agree with the said part of the first part, to charter and hire the said vessel as aforesaid, on the terms following, that is to say:—

First. The said part of the second part do engage to provide and furnish to the said vessel

Second. The said part of the second part do further engage to pay to the said part of the first part, or agent, for the charter or freight of the said vessel during the voyage aforesaid, in the manner following, that is to say:—

It is further agreed between the parties to this instrument, that the said part of the second part shall be allowed, for the loading and discharging of the vessel at the respective ports aforesaid, lay days as follows, that is to say:—

and in case the vessel is longer detained, the said part of the second part agree to pay to the said part of the first part, demurrage at the rate of Spanish milled dollars per day for each and every day so detained, provided such detention shall happen by default of the said part of the second part, or agent.

It is further understood and agreed, that the cargo shall be received and delivered alongside within reach of the vessel's tackles.

It is also further understood and agreed, that this charter shall commence when the vessel is ready to receive cargo at her place of loading, and notice thereof is given to the part of the second part, or to agent

To the true and faithful performance of all the foregoing covenants and agreements, the said parties, each to the other, do hereby bind themselves, their executors, administrators and assigns, and also the said vessel, freight, tackle, and appurtenances; and the merchandise to be laden on board, each to the other, in the penal sum of

In Witness Whereof, The said parties have hereunto interchangeably set their hands and seals this day of 185

(Signatures.) *(Seals.)*

Signed, Sealed and Delivered in the Presence of
(Witnesses.)

(94.)

A Bill of Lading.

Shipped, in good order and well conditioned, by (*name of the shipper*) on board the called the whereof is master, now lying in the port of and bound for To say :— (*here describe or enumerate the parcels*)

being marked and numbered as in the margin, and are to be delivered in the like good order and condition, at the aforesaid port of (the dangers of the seas only excepted), unto (*the name of the consignee*) or to assigns, he or they paying freight for the said
(*here specify the rate of freight agreed to be paid*)
with primage and average accustomed.

In Witness Whereof, The master or purser of the said vessel hath affirmed to bills of lading, all of this tenor and date; one of which being accomplished, the others to stand void.

Dated in the day of 185

(*Signature.*)

(95.)

Shipping Articles, in Common Use.

United States of America. It is agreed, between the master and seamen, or mariners, of the (*name of the vessel*) of whereof is at present master, or whoever shall go for master, now bound from the port of , to

And it is hereby expressly agreed, that should the said ship on the said voyage be seized, detained, or fined, for smuggling tobacco, or any other article, by one or more of the undersigned sailors, cooks, or stewards, they shall all be responsible for the damages thence resulting, and shall severally forfeit their wages, and all their goods and chattels on board, to the amount of such damage, and that the certificate of the person or persons who may seize, detain, or fine the said ship for smuggling, signed by him or them, and verified by the American consul at under his seal of office, shall be conclusive evidence of the facts therein stated, in all courts whatsoever, especially and as to the fact that smuggling had been committed, the individual or individuals by whom the same had been committed, the amount of the fine imposed therefor upon the said ship, the incidental expenses thereon, and the number of days the said ship was detained in consequence thereof. No grog allowed, and none to be put on board by the crew; and no profane language allowed, nor any sheath-knives permitted to be brought or used on board.

That, in consideration of the monthly or other wages against each respective seaman or mariner's name hereunder set, they severally shall and will perform the above-mentioned voyage: And the said master doth hereby agree with and hire the said seamen or mariners for the said voyages, at such monthly wages or prices, to be paid pursuant to this agreement, and the laws of the Congress of the United States of America: And they, the said seamen or mariners, do severally hereby promise and oblige themselves to do their duty, and obey the lawful commands of their officers on board the said vessel, or the boats thereunto belonging, as become good and faithful seamen or mariners; and at all places where the said vessel shall put in, or anchor at, during the said voyage, to do their best endeavors for the preservation of the said vessel and cargo, and not to neglect or refuse doing their duty by day or night, nor shall go out of the said vessel on board any other vessel, or be on shore, under any pretence whatsoever, until the above-said voyage be ended, and the said vessel be discharged of her loading, without leave first obtained of the captain or commanding officer on board: that in default thereof, he or they will be liable to all the penalties and forfeitures mentioned in the Marine Law, enacted for the government and regulation of seamen in the merchants' service, in which it is enacted, "That if any seaman or mariner shall absent himself from on board the ship or vessel, without leave of the master or officer commanding on board, and the mate or other officer having charge of the log-book, shall make an entry therein of the name of such seaman or mariner, on the day on which he shall so absent himself; and if such seaman or mariner shall return to his duty within forty-eight hours, such seaman or mariner shall forfeit three days' pay for every day which he shall so absent himself, to be deducted out of his wages; but if any seaman or mariner shall absent himself for more than forty-eight hours at one time, he shall forfeit all wages due to him, and all his goods and chattels which were on board the said ship or vessel, or in any store where they may have been lodged at the time of his desertion, to the use of the owner or owners of the said ship or vessel, and moreover shall be liable to pay him or them all damages which he or they may sustain by being obliged to hire other seamen or mariners in his or their place."

And it is further agreed, that in case of desertion, death, or imprisonment, the wages are to cease.

And it is further agreed by both parties, that each and every lawful command which the said master or other officer shall think necessary hereafter to issue for the effectual government of the said vessel, suppressing immorality and vice of all kinds, shall be strictly complied with, under the penalty of the person or persons disobeying forfeiting his or their whole wages or hire, together with every thing belonging to him or them on board the said vessel.

And it is further agreed on, that no officer or seaman belonging to the said vessel shall demand or be entitled to his wages, or any part thereof, until the arrival of said vessel at the said vessel's final port of discharge, and her cargo delivered.

And it is hereby further agreed, between the master, officers, and seamen of the said vessel, that whatever apparel, furniture, and stores each of them may receive into their charge, belonging to the said vessel, shall be accounted for on her return; and in case any thing shall be lost or damaged, through their carelessness or insufficiency, it shall be made good by such officer or seaman, by whose means it may happen, to the master and owners of the said vessel.

And whereas, it is customary for the officers and seamen, while the vessel is in port, or while the cargo is delivering, to go on shore at night to sleep, greatly to the prejudice of such vessel and freighters, be it further agreed by the said parties, that neither officer nor seaman shall, on any pretence whatever, be entitled to such indulgence, but shall do their duty by day in discharge of the cargo, and keep such watch by night as the master shall think necessary to order relative to said vessel or cargo; and whereas it frequently happens that the owner or captain incurs expenses while in a foreign port, relative to the imprisonment of one or more of his officers or crew, or in the attendance of nurses, or in the payment of board on shore for the benefit of such person or persons: now it is understood and agreed by the parties hereunto, that all such expenditures as may be incurred by reason of the foregoing premises shall be charged to, and deducted out of the wages of, any officer or such one of the crew by whose means or for whose benefit the same shall have been paid.

And whereas, it often happens that part of the cargo is embezzled after being safely delivered into lighters, and as such losses are made good by the owners of the vessel, be it therefore agreed by these presents, that whatever officer or seaman the master shall think proper to appoint, shall take charge of her cargo in the lighters, and go with it to the lawful quay, and there deliver his charge to the vessel's husband, or his representative, to see the same safely landed.

That each seaman or mariner who shall well and truly perform the above-mentioned voyage (provided always that there be no desertion, plunderage, embezzlement, or other unlawful acts committed on the said vessel's cargo or stores) shall be entitled to the payment of the wages or hire that may become due to him pursuant to this agreement, as to their names is severally affixed and set forth: *Provided, nevertheless*, that if any of the said crew disobey the orders of the said master or other officer of the said vessel, or absent himself at any time without liberty, his wages due at the time of such disobedience or absence shall be forfeited; and in case such person or persons so forfeiting wages shall be reinstated or permitted to do further duty, it shall not do away such forfeiture. It being understood and agreed, by the said parties, that parol proof of the misconduct, absence, or desertion of any officer or any of the crew of said vessel, may be given in evidence at any trial between the parties to this contract, any act, law, or usage to the contrary thereof notwithstanding.

In Testimony Whereof, and for the due performance of each and every of the above-mentioned articles and agreements, and acknowledgment of their being voluntarily, and without compulsion or any other clandestine means being used, agreed to and signed by us, we have each and every of us hereunto affixed our hands, the month and day against our names as hereunder written.

And it is hereby understood, and mutually agreed, by and between the parties aforesaid, that they will render themselves on board the said vessel, on or before the day of 18 at o'clock in the noon.

This is signed by all the officers and crew, under seventeen columns, which give the following particulars: Date of entry, names, stations, birthplace, age, height in feet and inches, wages per month, advance wages, advance abroad, hospital money, time of service in months and days, whole wages, wages due, sureties, witness. On the back of this instrument is usually a receipt in full in the following words. It should be remarked, however, that the sailor's discharge of all demands for assault and battery or imprisonment, &c., is of little, if any, legal force.

We, the undersigned, late mariners on board the on her late voyage described on the other side of this instrument, and now performed to this place of payment, do hereby, each one for ourselves, with our signatures, acknowledge to have received of agent or owner of said the full sum hereunder set against our names; being in full amount of our wages for our services, and all demands for assault and battery, or imprisonment, of whatever name or nature, against said her owners or officers, to the day or date hereunder also set against our names.

(*Signatures.*)

(96.)

A Bottomry Bond.

Know all Men by these Presents, That I (*name of the master, or of the owner if the Bond is made by him*) now master and commander of the or vessel called the of the burden of tons, or thereabouts, now lying in the port of am held and firmly bound unto (*name of the lender, who is the obligee of the Bond*) in the sum of lawful money of the United States of America, to be paid to the said or to certain attorney executors, administrators, or assigns; for which payment, well and truly to be made, I bind myself, my heirs, executors, and administrators, and also the said vessel, her tackle, apparel, and furniture, firmly by these presents. Sealed with my seal, at this day of in the year of our Lord one thousand eight hundred and

Whereas, The above bounden (*name of the obligor*) has been obliged to take up and borrow, and hath received of the said for the use of the said vessel, and for the purpose of fitting the same for sea, the sum of lawful money of the United States of America, which sum is to be and remain as a lien and bottomry on the said vessel, her tackle, apparel, and furniture,

at the rate or premium of (*state the rate of the maritime interest*) for the voyage. In consideration whereof, all risks of the seas, rivers, enemies, fires, pirates, &c., are to be on account of the said (*name of the lender*). And for the better security of the said sum and premium, the said master doth, by these presents, hypothecate and assign over to the said heirs, executors, administrators, and assigns, the said vessel, her tackle, apparel, and furniture,
And it is hereby declared, that the said vessel, is thus hypothecated and assigned over for the security of the money so borrowed, and taken up as aforesaid, and shall be delivered for no other use or purpose whatever, until this bond is first paid, together with the premium hereby agreed to be paid thereon.

Now the Condition of this Obligation is such, That if the above bounden (*the borrower*) shall well and truly pay, or cause to be paid, unto the said (*the lender*)
the just and full sum of lawful money as aforesaid, being the sum borrowed, and also the premium aforesaid, at or before the expiration of days after the arrival of the said vessel at

then this obligation, and the said hypothecation, to be void and of no effect, otherwise to remain in full force and virtue. Having signed and executed two bonds of the same tenor and date, one of which being accomplished, the other to be void and of no effect.

(*Signature.*) (*Seal.*)

Signed, Sealed and Delivered in the Presence of

I do not give the form of a Respondentia Bond. This contract is now unusual, and is made only when some special emergency calls for it, and must then be framed to suit that emergency, and express the special terms of the bargain. The foregoing form, in connection with what is said of Respondentia Bonds in the text, and the points in which they resemble Bottomry Bonds and those in which they differ from them, will enable any one to frame a Respondentia Bond suited to most cases.

(97.)

Oath or Affirmation of Consignee or Agent.

District and Port of Philadelphia. I (*name of the consignee*) do solemnly and truly swear (*or affirm*) that the invoice and bill of lading now presented by me to the collector of , are the true and only invoice and bill of lading by me received, of all the goods, wares, and merchandise, imported in the (*name of the vessel*) whereof is master, from for account of any person whomsoever, for whom I am authorized to enter the same: that the said invoice and bill of lading are in the state in which they were actually received by me, and that I do not know nor believe in the existence of any other invoice, or bill of lading of the said goods, wares, and merchandise; that the entry now delivered to the collector contains a just and true account of the said goods, wares, and merchandise according to the said invoice and bill of lading: that nothing has been, on my part, nor to my knowledge, on the part of any other person, concealed or suppressed, whereby the United States may be defrauded of any part of the duty lawfully due on the said goods, wares, and merchandise, and that if, at any time hereafter, I discover any error in the said invoice, or in the account now rendered of the said goods, wares, and merchandise, or receive any other invoice of the same, I will immediately make the same known to the collector of the district

And I do further solemnly and truly swear (*or affirm*) that, to the best of my knowledge and belief, (*name and residence of the owner of the goods*) is owner of the goods, wares, and merchandise, mentioned in the annexed entry; that the invoice now produced by me exhibits the actual cost, or fair market-value, of the said goods, wares, and merchandise, all the charges thereon, and no other or different discount, bounty, or drawback, but such as has been actually allowed on the same.

this day of 18

(*Signature.*)

Before me, *Collector.*

(98.)

Custom House Power of Attorney. No. 201.

Know all Men by these Presents, That I (*name of principal*) do make, constitute, and appoint (*name of attorney*) my true and lawful attorney for me and in my name and stead to enter in due form of law, at the Custom House in the city of all goods, wares, and merchandise, which have been imported or may hereafter be imported by or which have arrived, consigned, or may hereafter arrive, consigned to or in which or may be interested or concerned.

And for me and in my name and stead to sign, seal, execute, and deliver all and every bond and bonds which may be required to secure the duties thereon, or for the transportation or exportation of the same; or any other bond or bonds required by the revenue laws or the regulations of the Treasury Department of the United States, or the collector of the customs of the district of relative to any such merchandise; or which may be necessary to obtain the debenture and debentures, upon such of the said goods, wares, and merchandise as may be exported for me or on my account. To have, take, and receive all debenture certificates to be issued thereupon for me and in my name to indorse, assign, and transfer the same; or have, take, and receive the moneys due and to grow due thereon: And generally, as my attorney to do, transact, and perform all custom-house business, of what kind soever, in which I am or may be interested or concerned, as fully and effectually, to all intents and purposes, as I if present there in person, could do; also to set my seal to any instrument which may be necessary in the premises, and the same to acknowledge for me to be my deed; and generally to do and perform all things relating to the premises, which I could lawfully do, if personally present, and as fully and effectually to every intent and purpose, although the same should seem to require more precise or special authority than is herein expressed. And especially authorizng and empowering my said attorney, for me and in my name and stead to sign, seal, execute, and deliver all bonds of indemnity and other specialities, and also all other documents which may be necessary for effecting the premises; hereby ratifying all and whatsoever my said attorney may lawfully do by virtue hereof.

And I hereby further authorize my said attorney at any time, and from time to time at his discretion, by proper letters of attorney, to substitute any other person or persons for himself in my place, and the same at his pleasure to revoke; hereby giving to the substitute or substitutes, as full power and authority in the premises, as is hereby given to my said attorney. And also hereby ratifying and confirming all and every act, matter, and thing, that my said attorney or his substitute or substitutes may do in the premises, by virtue of these presents.

And it is hereby declared and understood, that this power shall be and remain in full force and virtue until revoked by written notice given to the collector.

In Witness Whereof, I have have hereunto set my hand and seal this day of 18

(*Signature.*) (*Seal.*)

Signed, Sealed and Delivered in Presence of

STATE OF

Be it Known, That on the day of 18 personally appeared and acknowledged before me the foregoing power of attorney to be free act and deed.

In Testimony Whereof, I have hereunto set my hand and seal of office the day of 18

(99.)

Maritime Protest.

UNITED STATES OF AMERICA.

Notary.

STATE OF COUNTY OF

By this Public Instrument of Protest, Be it known, that on the day of in the year of our Lord one thousand eight hundred and before me, a Notary Public in and for the State of County of and dwelling in the city of , State of , duly commissioned and sworn, personally came and appeared (*names of all the parties who make the protest, with a description of each of them, as to occupation and residence*) which said appearers, after having been duly sworn by me, the said notary, upon the Holy Evangelists of Almighty God, voluntarily, freely and solemnly declare and depose as follows, to wit: that the (*name of the vessel, describing her generally*) on the day of in the year 18 sailed from the port of bound for the port of with a cargo of that when they started, as aforesaid, the said was stout, stanch and strong; had her cargo well and sufficiently stowed and secured; was well manned, tackled, victualled, apparelled and appointed; and was in every respect fit for the voyage she was about to undertake: And thereafter, on the day of in the year 18 (*here must be set forth with some minuteness the place of any accident or loss, and the circumstances of the occurrence*)
Now, therefore, because of the premises, and as all the loss, damage and injury which already have or may hereafter appear to have happened or accrued to the said or her said cargo, has been occasioned solely by the circumstances hereinbefore stated, and cannot nor ought not to be attributed to any insufficiency of the said or default of him, the said his officers or crew; he now requires me, the said notary, to make his protest and this public act thereof, that the same may serve and be and remain in full force and virtue, as of right shall appertain. And thereupon the said doth protest, and I, the said notary, at his special instance and request, do, by these presents, publicly and solemnly protest against winds, weather (*and whatever else caused the loss, as fire, or pirates, &c.*), and against all and every accident, matter and thing, had and met with as aforesaid, whereby or by means whereof the said or her cargo, already has, or hereafter shall appear to have suffered or sustained damage or injury, for all losses, costs charges, expenses, damages, and injury, which the said the owner or owners of the said or the owners, freighters or shippers of her said cargo, or any other person or persons concerned in either, already have

or may hereafter pay, sustain, incur, or be put unto by, through, or on account of the premises, or for which the insurer or insurers of the said or her cargo, is or are respectively liable to pay, or make contribution or average, according to custom, or their respective contracts or obligations; so that no part of such losses and expenses already incurred, or hereafter to be incurred, do fall upon him, the said his officers and crew.

We, (*repeat here the names of the appearers*) do solemnly swear that the foregoing statement is correct, and contains a true account of all the facts and circumstances of the case, to the best of our knowledge.

(*Signatures of all the appearers.*)

Thus Done and Protested, at my office, in the city of , this day of in the year of our Lord one thousand eight hundred and sixty

Notary Public, County of State of

To all to whom these Presents shall come: I, Notary Public, duly commissioned and qualified, residing at , in the County of and State of , do hereby certify that the foregoing, purporting to be a copy of the protest of the master and a part of the crew of the bearing date the day of last, is a true and correct copy of said protest, which was made before me, examined and compared with the original draft of the same, drawn up and recorded in my office, in Book page and following:

In Testimony Whereof, I have hereunto set my hand, and affixed my notarial seal, this day of A.D. 18

(*Signature.*) (*Seal.*)

(100.)

A Steamboat Warrant, as used in the Western States.

Know all Men by these Presents, That we (*name of debtor*) as principal, and (*names of owners of the steamboat*) owners of the steamboat as security, are held and firmly bound unto (*name of creditor*) in the sum of dollars, for the payment of which we bind ourselves, our heirs, executors, and administrators, firmly by these presents. Sealed with our seals, and dated this day of eighteen hundred and sixty

The Condition of the above Obligation is such, That, whereas, the said (*name of creditor*) as plaintiff has sued out of the office of justice of the peace, a warrant against the steamboat (*name of the steamboat*) returnable forthwith; being on a demand for the sum of dollars, and cents.

Now, if the said (*name of the debtor*) shall satisfy the amount which shall be adjudged to be owing and due to the said plaintiff in the determination of said suit, together with all costs accruing, then this obligation to be void, otherwise to remain in full force.

(*Signatures.*) (*Seals.*)

Approved, Sheriff (*or Constable*)

CHAPTER XXVI.

MARINE INSURANCE.

SECTION I.

HOW THE CONTRACT OF INSURANCE IS MADE.

At the present day insurance is seldom made by individuals. Formerly, this was the universal custom in our commercial cities. Afterwards, companies were incorporated for the purpose of making insurance on ships and their cargoes; and the manifold advantages of this method have caused it to supersede the other. But an insurance company is not bound to insure for all who offer, and it has been held that an action will not lie against insurers for combining not to insure for a certain person, however malicious their motive may be.

The contract of insurance binds the insurer to indemnify the insured against loss or injury to certain property or interests which it specifies, from certain perils which it also specifies. The consideration for this obligation on the part of the insurer is the premium paid to the insurer, or promised to be paid to him, by the insured.

The instrument in which this contract is expressed is called a Policy of Insurance. But no instrument is essential to the validity of the contract; for if the proposals of the insured are written in the usual way in the proposal book of the insured, and signed by their officer with the word "done" or "accepted," or in any usual way to indicate that the bargain is made, it is valid, although no policy be delivered; and it would be construed as an insurance upon the terms expressed in the policy commonly used by that company.

If proposals are made, on either side, by letter, and accepted by the other party, also by letter, this is a valid contract of insurance as soon as the party accepting has mailed his letter to that effect, if he have not previously received notice of a withdrawal of the proposals.

The form of the policy is generally that which has been used for many years both in England and in this country, with such changes and modifications only as will make it express more accurately the bargain between the parties. And for this purpose it may be and is varied at pleasure.

It is subscribed only by the insurers; but binds both parties. The insured are bound for the premium, although no note is given. The date may be controlled by evidence showing when it was made and delivered; but if delivered after its date, it takes effect at and from its date, if that were the intention of the parties.

It may be effected on application of an agent of the insured, if he have full authority for this purpose; which need not be in writing. But a mere general authority, even if it related to commercial matters, or to a ship itself, as that of a "ship's husband," is not sufficient.

A party may be insured who is not named, if "for whom it may concern," or words of equivalent import, are used. But a party who seeks to come in under such a clause must show that he was interested in the property insured at the time the insurance was made, and that he was in the contemplation of the party asking insurance. The phrase "on account of owners at the time of loss," or an equivalent phrase, will bring in those who were intended, if they owned the property when the loss occurred, although there were assignments and transfers between the time of insurance and the loss.

Each person whose several interest is actually insured by any such general phrase may demand or sue in his own name.

If the nominal insured is described as "agent" generally, this is equivalent to "for all whom it may concern." And an insurance "for ——" will be read as for all whom it may concern, if that were intended. So, if the designation of the insured be common to many persons, the intention of the parties must decide for whom it is made. Whatever is written on any part of the sheet containing the policy, or even on a separate paper, if referred to or signed by the parties as a part of the policy, is thereby made a part of it.

But things said by either party while making their bargain, or written on other paper, and not so referred to or signed, form no part of it. The policy may expressly provide that its terms shall be made definite, especially as to the property insured, by subsequent indorsements or additions. Thus, it is very common to insure property to a certain amount, "from A to B, on board ship or ships, as shall hereafter be indorsed on this policy." And when this or any equivalent phrase is used, the insured requests the insurers to indorse on the policy the name of the vessel, and the amount shipped, as soon as he has notice of it.

Alterations may be made at any time by consent. But a material alteration by either party, without the consent of the other, renders the contract void; although it was made honestly, in the hope or belief of its being assented to. A court of equity will correct a material mistake of fact.

A policy may be assigned, and the assignee may sue in the name of the assignor. If the loss is made by the policy payable "to order" or "to bearer," it will then be negotiable by indorsement or delivery, but it is not certain that the transferee can even then sue in his own name. In New York and some other States, not only these assignees, but other assignees of debts or contracts, may sue in their own names.

If the insured transfers the property, unaccompanied by a transfer of the policy with consent of the insurer, this discharges the policy, unless it was expressly made for the benefit of whoever should be owner at the time of the loss, as before stated. There is usually a clause to the effect that the policy is void if assigned without the consent of the insurers. But this does not apply to an assignment by force of law, as in a case of insolvency, or in a case of death. And after a loss has occurred, the claim against the insurers is always assignable like any other debt. And a seller who remains in possession of the property as trustee for the purchaser, or a mortgagor retaining possession, may retain the policy, and preserve his rights.

SECTION II.

THE INTEREST OF THE INSURED.

THE contract of Insurance is a contract of indemnity for loss. The insured must therefore be interested in the property at the time of the loss. The value to be paid for may be agreed upon beforehand, and expressed in the policy, which is then called a *valued policy;* or left to be ascertained by proper evidence, and the policy is then called an *open policy.*

This valuation, if in good faith, is binding on both parties, even if it be very high indeed. But a *wager policy*, that is, one without interest, is void; and although there be some interest, the valuation may still be so excessive as to be open to the objection that the interest is a mere cover, and that the contract is void because only one cf wager. The valuation is void if fraudulent in any respect; as if it cover an illegal interest or peril. And in this case the fraud vitiates and avoids the whole contract, and the insured recovers nothing. And if the valuation is gross and excessive, fraud may be presumed.

The insured may apply his valuation to the whole property, or to that part of it which he wishes to insure; thus he may cause himself to be insured for one-half of a cargo, the whole of which is valued at $20,000, or for one-half, which half is valued at $20,000; and if the policy says, "Insured $15,000 on half the ship Scipio (or on her cargo), valued at $20,000," whether it is meant that the whole ship (or cargo) is valued at $20,000, or the half only that is insured, will be determined by a reasonable construction of the language used. If he owns the whole, the valuation, in general, will be held to apply to the whole; and only to a part, if he owns only a part.

He may value one thing insured, and not another; or may value the same thing in one policy, and not in another, and then the valuation does not affect the policy which does not contain it. If only a part of the goods included in the valuation are on board and at risk, it applies to them in due proportion to their value.

A valuation of an outward cargo may be taken as a valuation of a return cargo, substituted for the other by purchase, and covered by the same policy. And a valuation will cover the insured's whole interest in the thing valued, including the premium, unless a different purpose is expressed or indicated.

A valuation of freight applies to the freight of the whole cargo; and, if a part only be at risk, it applies in proportion. And it applies either to the whole voyage, or to freight earned by voyages which form parts of the whole, as may be intended and expressed.

If profits are insured as such, they are generally valued, but may be insured by an open policy. If they are valued, the loss of the goods on which the profits were to have been made implies in this country a loss of the valued profits, without proof that there would have been any profit whatever; it seems to be necessary in England to show that there would have been some profit, and then the valuation attaches.

It is very common to insure profits, in fact, without saying any thing about them, by a valuation of the goods sufficiently high to include all the profits that can be made upon them.

In an open policy, where the value insured is to be determined by evidence, the value of the property — whether ship or goods — which is insured, is its value when the insurance took effect, including the premium of insurance; as the law of insurance intends indemnifying the assured as accurately as may be for all his loss. If a ship be insured, its value throughout the insurance is the same as at the beginning, without allowance for the effect of time upon it. And all its appurtenances, in a mercantile sense of this phrase, enter into this value.

While the *value* of the property does not vary with time, the *interest* of the insured at the time of the loss (which may be the whole, or half, or any other part) is that on which he founds his claim. Thus, if an owner of a ship is insured $20,000 on ship A. B., valued at $30,000, and afterwards sells half of the ship, and it is subsequently lost, he recovers only $10,000. But if he owned half originally, and insured that, and before the loss acquired the other half, he recovers only for the half insured.

Generally, the value of goods is their invoice price, with all those charges, commissions, wages, &c., which enter into the cost to the owner, when the risk commences. The drawback is not deducted; and the expenses incurred after the risk begins, as for freight, &c., are not included. And the rate of exchange at the beginning of the risk is taken.

SECTION III.

THE INTEREST WHICH MAY BE INSURED.

A MERE possibility or expectation cannot be insured; but any actual interest may be. If one has contracted to buy goods, he may insure them, and will recover if the property be in him at the time of the loss; for if they are then destroyed, it will be his loss. (For what is meant by the property being in him, see the chapter on Sales.)

If one has taken on himself certain risks, or agreed to indemnify another for them, he may insure himself against the same risks. The policy may express and define the interest in such a way that any change in the nature of it will discharge the insurance. If it is not so defined and declared, a change, as from the interest of an owner to that of a mortgagor, or of a mortgagee, will not defeat the policy.

A mere indebtedness to a party on account of property gives the creditor no insurable interest; thus, one who repaired a house or a ship cannot insure the house or ship merely because the owner owes him; but if the creditor has a lien on the property, this is an insurable interest. And, generally, every bailee or party in possession of goods, with a lien on them, may insure them. And a lender on bottomry or respondentia may insure the ship or goods. And any persons who have possession of property, or a right to possession, and may legally make a profit out of it, as factors on commission, consignees, or carriers, may insure their interest.

If a mortgagee be insured, and recovers from the insurers, he, generally at least, transfers to them the security for his debt, or accounts with them for its value; because, to the extent of that security, he has met with no loss, and, if he did not transfer it, would recover his money twice. It should, however, be added that where a mortgagee, or one having a lien, insures his own interest in property, a payment of a loss to him by the insurers does not discharge the debt for which the mortgage or the lien is the security. Where, however, the mortgagee is trustee for the mortgagor, as where the mortgagor causes insurance to be made on the premises, payable to the mortgagee in case of loss, or where the mortgagee effects insurance at the expense of the mortgagor, with his consent, payment by the insurers would go in discharge of the debt.

A policy usually adds to the description of the property, "lost or not lost." This phrase makes the policy retrospective; and attaches it to the property if that existed when, by the terms of the policy, the insurance began, whether this were for a voyage or for a certain time, although it had ceased to exist when the policy was made.

An interest which was originally valid and sufficient cannot be defeated by that which threatens, but does not complete an actual divestment of the interest in property; therefore, not by attachment, or an execution for debt; nor by liability to seizure by government for forfeiture; nor a right in the seller to stop the goods *in transitu;* nor capture; because after all these the property may remain in or return to the insured. But sale on execution, actual seizure by government and forfeiture, stoppage *in transitu*, or condemnation by court as lawful prize, divest the property, and therefore discharge the insurance.

The insurance never attaches if the interest is illegal originally; and it is discharged if the interest becomes illegal subsequent to the insurance, or if an illegal use of the subject-matter of the insurance is intended. And any act is illegal which is prohibited by law, or made subject to a penalty. The effect would be the same if the policy opposes distinctly the principles and the purposes of law, as wagering policies do.

Mariners, or mates, are not permitted by the law-merchant to insure their wages, but may insure goods on board, bought with their wages; and one legally interested in the wages of a mariner may insure them; as one to whom they are assigned by order or otherwise. A master may insure his wages, commissions, or any profit he may make out of his privilege.

An unexecuted intention of illegality, if not distinctly acted upon, will not defeat a policy; nor a remote and incidental illegality; as smuggling stores on board, or not having on board the provisions required by law; nor a change from legality to illegality, which cannot be proved or supposed to be known to the insured. And upon these questions, the court, if the case be balanced, will incline to the side of legality. A cargo may be insured which is itself lawful, but was purchased with the proceeds of an illegal voyage.

If a severable part of a cargo or a voyage is legal, it may be insured, by itself, although other parts are illegal. But if a part of the whole property insured together is illegal, this avoids the whole policy.

A compliance with foreign registry laws is not necessary, and with our own probably is not, to sustain the insurance of an actual owner in good faith.

Freight is a common subject of insurance. In common conversation, this word means sometimes the cargo carried, and sometimes the earnings of the ship by carrying the cargo. The latter is the meaning in mercantile law, and especially in the law of insurance. It includes in insurance law the money to be paid to the owner of a ship by the shipper of goods, and also the earnings of an owner by carrying his own goods; and the amount to be paid to the owner by the hirer of his ship, and also the profits of such hirer, either by carrying his own goods, or by carrying, for pay, the goods of others.

An interest in freight begins as soon as the voyage is determined upon, and the ship is actually ready for sea, and goods are on board, or are ready to be put on board, or are promised to be put on board by a contract which binds the owner of the goods to put them on board, for that voyage.

If a ship is insured on a voyage which is to consist of many passages, and sails without cargo, but a cargo is ready for her, or contracted for her at the first port she is to reach and sail from, the owner has an insurable interest in the freight from the day on which she sails from his home port.

If one makes advances towards the freight he is to pay, and this is to be repaid to him by the ship-owner if the freight is not earned, the advancer has no insurable interest in what he advances; but if he is to lose it, without repayment, if the ship be lost or the freight not earned, he has an insurable interest.

SECTION IV.

PRIOR INSURANCE.

OUR marine policies generally provide for this by a clause to the effect that the insurer shall be liable only for so much of the property as a prior insurance shall not cover. The second covers what the first leaves, the third what the second leaves, and so on; and as soon as the whole value of the property is covered, the remainder of that policy, and the subsequent policies, have no effect. This priority relates not merely to the date of the instrument, but to the actual time of insurance. Sometimes the policy provides that the insured shall recover only the same proportion of the whole loss which the amount insured in that policy is of the whole amount insured by all the policies on the whole property.

Where no provision is made in the policies as to priority, all are insurers alike, but all together only of the whole value at risk. The insured, therefore, may recover of any one insurer at his election, and this insurer may compel the others to contribute to him in proportion to their respective insurances.

Insurances may be not successive, but simultaneous, and then no clause as to prior policies has any application, for then no policy is *prior* to another, and all the insurances are liable *pro rata*. They are simultaneous, if said to be so in the policies, which is common; or if made on the same day, and bearing the same date, and there is no evidence as to which was, in fact, first made.

SECTION V.

DOUBLE INSURANCE AND RE-INSURANCE.

If there be double insurance, either simultaneously or by successive policies in which priority of insurance is not provided for, we have seen that all are insurers, and liable each in proportion; thus, if all the policies cover twice the value of the property insured, each policy is valid for one-half of its own amount.

But there is no double insurance, unless all the policies insure the very same subject-matter, against the same risks, and, taken together, exceed its whole value.

Many insurances of the same subject-matter, for the benefit of different parties, do not constitute double insurance.

Re-insurance is lawful; for whoever insures another has assumed a risk against which he may cause himself to be insured. This is often done by companies who wish to close their accounts, to lessen their risks, or get rid of some especial risk.

SECTION VI.

THE MEMORANDUM.

This word is retained, because the English policies have attached to them a note or memorandum providing that the insurers shall not be liable for any loss upon certain articles therein enumerated (and thence called memorandum articles), unless it be total, or greater than a certain percentage. In our policies, the same thing is provided for, but usually by a clause contained in the body or in the margin of the policy. The general purpose is to guard against a liability for injuries which may very probably not arise from maritime peril, because the articles are in themselves perishable; but which injuries it might not be easy to refer to the precise causes which produced them. Thus, grain, fish, hides, fruit, &c., are very liable to be somewhat injured on the voyage, and if there has been bad weather, or a greater leak than usual, it is impossible to say whether these goods have lost value from their own decay, or from a peril of the sea. It is therefore provided, that the insurers shall not pay unless there be a total loss by a sea-peril, which ends all question, or so large a loss as ten or twenty per cent; for this could hardly happen without visible and certain cause. And then, if the cause was shown to be not a peril insured against, the insurers would not be liable.

The perishable articles thus excepted, and the percentage of loss necessary to charge the insurers, vary very much at different times and in different States.

SECTION VII.

EXPRESS WARRANTIES.

A STIPULATION or agreement *in the policy*, that a certain thing shall be or shall not be, is an express warranty. And every warranty must be, if not strictly, at least accurately complied with. Nor is it an excuse that the thing is not material; or that the breach was not intended, or not known; or that it was caused by an agent of the insured. A warranty is equally effectual if written upon a separate paper, but referred to in the policy itself as a warranty. And the direct assertion or allegation of a fact may constitute a warranty.

If the breach of the warranty exists at the commencement of the risk, it avoids the whole policy, although the warranty was complied with afterwards and before a loss, and although all other risks were distinct from that to which the warranty related. Thus, if a vessel is warranted "coppered," and she is not coppered, and is lost by the ignition of cotton in the hold. Here, the breach of the warranty, that is, the want of the copper, has nothing to do with the loss; but the insurers would be discharged.

If the breach occur after the risk begins, and before a loss, and is not caused or continued by the fault of the insured, the insurers are held; and so they are if a compliance with the warranty becomes illegal after the policy attaches, and it is therefore broken.

The usual subjects of express warranty are, first, the ownership of the property, which is chiefly important as it secures the neutrality, or freedom from war-risks, of the property insured. The neutrality of the ship and of the cargo must be proved by the ship's having on board all the usual and regular documents. False papers may, however, be carried for commercial purposes, either when leave is given by the insurers, or when it is permitted by a known and established usage.

If neutrality is warranted, it must be maintained by a strict adherence to all the rules and usages of a neutral trade or employment. Without warranty, every neutral ship is bound to respect a blockade which legally exists by reason of the presence of an armed force sufficient to preserve it, and of which the neutral has knowledge.

The second most common express warranty is that of the time of the ship's sailing. She sails when she weighs anchor or casts off her fastenings, and gets under way, if the intention be to proceed at once to sea without further delay. She must have been actually under way. But if she moves with the intention of prosecuting her voyage, this is sufficient. But if not entirely ready for sea, she has not sailed by merely moving down the harbor. If she moves, being ready and intended for sea, but is afterwards accidentally and compulsorily delayed, this is a sailing. Nor is the warranty complied with by leaving a place to return to it immediately; or by going from one port of the coast or island, which she is warranted to leave, to another. If the ship is warranted "in such a harbor or port," or "where the ship now is," this means at the time of the insurance. And "warranted in port" means the port of insurance, unless another port is expressed or distinctly indicated.

SECTION VIII.

IMPLIED WARRANTIES.

The most important of these warranties — which the law implies, or makes for the parties without their saying any thing about them, although they may, if they please, make them for themselves — is that of *sea-worthiness.* By this is meant, that every person who asks to be insured upon his ship, by the mere force and operation of law, warrants that she is, in every respect, — hull, sails, rigging, officers, crew, provisions, implements, papers, and the like, — competent to enter upon and prosecute that voyage at the time proposed, and encounter safely the common dangers of the sea. If this warranty be not complied with, the policy does not attach, whether the breach be known or not, unless there is some peculiar clause in the policy waiving this objection.

If the ship be seaworthy and the policy attaches, no subsequent breach discharges the insurers from their liability for a loss previous to the breach. Even if the policy does not attach at the beginning of the voyage, if the unseaworthiness be capable of prompt and effectual remedy, and be soon and entirely remedied, the policy may then attach. If the insurance is " at and from " a port, there is no implied warranty in the nature of a condition precedent to the attaching of the policy, that the vessel shall be then seaworthy in the sense of being fit for sea, and it is sufficient if she is portworthy. But the policy is avoided if she goes to sea in an unseaworthy condition. The general rule is, that, if unseaworthiness prevents the policy from attaching at the proper commencement of the *risk*, the contract becomes a nullity.

If she becomes unseaworthy in the course of the voyage, from a peril insufficient to produce it in a sound vessel, this may be evidence of inherent weakness and original unseaworthiness; and then the policy never attached. But if originally seaworthy, and by any accident made otherwise, the policy continues to attach until she can be restored to a seaworthy condition by reasonable endeavors. And the general rule is, that she must be so restored as soon as she can be. It is the duty of the master to repair her as soon as he can; by the aid of another ship if that may be, but if otherwise, not to keep her at sea if she can readily make a port where she can be made seaworthy; and not to leave that port until she is seaworthy. It is the rule that a ship must not leave a port in an unseaworthy condition, if she could there be made seaworthy; if she does, the insurers are no longer held. But their liability may be, not destroyed, but only suspended, if the seaworthiness be cured at the next port, especially if that be not a distant port.

There cannot possibly be a definite and universal standard for seaworthiness. The ship must be fit for her voyage or for her place. But a coasting schooner needs one kind of fitness, a freighting ship to Europe another, a whaling ship another, a ship insured only while in port another. So as to the crew, or provisions, or papers, or a pilot, or certain furniture, as a chronometer or the like; or the kind of rigging or sails. In all these respects, much depends upon the existing and established usage. There is, perhaps, no better test than this; the ship must have all those things, and in such quantity and of such quality as the law requires, provided there is any positive rule of law affecting them; and otherwise such as would be deemed requisite according to the common consent and usage of persons engaged in that trade. And the reason for this rule is, that this is exactly what the insurers have a right to expect, and if the insured intend any thing less, or the insurers desire any thing more, it should be the subject of special bargain.

If a policy be intended to attach when a ship is at sea, the ship must be seaworthy in that sense and in that way in which a ship of her declared age, size, employment, and character, after being at sea for that time, under ordinary circumstances, ought to be in, and may be expected to be in by all concerned. The standard of seaworthiness is to be found from the usage and understanding of merchants, at the place where the ship belongs, and not at that where the ship is insured.

SECTION IX.

REPRESENTATION AND CONCEALMENT.

If there be an affirmation or denial of any fact, or an allegation which would lead the mind to a conclusion, whether made orally or in writing, or by exhibition of any written or printed paper, or by a mere inference from the words of the policy, before the making of the policy, or at the making, and the same be false, and tend to procure for him who makes it the bargain, or some advantage in the bargain, it is a *misrepresentation*. And it is the same thing, whether it refers to a subject concerning which some representations were necessary, or otherwise.

Concealment is the suppression of a fact not known to the other party, referring to the pending bargain, and material thereto.

A misrepresentation or a concealment discharges the insurers. To have this effect, it must continue until the risk begins, and then be material.

It is no defence, that it was innocent, and arose from inadvertence or misapprehension, because the legal obligation of a full and true statement is absolute; nor that the insurers were not influenced by it, if it were wilfully made with intention to deceive.

If it be in its nature temporary, and begins after the risk begins, and ends before a loss happens, the insurers are not discharged. And if it relate to an entirely separate subject-matter of insurance, as the goods only, and has no effect upon the risk as to the rest, as the ship, for example, it discharges the insurers only as to that part. Ignorance is never an excuse, if it be wilful and intentional. If one says only he believes so and so, the fact of his belief in good faith is sufficient for him. But if he says that is true of which he does not know whether it be true or false, and it is actually false, it is the same misrepresentation as if he knew it to be false. If a statement relate to the future, a future compliance or fulfilment is necessary.

Any statement in reply to a distinct inquiry will be deemed material; because the question implies that the insurer deems it material. On the other hand, the insured is not bound to communicate any mere expectation or hope or fear; but only all the facts material to the risk.

SECTION X.

WHAT THINGS SHOULD BE COMMUNICATED.

Not only ascertained facts should be stated by the insured, but intelligence, and mere rumors, if of importance to the risk; and it has been held that intelligence known to his clerks would be generally presumed to be known to him; and it is no defence, that the things have been found to be false. It has been held that an agent was bound to state that his directions were sent him by express; because this indicated an emergency. If the voyage proposed would violate a foreign law not generally known, this should be stated.

It is impossible to give any other criterion to determine what should be communicated than the rule that every thing should be stated which might reasonably be considered in estimating the risk. And so every thing of any kind which the insurer might reasonably wish to take into consideration in estimating the value of the risk which he is invited to assume.

The question, however, being one of concealment as it affects the estimation of the risk, it is obvious that the insured need not state to the insurer things which he already knows; and by the same reason, he is not bound to state things which the insurer ought to know, and might be supposed to know.

If either party says to the other so much as should put the other upon inquiry in reference to a matter about which inquiry is easy and would lead to information, and the other party makes no inquiry, his ignorance is his own fault, and he must bear the consequences of it.

An intention, which, if carried into effect, would discharge the insurers, as, for example, an intention to deviate, need not be stated, unless the intention itself can be shown to affect the risk. So a past damage to the property need not be stated, unless it affects its present probability of safety.

A false statement that other insurers have taken the risk on such or such terms is a misrepresentation; but a false statement by the insured that he thinks they would take it on such terms is not one, for of this the insurers can judge for themselves.

Every statement or representation will be construed rationally, and so as to include all just and reasonable inferences. A substantial compliance with it will be sufficient; and a literal compliance which is not a substantial one will not be sufficient.

SECTION XI.

THE PREMIUM.

THIS is undoubtedly due when the contract of insurance is completed; but in practice in this country, the premium in marine insurance is usually paid by a premium note on time, which is given at or soon after the delivery of the policy. If the policy acknowledge the receipt of the premium, and it is not paid, this receipt would be no bar to an action for it.

The premium is not due, if the risk is not incurred; whether this be caused by the non-sailing of the ship; or by one insured on goods not having goods on board; or not so much cargo as he is insured for; or by any error or falsity in the description which prevents the policy from attaching.

If the premium be not earned, or not wholly earned, it must be returned in whole or in part by the insurers if it have been paid; and not charged in account with the insured, if it be unpaid.

The premium may be partially earned; and then there must be a part return only. As if the voyage consist of several passages, or of "out and home" passages, and these are not connected by the policy as one entire risk; or if the insured has some goods at risk, but not all which he intended to insure.

It is, however, an invariable rule, that if the whole risk attaches at all, that is, if there be a time, however short, during which the insurers might, in case of loss from a sea-peril, be called on for the whole amount they insure, there is to be no return of premium.

In this country, insurers usually retain one-half of one per cent of a returnable policy. And our policies contain a clause permitting the insurers to set off the premium due against a loss, whether the note be signed by the insured or by another person.

SECTION XII.

THE DESCRIPTION OF THE PROPERTY INSURED.

The description must be such as will distinctly identify the property insured, as by quantity, marks, and numbers, or a reference to the fact of shipment, or the time of shipment, or the voyage, or the consignee; or in some similar and satisfactory way; and no mere mistake in a name, or otherwise, vitiates the description if it leaves it sufficiently certain. If different shipments come within the policy, the insured may attach it to either by his declaration, which may be done after the loss, provided this appears to have been the intention of the parties. "Cargo," "goods on board," "merchandise," mean much the same thing; and do not attach to ornaments, clothing, or the like, owned by persons on board and not intended for commercial purposes. "Property" is the word of widest and almost unlimited meaning. "Ship" or "vessel" includes all that belongs to it at the time, — even sextants or chronometers belonging to the ship-owner, and by him appropriated to the navigation of the ship. So it includes all additions or repairs made during the insurance.

The phrase "a return cargo" will generally apply to a homeward cargo of the party insured in the same ship, however it be procured; but the phrases "proceeds" and "returns" are generally regarded as limited to a return cargo bought by means of the outward cargo. And neither of these, or any similar phrases, will apply to the same cargo brought back again, unless it can be shown, by the usage, or other admissible evidence, that this was the intention of the parties.

The nature of the interest of the insured need not be specified, unless peculiar circumstances, closely connecting this interest with the risk, make this necessary. But either a mortgagor or a mortgagee, a charterer, an assignee, a consignee, a trustee, or a carrier, may insure as on his own property, and without describing the exact nature of his interest.

SECTION XIII.

THE PERILS COVERED BY THE POLICY.

THE policy enumerates, as the causes of loss against which it insures, Perils of the Sea, Fire, Piracy, Theft, Barratry, Capture, Arrests, and Detentions; and "all other perils," by which is meant, by construction of law, all other perils of a like kind with those enumerated.

It is a universal rule, that the insurers are liable only for *extraordinary* risks. The very meaning of "seaworthiness," which the insured warrants, is that the ship is competent to encounter with safety all ordinary perils. If she be lost or injured, and the loss evidently arose from an ordinary peril, as from common weather, or the common force of the waves, the insurers are not liable, because the ship should be able to withstand these assaults. And if the loss be unexplained, and no extraordinary peril be shown or indicated, this fact would raise a very strong presumption of unseaworthiness. As, for example, if the vessel went down while sailing with favorable winds on a calm ocean.

It is a universal rule, that the insurers are never liable for a loss which is caused by the quality of the thing lost. This rule applies to the ship, her rigging and appurtenances, when worn out by age or hard service. But its most frequent application is to perishable goods. The memorandum already spoken of provides for this in some degree. But the insurers are liable for the loss of no article of merchandise whatever, if that loss were caused by the inherent qualities or tendencies of the article, *unless* these qualities or tendencies were excited to action and made destructive by a peril insured against. Thus, if hemp rots from spontaneous fermentation, which cannot occur if it be dry, the insurers are not liable if the loss arose from the dampness which the hemp had when laden on board; but if the vessel were strained by tempest, and her seams opened, and the hemp was in this way wet, and then rotted, they are liable.

The insurers may take upon themselves whatever risks they choose to assume. And express clauses in a policy, or the uniform and established usage and construction of policies, may throw upon them, as in fact it does, a very large liability to the owner or shipper for the effects of the misconduct — wilful or otherwise — of the master and crew. The clause relating to barratry, to be spoken of presently, is of this kind.

If the cargo is damaged through the fault of the master or crew, the shipper of the cargo has a remedy against the owner of the ship. But this does not necessarily discharge the insurers. If, however, he enforces his claim against them, he is bound to transfer to them his claim against the ship-owner. For the insurers of the cargo, by paying a loss thereon, put themselves, as it were, in the position of the shippers, and acquire their rights.

SECTION XIV.

PERILS OF THE SEA.

By this phrase is meant all the perils incident to navigation; and especially those arising from the wind and weather, the state of the ocean, and its rocks and shores. But it will be remembered that the insurers take upon themselves only so many of these as are "extraordinary." Hence, destruction by worms or by rats is not such a peril as the insurers are liable for, because it is not extraordinary. It seems now settled that *fire* is not included among "perils of the sea," or "perils of the river." But it is usually mentioned in the policy, as one of the risks insured against.

If a vessel be not heard from, it will be supposed, after a reasonable interval, that she has perished; but the law has not determined the length of this interval with any exactness. The presumption of law will be, that she was lost by an extraordinary peril of the sea, and, of course, the insurers will be answerable for her. But this presumption may be rebutted by any sufficient evidence, as of unseaworthiness, or any other probable cause of loss.

SECTION XV.

COLLISION.

Collision is a peril of the sea which may deserve especial notice. In the chapter on Shipping, it has been stated, that, where a collision is caused by the fault of one of the ships, the ship in fault sustains the whole loss; that is, it must bear its own loss, and must indemnify the other ship for the injury that ship sustains. It has been held that the insurers of the ship in fault are liable for the whole of this loss, because it is all caused by collision, which is a peril of the sea. But the Supreme Court of the United States have recently decided that the insurers are not held for more than the loss *directly* sustained by the ship they insure, that is, *not* for the amount that ship pays to the other ship for injury done to it.

SECTION XVI.

FIRE.

THIS peril also must come under the common rule, that the insurers will not be held unless it be caused by something extraordinary, and not belonging to the inherent qualities of the thing which takes fire.

The insurers would be held for any direct and immediate consequences of the fire; and for loss caused by the endeavor to extinguish it. It is, indeed, a general rule, that the insurers are liable for the loss or injury which is the natural, direct, and proximate effect of any peril insured against, although the loss itself may be only the effect of a preceding loss; as, if a part of the cargo was burned up, and another part was injured by water used to arrest the fire, the insurers would be liable for both parts.

SECTION XVII.

PIRACY, ROBBERY, OR THEFT.

THERE can be no piracy or robbery without violence; but this is not necessary to constitute the crime of theft. Piracy and robbery are most usually committed by strangers to the ship; they may, however, be committed by the crew; and the insurers are answerable for such a loss, unless it arose from the fault of the owner. Our policies now usually have the phrase "assailing thieves." This excludes theft without violence, and all theft by those lawfully on board the vessel, as a part of the ship's company. If, after shipwreck, the property is stolen, the insurers are liable, and might be so if there were no insurance against theft, if this was a direct effect of the wrecking.

SECTION XVIII.

BARRATRY.

THIS word means any wrongful act of the master, officers, or crew, as any fraud, cheat, or trick done by them, or either of them, against the owner. If he directed the act, or consented to it, or by his negligence or default caused it,—whether he were actual owner, or apparent or temporary owner by hiring the vessel,—it is no barratry. But it is not necessary that it should be done with an intention hostile to him. For an act otherwise barratrous would be none the less so because the committer of it supposed it would be for the advantage of the owner.

The master being appointed by the owner, and controlled by him, many policies provide that they do not insure against barratry, *if the insured be the owner of the ship*. The purpose of this is obvious; it is to prevent an insurance of the owner against the acts of one for whom the owner ought to hold himself responsible. The effect of the clause is to limit the insurance against barratry to goods shipped by one who is not owner of the vessel.

As a general rule, the insurers are liable for the misconduct of the crew, when all usual and reasonable precautions have been taken by the owner, and his servant, the master, to prevent such misconduct.

SECTION XIX.

CAPTURE, ARREST, AND DETENTION.

THE phrase which refers to these perils is usually in these words: "Against all captures at sea, or arrests, or detentions of all kings, princes, and people." Almost every word of this sentence has been the subject of litigation or of discussion. The provision has been held to apply not only to captures, arrests, or detentions by public enemies, by foreign belligerent powers, but to those by the very government of which the insured is himself a subject, *unless* the same be for a breach of the law by the insured. Then the insurers are not liable, because they never are for the consequence of an illegal act of the insured. By the "people" are understood the sovereign power of a State, whatever be its form of government. "Capture" and "seizure" are equivalent; they differ from "detention" in this respect: the two former words mean a taking with intent to keep; the latter, a taking with intent to restore the property. "Arrest" is any taking possession of the property for any hostile or judicial purpose.

SECTION XX.

THE GENERAL CLAUSE.

THIS clause has a very limited operation. We have already remarked, that it is usually restricted to perils of a like kind with those already enumerated; and although this phrase has been declared to be substantial and material, it might be difficult to hold an insurer liable under this clause, when he would not have been liable under some one of the enumerated perils.

SECTION XXI.

PROHIBITED TRADE.

THIS is not the same with contraband trade (which belongs to war), although the words are sometimes used as if they were synonymous. It is perfectly lawful for a ship to break through a blockade if it can, or to carry arms or munitions of war to a belligerent. This would be contraband trade. And it is perfectly lawful for the State whose enemy is thus aided, to catch, seize, and condemn the vessel that does this, if it can. The vessel takes upon itself this risk; and it is not covered by a common policy, unless the purpose is disclosed and permitted. Prohibited trade belongs to a time of peace. It is either trade prohibited by the State to which the ship belongs, — and then it is wholly illegal, and the insurers are not only not answerable under a general policy for a loss occasioned by this breach of law, but an express bargain to that effect would itself be illegal and void; or it may be trade prohibited only by a foreign State. And then it is not an illegal act in the vessel by whose sovereign it is not prohibited. The intention to incur this extra risk should be communicated; because the insurers should be enabled to take it into consideration. But in practice, our policies generally, if not universally, except expressly the risks arising from prohibited trade.

The parties may always agree to add such risks, or except such, as they choose.

SECTION XXII.

DEVIATION.

As the insurers are entitled to know, either from information given them, or from the known course of the trade, what risks they assume, it is obvious that the insured have no right to change those risks, and that, if they do, the insurers are not held to the new risk. Such a change of risk is called a deviation; it certainly discharges the insurers; and although the word originally meant in law what it means commonly, a departure from the proper course of the voyage, it now means, in the law of insurance, any departure from or change of the risks insured against. And it discharges the insurers, although it does not increase the risk, as they have a right to stand by the exact bargain they have made. There may be a deviation while the ship is in port; or where the insurance is on time, and no voyage is indicated. And a very slight deviation may suffice to discharge the underwriters.

But no deviation discharges the insurers, or, in the language of the law, no change or risk is a deviation, unless it be voluntary, that is, not if there was or seemed to be a sufficient necessity for it.

The proper course — a departure from which is a deviation — is always the usual course, provided there be a usage; for a master is not bound to follow their track wherever one or two have gone before, but must be allowed his own reasonable discretion. If there be no course so well established that every one would be expected to follow it, the master must go to his destined port in the most natural, direct, safe, and advantageous way.

An extraordinary and unnecessary protraction of a voyage would be a deviation. But the mere length of the voyage, without other evidence, would not prove this.

Liberty policies, so called, are often made. That is, the insured is expressly permitted to do certain things, which, without such permission, would constitute a deviation. And a large proportion of the cases on the subject of deviation have arisen under these policies. Most of the phrases commonly used have been construed by the courts; and generally quite strictly. A liberty to "enter" a port, or "touch" at a place, permits a ship to go in and come out, but it permits little delay, because for delay the word "stay" or "remain" is necessary.

It is certain that no permission is necessary for any change of course or risk that is made for the saving of life, or even for the purpose of helping the distressed. Always provided, however, that the change of course, or the delay, was no greater and no longer continued than this cause for it, actually and rationally considered, required. It is, however, equally well settled, that a change of course or of risk for the purpose of saving property is a deviation not justified by its cause. A delay for the purpose of towing a vessel is certainly a deviation, unless there are persons on board the vessel which is towed, and they can be saved in no other way.

Sometimes it is intended that a ship shall visit many ports, and even go backwards and forwards, at places between the port from which she sails and that at which the voyage is finally to terminate. Such purposes as this are sometimes provided for by a policy on time; and sometimes by express permission to go to and trade at certain ports.

If permission be given to enter and stop at a dozen different ports, the vessel may omit any of them, or the whole, but must visit in the proper order all to which she does go. She cannot go back and forth.

The substitution of a new voyage for that agreed upon is of course a deviation, and one that can seldom or never be justified by any necessity, so as to carry the insurer's liability on the new voyage. If an entirely new voyage is intended, and a vessel sails upon it, but in the same direction in which she would have gone on the insured voyages, the policy never attaches, and the premium is never earned, because the ship never sails on the insured voyage. But if the ship is intended to pursue the insured voyage to its proper terminus, but at a certain point of the voyage to deviate by going into another port, there is no deviation until that point is reached, and the deviation actually begun; because it is certain that no mere intention to deviate discharges the insurers until it is carried into execution; and they are liable for a loss happening before the deviation.

SECTION XXIII.

THE TERMINI OF THE VOYAGE, AND OF THE RISK.

THESE must be distinctly stated, whether they be termini of time or place. A policy from ——— to ———, or from B to ———, or from ——— to B, would be void. Nor would it be any better if the termini were named with apparent distinctness, but in such wise as to mean nothing, or nothing sufficiently certain.

A policy takes effect from its date, if the bargain was then complete, although not delivered until afterwards. And it may be remarked, that, if there be an unreasonable delay in the sailing of the vessel, the policy never attaches, for the bargain is considered as annulled.

A policy on a vessel "at," such a place attaches when she is there in safety. But if there were a policy "to" a place, and another was made out between the same parties "at," or "at and from," the same place, the law would presume that the parties intended that the second policy should attach whenever the first one ceased by the arrival of the ship, without reference to the condition of the ship or her peril at the time.

A policy on goods attaches to them at the time when it would have attached to the vessel had she been insured. The extent which should be given to the meaning of the word "port" is sometimes a question of some difficulty; but in general all places are within a port which belong to it by mercantile usage and acceptance, although not within the same municipal or legal precinct.

"At and from" covers a vessel in a port, as well as after she leaves it. "From" only covers the vessel *after* she gets under way. "At and from," applied to goods, does not cover them in the port when they are on shore and warehoused, nor until they become subject to marine risk, by being water-borne. They are, however, covered, not only when they reach the ship, but as soon as they are put on board of boats or lighters, or any other usual water conveyance to the ship. And if insured to a port, they continue covered after they leave the ship by any usual conveyance for the shore, until they are safely landed. The word "at," applied to an island or a coast, may embrace all the ports therein, and cover the ship while sailing from one to another. "To a port and a market," covers a voyage to the port, and thence to every place to which, by mercantile usage or reasonable construction, a ship may go thence in search of a market; and even to return to that port, if honestly with intent to learn there where a market could be found.

If the insurance be to "a port of discharge," this does not terminate if the vessel goes to a port for inquiry, or for needful refreshment or repair. If it be "a final port of discharge," the insurance ceases upon such parts of the cargo as are left at one port or another, and continues on the ship, and on all the goods on board, until arrival at the port where they will be finally discharged.

It is generally provided in time policies, that, if the vessel be at sea at the expiration of the time agreed on, the risk shall continue until her arrival at a port of discharge, or at her port of destination. If then, before the expiration of the time, she is actually at sea, or has broken ground for the voyage, or if, when the time expires, she is in a port of necessity or restraint, she is considered at sea, but not otherwise.

The English policies and our own contain a provision that the insurance continues on the ship "until she shall be arrived and moored twenty-four hours in safety;" and on the goods until they be "landed," or "safely landed."

Under this clause, the ship is insured until moored in safety, so far as the perils insured against are concerned, but not against the peculiar and local dangers of the port, or the possibility that a tempest there might injure her when moored; for these dangers continue to exist as long as she stays there, and the liability of the insurers would never terminate. If she enters the harbor, and, before she is moored, is blown off, or ordered into quarantine, she is insured until this delay ceases and she is safely moored in port. And if before or within the twenty-four hours a dangerous storm begins, but does no damage to her until after the expiration of the twenty-four hours, the risk has terminated, and the insurers are not liable.

SECTION XXIV.

TOTAL LOSS AND ABANDONMENT.

THE law of insurance recognizes an actual total loss, and also a constructive total loss. It is actual when the whole property passes away, as by submersion or destruction by fire. It is a constructive total loss, when the ship or goods are partially destroyed, and the law permits the insured to abandon the salvage or whatever is saved, to the insurers, and claim from them a total loss. By "abandonment" is meant, in insurance law, the transferring of the property insured, or what is left of it, to the insurers. The word is used, because originally the insured gave up, renounced, or abandoned the property, saying to the insurers, we will have nothing more to do with it, and you may do with it what you like. And the word is still always used, although now it means a transfer. And in the law of insurance, a constructive total loss is a partial loss made total by an exercise of the right of abandonment. That is, the actual loss took from the insured a part, and the abandonment took the rest, and so they have lost all. A constructive total loss is sometimes called a "technical" total loss.

The abandonment, we say, transfers all that remains of the property to the insurers. If nothing remains, or if that which remains has no value, there need be no abandonment, and this is an actual total loss.

The insured never need make an abandonment if he chooses not to do so. And if from such choice or neglect he makes no abandonment, his claim against the insurers is still valid; but it is a different claim from that which it would have been if he had abandoned, because it is now to be settled as a partial loss, of which we shall speak hereafter. For it is the purpose and effect of an abandonment to convert an actual partial loss into a constructive total loss. And if he makes an abandonment when he has no right to make it, such abandonment is wholly inoperative, unless the insurers choose to accept it; but if they accept it, they must settle the loss as a total loss.

The topics in relation to this subject which we will consider are:—1. The necessity of abandonment. 2. The right of abandonment. 3. The exercise of this right. 4. The acceptance of the abandonment. 5. The effect of the abandonment, or of the absence of abandonment.

1. Of the Necessity of Abandonment.—It is said, that if a ship be completely wrecked, and reduced to "a mere congeries of planks and iron," or if she has not been heard from for a sufficiently long time, there need be no abandonment, and the insured may claim as for a total loss, without one. In either case, or any other case, if the insurers pay a total loss, they are entitled to whatever shall come to hand of the property insured. And it is usual, and we think more proper, to abandon in both of these cases.

2. Of the Right of Abandonment.—The insured cannot convert every partial loss, however small, into a total loss, by abandonment, transferring the damaged property to the insurers. But by a rule which is nearly universal in this country, and not unknown abroad, if the damage by a peril insured against exceed one-half of the value of the property insured,—whether ship, goods, or freight,—he may abandon the property to the insurers, and claim as for a total loss. But if the vessel actually reaches her destined port, she cannot be abandoned, although the repairs would cost more than half of her value.

When we speak in another section of partial loss, it will be seen that, by the established usage of this country, an allowance of "one-third, new for old," is always made. This means, that if a new thing were given for an old one because the old one had been injured, the insurer would be more than indemnified. The sails, for example, might be so new that they had lost little of their value; or so old, that they were of no value. To avoid inquiring into each case, usage has adopted, as a fair average to apply to all cases, that the thing injured has lost one-third of its value. When it is replaced by repairs, the insured therefore loses one-third of the cost of repair, and the insurers pay two-thirds.

Now our policies provide that there shall be no total loss by abandonment, unless the injury exceed fifty per cent when "estimated as for a partial loss;" that is, one-third off. Consequently, the repairs necessary to restore the vessel to a sound condition must amount to more than seventy-five per cent of her value when repaired (one-third of which, twenty-five per cent, being cast off, leaves fifty per cent), before there can be an abandonment, which the insurers are bound to accept, and settle the loss as a total loss.

The valuation in the policy, if there be one, generally determines the value on which this estimate is to be made. In New York and in Massachusetts this seems to be distinctly held; but the courts of the United States and of some of our States incline to say that, whether the policy be valued or open, the value of the ship, the loss of one-half of which authorizes abandonment, is the actual value of the ship at the time the loss occurs, and that this value is to be proved by proper evidence.

A loss by jettison, by salvage, by general average contribution, by wages of sailors paid while they assisted in making the repairs, should be included in the fifty per cent. If the insured have lost a part of his goods by jettison, and have a claim for contribution which is not yet paid, the whole of his loss is to be included to make up the fifty per cent, and the insurers take the claim to contribution by abandonment. Thus, if his loss be by jettison of eight-tenths of his goods, it is 80 per cent, and if he has a claim for contribution in general average for 35 per cent, this does not reduce his loss to 45 per cent, so that he cannot abandon; but he may call his loss 80 per cent, and abandon, and by the abandonment transfer to the insurers his claim for 35 per cent. The expense of repairs is to be taken at the place where actually made, or where they must have been made, if made at all.

If a sale be lawfully made by the master, under the authority from necessity which we have considered in the chapter on the Law of Shipping, this is a total loss and the insured must account for the proceeds.

3. Of the Exercise of the Right of Abandonment. — As an abandonment has the effect of an absolute transfer of the property to the insurers, and is intended for this purpose, it is obvious that it cannot be made by one who is not possessed of such title to the property, or such interest therein, as would enable him to make a valid transfer.

There is no especial form or method of abandonment. But the proper and safe way is to do it in writing, and to use the word "abandon," or "abandonment," although other words of entirely equivalent meaning might suffice. It must be distinct and unequivocal, and state, at least in a general way, the grounds of the abandonment.

The following would be a good and sufficient form: —

(101.)

Abandonment.

NEW YORK, Jan. 9, 1869, 10 o'clock, A.M.

I have this day learned that my (*or the*) ship (*or whatever the vessel is*), insured by you (*or of which you have insured the cargo or freight or profits, as the case may be*), has been wrecked on her voyage from   to   (*or has met with such or such a disaster, describing it generally*), and that she now lies at   (*or that said cargo or what remains of it is now at*   ). And I do now and hereby abandon to you the ship, with her cargo and freight (*or whichever of these interests was the subject of insurance*), and shall claim payment of you as for a total loss.

To the   Insurance Company.

(*Signature.*)

If the abandonment be deficient in form, the insurers will waive any objection of this kind if they call for further proof, and otherwise act as if the abandonment were altogether sufficient.

The insured may abandon at any time when the ship, by a peril insured, is taken for an uncertain period from the master's control, and the voyage is broken up and cannot be renewed, unless at a cost which of itself gives this right.

The existence of the right depends upon the actual state of facts at the time, and not upon the supposed facts. Nothing, however, gives the right of instant abandonment, without a faithful endeavor of the master to find, if he can, and use, if he can, some means of deliverance and safety. But if, when delivered and restored to the master or owner, her damage amounts to more than half of her value, estimated as above stated, "as a partial loss," she may then be abandoned. If the precise voyage insured be broken up by a peril insured against, this justifies an abandonment, although the vessel might be put in condition to pursue a different voyage or render a different service.

As the insurers, who take the salvage (or saved) property by abandonment, have a right to every possible opportunity to make the most of it, it follows as an invariable and universal rule, that the insured *must* make an abandonment immediately after he receives the intelligence which justifies it; and if he does not, he will be regarded as having elected not to abandon, and no subsequent abandonment will have any effect.

The abandonment may be made on information of any kind, if it be entitled to weight and credence. So even a general rumor, without specific intelligence to the insured, will authorize an abandonment, if the rumor seems to be well grounded and altogether credible.

4. Of the Acceptance of the Abandonment. — As there is no especial form or method of making an abandonment, so there is no regular and established form of accepting an abandonment. Indeed, an acceptance, merely as such, or in so many words, is seldom made. And as the insurer's accepting is not necessary to give full effect to an abandonment which has been made on proper grounds, and in the right way and time, it is seldom asked for.

The acceptance of the abandonment may be inferred from words, or acts. The question has arisen whether it could be inferred from mere silence; and, in general, it cannot. "An insurer is not bound," says Mr. Justice Story, "to signify his acceptance. If he says nothing, and does nothing, the proper conclusion is, that he does not mean to accept it."

The rule may be stated thus. If the insurer, with a sufficient knowledge of the facts, says or does that which induces an honest insured to believe that he has accepted the abandonment, and will pay the loss, and to act on that belief, it is an acceptance, and is so far binding on the insurer. But if he neither says nor does what ought to produce this belief, then he is at liberty to say and prove if he can that the insured had no right to make an abandonment, and that the claim is only one for a partial loss.

5. Of the Effect of Abandonment. — We regard it is an ancient, reasonable, and well-established rule, that, if insurers pay as for a total loss, this payment entitles them to full possession of all that remains of the property insured, and also of all rights, claims, or interests which the insured has in or to or in respect of the property lost, and which, if he valued or enforced them himself, would, if added to the amount paid by the insurers, give him a double indemnity. Hence, if the insured has lost his goods by jettison, and has a claim for a general average contribution, and the insurers pay him for all his goods, they stand in his place, and acquire that claim for contribution which the loss of the goods gave him. And we should, very generally at least, extend this rule to the claim which a mortgagee has on the mortgage for his debt. That is, if the insurers pay for the loss of the property which secures the debt, they acquire, to the extent of their payment, the mortgagee's claim against the debtor.

By the abandonment, both the owner and the master become, to some extent, the trustees and agents of the insurers, in respect to the property abandoned; and are bound to act, in relation to it, with care and honesty. Still, if the property, after abandonment, or after a loss for which there is to be an abandonment, be further lost or wasted, by the bad faith or neglect of the master, or of the consignee of the owner, while they continue to act as such, this loss must be made up by the owner, because, although they are, in a certain sense, agents of the insured, they are then agents of the owner, and he is responsible for them to the insured.

Goods are totally lost if destroyed, or if so injured as to have little or no value for the purpose for which they are intended; or if the voyage upon which the insurance on the goods was effected is entirely broken up. But a mere delay gives no right of abandonment. And, in addition to all this, the rule which permits abandonment if more than fifty per cent be lost, of which we have already spoken, is applicable to goods, in this country; subject, however, to the important qualification, that it does not apply if any substantial portion of the goods arrive at their destination uninjured; or if the goods are insured "free from average." And the rule of abandonment, salvage, and transfer to the insurers, is the same in relation to goods as to the ship.

If there be many several shipments all insured, there may be a total loss of one, a partial loss of another, and no loss of a third.

SECTION XXV.

GENERAL AVERAGE.

THIS subject belongs primarily to the law of shipping, and is treated of in the chapter on the Law of Shipping. It comes within the scope of the law of insurance only when any of the property which is lost or saved is insured.

If an owner of property is insured, and other property is sacrificed to save the insured property from a peril common to it and to the sacrificed property, the insured property must pay such indemnity to the owner of the sacrificed property as will make them suffer alike. And the amount thus paid or contributed by the insured property is a loss by a sea-peril, for which the insurers are liable.

On the one hand, the insurers of the sacrificed property are under an obligation to pay for the loss thus made or incurred voluntarily, because it was not only the right, but the duty, of the master and crew to destroy a part rather than let the whole perish. It was therefore a loss by a peril of the sea, although purposely caused for the benefit of others; and the insurers must pay for it.

On the other hand, the owners of the property sacrificed acquire by its sacrifice a claim for contribution and indemnity; and if the insurers pay them for their loss, they acquire their claim for contribution. And this they take advantage of, in some cases, by deducting it from the amount they pay, and in other cases by first paying all the loss, and then collecting all the contribution for their own benefit. We have already seen that the insurers cannot deduct the contribution for the purpose of bringing the loss below fifty per cent, and thereby preventing an abandonment.

SECTION XXVI.

PARTIAL LOSS.

A PARTIAL loss is simply a loss of a part, and not of the whole. The principal questions relating to it arise out of the rule of one-third off, new for old, which has been already spoken of. We repeat the rule, with the reason of it. A ship sails to-day with new copper. Another sails with her copper nearly worn out. Both meet with peril which requires new coppering. The first is new coppered, and the insurers pay for it, and the insured gains nothing, because the copper on her was worth as much as it is now. The second is also coppered, and the insurers pay for it. But this ship gains nearly the whole value of the copper put on, because the old copper was worth very little. Now the whole purpose and principle of the law of insurance is to *indemnify* the insured, or make his loss good, and no more. Formerly they tried to do it by finding out in each case how much the old materials had lost of their value. But this was found so difficult, that it was agreed upon by merchants and insurers to *average* all the cases, and consider that all old materials had lost one-third of their value. And the rule is found to work well in practice.

The first effect of this rule is, that the thing or the part lost or injured, whether it be new or old, worn out or not worn at all, must be replaced or repaired in adaptation and conformity with the vessel, in the same way in which it would be if she were properly repaired at the owner's port, by his orders.

This third part is generally deducted from dockage, moving the ship, and similar expenses, provided they are incidental to the main purpose of repair.

The value of the old materials should be deducted from the expense of repair, before the third " new for old " is taken off. If a sea-peril makes it necessary to recopper a vessel, and the cost will be $9,000, and her old copper is worth $3,000, we should say that this should be deducted, leaving $6,000, for two-thirds of which only ($4,000), one-third being off, new for old, the insurers would be liable. The other way would be, to say the cost of repair is $9,000 of which the insurers would pay two-thirds (" one-third off "), or $6,000; and then the insurers would be entitled to the $3,000 which her old copper brings. Then the loss of the insurers would be only $6,000 less $3,000, or $3,000, instead of $4,000, which the insurers would lose on the first way. Insurers have tried to make the second way the law; but the first way is now pretty well established.

If an owner effects insurance on a part only of the value of the property insured, — as if for $5,000 on a ship valued at $10,000, — he is insured for half, and is his own insurer for the other half, and he recovers in the same proportion from the insurers in case of a partial loss. Thus, if there be a partial loss of sails and rigging, or of repairs, amounting, after one-third is deducted, to $2,000, one-half of this is the loss of the insurers, and they pay it to him, and one-half is his own loss.

The insurer takes no part of the risk of the market, and his liability is the same whether that rises or falls, although this may make a great difference as to the amount lost by the insured. What goods have lost from their original invoice value is the amount which the insurer pays. Thus, if he insures $10,000 on goods of which that is the original value, and they are so far damaged by a sea-peril, that at the port of discharge they bring, or are worth, only half of what they would have brought if they had not been damaged, the insurers are liable for $5,000, or that half, although the goods thus damaged may bring in the market of arrival the whole of their invoice cost or more. And if they bring but a quarter of it, the insurers pay no more than one-half, because the rest of the loss is caused by the falling market.

If the goods have sustained damage or loss by leakage, or by breakage, or by natural decay, or from inherent defect in quality, — that is, not by a sea-peril, — before the partial loss occurs, a proportional deduction should be made from the partial loss, as the insurers are liable only for the injury resulting from that loss, and not for any part of that which already existed when the loss took place, or which has occurred since from causes against which they did not insure.

CHAPTER XXVII.

FIRE INSURANCE.

SECTION I.

THE USUAL SUBJECT AND FORM OF THIS INSURANCE.

This kind of insurance is sometimes made to indemnify against the loss by fire of ships in port; more often of warehouses, and mercantile property stored in them; or of personal property in stores or factories, in dwelling-houses or barns, as merchandise, furniture, books, and plate, or pictures, or live stock. But by far the most common application of this mode of insurance is to dwelling-houses.

Like marine insurance, it may be effected by any individual who is capable of making a legal contract. In fact, however, it is always, or nearly always, in this country, and we suppose elsewhere, made by companies.

There are stock companies, in which certain persons own the capital and take all the profits by way of dividends; and mutual companies, in which every one who is insured becomes thereby a member, and the net profits, or a certain proportion of them, are divided among all the members in such manner as the charter or by-laws of the company may direct. Sometimes both kinds are united, in which case there is a capital stock provided, as a permanent guaranty fund, over and above the premiums received, and a certain part or proportion of the net profits is paid by way of dividend upon this fund, and the residue divided among the insured.

Of late years the number of mutual fire-insurance companies has greatly increased in this country, and much the largest amount of insurance against fire is effected by them. The principal reason for this is, undoubtedly, their greater cheapness; the premiums required by them being, in general, much less than in the stock offices. For example, if the insurance is effected for seven years, which is a common period, an amount or percentage is charged, about the same as that charged by the stock companies, or a little more. Only a small part of this is taken in cash; for the rest a premium note or bond is given, promising to pay whatever part of the amount may be needed for losses which shall occur during the period for which the note is given. More than this, therefore, the insured cannot be bound to pay, and it frequently happens that no assessment whatever is demanded; and sometimes, where the company is well established and does a large business upon sound principles, a part of the money paid by him is refunded when the insurance expires, or credited to him on the renewal of the policy, if such be his wish.

The disadvantage of these mutual companies is, that the premiums paid and premium notes constitute the whole capital or fund out of which losses are to be paid for. To make this more secure, it is provided by the charter of some companies, that they shall have a lien on the land itself on which any insured building stands, to the amount of the premium. But while this adds very much to the trustworthiness of the premium notes, and so to the availability of the capital, it is, with some persons, an objection, that their land is thus subjected to a lien or incumbrance.

There is another point of difference which recommends the stock company rather than the mutual company. It is that the stock company will generally insure more nearly the full value of the property insured; while the mutual companies are generally restrained by their charters from insuring more than a certain proportion, namely, from one-half to three-fourths, of the assessed value of the property. It would follow, therefore, that one insured by a mutual company cannot be fully indemnified against loss by fire; and may not be quite so certain of getting the indemnity he bargains for as if he were insured by a stock company.

The method and operation of fire insurance have become quite uniform throughout this country; and any company may appeal to the usage of other companies to answer questions which have arisen under its own policy; only, however, within certain rules, and under some well-defined restrictions.

In the first place, usage may be resorted to for the purpose of explaining that which needs explanation, but never to contradict that which is clearly expressed in the contract. And no usage can be admitted even to explain a contract, unless the usage be so well established, and so well known, that it may reasonably be supposed that the parties entered into the contract with reference to it. And not only the terms of the contract must be duly regarded, but those of the charter or act of incorporation.

In regard to the execution of a fire policy, and what is necessary to constitute such execution, we say that delivery is not strictly necessary, and a signed memorandum may be sufficient, or, indeed, an oral bargain only, and that this insurance may be effected by correspondence, and that the contract is completed when there is a proposition and assent, as we have already said in reference to marine insurance.

It has been held in an action on a fire policy, as doubtless it would be on a marine policy, that a memorandum made on the application book of the company by the president, and signed by him, was not binding, where the party to be insured wished the policy to be delayed until a different adjustment of the terms could be settled, and after some delay was notified by the company to call and settle the business, or the company would not be bound, and he did not call; because there was here no consummated agreement. So, too, a subsequent adoption or ratification of a policy made by an agent is equivalent, either in a fire or marine policy, to the making originally of the contract.

SECTION II.

THE CONSTRUCTION OF POLICIES AGAINST FIRE.

It is sufficient if the words of the policy describe the persons, the location, and the property, with so much distinctness that the court and jury have no difficulty in determining their identity with a certainty which prevents any real and substantial doubt.

In the construction of this as of other contracts, the intention of the parties is a very important and influential guide; but it must be the intention *as expressed;* for otherwise, a contract which was not made would be substituted for that which was made; and evidence from without the contract would be permitted to vary and to contradict it. Thus, where stock in trade, household furniture, linen, wearing-apparel, and plate were insured in a policy, the court held that the term "linen" must be confined to "household linen," and would not include linen drapery goods purchased on speculation. In a case where the policy required that the houses, buildings, or other places where goods are deposited and kept, shall be truly and accurately described, and the place was described as the dwelling-house of the insured, whereas he occupied only one room in it, as a lodger, this description was held sufficient.

It was held in another case, that the insurance by an inn-keeper against fire of his "interest in the inn and offices," does not cover the loss of profits during the repair of the damaged premises. And in another, the words "stock in trade," when used in a policy of insurance in reference to the business of a mechanic, as a baker, were held to include not only the materials used by him, but the tools, fixtures, and implements necessary for the carrying-on of his business; and the words in question were held to have a broader application to the business of mechanics than to that of merchants.

A policy upon wearing-apparel, household furniture, and the stock of a grocery, covers linen sheets and shirts actually laid in for family use, and such as were laid in for sale or traffic in the usual way, in the store; but not such as, being smuggled, were concealed and intended for secret sale.

There is no material difference in respect to mistake, or the correction of it, betwen fire-policies and marine-policies; and the law on this subject in relation to the latter has already been stated. And the same remark may be extended to the rule respecting the admission, as a part of the contract, of a memorandum on the back of the policy, or attached to it by a wafer, and neither referred to in the policy itself, nor signed by the insurer.

It is a general rule with our mutual insurance companies, that every one who is insured becomes a member of the company.

And it follows, necessarily, that every insured party is bound by all the laws and rules of the company, as by laws and rules of his own making.

The mutual fire-insurance companies, by a law or rule which is perhaps universal, require that an application shall be made in writing; and this written application is after a peculiar form, prescribed by the rules. It always contains certain definite statements, which relate to those matters which affect the risk of fire importantly. In each form of application sundry questions are put, which are quite numerous and specific, and are those which experience has suggested as best calculated to elicit all the information needed by the insurers, for the purpose of estimating accurately the value of the risk they undertake. Specific answers must be given to all these questions. And this application, with all these statements, questions, and answers, is expressly referred to in the policy, and made a part of the contract.

It is common to state in the printed part of the formal application, that it is made on such and such conditions; and these usually follow those statements which are deemed the most material in estimating the risk. These would be considered as express conditions, and therefore the substantial truth of all of them is a *condition precedent* to any right of indemnity in the insured party. By the legal phrase *condition precedent*, is meant a condition which must be fully complied with before the contract can take effect. Hence, if any of these statements are false, the policy will be void.

Sometimes there is no distinct application in writing, but the policy itself states the facts relied upon. For this purpose it contains many blanks, which are filled up according to the circumstances of each case. It may happen that what is written in these places may be inconsistent with what is printed; and then it is a general rule that what is written prevails, as that is more immediately and specifically the act of the parties, and may be supposed to express their precise purpose better than the printed phrases which were prepared without especial reference to any particular case. But this rule would not be applied where it would obviously operate injustice.

Policies of fire insurance, especially of mutual companies, often contain a scale of premiums, as calculated upon different classes of buildings, of stocks in trade, or other property, in conformity with what is thought to be the greater or less risk of fire in each case. This is a matter of special importance; and if a statement were made by an applicant which put his building or property into a class of which the risk and premium were less than for the class to which the building or property actually belonged, and in that way an insurance was effected at such less premium, the policy would undoubtedly be void, even if the false statement were made innocently.

When certain trades or occupations, or certain uses of buildings, or kinds and classes of property, are enumerated as "hazardous," or otherwise specified as peculiarly exposed to risk, the rule, *The expression of one thing excludes what is not expressed*, is applied, and sometimes with severity. This is better illustrated by marine insurance. Thus, in a case in New York, precisely in point, dried fish were enumerated in the memorandum clause as free from average, and "all other articles perishable in their own nature." It was held that the naming of one description of fish implied that other fish were not intended; and that the subsequent words, "all other articles perishable in their own nature," were not applicable, and did not repel this implication. The same rule would be applied, for the same reason, and in the same way, to cases of fire insurance.

If the printed conditions represent one class of buildings, or goods, or property, as more hazardous than another, it would not be competent for the insured, whose property was of that kind, to prove by other testimony that it was not more hazardous in fact.

Moreover, a description of the property insured, as it is a description *for* a contract on time, is held to amount to an agreement that the property shall continue within the class where it is put, or at least shall not enter into another that is declared to be more hazardous, during the operation of the policy. There must, however, be a rational, and perhaps a liberal, construction of this rule. Thus, it does not apply where a single article, or one or two, are kept in a store as a part of the stock of goods, although that article, as cotton in bales, is among those enumerated as hazardous. So if the "storing of spirituous liquors" is prohibited, the keeping of wine or brandy in a private house for consumption, or even for sale by retail to boarders, would not discharge the insurers.

In New York it was held that where oils and turpentine, which were classed among hazardous or extra-hazardous articles, were introduced for the purpose of repairing and painting the dwelling insured, and the dwelling was burned while being so repaired, the insurers were liable. But if the building is generally appropriated to a more hazardous occupation than the proposals or the policy indicate, or if the jury find that the introduction of these goods materially increased the actual risk, evidence would be received as to the intention of the parties to the contract. And the true meaning of the contract and the intent of the parties would be considered. Thus, where the "storing" of certain goods was prohibited, as "hazardous," it was held that the having a pipe or two of such articles in the cellar, from which smaller vessels in the store were replenished, did not come within the meaning of the word "storing" in the policy, any more than would the keeping of such articles for home consumption in a dwelling-house insured by a similar policy. So a description of a house as "at present occupied as a dwelling-house, but to be hereafter occupied as a tavern, and privileged as such," is only permission that it should be a tavern, and creates no obligation to occupy and keep it as a tavern on the part of the insured. But if the language is, "to be occupied as so or so, but *not*" in some other certain way, this restriction is a part of the bargain; and, if the building is occupied in the way prohibited, the insurers are discharged.

So if the premises are described as a "private residence," the insurance is not avoided by the fact that the occupants moved out of the house, leaving it vacant, and not the "residence" of any one, unless the jury find that the risk was thereby materially increased. But where the property was represented as a "tavern barn," and the insured permitted its occupation as a livery-stable, the policy was held to be discharged, although the keeper of the livery-stable was removable at the pleasure of the insured. Where a building insured by a company was represented, at the time of effecting the insurance, as connected with another building on one side only, and before the loss happened it became connected on two sides, the policy was held not to be avoided unless the risk thereby became greater.

The general subject of alterations of property under insurance against fire is not without difficulty. On the whole, however, mere alterations, although expensive and important, do not necessarily and of themselves avoid the insurance or discharge the insurers; but they have this effect, if they are found by the jury to increase the risk materially; or if they are specifically prohibited in the policy.

Still other questions may arise where material alterations are made, all of which are not easily disposed of. The following are instances. Suppose one gets his dwelling-house insured for seven years, truly describing it as having a shingled roof. After two or three years he determines to take off the shingles, but says nothing to the insurers about it. If he now puts on slates, or a metallic covering which does not require soldering, he does not increase the risk; nor is the work of putting on the new covering hazardous, and we see no grounds for its having any effect on the policy. But suppose the new metallic covering is secured by soldering. This is certainly a hazardous operation. And if the building takes fire in consequence of this operation, the insurers are certainly discharged.

If the operation is conducted safely through, and the work is entirely finished, we consider it clear that this greater hazard for a time has no effect whatever on the policy after that time, and after all the greater hazard has expired. But let us suppose that while this operation is going forward, and the house is thereby certainly exposed to an increase of risk, the house is set on fire by an incendiary, — without the slightest reference to this alteration, — and burns down. It is not, perhaps, settled, either by authority or practice, whether the insurers are or are not discharged. I am, however, of opinion, that the principles of insurance would lead to the conclusion, that, if the house be burned from a perfectly independent cause, during an increase of risk incurred for good cause and in good faith, the insurers are not thereby discharged. It is, however, certain, that it is always prudent to obtain the consent of the insurers to any proposed alteration. If such consent be asked, and refused, we do not see that the insurers stand on any better footing, or the insured on any worse one; and if the alterations are made and a loss occurs, we should say that the insurers would not, generally at least, be discharged because of their refusal, unless they would have been discharged if the alteration had been made without their knowledge. For if they have a right to object or refuse, it could only be because the contract in effect prohibited this alteration; and then their refusal was not wanted for their defence. And if they have no right to refuse, they can acquire no rights by the refusal.

If the alteration be of a permanent character, and causes a material increase of the danger of fire, then it is a substantial breach of contract; and we should hold that the insurers were discharged as soon as the alteration was made, and indeed as soon as the making of it, or preparations for it, as scaffolding or carpenter's work, materially increased the risk. And they are discharged equally, whether the fire be caused by the alteration, or by the work done, or by some wholly independent matter.

The insured may make reasonable repairs without especial leave, and the insurers are liable, although the fire take place while the repairs are going on; and even if it be caused by the repairs.

It may be added, that our fire-policies now in use frequently give the insured the right of keeping the property in repair. The failure of the insured to repair a defect in the building, arising after the contract is made, does not prevent the insured from recovering unless he was guilty of gross negligence.

SECTION III.

THE INTEREST OF THE INSURED.

ANY legal interest is sufficient. And if it be equitable in the sense that a court of equity will recognize and protect it, that is sufficient; but a merely moral or expectant interest is not enough. So one has an insurable interest in a house placed on another's land with that other's consent, but not if placed there without license or shadow of title. So, too, one who has made only an oral bargain with another to purchase the other's house, cannot insure it; but if there be a valid contract in law, or if by writing or by part performance it is enforceable in a court of equity, the purchaser may insure. So, if a debtor assign his property to pay his debts, he has an insurable interest in it until the debts are paid, or until the property be sold.

A partner may have an insurable interest in a building purchased with partnership-funds, although it stands upon land owned by the other partner. A mortgagor may insure the whole value of his property, even after the possession has passed to the mortgagee, if the equity of redemption be not wholly gone. So he may if his equity of redemption is seized on execution, or even sold, so long as he may still redeem. And in case of loss he recovers the whole value of the building, if he be insured on it to that amount.

A mortgagor and a mortgagee may both insure the same property, and neither need specify his interest, but simply call it his property. The mortgagee has an interest only equal to his debt, and founded upon it; and if the debt be paid, the interest ceases, and the policy is discharged; and he can recover no more than the amount of his debt.

It has been held, that if a mortgagor is bound by his contract with the mortgagee to keep the premises insured for the benefit of the mortgagee, and does keep them insured in his own name, the mortgagee has an equitable interest in or lien upon the proceeds of the policy.

One who holds property only in right of his wife may insure the property, even if his wife be only a joint tenant. And a tenant for years, or from year to year, may insure his interest, but would recover only the value of his interest, and not the value of the whole property.

We have said that, generally, any one having any legal interest in property may insure it as his own. But there is one important exception to or modification of this rule. By the charters of many of our mutual insurance companies, the company has a lien, to the amount of the premium note, on all property insured. It is obvious, therefore, that no such description can be given, or no such language used, as would induce the company to suppose they had a lien when they could not have one, or would in any way deceive them as to the validity or value of their lien. In all such cases, all incumbrances must be stated, and the title or interest of the insured fully stated in all those particulars in which it affects the lien.

A trustee, agent, or consignee may insure against fire, as he may against marine loss. Generally, the consignee is not bound to insure against fire, but may, at his discretion. He may insure, expressly, his own interest in them for advances, or the owner's interest. It has been held that a consignee may, by virtue of his implied interest and authority, insure, in his own name, goods in his possession *against fire*, to their full value, and recover for the benefit of the owner. And if the interest be not expressed, the policy will be construed as not covering the interest of the owners, if, upon a fair construction of the words and facts, it seems to have been the intention of the parties only to secure the consignee's interest. And an insurance against fire upon merchandise in a warehouse, "for account of whom it may concern," protects only such interests as were intended to be insured at the time of effecting the insurance.

It is now common for a commission merchant to cover in one policy, in his own name, all the goods of the various owners who have consigned goods to him. It has been held, that the words "goods held on commission," in fire-policies, have an effect equivalent to the words "for whom it may concern," in marine-policies.

A person having a lien on a building under a State law has an insurable interest in the building.

A consignee of goods, sent to him, but not received, may insure his own interest in them. So, any bailee (which means any person to whom property has been delivered for any purpose) who has a legal interest in the chattels which he holds, although this be temporary and qualified, may insure the goods against fire. Thus a common carrier by land, who has a lien on the goods, and is answerable for them if lost by fire (unless it be caused by the act of God or the public enemy), may insure the goods to their full value against fire.

The insurers must know whom they insure; for they may have a choice of persons, and it is important to them to know whether they are to depend on the care and honesty of this man or that man. The insured must so describe the owner as not to deceive them on this point, and so he must the kind of ownership. Thus, if he aver an entire interest in himself, he cannot support this by showing a joint interest with another; and if in his action he declare the latter, proof of the former is not sufficient.

So, too, there must be actual authority to make the insurance. This may be express, or implied, in some cases, as it seems to be implied with the consignee, or the carrier, and perhaps, generally, with any one who has an actual possession of, interest in, and lien on, the property. But a tenant in common does not derive from his cotenancy authority to insure for his cotenant; nor could a master of a ship or a ship's husband, merely as such, insure the owner's interest against fire.

SECTION IV.

DOUBLE INSURANCE.

By this, the party orginally insured becomes again insured. If, by a double insurance, the insured could protect himself over and over again, he might recover many indemnities for one loss. This cannot be permitted, not only because it is opposed to the first principles of insurance, but because it would tempt to fraud, and make it very easy.

In this country, fire-policies usually contain express and exact provisions on this subject. They vary somewhat; but, generally, they require that any other insurance must be stated by the insured, and indorsed on the policy; and it is a frequent condition, that each office shall in that case pay only a ratable proportion of a loss; and it is often added, that, if such other insurance be not so stated and indorsed, the insured shall not recover on the policy. And it has been held that such a condition applies to a subsequent as well as to a prior insurance; or to an insurance of any part of the property covered by the other policy. Nor will a court of equity relieve, if sufficient notice and indorsement have not been made. But it has been held that a valid notice might be given to an agent of the company, who was authorized to receive applications and survey property proposed for insurance.

In some instances, the charter of the company provides that any policy made by it shall be avoided by any double insurance of which notice is not given, and to which the consent of the company is not obtained, and expressed by their indorsement in the policy. But this would not apply to a non-notice by an insured of an insurance effected by the seller on the house which the insured had bought, if this policy were not assigned to the buyer.

SECTION V.

WARRANTY AND REPRESENTATION.

A WARRANTY is a part of the contract; it must be distinctly expressed, and written either in or on the policy, or on a paper attached to the policy, or, as has been held, on a separate paper distinctly referred to and described as a part of the policy. Then it operates as a condition precedent; that is, as a condition of the policy, which if it be not performed, the policy never takes effect; if it be not performed, there is no valid contract; nor can the non-performance be helped by evidence that the thing warranted was less material than was supposed, or, indeed, not material.

It may be a warranty of the present time, or, as it is called, affirmative, or of the future, and then it is promissory. And it may be, although of the present and affirmative, a continuing warranty, rendering the policy liable to avoidance by a non-continuance of the thing which is warranted to exist. Whether it is thus continuing or not must evidently be determined by the nature of the thing warranted. A warranty that the roof of a house is slated, or that there are only so many fireplaces or stoves, would, generally at least, be regarded as continuing; but a warranty that the building was five hundred feet from any other building would not cause the avoidance of the policy if a neighbor should afterwards put up a house within one hundred feet, without any act or privity of the insured.

We have seen, that statements made on a separate paper may be so referred to as to make them a part of the policy. And it is usual to refer in this way to the written application of the insured, and to all the written statements, descriptions, and answers to questions, which he makes for the purpose of obtaining insurance. But a fair and rational, or, in some cases, a liberal construction, will be given to such statements.

It is quite certain that the word warranty need not be used, if the language is such as to import unequivocally the same meaning. And an indorsement made upon the policy before it is executed may take effect as a part of it.

A statement may be introduced into the policy itself, and be construed not as any warranty, but merely as a license or permission of the insurers that premises may be occupied in a certain way, or some other fact occur without prejudice to the insurance.

A representation, in the law of insurance, differs from a warranty, in that it is not a part of the contract. If made after the signing of the policy or the completion of the contract, it cannot of course affect it. If made before the contract, and with a view to effecting insurance, it is no part of the contract; but if it be fraudulent, it makes the contract void. And if it be false, and known to be false by him who makes it, it is his fraud. To have this effect, however, it must be material; and there is no better test or standard for this than the question, whether the contract would have been made, and in its present form or on its actual terms, if this statement had not been made and believed by the insurers. If the answer is, that the contract would not have been made if this statement had not been made, it is material; otherwise, not. The general rule is, that the statements in the application on a separate sheet have the effect only of representations, and do not avoid the policy unless void in a material point, or unless the policy makes them specially a part of itself, and gives them the effect of warranties. A representation may be more certainly and precisely proved if in writing; but it will have its whole force and effect if only oral.

In some instances, by the terms of the policies, any misrepresentations or concealments avoid the policy. And it is held that the parties have a right to make such a bargain, and that it is binding upon them; and the effect of it would seem to be to give to representations the force and influence of warranties.

There seems to be this difference between marine-policies and fire-policies. In the former, a material misrepresentation avoids the policy, although innocently made; in the latter, it has this effect only when it is fraudulent. This distinction seems to rest upon the greater capability, and therefore greater obligation, of the insurers against fire to acquaint themselves fully with all the particulars which enter into the risk. For they may do this either by the survey and examination of an agent, or by specific and minute inquiries. If a *warranty* is broken, however innocently, it avoids all policies, whether material or not. And this difference between a *warranty* and a *representation* is very important.

Concealment is the converse of misrepresentation. The insured is bound to state all that he knows himself, and all that it imports the insurer to know, for the purpose of estimating accurately the risk he assumes. A suppression of the truth has the same effect as an expression of what is false. And the rule as to materiality and as to a substantial compliance is the same.

Even the rumor of an attempt to set fire to a neighboring building should be communicated; because the insurer should be informed of any unusual fact, or any circumstance relating to the building materially enhancing the risk.

Insurers must be understood as knowing all those matters of common information, that are as much within their reach as in that of the insured; and these need not be especially stated. But any special circumstance, as a great number of fires in the neighborhood, and the probability or belief that incendiaries were at work, should certainly be communicated; and silence on such a point—especially if the place of business of the insurers was at a considerable distance from the premises—would operate as a fraud, and avoid the policy. And any questions asked must be answered, and all answers must be as full and precise as the question requires. If there were a provision in the policy, that a certain fact, if existing, must be stated, silence in reference to it would avoid the policy, however immaterial the fact. Concealment in an answer to a specific question can seldom or never be justified by showing that it was not material. Thus, in general, nothing need be said about title. But if it be inquired about, full and accurate answers must be made.

Where the insurance company has, by the terms of the policy, a lien upon or interest in the premises insured, to secure the premium note, here it is obvious that any concealment of incumbrance or defect of title would operate as a fraud, and defeat the policy. But in all such cases it is probable that specific questions are put respecting the estate and title of the insured.

It is often required that all buildings standing within a certain distance of the property insured shall be stated; but this might not always be considered as applicable to personal and movable property. Still, an insurance of chattels, described as in a certain place or building, would be held to amount to a warranty that they should remain there; or rather it would not cover them if removed into a another place or building, unless, by some appropriate phraseology, the parties expressed their intention that the insured was to be protected as to this property wherever it might be situated. It is not uncommon to insure goods that are in course of transit, against fire; but then it is usual to name the places from which and to which the goods are passing.

SECTION VI.

THE RISK INCURRED BY THE INSURERS.

At the time of the insurance, the property must be in existence, and not on fire, and not at that moment exposed to a dangerous fire in the immediate neighborhood; because the insurance assumes that no unusual risk exists at that time.

The risk taken is that of fire. And therefore the insurers are not chargeable if the property be destroyed or injured by the indirect effect of excessive heat; or by any effect which stops short of ignition or combustion, when this heat is purposely applied, and the injury is caused by the negligence of the person in charge of it. Where, however, an extraordinary fire occurs, the insurers are clearly liable for the direct effects of it, as where furniture or pictures are injured by the heat, although they do not actually ignite.

And they are liable for the injury from water used to extinguish the fire; and for injury to or loss of goods caused by their removal from immediate danger of fire; but not if removed from a mere apprehension from a distant fire, even if it be reasonable; and not if the loss or injury might have been avoided by even so much care as is usually given in times of such excitement and confusion.

In some instances, the policies require that the insured should use all possible diligence to preserve their goods; and such a clause would strengthen the claim for injury caused by an endeavor to save them by removal. So the insurers are liable for injury or loss sustained by the blowing up of buildings to arrest the progress of a fire.

Lightning is not fire; and if property be destroyed by lightning, the insurers are not liable, unless there was also ignition; or unless the policy expressly insures against lightning.

An explosion caused by gunpowder is a loss by fire; not so, is an explosion caused by steam.

Whether, when the negligence of the insured or his servants is to be considered as the sole or direct cause of the fire or loss, the insurers can be held, has been somewhat considered. And as this is the most common and universal danger, and the very one which induces most persons to insure, there has been some disposition to say that no measure or kind of mere negligence can operate as a defence. And in effect this is almost the law. But if the loss be caused by negligence of the insured himself, of so extreme and gross a character that it is hardly possible to avoid the conclusion of fraud, the defence might be a good one, although there were no direct proof of fraud. That the fire was caused by the insanity of the insured should be no defence.

SECTION VII.

VALUATION.

VALUATION, precisely as it is understood in a marine policy, seldom enters into a fire-policy, — never, perhaps, in a policy made by any of those mutual companies, who now do a very large part of the insurance of this country. And quite seldom is a building valued when insured by a stock company. If a loss happens, whether it be total or partial, the insurers are bound to pay only so much of the sum insured as will indemnify the assured. But, as care is always taken — and sometimes required by law — not to insure upon any house its whole value, it seldom happens, and, if the proper previous precautions are taken, should never happen, that any question of value arises in a case of a total destruction of a building by fire.

But mutual companies are usually forbidden by their charter to insure more than a certain proportion of the value of a building; and this requires a valuation in the policy, which is conclusive, for some purposes, against both parties. Of course, the insurers can never be held to pay more than the sum insured. And if their charter or by-laws permit a company to insure only a certain proportion of the value, as three-fourths, — on the one hand, if the company insure more than that proportion, as $3,500 on property valued at $4,000, they are held to pay only $3,000, and the assured cannot show that the building was really worth more than $4,000; and, on the other hand, the valuation, if not fraudulent, is conclusive against the insurers if the building is destroyed, and they cannot show, in defence, that the building was worth less.

I know nothing to prevent the parties from making a valued policy, if they see fit to do so, although this has been questioned. It is not uncommon for companies who insure chattels, — as plate, pictures, statuary, books, or the like, — to agree on what shall be the value in case of loss.

Sometimes the policy reserves to the insurers the right to have the valuation made anew by evidence, in case of loss. Then if a jury find a less valuation, the insurers pay the same proportion of the new value which they had insured of the former valuation.

The value which the insurers on goods must pay is their value at the time of the loss. And it has been held, that a fair sale at auction, with due precaution, will be taken to settle that value after the fire, provided the insurers have reasonable notice or knowledge that the auction is to take place.

The valuation determines the amount which the insurers must pay only in case of total destruction. If the building is only injured by fire, the insurers may either repair it, or pay the cost of repairing it.

SECTION VIII.

ALIENATION.

POLICIES against fire are personal contracts between the insured and the insurers, and do not pass to any other party, without the express consent of the insurers.

It is essential to the validity and efficacy of this contract, that the insured have an interest in the property when he is insured, and also when the loss takes place ; for otherwise it is not his loss, and he can have no claim for indemnity. If, therefore, he alienates the whole of his interest in the property before the loss, he has no claim; and if he alienates a part, retaining a partial interest, he has only a partial and proportionate claim.

After a loss has occurred, the right of the insured to indemnity is vested and fixed; and this right may be assigned for value, so as to give an equitable claim to the assignee, without the consent of the insurers.

Policies against fire contain a provision that an assignment of the property, or of the policy, shall avoid the policy. So, generally, it is hardly worth while to inquire what right an assignee, without consent, would acquire at common law, or in equity, where there is no such provision.

A dissolution of the partnership before loss, and a division of the goods, so that each partner owned distinct portions, was held to be in violation of a condition against "any transfer or change of title in the property insured."

A conveyance by one insured, intended to secure a debt, will be treated in a court of equity as a mortgage, and therefore it does not terminate the interest of the insured. A contract to convey is not an alienation. Nor is a conditional sale, where the condition must precede the sale, and is not yet performed. Nor is a mortgage, not even after breach, and perhaps entry for a breach, and not until foreclosure. Nor selling and *immediately* taking back. Sometimes alienation by mortgage is directly prohibited.

If several estates are insured in one policy, and one or more are aliened (or conveyed away), the policy is void as to those only which are aliened. If many owners are insured in one policy, a transfer by one or more to strangers, without the act or concurrence of the other owners, will avoid the policy for only so much as is thus transferred.

In practice, care should be taken to have all such transfers regularly made and notified, and the consent of the insurer obtained, fully authorized, and duly indorsed or certified, and all the rules or usages of the insurers in this respect complied with.

SECTION IX.

NOTICE AND PROOF.

WHERE the policy requires a certificate of the loss, the production of it is a condition precedent to any claim for payment. And it must be such a certificate as is required; but a substantial compliance with its requirements is sufficient. So, too, if the notice is to be given *forthwith*, there must be no unreasonable or unnecessary delay. And all the circumstances of the case are considered, in determining whether there was or was not due diligence. Where a certificate is required to be furnished "as soon as possible," it is still sufficient if it be furnished within a reasonable time. But where the fire took place in November, and the account of loss was not furnished till the March following, it was held not to be a compliance with the conditions. Generally, this is a question for the jury.

In fire-policies, as the premises may be supposed always open to the inspection of the agents of the insurers, a general notice of the fire will be enough.

SECTION X.

ADJUSTMENT AND LOSS.

INSURERS against fire are not held to pay for loss of profits, gains of business, or other indirect and remote consequences of a loss by fire. We do not know, however, why profits may not be expressly insured against fire, where it is not forbidden by, or inconsistent with, the charter of the insurers.

There is one wide difference between the principle of adjustment of a marine-policy and of a fire-policy. In the former, if a proportion only of the value is insured, the insured is considered as his own insurer for the residue, and only an equal proportion of the loss is paid. Thus, if, on a ship valued at $10,000, $5,000 be insured, and there is a loss of one-half, the insurers pay only one-half of the sum they insure, just as if some other insurer had insured the other $5,000. But in a fire-policy, the insurers pay in all cases the whole amount which is lost by fire, provided only that it does not exceed the amount which they insure.

Most of the fire-policies used in this country give the insurers the right of rebuilding or repairing premises destroyed or injured by fire, instead of paying the amount of the loss. If, under this power, the insurers rebuild the house insured, at a less cost than the amount they insure, this does not exhaust their liability; they are now insurers of the new building for the difference between its cost and the amount they have insured. And if the new building burns down, or is injured while the policy continues, the insured may claim so much as, added to the cost already incurred, shall equal the sum for which he was insured.

It may be important to add, that, under our common mutual policies, the insured will also be liable for assessments for losses after the destruction of his building by fire, during the whole term of the policy.

There is no rule in fire-insurance similar to that which makes a deduction, in marine-insurance, of one-third, new for old. Still, the jury, to whom the whole question of damages is given, are to inquire into the greater value of a proposed new building, or of a repaired building, and assess only such damages as shall give the insured complete indemnity.

Where insurers reserved a right to replace articles destroyed, if the insured refused to permit them to examine and inventory the goods that they might judge what it was expedient for them to do, such conduct on the part of the insured would be evidence to the jury of great weight, to prove an overstatement of loss.

I have not thought it would be useful to give Forms of various policies. Applicants never make them, as they are always furnished by the insurance companies; each one having its own form, and using no other. But the following Forms, of immediate notice of loss, of a later and fuller statement under oath, with a magistrate's certificate, and assignments of policies, may be found useful. They must be all adapted, in practice, to the peculiar circumstances of each case.

(102.)

To the .... Fire-Insurance Company.

Take Notice, That on the day of inst. (or last) a fire broke out in the building No. in Street, in the city of (*or otherwise describe the location*), whereon I am insured by you, by your policy, No. the sum of dollars. I have not yet learned, and do not know, in what way the fire was caused; but, as soon as I am able, I will give you further information on the subject. (*If the insured or his agent knows, or has reasonable cause for supposing, how the fire was caught, he should say so, and state what particulars he can.*)

The house was wholly (*or partially*) destroyed by fire; and I shall claim a payment from you under your policy.

Written and sent this day of in the year

(*Signature.*) (*Seal.*)

Witness to the signature and sending.
(*Signature of Witness.*)

Some insurance companies, and, indeed, the express provisions of some policies, require that a sworn statement of the facts and circumstances of the loss, and the particulars of the claim, be given to the insurance company, with the certificate of a magistrate. I do not know that this course might not be always prudent. The form in which it is done must vary in each case, and be adapted to the peculiarities of that case. But the following Form will generally be a safe guide.

(103.)

To the .... Insurance Company.

Whereas the said Insurance Company, by their policy numbered , and dated on the day of in the year caused me to be insured in the sum of dollars against loss or damage by fire to the following-described building; that is to say (*here describe or designate the building sufficiently to show clearly where and what it was, taking the description from the policy, but not copying it at length*), Now, I, the said (*name of the assured*) having been solemnly sworn, do depose and say, —

1. That on the day of now last past, between the hours of and a fire broke out in said building, whereby the same was greatly damaged (*or destroyed*), and the said fire was, according to my best knowledge and belief, caused by (*here set forth the causes so far as they are known, or supposed on reasonable grounds*), and I aver that the said fire was not caused by me, or by my design and concurrence, or with any previous knowledge on my part, or in any manner attributable to me or to my agency, direct or indirect.

2. That I was interested in the said property in the following manner; that is to say (*here say whether the insured owned the property himself, or was a tenant of it, or a landlord, or mortgagor or mortgagee, or trustee, or how otherwise he was interested*)

3. That there was no other insurance against fire of the said property (*or, if there was any other, state what it was*)

4. That the occupants of the building at the time of the fire were, so far as is known to me, the following persons (*set forth the names of the occupants, the parts of the building occupied by each one, and the purpose for which it was occupied*)

5. That the actual value of the building in dollars at the time of the fire, was, according to my best belief and judgment, dollars. (*If the property was personal, as goods, furniture, or the like, say, as may appear by the schedule annexed.*)

6. That the whole of said value was lost by the fire; and being more than the sum insured thereon, I now claim of said insurance company said sum of

dollars. (*Or if the building was injured, and not destroyed, then say that so much of the value — stating the amount — of said building was lost by the fire, inasmuch as the building, if repaired, cannot be restored to as good a condition as before, for a less amount than that sum.*)

Witness my hand at this day of in the year

(*Signature.*)

(*Certificate to be appended to the Foregoing.*)

STATE OF , }
COUNTY OF . } ss.

I (*name of the magistrate*) a justice of the peace in and for said county (*or what else may be his office*), dwelling near to the property above mentioned, in the town (*or city*) of have investigated the circumstances attending the said fire, and am personally acquainted with the said (*name of insured*), whose character is good; and I believe that the above statement to which the said (*name of insured*) has made oath in my presence is true; that the loss cannot be imputed to fraud or misconduct on his part; and that he has suffered by the fire a loss of dollars. I am not in any way interested in the said property, or in the said policy, or any claim under the same.

In Witness of all which I have hereunto set my hand and my seal (*of office if he has an official seal*), at this day of in the year

(*Signature of Magistrate.*) (*Seal.*)

(104.)

Assignment of a Policy to be indorsed Thereon.

I (*name of the insured*) insured by the within policy, in consideration of a dollar paid to me by (*name of the assignee*) and for other good considerations, do hereby assign, and transfer to the said (*name of the assignee*) this policy, together with all the right, title, interest, and claim which I now have or hereafter may have, in, to, or under the same.

Witness my hand this day of in the year

(*Signature.*)

Witness.

It is always best to write this assignment on the policy itself; but it may sometimes happen that this is not convenient or possible;

the insured who wishes to make the assignment not having the policy within his possession or easy reach. Then the assured may use the following Form: —

(105.)

Whereas, the Insurance Company, by their policy, numbered and dated on day of in the year, caused me to be insured against loss or damage by fire on a certain building, being (*designate the building by location or otherwise*) in the sum of dollars; now, I the said (*name of the insured*), in consideration of one dollar paid to me by (*name of the assignee*) and for other good considerations, have transferred and assigned, and do by these presents transfer and assign unto the said (*name of the assignee*) the said policy of insurance, and all the right, title, interest or claim, which I now have or ever may have, in, to, or under the same, and in and to any sum of money which now is or shall ever be payable thereon.

Witness my hand this day of in the year

(*Signature.*)

(*Witness.*)

If the policy be on goods, or if it be not a fire-policy, but a marine-policy, or a life-policy, then the assignment must be made to conform to the facts.

It is *always* best to get the assent of the insurance company to the transfer *before it is made.* And always the assignment, when made, should be exhibited without loss of time, to them or to their agent authorized to give their assent, and this assent to the assignment be obtained and written upon the policy, or, if that cannot conveniently be, on the assignment, and in the books of the insurance company.

CHAPTER XXVIII.

LIFE-INSURANCE.

SECTION I.

THE PURPOSE AND METHOD OF LIFE-INSURANCE.

If A insures B a certain sum payable at B's death to B's representatives, we have only the insurer and insured, as in other cases of insurance. But if A insures B a sum payable to B or his representatives on the death of C, although C is often said to be insured, this is not quite accurate; more properly, B is the *insured* party and C is the *life-insured.*

Life-insurance is usually effected in this country in a way quite similar to that of fire-insurance by our mutual companies. That is, an application must be first made by the insured; and to this application queries are annexed by the insurers, which inquire, with great minuteness and detail, into every thing which can affect the probability of life. These must be answered fully; and if the insurer be other than the life-insured, there are usually questions for each of them. There are also, in some cases, questions which should be answered by the physician of the life-insured, and others by his friends or relatives; or other means are provided to have the evidence of the physician and friends.

These questions are not precisely the same in the forms given out by any two companies; and we do not speak of them in detail here. The rules as to the obligation of answering them, and as to the sufficiency of the answers, must be the same in life-insurance that we have already stated in the chapters on Fire and Marine Insurance; or rather must rest upon the same principles. And the same rules and principles of construction therein set forth would doubtless be applied to the question whether a contract had been made, or at what time it went into effect.

SECTION II.

THE PREMIUM.

If the insurance be for one year only, or less, the premium is usually paid in money, or by a note, at once. If for more than a year, it is usually payable annually. But it is common to provide or agree that the annual payment may be made quarterly, with interest from the day when the whole is due. Notes are usually given; but if not, the whole amount would be considered due. If A, whose premium of $100 is payable for 1856 on the 1st day of January, then pays $25, and is to pay the rest quarterly, but dies on the 1st of February, the $75 due, with interest from the 1st of January, would be deducted from the sum insured. If the policy provides that the risk shall "terminate in case the premium charged shall not be paid in advance on or before the day at noon on which the same shall become due and payable," and the day of payment falls on Sunday, the premium is not payable until Monday, although the assured dies on Sunday afternoon.

Provision is sometimes made that a part of the premium shall be paid in money, and a part in notes, which are not called in unless needed to pay losses. The greater the accommodation thus allowed, the more convenient it is, obviously to the insured, but the less certain will he be of the ultimate payment of the policy, because, in the same degree, the fund for the payment consists only of such notes, and not of payments actually made and invested. There is a great diversity among the life-insurance companies in this respect. But even the strictest, or those which require that all the premiums shall be paid in money, usually provide also that an amount may remain overdue, without prejudice, which does not exceed a certain proportion — say one-half or one-third — of the money actually paid in on the policy. This is considered, under all ordinary circumstances, safe for the company, because every policy is worth as much as this to the company. Or, in other words, it would always be profitable for the company to obtain a discharge of its obligation on a policy, by repaying the insured so small a proportion of what has been received from him.

Taking a note would certainly be a waiver of immediate payment, if not itself a payment.

The premiums, after the first, must be paid on the days on which they fall due. If no hour be mentioned, then it is believed that the insured would have the whole day, even to midnight. It is possible, however, that he might be restricted to the usual hours of business, and perhaps even to those in which the office of the insurers is open for business.

Practically, the utmost care is requisite on the part of the assured, to pay his premium as soon as it is due; and it is a wise precaution to pay it a little before. This is the only proper and safe course. But we believe it to be not unusual for the insurers to accept the premium if offered them a few days after, and continue the policy as if it were paid in season, provided no change in the risk has occurred in the mean time.

And sometimes the rules of the company, and in some States the statutes, provide, that, if a policy be defeated by a non-payment of the premium, the insured does not lose all that he has paid; but a certain proportion of the value which the policy then had shall be paid to him.

The time of the death is sometimes very important. If the policy be for a definite period, it must be shown that the death occurs within it. If there were an insurance on a man's life for a year, and some short time before the expiration of the term he received a mortal wound, of which he died one day after the year, the insurer would not be liable. And the terms of the policy may possibly make it necessary to determine which of two persons lived longest; as if a sum were insured on the joint lives of two persons, to be paid to the representatives of the survivor.

SECTION III.

THE RESTRICTIONS AND EXCEPTIONS IN LIFE-POLICIES.

Our policies usually contain certain restrictions or limitations as to place; the life-insured (he whose life is insured for his own or another's benefit) not being permitted to go beyond certain limits, or to certain places. But there is nothing to prevent a bargain permitting the life-insured to pass beyond these bounds, either in consideration of new and further payments, or of the common premium.

So certain trades or occupations, as of persons engaged in making gunpowder, or of engineers or firemen about steam-engines, are considered extra-hazardous, and as therefore prohibited, or requiring an extra premium.

The exception, however, which has created most discussion, is that which makes death by suicide an avoidance of the policy. The clause respecting duelling is plain enough; and no one can die in a duel without his own fault. But it is otherwise with regard to self-inflicted death. This may be voluntary and wrongful, or the result of insanity and disease, for which the suffering party should not be held responsible.

The general principles of the law of contracts, and of the law of insurance particularly, would lead to the conclusion that "death by his own hands," but without the concurrence of a responsible will or mind, would not discharge the insurers, without a positive provision to that effect. We should put such a death on the same footing with one resulting from a mere accident, brought about by the agency, but without the intent, of the life-insured. As if poison were sent to him by mistake for medicine, and he swallowed it under the same mistake.

Much question has been made, *when* a man may be believed to be dead, simply because nothing is known about him, or has been known for a long period. But there is not and cannot be any other presumption of law on the subject than that, after a certain period of absence and silence, there is a presumption of death; and seven years has been mentioned in England and in this country as this period, and even sanctioned by legislation in New York. But all questions of this kind we regard as pure questions of fact. Whichever party rests his case upon the death or the life of a certain person, at a certain time, must satisfy the jury upon this point by such evidence as may be admissible and sufficient.

SECTION IV.

THE INTEREST OF THE INSURED.

EVERY one insured in any way must have an interest in the subject-matter of the insurance. A person may effect insurance on his own life in the name of a creditor, for a sum beyond the amount of the debt, the balance to enure to his family, and the policy will be valid for the whole amount insured. Any one may insure his own life; but if the insured and the life-insured are not the same, that is, if the insured be insured on some other life than his own, interest must be shown.

A father has an insurable interest in the life of his minor son. And the general rule is, that any substantial pecuniary interest is sufficient, although not strictly legal nor definite. This has been held in the case of a sister dependent on a brother for support; and the rule would be held to apply not only to all relations, but where there was no relationship, if there were a positive and real dependence. That is, any one may insure a sum on the life of any other person on whom he or she really depends for support or for comfort. And generally, it is said to be enough, if, according to the ordinary course of events, pecuniary loss or disadvantage will naturally and probably result from the death of the one whose life is insured.

So an existing debt gives the creditor an insurable interest in the life of a debtor. But if the debt be not founded on a legal consideration, it does not sustain the policy. And if the debt be paid before the death of the debtor, the insurers are discharged.

SECTION V.

THE ASSIGNMENT OF A LIFE-POLICY.

LIFE-POLICIES are assignable at law, and are very frequently assigned in practice. And the assignee of a policy is entitled on the death of the party insured, to recover the full sum insured without reference to the amount of the consideration paid by him for the assignment. A large proportion of the policies which are effected are made for the purpose of assignment; that is, for the purpose of enabling the insured to give this additional security to his creditor. If the rules of the company or the terms of the policy refer to an assignment of it, they are binding on the parties. On the one hand, an assignment would operate as a discharge of the insurers, provided a rule or expressed provision gave this effect to the assignment. And, on the other, if the agreement were that the policy should continue in favor of the assignee, even after an act which discharged it as to the insured himself, — as, for example, his suicide, — the insurers would be bound by it.

It is an important question what constitutes an assignment. The general answer must be, any act distinctly importing an assignment. And, therefore, a delivery and deposit of the policy, for the purpose of assignment, will operate as such, without a formal written assignment. So will any transaction which gives to a creditor of the insured a right to payment out of the insurance.

It seems, however, that delivery is necessary. And where an assignment was indorsed on the policy, and notice given to the insurer, but the policy remained in the possession of the insured, it was held that there was no assignment. Where, however, the assignment is by a separate deed, which is duly executed and delivered, this is an assignment of the policy, without actual delivery of the policy itself.

SECTION VI.

WARRANTY, REPRESENTATION, AND CONCEALMENT.

THE general principles on this subject are the same which we have already stated in reference to other modes of insurance. In life-policies, however, the questions which must be answered are so minute, and cover so much ground, that difficulty seldom arises except in relation to the answers. One advisable precaution is for the answerer to discriminate carefully between what he knows and what he believes. If he says simply "yes" or "no," or gives an equivalent answer, this is in most cases a strict warranty, and avoids the policy if there be any material mistake in the reply. But where the answerer adds the words "to the best of my knowledge and belief," he *warrants* only the fact of his belief, or, in other words, nothing but his own entire honesty.

The cases which turn upon the answers to the questions are very numerous; but they necessarily rest upon the especial facts of each case, and hardly permit that general rules should be drawn from them. Some, however, may be stated.

The first is, that perfect good faith should be observed. The want of it taints a policy at once; and the presence of it goes far to protect one. Thus, where the life-insured was beginning to be insane, but was wholly unconscious of it, the policy was not vitiated by the concealment, although two doctors in attendance upon him knew how the case stood.

Most of the policies of the present day provide that the policy is made on the faith of the statements in the application for insurance with the stipulation, and that, if they shall be found in any respect untrue, the policies shall be avoided. Then the stipulations are considered as warranties, and if untrue, even in a point immaterial to the risk, avoid the policies.

There is a warranty, or statement, usually making a part of nearly all life-policies; it is that the life-insured is in good health. But this does not mean perfect health, or freedom from all symptoms or seeds of disease. It means reasonably good health; and loose as this definition, or rule, may be, it would be difficult to give any other. And if a jury on the whole are satisfied that the constitution of one warranted to be "in good health" is radically impaired, and the life made unusually precarious, there is a breach of the warranty, although no specific disease is shown which must have that effect. On the other hand, this warranty is not broken by the presence of a disease, if that be one which does not usually tend to shorten life (in one English case dyspepsia was said to be such a disease), unless it were organic, or had increased to that extreme degree as to be of itself dangerous.

Consumption is the disease which is most feared in this country, as well as in England. And the questions which relate to the symptoms of it, as spitting of blood, cough, and the like, are exceedingly minute. But here also there must be a reasonable construction of the answers. Thus, if spitting of blood be positively denied, there may be no falsification in fact, though literally speaking the life-insured may have spit blood many times, as when a tooth was drawn, or from some accident. If there be an action on the policy, and the insurers rest their defence on any falsification of this kind, the question usually put to the jury is, Was the party affected by any of these or similar symptoms, in such wise that they indicated a disorder tending to shorten life? And any symptom of this kind, however slight, — as a drop or two of blood having ever flowed from inflamed or congested lungs, — should be stated. Statements materially untrue on these points avoid the policy, although the insured, at the time of his application, did not believe that he had any pulmonary disease, and the statement made by him was not intentionally false, but, according to his belief, true.

The insurers always ask who is the physician of the life-insured, that they may make inquiries of him if they see fit. And his name must be stated fully and accurately. It is not enough to give the name of the usual attendant; but every physician really consulted should be named, and every one consulted as a physician, although he is an irregular practitioner or quack.

If the warranty be that the life-insured is a person of sober and temperate habits, it has been held, in an action on such a policy, that the jury are not to inquire whether his habits of drinking are such as might injure his health; for if he has any "habits of drinking," this would discharge the insurers, because they have a perfect right to say that they will insure only those who are temperate. But it may be answered, that although the insurers have this right, and there may be good reasons why this should be the general practice, yet unless they use the word "abstinence," or something equivalent, they have no right to say that any one is not "temperate" who does not drink enough to affect his health; for as, generally, all intemperance must affect health injuriously, if there be no such injury, the presumption would be that there was no intemperance; and there is clearly a broad distinction between temperance and total abstinence.

An answer, "not subject to fits," is not necessarily falsified by the fact that the life-insured has had one or more fits. But if the question had been, "Have you ever had fits?" then it is said that any fit of any kind, and however long before, must be stated. But if a man had a fit when a young child, and forgot to mention it, or considered it wholly unimportant, and it had nothing to do with his state of health, it would hardly be held a falsification which would avoid the policy.

As there is always a general question as to any facts affecting health not particularly inquired of, a concealment of such a fact goes to a jury, who are to judge whether the fact was material, and whether the concealment were honest. As when a life-insured was a prisoner for debt, and so without the benefit of air and recreation, and this was not told; and where a woman whose life was insured had become the mother of a child under disgraceful circumstances some years before, and this fact was concealed; the plaintiff was non-suited.

If the policy, and the papers annexed or connected, put no limits on the location of the life-insured, he may go where he will. But if, when applying for insurance, he intends going to a place of peculiar danger, and this intention is wholly withheld, it would be a fraudulent concealment.

If facts be erroneously but honestly misrepresented, and the insurers, when making the policy, knew the truth, the error does not affect the policy. Nor does the non-statement of a fact which diminishes the risk.

If upon a proposal for a life insurance, and an agreement thereon, a policy be drawn up by the insurers, and presented to the insured and accepted by them, which differs from the terms of the agreement, and varies the rights of the parties concerned, equity will interfere and deal with the case on the footing of this agreement, and not of the policy. But it may be shown by evidence and circumstances, that it was intended by the insurers to vary the agreement, and propose a different policy to the insured, and that this was understood by the insured, and the policy so accepted.

SECTION VII.

INSURANCE AGAINST ACCIDENT, DISEASE, AND DISHONESTY OF SERVANTS.

Of late years, both of these forms of insurance have come into practice, but not so long or so extensively as to require that we should speak of them at length. In general it must be true, that the principles already stated as those of insurance against marine peril, or fire, or death, must apply to these other — and indeed to all other — forms of insurance, excepting so far as they may be qualified by the nature of the contract.

From one interesting case which has occurred in England, it seems that, when an application is made for insurance, or guaranty, against the fraud or misconduct of an agent, questions are proposed, as we should expect, which are calculated to call forth all the various facts illustrative of the character of the agent, and all which could assist in estimating the probability of his fidelity and discretion. But a declaration of the applicant as to the course or conduct he was to pursue was distinguished from a warranty. He may recover on the policy, although he changes his course, provided the declaration was honest when made, and the change of conduct was also in good faith. In this case the application was for insurance of the fidelity of the secretary of an institution. There was a question as to when, and how often, the accounts of the secretary would be balanced and closed; and the applicant answered that these accounts would be examined by the financial committee once a fortnight. A loss ensued from the dishonesty of the secretary; and it appeared to have been made possible by the neglect of the committee or the directors to examine his accounts in the manner stated in the policy. But the insurers were held, on the ground that there was no warranty.

CHAPTER XXIX.

DEEDS CONVEYING LAND.

SECTION I.

WHAT IS ESSENTIAL TO SUCH DEEDS.

By the old law, no instrument was considered made until it was sealed; then it was thought to be *done*, and the word *deed*, which literally means only something done, was given to every written instrument to which a seal was affixed; and that is the legal meaning now. But the common meaning of the word is an instrument for the sale of lands; and it is of this that we would now treat.

By the statutes and usage of this country, generally, no lands can be transferred excepting by a deed, which is signed, sealed, acknowledged, delivered, and recorded.

What the deed should be, that is, in what words it should be expressed, we can best show by the forms appended to this chapter, and do not propose to say more about it than this. It is not safe to depart from forms, and established phrases, which have passed before the courts so often, that their exact meaning is certainly known. There are things which seem to be and perhaps are vain repetitions; and for the usual words it may be thought that others of the same or better meaning may be substituted. Such changes may be made, *perhaps*, without detriment; but *perhaps, also*, with ruinous results; and it is not wise to run the risk.

It should be signed; and this means, properly, that the seller or grantor should write his name in the usual way, in the proper place, and with ink. If the grantor cannot write his name, he may merely make his mark. It has been said that writing with a lead pencil is enough, but it would not be safe to trust to it. The name of the grantee should be distinctly written in the proper place, in ink. Sometimes, in our large cities, an agent buys land for a principal who does not wish to be known, and the agent's name is inserted as grantee, *in pencil*, and the deed is so executed and acknowledged and delivered; and some time afterwards the agent rubs his name out, and writes the name of his principal, the actual buyer, instead. But this is a very unsafe and reprehensible practice, and the deed cannot be considered satisfactory.

The deed of a corporation must be signed by an agent or attorney, who should be careful to execute it in the manner indicated in some of the forms appended. In one case, in Massachusetts, where a deed was written throughout as the deed of a corporation, and their treasurer signed it thus: "In witness whereof, I, the said C C, in behalf of the said company, and as their treasurer, have hereunto set *my hand and seal*," — it was held that this was the deed of the treasurer, and not the deed of the corporation, and did not transfer the lands. This is an extreme case, and the law might not always be applied with so much severity; but it is best not to incur any such risk. So, too, the rule that a person who is to be authorized to affix the seal of another should be authorized under the seal of the principal, is so general, that, although it has important exceptions, it should always be observed.

The seal is properly a piece of paper wafered on, or sealing-wax pressed on. In the New England States generally, and in New York, nothing else satisfies the legal requirement of a seal. In the Southern and Western States generally, a scrawl, intended for a seal, usually made by writing the word "seal" within a square or diamond, is regarded in law as a seal. If there be but one seal on an instrument, and many parties, all of whom should seal it, this seal will be taken generally for the seal of each one; although, properly, each signer should put a seal against his own name.

The deed should be delivered. If a man makes a deed, and acknowledges it, and keeps it in his possession, and dies, the deed has no effect whatever; no more than if the grantor had put it in the fire. Even where it was recorded, and then taken back by the grantor and kept by him, with words going to show that the grantor did not wish the grantee to know of it, it was held not to have been delivered. But there are no especial words or form necessary for delivery. If the deed, in any way whatever, gets into the possession of the grantee, with the knowledge and consent of the grantor, it is a delivery.

The grantor may deliver it by his agent, and it may be delivered to the agent of the grantee, authorized by him to receive it. Moreover, the law permits a kind of conditional delivery. Thus, the grantor may deliver the deed to a third person, to be delivered by him to the grantee on a certain condition, or when a certain thing is done; and when that condition is performed, or the thing is done, the deed belongs to the grantee, and takes effect in the same way as if it had been delivered to him personally. In legal language, the deed is said to be delivered to the third person, as an *escrow*.

So the grantor may put the deed in the hands of the third person, with directions to give it to the grantee after the death of the grantor, provided the grantor does not reclaim it in the mean time. Then the grantor can reclaim it whenever he will, which he cannot do after he has delivered it to the grantee; but if he does not reclaim it during his life, at his death it becomes the property of the grantee, and the law now considers that it was delivered to him when first delivered to that third party. So that deed is good even against creditors, provided that the grantor was perfectly solvent when he put the deed in the hands of the third party, and acted altogether in good faith.

If a deed to a married woman be delivered either to her or to her husband, it is sufficient.

As there must be delivery to the grantee, or to some one for him, so there must be assent and acceptance on his part. The law will help any evidence tending to show such assent, by presuming in favor of the grantee's assent if the deed be wholly and only favorable to him. But not if there is money to be paid by him, or any thing important to be done if he accept the deed.

It is usual and proper that the execution of the deed should be attested by witnesses. In many of our States, two witnesses are required by statute. In New York, one is enough. In the greater number, witnesses are not absolutely required by statutes, nor by strict law of any kind; but even there it is usual and safer to have them.

The witness should see the party sign; but if the deed is signed near him, and is immediately brought to him by the grantor, who tells him that is his signature, and asks him to witness, this would be sufficient in law.

It is desirable that witnesses, when called on to testify, should remember the signature, sealing, &c.; but it is sufficient in law that they are certain of their handwriting, and can declare under oath that they should not have attested the execution and delivery if they had not seen it. If witnesses are dead, proof of their handwriting is sufficient; and if this cannot be offered, then proof of the handwriting of the grantor is enough. If witnesses attest the signing, sealing, and delivery, in the common form, proof of their handwriting, in case of their death or absence, is proof of the execution and delivery of the deed.

The witness should, properly, be of sufficient age and understanding, but may be a minor. He should have no interest in the deed. Hence a wife is not a proper witness of a deed to her husband. But the courts, and especially a court of equity, would seldom permit a deed to be avoided through the incompetence of a witness, if there were no suspicion of wrong.

Generally a deed is valid as between the parties, although not acknowledged; but, to entitle it to be recorded, it must be acknowledged. For this purpose the grantor must go before a person qualified by law to receive acknowledgments, and exhibit the deed to him, and acknowledge it as his free act and deed; and the person receiving the acknowledgment then certifies that he has received this acknowledgment, under the proper date.

In general an acknowledgment may be made before any justice of the peace, or a commissioner appointed for the State in which the land to be conveyed is situated, if the deed is executed in another State, or any consul or consular agent of the United States if the deed is executed in a foreign country. This acknowledgment must be made, or the deed cannot be recorded. And the deed is invalid, as notice, if the acknowledgment is defective, although it is actually recorded.

Formerly, all the grantors acknowledged the deed; and this continues to be usual in most places, and is the safest practice. But, in some places, it is now sufficient in law, if either of the grantors acknowledge it.

In many States, if a wife, separately or joining with her husband, conveys away her land, a particular form and mode of acknowledgment is required, in order to ascertain that she does it of her own free will; and any such directions or requirements should be followed with great care. The Forms added to this chapter will show how this is done.

An attorney, A B, who executes a deed for another, C D, should acknowledge it as "the free act and deed of the said C D," and not as his own.

The justice taking the acknowledgment must be careful to state it in his certificate, exactly as it was made before him.

In some of our States, recent laws have in effect required the assent of the wife to a transfer of the husband's real estate; not merely to convey her dower, but to pass the property to the grantee. We do not enumerate or specify these States here; having given previously an abstract of the law of husband and wife in all the States.

In all our States, we have the excellent system of registering (or recording, as it is more frequently called) all deeds of land in the public registers of the county in which the land lies. This was adopted for the purpose of giving certainty and notoriety to title, and it works admirably well. The investigation of title is usually easy to those accustomed to this mode; and every purchaser of land should ascertain that the deed will give him good title before he takes it.

The law generally requires that a deed of lands should be acknowledged and recorded, to have full effect; but judicial decisions have everywhere qualified the force of these words, and in some instances the language of the statutes varies. But the rules of law in reference to the recording are quite uniform in all the States, and are as follows.

In the first place, every acknowledged deed is considered as recorded as soon as it is in the hands of the recording officer; and therefore he generally minutes upon it the day, hour, and minute when it was received by him. This may be very important; for if A makes his deed and delivers it to B, who presents it for record at five minutes past noon, and C, a creditor of A, attaches the same estate at four minutes past noon of the same day, the grantee loses the land and the creditor gets it; but the grantee saves it, if he presents it to the office three minutes and fifty seconds after noon.

In the next place, as the purpose of public registration is general notoriety, a deed is perfectly good without record against the grantor himself and his heirs, because the grantor himself could not but know of the deed, and, as all title passed out of him by it, his heirs could take none from him.

And finally, a deed not recorded is just as good as if it had been recorded, against any parties, or the heirs of any parties, who took the land from the grantor by a subsequent deed, even for a full price, if they had at the time notice or knowledge of the prior and unrecorded deed. Many wise persons have doubted the expediency of this last rule, because it tends to raise troublesome questions, and to make grantees careless about recording their deeds. But the rule itself is universally and firmly established, and in some statutes requiring record this exception is expressed.

A deed should be dated; but, if it have no date, it will take effect from delivery. Any erasures or alterations should be noticed and stated above the names of the witnesses, as having been made before the execution of the instrument. Any material alteration by a grantee, or by his procurement, makes the deed void in most cases, so far as he is concerned.

It is usual, and therefore proper, to name executors, administrators, &c., as in the forms appended; but, generally, the rights and obligations of the deceased fall by law on their legal representatives.

SECTION II.

THE USUAL CLAUSES IN DEEDS.

It is customary to recite in all deeds the consideration on which they are made. This is usually the price paid for them. Sometimes it is this price in part, and other things in part. Sometimes there is no price paid, the land being either a gift, or conveyed for other considerations. In the great majority of deeds, the language used is, "in consideration of (so much money) paid me by the said (grantee), the receipt whereof I acknowledge." Or it is, "in consideration of one dollar paid me, the receipt of which I acknowledge, and divers other considerations;" or, "in consideration of one dollar to me paid, the receipt of which I acknowledge, and of the love and good-will I bear to the said (grantee)." It is always customary, although not necessary, to put in "one dollar," or some other nominal sum, although no price is paid.

Although the price is inserted, and the receipt thereof be acknowledged, the seller is not bound by his receipt. It is a general rule, as has been stated, that all written receipts of money are open to evidence, as written contracts generally are not. Under this rule, the seller may sue for the whole or any part of the money of which he has acknowledged the receipt, if he can prove that the money he demands has not been paid to him. He cannot, however, say that the money has not been paid, and *therefore the deed is void*, and the land has not passed to the grantee. For only that part of the deed which is a receipt is open to denial or evidence.

Of the words of conveyance, which are usually "give, grant, sell, and convey," it needs only be said, that it is best to use them, *because* it is usual, but that other words, or these with some change, would be sufficient in law.

The description of the land should be minute and accurate, to an extreme degree. In this country, it is customary and well to refer to the previous deeds by which the grantor obtained his title. This is done by describing them by their parties, date, and book and page of registry. It may be well to remark, that a deed referred to in a deed becomes, for most purposes in law, a part of the deed referring.

By the law of England and of America, if land is conveyed by deed to "A B," the grantee takes it for his life only. Nor will he take it in full property (or, to use the technical law-term, in fee simple), that is, with full power of disposing of it during his life or at his death, with a right on the part of his heirs to it if he does not dispose of it, unless it is given to "A B and his heirs." These last words, which are commonly called words of inheritance, must always be added; for although there are some qualifications to this rule, which might help those who take such a deed inadvertently, there are none to which it would be safe to trust.

The deed is terminated by this clause of execution: "In witness whereof, I, the said A B, on the —— day of —— in the year ——, have hereunto set my hand and seal," or "subscribed (or written) my name and affixed my seal." And there should be no departure from this, although an exact adherence to this formula may not be necessary to the validity of the deed. This clause is often called the "In Testimonium clause."

If the deed contains nothing but what has now been said, it will convey the land, or all the right, title, and interest in and to the land, possessed by the grantor. But it is only what is called a *quit-claim deed.* That is, it is *not* a *warranty deed.* These phrases, which are in common use, explain themselves. Originally, a quitclaim deed was intended, and indeed operated, only where the grantee already held possession of the land, or some title to it, and the grantor intended to renounce all his right or title in favor of the grantee. But it was soon used where a man intended to sell and convey land, but not to give any warranty. And now, because there is some question, in some of our States, as to the effect of the words "give, grant, sell, and convey," although there be no express warranty in the deed, it is best, and it is usual, when only a quitclaim is intended, without any warranty whatever, to substitute for the words of conveyance above mentioned the words "grant and quit-claim," or, more accurately, "release and quitclaim." Then, if the grantee afterwards loses the land because the grantor had no title to it, the grantor is nevertheless under no responsibility, provided the transaction was an honest one on his part.

All purchasers, therefore, desire to have a warranty deed if they can get one. And a deed becomes a warranty deed, when clauses like those which follow are inserted just before the clause of execution: —

"And I, the said A B (the grantor), for myself, my heirs, executors, and administrators, do covenant with the said C D (the grantee), his heirs and assigns, that I am lawfully seised in fee of the afore-granted premises; that they are free from all incumbrances; that I have good right to sell and convey the same to the said C D as aforesaid; and that I will, and my heirs, executors, and administrators shall, warrant and defend the same to the said C D, his heirs and assigns forever, against the lawful claims and demands of all persons."

It will be noticed that this paragraph contains four different agreements or warranties, — covenants the law calls them. The cases are multitudinous, and the law excessively nice, as to their exact meaning and operation. None of this technical learning is it worth while to spread before the general reader. But the general purpose and effect of all of them together should be stated. It is, that if "the said C D," that is, the grantee, or his heirs or assigns, are turned out of that estate (ousted or evicted, the law says), on the ground that the grantor had no title, or an incumbered title, and could not convey any good and clear title, he or they may fall back on the grantor or his heirs, and demand damages for the loss of the land.

It is a question how much damage a grantee thus ousted shall recover. In most of our States, it seems to be the money paid for it, with interest (deducting rents and profits), and the legal costs and charges (not including counsel fees) for defending against the suit which has ousted him from the land, and no more. But in other States, as generally in New England, the party ousted recovers the actual value of the land, with his improvements, which he loses by the defect of the grantor's title; although this may be much more than he paid for it. It is not, however, settled uniformly what the measure of damages is.

In forms of deeds there is usually a blank of a few lines left after the word "incumbrances;" and this is intended for the insertion of any mortgage, or other incumbrance, which may exist; thus, "excepting a mortgage to, &c., dated, &c., to secure the sum of, &c." Or, "excepting a right in the owners of the adjoining land to have and maintain a drain running, &c."

Sometimes quitclaim deeds are made with this warranty: "And I will, and my heirs, &c., shall, warrant and defend, &c., to the said C D, &c., against all claims and demands of myself, or of any persons deriving title by or through me." Such a warranty will hold the grantor and his heirs liable for any incumbrance made or suffered by him, but not for any other.

As the usual covenants of a warranty deed are made with the grantee, " his heirs and assigns," if such grantee conveys the land only by grant and quitclaim, without warranty, *his* grantee takes the benefit of all the previous warranties to which this last grantor was entitled. Thus, A sells with warranty to B; B quitclaims to C; C is ousted by D, who proves that he has a better title than A. C cannot sue B because he got no warranty from B; but he can sue A on A's warranty to B, which was transferred to C.

Sometimes estates are conveyed on condition; but this is a very catching thing, and nobody should ever take such a deed if he can help it. It is hardly safe to have the word *condition* in any deed but a mortgage. The reason is, that if an estate is conveyed on condition, and the condition is broken, the estate is lost. Thus if land is sold on a certain street with this clause: " And the land aforesaid is sold on condition that neither the grantee, nor any one deriving title from or through him, shall build within ten feet of the street." If any owner build six inches over the line, by mistake, or extend his building by an addition of a foot or so in any part, the whole land, house and all, *might* be lost and forfeited to the grantor. And the grantor can always secure the proper effect of such a condition by a clause like this: " Provided, however, and it is agreed, that if the said C D, &c., shall build, &c., the said A B, or his heirs or assigns, may enter upon the land hereby conveyed, and abate and remove any and all buildings or parts of buildings, which stand nearer said street than the limit of ten feet aforesaid;" — or some similar clause, as might be framed to suit the case. This would be just as good for the grantor and a great deal safer for the grantee.

By a rule of law which originated in this country, and is now universal here, if a married woman holds lands, the husband and the wife, joining in one deed, may convey them. In some of our States such a deed is regulated by statutes, which of course are to be followed. And in many of them the wife now has peculiar powers by statute, as stated in Chapter V. on Married Women. It may be necessary that she should renounce or release certain rights, as of homestead, &c., under these statutes, if it is intended that the grantee should take a clear title; and in such case proper words should be inserted. This is now the custom, for example, in Massachusetts. She should always release her right of dower, unless it is intended that she should preserve it. In some States her signing the deed with her husband does not release any thing, even if it could be proved that such was her intention, unless the deed contain words expressing her intention to release or convey such or such a right or interest. In most printed forms there is a blank left to be filled up for this purpose. As this differs in different States I shall refer to it again.

It may be well to remark that bargains are often made for the purchase and sale of real property. If the contract be oral only, it has no force in any court. If it be in writing, either party may, in a court of law, recover damages from the other if he refuses to perform his contract. Or, in a court of equity, he may compel the other to execute his contract. Not, however, if there was fraud in the contract, or oppression, or gross misrepresentation, or intentional and important concealment. But a mere inadequacy of price — all things being honest — will not prevent a court of equity from enforcing such an agreement.

Deeds conveying land are of vast variety. They not only differ that they may suit the particular purposes of the parties and the terms of their bargain, but those used in each section of the country differ somewhat in form from those used in another; and different conveyancers in the same State prefer one form to another. But these differences are generally, if not always, differences only of form, and are seldom essential to the meaning and effect of the deeds. I give here forms of all the kinds most in use; and in such variety, and so selected and prepared, that it is believed that any person in any part of this country will be able to find a form, which, either as it stands, or with such alterations as can be readily seen to be required by the use he would make of it, will be safe, and sufficient for his purpose.

As acknowledgments differ much in form, enough of them are given to show the kinds that are used. The fuller and more particular are the safer, although the shorter and more general might be sufficient.

In New England, a deed of land is usually what is called in law a Deed Poll; by which is meant a deed *of* one party, and *from* him to another. In the other States generally, a deed of lands is more commonly in the form of an Indenture, which, as has been said before, is an instrument *between two or more parties*. The difference between them will be seen in the forms given. The first one is a Deed Poll. But most of them are Indentures, as they are most frequently used; although a Deed Poll that was satisfactory in other respects would generally suffice to give good title to land anywhere.

A form of a Deed Poll may be converted into an Indenture by changing the beginning of it in the manner shown in the forms, and, whenever the word "grantor" comes, changing that into "the party of the first part." And a deed by Indenture is made a Deed Poll by changes of an opposite kind. How to make these changes will be seen by comparing the deeds of the two kinds as herein given.

Another difference between the Deeds Poll in common use in the New-England States, and the deeds by Indenture in use elsewhere, must be noticed.

If the grantor by a Deed Poll has a wife, and it is intended that she shall relinquish her dower, she is not mentioned as grantor, but in the "In Testimonium," so called, which is that part of the deed which begins with "In witness (or in testimony) whereof," her name is mentioned, and it must be distinctly said that she signs the deed in token of her relinquishment or release of dower. This is shown in Form 106. But where deeds by Indenture are used, there she is joined with her husband, and named as grantor; he and she being "parties of the first part." It is, however, *not* necessary that any thing should be said in the deed about her release of dower, or homestead; but she signs and seals the deed, and, in the acknowledgment, express mention is made of her release of dower and homestead, and also that she was separately examined. Some of the forms are drawn in this way. Other forms are written as if the grantor was unmarried, or as if his wife, if he had one, did not intend to give up her dower. But all these forms can be readily altered, and made to resemble either of the forms accordingly as there is or is not a wife, or as, if there be a wife, it is intended that she should join in the conveyance and relinquish her dower, or that the husband should convey subject to the wife's dower. If this last be the intention, it is not necessary to say so, as the mere fact that she is not a party to the deed preserves for her her right of dower.

(106.)

A Deed Poll of Warranty, in Common Use in New England.

Know all Men by these Presents, That I, (*the grantor*) of (*residence, town or city, county and state*), (*occupation*), in consideration of (*the amount paid*) to me paid by (*here name the grantee or purchaser, giving in like manner his residence and occupation*), the receipt whereof is hereby acknowledged, do hereby give, grant, bargain, sell, and convey unto the said (*name the grantee, and then describe the premises granted, minutely and accurately*) : —

To Have and to Hold the above-granted premises, to the said (*name the grantee*), his (*or hers or their*) heirs and assigns, to his (*or hers or their*) use and behoof forever. And I, the said (*name of the grantor*), for (*myself*) and (*my*) heirs, executors, and administrators, do covenant with the said (*name of the grantee*), and with his heirs and assigns, that I am lawfully seised in fee simple of the aforegranted premises; that they are free from all incumbrances (*if there be any incumbrances, as a mortgage or lien, or right of way, or drain, or air, or light, say* excepting, *and then describe the incumbrance*), that I have good right to sell and convey the same to the said (*name of the grantee*), and his (*or her*) heirs and assigns forever as aforesaid; and that I will, and my heirs, executors, and administrators shall, warrant and defend the same to the said (*name of the grantee*), and his heirs and assigns forever, against the lawful claims and demands of all persons.

In Witness Whereof, I, the said (*name of the grantor*), and (*name of his wife*), wife of said grantor, in token of her release of all right and title of or to dower in the granted premises, have hereunto set our hands and seals this day of in the year of our Lord eighteen hundred and

Signed, Sealed and Delivered in Presence of (*Seals.*)

In those States in which a homestead law exists, the signature of the wife, with a clause like that above, would not release the homestead. To effect this the following clause should be inserted before the words, " In token of : " —

" In token of her release to the said (*name of the grantee*), of all her right, interest, and estate to or in the premises herein conveyed, under the homestead laws of this State; and also," &c.

Some conveyancers think this hardly sufficient, and prefer the following method, which would undoubtedly be effectual in every one of these States. Insert before the paragraph beginning "In witness whereof," this paragraph: —

"And I, (*name of the wife*) wife of the said (*the name of the grantor*), in consideration of one dollar to me paid by the said (*the name of the grantee*), the receipt whereof is acknowledged, do hereby release and assign to the said (*the name of the grantee*), and his heirs and assigns, all my right, interest, claim, and estate in or to the premises within granted, under the homestead laws of this State, or any other statutory provisions thereof."

It is to be remembered that, whether the deed be a warranty deed like that above given, or a release or quitclaim, or a mortgage deed, it is equally necessary and proper that the wife should release her homestead right and her dower, unless it is intended that she should retain them.

Below the deed comes the acknowledgment.

Commonwealth (*or State*) of (*County*) ss. (*Town, Month, and Date.*)
Then personally appeared the above-named and acknowledged the above instrument to be free act and deed; before me,

Justice of the Peace.

(107.

Deed of Gift by Indenture, without any Warranty whatever.

This Indenture, Made the day of in the year one thousand eight hundred and between (*name, residence, and occupation of the grantor*) of the first part, and (*name, residence, and occupation of the grantee*) of the second part, witnesseth, that the said (*the grantor*) as well for and in consideration of the love and affection which he has and bears towards the said (*the grantee*) as for the sum of one dollar, lawful money of the United States, to him in hand paid by the said party of the second part, at or before the ensealing and delivery of these presents, the receipt whereof is hereby acknowledged, has given, granted, aliened, enfeoffed, released, conveyed and confirmed, and by these presents does give, grant, alien, enfeoff, release, convey and confirm, unto the said party of the second and his heirs and assigns forever, all (*here describe carefully the land or premises granted, by metes and bounds, and dimensions, contents or quantity, or boundary marks or monuments, and refer by volume and page to the deed of the land to the grantor, under which he holds it*)

Together with all and singular the tenements, hereditaments and appurtenances thereunto belonging or in any wise appertaining, and the reversion and reversions, remainder and remainders, rents, issues and profits thereof. And also, all the estate, right, title, interest, property, possession, claim and demand whatsoever, of the said party of the first part, of, in and to the same, and every part and parcel thereof, with their and every of their appurtenances. To have and to hold the said hereby granted and described premises and every part and parcel thereof with the appurtenances unto the said party of the second part, and his heirs and assigns, to his and their only proper use, benefit and behoof forever.

In Witness Whereof, The said party of the first part has hereunto set his hand and seal the day and year first above written.

Sealed and Delivered in the Presence of (*Signature.*) (*Seal.*)

(108.)

Deed of Bargain and Sale without any Warranty.

This Indenture, Made the day of in the year one thousand eight hundred and between (*name, residence, and occupation of the grantor*) of the first part, and (*name, residence and occupation of the grantee*) of the second part, witnesseth, that the said party of the first part, for and in consideration of the sum of lawful money of the United States of America, to him in hand paid, by the said party of the second part, at or before the ensealing and delivery of these presents, the receipt whereof is hereby acknowledged, has granted, bargained, sold, aliened, remised, released, conveyed and confirmed, and by these presents does grant, bargain, sell, alien, remise, release, convey and confirm, unto the said party of the second part, and to his and assigns forever, all (*here describe carefully the land or premises granted, as directed in Form* 107)

Together with all and singular the tenements, hereditaments and appurtenances thereunto belonging or in any wise appertaining, and the reversion and reversions, remainder and remainders, rents, issues and profits thereof. And also all the estate, right, title, interest, property, possession, claim and demand whatsoever, as well in law as in equity, of the said party of the first part, of, in, or to the above-described premises, and every part and parcel thereof, with the appurtenances. To have and to hold all and singular the above mentioned and described premises, together with the appurtenances, unto the said party of the second part, and his heirs and assigns forever.

In Witness Whereof, The said party of the first part has hereunto set his hand and seal the day and year first above written.

Sealed and Delivered in the Presence of (*Signature.*) (*Seal.*)

STATE OF } ss.
COUNTY OF }

On this day of in the year one thousand eight hundred and before me personally came (*the name of the party of the first part, who is the grantor*) who is known by me to be the individual described, and who executed the foregoing instrument, and then and there acknowledged that he executed the same as and for his own deed.

(*Signature.*)

(109.)

Quitclaim Deed without any Warranty.

This Indenture, Made the day of in the year one thousand eight hundred and between (*name, residence, and occupation of the grantor*) of the first part, and (*name, residence, and occupation of the grantee*) of the second part, witnesseth, that the said party of the first part, for and in consideration of the sum of lawful money of the United States of America, to him in hand paid, by the said party of the second part, at or before the ensealing and delivery of these presents, the receipt whereof is hereby acknowledged, has remised, released and quitclaimed, and by these presents does remise, release and quitclaim, unto the said party of the second part, and to his heirs and assigns forever, all (*here describe carefully the land or premises granted, as directed in Form* 107)

Together with all and singular the tenements, hereditaments and appurtenances thereunto belonging or in any wise appertaining, and the reversion and reversions, remainder and remainders, rents, issues and profits thereof. And also all the estate, right, title, interest, property, possession, claim and demand whatsoever, as well in law as in equity, of the said party of the first part, of, in, or to the above-described premises, and every part and parcel thereof, with the appurtenances. To have and to hold all and singular the above mentioned and described premises, together with the appurtenances, unto the said party of the second part, and his heirs and assigns forever.

In Witness Whereof, The said party of the first part has hereunto set his hand and seal the day and year first above written.

(*Signature.*) (*Seal.*)

Sealed and Delivered in the Presence of

STATE OF } ss.
COUNTY OF }

On this day of in the year one thousand eight hundred and before me personally came (*the name of the grantor*) who is known by me to be the individual described, and who executed the foregoing instrument, and acknowledged that he executed the same.

(*Signature.*)

(110.)

Deed Poll of Release and Conveyance, Short Form.

Know all Men by these Presents, That I (*the name of releasor*) of the County of and State of for and in consideration of one dollar, to me in hand paid, and for other good and valuable considerations, the receipt whereof is hereby confessed, do hereby grant, bargain, remise, convey, release and quitclaim unto (*the name of the releasee*) of the County of and State of all the right, title, interest, claim or demand whatsoever, I may have acquired in, through or by a certain indenture or deed, bearing date the day of A.D. 18 and recorded in the office of County, and State of in book of page to the premises therein described, to wit (*here describe carefully the land or premises granted, as directed in Form* 107)

Witness my hand and seal this day of A.D. 18

(*Signature.*) (*Seal.*)

STATE OF
COUNTY. } ss.

I, in and for said county, in the State aforesaid, do hereby certify, that (*the name of the releasor*) personally known to me as the same person whose name is subscribed to the foregoing deed, appeared before me this day, in person, and acknowledged that he signed, sealed and delivered the said instrument of writing as his own free and voluntary act, for the uses and purposes therein set forth.

Given under my hand and seal, this day of A.D. 18

(*Signature.*) (*Seal.*)

(111.)

Deed, with Special Warranty against the Grantor only.

This Indenture, Made this day of in the year of our Lord one thousand eight hundred and sixty- between (*the name of the grantor*) and (*name of the wife of grantor*) wife of the said (*name of the grantor*) of the County of and State of parties of the first part, and (*name and residence of the grantee*) party of the second part: Witnesseth, that the said parties of the first part, for and in consideration of the sum of to them paid by the said party of the second part, the receipt of which is hereby acknowledged, do by these presents, grant, bargain, and sell unto the said party of the second part, and his heirs and assigns, the following-described tract or parcel of land, situate in (*here describe carefully the land or premises granted, as directed in Form* 107)

Together with all and singular the tenements, hereditaments, and appurtenances thereto belonging, or in any wise appertaining, and the reversion and reversions, remainder and remainders, rents, issues, and profits thereof; and also all the estate, right, title, interest, property, possession, claim, and demand whatsoever, as well in law as in equity, of the said parties of the first part, of, in, or to the above-described premises, and every part and parcel thereof, with the appurtenances: To have and to hold all and singular the above mentioned and described premises, together with the appurtenances, unto the said party of the second part and his heirs and assigns forever.

And the said the said parties of the first part, hereby expressly waive, release, and relinquish unto the said party of the second part, and his heirs, executors, administrators, and assigns, all right, title, claim, interest, and benefit whatever, in and to the above-described premises, and each and every part thereof, which is given by or results from all laws of this State pertaining to the exemption of homesteads.

And the said parties of the first part, for themselves and their heirs, executors, and administrators, do hereby covenant, promise, and agree to and with the said party of the second part, his heirs and assigns, that the said premises against the claim of all persons, claiming or to claim by, through or under him only, he will forever warrant and defend.

In Testimony Whereof, The said parties of the first part have hereunto set their hands and seals the day and year first above written.

(*Signature of grantor.*) (*Seal*)
(*Signature of wife of grantor.*) (*Seal.*)

Sealed and Delivered in Presence of

STATE OF , }
COUNTY. } SS.

I, in and for said county, in the State aforesaid, do hereby certify that (*name of the grantor*) personally known to me as the same person whose name is subscribed to the annexed deed, appeared before me this day in person, and acknowledged that he signed, sealed, and delivered the said instrument of writing as his free and voluntary act, for the uses and purposes therein set forth.

And the said (*name of the grantor's wife*) wife of the said (*name of the grantor*) having been by me examined, separate and apart and out of the hearing of her husband, and the contents and meaning of the said instrument of writing having been by me fully made known and explained to her, and she also by me being fully informed of her right under the Homestead Laws of this State, acknowledged that she had freely and voluntarily executed the same, and relinquished her dower to the lands and tenements therein mentioned, and also all her rights and advantages under and by virtue of all laws of this State relating to the exemption of homesteads, without compulsion of her said husband, and that she does not wish to retract the same.

Given under my hand and seal, this day of A.D. 186

(*Signature.*) (*Seal.*)

(112.)

Quit-Claim Deed. — Long Form Homestead Waiver.

This Indenture, Made the day of in the year of our Lord one thousand eight hundred and sixty- between (*name, residence, and occupation of the grantor, and name of the grantor's wife*) parties of the first part, and (*name, residence, and occupation of the grantee*) party of the second part,

Witnesseth, That the said party of the first part, for and in consideration of dollars in hand paid by the said party of the second part, the receipt whereof is hereby acknowledged, and the said party of the second part, forever released and discharged therefrom, have remised, released, sold, conveyed, and quit claimed, and by these presents do remise, release, sell, convey, and quit claim, unto the said party of the second part, his heirs and assigns forever, all the right, title, interest, claim, and demand which the said party of the first part have in and to the following-described lot , piece , or parcel of land, to wit (*here describe carefully the land or premises granted, as directed in Form* 107)

To Have and to Hold the Same, Together with all and singular the appurtenances and privileges thereunto belonging, or in any wise thereunto appertaining; and all the estate, right, title, interest, and claim whatever of the said party of the first part, either in law or equity, to the only proper use, benefit, and behoof of the said party of the second part, his heirs and assigns forever.

And the said parties of the first part hereby expressly waive, release, and relinquish unto the said party of the second part, his heirs, executors, administrators, and assigns, all right, title, claim, interest, and benefit whatever, in and to the above-described premises, and each and every part thereof, which is given by or results from all laws of this State pertaining to the exemption of homesteads.

And the said parties of the first part, for themselves and their heirs, executors, and administrators, do covenant, promise, and agree, to and with the said party of the second part, their heirs, executors, administrators, and assigns, that they have not made, done, committed, executed, or suffered any act or acts, thing or things, whatsoever, whereby, or by means whereof, the above mentioned and described premises, or any part or parcel thereof, now are, or at any time hereafter shall or may be, impeached, charged, or incumbered, in any way or manner whatsoever.

In Witness Whereof, The said party of the first part hereunto set their hands and seals the day and year above written.

(*Signature of grantor.*) (*Seal.*)
(*Signature of wife of grantor.*) (*Seal.*)

Signed, Sealed and Delivered in Presence of

STATE OF , }
COUNTY. } ss.

I in and for said county, and the State aforesaid, do hereby certify, that (*name of the grantor*) being personally known to me as the same person whose name is subscribed to the foregoing instrument of writing, appeared before me this day, in person, and acknowledged that he signed, sealed, and delivered the said instrument of writing as his free and voluntary act, for the uses and purposes therein set forth.

And the said (*name of the wife*) wife of the said (*name of the grantor*) having been by me examined separate and apart, and out of the hearing of her husband, and the contents and meaning of the said instrument of writing having been by me fully made known and explained to her, and she also by me being fully informed of her rights under the Homestead Laws of this State, acknowledged that she had freely and voluntarily executed the same, and relinquished her dower to the lands and tenements therein mentioned, and also all her rights and advantages under and by virtue of all laws of this State relating to the exemption of homesteads, without the compulsion of her said husband, and that she does not wish to retract the same.

Given under my hand and official seal, this day of A.D, 186 .

(*Signature.*) (*Seal.*)

(113.)

Deed, with Covenant against Grantor, without Release of Homestead or Dower.

This Indenture, Made the day of in the year one thousand eight hundred and between (*name of the grantor*) (*name of the grantee*) of the second part, witnesseth, That the said party of the first part, for and in consideration of the sum of lawful money of the United States of America, to him in hand paid, by the said party of the second part, at or before the ensealing and delivery of these presents, the receipt whereof is hereby acknowledged, ha granted, bargained, sold, aliened, remised, released, conveyed, and confirmed, and by these presents do grant, bargain, sell, alien, remise, release, convey, and confirm, unto the said party of the second part, and to his heirs and assigns forever, all (*here describe carefully the land or premises granted, as directed in Form* 107)

Together with all and singular the tenements, hereditaments, and appurtenances thereunto belonging or in any wise appertaining, and the reversion and reversions, remainder and remainders, rents, issues, and profits thereof. And also all the estate, right, title, interest, property, possession, claim, and demand whatsoever, as well in law as in equity, of the said party of the first part, of, in, or to the above-described premises, and every part and parcel thereof, with the appurtenances. To have and to hold all and singular the above mentioned and described premises, together with the appurtenances, unto the said party of the second part, and his heirs and assigns forever.

And the said (*name of the grantor*) for himself and his heirs, executors, and administrators, does hereby covenant, promise, and agree to and with the said party of the second part, and his heirs and assigns, that he has not made, done, committed, executed, or suffered any act or acts, thing or things whatsoever, whereby or by means whereof, the above mentioned and described premises, or any part or parcel thereof, now are, or at any time hereafter shall or may be, impeached, charged, or incumbered in any manner or way whatsoever.

In Witness Whereof, The said party of the first part has hereunto set his hand and seal the day and year first above written.

(*Signature.*) (*Seal.*)

Sealed and Delivered in the Presence of

STATE OF , }
COUNTY. } ss.

I in and for said county, and the State aforesaid, do hereby certify, that (*name of the grantor*) being personally known to me as the same person whose name is subscribed to the foregoing instrument of writing, appeared before me this day, in person, and acknowledged that he signed, sealed, and delivered the said instrument of writing as his free and voluntary act, for the uses and purposes therein set forth.

Given under my hand and official seal, this day of A.D. 186 .

(*Signature.*) (*Seal.*)

(114.)

Separate Relinquishment of Homestead and Dower in Land sold under Execution.

Know all Men by these Presents, That we (*name and residence of the debtor*) and (*name of his wife*) wife of the said of the County of and State of , parties of the first part, for the sum of one dollar to us paid by (*name of the purchaser*) of the County of and State of party of the second part, the receipt whereof is hereby acknowledged, do hereby agree and consent to let the said party of the second part levy and sell, under a certain execution, in favor of them, the said party of the second part, and against (*name of the creditor, or the defendant in the suit in which the execution issued*) now in the hands of the sheriff of the County of and State of , and dated the day of A.D. 186 , the following-described tract of land, situated in the County of and State of , to wit (*here describe carefully the land or premises granted, as directed in Form* 107), (and being the same land heretofore held, used, and occupied by the said parties of the first part, as a homestead) hereby waiving, releasing, relinquishing, and surrendering to and in favor of said party of the second part, under the said levy and sale on said execution, all the right, title, claim, interest, and benefit which we, the said parties of the first part, and each of us, have in and to said premises, by virtue of any and all homestead-exemption laws, now or heretofore in force in the State of , and more especially "An Act to exempt Homesteads from Sale on Execution," now in force in the State of .

Witness our hands and seals this the day of A.D. 186 .

(*Signature.*) (*Seal.*)
(*Signature.*) (*Seal.*)

STATE OF , }
COUNTY. } ss.

I in and for said county, in the State aforesaid, do hereby certify that personally known to me as the same persons whose names are subscribed to the annexed instrument, appeared before me this day in person, and acknowledged that they signed, sealed, and delivered the said instrument of writing as their free and voluntary act, for the uses and purposes therein set forth.

And the said (*the name of the wife*) wife of the said having been by me examined, separate and apart, and out of the hearing of her husband, and the contents and meaning of the said instrument of writing having been by me fully made known and explained to her, and she also by me being fully informed of her rights under the Homestead Laws of this State, acknowledged that she had freely and voluntarily executed the same, and relinquished her dower to the lands and tenements therein mentioned, without compulsion of her said husband, and that she does not wish to retract the same.

Given under my hand and seal this day of A.D. 186 .

(*Signature.*) (*Seal.*)

(115.)

Full Warranty Deed, by Indenture, without Release of Homestead or Dower.

This Indenture, Made the day of in the year one thousand eight hundred and between (*name, residence, and occupation of the grantor*) party of the first part, and (*name, residence, and occupation of the grantee*) party of the second part, witnesseth, that the said party of the first part, for and in consideration of the sum of lawful money of the United States, to him in hand paid by the said party of the second part, at or before the ensealing and delivery of these presents, the receipt whereof is hereby acknowledged, and the said party of the second part, and his heirs, executors, and administrators, forever released and discharged from the same, by these presents, has granted, bargained, sold, aliened, remised, released, conveyed and confirmed, and by these presents does grant, bargain, sell, alien, remise, release, convey and confirm, unto the said party of the second part, and to his heirs and assigns forever, all (*here describe carefully the land or premises granted, as, directed in Form* 107.)

Together with all and singular the tenements, hereditaments and appurtenances thereunto belonging, or in any wise appertaining, and the reversion and reversions, remainder and remainders, rents, issues and profits thereof. And also all the estate, right, title, interest, property, possession, claim and demand whatsoever, as well in law as in equity, of the said party of the first part, of, in, and to the same, and every part and parcel thereof with the appurtenances: To have and to hold the above granted, bargained and described premises, with the appurtenances, unto the said party of the second part, and his heirs and assigns, to his and their own proper use, benefit, and behoof forever.

And the said (*name of the grantor*) for himself and his heirs, executors, and administrators, does covenant, grant and agree to and with the said party of the second part, and his heirs and assigns, that the said (*name of the grantor*) at the time of the sealing and delivery of these presents, is lawfully seised, in his own right, of a good, absolute, and indefeasible estate of inheritance, in fee simple, of, and in all and singular the above granted and described premises, with the appurtenances thereunto belonging, and has good right, full power, and lawful authority to grant, bargain, sell, and convey the same, in manner aforesaid: And that the said party of the second part, and his heirs and assigns, shall and may at all times hereafter, peaceably and quietly, have, hold, use, occupy, possess and enjoy the above-granted premises, and every part and parcel thereof, with the appurtenances, without any let, suit, trouble, molestation, eviction, or disturbance of the said party of the first part, or his heirs or assigns, or of any other person or persons lawfully claiming or to claim the same: and that the same now are free, clear, discharged and unincumbered, of and from all former and other grants, titles, charges, estates, judgments, taxes, assessments and incumbrances of what nature or kind soever.

And also that the said party of the first part, and his heirs, and all and every person or persons whomsoever, lawfully or equitably deriving any estate, right, title, or interest, of, in, or to the hereinbefore granted premises, by, from, under, or in trust for him or them, shall and will, at any time or times hereafter, upon the reasonable request, and at the proper costs and charges in the law, of the said party of the second part, his heirs and assigns, make, do, and execute, or cause to be made, done, and executed, all and every such further and other lawful and reasonable acts, conveyances and assurances in the law, for the better and more effectually vesting and confirming the premises hereby granted or so intended to be, in and to the said party of the second part, his heirs and assigns, forever, as by the said party of the second part, his heirs or assigns, or his or their counsel learned in the law shall be reasonably advised or required: And the said party of the first part, for himself and his heirs, the above-described and hereby granted and released premises, and every part and parcel thereof, with the appurtenances, unto the said party of the second part, and his heirs and assigns, against the said party of the first part, and his heirs, and against all and every person and persons whomsoever, lawfully claiming or to claim the same, shall and will warrant and by these presents forever defend.

In Witness Whereof, the said party of the first part has hereunto set his hand and seal the day and year first above written.

(*Signature.*) (*Seal.*)

Sealed and Delivered in the Presence of

STATE OF , }
COUNTY OF . } SS.

On the day of in the year one thousand eight hundred and before me personally came (*the name of the grantor*), who is known to me to be the individual described in, and who executed, the foregoing instrument, and acknowledged that he executed the same, as his own free act and deed.

(*Signature.*)

(116.)

Warranty Deed, Short Form, with Release of Homestead and Dower.

This Indenture, Made this day of in the year of our Lord one thousand eight hundred and between (*name, residence, and occupation of grantor, and name of his wife*) of the first part, and (*name, residence, and occupation of grantee*) of the second part, witnesseth, that the said party of the first part, in consideration of the sum of dollars in hand paid (the receipt whereof is hereby acknowledged), have granted, bargained and sold, and by these presents do grant, bargain, and sell, unto the said party of the second part, his heirs and assigns, all that piece or parcel of land situate in in the County of and State of to wit (*here describe carefully the land or premises granted, as directed in Form* 107.)

Together with the appurtenances thereunto belonging; and all the estate, right, title, interest, claim, and demand of the said party of the first part herein.

And the said (*names of grantor and of his wife*) parties of the first part, hereby expressly waive, release, relinquish, and convey unto the said party of the second part, and his heirs, executors, administrators and assigns, all right, title, claim, interest and benefit whatsoever, in and to the above-described premises, and each and every part thereof, which is given by or results from any and all laws of this State, pertaining to the exemption of homesteads.

And the said (*names of grantor and of his wife*) for themselves and their heirs, executors, and administrators, do covenant, grant, bargain, and agree to and with the said party of the second part, and with his heirs and assigns, that the above-bargained premises in the quiet and peaceable possession of the said party of the second part, and his heirs and assigns, the said party of the first part shall and will warrant and forever defend.

In Witness Whereof, The said parties of the first part have hereunto set their hands and seals the day and year first above written.

(*Signature of grantor.*) (*Seal.*)
(*Signature of wife of grantor.*) (*Seal.*)

Signed, Sealed and Delivered in Presence of

STATE OF } ss.
COUNTY. }

I, in and for said county, do hereby certify that (*name of grantor*) who is personally known to me as the same person whose name is subscribed to the annexed deed, appeared before me this day, in person, and acknowledged that he signed, sealed, and delivered the said instrument of writing, as his free and voluntary act, for the uses and purposes therein set forth.

And the said (*name of the wife of grantor*) wife of the said (*name of the grantor*) having been by me examined separate and apart, and out of the hearing of her husband, and the contents and meaning of the said instrument of writing been by me fully made known and explained to her, and she also by me having been fully informed of her rights, under the Homestead Laws of this State, acknowledged that she had freely and voluntarily executed the same, and relinquished her dower to the lands and tenements therein mentioned, and also all her rights and advantages, under and by virtue of any and all laws of this State relating to the exemption of homesteads, without compulsion of her said husband, and that she does not wish to retract the same.

Given under my hand and official seal, this day of A.D. 186 .

(*Signature.*) (*Seal.*)

(117.)

Warranty Deed, with Covenant against Nuisances, without Release of Homestead or Dower.

This Indenture, Made the day of in the year one thousand eight hundred and between (*name, residence and occupation of the grantor*) party of the first part, and (*name, residence and occupation of the grantee*) party of the second part, witnesseth, that the said party of the first part, for and in consideration of the sum of lawful money of the United States, to him in hand paid by the said party of the second part, at or before the ensealing and delivery of these presents, the receipt whereof is hereby acknowledged, and the said party of the second part, his heirs, executors, and administrators, forever released and discharged from the same, by these presents, has granted, bargained, sold, aliened, remised, released, conveyed and confirmed, and by these presents does grant, bargain, sell, alien, remise, release, convey and confirm, unto the said party of the second part, and to his heirs and assigns forever, all (*here describe carefully the land or premises granted, as directed in Form* 107.)

Together with all and singular the tenements, hereditaments and appurtenances thereunto belonging, or in any wise appertaining, and the reversion and reversions, remainder and remainders, rents, issues and profits thereof: And also all the estate, right, title, interest, property, possession, claim and demand whatsoever, as well in law as in equity, of the said party of the first part, of, in, and to the same, and every part and parcel thereof, with the appurtenances: to have and to hold the above granted, bargained and described premises, with the appurtenances, unto the said party of the second part, and his heirs and assigns, to his and their own proper use, benefit, and behoof forever.

And the said party of the first part, for himself and for his heirs, executors and administrators, does hereby covenant, grant and agree to and with the said party of the second part, and his heirs and assigns, that the said party of the first part, at the time of the sealing and delivery of these presents, is lawfully seised in his own right of a good, absolute and indefeasible estate of inheritance, in fee simple, of, and in all and singular the above-granted and described premises, with the appurtenances to them belonging; and has good right, full power, and lawful authority, to grant, bargain, sell, and convey the same, in manner aforesaid.

And that the said party of the second part, and his heirs and assigns, shall and may at all times hereafter, peaceably and quietly have, hold, use, occupy, possess, and enjoy the above-granted premises, and every part and parcel thereof, with the appurtenances, without any let, suit, trouble, molestation, eviction, or disturbance of the said party of the first part, or his heirs or assigns, or of any other person or persons lawfully claiming or to claim the same: And that the same now are free, clear, discharged, and unincumbered, of and from all former and other grants, titles, charges, estates, judgments, taxes, assessments, and incumbrances of what nature or kind soever.

And also that the said party of the first part, and his heirs, and all and every person or persons whomsoever, lawfully or equitably deriving any estate, right, title, or interest, of, in, or to the hereinbefore granted premises, by, from, under or in trust for him or them, shall and will, at any time or times hereafter, upon the reasonable request, and at the proper costs and charges in the law, of the said party of the second part, his heirs and assigns, make, do, and execute, or cause to be made, done, and executed, all and every such further and other lawful and reasonable acts, conveyances, and assurances in the law, for the better and more effectually vesting and confirming the premises hereby granted, or so intended to be, in and to the said party of the second part, his heirs and assigns, forever, as by the said party of the second part, his heirs or assigns, or his or their counsel learned in the law, shall be reasonably advised or required: And the said party of the first part, for himself and for his heirs, the above-described and hereby granted and released premises, and every part and parcel thereof, with the appurtenances, unto the said party of the second part, and his heirs and assigns, against the said party of the first part, and his heirs, and against all and every person and persons whomsoever, lawfully claiming or to claim the same, shall and will warrant and by these presents forever defend.

And the said party of the second part, for himself and for his heirs and assigns does hereby covenant to and with the said party of the first part, and with his heirs, executors, and administrators, that neither the said party of the second part, nor his heirs or assigns, shall or will at any time hereafter erect or permit upon any part of the said lot, any slaughter-house, smith-shop, forge, furnace, steam-engine, brass-foundry, nail or other iron factory, or any manufactory of gunpowder, glue, varnish, vitriol, ink, or turpentine, or for the tanning, dressing, or preparing skins, hides, or leather, or any brewery, distillery, livery-stable, or buildings for any noxious or dangerous trade or business.

In Witness Whereof, the parties to these presents have hereunto interchangeably set their hands and seals the day and year first above written.

(*Signature.*) (*Seal.*)

Sealed and Delivered in Presence of (*Signature.*) (*Seal.*)

STATE OF
COUNTY OF } ss.

On this day of in the year one thousand eight hundred and before me personally came (*the name of the party of the first part, who is the grantor*) who is known by me to be the individual described, and who executed the foregoing instrument, and then and there acknowledged that he executed the same as and for his own deed.

(*Signature.*)

(118.)

Bond for a Deed.

Know all Men by these Presents, That I (*name of the obligor*) of the County of and State of am held and firmly bound to (*name of the obligee*) of the County of and State of in the sum of dollars, to be paid to said (*name of obligee*) or his executors, administrators, or assigns, to the payment whereof I bind myself, my heirs, executors, and administrators, firmly by these presents. Sealed with my seal and dated the day of , A. D. 18

The Condition of this obligation is that if I the said (*name of the obligor*) upon payment of dollars, and interest thereon, as agreed and promised by said (*name of the obligee*) agreeably to his promissory note, dated 18 , and made payable as follows, to wit (*here set forth the note. If there be no note from the obligee, omit this part*) shall convey to said (*name of the obligee*) or his heirs, executors, or assigns, forever, the following-described real estate, situate, lying and being in the County of and State of to wit (*here describe carefully the land or premises granted, as described in Form* 107) deed or deeds in common form, duly executed and acknowledged, and in the mean time shall permit said (*name of the obligee*) to occupy and improve said premises for his own use, then this obligation shall be void, otherwise it shall remain in full force.

(*Signature.*) (*Seal.*)

Signed, Sealed and Delivered in Presence of

STATE OF } ss.
COUNTY OF }

Be it Remembered, That on this day of A.D. 18 , before the undersigned, a Notary Public (*or other magistrate*), within and for the County of aforesaid, personally came (*name of the obligor*) who is personally known to me to be the same person whose name is subscribed to the foregoing instrument of writing, as the obligor therein, and acknowledged the same to be his free act and deed, for the purposes therein mentioned.

In Testimony Whereof, I have hereunto set my hand and affixed my official seal at my office in the day and year first above written.

(*Signature.*) (*Seal.*)

(119.)

Contract for Sale of Land, with Penal Obligation.

Articles of Agreement, Made and concluded this day of A.D. 18 , between of the County of and State of of the one part, and of the County of and State of of the other part as follows: —

The said (*name of the party of the first part*), for the consideration hereinafter mentioned, does for himself and for his heirs, covenant and agree with the said (*name of the party of the second part*) and his heirs and assigns, by these presents, that he the said party of the first part, shall and will, on or before the day of A.D. 18 , at the proper costs and charges of the said party of the first part (*or of the second part if that is agreed*), his heirs and assigns, by good and lawful deed or deeds, well and sufficiently grant, convey and assure unto the said party of the second part, his heirs and assigns, in fee simple, clear of all incumbrances, all that certain tract or parcel of land lying, being and situate in the County of State of , as follows, to wit (*here describe carefully the land or premises granted, as directed in Form* 107.)

In Consideration Whereof, The said (*here the name of the party of the second part*), for himself and his heirs, does covenant and agree with the said party of the first part, and with his heirs and assigns, by these presents, that he the said party of the second part, and his heirs, or some of them, shall and will on the execution and delivery of the said deed or deeds as aforesaid, well and truly pay, or cause to be paid, unto the said party of the first part, or his heirs and assigns, the sum of dollars, in the manner following, to wit (*set forth the terms and times of payment as agreed on*). And upon (*set forth the time agreed on*) the said party of the first part shall give to the said party of the second part possession of the aforesaid premises.

And for the true performance of all and every the covenants and agreements aforesaid, each of the said parties bindeth himself, his heirs, executors and administrators unto the other, his executors, administrators and assigns, in the penal sum of dollars.

In Witness Whereof, The said parties have hereunto set their hands and seals the day and year first above written.

(*Signature.*) (*Seal.*)
(*Signature.*) (*Seal.*)

Signed, Sealed and Delivered in Presence of us,

(*If it is intended that this contract should be recorded, in almost all cases it should be, an acknowledgment by both parties should follow; and the record should be like that in the next Form.*)

(120.)

Power of Attorney to Sell Lands.

Know all Men by these Presents, That I, the undersigned (*name of the selling party*) of the town (*or city*) of , County of , and State of , have this day made, constituted and appointed, and do by these presents make, constitute and appoint (*name of attorney*) of the town (*or city*) of , in the County of and State of , my true and lawful attorney, for me and in my name, to sell and dispose of, absolutely, in fee simple, the following-described lot, tract or parcel of land, or any part thereof, situate, lying and being in the County of and State aforesaid, to wit (*here describe carefully the land or premises granted, as directed in Form* 107) for such price or sum of money, and to such person or persons as he shall think fit and convenient; and also for me and in my name, and as my act and deed, to sign, execute, acknowledge and deliver, such deed or deeds, and conveyance or conveyances, for the absolute sale and disposal thereof, or of any part thereof, with such clause or clauses, covenant or covenants, and agreement or agreements, to be therein contained, as my said attorney shall think fit and expedient; hereby ratifying and confirming all such deeds, conveyances, bargains and sales which shall at any time hereafter be made by said attorney touching or concerning the premises.

In Testimony Whereof, I have hereunto set my hand and seal, on this day of , A.D. 18

(*Signature.*) (*Seal.*)

STATE OF
} ss.
COUNTY OF

Be it Remembered, That on this day A.D. 18 , before the undersigned, a notary public (*or other magistrate*), within and for the County of and State of , personally came (*the name of the principal*) who is personally known to me to be the same person whose name is subscribed to the foregoing instrument of writing, and acknowledged the same to be his free act and deed, for the purposes therein mentioned.

In Witness Whereof, I have hereto set my hand and affixed my official seal, at my office in the day and year first above written.

(*Signature.*) (*Seal.*)

STATE OF
} ss. IN THE RECORDER'S OFFICE.
COUNTY OF

I, , Clerk of the Circuit Court, and ex-officio Recorder of said county (*or whoever else is the recording officer*) do hereby certify that the within instrument of writing was on the day of A.D. 186 , duly filed for record in this office, and is recorded in the Records of this office in Book at page

In Witness Whereof, I have hereunto set my hand and affixed the seal of said court, at this day of A.D. 186

Recorder.

Per *Deputy.*

(121.)

Trust Deed for the Benefit of a Wife, or some other Person.

This Deed, Made and entered into this day of eighteen hundred and sixty by and between (*name, residence and occupation of the grantor*) party of the first part, and (*the name, residence and occupation of the trustee*) party of the second part, and (*name of the wife or any person who is to have the benefit of the trust*) party of the third part, witnesseth: That the said party of the first part, in consideration of the sum of dollars, to him in hand paid by the said party of the third part, the receipt of which is hereby acknowledged, and the further sum of one dollar to him paid by the said party of the second part, the receipt of which is hereby also acknowledged, do, by these presents, give, grant, sell, transfer, convey and assign unto the said party of the part, the following-described tract or parcel of land, that is to say (*here describe the premises carefully, as directed in Form* 107).

To Have and to Hold the Same, With all the rights, privileges, and appurtenances thereto belonging, or in any wise appertaining, unto him the said party of the second part, his heirs and assigns forever: In trust, however, to and for the sole and separate use, benefit, and behoof of wife of the said (*or the name of the son or daughter, or any other person, may be substituted for that of the wife*) and the said party of the second part hereby covenants and agrees to and with the said the party of the third part, that he will suffer and permit her (*or him*), without let or molestation, to have, hold, use, occupy, and enjoy the aforesaid premises, with all the rents, issues, profits and proceeds arising therefrom, whether from sale or lease, for her own sole use and benefit, separate and apart from her said husband, and wholly free from his control and interference, debts and liabilities, courtesy, and all other interests whatsoever; and that he will, at any and all times hereafter, at the request and direction of the said (*name of the party of the third part*) expressed in writing, signed by her (*or him*) or by her (*or his*) authority, bargain, sell, mortgage, convey, lease, rent, convey by deed of trust for any purpose, or otherwise dispose of said premises, or any part thereof, to do which full power is hereby given, and will pay over the rents, issues, profits and proceeds thereof to the said party of the third part, and that he will, at the death of the said party of the third part, convey or dispose of the said premises, or such part thereof as may then be held by him under this deed, and all profits and proceeds thereof, in such manner, to such person or persons, and at such time or times, as the said party of the third part shall, by her (*or his*) last will and testament, or any other writing signed by her, or by her authority, direct or appoint; and in default of such appointment, that he will convey such premises to (*here state what it is intended shall be done with the property at the death of the party of the third part if he or she die intestate*). And the said party of the third part shall have power at any time hereafter, whenever she (*or he*) shall from any cause deem it necessary or expedient, by an instrument in writing under her (*or his*) hand and seal, and by her (*or him*) acknowledged, to nominate and appoint a trustee, or trustees, in the place and stead of the party of the second part above named; which trustee or trustees, or the survivor of them, or the heirs of such survivor, shall hold the said real estate upon the same trust as above recited; and upon the nomination and appointment of such new trustees, the estate in trust hereby vested in said party of the second part, shall thereby be fully transferred and vested in the trustee or trustees so appointed by the said party of the third part. And said party of the first part, hereby covenants to warrant and defend the title to the said real estate against the lawful claims of all persons whomsoever, to the said parties of the second and third parts, their heirs and assigns. And the said party of the second part covenants faithfully to perform and fulfil the trust herein created.

In Testimony Whereof, The said parties have hereunto set their hand and seal the day and year first above written.

(*Signature.*) (*Seal.*)
(*Signature.*) (*Seal.*)
(*Signature.*) (*Seal.*)

THE STATE OF }
COUNTY OF } ss.

Be it Remembered, That on the day of eighteen hundred and sixty , before me, the undersigned came (*the persons who execute the instrument*) who are personally known to me to be the same persons whose names are subscribed to the foregoing instrument of writing, as parties thereto, and severally acknowledged the same to be their free act and deed for the purposes therein mentioned.

(*Signature.*)

(122.)

Trust Deed to secure Payment of a Note, without Release of Homestead or Dower.

This Deed, Made and entered into this day of eighteen hundred and , by and between (*name and occupation of the grantor who is the debtor*) of the County of State of , part of the first part, and (*name and occupation of the trustee*) of the County of State of , part of the second part, and (*name and occupation of the creditor for whose benefit the deed is made*) of the County of State of , part of the third part:

Witnesseth, That the said party of the first part, in consideration of the debt and trust hereinafter mentioned and created, and of the sum of one dollar to him paid by the said party of the second part, the receipt of which is hereby acknowledged, does by these presents grant, bargain and sell, convey and confirm, unto the said party of the second part, the following-described real estate, situate, lying and being in the County of and State of , to wit (*here describe carefully the land or premises granted, as described in Form* 107).

To Have and to Hold the same, with the appurtenances, to the party of the second part, and to his successor or successors in this trust, and to him and his heirs and his and their grantees and assigns, forever.

In Trust, However, for the following purposes: Whereas the said party of the first part has this day made, executed and delivered to the said party of the third part, his promissory note , of even date herewith, by which he promises to pay to the said (*name of the creditor*), or order, for value received, $\overline{100}$ dollars, in (*the days or months when the note is payable*)

Now Therefore, If the said party of the first part, or any one for him, shall well and truly pay off and discharge the debt and interest expressed in the said note and every part thereof, when the same becomes due and payable according to the true tenor, date and effect of said note, then this deed shall be void, and the property hereinbefore conveyed shall be released at the cost of the said party of the first part; but, should the said first party fail or refuse to pay the said debt, or the said interest, or any part thereof, when the same or any part thereof shall become due and payable, according to the true tenor, date and effect of said note , then the whole shall become due and payable, and this deed shall remain in force; and the said party of the second part, or in case of his absence, death, refusal to act, or disability in any wise, the (then) acting sheriff of County, , at the request of the legal holder of the said note, may proceed to sell the property hereinbefore described, or any part thereof, at public vendue, to the highest bidder, at , in the of County, , for cash, first giving days' public notice of the time, terms and place of sale, and of the property to be sold, by advertisement in some newspaper printed and published in the of , and upon such sale shall execute and deliver a deed in fee simple of the property sold to the purchaser or purchasers thereof, and receive the proceeds of said sale; and any statement of facts or recital by the said trustee, in relation to the non-payment of the money secured to be paid, the advertisement, sale, receipt of the money, and the execution of the deed to the purchaser, shall be received as *primâ facie* evidence of such fact; and such trustee shall, out of the proceeds of said sale, pay, first, the cost and expenses of executing this trust, including legal compensation to the trustee for his services, and next shall apply the proceeds remaining over to the payment of said debt and interest, or so much thereof as remains unpaid, and the remainder, if any, shall be paid to the said party of the first part, or his legal representatives. And the said party of the second part covenants faithfully to perform and fulfil the trust herein created, not being liable or responsible for any mischance occasioned by others.

In Witness Whereof, The said parties have hereunto set their hands and seals the day and year first above written.

(*Signature of party of the first part.*) (*Seal.*)
(*Signature of party of the second part.*) (*Seal.*)
(*Signature of party of the third part.*) (*Seal.*)

Signed, Sealed and Delivered in Presence of us

STATE OF
COUNTY OF } SS.

Be it Remembered, That on this day of A.D. 186 , before the undersigned, a within and for the County of and State of , personally came (*names of all the parties executing the deed*) who are personally known to me to be the same persons whose names are subscribed to the foregoing instrument of writing, as parties thereto, and acknowledged that they executed the same for the uses and purposes therein mentioned.

In Testimony Whereof, I have hereto set my hand and affixed my official seal at my office in the day and year first above written.

(*Signature.*) (*Seal.*)

(123.)

Deed of Trust to Secure a Debt; Fuller Form, and with Release of Dower.

This Deed, Made and entered into this day of , eighteen hundred and sixty- , by and between (*name and occupation of the debtor who is grantor*) and (*name of the wife of the grantor*) of (*residence*) parties of the first part, and (*name of the grantees who are the trustees*) of (*residence*) parties of the second part, and (*name, residence, and occupation of the creditor for whose benefit the trust is created*) of party of the third part, witnesseth, that the said parties of the first part, in consideration of the debt and trust hereinafter mentioned and created, and of the sum of one dollar to them paid by the said parties of the second part, the receipt of which is hereby acknowledged, do by these presents grant, bargain and sell, convey and confirm, unto the said parties of the second part, the following-described real estate, to wit (*here describe carefully the land or premises granted, by metes and bounds, as directed in Form* 107).

To Have and to Hold the same with the appurtenances, to the said parties of the second part, and to the survivor of them, and to their successor hereinafter designated, and to the assigns of the said parties of the second part, or of said survivor, or of said successor and his heirs forever.

In Trust, however, for the following purpose: Whereas the said (*name of the grantor and debtor*) (*here describe the debt, and if a promissory note is given, describe that, or set forth a copy of it* (and has also agreed and covenanted, to and with the said party of the third part and his indorsees or assignees, to cause all taxes and assessments, general and special, to be paid within the times required by law, whenever imposed upon said property, and has also further covenanted and agreed, to and with said party of the third part, his indorsees or assignees, that he will keep the improvements upon said property constantly insured in some good and responsible insurance office or offices, to be approved by said party of the third part, his indorsees or assignees, in a sum not less than dollars, until said notes are (*or note is*) fully paid, and will assign the policy or policies of insurance to said party of the third part, his indorsees or assignees, with full power to demand, receive, and collect, any and all moneys accruing under said insurance, and the same to apply to the payment of said notes and the interest that may accrue thereon, unless otherwise paid, when the same become due, and has also covenanted and agreed, to and with said party of the third part, his indorsees or assignees, that there shall not, at any time while said notes remain unpaid, be any mechanics' liens filed or taken, upon the real estate herein described, or upon the buildings which now are, or may hereafter be, erected upon said real estate, and that should said party of the first part fail or neglect to pay said taxes, when the same are by law due and payable, or fail or neglect to effect insurance and assign the policy or policies as above provided, or fail or neglect to keep said real estate free from mechanics' liens, the said party of the third part, his indorsees or assignees, may, at his option, consider the notes above mentioned and described, as having each and all become due and payable, though not then due by the tenor and effect thereof, and may require the said parties of the second part, or the survivor of them, or their successor in trust, to sell the property above described as hereinafter provided, or may pay said taxes, or the premium for such insurance, or the amount of said mechanics' liens, and the amount or amounts so paid, together with interest thereon, at the rate of ten per cent per annum, shall be taken and considered as a part of the amount secured hereby, and to be paid and refunded out of the proceeds of sale, should such sale be made, as hereinafter provided.

Now, if the said notes be well and truly paid, as the same severally become due and payable, according to the tenor and effect of said notes, and each of them, and if the said covenants and agreements in regard to taxes, insurance, and mechanics' liens be faithfully kept and performed, and all moneys paid by said third part, his indorsees or assignees, on account of said taxes, insurance, and mechanics' liens, are refunded, with the interest thereon, as above provided, then this deed shall be void, and the property hereinbefore conveyed shall be released at the cost of the said parties of the first part; but should default be made in the payment of the said notes, or either of them, or any part of either of them, or of the interest that may accrue thereon, or any part thereof, as the same severally become due and payable, or if the said parties of the first part fail or neglect to pay said taxes, when due and payable, or to insure the buildings on said property, or to keep the same free from mechanics' liens, as provided in the foregoing covenants and agreements, or to refund to said party of the third part, his indorsees or assignees, the amount paid by him or them for said taxes, insurance, or mechanics' liens, with interest thereon, as above provided, then this deed shall remain in force, and the said parties of the second part, or either of them, or the survivor of them, or in the event of the death of both of them, or absence from this State, or their refusal to act, or other disqualification for the performance of the duties of this trust, then, at the request of the holder of said notes, the sheriff of she county of for the time being (who shall thereupon become the successor of said trustees, and of the survivor of them, to the title of said property, and the same become vested in him, in trust, for the purposes and objects of these presents, with all the powers, duties and obligations thereof), may proceed to sell said described property, or any part thereof, at public vendue, to the highest bidder, for cash, at the *(state the place of sale)* first giving twenty days' public notice of the time, terms, and place of said sale, and the property to be sold, by advertisement in some newspaper printed in the English language, and published in the county of and upon such sale, the said parties of the second part, or either of them, or the survivor of them, or their successor in trust, the sheriff of said county, as the case may be, shall execute and deliver a deed or deeds, in fee simple, of the property sold, to the purchaser or purchasers thereof (a recital wherein of the request of the holder of said notes that they should proceed to sell, of the publication of said notice, and in case of sale by the sheriff of said county, of the happening of any or either of the events making him successor in this trust, shall be received in all courts of law or equity, and to all intents and purposes, as full and sufficient proof thereof), and shall receive the proceeds of said sale, out of which shall be paid, first, the cost and expenses of executing this trust, including compensation to said trustee, or said sheriff, for their or his services, next the amount paid by said party of the third part, or his indorsees or assignees for taxes, insurance, or mechanics' liens, with ten per cent per annum interest thereon, from the date of the payment thereof, and next, the amount remaining unpaid upon the principal note above described, together with all of the interest notes then due, and so much of the interest note, next falling due, as may be necessary to satisfy the interest on said principal note at the rate of per cent per annum from the date when the preceding interest note became due, up to the day of sale, it being distinctly understood and agreed between the parties hereto, that the failure to pay any one of said notes, principal or interest, when due and payable, shall cause the principal note to become immediately due and payable, though not then due by the terms, tenor, or effect thereof, and the remainder, if any, shall be paid to the said parties of the first part or their legal representatives.

And the said parties of the second part covenant faithfully to perform and fulfil the trust herein created.

In Witness Whereof, The said parties have hereunto set their hands and seals the day and year first above written.

(Signature of grantor.) *(Seal.)*
(Signature of grantor's wife.) *(Seal.)*
(Signature of trustee.) *(Seal.)*
(Signature of other trustee.) *(Seal.)*
(Signature of creditor.) *(Seal.)*

Signed, Sealed and Delivered in the Presence of

STATE OF } ss.
COUNTY OF }

Be it Remembered, That on this day of eighteen hundred and sixty- before me, the undersigned, came *(names of the parties who execute the deed)* who are personally known to me to be the same persons whose names are subscribed to the foregoing instrument of writing, as parties thereto, and acknowledged the same to be their act and deed for the purposes therein mentioned.

And the said having been by me first made acquainted with the contents of said instrument, on an examination separate and apart from her husband, acknowledged that she executed the same freely and without compulsion or undue influence of her said husband.

In Testimony Whereof, I have hereunto set my hand and seal of office the day and year first above written.

(124.)

Trust Deed to Secure a Note, Shorter Form, but with Warranty, and Release of Homestead and Dower.

This Indenture Witnesseth, that *(name, residence, and occupation of grantor)* and *(name of the wife of grantor)* wife of the grantor herein, in consideration of the indebtedness hereinafter mentioned, and one ($1) dollar to them paid by *(name, residence, and occupation of the trustee)* grantee , the receipt whereof is hereby acknowledged, do hereby grant, bargain, sell, remise, release and convey unto the said grantee , the following-described lot , piece , or parcel of land, situate in the county of and State of to wit (*here describe carefully the land or premises granted, as directed in Form* 107)

To Have and to Hold the same, with all the privileges thereunto or in any wise appertaining, and all the estate, right, title, interest, claim, or demand in and to the same, either now or which may be hereafter acquired unto the said grantee, his heirs and assigns. In trust, nevertheless, for the following purposes:

Whereas, the said (*name of the grantor*) grantor, herein, is justly indebted upon a certain promissory note, bearing even date herewith, payable to the order of (*here describe the note*)

Now, in case of default in the payment of said note or any part thereof, or the interest accruing thereon, according to the tenor and effect thereof, or in the payment of any taxes or assessments, ordinary or special, which may be levied or assessed against said premises during the continuance hereof, on the application of the legal holders of the said note, the said grantee (full power being hereby given), or his legal representatives, after having advertised such sale days in a newspaper published in or by posting up written or printed notices in four (4) public places in the county where said premises are situate (personal notice being hereby expressly waived), shall sell the said premises or any part thereof, and all the right and equity of redemption of the said grantor, or his heirs, executors, administrators, or assigns therein, at public vendue, to the highest bidder for cash, at at the time appointed in the said advertisement, or may adjourn the sale from time to time at discretion and as the attorney of the said grantor, for such purpose hereby constituted irrevocable, or in the name of the said grantee or his legal representatives, shall execute and deliver to the purchaser or purchasers thereof, deeds for the conveyance in fee of the premises sold, and shall apply the proceeds of sale (1st) to the payment of all advances made by the said party of the second part for taxes and assessments; and expenses for advertising, selling and conveying as aforesaid, including attorney's fees, and (2d) the amount due on said note, (3d) rendering the overplus, if any there be, to the said grantor or legal representatives, at the office of the said grantee in and it shall not be the duty of the purchaser to see to the application of the purchase money.

And the said (*names of the grantor and of his wife*) parties of the first part, hereby expressly waive, release, and relinquish unto the said party of the second part, the said grantee, his heirs, executors, administrators, and assigns, all right, title, claim, interest, and benefit whatever, in and to the above-described premises and each and every part thereof, which is given by or results from all laws of this State pertaining to the exemption of homesteads: Provided, that the said grantor and his heirs and assigns may hold and enjoy said premises, and the rents, issues, and profits thereof, until default shall be made as aforesaid, and that when the said note and all expenses accruing hereby shall be fully paid, the said grantee or his legal representatives, shall reconvey all the estate acquired hereby in the said premises, or any part thereof, then remaining unsold, to (and at the cost of) the said grantor, or his heirs or assigns.

And the said grantor covenants with the said grantee and with his legal representatives and assigns that he is seized in fee of the said premises, and has good right to convey the same in form aforesaid, that they are free from all liens or incumbrances of whatever name or nature, and that he will warrant and defend the same against all claims whatsoever, and will pay all taxes or assessments levied or assessed on the said premises, or any part thereof, during the continuance hereof, and pay the same ten days before the day of sale thereof.

Witness the hands and seals of the said (*names of grantor and his wife*) this day of A.D. 186

(*Signature of grantor.*) (*Seal.*)
(*Signature of wife of grantor.*) (*Seal.*)

In Presence of

STATE OF , }
COUNTY. } ss.

On the day of eighteen hundred and sixty- before me of the county of in the State of appeared (*name of the grantor*) personally known to me to be the real person whose name subscribed to the foregoing deed of trust, as having executed the same, and then acknowledged the execution thereof as free act and deed for the uses and purposes herein mentioned.

And the said (*name of the wife of grantor*) (who is personally known to me to be the same person who subscribed the said instrument of writing), having had the contents of the said instrument made known and fully explained to her, and she also by me being fully informed of her rights under the Homestead Laws of the State, and being by me examined, separate and apart from her said husband, did acknowledge said instrument to be her free act and deed; that she executed the same, and relinquished her dower in the lands and tenements therein mentioned, and also all her rights and advantages under and by virtue of all laws of this State relating to the exemption of homesteads, voluntarily and freely, and without the compulsion of her husband, and that she does not wish to retract.

Given under my hand and official seal, this day of A.D. 186

(*Signature.*) (*Seal.*)

(125.)

Deed from Trustees.

This Deed, Made and entered into this day of A.D. eighteen hundred and by and between (*names of trustees*) party of the first part, and (*name, residence, and occupation of grantee*) party of the second part, witnesseth, that whereas (*name of the party who conveyed the estate to the trustees*) by deed dated the day of 186 recorded in the Recorder's office of County, State of in book conveyed the property hereinafter described in trust to said (*name of trustees*) to secure the payment of certain promissory notes in said deed described, and whereas (*here describe the non-payment or other default which has authorized the sale by the trustees*) and the party herein of the first part, at the request of the legal holder of said promissory notes acting in pursuance of the provisions of said deed of trust, and having first given days' public notice of the time, terms, and place of sale, and of the property to be sold, by an advertisement inserted on the day of A.D. in the a daily newspaper printed in the city of and continued to the day of sale (as will appear by the copy of said advertisement and affidavit of publication thereof hereto annexed as a part of this deed) did proceed to sell the property described in said deed at public vendue to the highest bidder for cash at in the city of on the day of 186 between the hours of ten o'clock in the morning and five o'clock in the afternoon of said day, when and where the same was struck off to (*the name of the purchaser who is the grantee*) as the highest and last bidder therefor, at the price and sum of dollars, full payment whereof is hereby acknowledged; now, said party of the first part, by virtue of the proceedings aforesaid, and in consideration of the sum of dollars to him in hand paid by said party of the second part, does by these presents bargain, sell, and convey to said (*name of the grantee*) all the right, title, and interest (which by virtue of said trust deed and the proceedings aforesaid he may or can bargain, convey or sell) in and to the property described in said deed of trust, to wit (*here describe the land or premises granted in the same way in which they are described in the deed of trust under which the trustees act*)

To Have and to Hold the said described premises unto said (*name of the purchaser*) and unto his heirs and assigns forever.

In Witness Whereof, the said party of the first part has hereto set his hand and seal the day and year first herein above written.

(*Signature.*) (*Seal.*)

In presence of (*Signature.*) (*Seal.*)

STATE OF , } ss.
COUNTY }

Be it Remembered, that on this day of A.D. 186 before me, the undersigned, personally came who are to me personally known to be the same persons whose names are subscribed to the foregoing instrument of writing as parties thereto, and they acknowledged the same to be their act and deed for the purposes therein mentioned.

(*Signature.*)

(126.)

Deed of Master in Chancery.

This Indenture, Made this day of A.D. 18 , between (*name of grantor*) Master in Chancery, in and for the County of and State of , of the first part, and (*name of grantee*) of the second part, witnesseth: That whereas, at the term of the court of the said County of and State of , in the year of our Lord A.D. 18 , in a certain suit and proceedings in chancery, pending in said court, wherein were complainant , and were defendant , to obtain a decree for the sale of the property hereinafter described, and for other relief, it was ordered, adjudged, and decreed by the court, that (*here set forth the decree under which the sale is made*) and the master in chancery, in and for the County of and State of , was appointed to execute the said decree, and to make, execute, and deliver to the complainant a deed to the said premises as aforesaid, conveying to (*the name, residence, and occupation of the grantee*) all the interest and title of the defendant to said premises.

Now, Therefore, Know all Men by this Deed, That I, Master in Chancery as aforesaid, in consideration of one dollar, to me paid by the said party of the second part, the receipt whereof I acknowledge before the execution hereof, and by virtue of the decree aforesaid, have granted, bargained, and sold, and do hereby grant, bargain, and sell unto the said party of the second part, his heirs and assigns forever, the following-described real estate, lying in the County of and State of to wit (*here describe carefully the land or premises granted, as directed in Form* 107)

To Have and to Hold the said premises, with all the appurtenances thereto belonging, unto the said party of the second part, his heirs and assigns forever.

In Testimony Whereof, The said Master in Chancery of County, in the State of , has hereto set his hand and seal the day and year first above written.

(*Signature.*) (*Seal.*)

In Presence of

State of , }
County. } ss.

I, clerk of the county court in and for the County of and State of , do hereby certify, that the above-named whose name appears signed to the foregoing deed, is personally known to me to be the same person described therein, and acknowledged to me that, as master in chancery aforesaid, he executed the said deed freely for the uses and purposes therein mentioned.

Given under my hand and official seal at this day of A.D. 18 .

(*Signature.*) *Clerk.* (*Seal.*)

(127.)

Sheriff's Deed on Execution, in Use in the Western States.

Whereas, (*the name of the plaintiff in the suit in which the execution issued*) did at the term, A.D. eighteen hundred and sixty- of the court for the County of in the State of , recover a judgment against (*name of the defendant in that suit*) for the sum of and costs of suit, upon which judgment an execution was issued, dated on the day of A.D. eighteen hundred and sixty- directed to the sheriff of County, to execute, and by virtue of said execution (*name of the sheriff*) of then sheriff of said county, levied upon the lands hereinafter described, and the same were struck off and sold to (*name of the purchaser at the sheriff's sale*) he being the highest and best bidder therefor, and the time and place of the sale thereof having been duly advertised according to law.

And the said (*name of the purchaser*) having duly assigned his certificate of purchase to (*name of the grantee*)

Now, Therefore, Know all by this Deed, That I (*name of the sheriff*) sheriff of said County of in consideration of the premises, have granted, bargained, and sold, and do hereby convey to the said (*name of the grantee*) his heirs and assigns, the following-described tract of land, to wit (*here describe carefully the land or premises granted, as directed in Form* 107)

To Have and to Hold the said described premises, with all the appurtenances thereto belonging, to the said (*name of the grantee*) and his heirs and assigns forever.

Witness my hand and seal, this day of in the year of our Lord one thousand eight hundred and sixty- .

(*Signature.*) (*Seal.*)

In Presence of

Sheriff of *County.*

STATE OF , }
COUNTY OF } SS.

I, clerk of the court of County, do certify that sheriff of County, personally known to me to be the real person whose name is subscribed to the within annexed deed, this day acknowledged before me that he executed the said deed, as such sheriff, voluntarily and freely, for the use and purposes therein set forth.

Given under my hand, and the seal of said court, this day of eighteen hundred and sixty- .

(*Signature.*) *Clerk.* (*Seal.*)

(128.)

Sheriff's Deed, in Use in New England.

Know all Men by these Presents, That I (*name of the deputy sheriff selling*) of in the County of and State of , and a deputy sheriff under (*name of the sheriff*), Esq., sheriff of said county, having, on the day of in the year of our Lord one thousand eight hundred and , by virtue of a writ of execution, which was issued upon a judgment, recovered at the term of the court holden at within and for the County of on the in the year of our Lord eighteen hundred and , by (*name of the plaintiff in the suit*) of in the County of against (*name of the defendant in that suit*) of in the County of for the sum of dollars and cents damage and costs of suit taxed at dollars and cents, seized and taken all the right in equity which the said had on the day of in the year of our Lord eighteen hundred and being the time when the same was attached on mesne process of redeeming the following-described mortgaged real estate, to wit (*here describe carefully the land or premises granted, as directed in Form* 107) and having on the day of last, being thirty days at least before the time of the sale hereinafter mentioned, given notice in writing, to the said (*name of the defendant*) of the time and place of sale, and having posted up notifications thereof in one public place in said town of and in one public place in each of the towns of and being two towns adjoining said town of and also having caused an advertisement of the time and place of sale, to be published three weeks successively, before the day of sale, in the public newspaper called the printed at in said County of on the day of in the year of our Lord eighteen hundred and made sale of said right in equity of redemption at public auction, to (*name of the purchaser*) of in ; he being the highest bidder for the same, for the sum of dollars. Now, therefore, in consideration of said sum of dollars to me paid by the said (*name of the purchaser*) the receipt whereof I do hereby acknowledge, I have gi··en, granted, bargained, and sold, and do, by these presents, give, grant, bargain, sell, and convey to the said (*name of the purchaser*) his heirs and assigns forever, all the right in equity which the said (*name of the defendant*) had of redeeming the aforesaid mortgaged real estate, at the time aforesaid. To have and to hold the same to the said (*name of purchaser*) his heirs and assigns, to his and their use forever; subject, however, to be redeemed agreeably to the law in such case made and provided. And I, the said (*name of grantor*) in my said capacity of deputy sheriff, do covenant with the said (*name of purchaser*) as aforesaid, that, in making said sale, and in every thing concerning the same, I have complied with, and observed the rules and requisitions of the law for making sales of rights in equity to redeem real estate. But I do not warrant or defend to the said (*name of the purchaser*) that the said (*name of the defendant*) had any right, title, or interest in said estate at the time aforesaid.

In Witness Whereof, I, the said in my said capacity of deputy sheriff, have hereunto set my hand and seal this day of in the year of our Lord one thousand eight hundred and

(*Signature.*) (*Seal.*)

Signed, Sealed and Delivered in Presence of

ss. 18 . Then the above-named personally appeared, and acknowledged the above instrument by him signed, to be his free act and deed. Before me,

Justice of the Peace.

(129.)

Sheriff's Tax Deed, in Use in the Western States.

Know all Men by these Presents, That whereas, at the Term, A.D. 18 , of the Court of County, a judgment was obtained in said court, in favor of the State of against the following-described lot , piece or parcel of land, for the sum herein specified, to wit, the sum of (*here state in writing the amount of the tax*); said sum being the whole amount of taxes, interest, and costs assessed upon said lot , piece, or parcel of land, for the year 18

And whereas, on the day of A.D. 18 (*name of the collector of taxes*) then collector of taxes of the county aforesaid, by virtue of a precept or order issued out of the Court of the county aforesaid, dated the day of A.D. 18 , and directed to the said as aforesaid, did expose at public sale, at the Court-House, in the county aforesaid, in conformity with all the requirements of the statutes in such case made and provided, the said lot , tract, or parcel of land above described, for the satisfaction of the judgment so rendered, as aforesaid. And whereas, at the time and place aforesaid (*name of the purchaser*) of the County of and State of having offered to pay the aforesaid sum, amounting to the sum of dollars, and cents, for the (*here state what part or portion of the land was sold*) of said lot , piece, or parcel of land, as follows, to wit, the sum of dollars cents, which was the least quantity of said lot , piece, or parcel of land bid for, the said lot , tract, or parcel of land was stricken off to (*name of the purchaser*) at that price. And whereas, the said purchaser has now made and delivered to me an affidavit of having complied with all the requirements of the statute and constitution of the State of necessary to entitle said purchaser to a deed for the premises so sold to him as aforesaid; and whereas the said (*name of the purchaser*) has duly assigned the certificate of purchase of the land above described, unto (*the name of the grantee*): Now, therefore, I, sheriff of the county of for and in consideration of the said above-named sum, amounting to the sum of dollars, and cents, paid to (*the collector of taxes*) of said county of by the said (*the name of the purchaser*) at the time of the aforesaid sale, and in consideration of (*the amount of costs and fees*) $\frac{}{100}$ dollars to me paid by said (*name of grantee*) and by virtue of the statute in such case made and provided, have granted, bargained and sold, and by these presents do grant, bargain and sell unto the said (*name of the grantee*) his heirs and assigns, the premises so sold as aforesaid, situated in the County of and State of to wit (*here describe carefully the land or premises granted, by metes and bounds, and contents or quantity, or boundary marks or monuments*)

To Have and to Hold unto him, the said (*the name of the grantee*) his heirs and assigns forever, subject, however, to all the rights of redemption provided by law.

In Witness Whereof, I, sheriff as aforesaid, by virtue of the authority aforesaid, have hereunto subscribed my name and affixed my seal this day of A.D. 18 .

(*Seal.*)

Sheriff of County.

STATE OF
} ss.
COUNTY OF

I, in and for said County and State, do certify that sheriff of said county, who is personally known to me to be the real person who executed and subscribed his name to the foregoing deed, appeared before me this day, and acknowledged that he had executed the same as such sheriff, freely and voluntarily for the uses and purposes therein set forth.

In attestation whereof, I have hereunto set my hand and attached the seal of our said court, at my office in in said County and State, this day of A.D. 18 .

(*Signature*) Clerk. (*Seal.*)

(130.)

Deed of Executor, in Use in the Eastern States.

Know all Men by these Presents, That whereas (*name of the executor*) in the County of and State of executor of the last will of (*name of the testator*) late of deceased, by an order of the Court of Probate, held at within and for the County of on the day of in the year one thousand eight hundred and was licensed and empowered to sell and pass deeds to convey certain real estate of the said deceased; and whereas, the said executor having given public notice of the intended sale, by causing notifications thereof to be published once a week, for three successive weeks, prior to the time of sale, in the newspaper called the printed at and having first taken the oath and given the bond by law in such cases required, did on the day of in the year one thousand eight hundred and pursuant to the order and notice aforesaid, sell by public auction the real estate of the said deceased hereinafter described, to (*name, residence, and occupation of the purchaser*) for the sum of dollars $\frac{}{100}$ he being the highest bidder therefor.

Now therefore, Know ye, That I the said executor as aforesaid, by virtue of the power and authority in me vested as aforesaid, and in consideration of the aforesaid sum of dollars $\frac{}{100}$ paid by the said (*name of purchaser*) the receipt whereof is hereby acknowledged, do, by these presents, give, grant, sell and convey unto the said (*here describe carefully the land or premises granted, by metes and bounds, and contents or quantity, or boundary marks or monuments, and refer to the deed of the land to the testator, under which he held it*)

To Have and to Hold the afore-granted premises, with all the privileges and appurtenances to the same belonging, to him the said (*name of purchaser*) and his heirs and assigns, to his and their use and behoof forever. And I the said (*name of executor*) for myself and my heirs, executors, and administrators, do hereby covenant with the said (*name of purchaser*) and his heirs and assigns, that in pursuance of the order aforesaid, I gave public notice of the said intended sale, in manner aforesaid, and that I took the oath and gave the bond by law required, previous to fixing on the time and place of sale.

In Witness Whereof, I the said executor as aforesaid, have hereunto set my hand and seal this day of in the year of our Lord one thousand eight hundred and sixty

(*Signature.*) (*Seal.*)

Signed, Sealed and Delivered in presence of

ss. A.D. 186 . Then personally appeared the above-named execut and acknowledged the foregoing instrument to be free act and deed.

Before me,

Justice of the Peace.

(131.)

Deed of Executor, in Use in the Middle States.

This Indenture, Made the day of in the year one thousand eight hundred and between (*name of executor*) executor of the last will of (*name and residence of testator*) of the first part, and (*name, residence, and occupation of the purchaser, who is the grantee*) of the second part, witnesseth, that the said party of the first part, by virtue of the power and authority to him given in and by the said last will and testament, and for and in consideration of the sum of lawful money of the United States of America, to him in hand paid at or before the ensealing and delivery of these presents, by the said party of the second part, the receipt whereof is hereby acknowledged, and the said party of the second part, his heirs, executors, and administrators, forever released and discharged from the same by these presents, have granted, bargained, sold, aliened, released, conveyed and confirmed, and by these presents do grant, bargain, sell, alien, release, convey and confirm, unto the said party of the second part, and his heirs and assigns forever, all (*here describe carefully the land or premises granted, by metes and bounds, and contents or quantity, or boundary marks or monuments, and refer to the deed of the land to the testator, under which he held it*)

Together with all and singular the edifices, buildings, rights, members, privileges, advantages, hereditaments, and appurtenances to the same belonging or in any wise appertaining; and the reversion and reversions, remainder and remainders, rents, issues and profits thereof. And also all the estate, right, title, interest, claim, and demand whatsoever, both in law and equity, which the said testator had in his lifetime, and at the time of his decease, and which the said party of the first part hath, by virtue of the said last will and testament, or otherwise, of, in, and to the same, and every part and parcel thereof, with the appurtenances: To have and to hold the said premises above mentioned and described, and hereby granted and conveyed, or intended so to be, with the appurtenances, unto the said party of the second part, and his heirs and assigns, to his and their only proper use, benefit and behoof forever. And the said party of the first part, for himself and for his heirs, executors, and administrators, does for himself and for his heirs, executors, and administrators, covenant, grant, promise and agree to and with the said party of the second part, and his heirs and assigns, that the said party of the second part, his heirs and assigns, shall and lawfully may from time to time, and at all times forever hereafter, peaceably and quietly have, hold, use, occupy, possess, and enjoy, all and singular the said hereditaments and premises hereby granted and conveyed, or intended so to be, with their and every of their appurtenances, and receive and take the rents, issues, and profits thereof, to and for his and their own use and benefit, without any lawful let, suit, hindrance, molestation, interruption or denial whatsoever, of, from, or by them the said party of the first part, his heirs or assigns; or of, from, or by any other person or persons whomsoever lawfully claiming, or who shall or may lawfully claim hereafter, by, from, or under him, or by, from, or under his right, title, interest, or estate. And that free and clear, and freely and clearly discharged, acquitted and exonerated, or otherwise well and sufficiently saved, defended, kept harmless, and indemnified by them, the said party of the first part, his heirs and assigns, of, from, and against all and all manner of former and other gifts, grants, bargains, sales, mortgages, judgments, and all other charges and incumbrances whatsoever, had, made, committed, executed, or done by him the said party of the first part, or by, through, or with his acts, deeds, means, consent, procurement, or privity.

In Witness Whereof, the parties to these presents have hereunto interchangeably set their hands and seals the day and year first above written.

(*Signature of party of the first part.*) (*Seal.*)

(*Signature of party of the second part.*) (*Seal.*)

Sealed and Delivered in the Presence of

STATE OF , } ss.
COUNTY. }

This day personally appeared before the undersigned, (*name and office of the magistrate*) within and for the county and State aforesaid, (*name of the executor*) executor of the estate of (*name of deceased*) deceased, who personally known to me to be the person whose name as such is subscribed to the foregoing deed, as having executed the same, and acknowledged that he had as such executor subscribed to the foregoing deed, as having executed the same, and acknowledged that he had as such executor executed the same for the uses and purposes therein expressed.

In Witness Whereof, I have hereunto set my hand and seal, at my office in said county, this day of A.D. 18

(*Signature.*) (*Seal.*)

(132.)

Deed of Administrator of Intestate.

This Indenture, Made this day of in the year of our Lord one thousand eight hundred and between *(name and residence of administrator)* administrator of the goods and estate of *(name of intestate)* of who died intestate, party of the first part, and *(name, residence, and occupation of the grantee)* of the County of and State of party of the second part:

Whereas, at the term, A.D. 18 of the court, within and for the County of and State of , in a certain petition or cause therein pending, in which the said *(name of the grantor)* administrator of the goods and estate of *(name of the deceased)* deceased, was petitioner and *(names of the defendants who are minor children of the deceased, and of the widow of deceased, and of the guardian of the minors)* were defendants, the following order and decree were rendered, that is to say:

STATE OF , }
COUNTY. } SS.

In Court Term A.D. 186

(name of the administrator) administrator of the goods and estate of *(name of deceased)* deceased, *vs.* *(names of the defendants, who should be the widow and heirs of the deceased)*

And now comes the petitioner by his solicitor and presents his petition herein, and it satisfactorily appearing to the court that the defendants have been duly served with summons herein by the sheriff of . County, and that the defendants are non-residents of the State of , and have been duly notified of this proceeding by publication as required by law, it is therefore ordered by the court, that the said defendants be called. And they, being three times solemnly called, came not, nor any one for them, but herein failed and made default; which it ordered to be entered of record; and it further appearing to the court that the said *(names of defendants who are minors)* are minors and have a guardian, to wit, the said *(name of the guardian)* And afterwards the said *(name of guardian)* as such guardian comes and files his answer herein, neither admitting nor denying the allegations in said petition contained, but reserving the right of said minor by requiring proof. And this cause having been brought on to be heard upon the petition herein taken as confessed by the answer of said guardian and the exhibits and proofs, and the testimony of *(name of the witness or witnesses called in the case)* witness duly sworn, who testified herein in open court, and it satisfactorily appearing to the court from the evidence that the said *(name of the deceased)* departed this life on or about the day of A.D. 18 , leaving *(name of his widow)* his widow and *(names of his children)* his children and only heirs at law; that the petitioner herein was duly appointed administrator of the goods and estate of said (*name of deceased*) deceased, and that letters of administration were duly granted to him by this court, bearing date on the day of A.D. 186 , and the court having ascertained that said petitioner as aforesaid, has made a just and true account of the condition of the estate of said deceased to this court, and that the personal estate of said deceased is not sufficient for the payment of the debts of the said (*name of the deceased*) deceased; and the court having found the amount of the deficiency aforesaid to be the sum of dollars, besides interest and costs, and it further appearing to the court that the said (*name of the deceased*) died seized of the following-described real estate, situate in the County of and State of , to wit (*here describe carefully the land or premises granted, by metes and bounds, and contents or quantity, or boundary marks or monuments, and refer to the deed of the land to the deceased, under which he held it*) and the court having ascertained that it will be necessary to sell the said real estate to pay the deficiency aforesaid, with the expenses of administration now due and to accrue; it is therefore ordered, adjudged, and decreed that the said petitioner proceed, according to law, to advertise and make sale of the real estate above described, or so much thereof as may be necessary to pay the debts now due from said estate, and the costs of administration now due and to accrue. And it is ordered and decreed by the court, that said sale shall be made on the following terms; viz. (*here set forth the terms, place, time, and manner of the sale as prescribed in the decree*) which terms shall be distinctly set forth in all the advertisements of said sale.

It is further ordered that upon such a sale being made, that said (*name of the administrator*) shall make and execute to the purchaser or purchasers of said real estate, good and sufficient deed or deeds to convey the interest of said deceased therein at the time of his disease, and that said (*name of the administrator*) report his action in the premises with all convenient speed. And it is further ordered, that his cause stand continued for said report.

And Whereas, in pursuance of said order and decree, the said party of the first part did on the day of A.D. 18 , between the hours of ten o'clock in the forenoon, and five o'clock in the afternoon of such day, at (*place of sale*) expose to sale by public vendue, to the highest bidder, the lands and real estate so ordered to be sold, in said decree, having first given notice of the time, terms, and place of such sale, with a description of such lands and real estate, according to the terms and requirements of said order and decree, and of the statute regulating such sales, as will more fully and at large appear by the report of such sale, made by said party of the first part, as administrator as aforesaid to the said court.

And Whereas, at such sale, the said party of the second part became the purchaser of the following-described lands and real estate, being the highest bidder therefor, at the following price; that is to say (*here state what part, or the whole, of the above-described lands were sold, and at what price*)

Now, Therefore, This indenture witnesseth that the said party of the first part, by virtue of the order and decree aforesaid, and in consideration of the premises, and for the further consideration of the sum of dollars, to him in hand paid by the said party of the second part, the receipt of which is hereby acknowledged, has granted, bargained, sold, and conveyed, and by these presents does grant, bargain, sell, and convey unto the said party of the second part, heirs and assigns, the lands and real estate last above described as having been sold to the said party of the second part, to have and to hold the same with all the appurtenances thereunto belonging, or in any wise appertaining, to the only proper use, benefit, and behoof, of the said party of the second part, and his heirs and assigns forever. And the said party of the first part, for the consideration aforesaid, covenants with the said party of the second part, and his heirs and assigns, that he has in all respects complied with the order and decree aforesaid, and with the directions of the law generally in such case made and provided.

In Witness Whereof, The said party of the first part, as administrator as aforesaid, has hereunto set his hand and seal the day and year first above written.

(*Signature.*) (*Seal.*)

Administrator of (*name of deceased*) as aforesaid.

In Presence of

STATE OF ,
COUNTY. } ss.

This day personally appeared before the undersigned, within and for the county and State aforesaid, executor of the estate of (*name of deceased*) deceased, who personally known to me to be the person whose name as such is subscribed to the foregoing deed, as having executed the same, and acknowledged that he had as such executor subscribed to the foregoing deed, as having executed the same, and acknowledged that he had as such executor executed the same for the uses and purposes therein expressed.

In Witness Whereof, I have hereunto set my hand and seal, at my office in said county, this day of A.D. 18

(*Signature.*) (*Seal.*)

(133.)

Deed Poll of Guardian of a Minor.

Know all Men by these Presents, That whereas (*name of guardian and grantor*) of in the County of and State of , guardian of (*name of the ward*) a minor child of (*name of the father of the minor*) by an order of the probate court, held at within and for County of on the day of in the year one thousand eight hundred and was licensed and empowered to sell and pass deeds to convey certain real estate of the said minor; and whereas, I, the said guardian, having given public notice of the intended sale, by causing notifications thereof to be published once a week, for three successive weeks, prior to the time of sale, in the newspaper called the printed at and having first taken the oath and given the bond by law in such cases required, did on the day of in the year one thousand eight hundred and pursuant to the order and notice aforesaid, sell by public auction the real estate of the said minor hereinafter described, to (*the name, residence, and occupation of the purchaser and grantee*) for the sum of dollars $\frac{}{100}$ he being the highest bidder therefor.

Now, Therefore, Know ye, That I, the said (*name of the guardian and grantor*) guardian as aforesaid, by virtue of the power and authority in me vested as aforesaid, and in consideration of the aforesaid sum of dollars $\frac{}{100}$ to me paid by the said the receipt whereof is hereby acknowledged, do, by these presents, give, grant, sell, and convey unto the said (*name of the purchaser and grantee*) a certain lot or parcel of land, situated, bounded, and described as follows (*here describe the premises as directed in Form* 107)

To Have and to Hold the aforegranted premises, with all the privileges and appurtenances to the same belonging, to him the said (*purchaser's name*) and his heirs and assigns, to his and their use and behoof forever. And I, the said (*name of guardian*) for myself, my heirs, executors, and administrators, do hereby covenant with the said (*name of purchaser*) and his heirs and assigns, that in pursuance of the order aforesaid, I gave public notice of the said intended sale, in manner aforesaid, and that I took the oath by law required, previous to fixing on the time and place of sale, and gave the bond previous to said sale.

In Witness Whereof, I, the said guardian as aforesaid, have hereunto set my hand and seal, this day of in the year of our Lord one thousand eight hundred and

(*Signature.*) (*Seal.*)

Signed, Sealed and Delivered in Presence of

ss. A.D. 18 . Then personally appeared the above-named guardian, and acknowledged the foregoing instrument to be free act and deed.

Before me, *Justice of the Peace.*

(134.)

Deed of Referee on Foreclosure, in Use in the Middle States.

This Indenture, Made the day of in the year one thousand eight hundred and between (*name and residence of the referee and grantor*), a referee duly appointed as hereinafter mentioned, of the first part, and (*name, residence, and occupation of the grantee*) of the second part.

Whereas at a Term of the (*name of the court*) court, on the day of one thousand eight hundred and it was among other things ordered and adjudged by the said court, in a certain action then pending in the said court, between (*names of plaintiff and defendant in the action*)

That all and singular the mortgaged premises mentioned in the complaint in said action, and in said judgment described, or so much thereof as might be sufficient to raise the amount due to the plaintiff for principal, interest, and costs in said action, and which might be sold separately, without material injury to the parties interested, be sold at public auction, according to the course and practice of said court, by or under the direction of the said party of the first part as referee thereby, duly appointed for that purpose: that the said sale be made (*here state the directions in the order of court as to the place and time of the sale*) that the said referee give public notice of the time and place of such sale, according to the course and practice of said court, and that any of the parties in said action might become a purchaser or purchasers on such sale; that the said referee execute to the purchaser or purchasers of the said mortgaged premises, or such part or parts thereof as should be sold, a good and sufficient deed or deeds of conveyance for the same:

And Whereas, the said referee, in pursuance of the said judgment of the said court, did on the day of one thousand eight hundred and sell at public auction at (*the place of sale*) the premises in the said judgment mentioned, due notice of the time and place of such sale being first given, agreeably to the said judgment; at which sale the premises hereinafter described were struck off to the said party of the second part for the sum of dollars, that being the highest sum bidden for the same. Now this indenture witnesseth, that the said referee, the party of the first part to these presents, in order to carry into effect the sale so made by him as aforesaid, in pursuance of the judgment of the said court, and in conformity to the statute in such case made and provided, and also in consideration of the premises, and of the said sum of money so bidden as aforesaid, being first duly paid by the said party of the second part, the receipt whereof is hereby acknowledged, hath bargained and sold, and by these presents doth grant and convey unto the said party of the second part, the premises aforesaid, situate, bounded, and described as follows (*describe here the premises sold as directed in Form* 107)

To Have and to Hold all and singular the premises above mentioned and described, and hereby conveyed, or intended so to be, unto the said party of the second part, his heirs and assigns, to and for his and their only proper use, benefit, and behoof.

In Witness Whereof, The said referee as aforesaid, hath hereunto set his hand and seal, the day and year first above written.

(*Signature.*) (*Seal.*)

Sealed and delivered in the presence of

STATE OF , } ss.
COUNTY. }

On the day of one thousand eight hundred and before me came known to me to be the individual described in, and who executed the above conveyance, and acknowledged that he executed the same.

(*Signature.*)

(135.)

Deed of Collector of Taxes.

To all Persons to whom these Presents shall come, I, (*name of collector*) of in the county of and State of collector of taxes for said town of duly chosen and qualified at the last annual meeting of the inhabitants of said town, held on the day of last past sends greeting:

Whereas, the assessors of said town of (*name of the town*) in their list of assessments committed to me, the said (*name of the collector*) to collect, have assessed (*name of the party for whose taxes the land is sold*) a resident owner of a certain tract of land situated in said bounded and described as follows, viz. (*describe the premises as directed in Form* 107) the sum of (*amount of tax*) and $\frac{}{100}$ dollars, as a tax on said premises for the year eighteen hundred and

And Whereas I, the said (*name of collector*) have demanded payment of said tax of (*name of party taxed*) more than fourteen days before proceeding to advertise and sell as hereinafter set forth.

And Whereas the said (*name of the party taxed*) has given no written authority to any inhabitant of said town, as his attorney to pay the tax imposed on said land, and no mortgagee of said land has given written notice to the clerk of said town, that he the said mortgagee holds a mortgage thereon, nor given written authority to any inhabitant of said town as his attorney, to pay said tax.

And Whereas I, the said having given public notice of the time and place of sale of the said land, for the non-payment of said tax, by an advertisement thereof three weeks successively, in the newspaper called the printed and published in in said county, the last publication of said advertisement being one week before the time of said sale: also by posting a like notice on said land three weeks before the time of said sale: and also by posting a like notice (*here state whatever other places the notice was posted at*) being two public places in said town, three weeks before the time of said sale, which notices severally contained the name of the said (*name of the party taxed*) and the amount of the tax assessed on said land; also a substantially accurate description of said land, did, on the day of instant, pursuant to the authority and notice aforesaid, no person appearing to pay said tax, and it being the opinion of me, that the said land could not be conveniently divided and a part theroof set off without injury to the residue, and judging it to be most for the public interest to sell the whole of said land, sell, at public auction, the said land above described, to (*name of purchaser and grantee*) for the sum of and $\frac{}{100}$ dollars, he being the highest bidder therefor.

Now Therefore, Know Ye, that I the said (*name of the collector*) by virtue of the authority in me vested as aforesaid, and in consideration of the aforesaid sum of and $\frac{}{100}$ dollars, to me paid by the said (*name of the purchaser*) the receipt whereof is hereby acknowledged, do hereby give, grant, bargain, sell, and convey unto the said all that said tract or parcel of land above mentioned and described, with the appurtenances thereto belonging.

To Have and to Hold the same to him, the said grantee, his heirs and assigns, to his and their use and behoof forever; subject, nevertheless, to the right of redemption, according to law.

And I, the said grantor, do covenant with the said grantee, his heirs and assigns, that in making the said sale as above set forth, I have complied with, observed, and obeyed all the provisions of law for the sale of real estate for the non-payment of taxes.

In Witness Whereof, I, the said collector, have hereto set my hand and seal, this day of in the year eighteen hundred and

(*Signature.*) (*Seal.*)

Executed and delivered in the presence of

STATE OF , } ss.
COUNTY. } A.D. 18

Then personally appeared the above-named collector, and acknowledged the above instrument to be his free act and deed.

Before me, *Justice of the Peace.*

(136.)

Deed of Assignee, in Use in the Western States.

This Indenture, Made this day of in the year of our Lord one thousand eight hundred and (A.D. 18) between (*name, residence and occupation of the assignee who is the grantor*) as assignee of (*name, residence and occupation of the assignor*) of the one part, and (*name, residence and occupation of the purchaser who is grantee*) of the other part:

Whereas, The said (*name of the assignor*) being lawfully seized in his demesne, as of fee, among other things, of and in a certain lot, piece or parcel of ground, situate in the County of and State of , known and described as follows, to wit (*here describe the premises as in Form* 107). And being so thereof seized, did, on or about the day of A.D. one thousand eight hundred and (A.D. 18), enter into a written contract with the said party of the second part for the sale of the above-described premises for the sum of dollars.

And Whereas, The said (*name of the assignor*) did, by his certain deed of assignment, bearing date the day of A.D. 18 , grant, bargain, sell, alien, remise, release, convey, assign, transfer and set over (with other property) the above-described lot, piece or parcel of ground unto the said party of the first part, his successors, executors, administrators and assigns forever, in trust nevertheless, to and for the uses and intent and purposes in said deed of assignment mentioned and set forth, reference thereto being had may fully and at large appear; which said deed of assignment is recorded in Book page of deeds, in the office of the clerk of the Circuit Court of said county, and ex-officio recorder of deeds.

And Whereas, The said assignor did not comply with the said contract before the execution and delivery of the said deed of assignment to the said party of the first part,

Now this Indenture Witnesseth, That the said (*name of the assignee and grantor*) assignee of said (*name of the assignor*) for and in consideration of the sum of dollars (being the balance of the purchase money and interest due on said contract), unto him in hand paid by the said party of the second part, at and before the ensealing and delivery hereof, the receipt whereof is hereby acknowledged, by these presents does grant, bargain, sell, alien, release and confirm unto the said party of the second part, and his heirs and assigns, all the above mentioned and described lot, piece or parcel of ground, together with all and singular the rights, hereditaments and appurtenances thereunto belonging or in any wise appertaining, and all the estate, right, title, interest, property, claim and demand whatever, that he the said assignor had and held at and immediately before the execution and delivery of the said deed of assignment to said party of the first part, and also all the right, title, interest, property, claim and demand whatever, that the said party of the first part acquired in, under or by virtue of the said deed of assignment by said assignor, to him, the said party of the first part. To have and to hold the same, together with all and singular the appurtenances and privileges thereunto belonging, or in any wise appertaining, and all the estate, right, title, interest and claim whatsoever, either in law or equity, that said assignor had and held at the time of and immediately preceding the execution and delivery of said deed of assignment to the said party of the first part, and all the right, title interest and claim whatsoever of the said party of the first part, either in law or equity, to the only proper use, benefit and behoof of the said party of the second part, his heirs and assigns forever.

In Witness Whereof, The said party of the first part has hereunto set his hand and seal the day and year first above written.

(*Signature of assignee.*) (*Seal.*)

STATE OF , } ss.
COUNTY.

I, a in and for said county, in the State aforesaid, do hereby certify that who is personally known to me as the real person whose name is subscribed to the within deed, appeared before me this day, in person, and acknowledged that he executed and delivered the said deed, as his free and voluntary act for the uses and purposes therein set forth.

Given under my hand and seal this day of in the year of our Lord one thousand eight hundred and (A.D. 18).

(*Signature.*) (*Seal.*)

(137.)

Acknowledgment of Grantor and Wife identified, before Commissioner for another State.

STATE OF } ss.
COUNTY OF

Be it Remembered, That on the day of one thousand eight hundred and before me, commissioner for the State of (*name of the State of which he is commissioner*) resident in the of , duly appointed, commissioned, and sworn to take acknowledgments and proof of deeds and other writings in the State of , to be used or recorded in the said State of (*name of the State of which he is commissioner*) and to administer oaths and affirmations, and to take depositions in the said State of , to be used within the said State of appeared (*name of grantor*) and (*name of wife of grantor*) his wife, who are satisfactorily proven to me to be the individuals described in, and who executed the within deed, from said (*name of grantor*) and wife to (*name of grantee*) by the oath of (*witnesses to their identity*) who being by me duly cautioned and sworn, deposed that he knew them, the individuals, then present, to be the persons described in, and who executed the within deed. The said and his wife, then and there acknowledged to me that they executed the said deed for the purposes therein mentioned; and the said (*name of the wife*) being examined by me privily, and apart from her said husband, and the contents and effect of the said deed being by me first duly explained to her, did then and there acknowledge that she executed the same for the purposes therein mentioned, freely and without compulsion of or from her said husband.

In Witness Whereof, I have hereunto set my hand and affixed the seal of my office, on the day of in the year of our Lord one thousand eight hundred and

(*Signature.*) (*Seal.*)

CHAPTER XXX.

MORTGAGES OF LAND.

THE purpose of a mortgage is to give to a creditor the security of property. It is very similar to a pledge, although not the same thing.

Mortgages are now made of personal property, as well as of real property; but we will consider in this chapter a mortgage of real property; or, as it is usually called, a mortgage deed.

This is a deed conveying the land to the creditor as fully, and in precisely the same way, as if it were sold to him outright; but with an addition. This consists of a clause inserted before the clause of execution, to the effect, that if the grantor (the mortgagor) shall pay to the grantee (the mortgagee) a certain amount of money at a certain time, then the deed shall be void. It is usually expressed in words substantially like these: —

"Provided, nevertheless, that if the said A B (the grantor), his heirs, executors, or administrators, shall pay to the said C D (the grantee), his executors, administrators, or assigns, the sum of $——— with interest (semi-annually, or otherwise as agreed on), on or before the —— day of ——, then this deed, and also a certain promissory note signed by said A B, whereby said A B promised to pay said C D, or his order, the said sum at the said time, shall both be void; and otherwise shall remain in full force."

In some States it is more frequent to make a bond, instead of a note, to be secured by the mortgage; and the proviso should be altered accordingly; and it should also be made to express any other terms agreed on. Some of these will be spoken of presently.

In law, every thing is a mortgage which consists of a valid conveyance, and a promise, or agreement, which may be on the same or on a different piece of paper or instrument, providing that the conveyance shall be void when a certain debt is paid, or the act performed for which the mortgage is security.

The mortgagee has now a title to the land; but it is subject to avoidance by payment of the debt. Until such payment, the land is his; and all the mortgagor owns in relation to it is a right to pay the debt and redeem the land. Hence, a mortgagee has instantly as good a right to take possession of the land (unless, as is now common, the deed provides that the mortgagor may retain possession) as if he were an outright purchaser.

Formerly, a mortgagor had a right to redeem his land only before or when the debt became due; for, if he did not pay the money when it was due, he had no further right. But courts of equity, deeming this too hard, allowed him a further time to redeem it. And courts of law adopted the same rule, which is also contained in the statutes of all our States. This right to redeem is called a right in equity to redeem, or, more briefly and commonly, an equity of redemption; which all courts now regard and protect. The mortgagor may sell this equity of redemption, or he may mortgage it by making a second or other subsequent mortgage of the land, and it may be attached by creditors, and would go to assignees as a part of his property if he became insolvent. The time within which a mortgagor may thus redeem his land is usually three years.

The law regards this equity as so important, that it will not permit a party to lose it by his own agreement. Thus, if a mortgagor agrees with the mortgagee, in the most positive terms, or in any way he can contrive, or for any consideration, that he will have no equity of redemption, and that the mortgagee may have possession and absolute title as soon as the debt is due and unpaid, the law sets aside all such agreements, and gives the debtor his equity of redemption for three years.

Within a few years, however, a way has been found to effect this purpose indirectly, which the law sanctions. Many persons object to lending their money on mortgage, because they will have to wait three years after the debt is due before the land can be certainly theirs. But it is now quite common for the mortgage deed to contain an agreement of the parties, that, if the money is not paid when it is due, the mortgagee may, in a certain number of days thereafter, sell the land (providing also such precautions to secure a fair price as may be agreed on), and, reserving enough to pay his debt and charges, pay over the balance to the mortgagor. This is called a power of sale mortgage.

The three years of redemption do not begin from the day when the debt is due and unpaid, unless the mortgagee then enters and takes possession for the purpose of *foreclosing* the mortgage, as the legal phrase is; by which phrase is meant extinguishing the equity of redemption. If the debt has been due a dozen years, the mortgagor may still redeem, unless the mortgagee has entered *to foreclose*, and three years have elapsed afterwards.

He may make entry for this purpose in a peaceable manner, before witnesses, as pointed out in the statutes regulating mortgages, or by an action at law.

If the mortgagor redeems, he must tender the debt, with interest, and the lawful costs and charges of the mortgagee; but he will be allowed such rents and profits as the mortgagee has actually received, or would have received but for his own fault.

It is commonly thought that the mortgagor has a right to retain possession until the debt is due and unpaid, and in fact he usually does so. But we have seen that the mortgagee has just as much right of immediate possession as a buyer; and therefore, if it is not intended that he should have possession at once, the mortgage deed ought to contain a clause to the effect, that the mortgagor may retain possession as long as he pays instalments and interest as due, and complies with his other agreements.

One of these other agreements, which is now very common, is that the mortgagor shall keep the premises insured in a certain sum for the security of the mortgagee; and, if there be such an agreement, it should be expressed in the deed. Otherwise, if the mortgagee insures the house, he cannot charge the premium to the mortgagor.

If a mortgagor erects buildings on the mortgaged land, or puts fixtures there, and the mortgagee takes possession of the land, and *forecloses* the mortgage, he gets all these additions. If the mortgagee puts them on the land, and the mortgagor redeems, he gets the benefit of them all, without paying the mortgagee for them. Such is the effect of the law if there be no bargain between the parties about these things. But they may make any bargain about them they choose to make.

The remarks which were made at the close of the preceding chapter (just before the forms), concerning the various Forms of deeds conveying land, apply with equal force to deeds of mortgage of land; and I refer to them now because they are equally necessary to the proper understanding and use of the following Forms.

(138.)

A Promissory Note, to be secured by Mortgage.

18

for value received promise to pay to dollars, at with interest at the rate of per cent per annum

This note is secured by a deed of mortgage of even date herewith, from to which is duly stamped according to the internal revenue law.

$

(*Signature.*)

(139.)

Bond, to be secured by a Mortgage.

Know all Men by these Presents, That I (*name of obligor*) of in the County of and State of , am held, bound and obliged unto (*name of obligee*) of in the County of and State of , in the sum of (*penalty, usually twice as much as the actual debt*) to be paid to the said (*the obligee*) his executors, administrators, heirs or assigns, and to this payment I hereby bind myself, my heirs, executors and administrators, firmly by these presents.

Sealed with my seal, this day of in the year

The Condition of the above obligation is such, that if I the said (*name of the obligor*) or my heirs, executors or administrators, shall pay or cause to be paid unto the said (*name of the obligee*) the sum of (*here insert the amount of the debt or sum to be secured*) on the day of in the year , with interest at per cent, payable six months from the date hereof, and every six months afterwards, until the said sum is paid, then the above obligation shall be void and of no effect; and otherwise it shall remain in full force. And I further agree and covenant, that if any payment of interest be withheld or delayed for days after such payment shall fall due, the said principal sum and all arrearage of interest thereon, shall be and become due immediately on the expiration of days, at the option of said (*name of the obligee*) or his executors or administrators.

(*Signature.*) (*Seal.*)

(*Witness.*)

(140.)

Mortgage without Power of Sale and without Warranty, but with release of Homestead and of Dower.

This Indenture, Made this day of in the year of our Lord one thousand eight hundred sixty- between (*name, residence and occupation of mortgagor*) and (*name of wife*) wife of said (*name of mortgagor*) parties of the first part, and (*name, residence and occupation of mortgagee*) party of the second part,

Whereas, The said party of the first part is justly indebted to the said party of the second part, in the sum of secured to be paid by a certain promissory note (*or bond*) (*describe the note or bond*)

Now, Therefore, this Indenture Witnesseth, That the said parties of the first part, for the better securing the payment of the money aforesaid, with interest thereon, according to the tenor and effect of the said note (*or bond*) above mentioned; and also in consideration of the further sum of one dollar to us in hand paid by the said party of the second part, at the delivery of these presents, the receipt whereof is hereby acknowledged, have granted, bargained, sold and conveyed, and by these presents do grant, bargain, sell and convey unto the said party of the second part, his heirs and assigns forever, all that (*here describe the premises as directed in Form* 107 *of deeds of land*)

To Have and to Hold the Same, Together with all and singular the tenements, hereditaments, privileges and appurtenances thereunto belonging or in any wise appertaining. And also all the estate, interest and claim whatsoever in law as well as in equity, which the parties of the first part have in and to the premises hereby conveyed unto the said party of the second part, and his heirs and assigns, and to their only proper use, benefit and behoof. And the said parties of the first part hereby expressly waive, release, relinquish and convey unto the said party of the second part and his heirs, executors, administrators and assigns, all right, title, claim, interest and benefit whatever, in and to the above-described premises, and each and every part thereof, which is given by or results from all laws of this State pertaining to the exemption of homesteads.

Provided Always, and these Presents are upon this Express Condition, That if the said party of the first part, or his heirs, executors or administrators shall well and truly pay or cause to be paid to the said party of the second part or his heirs, executors, administrators or assigns, the aforesaid sum of money, with such interest thereon, at the time and in the manner specified in the above-mentioned note (*or bond*) according to the true intent and meaning thereof, then in that case, these presents and every thing herein expressed shall be absolutely null and void.

In Witness Whereof, The said parties of the first part hereunto set their hand and seal the day and year first above written.

(Signature of mortgagor.) *(Seal.)*
(Signature of wife of mortgagor.) *(Seal.)*

Signed, Sealed and Delivered in Presence of

STATE OF
COUNTY. } ss.

I in and for the said county, in the State aforesaid, do hereby certify that *(name of mortgagor)* personally known to me as the same person whose name is subscribed to the foregoing mortgage, appeared before me this day in person, and acknowledged that he signed, sealed and delivered the said instrument of writing as his free and voluntary act, for the uses and purposes therein set forth.

And the said *(name of wife)* wife of the said *(name of mortgagor)* having been by me examined, separate and apart, and out of the hearing of her husband, and the contents and meaning of said instrument of writing having been by me made known and fully explained to her, and she also by me being fully informed of her rights under the homestead laws of this State, acknowledged that she had freely and voluntarily executed the same, and relinquished her dower to the lands and tenements herein mentioned, and also all her rights and advantages under and by virtue of all laws of this State relating to the exemption of homesteads, voluntarily and freely and without the compulsion of her said husband, and that she does not wish to retract the same.

Given under my hand and official seal this day of A.D. 186

(Signature.) *(Seal.)*

(141.)

Mortgage, with Power of Sale, to secure a Bond, without Release of Dower.

This Indenture, Made the day of in the year one thousand eight hundred and between *(name, residence, and occupation of mortgagor)* party of the first part, and *(name, residence, and occupation of mortgagee)* party of the second part; Whereas, the said *(name of mortgagor)* is justly indebted to the said party of the second part, in the sum of lawful money of the United States, secured to be paid by a certain bond or obligation bearing even date with these presents, in the penal sum of dollars, lawful money as aforesaid, conditioned for the payment of the said first-mentioned sum of *(here state the amount due on the bond,* *and the time and terms of payment*) as by the said bond or obligation, and the condition thereof, reference being thereunto had, may more fully appear.

Now this Indenture Witnesseth, That the said party of the first part, for the better securing the payment of the said sum of money mentioned in the condition of the said bond or obligation, with interest thereon, according to the true intent and meaning thereof, and also for and in consideration of the sum of one dollar to him in hand paid by the said party of the second part, at or before the ensealing and delivery of these presents, the receipt whereof is hereby acknowledged, has granted, bargained, sold, aliened, released, conveyed, and confirmed, and by these presents does grant, bargain, sell, alien, release, convey, and confirm unto the said party of the second part, and to his heirs and assigns forever, all (*here describe the premises as directed in Form* 107, *deeds of land*)

Together with all and singular the tenements, hereditaments, and appurtenances thereunto belonging, or in any wise appertaining, and the reversion and reversions, remainder and remainders, rents, issues, and profits thereof: and also all the estate, right, title, interest, property, possession, claim, and demand whatsoever, as well in law as in equity, of the said party of the first part, of, in, and to the same, and every part and parcel thereof with the appurtenances: To have and to hold the above granted, bargained, and described premises, with the appurtenances, unto the said party of the second part, and his heirs and assigns, to his and their own proper use, benefit, and behoof forever.

Provided Always, and these presents are upon this express condition, that if the said party of the first part, or his heirs, executors, or administrators, shall well and truly pay unto the said party of the second part, or his executors, administrators, or assigns, the said sum of money mentioned in the condition of the said bond or obligation and the interest thereon, at the time and in the manner mentioned in the said condition according to the true intent and meaning thereof, that then these presents, and the estate hereby granted, shall cease, determine, and be void. And the said (*name of mortgagor*) for himself and his heirs, executors, and administrators, does covenant and agree, to pay unto the said party of the second part, or his executors, administrators, or assigns, the said sum of money and interest as mentioned above and expressed in the condition of the said bond. And if default shall be made in the payment of the said sum of money above mentioned, or the interest that may grow due thereon, or of any part thereof, that then and from thenceforth, it shall be lawful for the said party of the second part, or his executors, administrators, or assigns, to enter into and upon all and singular the premises hereby granted or intended so to be, and to sell and dispose of the same, and all benefit and equity of redemption of the said party of the first part, or his heirs, executors, administrators, or assigns therein, at public auction. And out of the money arising from such sale, to retain the principal and interest, which shall then be due on the said bond or obligation, together with the costs and charges of advertisement and sale of the same premises, rendering the overplus of the purchase-money (if any there shall be), unto the said (*name of mortgagor*) party of the first part, or his heirs, executors, administrators, or assigns, which sale, so to be made, shall forever be a perpetual bar, both in law and equity, against the said party of the first part, and his heirs and assigns, and all other persons claiming or to claim the premises, or any part thereof, by, from, or under him or them, or any of them.

In Witness Whereof, The parties to these presents have hereunto interchangeably set their hands and seals the day and year first above written.

(*Signature of mortgagor.*) (*Seal.*)
(*Signature of mortgagee.*) (*Seal.*)

Sealed and Delivered in the Presence of

STATE OF } ss.
COUNTY OF }

On the day of in the year one thousand eight hundred and before me personally came (*names of both parties*) who are known to me to be the individuals described in, and who executed the foregoing instrument, and acknowledged that they executed the same.

(*Signature.*)

(142.)

Mortgage to secure a Debt, with Power of Sale. Short Form.

This Indenture, Made the day of in the year one thousand eight hundred and between (*name, residence, and occupation of mortgagor*) party of the first part, and (*name, residence, and occupation of mortgagee*) party of the second part, witnesseth, that the said party of the first part, in consideration of the sum of (*the amount of the debt*) to him duly paid before the delivery hereof, has bargained and sold, and by these presents does grant and convey to the said party of the second part, and his heirs and assigns forever, all (*here describe the premises as directed in Form* 107 *of deeds of land*) with the appurtenances, and all the estate, right, title, and interest of the said party of the first part therein.

This Grant is intended as a security for the payment of (*here describe the debt*) which payments, if duly made, will render this conveyance void. And if default shall be made in the payment of the principal or interest above mentioned, then the said party of the second part, or his executors, administrators, or assigns, are hereby authorized to sell the premises above granted, or so much thereof as will be necessary to satisfy the amount then due, with the costs and expenses allowed by law.

In Witness Whereof, the said party of the first part has hereunto set his hand and seal the day and year first above written.

(*Signature.*) (*Seal.*)

Sealed and Delivered in the Presence of

STATE OF , }
COUNTY OF . } ss.

On the day of in the year one thousand eight hundred and before me personally came (*name of mortgagor*), who is known to me to be the individual described in, and who executed, the foregoing instrument, and acknowledged that he executed the same, as his free act and deed.

(*Signature.*)

(143.)

Mortgage to secure a Debt, fuller Form, with Power of Sale.

This Indenture, Made the day of in the year one thousand eight hundred and between (*name, residence, and occupation of mortgagor*) party of the first part, and (*name, residence, and occupation of the mortgagee*) party of the second part:

Whereas, the said party of the first is justly indebted to the said party of the second part in (*here describe the amount and terms of the debt, or note, or bond*)

Now this Indenture Witnesseth, That the said party of the first part, for the better securing the debt (*or note, or bond*) above described, according to the true intent and meaning thereof, and also for and in consideration of the sum of one dollar to him in hand paid by the said party of the second part, at or before the ensealing and delivery of these presents, the receipt whereof is hereby acknowledged, has granted, bargained, sold, aliened, remised, released, conveyed, and confirmed, and by these presents does grant, bargain, sell, alien, remise, release, convey, and confirm, unto the said party of the second part, and to his heirs and assigns forever, all (*here describe the premises as directed in Form* 107, *deeds of land*)

Together with all and singular the tenements, hereditaments and appurtenances thereunto belonging, or in any wise appertaining, and the reversion and reversions, remainder and remainders, rents, issues and profits thereof. And also all the estate, right, title, interest, property, possession, claim and demand whatsoever, as well in law as in equity, of the said party of the first part, of, in, and to the same, and every part and parcel thereof with the appurtenances: To have and to hold the above granted, bargained and described premises, with the appurtenances, unto the said party of the second part, and his heirs and assigns, to his and their own proper use, benefit, and behoof forever.

Provided Always, and these presents are upon this express condition, that if the said party of the first, or his heirs, executors, or administrators, shall well and truly pay to the said party of the second part, or his heirs, executors, administrators, or assigns, the above-described debt (*or note, or bond*) according to terms and tenor thereof, then this deed (*and also said debt or note or bond*) shall be wholly discharged and void; and otherwise shall remain in full force and effect. And if default shall be made in the payment of the said sum of money above mentioned, or the interest that may grow due thereon, or of any part thereof, that then and from thenceforth it shall be lawful for the said party of the second part, or his executors, administrators, and assigns, to enter into and upon all and singular the premises hereby granted, or intended so to be, and to sell and dispose of the same, and all benefit and equity of redemption of the said party of the first part, or his heirs, executors, administrators, or assigns, therein, at public auction, according to the act in such case made and provided. And as the attorney of the said party of the first part, for that purpose by these presents duly authorized, constituted, and appointed, to make and deliver to the purchaser or purchasers thereof, a good and sufficient deed or deeds of conveyance in the law for the same, in fee simple, and out of the money arising from such sale, to retain the principal and interest which shall then be due on the said debt (*or note or bond*) together with the costs and charges of advertisement and sale of the said premises, rendering the overplus of the purchase-money (if any there shall be), unto the said party of the first part, or his heirs, executors, administrators, or assigns; which sale, so to be made, shall forever be a perpetual bar, both in law and equity, against the said party of the first part, or his heirs and assigns, and all other persons claiming or to claim the premises or any part thereof, by, from, or under him, them, or either of them.

In Witness Whereof, The parties to these presents have hereunto set their hands and seals the day and year first above written.

(*Signature of mortgagor.*) (*Seal.*)
(*Signature of mortgagee.*) (*Seal.*)

Sealed and Delivered in the Presence of

STATE OF } ss.
COUNTY OF }

On the day of in the year one thousand eight hundred and before me personally came (*names of both parties*) who are known to me to be the individuals described in, and who executed the foregoing instrument, and acknowledged that they executed the same.

(*Signature.*)

(144.)

Deed Poll of Mortgage, with Power to sell, and Insurance Clause, and Release of Dower and Homestead.

Know all Men by these Presents, That I (*name, residence and occupation of mortgagor*) in consideration of to me paid by (*name, residence and occupation of mortgagee*) the receipt whereof is hereby acknowledged, do hereby give, grant, bargain, sell, and convey unto the said (*name of mortgagee*) all that lot or parcel of land, with all the buildings thereon standing, situated in the town (*or city*) of County, of State of and bounded and described as follows; that is to say (*here describe the premises as directed in Form* 107, *in chapter on deeds of land*)

To Have and to Hold the afore-granted premises, with the privileges, easements and appurtenances thereto belonging, to the said grantee, and to his heirs and assigns, to their use forever.

And I the said grantor, for myself and my heirs, executors and administrators, do covenant with the said grantee, and his heirs and assigns, that I am lawfully seized in fee of the afore-granted premises; that they are free from all incumbrances (*if any incumbrance exists, say* "*except as follows,*" *and describe the incumbrance*), that I have good right to sell and convey the same to the said grantee, and his heirs and assigns as aforesaid; and that I will, and my heirs, executors, and administrators shall warrant and defend the same to the said grantee, and his heirs and assigns forever, against the lawful claims of all persons.

Provided Nevertheless, That if the said grantor, or his heirs, executors, or administrators, shall pay unto the said grantee, or his executors, administrators, or assigns, the sum of dollars $\frac{}{100}$ in days (*or months*) from the day of the date hereof, with interest on said sum at the rate of per centum, per annum, payable (*semi-annually*) and until such payment keep the buildings standing on the land aforesaid insured against fire, in a sum not less than dollars, for the benefit of said mortgagee and payable to him in case of loss, at some insurance office approved by said mortgagee; or in any default thereof, shall on demand pay to said mortgagee all such sums of money as the said mortgagee shall reasonably pay for such insurance, with interest, and also pay all taxes levied or assessed upon the said premises, then this deed, as also (*a certain bond or*) a certain promissory note, bearing even date with these presents, signed by the said mortgagor, whereby for value received he promises to pay the said mortgagee or his order, the said sum and interest, at the time aforesaid, shall both be absolutely void to all intents and purposes.

But if default shall be made in the payment of the money above mentioned, or the interest that may grow due thereon, or of any part thereof, then it shall be lawful for the said grantee, or his executors, administrators, or assigns to sell and dispose of all and singular the premises hereby granted or intended to be granted, and all benefit and equity of redemption of the said (*name of the mortgagor*) the grantor, his heirs, executors, administrators, or assigns therein, at public auction; such sale to be on or near the premises hereby granted; first giving notice of the time and place of sale, by publishing the same once each week, in three successive weeks, in (*name of the newspaper*) a newspaper printed in the county of aforesaid; and in his or their own names, or as the attorney of the said (*name of mortgagor*) the grantor, for that purpose by these presents duly authorized, constituted and appointed, to make and deliver to the purchaser or purchasers thereof, a good and sufficient deed or deeds of conveyance for the same in fee simple; and out of the money arising from such sale, to retain the said sum of dollars, or the part thereof remaining unpaid, and also the interest then due on the same, together with the costs and charges of advertising and selling the same premises; rendering the surplus of the purchase-money, if any there be, over and above said sum and interest as aforesaid, together with a true and particular account of said sale and charges, to the said (*name of the mortgagor*) the grantor, his heirs, executors, administrators, or assigns; which sale, so to be made, shall forever be a perpetual bar, both in law and equity, against the said (*name of the mortgagor*) the grantor, and his heirs and assigns, and all other persons claiming or to claim the premises, or any part thereof, by, from, or under him, them, or any of them.

And Provided Also, That until some breach of the condition of this deed, the grantee shall have no right to enter and take possession of the premises, and hold the same.

In Witness Whereof, We the said (*name of mortgagor*) and (*name of his wife*) wife of the said (*name of mortgagor*) in token of her release of all right and title of or to both dower and homestead in the granted premises, have hereunto set our hands and seals this day of in the year of our Lord eighteen hundred and

(*Signature of mortgagor.*) (*Seal.*)
(*Signature of wife of mortgagor.*) (*Seal.*)

Executed and Delivered in Presence of

ss. 18

Then personally appeared the above-named and acknowledged the above instrument to be free act and deed, before me,

Justice of the Peace.

(145.)

Mortgage by Indenture, with Power of Sale and Interest and Insurance Clause, to secure a Bond.

This Indenture, Made the day of in the year one thousand eight hundred and between (*name, residence, and occupation of the mortgagor*) party of the first part, and (*name, residence, and occupation of the mortgagee*) party of the second part:

Whereas, The said party of the first part is justly indebted to the said party of the second part, in the sum of (*amount of debt due on the bond*) dollars lawful money of the United States, secured to be paid by his certain bond or obligation bearing even date with these presents, in the penal sum of (*amount of penalty*) lawful money as aforesaid, conditioned for the payment of the said first-mentioned sum of (*amount of debt due on the bond*) lawful money as aforesaid, to the said party of the second part, or his executors, administrators, or assigns, on the day of which will be in the year one thousand eight hundred and and interest thereon to be computed from at and after the rate of per cent per annum, and to be paid (*here set forth the time and terms of the payment*)

And it is Thereby Expressly Agreed, That should any default be made in the payment of the said interest, or of any part thereof, on any day whereon the same is made payable, as above expressed, and should the same remain unpaid and in arrear for the space of days, then and from thenceforth, that is to say, after the lapse of the said days, the aforesaid principal sum of (*amount of the debt*) with all arrearage of interest thereon, shall, at the option of the said party of the second part, or his executors, administrators, or assigns, become and be due and payable immediately thereafter, although the period above limited for the payment thereof may not then have expired, any thing thereinbefore contained, to the contrary thereof in any wise notwithstanding:

As by the said bond or obligation, and the condition thereof, reference being thereunto had, may more fully appear. Now this indenture witnesseth, that the said party of the first part, for the better securing the payment of the said sum of money mentioned in the condition of the said bond or obligation, with interest thereon, according to the true intent and meaning thereof, and also for and in consideration of the sum of one dollar to him in hand paid by the said party of the second part, at or before the ensealing and delivery of these presents, the receipt whereof is hereby acknowledged, has granted, bargained, sold, aliened, released, conveyed, and confirmed, and by these presents does grant, bargain, sell, alien, release, convey, and confirm unto the said party of the second part, and to his heirs and assigns forever, all (*here describe carefully the land or premises granted, as directed in Form* 107, *deeds of land*)

Together with all and singular the tenements, hereditaments, and appurtenances thereunto belonging, or in any wise appertaining, and the reversion and reversions, remainder and remainders, rents, issues, and profits thereof: and also all the estate, right, title, interest, property, possession, claim, and demand whatsoever, as well in law as in equity, of the said party of the first part, of, in, and to the same, and every part and parcel thereof with the appurtenances: to have and to hold the above granted, bargained, and described premises, with the appurtenances, unto the said party of the second part, his heirs and assigns, to his and their own proper use, benefit, and behoof forever:

Provided Always, and these presents are upon this express condition, that if the said party of the first part, his heirs, executors, or administrators, shall well and truly pay unto the said party of the second part, his executors, administrators or assigns, the said sum of money mentioned in the condition of the said bond or obligation and the interest thereon, at the time and in the manner mentioned in the said condition according to the true intent and meaning thereof, that then these presents, and the estate hereby granted, shall cease, determine, and be void. And the said (*name of the mortgagor*) for himself and his heirs, executors, and administrators, does covenant and agree, to pay unto the said party of the second part, or his executors, administrators, or assigns, the said sum of money and interest as mentioned above and expressed in the condition of the said bond. And if default shall be made in the payment of the said sum of money above mentioned, or the interest that may grow due thereon, or of any part thereof, that then and from thenceforth it shall be lawful for the said party of the second part, or his executors, administrators, and assigns, to enter into and upon all and singular the premises hereby granted or intended so to be, and to sell and dispose of the same, and all benefit and equity of redemption of the said party of the first part, or his heirs, executors, administrators, or assigns, therein, at public auction, according to law. And as the attorney of the said party of the first part, for that purpose by these presents duly authorized, constituted, and appointed, to make and deliver to the purchaser or purchasers thereof, a good and sufficient deed or deeds of conveyance in the law for the same, in fee simple, and out of the money arising from such sale, to retain the principal and interest which shall then be due on the said bond or obligation, together with the costs and charges of advertisement and sale of the said premises, rendering the overplus of the purchase-money (if any there shall be), unto the said party of the first part, his heirs, executors, administrators, or assigns; which sale, so to be made, shall forever be a perpetual bar, both in law and equity, against the said party of the first part, and his heirs and assigns, and all other persons claiming or to claim the premises or any part thereof, by, from, or under him or them, or either of them.

And it is Expressly Agreed by and between the parties to these presents, that the said party of the first part shall and will keep the buildings erected and to be erected upon the lands above conveyed, insured against loss and damage by fire, by insurers approved by the said party of the second part, and in an amount approved by the said party of the second part, and assign the policy and certificates thereof to the said party of the second part; and in default thereof, it shall be lawful for the said party of the second part to effect such insurance, and the premium and premiums paid for effecting the same shall be a lien on the said mortgaged premises, added to the amount of the said bond or obligation, and secured by these presents, and payable on demand with interest at the rate of per cent per annum.

In Witness Whereof, the parties to these presents have hereunto interchangeably set their hands and seals the day and year first above written.

(*Signature of mortgagor.*) (*Seal*)

(*Signature of mortgagee.*) (*Seal*)

Sealed and Delivered in the Presence of

STATE OF , }
COUNTY. } ss.

On the day of in the year one thousand eight hundred and before me personally came to be the individuals described in, and who executed the foregoing instrument, and acknowledged that they executed the same as their free act and deed.

(*Signature.*)

(146.)

Mortgage to Executors, with Power of Sale.

This Indenture, Made the day of in the year one thousand eight hundred and between (*name, residence, and occupation of the mortgagor*) party of the first part, and (*name and residence of the mortgagee*) executor of the last will and testament of (*name and residence of the testator*) deceased, of the second part; whereas, the said party of the first part is justly indebted to the said party of the second part in the sum of lawful money of the United States of America, secured to be paid by a certain bond or obligation bearing even date with these presents, in the penal sum of lawful money as aforesaid, conditioned for the payment of the said first-mentioned sum (*state the terms of the payment; and if the bond was made to the testator, state that*) as by the said bond or obligation and the condition thereof, reference being thereunto had, may more fully appear.

Now this Indenture Witnesseth, That the said party of the first part, for the better securing the payment of the said sum of money mentioned in the condition of the said bond or obligation with interest thereon, according to the true intent and meaning thereof, and also for and in consideration of the sum of one dollar, to him in hand paid by the said party of the second part, at or before the ensealing and delivery of these presents, the receipt whereof is hereby acknowledged, has granted, bargained, sold, aliened, released, conveyed, and confirmed, and by these presents does grant, bargain, sell, alien, release, convey, and confirm, unto the said party of the second part, and his successors and assigns forever, all (*here describe carefully the land or premises granted, as directed in Form* 107, *deeds of land*)

Together with all and singular the tenements, hereditaments, and appurtenances thereunto belonging or in any wise appertaining, and the reversion and reversions, remainder and remainders, rents, issues, and profits thereof: and also all the estate, right, title, interest, property, possession, claim, and demand whatsoever, as well in law as in equity, of the said party of the first part, of, in, and to the same, and every part and parcel thereof with the appurtenances. To have and to hold the above granted, bargained, and described premises, with the appurtenances, unto the said party of the second part, his successors and assigns, to their only proper use, benefit, and behoof forever. Provided always, and these presents are upon this express condition, that if the said party of the first part, or his heirs, executors, or administrators, shall well and truly pay unto the said party of the second part, or his successors or assigns, the said sum of money mentioned in the condition of the said bond or obligation, and the interest thereon, at the time, and in the manner mentioned in the said condition, according to the true intent and meaning thereof, that then these presents, and the estate hereby granted, shall cease, determine, and be null and void. And the said party of the first part, for himself and his heirs, executors, and administrators, does covenant and agree to pay unto the said party of the second part, his successors or assigns, the said sum of money and interest, as mentioned above, and expressed in the condition of the said bond. And if default shall be made in the payment of the said sum of money above mentioned, or the interest that may grow due thereon, or of any part thereof, that then and from thenceforth it shall be lawful for the said party of the second part, his successors and assigns, to enter into and upon all and singular the premises hereby granted, or intended so to be, and to sell and dispose of the same, and all benefit and equity of redemption of the said party of the first part, or his heirs, executors, administrators, or assigns therein, at public auction, according to law. And as the attorney or attorneys of the said party of the first part, for that purpose by these presents duly authorized, constituted, and appointed, to make and deliver to the purchaser or purchasers thereof a good and sufficient deed or deeds of conveyance in the law for the same, in fee simple, and out of the money arising from such sale, to retain the principal and interest which shall then be due on the said bond or obligation, together with the costs and charges of advertisement and sale of the said premises, rendering the overplus of the purchase-money (if any there shall be) unto the said party of the first part, his heirs, executors, administrators, or assigns; which sale, so to be made, shall forever be a perpetual bar, both in law and equity, against the said party of the first part, his heirs and assigns, and all other persons claiming or to claim the premises, or any part thereof, by, from, or under him, them, or any of them.

In Witness Whereof, the parties to these presents have hereunto set their hands and seals the day and year first above written

(*Signature.*) (*Seal.*)
(*Signature.*) (*Seal.*)

Signed, Sealed and Delivered in the Presence of

STATE OF , } ss.
COUNTY. }

On the day of in the year one thousand eight hundred and before me personally came to be the individuals described in, and who executed the foregoing instrument, and acknowledged that they executed the same as their free act and deed.

(*Signature.*)

(147.)

Mortgage of a Lease.

This Indenture, Made the day of in the year one thousand eight hundred and between *(name, residence, and occupation of mortgagor)* party of the first part, and *(name, residence, and occupation of mortgagee)* party of the second part: Whereas, *(name, residence, and occupation of the lessor of the lease to be mortgaged)* did, by a certain indenture of lease, bearing date the day of in the year one thousand eight hundred and demise, lease, and to farm let, unto the said party of the first part, and to his executors, administrators and assigns, all and singular the premises hereinafter mentioned and described, together with their appurtenances: To have and to hold the same unto the said party of the first part, and to his executors, administrators and assigns, for and during and until the full end and term of years, from the day of and fully to be complete and ended, yielding and paying therefor unto the said *(name of the lessor)* and to his heirs, executors, administrators or assigns, the yearly rent or sum of *(state the rent, and the times, or terms of the payments)*

And Whereas, The said party of the first part is justly indebted to the said party of the second part, in the sum of dollars, lawful money of the United States of America, secured to be paid by his certain bond or obligation bearing even date with these presents, in the penal sum of dollars, lawful money as aforesaid, conditioned for the payment of the said first mentioned sum of *(here give the amount of the debt to be paid)* as by the said bond or obligation and the condition thereof, reference being thereunto had, may more fully appear.

Now this Indenture Witnesseth, That the said party of the first part, for the better securing the payment of the said sum of money mentioned in the condition of the said bond or obligation, with interest thereon, according to the true intent and meaning thereof, and also for and in consideration of the sum of one dollar, to him in hand paid, by the said party of the second part, at or before the ensealing and delivery of these presents, the receipt whereof is hereby acknowledged, has granted, bargained, sold, assigned, transferred and set over, and by these presents does grant, bargain, sell, assign, transfer and set over unto the said party of the second part, the estate or premises leased and transferred by said indenture of lease, that is to say *(here describe the premises in the same manner in which they are described in the lease)*, together with all and singular the edifices, buildings, rights, members, privileges and appurtenances thereunto belonging, or in any wise appertaining; and also all the estate, right, title, interest, term of years yet to come and unexpired, property, possession, claim and demand whatsoever, as well in law as in equity, of the said party of the first part, of, in, and to the said demised premises, and every part and parcel thereof, with the appurtenances; and also the said indenture of lease, and every clause, article and condition therein expressed and contained.

To Have and to Hold the said indenture of lease, and other hereby granted premises, unto the said party of the second part, his executors, administrators and assigns, to his and their only proper use, benefit and behoof, for and during all the rest, residue, and remainder of the said term of years yet to come and unexpired; subject, nevertheless, to the rents, covenants, conditions and provisions in the said indenture of lease mentioned. Provided always, and these presents are upon this express condition, that if the said party of the first part shall well and truly pay unto the said party of the second part the said sum of money mentioned in the condition of the said bond or obligation, and the interest thereon, at the time and in the manner mentioned in the said condition, according to the true intent and meaning thereof, that then and from thenceforth these presents, and the estate hereby granted, shall cease, determine, and be utterly null and void, any thing hereinbefore contained to the contrary in any wise notwithstanding. And the said party of the first part does hereby covenant, grant, promise and agree to and with the said party of the second part, that he shall well and truly pay unto the said party of the second part the said sum of money mentioned in the condition of the said bond or obligation, and the interest thereon, according to the condition of the said bond or obligation. And that the said premises hereby conveyed now are free and clear of all incumbrances whatsoever, and that the said party of the first part has good right and lawful authority to convey the same in manner and form hereby conveyed. And if default shall be made in the payment of the said sum of money above mentioned, or in the interest which shall accrue thereon, or of any part of either, that then and from thenceforth it shall be lawful for the said party of the second part, and his assigns, to sell, transfer, and set over, all the rest, residue and remainder of the said term of years then yet to come, and all other the right, title and interest of the said party of the first part, of, in and to the same, at public auction, according to the act in such case made and provided: and as the attorney of the said party of the first part, for that purpose by these presents duly authorized, constituted and appointed, to make, seal, execute and deliver to the purchaser or purchasers thereof, a good and sufficient assignment, transfer, or other conveyance in the law, for the same premises, with the appurtenances; and out of the money arising from such sale, to retain the principal and interest which shall then be due on the said bond or obligation, together with the costs and charges of advertisement and sale of the same premises, rendering the overplus of the purchase-money (if any there shall be), unto the said party of the first part, or his assigns; which sale, so to be made, shall be a perpetual bar, both in law and equity, against the said party of the first part, and against all persons claiming or to claim the premises, or any part thereof, by, from, or under him or them, or any of them.

In Witness Whereof, The said party of the first part to these presents has hereunto set his hand and seal the day and year first above written.

(Signature.) *(Seal.)*

Signed, Sealed and Delivered in the Presence of

STATE OF } ss.
COUNTY OF }

On the day of in the year one thousand eight hundred and before me personally came who is known to me to be the individual described in, and who executed the foregoing instrument, and acknowledged that he executed the same as his free act and deed.

(*Signature.*)

(148.)

Mortgagee's Deed, under a Power of Sale.

This Indenture, Made this day of in the year of our Lord one thousand eight hundred and between (*name and occupation of the mortgagee*) of the County of and State of party of the first part, and (*name and occupation of the grantee*) of the County of and State of of the second part.

Witnesseth, That whereas (*name and occupation of the owner and mortgagor who gave to the mortgagee the power now exercised*) of the County of and State of did, by a certain deed, dated the day A.D. 18 , which deed is recorded in the recorder's office of the County of in the State of on the day of A.D. 18 , in book of at page , grant, sell and convey to the said party of the first part all the premises hereinafter described, to secure the payment of a certain debt (*or note, or bond*) in said deed particularly mentioned, and upon certain terms in said deed particularly declared; and whereas default hath been made in the payment of said debt (*note or bond*), the said premises were, by said party of the first part, duly advertised for public sale at the door of the court house in the County of and State of on the day of A.D. 18 in the manner prescribed by said deed, and were, upon the day and year and at the place last mentioned aforesaid, in pursuance of said notice, sold at public sale, and at said sale the said party of the second part was the highest and best bidder therefor, and bid for the tract first hereinafter named, the sum of dollars

Now Therefore These presents witness, that the said party of the first part, in pursuance of the power and authority in him vested in and by the said deed, and in consideration of the sum of dollars, to the said party of the first part paid by the said party of the second part, the receipt whereof is hereby acknowledged, hath released and quitclaimed, and doth hereby convey, remise, release and quitclaim to the said party of the second part, his heirs and assigns forever, all the right, title and interest, as well in law as in equity, which the said party of the first part hath acquired by virtue of the deed above mentioned, of, in and to all that certain tract , piece or parcel of land situated in the County of and State of and described as follows, to wit (*here describe the premises as directed in Form* 107, *of deeds of lands*).

Together with all and singular the tenements, hereditaments and appurtenances thereunto belonging or in any wise appertaining, and the reversions, remainders, rents, issues and profits thereof; and also all the estate, right, title, interest, claim and demand whatsoever, as well in law as in equity, of the said party of the first part, of, in and to the same and any and every part thereof, with the appurtenances, which the said party of the first part acquired by virtue of said deed:

To Have and to Hold the aforesaid right, title and interest of the said party of the first part, unto the said party of the second part, his heirs and assigns forever, as full and absolutely as the said party of the first part can, by virtue of the power and authority in him by said deed vested, convey the same.

In Witness Whereof, The party of the first part hath hereto set his hand and seal the day and year first above written.

(*Signature of seller.*) (*Seal.*)

Signed, Sealed and Delivered in Presence of

STATE OF
COUNTY. } ss.

On the day of eighteen hundred and sixty- , before me of the County of in the State of appeared who is personally known to me to be the real person whose name is subscribed to the foregoing instrument of writing, as having executed the same, and then acknowledged the execution thereof as his free act and deed, for the uses and purposes herein mentioned.

(*Signature.*)

(149.)

Assignment of Mortgage, Short Form.

Know all Men by these Presents, That I, (*name, residence and occupation of the assignor*) the mortgagee named in a certain mortgage deed, given by (*name, residence, and occupation of the mortgagor*) to said (*name of assignor*) to secure the payment of dollars $\frac{}{100}$, dated the day of in the year of our Lord eighteen hundred and recorded in the registry of deeds for the County of lib. fol. in consideration of the sum of dollars $\frac{}{100}$ to me paid by (*name, residence, and occupation of buyer and assignee*) the receipt whereof is hereby acknowledged, do hereby sell, assign, transfer, set over and convey unto said (*name of assignee*) and his heirs and assigns, said mortgage deed, the real estate thereby conveyed, and the promissory note, debt and claim thereby secured, and the covenants therein contained.

To Have and to Hold the same to him the said (*name of assignee*) and his heirs and assigns, to his and their use and behoof forever; subject nevertheless to the conditions herein contained, and to redemption according to law.

In Witness Whereof, I the said have hereunto set my hand and seal this day of in the year of our Lord eighteen hundred and

(*Signature.*) (*Seal.*)

Executed and Delivered in Presence of

ss. A.D. 18

Then personally appeared the above-named and acknowledged the above instrument to be his free act and deed. Before me,

(*Signature.*)

(150.)

Assignment of Mortgage, with Power of Attorney.

Know all Men by these Presents, That I, (*name, residence, and occupation of assignor*) party of the first part, in consideration of the sum of lawful money of the United States, to me in hand paid by (*name, residence, and occupation of assignee*) of the second part, at or before the ensealing and delivery of these presents, the receipt whereof is hereby acknowledged, have granted, bargained, sold, assigned, transferred, and set over, and by these presents do grant, bargain, sell, assign, transfer, and set over unto the said party of the second part, his executors, administrators, and assigns, a certain indenture of mortgage, bearing date the day of one thousand eight hundred and sixty- made by (*here state the name of the mortgagor, and briefly describe the mortgage deed, and state the volume and page where it is registered*) to which reference may be made, together with all the right, title, interest, and estate of said party of the first part, in and to the premises described and conveyed in and by said indenture of mortgage.

Together with the bond (or note) therein described and the money due and tc grow due thereon, with the interest accruing or accrued, to have and to hold the same, unto the said party of the second part, his executors, administrators, and assigns, for his and their use, subject only to the proviso in the said indenture of mortgage mentioned: and I do hereby make, constitute, and appoint the said party of the second part, my true and lawful attorney, irrevocably in my name or otherwise, but at his own proper costs and charges, to have, use, and take all lawful ways and means for the recovery of the said money and interest; and in case of payment, to discharge the same as fully as I might or could do if these presents were not made.

In Witness Whereof, I have hereunto set my hand and seal the day of one thousand eight hundred and sixty-

(*Signature.*) (*Seal.*)

Signed, Sealed and Delivered in the Presence of

STATE OF , } ss.
COUNTY. }

On this day of eighteen hundred and sixty- personally appeared before me known to me to be the person who signed and sealed the foregoing assignment of mortgage, and acknowledged the execution of the same for the uses and purposes therein set forth.

Given under my hand and seal at in said county aforesaid.

(*Signature.*) (*Seal.*)

(151.)

Assignment of Mortgage by a Corporation.

Know all Men by these Presents, That the (*legal name of the corporation assigning*) existing as a corporate body, in and under the laws of the State of of the first part, for and in consideration of the sum of lawful money of the United States, to the said corporation paid by (*name, residence, and occupation of assignee*) of the second part, at or before the ensealing and delivery of these presents, the receipt whereof is hereby acknowledged, have granted, bargained, sold, assigned, transferred, and set over, and by these presents do grant, bargain, sell, assign, transfer, and set over unto the said party of the second part, a certain indenture of mortgage, bearing date the day of one thousand eight hundred and made by (*here state the name of the mortgagor, and briefly describe the mortgage deed*) the same being duly registered in the office of the register of deeds for the County of and State of to which said indenture of mortgage, reference may be had.

Together with the bond or obligation therein described, and the moneys due, and to grow due thereon, with the interest: to have and to hold the same unto the said party of the second part, his heirs and assigns, for his and their own use, subject only to the proviso in the said indenture of mortgage mentioned. And the said parties of the first part do hereby make, constitute, and appoint the said party of the second part their true and lawful attorney, irrevocable, in the name of the said parties of the first part, or otherwise, but at the proper costs and charges of the said party of the second part, to have, use, and take all lawful ways and means for the recovery of the said money and interest, and in case of payment to discharge the same as fully as the said parties of the first part might or could do if these presents were not made.

In Witness Whereof, the said parties of the first part have caused their common seal to be affixed to these presents, and the same to be signed by their attorney and president (*or other officer*) the day of in the year one thousand eight hundred and

(*Signature.*) (*Seal of the Corporation.*)

Signed, Sealed and Delivered in Presence of

STATE OF , }
COUNTY. } ss.

On the day of in the year one thousand eight hundred and before me came with whom I am personally acquainted, and known to me to be the attorney and of the within named corporation, who being by me duly examined says, that the seal which is affixed to the within assignment is the corporate seal of the said corporation, and was so affixed by their authority, and acknowledged that he executed the same as their act and deed.

(*Signature.*)

(152.)

Discharge of Mortgage, Short Form.

The Debt secured by the mortgage, dated and recorded with deeds, lib. fol. has been paid to me by (*name of mortgagor*) and in consideration thereof I do discharge the mortgage and release the mortgaged premises to said (*name of mortgagor*) and his heirs.

Witness my hand and seal A.D. 18

(*Signature.*) (*Seal.*)

Executed and Delivered in Presence of

ss. A.D. 186 Then said acknowledged the foregoing instrument to be free act and deed.

Before me, (*Signature.*)

(153.)

Release and Quitclaim of Mortgage, as Used in the Western States.

Know all Men by these Presents, That I (*name of mortgagee*) of the County of and State of for and in consideration of one dollar, to me in hand paid, and for other good and valuable considerations, the receipt whereof is hereby confessed, do hereby grant, bargain, remise, convey, release, and quitclaim unto (*name of assignee or releasee*) of the County of and State of all the right, title, interest, claim, or demand whatsoever I may have acquired in, through, or by a certain indenture or mortgage deed, bearing date the day of A.D. 186 , and recorded in the recorder's office of County, in book of page to the premises therein described, and which said deed was made to secure a certain promissory note (*or bond*) bearing even date with said deed, for the sum of dollars and cents.

Witness my hand and seal this day of A.D. 186

(*Signature.*) (*Seal.*)

STATE OF , }
COUNTY. } ss.

I, in and for said county in the State aforesaid, do hereby certify that who is personally known to me as the same person whose name is subscribed to the foregoing deed, appeared before me, this day, in person, and acknowledged that he signed, sealed, and delivered the said instrument of writing as his free and voluntary act, for the uses and purposes therein set forth.

Given under my hand and seal this day of A.D. 186

(*Signature.*) (*Seal.*)

(154.)

Discharge of Mortgage, as used in the Middle States.

STATE OF }
COUNTY OF } ss.

I, (*name, residence, and occupation of mortgagee*) do hereby certify that a certain indenture (*or deed*) of mortgage bearing date the day of one thousand eight hundred and made and executed by (*here state the name of the mortgagor, and describe the deed briefly*) and recorded in the office of County of in lib. of mortgages, page on the day of in the year one thousand eight hundred and o'clock, in the is paid. And I do hereby consent that the same be discharged of record.

Dated the day of 18

(*Signature.*) (*Seal.*)

In Presence of

STATE OF } ss.
COUNTY OF

On the day of in the year one thousand eight hundred and before me personally came who is known to me to be the individual described in, and who executed the foregoing instrument, and acknowledged that he executed the same as his free act and deed.

(*Signature.*)

(**155.**)

Discharge and Satisfaction of Mortgage by a Corporation.

We, (*the legal name of the corporation*) a corporate body existing within and under the laws of the State of

Do hereby Certify, That a certain mortgage, bearing date the day of in the year one thousand eight hundred and made and executed by (*here state the name of the mortgagor, and describe the mortgage briefly*) and recorded in the office of the register in and for the County of in lib. of mortgages, page on the day of is paid.

In Witness Whereof, The said corporation has caused its corporate seal to be hereunto affixed, this day of in the year one thousand eight hundred and

(*Signature of attorney.*) (*Seal of corporation.*)

Witnessed by

STATE OF } ss.
COUNTY OF

On the day of in the year one thousand eight hundred and before me personally came to me known, who, being by me duly sworn, did depose and say, that he resided in the city (*or town*) of that he is the attorney and president (*or other officer*) of the said corporation; that he knew the corporate seal of the said corporation, and that the seal affixed to the foregoing instrument was such corporate seal; that it was affixed by him by order of the said corporation, and that he signed his name thereto by the like order.

(*Signature.*)

(**156.**)

Release of a Part of the Mortgaged Premises.

This Indenture, Made the day of in the year of our Lord one thousand eight hundred and between (*name, residence and occupation of the mortgagee and releasor*) party of the first part, and (*name, residence and occupation of the mortgagor to whom the release is given*) party of the second part:

Whereas, The said party of the second part, by indenture of mortgage, bearing date the day of one thousand eight hundred and for the consideration therein mentioned, and to secure the payment of the money therein specified, did convey certain lands and tenements, of which the lands hereinafter described are part, unto the said party of the first part,

And Whereas, The said party of the first part, at the request of the said party of the second part, has agreed to give up and surrender the lands hereinafter described unto the said party of the second part, and to hold and retain the residue of the mortgaged lands as security for the money remaining due on the said mortgage: Now this indenture witnesseth, that the said party of the first part, in pursuance of the said agreement, and in consideration of to him duly paid at the time of the ensealing and delivery of these presents, the receipt whereof is hereby acknowledged, has granted, released, quitclaimed and set over, and by these presents does grant, release, quitclaim, and set over, unto the said party of the second part, all that part of the said mortgaged land (*here describe carefully and accurately all that part of the mortgaged land which it is intended to release, distinguishing it from that which is retained*)

Together with the hereditaments and appurtenances thereto belonging; and all the right, title and interest of the said party of the first part, of, in and to the same, to the intent that the lands hereby conveyed may be discharged from the said mortgage, and that the rest of the lands in the said mortgage specified may remain to the said party of the first part as heretofore. To have and to hold the lands and premises hereby released and conveyed, to the said party of the second part, and his heirs and assigns to his and their only proper use, benefit and behoof forever, free, clear and discharged of and from all lien and claim, under and by virtue of the indenture of mortgage aforesaid.

In Witness Whereof, The said party of the first part has hereunto set his hand and seal on the day of in the year

(*Signature.*) (*Seal.*)

Executed and delivered in presence of

STATE OF }
COUNTY OF } ss.

On the day of in the year one thousand eight hundred and before me personally came who is known to me to be the individual described in, and who executed the foregoing instrument, and acknowledged that he executed the same as his free act and deed.

(*Signature.*)

(157.)

Deed extending a Mortgage.

This Indenture, Made this day of A.D. 18 by and between (*name, residence, and occupation of the mortgagee*) the owner and holder of a certain promissory note (*or bond*) for the principal sum of dollars, given by (*name of mortgagor*) and secured by a mortgage of certain real estate in in the County of and State of dated day A.D. 18 , and recorded in Registry of Deeds, for the County of lib. fol. party of the first part, and the said (*name of mortgagor*) party of the second part,

Witnesseth, That the said parties, for themselves and their representatives, hereby mutually agree that the time for the payment of the principal of said note and mortgage debt shall be and the same is hereby extended for the term of years from the day of A.D. 18 , and that the same is to bear interest from said date at the rate of per cent per annum, payable on the day of and the day of in every year, until said principal sum shall be fully paid.

And the said party of the second part hereby covenants and agrees that he will not require the holders of said note and mortgage to receive payment of said mortgage debt during said extended term; that he will punctually pay the interest now due, and to grow due thereon, at the times and at the rate aforesaid; that he will keep the mortgaged premises in good repair, and insured against fire, and the taxes thereon duly paid, according to the provisions of said mortgage, and that at the expiration of said extended term he will pay the said mortgage debt, with all interest then due thereon.

It is expressly understood and agreed that nothing herein contained shall be construed to impair the security of said party of the first part, or his executors, administrators, or assigns, under said mortgage, or to affect or impair the lien on the real estate therein described which he has by virtue of said mortgage, nor affect or impair any rights or powers which he may have under the said note and mortgage for the recovery of the mortgage debt, with interest, in case of non-fulfilment of this agreement, or of any of the provisions hereof, by said party of the second part.

In Witness Whereof, The said parties have hereunto set their hands and seals the day and year first above written.

(*Signature of mortgagee.*) (*Seal.*)
(*Signature of mortgagor.*) (*Seal.*)

Signed, Sealed and Delivered in Presence of

Commonwealth of ss. 18 . Personally appeared the above-named and acknowledged the above instrument to be their free act and deed.

Before me, (*Signature.*)

CHAPTER XXXI.

LEASES.

A LEASE is a contract whereby one party (the tenant) takes the possession of the land and all that is on it, and the other party (the landlord) gives possession of the land, and reserves (that is, agrees to take) a rent, which the tenant pays him by way of compensation.

All things usually comprehended under the words "house," "farm," "land," "store," &c., pass to the tenant, where such words are used, unless there be an express exception. And inaccuracies as to qualities, names, measurements, or amounts, will be corrected, if there be enough in the lease to make the purposes and intentions of the parties certain. And letting to hire any thing to be used carries with it all those appurtenances and accompaniments necessary for the proper use and enjoyment of the thing which belong to the letter.

A landlord is bound to put his lessee into possession with good title. If he covenants "to renew" generally, this means a renewal of the lease on the same terms, but without inserting in the new lease another covenant of renewal.

A landlord is under no legal obligation to repair the house, unless he expressly agrees to do so. If the house is never so much dilapidated and disfigured as to paper, paint, &c., and locks and blinds and doors and windows are out of order, and the like, the tenant can claim nothing of the landlord. Even if it becomes wholly uninhabitable by no fault of the house or of the landlord, as if it burns up, or is blown down, or if the overflow of a stream ruins a field or a farm, still the landlord is not bound to do any thing, unless by special agreement.

But if the house is uninhabitable by its own fault, as if it has a noisome and unwholesome stench, or, according to one case, if it be overrun with rats, or so decayed as to be open to the weather, it would seem to be the law of this country, that the tenant may leave the house; always provided, however, that the objection or defect be not one which the tenant knew or anticipated, or would have known or expected if he had made reasonable inquiry and investigation before he took his lease. And perhaps no tenant can leave his house, or refuse or abate his rent, for any objection or difficulty arising *after* he hires the house. But, strange to say, the important question what the tenant's rights are in such a case is still uncertain.

If the house be wholly destroyed, the tenant must still pay rent, under an ordinary lease; because the law looks upon the land as the principal thing, and the house as secondary. And not only so, but if the tenant covenants "to return and redeliver the house at the end of the term, in good order and condition, reasonable wear and tear only excepted," he would be bound under this agreement to rebuild the house if it were burned down. But recently all well-drawn leases have clauses providing that the rent shall cease or be abated while the premises are uninhabitable from fire or any other unavoidable calamity. A similar exception is added to the clause about returning the house, at the end of the lease. If this exception be in, a tenant is not bound to rebuild, even if the house be burned through the carelessness of himself or his servants.

A tenant of a room, or of a suite of chambers, is entitled to the use of all the appurtenances and accommodations which fairly go with it, as of the front door and entry, water-closets, and of all windows, &c., proper to the enjoyment of what he hires. But an express agreement about all these things, and cellar-room, pump, and the like, is always safest.

The tenant is not bound to make general repairs without an express agreement. But he must make such as are necessary to preserve the house from injury, as from rain, if shingles or slates are blown off or glass broken. And he would be bound even for ornamental repairs, as paper and paint, under a covenant to return "in good order."

The tenant of a farm is bound, without express covenants, to manage and cultivate the same in such a manner as good husbandry and the usual course of management of such farms in his vicinity would require.

The times for payment of rent are usually specified in the lease; if not, they would be governed by the usage of the country, if there were any of sufficient distinction and force.

A tenant under a lease which says nothing about underletting has a perfect right to underlet, remaining himself bound for his rent to his landlord.

A tenant is not responsible for taxes, unless it is expressly agreed in the lease that he shall be.

If there be a clause prohibiting him from underletting or assigning, and he agrees not to, nevertheless he may do so without forfeiting the land; but he will be, as before, liable for rent; and besides this, he will be responsible in an action for any damages which the landlord can show that he has sustained by such underletting.

It is usual to go further in the lease than this, and provide that such underletting shall make a forfeiture of the lease, and authorize the landlord to enter upon the premises and turn the tenant out. Where there is this covenant, if the tenant now underlets, the landlord cannot avail himself of the clause of forfeiture and afterwards hold the tenant for his rent. He may either hold him for his rent, and also for damages, or he may terminate the lease; but cannot do both. That is, if he continues to hold the tenant responsible for rent, he cannot prevent the tenant's letting somebody else occupy the house and pay to him (the tenant) the rent which he pays over.

A tenant of a farm, if his lease is terminated by any event which was uncertain, and which he could neither foresee nor control, is entitled to the annual crop which he sowed while his interest in and right to the farm continued.

If a lease be for a certain time, the tenant loses all right or interest in the land or premises when that time comes, and he must leave, or the landlord may turn him out at once. But he is a tenant at will, if he holds over after a lease with consent, or occupies the land or house or store without a lease but with consent and an oral bargain; and a tenant at will cannot leave, nor can he be turned out, without a notice to quit. The law on this subject is not uniform. In general, however, it is this. If rent is payable quarterly, or not more frequently, then there must be a quarter's notice. If rent is payable oftener, then the notice must be as long as the period of payment. Thus, if rent is payable monthly, there must be a month's notice; if weekly, a week's notice. But the notice must terminate on a day when the rent is payable. It may be given at any time, but operates only after the required interval or period between two payments. Thus, if a tenant whose lease terminates on the 31st of December holds over by consent, and pays rent quarterly, and the landlord wishes that he should leave the house on the last day of September, he may give notice on the preceding 30th day of June, or any day preceding that. But if he gives notice on any day before the 30th of June, the tenant will still have a right to stay until the 30th of September. Properly, the notice should specify the day, and the right day, when the tenant must leave; and should be in writing.

Where the rent is in arrear, the notice to quit may be more brief; the statutes of the different States vary on this point, but a frequent period is fourteen days. And if notice to quit is given because the rent is unpaid, it may be given at any time, and will operate at the end of the period which the law designates; but it should specify the day on which the tenant must quit.

A tenant may give notice of his intention to quit, and generally it will be subject to the same rules already stated in reference to the notice given by a landlord. A tenant should give his notice to the party to whom he is bound to pay rent, or to an authorized agent of that party.

Fixtures.

It is quite important that both tenant and landlord should have some knowledge of the law of fixtures; for this tells them what things the tenant may take away and what he cannot. For there are many things which a tenant may add, and afterwards remove, and many which he cannot remove. The method of affixing them may be a useful criterion, as it indicates the purpose of removal or otherwise. If with screws, or in such a way as to show that removal was intended, things may be taken away, when, if the same things were fastened more permanently, they could not be. In modern times the rule in favor of the tenant seems to extend as far as this: whatever he has added, and can remove, leaving the premises entirely restored and in as good order as if he had not removed it, that he may take away. Among the things held to be removable, in different adjudged cases, are these: ornamental chimney-pieces; coffee-mills; cornices screwed on; furnaces; fire-frames; stoves; iron backs to chimneys; looking-glasses; pumps; gates; rails and posts; barns or stables on blocks.

Among those held not removable are these: barns fixed in the ground; benches fastened to the house; trees, plants, and hedges, not belonging to a gardener by trade; conservatory strongly affixed; glass windows; locks and keys.

But almost every one of these might be removable, or not, according to the intent of the parties, and the rule above stated, of removableness with or without injury.

If a man sells a house, the law of fixtures is construed far more severely against him than against a tenant who leaves a house; that is, the seller must permit the buyer to hold a great many things which an outgoing tenant might remove. Of course, a seller may take what he will from his house before he sells it, or make what bargain the parties choose to make about the fixtures. But if he makes no such bargain, and sells the house, he cannot then take from the house what a tenant who put them there might take.

In favor of trade and manufactures, the law permits almost any thing which was put in by a tenant for such purposes to be taken away, if the premises can be restored substantially to their original condition.

The remarks in respect to the variety of forms which will be found at the close of the chapter on deeds of land, are equally applicable to forms of leases, and should be read in connection with the following forms.

(158.)

A Short Form of a Lease.

This Indenture, Made the day of in the year of our Lord one thousand eight hundred and sixty-

Witnesseth, That I, (*name and residence of the lessor*) do hereby lease, demise, and let unto (*name and residence of lessee*) a certain parcel of land, in the city (or town) of County of and State of with all the buildings thereon standing, and the appurtenances to the same belonging, bounded and described as follows (*or, a certain house in said city, giving the street and number, with the land under and adjoining the same*)

(*The premises need not be described quite so minutely or fully as is proper in a deed or mortgage of land, but must be so described as to identify them perfectly, and make it certain just what premises are leased.*)

To Hold for the term of from the day of yielding and paying therefor the rent of

And said lessee does promise to pay the said rent in four quarterly payments, on the day of , (*or state otherwise just when the payments of rent are to be made*) and to quit and deliver up the premises to the lessor or his attorney, peaceably and quietly, at the end of the term, in as good order and condition, reasonable use and wearing thereof, fire and other unavoidable casualties excepted, as the same now are or may be put into by the said lessor, and to pay the rent as above stated, and all taxes and duties levied or to be levied thereon, during the term, and also the rent and taxes, as above stated, for such further time as the lessee may hold the same, and not make or suffer any waste thereof; nor lease, nor underlet, nor permit any other person or persons to occupy or improve the same, or make or suffer to be made any alteration therein but with the approbation of the lessor thereto, in writing, having been first obtained; and that the lessor may enter to view, and make improvements, and to expel the lessee, if he shall fail to pay the rent and taxes as aforesaid, or make or suffer any strip or waste thereof.

In Witness Whereof, The said parties have hereunto interchangeably set their hands and seals the day and year first above written.

(*Signature.*) (*Seal.*)
(*Signature.*) (*Seal.*)

Signed, Sealed and Delivered in Presence of

(159.)

A fuller Form, with a Provision for Abatement of Rent.

This Indenture, Made this day of in the year of our Lord one thousand eight hundred and by and between (*name and residence of lessor*) and (*name and residence of lessee*)

Witnesseth, That the said (*name of lessor*) does hereby lease, demise, and let unto the said (*name of lessee*) (*describe the premises as directed in Form* 158, *leases*)

To Hold for the term of commencing the day of A.D. one thousand eight hundred and the said lessee or those claiming under him, yielding and paying rent therefor, the sum of for each and every year, and after the same rate for any part of a year.

And the said lessee for himself, his heirs, executors and administrators, does hereby covenant to and with the said lessor, and his heirs and assigns, that he or they will pay the said rent of in equal sums of the first of which payments shall be made on the day of A.D. one thousand eight hundred and and that he or they will pay rent after the same rate for such further time as he the said lessee, or those claiming under him, may hold the premises; that he or they will from time to time, upon request by the lessor, or his heirs or assigns, pay to them such sum or sums of money as shall be equal to the amount of the taxes and duties, and water-taxes, that shall be levied or assessed on the demised premises for each year and part of a year during the term aforesaid, and during such further time as the said lessee and those claiming under him may hold the premises; that he or they will not suffer nor commit any strip or waste in the premises; that he or they will not assign this lease, nor underlet the whole or any part of the premises, to any person or persons; and that no alterations or additions shall be made during the term aforesaid, in or to the same, without the consent of the said lessor, or of those having his estate in the premises, being first obtained in writing, allowing thereof; and also that it shall be lawful for the said lessor, and those having his estate in the premises, at seasonable times to enter into and upon the same to examine the condition thereof; and further, that he the said lessee, and his representatives, shall and will, at the expiration of said term, peaceably yield up unto the said lessor, or those having his estate therein, all and singular the premises, and all future erections and additions to or upon the same, in as good order and condition, in all respects, (reasonable wearing and use thereof, and damage by fire, and other unavoidable casualties excepted) as the same now are, or may be put into by the said lessor or those having his estate in the premises.

Provided always, and these presents are upon this condition, that if the said rent shall be in arrear, or the said lessee or his representatives or assigns do or shall neglect or fail to perform and observe any or either of the above covenants hereinbefore contained, which on his or their part are to be performed, then and in either of said cases, the said lessor or those having his estate in the said premises, lawfully may, immediately or at any time thereafter, and while such neglect or default continues, and without further notice or demand, enter into and upon the said premises, or any part thereof, in the name of the whole, and repossess the same as of his former estate, and expel the said lessee and those claiming under him, and remove his or their effects (forcibly if necessary) without being taken or deemed guilty of any manner of trespass, and without prejudice to any remedies which might otherwise be used for arrears of rent, or preceding breach of covenant.

And Provided also, that in case the premises, or any part thereof, shall, during said term, be destroyed or damaged by fire or other unavoidable casualty, so that the same shall be thereby rendered unfit for use and habitation, then, and in such case, the rent hereinbefore reserved, or a just and proportionate part thereof, according to the nature and extent of the injuries sustained, shall be sus-

35

pended or abated until the said premises shall have been put in proper condition for use and habitation by the said lessor, or these presents shall thereby be determined and ended at the election of the said lessor or his legal representatives.

In Testimony Whereof, the said parties have set their hands and seals, on the day and year first above written, to this and to another instrument of like tenor and date.

(Signature.) *(Seal.)*
(Signature.) *(Seal.)*

Signed, Sealed and Delivered in Presence of

(160.)

A Short Form of Lease, in Use in the Western States.

This Indenture, Made this day of , 186 between *(name and residence of the lessor)* party of the first part, and *(name and residence of the lessee)* party of the second part, witnesseth, that the said party of the first part, in consideration of the covenants of the said party of the second part, hereinafter set forth, do by these presents lease to the said party of the second part the following-described property, to wit (*describe the property as directed in Form* 158.)

To Have and to Hold the same to the said party of the second part, from the day of 186 , to the day of 186 , And the said party of the second part, in consideration of the leasing the premises as above set forth, covenants and agrees with the party of the first part to pay the said party of the first part, as rent for the same, the sum of dollars, payable as follows, to wit (*here state the times and terms of payment, much as in Form* 158.)

The said party of the second part further covenants with the said party of the first part, that at the expiration of the time mentioned in this lease, peaceable possession of the said premises shall be given to said party of the first part, in as good condition as they now are, the usual wear, inevitable accidents, and loss by fire excepted; and that upon the non-payment of the whole or any portion of the said rent at the time when the same is above promised to be paid, the said party of the first part may, at his election, either distrain for said rent due, or declare this lease at an end, and recover possession as if the same was held by forcible detainer: the said party of the second part hereby waiving any notice of such election, or any demand for the possession of said premises.

The covenants herein shall extend to and be binding upon the heirs, executors, and administrators of the parties to this lease.

Witness the hands and seals of the parties aforesaid.

(Signature of lessor.) *(Seal.)*
(Signature of lessee.) *(Seal.)*

(161.)

A Lease of City Property, in Use in Chicago.

This Indenture, Made this day of in the year of our Lord one thousand eight hundred and sixty between (*name of the lessor*) of the city of in the County of and State of party of the first part, and (*name and residence of the lessee*) of the second part,

Witnesseth, That the said party of the first part, for and in consideration of the covenants and agreements hereinafter mentioned, to be kept and performed by the said party of the second part, or his executors, administrators and assigns, has demised and leased to the said party of the second part all those premises situate, lying and being in the city of Chicago, in the County of Cook, and State of Illinois, and known and described as follows, to wit (*here describe the premises as directed in Form* 158)

To Have and to Hold The said above-described premises, with the appurtenances, unto the said party of the second part, and his executors, administrators, and assigns, from the day of in the year of our Lord one thousand eight hundred and sixty for and during, and until the day of in the year of our Lord one thousand eight hundred and the said party of the second part paying rent therefor, as hereinafter stated.

And the said party of the second part, in consideration of the leasing the premises aforesaid, by the said party of the first part, to the said party of the second part, does covenant and agree with the said party of the first part, and his heirs, executors, administrators, and assigns, to pay the said party of the first part, at the house (*or office or store*) of the said party of the first part, numbered in Street, Chicago, or at the house or office of his assigns, as rent for the said demised premises, the sum of (*state the whole annual rent*) payable as follows (*here state the times and terms of the payments of rent*)

And it is further agreed by the said party of the second part, in consideration of the leasing of the premises, that the said party of the second part shall and will pay, or cause to be paid, promptly, as soon as the same becomes due, all assessments for water-rents that may be levied upon said demised premises, during the continuance of this lease, by the Board of Water Commissioners of the city of Chicago, and save the said premises and the said party of the first part harmless therefrom, and that he will keep said premises in a clean and healthy condition, in accordance with the ordinances of the city and the direction of the Sewerage Commissioners.

And the said party of the second part hereby covenants and agrees, in case of delay in payment of any water-rent levied upon said premises during said term, to pay said party of the first part, as liquidated damages for such breach of covenant, double the sum of such rent so assessed upon said premises as aforesaid.

And the said party of the second part further covenants with the said party of the first part, that at the expiration of the time in this lease mentioned, he will yield up the said demised premises to the said party of the first part, in as good condition as when the same were entered upon by the said party of the second part, loss by fire or inevitable accident, and ordinary wear excepted.

It is further agreed by the said party of the second part, that neither he nor his legal representatives will underlet said premises, or any part thereof, or assign this lease, without the written assent of said party of the first part, first had and obtained thereto.

It is Expressly Understood and Agreed, By and between the parties aforesaid, that if the rent above reserved, or any part thereof, shall be behind or unpaid on the day and at the place of payment whereon the same ought to be paid, as aforesaid, or if default shall be made in any of the covenants herein contained, to be kept by the said party of the second part, or his executors, administrators, and assigns, it shall and may be lawful for the said party of the first part, or his heirs, executors, administrators, agent, attorney, or assigns, at his or their election, to declare said term ended, and the said demised premises, or any part thereof, either with or without process of law, to re-enter, and the said party of the second part, or any other person or persons occupying, in or upon the same, to expel, remove, and put out, using such force as may be necessary in so doing, and the said premises again to repossess and enjoy as in his or their first and former estate; and it shall be the duty of the said party of the second part, his executors, administrators, or assigns, to be and appear at the said place above specified for the payment of said rent, and then and there tender and pay the same as the same shall fall due from time to time, as above, to the said party of the first part, or his agent or assigns; or in his or their absence, if the party of the second part or his legal representatives shall offer to pay the same then and there, such offer shall prevent such forfeiture.

And it is expressly understood that it shall not be necessary in any event for the party of the first part, or his assigns, to go on or near the said demised premises to demand said rent, or elsewhere than at the place aforesaid. And in the event of any rent being due and unpaid, whether before or after such forfeiture declared, to distrain for any rent that may be due thereon, upon any property belonging to the said party of the second part, whether the same be exempt from execution or distress by law or not, and the said party of the second part, in that case, hereby waives all legal rights which he may have to hold or retain any such property, under any exemption laws now in force in this State, or in any other way. Meaning and intending hereby to give to the said party of the first part, and his heirs, executors, administrators, and assigns, a valid and first lien upon any and all the goods, chattels, or other property belonging to the said party of the second part, as security for the payment of said rent, in manner aforesaid, any thing hereinbefore contained to the contrary notwithstanding. And if at any time said term shall be ended at such election of said party of the first part, or his heirs, executors, administrators, or assigns, as aforesaid, or in any other way, the said party of the second part, for himself and his executors, administrators, and assigns, does hereby covenant, promise and agree to surrender and deliver up said above-described premises and property, peaceably to the said party of the first part, or his heirs, executors, administrators, and assigns, immediately upon the determination of said term as aforesaid; and, if he shall remain in the possession of the same days after notice of such default, or after the termination of this lease, in any of the ways above named, he shall be deemed guilty of a forcible detainer of said demised premises under the statute, and shall be subject to all the conditions and provisions above named, and to eviction and removal, forcibly or otherwise, with or without process of law, as above stated; and in order to enforce a forfeiture of this lease for non-payment of rent when due, no demand for rent when due shall be required, any demand being hereby expressly waived.

And it is further covenanted and agreed by and between the parties, that the party of the second part shall pay and discharge all costs and attorney's fees and expenses that shall arise from enforcing the covenants of this indenture by the party of the first part.

In Testimony Whereof, The said parties have hereunto set their hands and seals the day and year first above written.

(*Signature of lessor.*) (*Seal.*)
(*Signature of lessee.*) (*Seal.*)

In Presence of

(162.)

A Lease, with Provisions for Taxes and Assessments.

This Indenture, Made the day of in the year one thousand eight hundred and between (*name and residence of lessor*) of the first part, and (*name and residence of lessee*) of the second part, witnesseth, that the said party of the first part, for and in consideration of the rents, covenants, and agreements hereinafter mentioned, reserved, and contained, on the part and behalf of the said party of the second part, his executors, administrators, and assigns, to be paid, kept, and performed, has granted, demised, and to farm letten, and by these presents does grant, demise, and to farm let, unto the said party of the second part, and his executors, administrators, and assigns, all (*describe the premises as in Form* 158)

To Have and to Hold the said above mentioned and described premises, with the appurtenances, unto the said party of the second part, his executors, administrators, and assigns, from the day of one thousand eight hundred and for and during, and until the full end and term of thence next ensuing: and fully to be complete and ended, yielding and paying therefor unto the said party of the first part, his heirs or assigns, yearly, and every year during the said term hereby granted, the yearly rent or sum of lawful money of the United States of America, in equal quarter-yearly payments, to wit: on the first day of (*name *the months*) in each and every of the said years: provided always nevertheless, that if the yearly rent above reserved, or any part thereof, shall be behind or unpaid on any day of payment whereon the same ought to be paid as aforesaid; or if default shall be made in any of the covenants herein contained, on the part and behalf of the said party of the second part, his executors, administrators, and assigns, to be paid, kept, and performed, then and from thenceforth it shall and may be lawful for the said party of the first part, his heirs or assigns, into and upon the said demised premises, and every part thereof, wholly to re-enter and remove all persons therefrom, and the same to have again, repossess, and enjoy, as in his or their first and former estate, any thing hereinbefore contained to the contrary thereof in any wise notwithstanding. And the said party of the second part, for himself and his heirs, executors, and administrators, does covenant and agree, to and with the said party of the first part, his heirs and assigns, by these presents, that the said party of the second part, his executors, administrators, or assigns, shall and will yearly, and every year during the said term hereby granted, well and truly pay, or cause to be paid, unto the said party of the first part, his heirs or assigns, the said yearly rent above reserved, on the days and in manner limited and prescribed as aforesaid, for the payment thereof, without any deduction, fraud, or delay, according to the true intent and meaning of these presents. And that the said party of the second part, his executors, administrators, or assigns, shall and will, at their own proper costs and charges, bear, pay, and discharge all such taxes, duties, and assessments whatsoever, as shall or may, during the said term hereby granted, be charged, assessed, or imposed upon the said demised premises.

And that on the last day of the said term, or other sooner determination of the estate hereby granted, the said party of the second part, his executors, administrators, or assigns, shall and will peaceably and quietly leave, surrender and yield up unto the said party of the first part, his heirs or assigns, all and singular the said demised premises.

And the said party of the first part, for himself and his heirs, executors, and administrators, does covenant and agree to and with the said party of the second part, his executors, administrators, and assigns, by these presents, that the said party of the second part, executors, administrators, or assigns, paying the said yearly rent above reserved, and performing the covenants and agreements aforesaid on his and their part, the said party of the second part, his executors, administrators, and assigns, shall and may at all times during the said term hereby granted, peaceably and quietly have, hold and enjoy the said demised premises, without any manner of let, suit, trouble or hinderance of or from the said party of the first part, his heirs or assigns, or any other person or persons whomsoever.

In Witness Whereof, the said have hereunto set their hands and seals, interchangeably, to two copies of this indenture.

(*Signature of lessor.*) (*Seal.*)
(*Signature of lessee.*) (*Seal.*)

In Presence of

(163.)

A Lease, With Covenants about Water-Rate, and Injury by Fire, in Use in New York.

This Agreement, Made between (*name and residence of lessor*) party of the first part, and (*name and residence of lessee*) party of the second part, witnesseth, that the said party of the first part has agreed to let, and hereby does let, and the said party of the second part has agreed to take, and hereby does take, the following-described premises (*here describe the premises, as in Form* 158) for the term of to commence and to end to be occupied (*describe the intended occupation*) and not otherwise. And the said party of the second part hereby covenants and agrees to pay unto the said party of the first part the annual rent or sum of dollars, payable (*state the times and terms of the payments*)

And shall also pay the Croton water-rate, and will keep the plumbing work, pipes, glass, and the premises generally in repair, and will surrender them at the expiration of the said term, in as good state and condition as reasonable use and wear thereof will permit.

And the said party of the second part further covenants that he will not assign, let, or underlet the whole or any part of the said premises, nor make any alteration therein without the written consent of the said party of the first part, under the penalty of forfeiture and damages; and that he will not occupy the said premises, nor permit the same to be occupied for any business deemed extra-hazardous without the like consent, under the like penalty. And the said party of the second part further covenants that he will permit the said party of the first part, or his agent, to show the premises to persons wishing to hire or purchase, and three months next preceding the expiration of the term will permit the usual notices of "to let," or "for sale," to be placed upon the windows, walls, or doors of said premises, and remain thereon without hinderance or molestation.

And also, that if default be made in any of the covenants herein contained on the part of the party of the second part, or if the said premises or any part thereof shall become vacant during the said term, the said party of the first part may re-enter the same, either by force or otherwise, without being liable to any prosecution therefor; and re-let the said premises or any part thereof in one or more parcels, as the agent of the said party of the second part, and receive the rent thereof, applying the same, first to the payment of such expense as he may be put to in re-entering, and then to the payment of the rent due by these presents; and the balance (if any) to be paid over to the said party of the second part; and, in case of deficiency, said party of the second part will pay the same.

And the said party of the second part hereby further covenants that if any default be made in the payment of the said rent or any part thereof, at the times above specified, or if default be made in the performance of any of the covenants or agreements herein contained, the said hiring, and the relation of landlord and tenant, at the option of the said party of the first part, shall wholly cease and determine; and the said party of the first part shall and may re-enter the said premises, and remove all persons therefrom; and the said party of the second part hereby expressly waive, the service of any notice in writing of intention to re-enter, as provided for in the third section of an act entitled "An Act to abolish Distress for Rent, and for other Purposes," passed May 13, 1846.

And it is further agreed between the parties to these presents, that, in case the building hereby leased shall be partially damaged by fire, the same shall be repaired as speedily as possible by the party of the first part; that, in case the damage shall be so extensive as to render the building untenantable, the rent shall cease until the same be repaired; provided the damage be not caused by the carelessness or negligence of the party of the second part, or his agents or servants.

If the building be so damaged that the owner shall decide to rebuild, the term shall cease, the premises be surrendered, and the accrued rent be paid up to the time of the fire.

In consideration of the letting of the premises above mentioned to the above named (*name of the lessee*) and of the sum of one dollar to him paid by the said party of the first part, the said party of the second part does hereby covenant and agree to and with the party of the first part above named, and his legal representatives, that if default shall at any time be made by the said party of the second part, in the payment of the rent and performance of the covenants above contained on his part to be paid and performed, that he will well and truly pay the said rent or any arrears thereof, that may remain due unto the said party of the first part and also all damages that may arise in consequence of the non-performance of said covenants, or either of them, without requiring notice of any such default from the said party of the first part.

Witness our hands and seals this day of in the year of our Lord one thousand eight hundred and

(*Witness.*)

(*Signature of lessor.*) (*Seal.*)
(*Signature of lessee.*) (*Seal.*)

(164.)

A Lease by Grant, in Use in the Western States.

This Indenture, Made and entered into on the day of one thousand eight hundred and sixty- by and between (*name of lessor*) of (*residence of lessor*) party of the first part, and (*name of lessee*) of (*residence of lessee*) party of the second part, witnesseth, That the said party of the first part, in consideration of the rents reserved, and the covenants hereinafter contained, does hereby grant, demise, and to farm let, unto the said party of the second part (*describe the premises as in Form* 158)

To Have and to Hold the Same, With all the rights, immunities, privileges and appurtenances thereto belonging, unto the said party of the second part, and his executors, administrators and assigns, for and during the full end and term of commencing on the day of 186 , and ending on the day of 186 , under and subject to the stipulations hereinafter contained, the said party of the second part yielding and paying to the said part of the first part, for the said premises, the annual rent of payable in equal quarterly (*or monthly*) payments; that is to say on the during said term; which rent the said party of the second part, for himself and his executors, administrators and assigns, covenants well and truly to pay, at the times aforesaid.

And the said party of the second part covenants and agrees that if the rent aforesaid should at any time remain due and unpaid, the same shall bear interest at the rate of per cent per annum, from the time it so becomes due, until paid. And the said party of the second part further covenants and agrees that it shall be lawful for the said party of the first part, and those having freehold estate in the premises, at reasonable terms, to enter into and upon the same, to examine the condition thereof; and also that the said party of the second part and his legal representatives shall and will, at the expiration of this lease, whether by limitation or forfeiture, peaceably yield up to the said party of the first part, or his legal representatives, the said premises, in the condition received, only excepting natural wear and decay, and the effects of fire; and that the said party of the second part, for and during all the time that he or any one else in his name, shall hold over the premises after the expiration of this lease, in either of said ways, shall and will pay to said party of the first part double the rent hereinbefore reserved. Also the said party of the second part further covenants and agrees that any failure to pay the rent hereinbefore reserved, when due and within days after a demand of the same, shall produce an absolute forfeiture of this lease, if so determined by said party of the first part, or his legal representatives. Also that this lease shall not be assigned, nor the said premises, or any part thereof, underlet, without the written consent of the said party of the first part, or his legal representatives, under penalty of forfeiture. And that all repairs of a temporary character, deemed necessary by said party of the second part, shall be made at his own expense, with the consent of the said party of the first part, or his legal representatives, and not otherwise.

Provided Always, And these presents are on this express condition, that if the said party of the second part, or his legal representatives, shall fail to pay the rent hereinbefore reserved, for the space of days after the same shall have become due, or shall fail to perform any of the covenants hereinbefore entered into on h's and their part, then the said party of the first part shall be at liberty to declare this lease forfeited, by serving a written notice to that effect on the said party of the second part, or his legal representatives, and to re-enter upon and take possession of the demised premises, free from any claim of the lessee or any one claiming under him. And all estate herein granted shall, upon service of such notice, forthwith cease, and said lessor, his heirs, legal representatives or assigns, shall be forthwith entitled to the possession of the demised premises without any further proceeding at law or otherwise, to recover possession thereof. And the said party of the first part covenants and agrees with the said party of the second part, and his legal representatives, that, the covenants herein contained being faithfully performed by the said party of the second part, he shall peaceably hold and enjoy the said demised premises, during the term aforesaid, without hinderance or interruption by the said lessor or any other person.

In Witness Whereof, The said parties have executed this indenture in duplicate, signing their names and affixing their seals to both parts thereof, the day and year in this behalf above written.

(*Signature of lessor.*) (*Seal.*)
(*Signature of lessee.*) (*Seal.*)

In Presence of

(165.)

A Lease by Certificate, with Surety.

This is to Certify, That I have let and rented unto (*name of lessee*) (*describe the premises, as in Form* 158) for the term of from the day of 18 at the annual rent of dollars, payable (*state the times of payment*). The premises above mentioned, or any part thereof, shall not be let or underlet without the written consent of the landlord, under penalty of forfeiture and damages; nor shall the same be used or occupied for any business deemed extra hazardous on account of fire, without the like consent under the like penalty.

Given under my hand and seal the day of 18

(*Signature.*) (*Seal.*)

(*Witnesses.*)

This is to Certify, That I have hired and taken from (*name of lessor*) (*describe the premises in the same way as in the preceding part*) for the term of from the day of 18 at the rent of dollars, payable And I hereby promise to make punctual payment of the rent in manner aforesaid, and to quit and surrender the premises, at the expiration of said term, in as good state and condition as reasonable use and wear thereof will permit, damages by the elements excepted, and engage not to let or underlet the whole or any part of the said premises, without the written consent of the landlord, under the penalty of forfeiture and damages; and also not to use or occupy the said premises for any business deemed extra hazardous, on account of fire, without the like consent, under the like penalty.

Given under my hand and seal the day of 18

(*Signature.*) (*Seal.*)

(*Witnesses.*)

In Consideration of the letting of the premises above described, and for the sum of one dollar, I do hereby become surety for the punctual payment of the rent, and performance of the covenants, in the above-written agreement mentioned, to be paid and performed by (*name of lessee*) and if any default shall be made therein, I do hereby promise and agree to pay unto (*name of lessor*) such sum or sums of money as will be sufficient to make up such deficiency, and fully satisfy the conditions of the said agreement, without requiring any notice of non-payment, or proof of demand being made.

Given under my hand and seal the day of 18

(*Signature.*) (*Seal.*)

(*Witnesses.*)

(166.)

A Lease of City Property, in Use in St. Louis.

This Indenture, Made the day of in the year of our Lord eighteen hundred and sixty- between (*name and residence of the lessor*) of the first part, and (*name and residence of lessee*) of the second part, witnesseth, That the said party of the first part, in consideration of the rents, covenants and stipulations hereinafter mentioned, and hereby agreed to be paid, kept and performed by the said party of the second part, his executors, administrators and assigns, hath leased, and by these presents doth lease, to the said party of the second part the following-described premises (*here describe the house, as of brick, or stone, number of stories, and number in the block*) in block No. in the city of St. Louis, to commence on the day of , 186 for and during the term of at the annual rent of payable in four equal quarterly payments, beginning three months from the date hereof. Any failure to pay each payment of rent when due, to produce a forfeiture of this lease, if so determined by said lessor or his successors. The lease of said tenement or any part of it is not assignable, nor is said tenement or any part of it to be underlet, without the written consent of said lessor, under penalty of forfeiture. And it is hereby covenanted, that, at the expiration of this lease, the said tenement and premises are to be surrendered to said lessor, his heirs, assigns, or successors, in the condition received, only excepting its natural wear and decay, or the effects of accidental fire. All repairs deemed necessary by said lessee to be made at his expense. All fixtures shall be bound for the rent.

The said lessee and all holding under him hereby engaging to pay the rent above reserved, and double rent for every day when he or any one else in his name shall hold on to the whole or any part of said tenement, after the expiration of this lease, or of its forfeiture for non-payment of rent, &c. This tenement and premises to be kept free of any nuisance in or adjacent thereto, at the expense of the said lessee.

(*Signature of lessor.*) (*Seal.*)
(*Signature of lessee.*) (*Seal.*)

(*Witness.*)

(167.)

What is called a Country Lease, in Use in the Western States.

This Indenture, Made this day of in the year of our Lord one thousand eight hundred and between (*name of lessor*) of the of in the County of and State of party of the first part, and (*name and residence of lessee*) party of the second part, witnesseth, That the said party of the first part for and in consideration of the covenants and agreements hereinafter mentioned, to be kept and performed by the said party of the second part, his executors, administrators, and assigns, has demised and leased to the said party of the second part all those premises situate, lying and being in the township of County of State of known and described as follows, to wit (*describe the premises in such way as to identify them perfectly by situation, metes, and bounds, or otherwise*)

To Have and to Hold the said above-described premises, with the appurtenances, unto the said party of the second part, and his executors, administrators, and assigns, from the day of in the year of our Lord one thousand eight hundred and for and during, and until the day of in the year of our Lord one thousand eight hundred and paying rent therefor as hereafter stated.

And the said party of the second part, in consideration of the leasing of the premises aforesaid, by the said party of the first part, to the said party of the second part, does covenant and agree with the said party of the first part, and his heirs, executors, administrators, and assigns, to pay the said party of the first part, as rent for the said demised premises, the sum of dollars, annual rent, payable quarterly, in four equal quarterly payments, the first payment to be due and made in three months from the date of this lease, payable at the (*here state the place where the rent should be paid*)

And the said party of the second part further covenants with the said party of the first part, that at the expiration of the time in this lease mentioned, he will yield up the said demised premises to the said party of the first part, in as good condition as when the same were entered upon by the said party of the second part, loss by fire or inevitable accident, and ordinary wear excepted.

It is further agreed by the said party of the second part, that neither he nor his legal representatives will underlet said premises, or any part thereof, or assign this lease, without the written assent of said party of the first part, first had and obtained thereto.

It is Expressly Understood and Agreed by and between the parties aforesaid, that if the rent above reserved, or any part thereof, shall be behind or unpaid, on the day and at the place of payment, whereon the same ought to be paid, as aforesaid, or if default shall be made in any of the covenants herein contained, to be kept by the said party of the second part, his executors, administrators, and assigns, it shall and may be lawful for the said party of the first part, his heirs, executors, administrators, agent, attorney, or assigns, at his or their election, to declare said term ended, and the said demised premises, or any part thereof, either with or without process of law, to re-enter, and the said party of the second part, or any other person or persons occupying, in or upon the same, to expel, remove, and put out, using such force as may be necessary in so doing, and the said premises again to repossess and enjoy, as in his or their first and former estate; and it shall be the duty of the said party of the second part, his executors, administrators, or assigns, to be and appear at the said place above specified, for the payment of said rent, and then and there tender and pay the same as the same shall fall due from time to time, as above, to the said party of the first part, or his agent or assigns; or in his or their absence, if the said party of the second part shall offer to pay the same then and there, such offer shall prevent said forfeiture.

And it is expressly understood that it shall not be necessary in any event for the party of the first part or his assigns, to go on or near the said demised premises to demand said rent, or elsewhere than at the place aforesaid. And in the event of any rent being due and unpaid, whether before or after such forfeiture declared, to distrain for any rent that may be due thereon, upon any property belonging to the said party of the second part, whether the same be exempt from execution or distress by law or not, and the said party of the second part, in that case, hereby waives all legal rights which he now has or may have to hold or retain any such property, under any exemption laws now in force in this State, or in any other way. Meaning and intending hereby to give to the said party of the first part and his heirs, executors, administrators, and assigns, a valid and first lien upon any and all the goods, chattels, or other property belonging to the said party of the second part, as security for the payment of said rent in manner aforesaid, any thing hereinbefore contained to the contrary notwithstanding. And if at any time said term shall be ended at such election of said party of the first part, or his heirs, executors, administrators, or assigns, as aforesaid, or in any other way, the said party of the second part, for himself and his executors, administrators, and assigns, does hereby covenant, promise, and agree to surrender and deliver up said above-described premises and property, peaceably, to said party of the first part, or his heirs, executors, administrators, and assigns, immediately upon the determination of said term as aforesaid; and if he shall remain in the possession of the same days after notice of such default, or after the termination of this lease, in any of the ways above named, he shall be deemed guilty of a forcible detainer of said demised premises, and shall be subject to all the conditions and provisions above named, and to eviction and removal, forcibly or otherwise, with or without process of law, as above stated.

And it is further covenanted and agreed by and between the parties, that the party of the second part shall pay and discharge all costs and attorney's fees and expenses that shall arise from enforcing the covenants of this indenture by the party of the first part.

In Testimony Whereof, The said parties have hereunto set their hands and seals the day and year first above written.

(*Signature of lessor.*) (*Seal.*)
(*Signature of lessee.*) (*Seal.*)

In Presence of

(168.)

A Ground Lease.

This Indenture, Made this day of in the year of our Lord one thousand eight hundred and sixty between (*name and residence of lessor*) party of the first part, and (*name and residence of lessee*) party of the second part, witnesseth, That the said party of the first part, for and in consideration of the covenants and agreements hereinafter mentioned, to be kept and performed by the party of the second part, hath demised and leased to the party of the second part all those premises situate in the of in the County of and State of known and described as follows, to wit (*here give such description of the premises as shall identify them, and distinguish them from any other*)

To Have and to Hold The above-described premises, with the appurtenances, unto the party of the second part, from the day of in the year of our Lord one thousand eight hundred and for and during, and until the

And the party of the second part, in consideration of the leasing of the premises aforesaid, does covenant and agree with the party of the first part to pay to the party of the first part as rent for said demised premises, at the office of in the sum of (*state the sum to be paid as annual rent*) in four equal quarterly payments, each of them the sum of dollars, to be paid on the first (*or other*) day of the months of (*the four months in which the rent is payable*) in each year (*or describe otherwise the terms and times of the payments as they may have been agreed upon*); and also that the said party of the second part will pay, or cause to be paid, all water-rates, and all taxes and assessments that may be laid, charged or assessed on said demised premises, pending the existence of this lease; or if at any time after any tax, assessment, or water-rate shall have become due or payable, the party of the second part, or his legal representatives, shall neglect to pay such water-rates, tax, or assessment, it may be lawful for the party of the first part to pay the same at any time thereafter, and the amount of any and all such payments so made by the party of the first part shall be deemed and taken, and are hereby declared to be, so much additional and further rent, for the above-demised premises, due from and payable by the party of the second part; and may be collected in the same manner, by distress or otherwise, as is hereinafter provided for the collection of other rents to grow due thereon.

And it is expressly understood and agreed by the said party of the second part hereto, for himself and his heirs, executors, administrators, and assigns, that the whole amount of rent reserved, and agreed to be paid for said above-demised premises, and each and every instalment thereof, shall be and is hereby declared to be a valid and first lien upon any and all buildings and improvements on said premises, or that may at any time be erected, placed, or put on said premises by said party of the second part, or his heirs, executors, and administrators, or assigns, and upon his or their interest, in this lease, and the premises hereby demised; and that whenever, and as often as any instalment of rent or any other amount above declared to be deemed and taken as rent, shall become due and remain unpaid for one day after the same becomes due and payable, said party of the first part, his heirs, executors, administrators, agent, attorney, or assigns, may sell at public auction to the highest bidder for cash, after having first given ten days' notice of the time and place of such sale in some newspaper published in all the buildings and improvements on said premises, and all the right, title, and interest acquired by said party of the second part, under this lease, to the premises herein described, and as the attorney of said party of the second part — hereby irrevocably constituted — may make to the purchaser or purchasers thereof a suitable and proper transfer bill of sale or deed of the same — and out of the proceeds arising from such sale, after first paying all costs and expenses of such sale, including commissions and attorney's fees — retain to himself the whole amount due on said lease, up to the date of said sale, rendering the surplus (if any) to said party of the second part, his heirs, executors, administrators, agent, attorney, or assigns, which sale shall be a perpetual bar to and against all rights and equities of said party of the second part, his heirs and assigns in and to the property sold.

And the party of the second part further covenants with the party of the first part, that, at the expiration of the time in this lease mentioned, he will yield up said demised premises to the party of the first part, in as good condition as when the same were entered upon by the party of the second part, loss by fire, or inevitable accident and ordinary wear excepted.

It is further agreed, by the party of the second part, that neither he nor his legal representatives will underlet said premises, or any part thereof, or assign this lease, without the written assent of said party of the first part, first had and obtained thereunto, nor use or suffer them to be used for any purpose calculated to injure the reputation of the premises, or of the neighborhood, or to impair the value of the surrounding neighborhood property for present use or otherwise.

It is Expressly Understood and Agreed, By and between the parties aforesaid, that if the rent above reserved, or any part thereof, shall be behind or unpaid, on the day of payment, whereon the same ought to be paid, as aforesaid, or if default shall be made in any of the covenants herein contained to be kept by the party of the second part, his executors, administrators, or assigns, it shall and may be lawful for the party of the first part, or his heirs, executors, administrators, agent, attorney, or assigns, at his or their election, to declare said term ended, and into the said demised premises, or any part thereof, either with or without process of law, to re-enter, and the party of the second part or any other person or persons occupying, in or upon the same, to expel, remove, and put out, using such force as may be necessary in so doing, and the said premises again to repossess and enjoy, as of his or their first and former estate; and to distrain for any rent that may be due thereon, upon any property belonging to the party of the second part, whether the same be exempt from execution and distress by law or not; and the party of the second part, in that case, hereby waives all legal rights which he now has, or may have, to hold or retain any such property under any exemption laws now in force in this State, or in any other way; meaning and intending hereby to give the party of the first part, his heirs, executors, administrators, agent, attorney, or assigns, a valid and first lien, upon any and all the goods, chattels, or other property belonging to the party of the second part, as security for the payment of said rent, in manner aforesaid, any thing hereinbefore contained to the contrary notwithstanding. And if at any time said term shall be ended at such election of said party of the first part, or his heirs, executors, administrators, agent, attorney, or assigns, as aforesaid, or in any other way, the party of the second part does hereby covenant and agree to surrender and deliver up said above-described premises and property, peaceably, to the party of the first part, or his heirs, executors, administrators, agent, attorney, or assigns, immediately upon the determination of said term, as aforesaid; and if the said party of the second part, or his legal representatives, shall remain in possession of the same one day after notice of such default, or after the termination of this lease, in any of the ways above named, he or they shall be deemed guilty of a forcible detainer of the premises, and shall be subject to all the conditions and provisions above named, and to eviction and removal, forcibly or otherwise, with or without process of law, as above stated.

And it is further understood and agreed by the said party of the second part, that neither the right given in this lease, to said party of the first part, to collect the rent that may be due under the terms of this lease by sale, or any proceedings under the same, shall in any way affect the right of said party of the first part to declare this lease void and the term hereby created ended, as above provided upon default made by said party of the second part.

And the said party of the first part hereby waives his right to any notice from said party of the second part, of his election to declare this lease at an end, under any of its provisions, or any demand for the payment of rent, or the possession of premises leased herein; but the simple fact of the non-payment of the rent reserved shall constitute a forcible entry and detainer as aforesaid.

The said party of the second part further agrees not to remove any buildings or other improvements from said premises, without written consent of said party of the first part, and that the said second party shall pay and discharge all costs and attorney's fees and expenses that shall arise from enforcing the covenants of this indenture, by the party of the first part.

It is further understood and agreed, That all the conditions and covenants contained in this lease shall be binding upon the heirs, executors, administrators, and assigns of the parties to these presents respectively.

In Testimony Whereof, The said parties have hereunto set their hands and seals the day and year first above written.

(*Signature of the lessor.*) (*Seal.*)
(*Signature of the lessee.*) (*Seal.*)

Signed, Sealed and Delivered in Presence of

(169.)

An Assignment of Lease, and Ground-Rent.

This Indenture, Made the day of in the year of our Lord one thousand eight hundred and between (*name and residence of the assignor*) party of the first part, and (*name and residence of the assignee*) party of the second part, witnesseth, That the said party of the first part, for and in consideration of the sum of dollars, lawful money of the United States of America, unto him in hand well and truly paid by the said party of the second part, at the time of the execution hereof, the receipt whereof is hereby acknowledged, by these presents does grant, bargain, sell, assign, release, and confirm unto the said party of the second part a certain indenture, made and executed on the day of in the year of our Lord eighteen hundred and whereby the said party of the first part leased to one (*name of the lessee in the lease here assigned*) certain premises therein described as follows (*here copy the description of the premises in that lease*) reserving a certain rent, payable to said party of the first part; that is to say (*here state the rent reserved in that lease*) payable (*here state the times and terms of payment*) together with the said rent to the said party of the first part, payable as aforesaid.

Together with all right and power of entry and distress and of re-entry, and all other the covenants, ways, means, and remedies for the recovery thereof, and all and singular the rights, incidents, and appurtenances whatsoever, thereunto belonging, and the reversions and remainders thereof, and all the estate, right, title, nterest, property, claim, and demand whatsoever, of him the said party of the first part, or his legal representatives, either in law or equity, as well of, in, and to the said yearly rent or sum hereby granted and assigned, as also of, in, and to the said lot or piece of ground, with the appurtenances, for and out of which the same rent is issuing and payable. To have and to hold, receive and take, all and singular the hereditaments and premises hereby granted and assigned, with the rights, remedies, incidents, and appurtenances, unto the said party of the second part, his heirs and assigns, to and for the only proper use and behoof of him the said party of the second part, his heirs and assigns, forever. And the said party of the first part, and his heirs, all and singular the hereditaments and premises hereby granted and assigned, with the rights, remedies, incidents, and appurtenances, unto the said party of the second part, and his heirs and assigns, against him the said party of the first part and his heirs, and against all and every other person and persons whomsoever, lawfully claiming or to claim, by, from, or under him or them, or any of them, shall and will warrant and forever defend by these presents.

In Witness Whereof, The said parties to these presents have hereunto interchangeably set their hands and seals the day and year hereinbefore first written.

(*Signature of the assignor.*) (*Seal.*)
(*Signature of the assignee.*) (*Seal.*)

Sealed and Delivered in the Presence of us,
(*Witnesses.*)

Received the day of the date of the above indenture of the above-named the sum of being the full consideration money above mentioned.

(*Signature of the assignor.*)

(*Witness.*)

On the day of Anno Domini, 18 before me, personally appeared the above-named (*name of the assignor*) and in due form of law acknowledged the above indenture to be his free act and deed, and desired the same might be recorded as such.

Witness my hand and seal the day and year aforesaid.

(*Signature.*) (*Seal.*)

(170.)

A Lease containing Chattel Mortgage Covenants, to secure the Rent.

This Indenture, Made this day of in the year of our Lord one thousand eight hundred and between (*name and residence of lessor*) of the first part, and (*name and residence of the lessee*) of the second part, witnesseth, That the said party of the first part, for and in consideration of the covenants and agreements hereinafter mentioned, to be kept and performed by the said party of the second part, his executors, administrators, and assigns, has demised and leased to the said party of the second part all those premises situate, lying, and being in the City of in the County of and in the State of known and described as follows, to wit (*here describe the premises as in Form* 158)

To Have and to Hold The said above-described premises, with the appurtenances, unto the said party of the second part, his executors, administrators, and assigns, from the day of in the year of our Lord one thousand eight hundred and for and during, and until the day of in the year of our Lord one thousand eight hundred and And the said party of the second part, in consideration of the leasing of the premises aforesaid, by the said party of the first part to the said party of the second part, does covenant and agree with the said party of the first part, his heirs, executors, administrators, and assigns, to pay the said party of the first part, as rent for said demised premises, the sum of dollars, in four equal quarterly payments of dollars each ($), payable (*here state the days when the rent should be paid*) at the house (*or office or counting-room or store*) of said party of the first part, in said city of

And it is further agreed by the said party of the second part, in consideration of the leasing of the premises aforesaid, that the said party of the second part shall and will pay, or cause to be paid, promptly, as soon as the same becomes due, all assessments for water-rents that may be levied upon said demised premises during the continuance of this lease, and save said premises and the party of the first part harmless from all charges and expenses connected with the supply of water to said premises. And the said party of the second part hereby covenants and agrees, in case of default in the payment of any water-rent levied upon said premises during said term, to pay unto said party of the first part, as liquidated damages for such breach of covenant, double the sum of such rent so assessed upon said premises as aforesaid.

And the said party of the second part further covenants with the said party of the first part, that he will keep said premises in a clean and healthy condition, in accordance with the ordinances of the city, and directions of the proper authorities.

It is further agreed by the said party of the second part, that neither he nor his legal representatives will underlet said premises or any part thereof, or assign this lease, without the written assent of the said party of the first part first had and obtained thereto.

This Indenture Further Witnesseth, That the said party of the second part, for and in consideration of the sum of (*insert the whole sum to be paid under the lease*) dollars, in hand paid, the receipt whereof is hereby acknowledged, does hereby grant, sell, convey, and confirm unto the said party of the first part, his heirs and assigns, all and singular the following-described goods and chattels, to wit (*here give a schedule or list of the articles, describing them sufficiently*)

Together with all and singular the appurtenances thereunto belonging or in any wise appertaining: to have and to hold the same unto the said party of the first part, his heirs, executors, administrators, and assigns, to his and their sole use forever. And the said party of the second part, for himself and for his heirs, executors, and administrators, does covenant and agree with the said party of the first part and his heirs, executors, administrators, and assigns, that he is lawfully possessed of the said goods and chattels as of his own property; that the same are free from all incumbrances, and that he will, and his heirs, executors, and administrators shall, warrant and defend the same unto the said party of the first part, and his heirs, executors, administrators, and assigns, against the lawful claims and demands of all persons.

Provided, Nevertheless, That if the said party of the second part, or his heirs, executors, administrators, or assigns, shall well and truly pay, or cause to be paid, unto the said party of the first part or his heirs, executors, administrators, or assigns, the said sum of   dollars, rent, above reserved, punctually, and in the manner and at the times and place above mentioned, then and from thenceforth these presents, and every thing herein contained, shall cease, and be null and void.

And Provided Also, That it shall be lawful for the said party of the second part, his heirs, executors, and administrators, to retain possession of the said granted goods and chattels, and at his own expense to keep and to use and enjoy the same, until the said party of the second part, or his heirs, executors, administrators, or assigns, shall make default in the payment of said rent above specified, at the time or times, and in the manner hereinbefore contained, or unless the said party of the first part shall fear diminution, removal, or waste for want of proper care, or if the said party of the second part shall sell or assign, or attempt to sell or assign, said goods and chattels, or any part thereof, or if any writ issued from any court shall be levied on any part of the above-described goods and chattels — that then, and in any of the aforesaid cases, all of said sum of   dollars, above reserved as rent for said demised premises, shall become due and payable, and the said party of the first part, his heirs, executors, administrators, and assigns, agents, or attorneys, or any of them, may elect to take possession of the said property, and for that purpose may pursue the same or any part thereof, wherever it may be found, and also may enter any of the premises of the said party of the second part, with or without force or process of law, wherever the said goods and chattels may be or be supposed to be, and search for the same, and, if found, to take possession of and remove, and sell and dispose of said property, or so much thereof as may be necessary to pay the rent due, and the balance of rent for the whole unexpired term, whether due or not due, at public auction, to the highest bidder, after giving ten days' notice of the time, place, and terms of sale, together with a description of the property to be sold, either by publication in some newspaper in the city of or by similar notices posted up in three public places in the vicinity of such sale, or at private sale, with or without notice, for cash or on credit, as the said party of the first part, or his heirs, executors, administrators, or assigns, agents or attorneys, or any of them, may elect; and out of the money arising from such sale, to retain, first, all costs and charges for pursuing, searching, taking, removing, keeping, storing, advertising, and selling of such property, goods, chattels, and effects, and all prior liens, together with the rent due and the balance of rent for the whole unexpired term, whether due or not due, rendering the overplus of the money arising from such sale, and the remainder of said goods and chattels, if any there shall be, unto the said party of the second part, or his legal representatives.

It is Expressly Understood and Agreed, by and between the parties aforesaid, that if the rent above covenanted to be paid, or any part thereof, shall be behind or unpaid on the day of payment whereon the same ought to be paid, as aforesaid, or if default shall be made in any of the covenants herein contained, to be kept by the said party of the second part, his executors, administrators, and assigns, it shall and may be lawful for the said party of the first part, his heirs, executors, administrators, agent, attorney, or assigns, at his or their election, to declare said term ended, and into the said demised premises, or any part thereof, either with or without process of law, to re-enter, and that said party of the second part, or any other person or persons occupying, in or upon the same, to expel, remove, and put out, using such force as may be necessary in so doing, and the said premises again to repossess and enjoy, as in his or their first and former estate, and to distrain for any rent that may be due thereon, upon any property belonging to the said party of the second part, whether the same be exempt from execution or distress by law or not, and the said party of the second part, in that case, hereby agrees to waive all legal right which he may have to hold or retain any such property, under any exemption-law now in force in this State, or in any other way. And if at any time said term shall be ended at such election of said party of the first part, or his heirs, executors, administrators, or assigns, as aforesaid, or in any other way, the said party of the second part, or his executors, administrators, or assigns, does hereby covenant and agree to surrender and deliver up said above-described premises and property, peaceably, to said party of the first part, or his heirs, executors, administrators, and assigns, immediately upon the determination of said term as aforesaid, and if he shall remain in possession of the same after such default, or after the termination of this lease in any of the ways above named, he shall be deemed guilty of a forcible detainer of said demised premises, and shall be subject to all the conditions and provisions above named, and to eviction and removal, forcibly or otherwise, with or without process of law, as above stated.

In Testimony Whereof, The said parties have hereunto set their hands and seals the day and year first above written.

(*Signature of lessor.*) (*Seal.*)

(*Signature of lessee.*) (*Seal.*)

In Presence of

STATE OF } ss.
COUNTY OF

I, Justice of the Peace in and for said county, do hereby certify that this lease and mortgage was duly acknowledged before me by the above-named (*name of lessee*) this day of A.D. 18

(*Seal.*)

(171.)

A Building Lease.

This Deed of Lease, Made and entered into, in duplicate, this day of A.D. 186 , between (*name of lessor*) of County of and State of party of the first part, and (*name of lessee*) of County of and State of party of the second part:

Witnesseth, That the said party of the first part, in consideration of the covenants, agreements, and stipulations hereinafter mentioned, as well as the yearly rent of dollars, to be paid to him in four equal quarterly payments in each year (the first payment to be made on the day of A.D. 186), doth by these presents lease to the said party of the second part for the term of years, which said term begins on the day of 186 , the following-described lot of land, to wit (*here describe the premises as in Form* 158)

The said party of the second part, for himself and his heirs, hereby covenants with said lessor and his heirs to pay said rent as aforesaid, and also to pay all city, county, and State taxes, and all other taxes and demands of every description, nature, or kind whatever, which may from time to time be legally required or demanded of said premises, whether general tax or special tax.

Every failure, first, to pay the said rent, or any part thereof, when it is respectively made payable; or, second, to pay the said city, county, and State taxes, and all other taxes and demands, or any part thereof (legally required or demanded of said premises, within the year the same shall become due, assessed to either said lessor, his heirs or representatives, or to said lessee or his representatives); or, third, to keep and perform any of the other covenants, agreements, or stipulations herein mentioned, shall make and create a forfeiture of this lease, and a termination of the term for which the above premises were let, and all the estate hereby conveyed shall be absolutely void, if so determined, at any day or time however distant, after such failure, by notice in writing to that effect, given by said lessor, his heirs or assigns, to said lessee or his assigns; which said notice may be served by posting a copy or duplicate of the same up at one of the most public places on said premises, or by delivering a copy or duplicate of such notice to said lessee or his assigns.

This lease of said premises, or any part thereof, is not to be assigned, under penalty of forfeiture, without the written consent of said lessor, his heirs or assigns. At the expiration of this lease, the said premises to be delivered to said lessor, his heirs, or assigns. The said lessee, and all who hold under him, hereby engage to pay double rent for every day they or any one else in their name shall hold on to the whole or any part of said premises, after the expiration of this lease, or after forfeiture thereof.

The said lessee is, under penalty of forfeiture, bound to keep said premises free from any disorderly, bawdy, or gambling establishments, dram-shops, tippling-shops, beer-houses, or any nuisances whatsoever. And in case of any forfeiture of this lease, the said lessor, his heirs and assigns, may forthwith take possession of said premises, with all the improvements thereon, and shall be entitled to the same, any custom, usage, or law, to the contrary notwithstanding.

All improvements erected on said premises by said lessee or his assigns, or by any one who may claim under them, are bound for the payment of each quarterly instalment of rent, and for the city, county, and State taxes, and all other taxes and demands as aforesaid, and for any arrears of rent or taxes; and in case of the punctual payment of the rent and taxes, as herein specified, the said lessee or his assigns is hereby authorized to remove all such improvements (and no others), at the expiration of this lease, which he or any one who may claim under him, may have erected on said premises during said term.

In Testimony Whereof, The parties hereto have hereunto set their hands and seals to duplicate leases the day and year aforesaid.

(*Signature of lessor.*) (*Seal.*)
(*Signature of lessee.*) (*Seal.*)

In Presence of

(172.)

A Mining Lease.

This Indenture, Made this day of in the year of our Lord one thousand eight hundred and between (*name and residence of the lessor*) of the first part, and (*name and residence of the lessee*) of the second part, witnesseth, That the said party of the first part, for and in consideration of the covenants and agreements hereinafter contained on the part of the said party of the second part, and of one dollar in hand paid to the said party of the first part, the receipt whereof is hereby acknowledged, has granted and conveyed, and by these presents does grant and convey to the said party of the second part, his heirs, executors, administrators, and assigns, the right of entering in and upon the lands hereinafter described, for the purpose of searching for mineral and fossil substances, and of conducting mining and quarrying operations, to any extent he or they may deem advisable (but not to hold possession of any part of said lands for any other purpose whatsoever) paying for the site of buildings of any kind, necessary thereto, a reasonable rent.

The said lands are situated (*here state the situation of the premises leased, and describe them by metes and bounds, dimensions, and references to other boundaries, so as to distinguish them perfectly*)

And the said party of the second part hereby agrees that he or his heirs, executors, administrators, or assigns will pay or cause to be paid to the said party of the first part, his heirs or assigns, an annual rent of the amount of dollars, in four equal quarterly payments, payable severally on the following days (*here state the days when the payments are to be made, or whatever other terms or times are agreed upon*), and also covenants that no damage shall be done to or upon said lands and premises, other than may be necessary in conducting said operations. And it is agreed and covenanted by and between the parties hereunto, that this lease shall be and remain in full force and effect (subject to the proviso hereinafter stated) years, from the date hereof, and no longer. But the said parties of the first and the second part, each for themselves, their heirs, executors, administrators, and assigns, covenant and agree, and this indenture is made with this express proviso, that if no mineral or fossil substance be mined or quarried, as now contemplated by said parties, within the period of years, from the present time, then these presents, and every thing contained herein, shall cease and be forever null and void.

In Testimony Whereof, the parties to these presents have hereunto set their hands and seals the day and year first above written.

(*Signature of lessor.*) (*Seal.*)
(*Signature of lessee.*) (*Seal.*)

Signed, Sealed and Delivered in Presence of

(173.)

A Lease of Land supposed to contain Oil, Salt, or other Minerals.

Articles of Agreement, Made and concluded this day of A.D. 186 , between (*name of lessor*) of the township of County of and State of party of the first part, and (*name and residence of lessee*) party of the second part. Witnesseth, That the said party of the first part for himself and his heirs, executors, administrators and assigns, for and in consideration of the sum of one dollar, the receipt of which is hereby acknowledged, and for the further consideration hereinafter mentioned, and on account of covenants hereinafter contained, hereby leases to the said party of the second part, his heirs, executors, administrators and assigns, the following-described piece or parcel of land, situated in the township of County of and State of bounded and described as follows (*describe the premises as in the preceding Form.*) The said land more fully described in deed of conveyance by (*name of the grantor to the lessor*) to the said party of the first part, containing acres, more or less, for the purpose of boring, mining, and operating for oil, salt, and other minerals on said land, for the term of years.

Said second parties to have the exclusive right to mine for oil, salt, and other minerals, on said land, during the continuance of said term: to have the privilege of taking sufficient coal and wood for conducting said boring and mining operations, and timber for derricks and mill-frames and for refineries, and the right to erect all necessary buildings upon said premises for carrying on the business of boring for oil, and mining, refining and storing away oil and other minerals; and to have the necessary roads to and from any well or wells that may be bored, or any mines; and to have possession whenever they shall be ready to commence operations. And in case successful in obtaining oil or other minerals, agree to deliver to the said party of the first part (*here state the part or proportion which is to be given to the lessor*) of all oil, salt, or other minerals obtained. Said party of the first part to find his own barrels, and remove the oil and other minerals belonging to him, as often as required by the second parties. And in case said second parties should not be successful in obtaining oil or other minerals, they shall have the right to remove all engines, tools, machinery, and buildings. And further, it is agreed that said second parties have the right to sub-lease said land for the purpose of boring for oil or other minerals; the said lessee or lessees being granted all the rights and privileges herein granted to the said party of the second part.

Witness our hands and seals this day of 186 .

(*Signature of lessor.*) (*Seal.*)
(*Signature of lessee.*) (*Seal.*)

Witnesses.

Personally appeared before me, a Justice of the Peace in and for the township of within the County aforesaid and did acknowledge the signing and sealing of the above agreement to be act and deed.

Given under my hand this day of 186 .

Justice of the Peace.

(174.)

An Assignment of a Lease.

Know all Men by these Presents, That I, (*name and residence of assignor*) for and in consideration of the sum of dollars, lawful money of the United States, to me duly paid, by (*name and residence of assignee*) have sold, and by these presents do grant, convey, assign, transfer and set over, unto the said (*name of assignee*) a certain indenture of lease, bearing date the day of in the year one thousand eight hundred and made by (*name of the lessor in the lease assigned*) whereby he leases to me the following-described premises (*here* *describe the premises briefly*), with all and singular the premises therein mentioned and described, and the buildings thereon, together with the appurtenances.

To Have and to Hold the same unto the said (*the name of the assignee*) and his assigns, from the day of for and during all the rest, residue, and remainder yet to come of and in the term of years mentioned in the said indenture of lease, and all my rights and privileges in and under said lease; subject nevertheless to the rents, covenants, conditions and provisions therein also mentioned. And I do hereby covenant, grant, promise and agree, to and with the said (*name of the assignee*) that the said assigned premises now are free and clear of and from all former and other gifts, grants, bargains, sales, leases, judgments, executions, back rents, taxes, assessments, and incumbrances whatsoever.

In Witness Whereof, I have hereunto set my hand and seal this day of one thousand eight hundred and

(*Signature.*) (*Seal.*)

Sealed and Delivered in the Presence of

(175.)

Landlord's Notice to quit for Non-Payment of Rent; Short Form.

STATE OF ss. A.D. 186

To (*name of tenant*). You being in possession of the following-described premises, which you occupy as my tenant (*here describe the premises sufficiently to identify them*) in the city (*or township*) of and county aforesaid, are hereby notified to quit and deliver up to me the premises aforesaid, in fourteen days from this date, according to law, your rent being due and unpaid. Hereof fail not, or I shall take a due course of law to eject you from the same.

Witness. (*Signature.*)

(176.)

Landlord's Notice to quit for Non-Payment of Rent; another Form.

STATE OF CITY OF (*date*) 18

You are hereby notified to quit the premises situate (*state the situation of the premises, giving township or city, and street, and number*) which I have leased to you, reserving rent, or pay and satisfy the rent due and in arrear, being $ which amount was due on the day of 18 and is hereby demanded (you having neglected or refused to pay the amount so reserved, as often as the same has grown due, according to the terms of our contract, and there being no goods on the premises adequate to pay the rent so reserved, except such articles as are exempt from levy and sale by the laws of this State) within days from the date hereof, or I shall proceed against you as the law directs. Yours, &c.

(*Signature.*)

To (*name of tenant*)

(177.)

Landlord's Notice to pay Rent due, or quit.

STATE OF
} ss.
COUNTY OF

(*Name of landlord*) landlord, against (*name of tenant*) tenant.

Take Notice, That you are justly indebted unto me in the sum of for rent of (*home, store, or other premises, describing them generally*) from (*date when the rent was due and payable*), which you are required to pay on or before the expiration of three days from the day of the service of this notice, or surrender up the possession of the said premises to in default of which shall proceed under the provisions of law to recover the possession thereof.

Dated this day of 18

(*Name of the landlord*) Landlord.

To (*name of the tenant*) Tenant, in possession of the premises above specified.

(178.)

Landlord's Notice to leave at End of the Term.

To (*name and address of the tenant*)

SIR, — Being in the possession of a certain messuage or tenement, with the appurtenances, situate (*describe the premises briefly*) which said premises were demised to you by me for a certain term, to wit, from the day of A.D. 18 until the day of A.D. 18 and which said term will terminate and expire on the day and year last aforesaid, I hereby give you notice, that it is my desire to have again and repossess the said messuage or tenement, with the appurtenances, and I therefore do hereby require you to leave the same upon the expiration of the said hereinbefore mentioned term.

Witness my hand this day of city of A.D. 18.

(*Witness.*) (*Signature.*)

(179.)

Landlord's Notice to determine a Tenancy at Will.

STATE OF ss. A.D. 186

To (*name of tenant*). You being in possession of the following-described premises, which you occupy as my tenant at will (*describing them sufficiently to identify them*) in the (*city and street*) aforesaid, are hereby notified to quit and deliver up to me the premises aforesaid (*on such a day, stating here the day as far distant as is made necessary by the requisite length of notice*) according to law, it being my intention to determine your tenancy at will. Hereof fail not, or I shall take a due course of law to eject you from the same.

(*Witness.*) (*Signature.*)

(180.)

Receipt for Rent, in Use in New York.

Rent payable

The tenant mentioned below hereby agrees to pay the rent of the premises occupied and used by on the first day of the term; and engages to clean the entries, stairs, stoops, and privy thereof, weekly, in turn with other occupants, and not incumber the same with furniture, fuel, or rubbish, nor keep any hog, dog, or fowl, nor deposit ashes or garbage on said premises, nor in the sinks or privies, nor split wood on the hearth, floor, or yard.

NEW YORK, 186

Received from (*name of tenant paying*) dollars, for months' rent, from 18 to 18 for (*stone, brick, or other*) house, No Street, in the city of New York.

$

CHAPTER XXXII.

MORTGAGES OF GOODS AND CHATTELS, OR PERSONAL PROPERTY.

IT was said that mortgages are now often made of personal property. The instrument need not be so formal as a mortgage deed of land. Any instrument will answer the purpose, which would suffice as a bill of sale of the property, and which contains, in addition to the words of sale and transfer, a clause providing for the avoidance of it when the debt is paid. I append to this chapter forms for this purpose.

When the mortgagor of personal property retained possession, it was formerly doubtful what security the mortgagee had. Now, however, it is generally provided by statute, that the mortgagor may retain possession, if the mortgage be recorded.

These instruments should always be recorded according to the provisions of the statute of the State in which they are made; although the general rule would apply to them, that they would operate without record, as to all parties having notice or knowledge of them.

The statutes respecting mortgages of personal property always provide for an equity of redemption, which is usually very much shorter than that of land. A frequent period is sixty days. The requirements of the statute in respect to notice, foreclosure, &c., must be strictly followed.

It used to be thought that a personal mortgage might be made to cover property subsequently acquired by the mortgagee. Thus, a dealer in dry goods would mortgage all his stock to secure some creditor, and provide in the mortgage that it should operate upon all his goods and merchandise subsequently acquired by him. But it has been held that such a clause has no effect; because no man can make a mortgage of property which he does not own at the time.

The Pledge of Personal Property.

A PLEDGEE is bound to take ordinary (not extreme) care of the thing pledged; and if it be lost or injured for want of such care, he is answerable.

He cannot use it, except at his own peril; that is, he is liable for any injury caused by using it, even if it was not his fault. If the thing — as a horse — needs use for its own safety, then the pledgee may use it for this purpose, and is liable only for an injury caused by his negligence.

He must account with the pledgor for the income, increase, or profits.

One difference between a mortgagee and a pledgee is this. A mortgagee need not take possession, for the mortgagor may retain it, and now this is provided for, as we have seen, by recording the mortgage. But if a thing is given in pledge, the pledgee must have and keep possession of it.

The most important difference is this. A mortgagee may sell and transfer his mortgage, and his transferee may transfer it again, and so on; and when the debt is paid, the mortgagor reclaims it from whomsoever has it then. But if a pledgee sells the pledge before the debt is due, it is held that he is at once answerable to the pledgor for its full value, although the debt be not paid.

Some cases of this kind have been carried very far in New York. It is held there, — and on grounds which may perhaps suffice to make it law everywhere, — that if A lends money to B, and takes stocks in pledge, A cannot sell these stocks and keep the proceeds, and replace the stock and return it when the debt is paid. He can do nothing but keep the stock; and if he sells it, the pledgor may recover at once its full value, and the pledgee will have no security for his debt. In such a case, a pledgee, being sued, offered the testimony of brokers and others to prove a uniform and established usage in the city of New York thus to sell or use pledged stock until the debt was paid; but the court said the usage was illegal, and refused to receive the evidence.

It is certain that after the debt is due and payable, and after demand if it be payable on demand, the pledgee may have a decree in chancery for a sale of the pledge, or may sell it himself, *provided* he first gives a reasonable notice to the pledgor, and then sells it, after a reasonable delay, in a proper manner, by a public sale at auction; and uses all reasonable precautions to get its value, as by advertisement, &c.; and does not buy it himself, directly or indirectly; and conducts himself in all respects honestly; and then he must account for the proceeds.

Sometimes the parties agree, when the pledge is given, or afterwards, how the pledge shall be treated, or how sold if not redeemed, &c.; and such agreements, if fair and reasonable, would undoubtedly be binding on both parties.

It is agreed that negotiable paper is excepted from the common rule; and the pledgee of that may sell or discount it before the debt is due; and must account for it, or its proceeds, if the debt is paid and the paper redeemed, or for the balance if he applies it to payment of the debt.

A *loan* of stock is not like a *pledge* of stock, because it authorizes the borrower to sell or pledge it, or use it in any way, at any time; but he must replace and return the same quantity of the same stock, when it is called for. If he could not thus make use of the stock, the loan of it would be of no benefit whatever to the borrower. But he cannot thus use stock pledged to him, unless by a special agreement which permits this use.

A pledgee, who receives a pledge to secure one or more specific debts, cannot retain it to secure other and further debts of the pledgor, unless with his consent. This consent may be express, or implied from words or circumstances which show that such was the understanding of the parties.

(181.)

A Mortgage of Personal Property.

Know all Men by these Presents, That I, (*name of mortgagor*) of the town of County of and State of for and in consideration of dollars, to me in hand paid by (*name of mortgagee*) of the town of County of and State aforesaid, do sell and convey to the said (*name of mortgagee*) the following goods and chattels, to wit (*list or schedule of the articles, specifying them with sufficient distinctness to make it certain what they are*) warranted free of incumbrance, and against any adverse claims: Upon condition, that if the said (*name of the mortgagor*) pay to the said (*name of the mortgagee*) dollars and interest, in year, agreeably to a promissory note of this date, for that sum, payable to the said (*name of mortgagee*) or order, on demand, with interest, this deed shall be void, otherwise in full force and effect.

The aforesaid Parties Agree, That, until the condition of this instrument is broken, the said property may remain in possession of the said (*name of mortgagor*), but after condition broken the said (*name of mortgagee*) may at his pleasure take and remove the same, and may enter into any building or premises of the said (*name of the mortgagor*) for that purpose.

Witness our hands and seals this day of A. D. 18

(*Signature of mortgagor.*) (*Seal.*)
(*Signature of mortgagee.*) (*Seal.*)

Sealed and Delivered in Presence of

STATE OF } ss.
COUNTY OF }

Be it Remembered, That on this day of eighteen hundred and before me, the undersigned, Notary Public in and for said County and State, duly commissioned and qualified, came who is known to me to be the same person whose name is subscribed to the foregoing instrument of writing, as party thereto, and he acknowledged the same to be his act and deed, for the purpose therein mentioned.

In Testimony Whereof I have hereunto set my hand and affixed my official seal, at office, in the city of the day and year last aforesaid.

Notary Public.

(182.)

A Mortgage of Personal Property, with Warranty.

Know all Men by these Presents, That I, (*name and residence of mortgagor*) in consideration of the sum of to me in hand paid by (*name and residence of mortgagee*) the receipt whereof is hereby acknowledged, have granted, bargained, and sold, and by these presents do grant, bargain, and sell, unto the said (*name of mortgagee*) the following articles of personal property; that is to say (*list or schedule as in Form* 181)

To Have and to Hold, all and singular, the said goods and chattels, unto the said (*name of the mortgagee*) and his executors, administrators, and assigns, to his and their use forever. And I the said mortgagor for myself and for my executors and administrators do covenant to and with the said mortgagee and with his executors, administrators and assigns, that I am lawfully possessed of the said goods and chattels, as of my own property; that the same are free from all incumbrances, and that I will, and my executors and administrators shall, warrant and defend the same to the said mortgagee, his executors, administrators, and assigns, against the lawful claims and demands of all persons.

Provided Nevertheless, That if the said mortgagor, his executors or administrators, shall well and truly pay unto the said mortgagee, his executors, administrators, or assigns, the sum of dollars, in months from the date hereof (*or on a certain day, stating the day when the money is to be paid*) with interest at per cent, then this deed, as also a certain promissory note bearing even date herewith, signed by the said mortgagor, whereby he promises to pay the said mortgagee the said sum and interest at the time aforesaid, shall both be void; otherwise shall remain in full force and virtue.

And Provided Also, That until default by the said mortgagor, or his executors and administrators, in the performance of the condition aforesaid, or of some part thereof, it shall and may be lawful for him or them to keep possession of the said granted property, and to use and enjoy the same; but in case of such default, or if the same or any part thereof shall be attached, at any time before payment as aforesaid, by any other creditor or creditors of the said mortgagor, or if the said mortgagor or his executors or administrators, shall attempt to sell the same, or any part thereof, without notice to the said mortgagee or his executors, administrators, or assigns, and without his or their assent to such sale in writing expressed, or shall remove the same, or any part thereof, from the place in which they now are, without such notice and assent, then it shall be lawful for the said mortgagee or his executors, administrators, or assigns, to take immediate possession of the whole of said granted property, to his and their own use.

In Testimony Whereof, I have hereunto set my hand and seal this day of in the year of our Lord one thousand eight hundred and sixty-

(*Signature.*) (*Seal.*)

Executed and Delivered in Presence of

(183.)

A Mortgage of Personal Property, with a Power of Sale.

Know all Men by these Presents, That I, (*name of mortgagor*) of the town (*or city*) of in the County of and State of , in consideration of dollars, to me paid by (*name of mortgagee*) of the town (*or city*) of in the County of and State of the receipt whereof is hereby acknowledged, do hereby grant, bargain and sell unto the said (*name of mortgagee*) and his assigns, forever, the following goods and chattels, to wit (*list or schedule, as in Form* 181)

To Have and to Hold, All and singular the said goods and chattels unto the mortgagee herein, and his assigns, to their sole use and behoof forever. And the mortgagor herein, for himself and for his heirs, executors and administrators, does hereby covenant to and with the said mortgagee and his assigns, that said mortgagor is lawfully possessed of the said goods and chattels, as of his own property; that the same are free from all incumbrances, and that he will warrant and defend the same to him the said mortgagee and his assigns, against the lawful claims and demands of all persons.

Provided, Nevertheless, that if the said mortgagor shall pay to the mortgagee, on the day of in the year the sum of dollars, then this mortgage is to be void, otherwise to remain in full force and effect.

And Provided Further, That until default be made by the said mortgagor in the performance of the condition aforesaid, it shall and may be lawful for him to retain the possession of the said goods and chattels, and to use and enjoy the same; but if the same or any part thereof shall be attached or claimed by any other person or persons at any time before payment, or the said mortgagor or any person or persons whatever, upon any pretence, shall attempt to carry off, conceal, make way with, sell, or in any manner dispose of the same or any part thereof, without the authority and permission of the said mortgagee or his executors, administrators or assigns, in writing expressed, then it shall and may be lawful for the said mortgagee with or without assistance, or his agent or attorney, or his executors, administrators, or assigns, to take possession of said goods and chattels, by entering upon any premises wherever the same may be, whether in this county or State, or elsewhere, to and for the use of said mortgagee or his assigns. And if the moneys hereby secured, or the matters to be done or performed, as above specified, are not duly paid, done or performed at the time and according to the conditions above set forth, then the said mortgagee or his attorney, or agent, or his executors, administrators or assigns, may, by virtue hereof, and without any suit or process, immediately enter and take possession of said goods and chattels, and sell and dispose of the same at public or private sale, and after satisfying the amount due, and all expenses, the surplus, if any remain, shall be paid over to said mortgagor or his assigns. The exhibition of this mortgage shall be sufficient proof that any person claiming to act for the mortgagee is duly made, constituted and appointed agent and attorney to do whatever is above authorized.

In Witness Whereof, The said mortgagor has hereunto set his hand and seal this day of in the year of our Lord one thousand eight hundred and

(Signature of mortgagor.) *(Seal.)*

Signed, Sealed and Delivered in Presence of

STATE OF , }
COUNTY } ss.

This mortgage was acknowledged before me, by *(the mortgagor)*, this day of A.D. 18

(184.)

Mortgage of Personal Property, with Power of Sale: another Form.

Know all Men by these Presents, That I *(name and residence of mortgagor)* in consideration of the sum of to me paid by *(name and residence of mortgagee)* the receipt whereof is hereby acknowledged have granted, bargained, and sold, and by these presents do grant, bargain, and sell unto the said *(name of mortgagee)* the following named and described articles of personal property; that is to say *(here follows the list or schedule and description of the articles mortgaged, as in Form* 181)

To Have and to Hold All and singular, the said goods and chattels, unto the said (*name of mortgagee*) and his executors, administrators, and assigns, to his and their sole use forever. And I, the said mortgagor, for myself and my executors and administrators, do covenant to and with the said mortgagee and his executors, administrators, and assigns, that I am lawfully possessed of the said goods and chattels, as of my own property: that the same are free from all incumbrances; and that I will, and my executors and administrators shall, warrant and defend the same to the said mortgagee and his executors, administrators, and assigns, against the lawful claims and demands of all persons.

Provided Nevertheless, That if the said mortgagor or his executors, or administrators, shall well and truly pay unto the said mortgagee or his executors, administrators or assigns, the sum of then this deed, as also a certain promissory note bearing even date herewith, signed by the said mortgagor, whereby he promises to pay the said mortgagee the said sum and interest at the time aforesaid, shall both be void, and otherwise they shall remain in full force and virtue.

And Provided Also, That until default by the said mortgagor or his executors and administrators, in the performance of the condition aforesaid, or of some part thereof, it shall and may be lawful for him or them to keep possession of the said granted property, and to use and enjoy the same; but in case of such default, or if the same or any part thereof shall be attached at any time before payment as aforesaid, by any other creditor or creditors of the said mortgagor, or if the said mortgagor, his executors or administrators, shall attempt to sell the same or any part thereof without notice to the said mortgagee or his executors, administrators, or assigns, and without his or their assent to such sale in writing expressed; or shall remove the same, or any part thereof, from the place where they now are, without such notice and assent, then it shall be lawful for the said mortgagee, his executors, administrators, or assigns, to take immediate possession of the whole of said granted property to his or their own use, and to sell and dispose of the whole, or of so much of said granted property at public auction, as shall produce a sum of money sufficient to pay and discharge the above-mentioned debt or liability, with interest, and all costs and charges of keeping and selling the same, and all just and equitable liens then existing thereon, without further notice or demand, except giving days' notice of the time and place of said sale to said mortgagor or his legal representatives; and after the said debt or liability, with interest, costs, charges, and liens, shall be so discharged and satisfied, the surplus of the money arising from said sale, and the residue of said granted property, shall be paid and restored to said mortgagor or his legal representatives, discharged from all claim under this mortgage.

In Testimony Whereof, I, the said (*name of mortgagor*) have hereunto set my hand and seal this day of in the year of our Lord one thousand eight hundred and

(*Signature.*) (*Seal.*)

Executed and Delivered in Presence of

CHAPTER XXXIII.

THE LAW OF PATENTS.

What may be patented.

ANY new and useful art, machine, manufacture, or composition of matter, or any new and useful improvement thereof not before known or used by others in this country, and not at the time patented or described in any printed publication in this or any foreign country.

And any new and original design for a manufacture, bust, statue, alto relievo, or bass relief, or any new and original impression, ornament, pattern, print, or picture to be placed on or worked into any article of manufacture; or any new and original shape or configuration of any such article, the same not having been known or used by others before the application for a patent.

Who is entitled to a Patent.

Any person, whether citizen or alien, may obtain a patent for any invention or improvement made by him, and not before known.

In case of the death of the inventor, the patent may be applied for by, and will issue to, his legal representatives.

Joint inventors are entitled to a joint patent; but neither can claim one separately.

What will prevent the granting of a Patent.

Although an applicant may have actually made an invention, a patent therefor will not be granted him if the whole or any part of what he claims as new has been patented, or described in any printed publication in this or any foreign country, or been before invented or discovered in this country, nor if he has once abandoned his invention to the public, or for more than two years consented and allowed it to be in public use or on sale; but the mere fact of prior use, invention, or discovery abroad, will not prevent the issue of the patent, unless the invention has been there patented, or described in some printed publication.

Merely conceiving the idea of an improvement or machine is not such an "invention" or "discovery" as is above contemplated. The invention must have been reduced to a practical form, either by the construction of the machine itself or of a model thereof, or at least by making a full drawing of it, or in some other manner equally descriptive of its exact character, so that a mechanic would be enabled, from the description given, to construct a model thereof, before it will prevent a subsequent inventor from obtaining a patent.

Mode of proceeding to obtain a Patent.

APPLICATION.

All applications must be completed for examination within two years after the filing of the petition; and in default, all such will be regarded as abandoned, unless it be satisfactorily proved to the office that such delay was unavoidable. The application must be made by the actual inventor, if alive, even if the patent is to issue to an assignee; but, where the inventor is dead, the application and oath may be made by the executor or administrator. The application must be in writing, in the English language, signed by the applicant, and addressed to the Commissioner of Patents, Washington, D.C. The following is a suitable form, which may serve as a useful guide, but must be varied according to circumstances: —

(185.)

Form of Petition.

To the Commissioner of Patents: —

Your petitioner prays that a patent may be granted to him for the invention set forth in the annexed specification.

(*Signature.*)

SPECIFICATION.

The applicant must set forth in his specification the precise invention for which he claims a patent.

In all applications for mere improvements, the specification must distinguish between what is admitted to be old and what is described and claimed to be the improvement; so that the office and the public may understand exactly for what the patent is granted.

Two or more distinct and separate inventions may not be claimed in one application; but where several inventions have a necessary and dependent connection with each other, so that all co-operate in attaining the end which is sought, they may be so claimed. If more than one invention is claimed in a single application, and they are found to be such that a single patent may not be issued to cover the whole, the inventor must divide the application, and confine the claim to whichever invention he may elect.

The specification must be signed by the inventor (or by his executor or administrator, if the inventor be dead). It should describe the sections of the drawings (where there are drawings), and refer by letters and figures to the different parts. The following may be taken as a specimen of the proper form of a specification to accompany the petition: —

(186.)

Form of a Specification to accompany the Petition.

TO ALL WHOM IT MAY CONCERN: —

Be it known that I, of in the County of in the State of have invented a new and improved mode of preventing steam-boilers from bursting; and I do hereby declare that the following is a full and exact description thereof, reference being had to the accompanying drawings, and to the letters of reference marked thereon.

The nature of my invention consists in providing the upper part of a steam-boiler with an aperture in addition to that for the safety-valve, which aperture is to be closed by a plug or disk of alloy, which will fuse at any given degree of heat, and permit the steam to escape, should the safety-valve fail to perform its functions.

To enable others skilled in the art to make and use my invention, I will proceed to describe its construction and operation. I construct my steam-boiler in any of the known forms, and apply thereto gauge-cocks, a safety-valve, and the other appendages of such boilers; but, in order to obviate the danger arising from the adhesion of the safety-valve, and from other causes, I make a second opening in the top of the boiler, similar to that made for the safety-valve, as shown at A, in the accompanying drawing; and in this opening I insert a plug or disk of fusible alloy, securing it in its place by a metal ring and screws, or otherwise. In general, I compose this fusible metal of a mixture of lead, tin, and bismuth, in such proportions as will insure its melting at a given temperature, which must be that to which it is intended to limit the steam; it will, of course, vary with the pressure the boiler is intended to sustain.

I surround the opening containing the fusible alloy by a tube, B, intended to conduct off any steam which may be discharged therefrom. When the temperature of the steam in such a boiler rises to its assigned limit, the fusible alloy will melt and allow the steam to escape freely, thereby securing it from all danger of explosion.

What I claim as my invention, and desire to secure by letters patent, is the application to steam-boilers of a fusible alloy which will melt at a given temperature and allow the steam to escape, as herein described, using for that purpose the aforesaid metallic compound, or any other substantially the same, and which will produce the intended effect.

(*Signature.*)

(*Witnesses.*)

When the application is for a machine, the specification should begin thus: —

Be it known that I, (*name of inventor*) in the County of and State of have invented a new and useful machine for [stating the use and title of the machine; and, if the application is for an improvement, it should read thus: a new and useful improvement on a or on the machine, &c.] and I do hereby declare that the following is a full, clear, and exact description of the construction and operation of the same, reference being had to the annexed drawings, making a part of this specification, in which Figure 1 is a perspective view; Figure 2 a longitudinal elevation; Figure 3 a transverse section, &c. (thus describing all the sections of the drawings, and then referring to the parts by letters. Then follows the description of the construction and operation of the machine, and lastly the claim, which should express the nature and character of the invention, and identify the parts claimed separately or in combination. If the specification is for an improvement, the original invention should be disclaimed, and the claim confined to the improvement).

The specification must be signed by the inventor, and attested by two witnesses.

The applicant must make oath or affirmation, to be substantially as follows: —

(187.)

Form of Oath.

CITY (OR TOWN) OF COUNTY OF STATE OF } ss.

On this day of 186 , before me, the subscriber a personally appeared the within named and made solemn oath (or affirmation) that he verily believes himself to be the original and first inventor of the mode herein described for preventing steam-boilers from bursting, and that he does not know or believe the same was ever before known or used; and that he is a citizen of the United States [or citizen of other country, as the case may be].

(*Signature.*) *Justice of the Peace.*

Citizens of the British Provinces should state specifically the provinces of which they are citizens, and not merely that they are subjects of the crown of Great Britain. The oath may be taken before any person authorized by law to administer oaths. The oath may be taken in a foreign country before any minister plenipotentiary, chargé d'affaires, consul, or commercial agent, holding commission under the government of the United States, or before any notary public of the country in which the oath is taken, being attested in all cases by the proper official seal of such notary. Applicants for patents, upon paying the final fee, should notify the office how many copies of the specifications they desire to have furnished them.

DRAWINGS.

The applicant for a patent is required by law to furnish duplicate drawings where the nature of the case admits of them. They should be neatly and artistically executed, in fast colors, generally in perspective, and with such detached sectional and plain views as to clearly show what the invention is, its construction and operation. Each part must be distinguished by the same number or letter wherever it appears in the several drawings. The name of the invention should be written at the top, the shortest side being considered as such. Each sheet should be fifteen inches from top to bottom, and ten inches across, that being the size of the patent; or it may be twenty inches across, so as to be folded. One of the duplicates should be on thick drawing-paper, sufficiently stiff to support itself in the portfolios of the office, for which it is intended. Tracings upon cloth pasted on thick paper are not admitted. This must be signed by the applicant, and attested by two witnesses, and must be sent with the specification. The other duplicate need not be forwarded until the patent is ordered to issue, to which it is to be attached. It must have, for that purpose, a margin of one inch on the right hand, and should be on tracing-muslin, which will bear folding and transportation, and not on paper.

The above are the rules imposed by the office, being found necessary for the convenient transaction of their business. And applicants are advised to employ competent artists to make the drawings, as they will be returned if not executed in conformity with these rules. Thick drawings should never be folded for transmission.

MODEL.

A model is required in every case where the nature of the invention admits of such illustration. It must be neatly and substantially made of durable material, and not more than one foot in length or in height, unless a larger model is necessary to exhibit the invention. If made of pine or other soft wood, it should be painted, stained, or varnished. Models filed as exhibits, in interference and other cases, may be returned to the applicant, at the discretion of the commissioner.

A working model is always desirable, in order to enable the office fully and readily to understand the precise operation of the machine. The name of the inventor, and also of the assignee (if assigned), and also the title of the invention, must be affixed upon it in a permanent manner.

When the invention is a composition of matter, a specimen of each of the ingredients and of the composition must accompany the application, and the name of the inventor and of the assignee (if there be one) must be permanently affixed thereto.

When a work of design can be sufficiently represented by a drawing, a model will not be required.

Photographs are admitted for the illustration of works of design only, and must be pasted upon thick drawing-paper and tracing-muslin, of the size prescribed for drawings; but in every case where this mode of illustration is employed by an applicant, he will be required to deposit in this office the glass or other "negative" from which the photograph is printed, so that exact official copies may be made therefrom when desirable.

COMPLETION OF THE APPLICATION.

No application is examined, nor is the case placed upon the files for examination, until the fee is paid, the model or specimen deposited, and the specification, with the petition, oath, and drawings (when required), filed. It is desirable that every thing necessary to make the application complete should be deposited in the office at the same time.

Of the Examination.

All cases in the Patent Office are arranged in classes, which are taken up for examination in regular rotation; those in the same class being examined and disposed of, as far as practicable, in the order in which the respective applications are completed. When, however, the invention is deemed of peculiar importance to some branch of the public service, and when, for that reason, the head of some department of the government specially requests immediate action, the case will be taken up out of its order. These, with applications for re-issue, are the only exceptions to the rule above stated in relation to the order of examination.

When an application has been once rejected, either in whole or in part, and the applicant desires a second examination, either with or without amendment, he will be entitled to it with as little delay as may be practicable, so that he may be in condition to appeal, if desirable, without loss of time. When an application has been finally decided, the office will retain the original papers, furnishing the applicant copies — if he desires them — at the usual expense.

When a patent is granted, it will be transmitted to the patentee, or to his agent, having a full power of attorney authorizing him to receive it.

Protests.

The office cannot stay the regular proceedings on applications for letters-patent in consequence of protests founded upon mere *ex parte* statements; but, where affidavits of disinterested persons are received, they will be considered and allowed such weight as they may seem entitled to.

Withdrawals.

If an application filed prior to the 2d of March, 1861, be rejected, and the applicant shall relinquish his claim, he must notify the commissioner of the fact of such withdrawal, sending at the same time his receipt for two-thirds of the fee paid by him, which will be thereupon returned. The model and papers will be retained by the office. The applicant may, however, have the duplicate drawing if he desires it. But no money paid on any application filed subsequent to the second day of March, 1861, nor for a design, nor for a re-issue, can be withdrawn.

Retaining Patents in the Secret Archives.

An application upon which a patent has been allowed may, at the request of the applicant or of his assignee, made before the patent has been recorded, be retained in the secret archives of the office for a period not exceeding six months from the date of the order to issue, without reference to the time of payment of the final fee.

Appeals.

After an application for a patent has been twice rejected by the examiner having it in charge, it may, at the option of the applicant, be brought before the board of examiners-in-chief, on payment of a fee of ten dollars.

For this purpose, a petition in writing must be filed, signed by the party or his authorized agent or attorney.

(188.)

Form of Appeal to the Examiners-in-Chief.

To the Commissioner of Patents.

Sir, — I hereby appeal to the examiners-in-chief from the decision of the principal examiner in the matter of my application for a patent for an improvement in (*here state the subject of the invention*) rejected a second time on day of

Respectfully,

(*Signature.*)

The examiners-in-chief will consider the case as it was when last passed upon by the primary examiner, merely revising his decisions so far as they were adverse to the applicant.

All cases which have been acted on by the board of examiners-in-chief may be brought before the commissioner in person, upon a written request to that effect, and upon the payment of the fee of twenty dollars required by law. A decision deliberately made and approved by one commissioner will not be disturbed by his successor. The only remaining remedy will be by appeal in those cases allowed by law to the judges of the Supreme Court of the District of Columbia.

The mode of appeal from the decision of the office to the judges of the Supreme Court of the District of Columbia is by giving written notice thereof to the commissioner, filing in the patent office, within such time as the commissioner shall appoint, reasons of appeal, and paying to him the sum of twenty-five dollars. Printed forms of notice of appeal, of the reasons of appeal, of the petition, and copies of the rules of the Supreme Court of the District of Columbia, will be forwarded from the patent office to any one wishing to make an appeal, on his request. The following rules have been adopted by the Supreme Court in appeals from the decisions of the Commissioner of Patents: —

The party desiring to appeal from the decision of the commissioner of patents must give written notice thereof to the commissioner, accompanied with his petition to the Supreme Court of the District of Columbia to grant him a hearing, and file the reasons of appeal, and pay the fee of twenty-five dollars.

The appellant, previous to any action on, and preparatory to the hearing of any appeal, must comply with the requisites of the law in the patent office, and his petition must state concisely —

1. The application for the patent;
2. Its nature, and, if a case of interference,
3. The residence of the party interested;
4. The commissioner's refusal;
5. The prayer of appeal;
6. Notice thereof to the commissioner;
7. The filing of the reasons of appeal in the patent office; and,
8. The payment into the office of the sum required by law.

To every petition must be annexed a certificate of the proper officer that the requisitions of the law have been complied with, or an affidavit of the truth of the facts stated in the petition.

No notice to the commissioner will be issued until such certificate or affidavit be made or produced.

The appeal will be tried upon the evidence which was in the case and produced before the commissioner.

The appellant must file his argument, in writing, within five days after the commissioner shall send in his report, and the papers, models, and drawings or specimens, or within five days after the day of hearing, which argument must state the facts and law relied on, together with the authorities in support of the same.

In contested cases the appellee shall file his argument, in writing, within ten days after the appellant shall have filed his argument. At the hearing, oral arguments may be made, not to occupy more than one hour for each counsel engaged, and not more than two counsel in each case will in any case be heard, and in no case will oral argument be heard unless the opposite party shall have reasonable notice thereof, through the mail or otherwise, from the party desiring to be heard orally; or where oral arguments are ordered by the court, the appellant shall give the notice.

The court, having fully heard the appeal, shall return all the papers to the commissioner, with a certificate of its proceedings and decisions, which shall be entered of record in the patent office, and such decision, so certified, shall govern the further proceedings of the commissioner in such case.

Interferences.

When each of two or more persons claims to be the first inventor of the same thing, an "interference" is declared between them, and a trial is had before the examiner. Nor does the fact that one of the parties has already obtained a patent prevent such an interference; for, although the commissioner has no power to cancel a patent already issued, he may, if he finds that another person was the prior inventor, give him also a patent, and thus place them on an equal footing before the courts and the public. If an applicant for a re-issue embraces in his amended specification any new or additional description of his invention, or enlarges his claim, or makes a new one, and thereby includes therein any thing which has been claimed in any patent granted subsequent to the date of his original application, as the invention of another person, an interference will be declared between the application and any unexpired patent, or pending application, in which the same thing is claimed; but not where such pending application for re-issue claims only what was granted in the original patent.

When an application is found to conflict with a caveat, the caveator is allowed a period of three months within which to present an application, when an interference may be declared. In cases of interference, patentees have the same remedies by appeal as applicants in pending applications. In contested cases, whether of interference or of extension, parties may have access to the testimony on file, prior to the hearing, in presence of the officer in charge; or, when practicable, copies may be obtained by them at the usual charges.

In cases of interference, the party who first made oath to the invention will be deemed the first inventor in the absence of all proof to the contrary. A time will be assigned in which the other party shall complete his direct testimony, and a further time in which the adverse party shall complete the testimony on his side; and a still further time in which the first party shall close his rebutting testimony, but shall take no other. If there are more than two parties, the times for taking testimony shall be so arranged that each shall have a like opportunity in his turn, each being held to go forward and prove his case against those who made oath to their applications before him. If either party wishes the time for taking his testimony, or for the hearing, postponed, he must make application for such postponement, and must show sufficient reason for it by affidavit filed before the time previously appointed has elapsed, if practicable; and must also furnish his opponent with copies of his affidavits, and with seasonable notice of the time of hearing his application.

When an interference has been declared, and a new application claiming the invention in controversy comes into the office before the final determination of such interference, the new application will be included in the case, and the proper means will be taken to allow all the parties a fair hearing. The testimony taken by the original parties will be retained in the case, provided that due opportunity can be given the new applicant to cross examine the witnesses. If, however, on the original interference, an appeal has been taken to the examiners in chief, before the new application is filed, such new application will be suspended until the decision in the original case, after which a new interference may be declared with the successful party. After an interference has been declared, another interference will not be declared upon a new application filed by either party unless it is shown to the satisfaction of the office that such party has new testimony which he could not have procured in time for the hearing, and which might change the decision.

When an application is adjudged to interfere with a part only of another pending application, the interfering parties will be permitted to see or obtain copies of so much only of the specifications as refers to the interfering claims. And either party may, if he so elect, withdraw from his application the claims adjudged not to interfere, and file a new application therefor. In such case, the new application will be examined without reference to the interference from which it was withdrawn.

Re-issues.

A re-issue is granted to the original patentee, his heirs, or the assignees of the entire interest, when, by reason of an insufficient or defective specification, the original patent is invalid, provided the error has arisen from inadvertence, accident, or mistake, without any fraudulent or deceptive intention. The petition for a re-issue must show that all parties owning any undivided or territorial interest in the patent (irrespective of licenses) concur in the surrender. And a certified statement of the title of the party surrendering must be filed with the application. Whatever is really embraced in the original invention, and so described or shown that it might have been embraced in the original patent, may be the subject of a re-issue; but an applicant will not be allowed the benefit of proof that there was more in his invention than is shown in his original application, model, or specimens.

Re-issued patents expire at the same time that the original patent would have done. For this reason, applications for re-issue will be acted upon immediately after they are completed.

A patentee may, at his option, have in his re-issue a separate patent for each distinct part of the invention comprehended in his original application, by paying the required fee in each case, and complying with the other requirements of the law, as in original applications. Each division of a re-issue constitutes the subject of a separate specification descriptive of the part or parts of the invention claimed in such division; and the drawing may represent only such part or parts. One or more divisions of a re-issue may be granted, though other divisions shall have been postponed or rejected. In all cases of applications for re-issues, the original claim is subject to re-examination, and may be revised and restricted in the same manner as in original applications.

The following are appropriate forms of application for re-issue:—

(189.)

Form of Surrender of a Patent for Re-issue.

To the Commissioner of Patents:—

The petition of , of , in the county of and State of ,

Respectfully represents:

That he did obtain letters-patent of the United States, for which letters-patent are dated on the first day of March, 1850; that he now believes that the same are inoperative and invalid by reason of a defective specification, which defect has arisen from inadvertence and mistake. He therefore prays that he may be allowed to surrender the same, and requests that new letters-patent may issue to him, for the same invention, for the residue of the period for which the original patent was granted, under the amended specification herewith presented, he having paid thirty dollars into the treasury of the United States, agreeably to the requirements of the act of Congress in that case made and provided.

(*Signature.*)

(190.)

Form of Oath to be appended to Applications for Re-issue.

CITY (OR TOWN) OF COUNTY OF STATE OF } SS.

On this day of 186 , before the subscriber, a personally appeared the above-named and made solemn oath (or affirmation) that he verily believes that, by reason of an insufficient or defective specification, his aforesaid patent is not fully valid and available to him, and that the said error has arisen from inadvertence, accident, or mistake, and without any fraudulent or deceptive intention, to the best of his knowledge or belief.

(*Signed.*) (*Signature.*)

Applications for re-issues will not be kept secret; and information respecting the same will be furnished upon inquiry, as well as copies of the proposed claims for publication.

Disclaimers.

Where, by inadvertence, accident, or mistake, the original patent is too broad, a disclaimer may be filed either by the original patentee or by any of his assignees.

The following is a sufficient form for a disclaimer: —

(191.)

Form for a Disclaimer by an Assignee.

TO THE COMMISSIONER OF PATENTS: —

The petition of of in the County of and State of

Respectfully represents:

That he has, by grant, duly recorded in the patent office, become the owner of a right for the several States of Massachusetts, Connecticut, and Rhode Island, to certain improvements in the steam-engine, for which letters-patent of the United States were granted to of in the State of dated on the day of 18 ; that he has reason to believe that through inadvertence and mistake, the claim made in the specification of said letters-patent is too broad, including that of which the said patentee was not the first inventor. Your petitioner, therefore, hereby enters his disclaimer to that part of the claim in the aforenamed specification which is in the following words, to wit: "I also claim the particular manner in which the piston of the above-described engine is constructed, so as to insure the close fitting of the packing thereof to the cylinder, as set forth;" which disclaimer is to operate to the extent of the interest in said letters-patent vested in your petitioner, who has paid ten dollars into the treasury of the United States, agreeably to the requirements of the act of Congress in that case made and provided.

(*Signature.*)

The above form is for disclaimer by an assignee. When the disclaimer is made by the original patentee, it must, of course, be so worded as to express that fact.

Extensions.

The applicant for an extension must file his petition and pay in the requisite fee at least ninety days prior to the expiration of his patent. There is no power in the patent office to renew a patent after it has once expired.

The questions which arise on each application for an extension are: —

Is the invention *novel?*

Is it *useful?*

Is it *valuable* and *important* to the public?

Has the inventor been *adequately remunerated* for his time and expense in originating and perfecting it?

Has he used due diligence in introducing his invention into general use?

The first two questions will be determined upon the result of an examination in the patent office; as will also the third, to some extent.

To enable the commissioner to come to a correct conclusion in regard to the third point of inquiry, the applicant should, if possi ble, procure the testimony of persons disinterested in the invention, which testimony should be taken under oath. In regard to the fourth and fifth points of inquiry, in addition to his own oath showing his receipts and expenditures on account of the invention, by which its value is to be ascertained, the applicant should show, by testimony on oath, that he has taken all reasonable measures to introduce his invention into general use; and that, without default or neglect on his part, he has failed to obtain from the use and sale of the invention a reasonable remuneration for the time, ingenuity, and expense bestowed on the same, and the introduction thereof into use.

In case of opposition by any person to the extension of a patent, both parties may take testimony, each giving reasonable notice to the other of the time and place of taking said testimony, which shall be taken according to the rules prescribed by the Commissioner of Patents in cases of interference. All arguments submitted must be in writing.

A monopoly of his invention was secured by the law formerly in force to the inventor for the term of fourteen years, with a view to compensate him for his time and expense in originating and perfecting it. At the end of the time for which his patent runs his monopoly should cease, and the invention become public property, unless he can show good reason for the contrary. The presumption is always against his application; and if he cannot show that his invention is novel, useful, and valuable, and important to the public, and that having made all reasonable effort to introduce it into general use, he has not been adequately remunerated for his time and expense in discovering and perfecting it, the commissioner cannot grant an extension. Therefore, the applicant for an extension must furnish to the office a statement in writing, under oath, of the ascertained value of the invention, and of his receipts and expenditures. This statement should be made particular and in detail, unless sufficient reason is set forth why such a statement cannot be furnished. This statement must be filed within thirty days after filing his petition.

Any person who intends to oppose an application for extension may, at any time after such application has been made, give notice of such intention to the applicant. After this he will be regarded as a party in the case, and be entitled to notice of the time and place of taking testimony, as well as to a list of the names and residences of witnesses whose testimony may have been previously taken; but he must file his reasons in the patent office at least twenty days before the day of hearing. The person opposing the extension will be entitled to a copy of the application, and of any other papers on file, upon paying the costs of copying.

In contested cases, no testimony will be received, unless by consent, which has been taken within thirty days next after the filing of the petition or the extension. In the notice of the application for an extension, a day will be fixed for the reception of testimony; a day ten days later for the reception of arguments; and a day ten days after this for a hearing. Applications for a postponement of the hearing must be made and supported according to the same rules as are to be observed in the case of interferences. But they will not be granted in such a manner as to cause a risk of preventing a decision in season.

Designs.

Designs are provided for by the Act of March 2, 1861, Sect. 11, as follows: —

"Any citizen or citizens, or alien or aliens, having resided one year in the United States and taken oath of his or their intention to become a citizen or citizens, who, by his, her, or their own industry, genius, efforts, and expense, may have invented or produced any new and original design for a manufacture, whether of metal or other material or materials, an original design for a bust, statue, or bass-relief, or composition in alto or basso relievo, or any new and original impression or ornament, or to be placed on any article of manufacture, the same being formed in marble or other material, or any new and useful pattern, or print, or picture, to be either worked into or worked on, or printed, or painted, or cast, or otherwise fixed on any article of manufacture, or any new and original shape or configuration of any article of manufacture not known or used by others before his, her, or their invention or production thereof, and prior to the time of his, her, or their application for a patent therefor, and who shall desire to obtain an exclusive property of right therein to make, use, and sell and vend the same or copies of the same to others, by them to be made, used, and sold, may make application in writing to the Commissioner of Patents, expressing such desire; and the commissioner, on due proceedings had, may grant a patent therefor, as in the case now of application for a patent, for the term of three and one-half years, or for the term of seven years, or for the term of fourteen years, as the said applicant may elect in his application: *Provided*, That the fee to be paid in such application shall be for the term of three years and six months, ten dollars; for seven years, fifteen dollars; and for fourteen years, thirty dollars; *And provided*, That the patentees of designs under this act shall be entitled to the extension of their respective patents for the term of seven years from the day on which said patents shall expire, upon the same terms and restrictions as are now provided for the extension of letters-patent."

Trade-marks, merely, are not patentable; there must be some new design to authorize a patent.

The following forms are proper to be observed in applications of this nature.

(192.)

Form of Application for Patents or Designs.

To the Commissioner of Patents:—

The petition of of , in the County of and State of ,

Respectfully represents:

That your petitioner has invented or produced a new and original design for , which he verily believes has not been known prior to the production thereof by your petitioner. He therefore prays that letters-patent of the United States may be granted to him therefor, for the term of years, vesting in him and his legal representatives the exclusive right to the same, upon the terms and conditions expressed in the act of Congress in that case made and provided, he having paid dollars into the treasury, and complied with the other provisions of the said act.

(*Signature.*)

The following may be used as a form of specification for designs: —

(193.)

Form of Specification for Designs.

To ALL WHOM IT MAY CONCERN: —

Be it known that I , of the city of , in the County of , and State of , have originated and designed a new pattern for carpets or other fabrics (or design for a trade-mark) of which the following is a full, clear, and exact description, reference being had to the accompanying specimens or drawings, making part of this specification.

[Here follows a description of the design, with reference to the specimen or drawing, the specification to conclude as follows: —]

Claim.

What I claim as my invention and desire to secure by letters-patent is the design or pattern for carpets or other fabrics (or design for a trade-mark) herein set forth.

Witnesses. (*Signature.*)

(194.)

Form of Oath.

CITY (OR TOWN) OF AND COUNTY OF , STATE OF . } ss.

On this day of , 186 , before the subscriber, a , personally appeared the within-named and made solemn oath (or affirmation, as the case may be) that he verily believes himself to be the original and first inventor or producer of the design for a composition in alto-relievo, and that he does not know or believe that the same was ever before known or used, and that he is a citizen of the United States.

(*Signature.*)

Foreign Patents.

The taking-out of a patent in a foreign country does not prejudice a patent previously obtained here; nor does it prevent obtaining a patent here subsequently. When application is made for a patent for an invention which has been already patented abroad, the inventor will be required to make oath that, according to the best of his knowledge and belief, the same has not been introduced into public and common use in the United States. An applicant who has obtained a foreign patent should (temporarily) file in the office the patent so obtained, with the specifications (provisional or complete) attached, or a sworn copy of them. But where such papers or copies cannot be conveniently furnished, it will be sufficient if the reasons of such inability be set forth by affidavit; and the applicant shall also state the fact that a foreign patent has actually been obtained, giving its date, and showing clearly that the invention so patented covers the whole ground of his present application.

Caveats.

Any citizen of the United States, or alien who has resided for one year last past in the United States, and has made oath of his intention to become a citizen thereof, can file a caveat in the secret archives of the patent office on the payment of a fee of ten dollars therefor. And if, at any time within one year thereafter, another person applies for a patent for the same invention, the caveator will be entitled to notice to file his application, and to go into interference with the applicant for the purpose of proving priority of invention, and obtaining the patent if he succeed. He must file his application within three months from the day on which the notice to him is deposited in the post office at Washington, adding the regular time for the transmission of the same to him; and the day when the time for filing expires shall be mentioned in the notice or indorsed thereon. The caveator will not be entitled to notice of any application pending at the time of filing his caveat, nor of any application filed after the expiration of one year from the date of filing the caveat; but he may renew his caveat at the end of one year by paying a second caveat fee of ten dollars, which will continue it in force for one year longer, and so on from year to year as long as the caveator may desire.

No caveat can be filed in the secret archives of the office unless accompanied by an oath of the caveator that he is a citizen of the United States, or that he is an alien and has resided for one year last past within the United States, and has made oath of his intention to become a citizen thereof; nor unless the applicant also states, under oath, that he believes himself the original inventor of the art, machine, or improvement set forth in his caveat.

A caveat need not contain as particular a description of the in vention as is requisite in a specification; but still the description should be sufficiently precise to enable the office to judge whether there is a probable interference when a subsequent application is filed.

Caveat papers cannot be withdrawn from the office nor undergo alteration after they have once been filed; but additional papers relative to the invention may be appended to the caveat (their date being noted), provided they are merely amendatory of the original caveat. In the case of filing papers supplementary to an original caveat, the right to notice in regard to the subject of those papers expires with the caveat; and any additional papers not relating to the invention first caveated will receive no notice. The caveator, or any person properly authorized by him, can at any time obtain copies of the caveat papers at the usual rates.

The caveat should be accompanied by drawings or sketches.

The following is a proper form of a caveat: —

(195.)

Form of a Caveat.

To the Commissioner of Patents: —

The petition of , of , in the county of , and State of ,

Respectfully represents:

That he has made certain improvements in and that he is now engaged in making experiments for the purpose of perfecting the same, preparatory to his applying for letters-patent therefor. He therefore prays that the subjoined description of his invention may be filed as a caveat in the confidential archives of the patent office, agreeably to the provisions of the act of Congress in that case made and provided; he having paid ten dollars into the treasury of the United States, and otherwise complied with the requirements of the said act.

MARCH 1, 1856. (*Signature.*)

[Here should follow a description of the general principles of the invention so far as it has been completed.]

The caveator must make oath or affirmation substantially according to the form already given.

The Repayment of Money.

Money paid by actual mistake will be refunded, but a mere change of purpose after the payment of money will not entitle a party to demand such return.

Assignments and Grants.

The assignee of any invention may have the patent issue to him directly, but this is held to apply only to assignees of entire interests. Although, when the inventor assigns his *entire* interest to two or more, a patent will issue to them jointly, still, if he yet retain a portion in himself, a joint patent will not be issued to him and them; the inventor, however, may make himself an assignee of a part interest in his invention.

An inventor can assign his entire right before a patent is obtained, so as to enable the assignee to take out a patent in his own name; but the assignment must first be recorded, and the specification sworn to by the inventor. After a patent is obtained, a patentee may grant the right to make or use the thing patented in any specified portion of the United States. Every assignment or grant should be recorded within three months from its date; but, if recorded after that time, it will protect the assignee or grantee against any one purchasing after the assignment or grant is placed on record. When the patent is to issue in the name of the assignee, the entire correspondence should be in his name.

The receipt of assignments is not generally acknowledged by the office. They will be recorded in their turn within a few days after their reception, and then transmitted to persons entitled to them.

A five-cent stamp is required for each sheet or piece of paper on which an assignment may be written.

(196.)

Form of Assignment of the entire Interest in Letters-Patent before obtaining the same, and to be recorded preparatory thereto.

Whereas I, , of , in the County of and State of , have invented certain new and useful improvements in ploughs, for which I am about to make application for letters-patent of the United States; and whereas of , has agreed to purchase from me all the right, title, and interest which I have, or may have, in and to the said invention, in consequence of the grant of letters-patent therefor, and has paid to me, the said the sum of five thousand dollars, the receipt of which is hereby acknowledged: Now this indenture witnesseth, that, for and in consideration of the said sum to me paid, I have assigned and transferred, and do hereby assign and transfer, to the said , the full and exclusive right to all the improvements made by me, as fully set forth and described in the specification which I have prepared and executed preparatory to the obtaining of letters-patent therefor. And I do hereby authorize and request the Commissioner of Patents to issue the said letters-patent to the said , as the assignee of my whole right and title thereto, for the sole use and behoof of the said and his legal representatives.

In testimony whereof, I have hereunto set my hand and affixed my seal this 16th day of February, 1856.

(*Signature.*) (*Seal.*)

Sealed and Delivered in Presence of

(197.)

Form of a Grant of a Partial Right in a Patent.

Whereas I, of in the County of and State of did obtain letters-patent of the United States for , which letters-patent bear date the day of 18 ; and whereas , of is desirous of acquiring an interest therein: Now this indenture witnesseth, that for and in consideration of the sum of two thousand dollars, to me in hand paid, the receipt of which is hereby acknowledged, I have granted, sold, and set over, and do hereby grant, sell, and set over, unto the said all the right, title, and interest which I have in the said invention, as secured to me by said letters-patent for, to, and in the several States of New York, New Jersey, and Pennsylvania, and in no other place or places; the same to be held and enjoyed by the said for his own use and behoof, and for the use and behoof of his legal representatives, to the full end of the term for which said letters-patent are granted (if it is intended to grant for any extended term, then add — and for the term of any extension thereof), as fully and entirely as the same would have been held and enjoyed by me had this grant and sale not been made.

In Testimony Whereof, I hereunto set my hand and affix my seal this day of 18

(*Signature.*) (*Seal.*)

Sealed and Delivered in Presence of

The Office Fees, and how payable.

Nearly all the fees payable to the patent office are positively required by law to be paid in advance. For the sake of uniformity and convenience, the remaining fees are required to be paid in the same manner; that is to say, before the labor is performed for which they are to be received in payment.

The following is the tariff of fees established by law: —

On every application for a design, for three years and six months	$10.00
On every application for a design, for seven years	15.00
On every application for a design, for fourteen years	30.00
On every caveat	10.00
On every application for a patent	15.00
On issuing each original patent	20.00
On filing a disclaimer	10.00
On every application for a reissue	30.00
On every additional patent granted on a re-issue	30.00
On every application for an extension	50.00
On the grant of every extension	50.00
On the first appeal from a primary examiner to examiners in chief	10.00
On appeal to the commissioner from examiners in chief	20.00
On every appeal to the judges of the Supreme Court, D.C.	25.00

On every copy of a patent or other instrument, for every 100 words	10
On every copy of drawing the cost of having it made .	
For recording every assignment of 300 words or under .	1.00
For recording every assignment, if over 300 and not over 1,000 words	2.00
For recording every assignment, if over 1,000 words .	3.00

The final fee on issuing a patent must be paid within six months after the time at which the patent was allowed, and notice thereof sent to the applicant or his agent. And if the final fee for such patent be not paid within that time, the patent will be withheld, and the invention therein described become public property as against the applicant therefor, unless he shall make a new application therefor within two years from the date of the allowance of the original application.

The money for the payment of fees should be deposited with an assistant treasurer, or other officer authorized to receive the same, taking his certificate, and remitting the same to this office. When this cannot be done without inconvenience, the money may be remitted by mail; and in every case the letter should state the exact amount enclosed. Letters containing money should be registered at the post-office where mailed.

The following officers are authorized to receive patent fees on account of the treasurer of the United States, and to give receipts and certificates of deposit therefor, to wit:—

Assistant treasurer of the United States, Boston, Mass.
Assistant treasurer of the United States, New York, N.Y.
Treasurer of the mint, Philadelphia, Penn.
Surveyor and inspector, Pittsburg, Penn.
Collector of customs, Baltimore, Md.
Collector of customs, Buffalo Creek, N.Y.
Assistant treasurer of the United States, St. Louis, Mo.
Surveyor of the customs, Cincinnati, O.
Receiver of public moneys, Jeffersonville, Ind.
Receiver of public moneys, Chicago, Ill.
Receiver of public moneys, Detroit, Mich.

Assistant treasurer of the United States, San Francisco, Cal.

And any national bank which has been designated as a depository of the public moneys.

All money sent by mail, either to or from the patent office, will be at the risk of the owner. In no case, should money be sent enclosed with models. All payments to or by the office must be paid in specie or treasury-notes, or national bank-notes.

Taking and Transmitting Testimony.

The clerks of the circuit courts of the United States may issue subpœnas to compel the attendance of witnesses when depositions are to be read in evidence in any contested cases in the patent office.

In interferences and other contested cases, the following rules have been established for taking and transmitting evidence: —

1. That before the deposition of a witness or witnesses be taken by either party, notice shall be given to the opposite party, as hereinafter provided, of the time and place when and where such deposition or depositions will be taken, with the names and residences of the witness or witnesses, so that the opposite party, either in person or by attorney, shall have full opportunity to cross-examine the witness or witnesses. And such notice shall, *with proof of service of the same*, be attached to the deposition or depositions, whether the party cross-examine or not, and such notice shall be given in sufficient time for the appearance of the opposite party, and for the transmission of the evidence to the patent office before the day of hearing.

2. That, whenever a party relies upon a caveat to establish the date of his invention, a certified copy thereof must be filed in evidence, with due notice to the opposite party, as no notice can be taken by the office of a caveat filed in its secret archives.

3. That all evidence, &c., shall be sealed, and addressed to the Commissioner of Patents by the person before whom it shall be taken, and so certified thereon.

4. That the certificate of the magistrate taking the evidence shall be substantially in the following form, and written upon the envelope, viz.: —

(198.)

Form of Magistrate's Certificate.

I hereby certify that the depositions of A B, C D, &c., relating to the matter of interference between E F and G H, were taken, sealed up, and addressed to the Commissioner of Patents by me.

(*Signature.*)

5. In cases of extension where no opposition is made, the party's own testimony will be received from the applicant; and such testimony as may have been taken by the applicant prior to notice of opposition shall be received, unless taken within thirty days after filing the petition for the extension: but the applicant shall give prompt notice to the opposing party or parties of the names and residences of the witnesses whose testimony has thus been taken.

No evidence touching the matter at issue will be *considered* upon the day of hearing, which shall not have been taken and filed in compliance with these rules: *Provided*, Notice of the objection has been given to the other party. But if either party shall be unable, for good and sufficient reasons, to procure the testimony of a witness or witnesses within the stipulated time, then it shall be the duty of said party to give notice of the same to the Commissioner of Patents, accompanied by statements, *under oath*, of the cause of such inability, and of the names of such witnesses, and of the facts expected to be proved by them, and of the *steps* which have been taken to procure said testimony, and of *the time* or *times* when efforts have been made to procure it; which last-mentioned notice to the commissioner shall be received by him previous to the day of hearing aforesaid.

The notice for taking testimony must be served by delivering to the adverse party a copy. If he is not found, such service may be made upon his agent or attorney of record, or by leaving a copy at the party's usual place of residence, with some member of the family who has arrived at the years of discretion. This notice must be annexed to the deposition, with a certificate duly sworn to, stating the manner and time in which the service was made.

The testimony must (if either party desires it) be taken in

answer to interrogatories, having the questions and answers committed to writing in their regular order by the magistrate, or, under his direction, by some person not interested in the issue, nor the agent or attorney of one who is. The deposition, when complete must be signed by the witness. The magistrate must append to the deposition his certificate, stating the time and place at which it was taken, the names of the witnesses, the administration of the oath, at whose request the testimony was taken, the occasion upon which it is intended to be used, the names of the adverse party (if any), and whether they were present.

No notice will be taken, at the hearing, of any merely formal or technical objection, unless it may reasonably be presumed to have wrought a substantial injury to the party raising the objection; nor even then, unless, as soon as that party became aware of the objection, he immediately gave notice thereof to this office, and also to the opposite party, informing him at the same time, that, unless corrected, he should urge his objection at the hearing. Each party shall furnish at the hearing an abstract of the testimony filed by him, not exceeding in length one-sixth of the original.

The following are useful forms for the taking of depositions: —

(199.)

Form in Taking of Depositions.

A B, being duly sworn, doth depose and say, in answer to interrogatories proposed to him by C D, counsel for E F, as follows, viz.: —

1. *Interrogatory.* What is your name, your residence, and occupation?

1. *Answer.* My name is A B; I am a carpenter, and reside in Boston, Mass.

And in answer to cross-interrogatories proposed to him by G H, counsel for I K, as follows:—

1. *Cross-interrogatory, &c.*

(Signed) A B.

STATE OF } ss.
COUNTY OF }

At , in said county, on the day of , A. D. 18 . before me personally appeared the above-named A B, and made oath that the foregoing deposition, by him subscribed, contains the whole truth, and nothing but the truth.

The said deposition is taken at the request of E F, to be used upon the hearing of an interference between the claims of the said E F and those of I K, before the Commissioner of Patents of the United States, at his office, on the day of next. The said I K was duly notified, as appears by the original notice hereto annexed, and attended by G H, his counsel.

Certified by me: *(Signature.)*

The magistrate must then seal up the deposition when completed, and indorse upon the envelope a certificate according to the form before the last.

After a second rejection, none of the papers can be inspected, save in the presence of a sworn officer, nor will any of the papers be returned to the applicant or agent.

Whenever it shall be found that two or more parties whose interests are in conflict are represented by the same attorney, the examiner in charge will notify each of said principal parties of this fact.

The Filing and Preservation of Papers.

All claims and specifications filed in this office (including amendments) must be written in a fair, legible hand, without interlineations or erasures, except such as are clearly stated in a marginal or foot note, written on the same sheet of paper; or, failing in which, the office may require them to be printed. All papers filed in the office will be regarded as permanent records of the office, and must never, on any account, be changed, further than to correct mere clerical mistakes.

Amendments.

The applicant has a right to amend, of course, after the first rejection; and he may amend after the second, if the examiner therein present any new references, unless the devices claimed by him in the first amendment were entirely different from those originally relied upon, and not mere modifications of them. After a second rejection, and before appeal to the examiners in chief, the applicant may draw up special amendments, and present the same to the commissioner, together with an affidavit showing good cause why the amendments were not sooner offered, whereupon the commissioner may, in his discretion, grant leave to make such special amendments, and allow a reconsideration. No alterations or amendments, except of clerical errors, will be allowed after an appeal to the examiner in chief, or after the patent has been ordered to issue, unless the same are approved by the examiner in charge.

All amendments of the model, drawings, or specification, must conform to at least one of them as they were at the time of the filing of the application; and all amendments of specifications or claims must be made on separate sheets of paper from the original, and must be filed in the manner above directed. Even when the amendment consists in striking out a portion of the specification, or other paper, the same course should be observed. No erasure must be made. The papers must remain forever just as they were when filed, so that a true history of all that has been done in the case may be gathered from them.

The following are forms proper to be observed in such cases: —

(200.)

Form of Amendment of Specification.

"I hereby amend my specification by inserting the following words after the word , in the line of the page thereof" (here should follow the words that are to be inserted); or, "I hereby amend my specification by striking out the line of the page thereof;" or, "by striking out the first and fourth clauses of the claim appended thereto;" or whatever may be the amendment desired by the applicant.

In each case, the exact word to be stricken out or inserted should be clearly described, and the precise point indicated where any insertion is to be made.

The office may, at its option, return specifications for amendment; but in no other case will any person be allowed to take any papers, models, or samples from the office. If applicants have not preserved copies of such papers as they wish to amend, the office will furnish them on the usual terms. No application will be suspended merely because the applicant may refuse to amend as requested or advised by an examiner in charge; but in such case the application must be examined on its merits, as presented, and allowed or rejected, so that the inventor may take an appeal if the decision should be adverse.

Placing the affidavit of the applicant on one piece of paper and the specification on another, so that both may be detached and applied to other papers, will be looked upon with suspicion, and any such substitution will be carefully guarded against. No specification will be received unless the sheets are attached together, or unless the officer who administers the oath has subscribed his name upon each separate sheet of paper, so as to show that the specification presented is the same that was subscribed and sworn to.

References.

Upon the rejection of an application for a patent, for the want of novelty, the applicant will be furnished with a specific reference to the article or articles by which it is anticipated, so that he may be enabled to judge of the propriety of renewing his application, or of amending his specification to embrace only that part of the invention which is new. If he desires a copy of the cases so referred to, or of the plates or drawings connected with them, they will be forwarded to him, if in possession of the office, on payment of the cost of making such copies.

The examiners in charge will designate the class to which the references made by them belong; and, in asking for a copy of the patent referred to, the applicant must indicate the class, so as to facilitate the search.

Giving or witholding Information.

The caveats are required by law to be kept secret. In addition, all pending applications, except for re-issues, are, as far as practicable, preserved in like secrecy. No information will, therefore, be given those inquiring whether any particular case is before the office, or whether any particular person has applied for a patent. But information is given in relation to any case after a patent has issued, or after a patent has been refused, and the further prosecution of the application is abandoned. The models, in such cases, are so placed as to be subject to general inspection. The specifications and drawings in any particular case can be seen by any one having particular occasion to examine them, and copies thereof, as well as of patents granted, will be furnished to any one willing to pay the bare expense of making them. Copies will be made on parchment, at the request of the applicant, on his paying the additional cost.

Even after a case is rejected, the application is regarded as pending until after the decision of an appeal thereon, or until after the party has withdrawn the case from the further consideration of the office; but if a party, whose application has been rejected, allows the matter to rest for two years without taking any further steps therein, he will be regarded as having abandoned his application, so far, at least, that it will no longer be protected by any rule of secrecy. The specification, drawings, and model will then be subject to inspection in the same manner as those of patented or withdrawn applications.

Information in relation to pending cases is given so far as it becomes necessary in conducting the business of the office, but no further. Thus, when an interference is declared between two pending applications, each of the contestants is entitled to a knowledge of so much of his antagonist's case as to enable him to conduct his own understandingly.

An application will not be rejected upon a previously rejected one not withdrawn or abandoned, but the original references will be given. Should either applicant, in such case, take an appeal, and the decision be reversed, the other will be notified, so that an interference may be declared, if desired.

When an applicant claims a certain device, and the same device is found *described* but not *claimed* in another pending application which was previously filed, or on any unexpired patent, information of the filing of such second application is always given to the prior applicant, or patentee, with a suggestion that if he desires to claim a patent for that device he should forthwith modify his specification accordingly, or file an application for a re-issue, as the case may be.

But where the application, which thus describes a device without claiming it, is subsequent in date to that wherein such device is claimed, the general rule is that no notice of the claim in the previous application is given to the subsequent applicant. But where there are any special reasons to doubt whether the prior applicant is really the inventor of the device claimed, or where there are any other peculiar and sufficient reasons for departing from the rule above stated, the office reserves to itself the right of so doing without its being regarded as a departure from the established rule.

The office never responds to inquiries as to the novelty of an alleged invention, in advance of an application for a patent, nor to inquiries founded upon brief and imperfect descriptions propounded with a view of ascertaining whether such alleged improvements have been patented, and if so, to whom; nor can it act as an expounder of the patent law, nor as counsellor for individuals, except as to questions arising within the office.

All business with the office should be transacted in writing. Unless by the consent of all parties, the action of the office is predicated exclusively on the written record.

Rules of Correspondence.

All correspondence must be in the name of the Commissioner of Patents, and all letters and other communications intended for the office must be addressed to him. If addressed to any of the other officers, they will not be noticed, unless it should be seen that the mistake was owing to inadvertence. A separate letter should in every case be written in relation to each distinct subject of inquiry or application; the subject of the invention and the date of filing being always carefully noted. When an agent has filed his power of attorney, duly executed, the correspondence will, in ordinary cases, be held with him only. A double correspondence with him and his principal, if generally allowed, would largely enhance the labor of the office. For the same reason, the assignee of the entire interest in an invention is alone entitled to hold correspondence with the office, to the exclusion of the inventor. If the principal becomes dissatisfied, he must revoke his power of attorney, and notify the office, which will then communicate with him. All communications to and from the commissioner, upon official business, are carried in the mail free of postage.

The interests of inventors and of the public, and the proper transaction of the immense and complicated business of the patent office, absolutely require the rules we have above stated; and most of them are rigidly adhered to. The statements, rules, and forms above given are the same as those approved and prepared by the Commissioner of Patents, for the information and guidance of applicants. The experience of the author of this book authorizes him to say that all who deal with any of the officers of the patent office will meet with kindness and courtesy, and as much indulgence and assistance as the business and the rules of the office permit.

CHAPTER XXXIV.

THE LAW OF COPYRIGHT.

SECTION I.

WHAT MAY BE THE SUBJECT OF COPYRIGHT.

ANY citizen of the United States, or resident therein, who shall be the author, inventor, or designer of any book, map, chart, dramatic or musical composition, engraving, cut, print, or photograph, and his executors, administrators, or assigns, shall have the sole liberty of printing, reprinting, publishing, and vending the same; and, in the case of a dramatic composition, of publicly performing or representing it, or causing it to be performed or represented by others. And all copyrights are granted for the term of twenty-eight years from the time of recording the title thereof.

The author, inventor or designer, if he be still living and a citizen of the United States or resident therein, or his widow, or children, if he be dead, shall have the same exclusive right continued for the further term of fourteen years, upon recording the title of the work so secured a second time, and complying with all other regulations in regard to original copyrights, within six months before the expiration of the first term. And such persons shall, within two months from the date of said renewal, cause a copy of the record thereof to be published in one or more newspapers, printed in the United States, for the space of four weeks.

All copyrights are assignable in law, by an instrument of writing: this should be proved or acknowledged in such manner as deeds for the conveyance of land are required by law to be proved or acknowledged in the same State or district, and be recorded in the office where the original copyright is recorded; and every such instrument not so proved or acknowledged and recorded, within sixty days after its execution, shall be void, as against any subsequent purchaser or mortgagee for a valuable consideration, without notice.

SECTION II.

HOW COPYRIGHTS ARE TO BE OBTAINED.

No person is entitled to a copyright, unless he, before publication, deposits a printed copy of the title of the book or other article for which he desires a copyright, in the clerk's office of the district court of the district wherein the proprietor resides, and, within three months thereafter, causes to be delivered a copy of such copyright book or other article to said clerk.

It is the duty of the clerk of the court to record the name of such copyright book or other article, forthwith, in a book to be kept for that purpose, in these words: "District of , to wit: Be it remembered, that on the day of , Anno Domini , A B, of the said district, hath deposited in this office the title of a book (map, chart, or otherwise, as the case may be), the title of which is in the words following, to wit: (here insert the title) the right whereof he claims as author (or proprietor, as the case may be) in conformity with the laws of the United States respecting copyrights. C. D., clerk of the court." And he shall give a copy of the title, under the seal of the court, to said proprietor, whenever he shall require it. And he shall, once in each year, transmit a certified transcript of his records of copyright, with all the several copyright books or other articles deposited in his office, to the Secretary of the Interior, to be preserved in his department.

For recording the title of any copyright book or other article, the clerk of the court is entitled to receive from the other person claiming the same, fifty cents; and for every copy, under seal, actually given to such person or his assigns, fifty cents; and for recording any instrument of writing for the assignment of a copyright, fifteen cents for every one hundred words, and for every copy thereof, ten cents for every one hundred words.

It is the duty of every proprietor of any copyright book or other article, to deliver to the library of Congress at Washington, within one month after its publication, a complete printed copy thereof, and a copy of every subsequent edition wherein any changes shall be made. If he fails to make such delivery, he is liable to a penalty of twenty-five dollars, to be collected by the librarian of Congress, in the name of the United States, in any district or circuit court of the United States, within the jurisdiction of which the delinquent may reside or be found.

Any such copyright book or other article may be sent to the librarian of Congress by mail, free of postage, provided the words "copyright matter" are plainly written or printed on the outside of the package containing the same. It is the duty of the postmaster to give a receipt for such package if requested, and when delivered to him to see that it is safely forwarded to its destination without cost to the proprietor.

No person shall maintain an action for the infringement of his copyright, unless he has inserted in the several copies of every edition published, on the titlepage, or the page immediately following, if it be a book; or if a map, chart, musical composition, print, cut, engraving, or photograph, by causing to be impressed on the face; or if a volume, then upon the title or frontispiece thereof the following words, viz., "Entered according to act of Congress, in the year , by A B, in the clerk's office of the district court of " (as the case may be)

If any person inserts or impresses such notice, or words purporting the same, in any book, map, chart, musical composition, print, cut, engraving, or photograph, for which he has not obtained a copyright, every person so offending shall forfeit and pay one hundred dollars; one moiety thereof to the person who shall sue for the same, and the other to the use of the United States, to be recovered by action in any court of competent jurisdiction.

SECTION III.

PUNISHMENT FOR INFRINGEMENT OF COPYRIGHT.

If any person, after the due recording of the title of any book, shall, within the term limited, and without the consent of the proprietor of the copyright, first obtained in writing, signed in presence of two or more witnesses, print, publish, or import, or knowing the same to be so printed, published, or imported, shall sell or expose to sale, any copy of such book, such offender shall forfeit every copy thereof to said proprietor, and shall also forfeit and pay fifty cents for every sheet thereof which may be found in his possession, either printing, printed, published, imported, or exposed for sale; the one half thereof to the proprietor, and the other to the use of the United States.

If any person, after the recording of the title of any map, chart, musical composition, print, cut, engraving, or photograph, as herein provided, shall, within the term limited, and without the consent of the proprietor of the copyright, first obtained in writing, signed in presence of two or more witnesses, engrave, etch, work, copy, print, publish, or import, either in whole or in part, or by varying the main design with intent to evade the law, or knowing the same to be so printed, published, or imported, shall sell or expose to sale, any copy of such map or other article, as aforesaid, such offender shall forfeit to the said proprietor all the plates on which the same shall be copied, and every sheet thereof either copied or printed, and shall further forfeit one dollar for every sheet of the same found in his possession, either printing, printed, copied, published, imported, or exposed for sale; the one half thereof to the proprietor and the other to the use of the United States.

Any person publicly performing or representing any dramatic composition for which a copyright has been obtained, without the consent of the proprietor thereof, shall be liable for damages therefor, not less than one hundred dollars for the first, and fifty dollars for every subsequent performance, or more, as to the court shall appear to be just.

Any person who shall print or publish any manuscript whatever, without the consent of the author or proprietor first obtained (if such author or proprietor be a citizen of the United States, or resident therein), shall be liable to said author or proprietor for all damages occasioned by such injury, to be recovered by action in any court of competent jurisdiction. But no law prohibits the printing, publishing, importation, or sale of any book, map, chart, dramatic or musical composition, print, cut, engraving, or photograph, written, composed, or made by any person not a citizen of the United States, nor resident therein.

No action shall be maintained in any case of forfeiture or penalty under the copyright laws, unless the same is commenced within two years after the cause of action has arisen.

All actions and suits arising under the copyright laws of the United States are originally cognizable as well in equity as at law, whether civil or penal in their nature, by the circuit courts of the United States, or any district court having the jurisdiction of a circuit court. And the court has power, upon bill in equity, filed by any party aggrieved, to grant injunctions to prevent the violation of any right secured by said laws, on such terms as the court may deem reasonable. And it may be added, that at present, actions for infringement of copyright are generally brought in courts of equity.

A writ of error or appeal to the Supreme Court of the United

States shall lie from all judgments and decrees of any circuit court, in any suit touching copyrights originally commenced therein, without regard to the sum or value in controversy. In all recoveries under the copyright laws, either for damages, forfeitures, or penalties, full costs shall be allowed thereon.

I subjoin two forms of agreement between authors holding copyrights, with publishers, for the publication of the book. Every such agreement must express the particular terms of that bargain; but the following may serve as general guides. I add a form of assignment of copyright:—

(201.)

Agreement between Author and Publisher: short Form.

This agreement, made this day of in the year 18 , by and between (*name of author*) and (*name of publisher*) witnesseth as follows:

The said (*name of author*) being now preparing a work, to be called (*or on the subject of*) to be in volume , hereby agrees and promises to complete the same for the press as rapidly as practicable, and to sell to the same (*name of the publisher*) for the sum of dollars, to be paid as hereinafter mentioned, the exclusive right of printing, publishing, and selling the first edition thereof, to consist of copies. The copyright of said work to be secured and retained by said (*name of author*) as author and proprietor.

And the said (*name of publisher*) hereby agrees and promises to publish said edition of copies, and to pay to said (*name of author*) the said sum of dollars, by their promissory, negotiable notes, payable at average credit of months from the day of publication of said edition; and also to give him copies of said work, for presentation.

Witness Our hands, in duplicate, this day of

(*Signature of author.*)
(*Signature of publisher.*)

(202.)

Agreement between Author and Publishers: fuller Form.

Articles of Agreement, Made this day of A.D. 186 by and between of the first part, and of State of booksellers and publishers, of the second part, witnesseth, That the said (*name of the *author*) in consideration of the agreements of the said (*name of publishers*) hereinafter contained, hereby agrees with them and their representatives and assigns that he will deliver to them on or before the day of A.D. 186 the manuscript of a book now in course of preparation by him, to be entitled said manuscript to be properly prepared for the press, and to be sufficient in amount for volume of not less than pages, similar to those of that he will secure in his own name a good and valid copyright thereof for the United States, and any renewals or extensions of such copyright to which he may hereafter be entitled, and will defend the same from all infringements and adverse claims, and will save the said and their representatives and assigns harmless and indemnified from all such infringements and claims, and from all damage, costs, and expenses arising to them by reason thereof; that he will license and allow the said and their representatives and assigns, but no other party or parties, to print, publish, and sell the aforesaid book, and any revisions of the same, during the continuance of any copyrights or renewals thereof which he may obtain therefor; provided, however, that the said and their representatives and assigns, shall in substantial good faith keep and perform their agreements hereinafter contained; and that, during the continuance of the exclusive rights hereby granted, he will revise said book as occasion may require, and will with all reasonable diligence and speed superintend in the usual manner of authors the printing of all editions thereof; and will not prepare, edit, or cause to be published in his name or otherwise, any thing which may injure or interfere with the sale of the aforesaid book.

And the said (*name of the publishers*) in consideration of the foregoing agreements of the said author of the aforesaid book, hereby agree on their part that they will, upon the delivery to them of the manuscript thereof as aforesaid, proceed at once to print and publish an edition of said book, of at least copies, of which they will deliver to the said author for his own use without charge; that they will subsequently, from time to time, during the continuance of their enjoyment of the exclusive rights herein granted them, print and publish such other editions of said book as the demand for the same may require, copies of each of which they will deliver to said author for his own use without charge; that they will use their best exertions to secure the speedy sale of all such editions published by them as aforesaid; and that, upon the publication of each and every edition of said book, they will pay unto the said author, or his representatives or assigns, a sum equal to upon each and every copy of which said edition shall consist (excepting, however, said copies to be given to said author as aforesaid, and such other copies as may be used for presentation to editors and others for the purpose of obtaining reviews and notices, or otherwise to promote the sale of said book), which said sum shall be paid as follows (*state the manner and times of payment, as by cash or notes*) but from any sum so to be paid as aforesaid shall first be deducted the cost of any alterations or corrections, exceeding ten per cent of the cost of first setting up the type, made by the said author in said book after the portion altered or corrected is in type.

In Witness Whereof, The said parties have hereto, and to another instrument of like tenor, set their hands the day and year first above written.

(*Signature of author.*)

(*Signature of publishers.*)

(*Witnesses.*)

(203.)

An Assignment of a Copyright.

To all whom it may Concern: Whereas I (*name of assignor*) of in the County of and State of did obtain a copyright from the United States for a work entitled and the certificate of said copyright bears date A.D. eighteen hundred and

Now this Deed Witnesseth, That for a valuable consideration, viz. to me in hand paid, the receipt of which is hereby acknowledged, I have assigned, sold, and set over, and by these presents do assign, sell, and set over unto the said (*name of assignee*) all the right, title, and interest I have in the above book (*or design, &c.*) as secured to me by said copyright. The same to be held and enjoyed by the said (*name of assignee*) for his own use and behoof, and for the use and behoof of his legal representatives, to the full end of the term for which said copyright was issued, as fully and entirely as the same would have been held and enjoyed by me had this assignment and sale not been made.

In Testimony Whereof, I have hereunto set my hand and affixed my seal this day of in the year of our Lord one thousand eight hundred and

(*Signature.*) (*Seal.*)

Sealed and Delivered in Presence of

CHAPTER XXXV.

MEANS PROVIDED FOR THE RECOVERY AND COLLECTION OF DEBTS.

1. Arrest and Imprisonment.—In eight States, no person can be arrested or imprisoned for debt. These are Virginia, Maryland, North Carolina, Mississippi, Florida, Wisconsin, Arkansas, and Texas. In California no female, and in Louisiana no female, and no person who has not a domicil in the State, and in Ohio no female nor any officer or soldier of the Revolutionary army, can be arrested or imprisoned for debt. In all the States, the *intention* of the law is to limit imprisonment to those cases in which either fraud was committed in the contraction of the debt, or the debtor intends to abscond out of the reach of process. The provisions to effect this are very various. Generally, the plaintiff must file in the clerk's office, or indorse upon the writ, an affidavit of the facts on which he grounds the right of arrest. In some of the States, provision is made for the imprisonment on execution of a debtor who can be found to possess, and refuses to surrender, property or interest, real or personal, which might be made available for the payment of his debts.

2. The Trustee Process.—The trustee process, or garnishee process, or process of foreign attachment,—by all which names it is known,—is now nearly or quite universal. It is substantially this. A owes B a debt; but A has no property in his hands or possession which B can get at; but A has deposited in the hands of C goods or property or credits of some kind, or A has a valid claim against C for wages or services, or money loaned, or goods sold, or something else; and this B gets by suing A, *not* with a common writ, but with a *trustee* writ, so called, in which he declares that B is the *trustee* of A, for property, &c.; and on this writ, if B recovers payment against A, he will have an execution against all A's property in the hands of C, and all A's valid demands against C. But C, when notified, may come into court, and, in answer to all questions put to him, declare that he (C) has no property in his hands belonging to A, and that he does not owe A any thing. And then the plaintiff may shape the questions as he pleases, to draw out the truth.

No one is adjudged trustee, or made to pay to the creditor the debt due to the debtor, if he has given a negotiable note for it, because he might have to pay it again to an honest indorsee. Nor if the debt is not certainly due; nor, generally, if it is due from the trustee in any official capacity, which will require him to account over for the money in his hands; nor if the debtor has recovered a judgment against the trustee, on which execution may issue.

3. The Homestead. — In sixteen of the States, a *homestead* is protected from creditors, and exempted from all attachment or execution, excepting in some States for taxes, or wages of labor to a certain amount. In Maine, New Hampshire, Vermont, Massachusetts, Ohio, Tennessee, Alabama, and Iowa, it is limited to five hundred dollars in value. In Georgia, fifty acres, not to exceed two hundred dollars. In Florida, forty acres, not to exceed two hundred dollars. In New York, New Jersey, and Illinois, not to exceed one thousand dollars; in Michigan, fifteen hundred dollars; in Texas, two hundred acres, or two thousand dollars in value; in California, five thousand dollars.

Various provisions are made in each of these States to combine a due protection of the creditor with proper prevention of fraud. The most common means are by requiring that "the homestead" should be distinctly defined and set apart, and in many cases by the additional requirement, that the description and location of it should be put on public record.

In all the States there are also exemption laws. These provide very generally that bed and bedding and other necessary furniture, needful clothing, a Bible and school-books, and a certain amount of food and fuel, shall not be taken on attachment or execution. In some States, the tools of a trade, the uniform, arms, and equipments of soldiers or officers in the militia, the family burying-vault and gravestones, a team or yoke of oxen, bees with their hives and honey, a boat for fishing, &c., are exempted. The statutes often enumerate the articles exempted quite minutely, and then add, that necessary articles to a certain amount of value, usually one or two hundred dollars, are also exempted.

CHAPTER XXXVI.

THE LIENS OF MECHANICS AND MATERIAL MEN FOR THEIR WAGES AND MATERIALS.

In nearly all our States there are now some provisions for securing to mechanics, and to persons supplying materials (who are called "material men"), their wages and pay for their materials, by means of *liens*, as they are called in law. A *lien* is a *hold* upon or a valid claim against property. This means that every mechanic employed upon a house, and, in most of the States, upon a vessel, and in some upon any property whatever, as a railroad or canal, either in the construction or repair of it, has a *lien* upon the property on which he has labored or for which he has supplied materials, for the amount of his wages and the price of his materials. This lien or claim he has for a certain time; and during that time he may either sue for his wages, and make an attachment of the property, or, in some States, file a petition with the proper court; and in either may have the property sold to pay his wages, unless the owner redeems it.

The reason of these precautions is obvious enough. The purpose of the law is to assist and protect the mechanic, or material man, but not to enable him to commit a fraud or do an injury to his neighbors. And it would be an injury to a man to let him buy a house and pay full price for it, and then tell him that the mechanics who built it had a *lien* (which is much the same in effect as a mortgage) upon the house, without his knowing any thing about it. And it would be an injury to an owner, who had contracted with the master-workman to repair or change his house at great expense, to settle with this master-workman in due time, and pay him the full amount of his bill, without any notice to the owner that he was under an obligation to pay again for all the labor spent upon his house, or let the house go on execution.

Of all these laws for the recovery of debts, and the enforcement of the liens of mechanics, the provisions *now in force* are quite recent. Only of late years has imprisonment for debt been greatly mitigated or removed, and the trustee or garnishee process made what it now is, exceedingly convenient and useful. The homestead law and the lien law, though now so widely spread, are a modern invention, or, at least, of modern introduction. The effect of this recent origin is twofold. First, important practical questions still exist as to their construction, application, and effect, which only time can solve. Secondly, there is not only no general agreement as to their details, but, to all appearance, no permanent contentment with these details anywhere. The statutes on these subjects undergo very frequent changes of all degrees of importance, and we have no reasonable assurance, anywhere, that precisely what is law to-day will be law in the same place to-morrow.

I have thought it best, therefore, not to attempt to give all those statutory provisions of the several States in detail. Such a thing might be much worse than useless if it led to conduct grounded on a mistaken belief that the law of one time is just what it is at another. Nothing more has been attempted, therefore, than this. First, to give a general and accurate view of all those principles of the laws relating to creditor and debtor which are now generally agreed upon, and may be regarded as probably permanent. Secondly, to give such information as may be depended upon, to those who are caught in an emergency where they cannot at once seek counsel, or for any reason will not, and who may here be told, *in general,* how the law stands in relation to them. Thirdly, to indicate distinctly to the mechanic what rights he may possess and what securities he may hold, and how he may lose the rights and securities he possesses, and to the owner or buyer what liabilities he may incur, unless the one and the other take the proper course which the law has provided for their safety.

In the present state of the laws for the collection of debts or the exemption of property, it would be difficult for any one but a lawyer to learn or state all the exact provisions and effects of these laws. And even if this were possible, no mechanic would probably be willing to trust to himself to make out his writ, or file his petition, to enforce his claims or lien ; and any competent counsel whom he would employ for this purpose would be able to tell him what the law was *at that very time, in that very State, and on that precise question.*

For these reasons, little more is attempted in this chapter, because little more is thought possible, than to yield all available assistance to debtors or creditors who have not the means or opportunity of employing counsel, and of indicating to those who can consult them, the rights, security, and safety they may possess, by wise advice and accurate conformity with the law.

The forms to be used under the lien laws are not prescribed by statute. Those given below are in use in some of our principal cities; and the same, in substance, would be suitable anywhere.

(204.)

A Notice under Mechanic's Lien Law.

(To be filed with the Clerk of the County.)

To Esquire,
Clerk of the City and County of

Sir,

Please to take Notice, That I, residing at No. Street, in have a claim against amounting to the sum of due to me, and that the claim is made for and on account of (*here state the work or materials*) and that such work was done in pursuance of (*here describe the contract*) which building is owned by situated in the ward, of the city of on the side of Street, and is known as No. the following is a diagram of said premises (*or, the said premises being described as follows*)

And that I have and claim a lien upon said house or building and the appurtenances and lot on which the same shall stand pursuant to the provisions of an act of the Legislature of the State of to secure the payment of mechanics, laborers, and persons furnishing materials towards the erection, altering, or repairing of buildings.

Dated, this day of 18

(*Signature.*)

COUNTY OF } ss.
CITY OF }

(*The name of the party claiming the lien*) being duly sworn, says, that he is the claimant mentioned in the foregoing notice of lien, that he has read the said notice and knows the contents thereof, and that the same is true to his own knowledge, except as to the matters therein stated on information and belief, and as to those matters he believes it to be true.

to before me, this day of 18

(205.)

A Bill of Particulars of Mechanic's Claim.

(*To be served on owner.*)

A Bill of Particulars Of the amount claimed to be due from for and on account of (*work or materials*) and that such work was done (*or materials furnished*) in pursuance of (*state the contract or order*) which building is owned by situated in the ward of the city of on the side of Street, and is known as No. of said street.

M

To

18

(206.)

A Release and Discharge of a Mechanic's Lien.

I do Hereby Certify, That a certain mechanic's lien, filed in the office of the clerk of the county of the day of one thousand eight hundred and at o'clock, in the noon, in favor of claimant against the building and lot, situate side of street, and known as No. in said street, whereof is owner, and is contractor, is discharged.

ss. On the day of one thousand eight hundred and before me came who is known to me to be the individual described in, and who executed the above certificate, and acknowledged that he executed the same.

(207.)

Release and Discharge of a Mechanic's Lien; another Form.

Whereas, We, the subscribers, have erected and furnished materials for erecting on lot or piece of ground situate And have agreed to release all liens which we, or any or either of us have, or might have, on the said by reason of materials furnished, or work performed, for erecting the same. Now these presents witness, that we, the subscribers, for and in consideration of the premises, and of the sum of one dollar, to each of us at or before the sealing and delivery hereof by the said well and truly paid, the receipt whereof we do hereby acknowledge, have remised, released, and forever quit-claimed, and by these presents do remise, release, and forever quit-claim unto the said and to his heirs and assigns, all and all manner of liens, claims, and demands whatsoever, which we, or any or either of us now have, or might or could have, on or against the said and premises, for work done, or for materials furnished, for erecting and constructing the said building, or otherwise howsoever. So that he the said and his heirs and assigns, shall and may have, hold, and enjoy, the said and premises, freed and discharged from all liens, claims, and demands whatsoever, which we, or any or either of us, now have, or might or could have, on or against the same, if these presents had not been made.

In Witness Whereof, we have hereunto set our hands and seals the day of the date written opposite our respective signatures.

(*Date.*) (*Witnesses at signing.*) (*Signatures of Claimants.*)

CHAPTER XXXVII.

PENSIONS.

Congress has provided pensions for officers, soldiers, and sailors disabled in the service, and for the widows and children of officers, soldiers, and sailors who have died in the service. The statutes are very carefully drawn, and may be regarded as making, on the whole, wise and liberal provision.

The officers to whom application by officers, soldiers, or sailors, or their representatives, should be made in Washington, by letter or petition, are, by a soldier having his regular discharge-paper, to the Paymaster General; if the discharge-paper be lost, to the second Auditor of the Treasury; by those who claim as the representatives of a deceased person, to the same auditor; if for commutation of rations, to the same auditor; if for pensions, or in any especial question arising out of pensions, to the Commissioner of Pensions.

The officers having charge of these matters are disposed to do whatever can be done for the benefit and convenience of applicants, consistently with a due protection of the government and the country against fraud or mistake. And both fraud and mistake are so easy, that many precautions and precise regulations have been found necessary, and are carefully adhered to.

The Commissioner of Pensions has prepared instructions for all applicants, military or naval; which, being understood and regarded, will prevent all fraud or misunderstanding. They are substantially as follows: —

Instructions.

Under the act of Congress approved July 14, 1862, and acts amendatory thereof, pensions are granted to the following classes of persons: —

I. INVALIDS, disabled since March 4, 1861, in the military or naval service of the United States, in the line of duty.

II. WIDOWS of officers, soldiers, or seamen, dying of wounds received or of disease contracted in the military or naval service, as above.

III. CHILDREN, under sixteen years of age, of such deceased persons, if there is no widow surviving, or from the time of the widow's remarriage.

IV. MOTHERS of officers, soldiers, or seamen, deceased as aforesaid, provided the latter have left neither widow nor children under sixteen years of age; and provided, also, that the mother was dependent, wholly or in part, upon the deceased for support.

V. FATHERS, upon the same conditions, and subject to the same restrictions, as mothers, if there be no mother surviving.

VI. Brothers and Sisters, under sixteen years of age, of deceased officers, soldiers, or seamen, dependent on the latter wholly or in part for support, if there be neither widow, minor child under sixteen years of age, nor father surviving; all of such minor brothers and sisters to be pensioned jointly.

Only one full pension in any case will be allowed to the relatives of a deceased officer, soldier, or seaman, and in order of precedence, as set forth above.

The rates of pension to the several classes and grades are set forth in the First Section of the Act of July 14, 1862, as follows: —

Be it enacted by the Senate and House of Representatives of the United States of America in Congress assembled, That if any officer, non-commissioned officer, musician, or private of the army, including regulars, volunteers, and militia, or any officer, warrant or petty officer, musician, seaman, ordinary seaman, flotillaman, marine, clerk, landsman, pilot, or other person in the navy or marine corps, has been, since the fourth day of March, eighteen hundred and sixty-one, or shall hereafter be, disabled by reason of any wound received or disease contracted while in the service of the United States, and in the line of duty, he shall, upon making due proof of the fact according to such forms and regulations as are or may be provided by or in pursuance of law, be placed upon the list of invalid pensions of the United States, and be entitled to receive, for the highest rate of disability, such pension as is hereinafter provided in such cases, and for an inferior disability an amount proportionate to the highest disability, to commence as hereinafter provided, and continue during the existence of such disability. The pension for a total disability for officers, non-commissioned officers, musicians, and privates employed in the military service of the United States, whether regulars, volunteers, or militia, and in the marine corps, shall be as follows, viz., lieutenant-colonel, and all officers of a higher rank, thirty dollars per month; major, twenty-five dollars per month; captain, twenty dollars per month; first lieutenant, seventeen dollars per month; second lieutenant, fifteen dollars per month; and non-commissioned officers, musicians, and privates, eight dollars per month. The pension for total disability for officers, warrant or petty officers, and others employed in the naval service of the United States, shall be as follows, viz., captain, commander, surgeon, paymaster, and chief engineer, respectively, ranking with commander by law, lieutenant commanding, and master commanding, thirty dollars per month; lieutenant, surgeon, paymaster, and chief engineer, respectively, ranking with lieutenant by law, and passed assistant surgeon, twenty-five dollars per month; professor of mathematics, master, assistant surgeon, assistant paymaster, and chaplain, twenty dollars per month; first assistant engineers and pilots, fifteen dollars per month; passed midshipman, midshipman, captain's and paymaster's clerk, second and third assistant engineer, master's mate, and all warrant officers, ten dollars per month; all petty officers, and all other persons before named employed in the naval service, eight dollars per month; and all commissioned officers, of either service, shall receive such and only such pension as is herein provided for the rank in which they hold commissions.

Widows who have never applied for pension, and who are entitled to the additional allowance provided by the Second Section of the Act of July 25, 1866, should file an application in accordance with Form 215.

Army Pensions.

All declarations (including evidence of identity) are required to be made before a court of record, or before some officer of such court duly authorized to administer oaths, and having custody of its seal. *Testimony* other than that indicated above may be taken before a justice of the peace, or other officer having like authority to administer oaths; but in no case will any evidence be received that is verified before an officer who is concerned in prosecuting the claim, or has a manifest interest therein.

The subjoined forms should be exactly followed in the classes for which they are designated. No attorney will be regarded as having filed the necessary declaration and affidavits, unless the *forms*, as well as the instructions given in this pamphlet, are strictly complied with. In declarations of widows and mothers, the continuance of their widowhood must be averred.

In support of the allegations made in the claimant's declaration, testimony will be required in accordance with the following rules:—

1. The claimant's identity must be proved by two witnesses certified by a judicial officer to be respectable and credible, who are present and witness the signature of the declarant, and who state, upon oath or affirmation, their belief, either from personal acquaintance or for other reasons given, that he or she is the identical person he or she represents himself or herself to be.

2. Every applicant for an invalid pension must, if in his power, produce the certificate of the captain, or of some other commissioned officer under whom he served, distinctly stating the time and place of the said applicant's having been wounded or otherwise disabled, and the nature of the disability, and that the said disability

arose while he was in the service of the United States and in the line of his duty.

3. If it be impracticable to obtain such certificate, by reason of the death or removal of said officers, it must be so stated under oath by the applicant, and his averment of the fact proved by persons of known respectability, who must state particularly all the knowledge they may possess in relation to such death or removal; then secondary evidence can be received. In such case the applicant must produce the testimony of at least two credible witnesses (who were in a condition to know the facts about which they testify), whose good character must be vouched for by a judicial officer, or by some one known to the department. The witnessess must give a minute narrative of the facts in relation to the matter, and must show how they obtained a knowledge of the facts to which they testify.

4. The usual certificate of disability for discharge should show the origin, character, and degree of the claimant's disability; but, when that is wanting or defective, the applicant will be required to be examined by some surgeon regularly appointed, unless clearly impracticable.

5. The habits of the applicant, and his occupation since he left the service, should be shown by at least two creditable witnesses.

If the applicant claims a pension as the widow of a deceased officer or soldier, she must prove the legality of her marriage and the death of her husband. She must also furnish the names and ages of decedent's children under sixteen years of age at her husband's decease, and the place of their residence. On a subsequent marriage her pension will cease, and the minor child or children of the deceased officer or soldier, if any be living under the age of sixteen years, will be entitled to the same in her stead, from the date of such marriage, on the requisite proof, under a new declaration. Proof of the marriage of the parents and of the age of claimants will be required in all applications in behalf of minor children, if such evidence has not been filed in a prior claim. The legality of the marriage, in either case, may be ascertained by the affidavit of the clergyman or magistrate who joined them in wedlock, or by the testimony of respectable persons having knowledge of the fact, in default of record evidence, which must always be furnished, or its absence shown. The ages and number of children may be ascertained by the deposition of the mother, accompanied by the testimony of respectable persons having knowledge of them, or by transcripts from the parish or town registers, duly authenticated.

A mother or father, to be entitled to a pension, as having been wholly or partly dependent on a deceased officer, soldier, or seaman, must prove that the latter contributed to her or his support for a certain period, showing specifically in what manner and to what extent.

If the claimant be a brother or sister, like proof will be required of the marriage of parents, of relationship to the deceased, and of dependence.

Guardians of minor claimants must, in all cases, produce evidence of their authority as such, under the seal of the court from which their appointment is obtained.

Applicants of the last five classes heretofore enumerated, who have in any manner aided or abetted the Rebellion against the United-States Government, are not entitled to the benefits of these acts.

Invalid applicants who are minors must apply in their own behalf, without the intervention of a guardian.

Attorneys for claimants must have proper authority from those in whose behalf they appear. Powers of attorney must be signed in the presence of two witnesses, and acknowledged before a duly qualified officer, whose official character must be certified under seal.

In all cases the post-office address of the claimant must be distinctly stated over his or her proper signature.

Applications under this act will be numbered and acknowledged, to be acted on in their turn. In filing additional evidence, correspondents should always give the number of the claim, the name of the claimant, and the post-office address at the time the claim was originally filed.

Navy Pensions.

The foregoing instructions, with obvious variations, are applicable to navy cases. In addition thereto, the following is subjoined: —

The surgeon's certificate for discharge should show the character and degree of the claimant's disability; but when that is wanting, and when the certificate of a navy surgeon or of a board of survey is not obtainable, that fact must be satisfactorily explained, and the certificate of two respectable civil surgeons will be received, in accordance with Form 221. These surgeons must give in their certificate a particular description of the wound, injury, or disease, and specify how and in what manner his present condition and disability are connected therewith. The degree of disability for obtaining subsistence by manual labor must also be stated. The certificates of civil surgeons should be forwarded with the declaration.

ACT OF JULY 14, 1862.

The foregoing instructions comprise all explanations required by the Act of July 14, 1862.

ACT OF JULY 4, 1864.

Attention is especially directed to the following particulars, in which previous legislation and official practice have been modified: —

1. Biennial Examinations. — The biennial examinations of invalid pensioners, required by the Act of March 3, 1859, will hereafter be made by one surgeon only, if he is regularly appointed, or holds a surgeon's commission in the army. In no case will an examination by unappointed civil surgeons be accepted, unless it is satisfactorily shown by the affidavit of one or more disinterested and credible witnesses, giving the reasons for such asseveration, that an examination by a commissioned or duly appointed surgeon is impracticable. On such proof, the certificate of two unappointed civil surgeons will be accepted in the same manner as heretofore. Fees paid to unappointed examining surgeons will not be refunded. Fees of appointed surgeons will be paid directly by pension agents, under prescribed regulations, and not by the pensioner (to be afterwards refunded), as under the Act of 1862.

2. Declarations. — All declarations of claimants residing within twenty-five miles of any court of record must, without exception, be made before such court, or before some officer thereof having custody of its seal. For the convenience of persons residing more than

twenty-five miles distant from any court of record, officers qualified by law to administer oaths may be designated by the Commissioner of Pensions, before whom such declarations shall be executed.

3. Increased Pensions in Certain Cases.—A pension of twenty-five dollars per month is granted to those having lost both hands or both eyes in the military service of the United States, in the line of duty, and twenty dollars per month, to those who, under the same conditions, shall have lost both feet, if such parties were entitled to a lower rate of pension under the Act of 1862. This higher pension will date only from the 4th day of July, 1864, in the case of pensioners already enrolled, or of applicants discharged prior to that date.

4. Commencement of Pensions when Applications are delayed more than Three Years. — In all cases in which the application is filed more than three years after the discharge or decease of the person on whose acccount the claim is made, the pension, if allowed, will commence at the date of filing the last paper in support of such claim. Claims filed before July 4, 1864, must be prosecuted to a final issue within three years from that date, and those filed subsequently to July 4, 1864, must be prosecuted to a final issue within five years from the date of filing, or they will thereafter be rejected, in the absence of satisfactory record evidence from the War Department in support of such claim.

[By the Sixth Section of the Act of July 27, 1868, it is provided that in case the application is filed within *five* years after the title to pension accrued, the same shall commence from the discharge or from the death of the person on whose account the pension is claimed, if disability or death was incurred subsequent to March 4, 1861.]

5. Widow's Pension not Renewable after Remarriage. — The remarriage of a widow terminates all claim to the pension from the date of such remarriage, although she may again become a widow.

6. Special Examinations of Pensioners. — Special examinations of pensioners will be ordered at such times as the interests of the government may seem to require; and such examinations, subject to an appeal to a board of three appointed surgeons, will take precedence of all previous examinations.

7. Pensions to Unenlisted Men, or to their Dependents, in Certain Cases. — *Persons disabled by wounds received in battle* while temporarily serving with any regularly organized military or naval force of the United States, since March 4, 1861, but not regularly enlisted, and the widows, dependent mothers or sisters, or minor children under sixteen years of age, of those who, serving in like manner, have been or may be killed, are entitled, on satisfactory proof, to the benefits of the Act of July 14, 1862, on the conditions therein prescribed. Claims of this character must be filed and established prior to July 4, 1867.

[By the Eleventh Section of the Act of July 27, 1868, the limitation of the above provision is extended to July 4, 1872.]

Proof of service, in cases arising under the Ninth Section of the Act of July 4, 1864, must be furnished by a commissioned officer under or with whom such unenlisted person served, showing the nature, period, and circumstances of such service. Proof as to the disability or death of a person so serving must be shown in the same manner, when practicable, or by the affidavits of two non-commissioned officers or privates in the same service, with evidence that proof by a commissioned officer is impracticable. If the officer furnishing such evidence is not at the time in the service, his certificate must be duly sworn to and his signature authenticated.

8. Commencement of Widows' Pensions in Certain Cases. — When an applicant entitled to an invalid pension dies during the pendency of his claim, leaving a widow or dependent relative entitled to receive a pension by reason of his service and death, such pension will commence from the date at which the invalid pension would have commenced if admitted while the claimant was living.

9. Evidence of Muster-in. — In accordance with the Eleventh Section of the Act of July 4, 1864, evidence of the muster-in of the soldier will not be required in any case, but there must be positive record evidence of service, except in such cases as are embraced within the provisions of the ninth section of the said act. The eleventh section applies only to *enlisted soldiers*. Evidence of muster-in in the case of commissioned officers is still required.

10. Fees of Claim Agents. — Claim agents are prohibited, under severe penalty, from receiving more than ten dollars in all for their

services in prosecuting any pension claim, or from receiving any part of such fee in advance, or any percentage of any claim, or any portion thereof, for pension or bounty.

11. PROOF OF MARRIAGE OF COLORED SOLDIERS' WIDOWS.—To establish the marriage of the alleged widow of any colored soldier, evidence of habitual recognition of the marriage relation between the parties, for two years next preceding the soldier's enlistment, must be furnished by the affidavits of at least two credible witnesses; provided, however, if such parties resided in any State in which their marriage may have been legally solemnized, the usual evidence shall be required. The widow or children, claiming the benefits of this provision, must be free persons. (See Section 14, Act of June 6, 1866.)

ACT OF JUNE 6, 1866.

The First and Third Sections of the Act of March 3, 1865, are repealed by the Act of June 6, 1866.

1. ASSISTANT OR CONTRACT SURGEONS.—By the Second Section of the Act of March 3, 1865, acting assistant (or "contract") surgeons who, in certain specified cases and under certain limitations, become disabled, are entitled to the benefit of the pension laws the same as though they had been mustered into service with the rank of assistant surgeon.

The widows or dependent relatives of such officers are only entitled to the benefits of the pension laws, provided the said officers died while in the service.

The Fourth Section of the Act of March 3, 1865, provides for the allowance of pensions to minor children less than sixteen years of age, under certain circumstances not definitely provided for in the previous acts. The limitations dependent on the date of application and of filing the last proof are to be construed in connection with the sixth section of the Act of July 27, 1868.

2. PENSIONS TO CHAPLAINS.—The Second Section of the Act approved April 9, 1864, provides for pensions to chaplains and their widows and dependent relatives, and is as follows:—

"The act approved July 14, 1862, is hereby so amended as to include chaplains in the regular and volunteer forces of the army: *Provided,* That the pension to which chaplains shall be entitled for a total disability shall be twenty dollars per month, and all the provisions of the act to which this section is an amendment shall apply to and embrace the widows, children, mothers, and sisters of chaplains of the land forces who have died since the fourth day of March, 1861, or shall die of wounds or diseases contracted in the service of the United States, and while such chaplains are or shall be in the line of their duty."

ACT OF JUNE 6, 1866.

1. INCREASE OF PENSIONS. — The supplementary Pension Act, approved June 6, 1866, provides increased rates of pensions over those granted by the Act of July 14, 1862, in the following cases, viz., —

Twenty-five dollars per month to all those invalids entitled, under the Act of July 14, 1862, to a lower rate of pension, on account of service rendered since March 4, 1861, "who shall have lost the sight of both eyes, or who shall have lost both hands, or been permanently and totally disabled in the same, or otherwise so permanently and totally disabled as to render them utterly helpless, or so nearly so as to require the constant personal aid and attendance of another person."

[By the Twelfth Section of the Act of July 27, 1868, a pension of twenty-five dollars is allowed to those having totally lost their sight, although one eye had been lost prior to enlistment.]

Twenty dollars per month to those invalids, who, being entitled under like conditions to a lower rate of pension, "shall have lost both feet, or one hand and one foot, or been totally and permanently disabled in the same, or otherwise so disabled as to be incapacitated for performing any manual labor, but not so much so as to require constant personal aid and attention."

Fifteen dollars per month to those invalids, who, under like conditions, "shall have lost one hand or one foot, or been totally and permanently disabled in the same, or otherwise so disabled as to render their inability to perform manual labor equivalent to the loss of a hand or foot."

In order to obtain the benefits of the foregoing provisions, pensioners already enrolled will file an application in accordance with Form 213, appended to this chapter. Proof in addition to that on file with the previous application need not be forwarded, except as shall be specially required in each case, after the application is received. The applicant need only be examined by a pension surgeon when expressly required on due notice from this office. Applicants not already pensioned, who believe themselves entitled to the benefit of the foregoing provisions, will specifically set forth such claim in their declarations, carefully stating the nature of the disability on account of which such higher rate of pension is claimed. The declaration must be made before some officer of a court of record, or before a pension notary designated by this office, as provided by the Third Section of the Act of July 4, 1864.

The above-specified increased rates of pension will date only from the 6th day of June, 1866.

2. Pensions not assignable or Liable to Attachment. — The Second and Third Sections of the Act of June 6, 1866, are applicable to all pensions granted under the various acts of Congress. By the provisions of the Second Section, pensions are secured to the exclusive use and benefit of the pensioners. Any " pledge, mortgage, sale, assignment, or transfer of any right, claim, or interest in any pension," is declared void and of no effect. Any person other than the pensioner, who may receive any payment of a pension, is required to disclaim, under oath, any interest, by pledge, mortgage, sale, assignment, or transfer, in the money to be received, or any knowledge or belief that the same has been so disposed of to any person; and the penalty of perjury is affixed for falsely taking the oath so required.

The Third Section fixes a penalty for the offence of post-dating vouchers required in drawing pensions. It further provides that no pension-money shall be " liable to attachment, levy, or seizure by or under any legal or equitable process whatever, whether the same remains with the Pension Office, or any officer or agent thereof, or is in course of transmission to the pensioner entitled thereto, but shall inure wholly to the benefit of such pensioner."

3. Fees for drawing Pensions restricted. — The Fourth Section of the act prohibits, under penalty, the receiving of more than twenty-five cents for preparing the necessary vouchers for drawing a semi-annual payment of any pension, and fixes the fee receivable

by any pension agent for administering an oath to a pensioner, or his attorney-in-fact, at fifteen cents.

4. PENSIONS CONTINUED TO PENSIONERS ENTERING CIVIL SERVICE. — The Fifth Section unconditionally repeals that provision of the Act of March 3, 1865, by which pensions were withheld from certain pensioners in civil employment under the government. Persons desiring the benefit of this repeal will make application for a "renewal" of their pensions as in other cases, filing an examining surgeon's certificate showing their present disability, except in the case of those exempt from biennial examination. The restored pension will date only from the passage of this act.

5. INVALID PENSION CERTIFICATES ISSUED AFTER DEATH OF APPLICANTS. — The Sixth Section gives validity to a certificate issued after the death of an applicant for an invalid pension, if he left neither widow nor minor child entitled to a pension by reason of his death, provided the application was pending and the proof complete at the time of his death. This section is construed as retro-active in its operation, and consequently it applies to certificates already issued which come within the limitations specified, previous legislation having provided for the cases in which the deceased left a widow or minor children entitled to a pension on his behalf.

[By the Ninth Section of the Act of July 27, 1868, the parties above entitled may complete the proof after the death of the applicant, and receive the accrued pension.]

6. RANK RECOGNIZED WITHOUT MUSTER IN CERTAIN CASES. — The Seventh Section recognizes the rank conferred by a commission, so far as pensions are concerned, without an actual muster into such rank, provided the failure to be mustered was not through the neglect or refusal of the person commissioned. The proviso renders it necessary, that, before an application involving this question is allowed, the reason why the officer was not duly mustered should be shown, the best proof of which will be the affidavit of the proper mustering officer, or of a superior officer having personal knowledge of the facts.

7. OFFICERS AND ENLISTED MEN ON SICK FURLOUGH. — Officers absent on sick leave, and enlisted men on sick furlough, are, in accordance with the Eighth Section, to be regarded in the same

manner as if they were in the field or in hospital. This section will not be construed, however, as bringing within the intent of the pension laws any cause of disability or death altogether apart from the military or naval service, and resulting neither directly nor indirectly therefrom.

8. Constructive Extension of the Period of Service. — The Ninth Section treats the period of service, in the army or navy, as extending to the date of the actual disbandment of the organization to which the party belonged, except in the case of discharge for other cause than the expiration of the term of service of such organization.

9. Teamsters, Artificers, and other Enlisted Men, not embraced in the terms of the Act of July 14, 1862, or of acts supplementary thereto, are, by the Tenth Section of the Act of June 6, 1866, included in the administration of the pension laws, in the class of non-commissioned officers and privates.

10. Minor Children to be pensioned in Certain Cases instead of the Widow. — The Eleventh Section provides that when any widow entitled to a pension under previous acts has abandoned the care of a child or children of her deceased husband, under sixteen years of age, "or is an unsuitable person, by reason of immoral conduct, to have the custody of the same," the pension shall be paid to the duly authorized guardian of such child or children, while under the age of sixteen years, and not to the widow. The proper proof in such case, as provided by this section, is the certificate of the judge of any court having probate jurisdiction "that satisfactory evidence has been produced before such court" to the effect above indicated. In presenting an application under this section, the guardians of the minor child or children will make a declaration in accordance with the appended Form 214.

[By Section Eight of the Act of July 27, 1868, the provision requiring a certificate of a judge of a court, in order to suspend a claim, is annulled, and the matter left to the discretion of the Commissioner.]

11. Pensions granted to Dependent Fathers and to Dependent Orphan Brothers. — By the Twelfth Section, the provisions of the Act of July 14, 1862, are extended so as to include the dependent

brother or brothers of a deceased officer, soldier, or seaman, and the dependent father of such deceased persons, under like limitations as apply in the case of dependent sisters and mothers; but not more than one pension is granted on account of the same person, or to more than one of said classes. The forms prescribed for the latter cases may be used, with obvious variations, in applications made by dependent fathers, or on behalf of dependent brothers.

[By Section One of the Act of July 27, 1868, it is required that minor brothers and sisters shall be pensioned jointly, and that dependent fathers shall have precedence of both.]

12. LIMITATIONS AS TO NUMBER AND DATE OF PENSIONS. — The Thirteenth Section declares that but one pension shall be granted to any person at the same time; and that, when application is not made within three years after the death or discharge of the party on whose account a pension is claimed, such pension, if allowed, "shall commence from the date of filing the last paper in said case by the party prosecuting the same." This limitation applies to all classes of pensions.

[The above provision is annulled by the Sixth Section of the Act of July 27, 1868, and five years allowed after the death or discharge of said party, in which to make application.]

13. EVIDENCE OF MARRIAGE OF COLORED APPLICANTS. — The Fourteenth Section provides that habitual recognition of the marriage-relation between colored parties, — that is, in the absence of the usually required proof, — when shown by "proof satisfactory to the Commissioner of Pensions," shall be accepted as evidence of marriage, and the children of such parties shall be regarded as if born in lawful wedlock. When the usual proof of marriage can be furnished, it will be required as heretofore. When only evidence of cohabitation and mutual recognition can be adduced, as provided in this section, the testimony of two credible and disinterested witnesses will be required, who must state how long they have been personally acquainted with the parties, and for how long a period the latter are known to have recognized each other as man and wife. If such acquaintance is deemed to be of too recent date to warrant the acceptance of this testimony, or if there is reason to doubt, in any instance, that the marriage-relation existed in good

faith, more specific instructions will be issued, adapted to the circumstances of the particular case.

ACT OF JULY 25, 1866.

1. Provost-Marshals, Enrolling Officers, and Others, entitled to the Benefits of the Pension Laws. — The First Section of the Act of July 25, 1866, extends the benefits conferred by the pension laws to provost-marshals, deputy provost-marshals, and enrolling officers disabled in the line of official duty as such, and to the widows or dependents of such officers in like manner.

Declarations will be made in accordance with the instructions issued under the Pension Act of July 14, 1862, and supplementary acts. The grade of such officers, for the purpose of determining the rates of pensions under this section, is fixed as follows: provost-marshals will rank as captain, their deputies as first lieutenants, and enrolling officers as second lieutenants.

2. Increased Pensions to Widows and Orphan Children under Sixteen Years of Age. — The Second Section of this act allows to those who are or shall be pensioned as widows of soldiers or sailors, two dollars per month additional pension for each child (under sixteen years of age) of the deceased soldier or sailor, by the widow thus pensioned.

[By Section Four of the Act of July 27, 1868, provision is made for the extension of such increase to children by a former wife.]

On the death or remarriage of such widow, or on the denial of a pension to her, in accordance with the provisions of Section Eleven of the Act of June 6, 1866, the same amount to which she would otherwise be entitled, under this and previous provisions, is allowed to the minor children. The number and names of the children, with their ages, must be proved, as heretofore required in applications for minors by guardians.

The widows or minor children of officers are not entitled to this increase. Dependent mothers and minor sisters and brothers are also excluded.

Declarations for an increase under this section or its amendments, if for the widow, will be made in accordance with Form 215, appended to this chapter; and if for minor children, according to Form 216. In cases where no application for original pension has been made by the widow, her declaration should accord with Form 217.

3. Increase of Pensions under Acts prior to July 14, 1862. — All pensioners under acts approved prior to July 14, 1862, are, by the Third Section of the present act, granted the same rights as those pensioned under acts approved at or since that date, so far as said acts may be applicable, with the exception of soldiers of the Revolution, or their widows. This section applies only to pensioners who were such at the date of the approval of this act.

[By Section Thirteen of the Act of July 27, 1868, it is provided that widows of Revolutionary soldiers, now receiving a less sum, shall be entitled to eight dollars per month.]

Declarations of claimants under this section will be made in accordance with the forms herewith issued, with the necessary modifications, and the pension certificates will be returned.

4. Invalid Pensions of Claimants dying while their Applications are pending, the Evidence being completed. — The Fourth Section of this act is construed in connection with the Tenth Section of the Act of July 4, 1864, and the Sixth Section of the Act of June 6, 1866, to which it is supplementary. If an applicant for an invalid pension dies while his claim is pending, the evidence having been completed, the pension, under the provisions of this section, and of those sections of previous acts above referred to, is disposed of as follows: —

1. If he left a widow, or minor child or children under sixteen years of age, or other dependent relatives, and died of wounds received, or of disease contracted, in the service and in the line of duty, no invalid pension certificate will issue, but such widow or dependent relatives will receive a pension, in their own right, taking precedence in the order prescribed by law in other cases. (See Section 10, Act of July 4, 1864.)

2. If the claimant left a widow or dependent relatives, but did not die of wounds received or disease contracted in the service and in the line of duty, so that neither widow nor dependent relatives

would be entitled to a pension on his account, then the certificate will be issued in his name, and the pension paid to the widow, or to the dependent relatives, as the case may be, in the same order in which they would have been pensioned if entitled as set forth in the preceding paragraph.

3. If the claimant left no widow or dependent relatives, the certificate will issue in his name, and the pension will be drawn by his executor or administrator.

[The Ninth Section of the Act of July 27, 1868, provides that in case of a person entitled to pension dying subsequent to March 4, 1861, while an application is pending, and leaving no widow or minor child, the requirement of completion of proof *before death* is dispensed with.]

5. CERTAIN ACCRUED RIGHTS RESERVED UNDER REPEALED ENACTMENTS. — The Fifth Section reserves all rights that may have accrued under the Fifth Section of the Pension Act of July 4, 1864, and the Third Section of the Pension Act of March 3, 1865, though repealed by the First Section of the Act of June 6, 1866.

WIDOWS WHO REMARRY WHILE THEIR CLAIMS ARE PENDING are entitled, under the Sixth Section, if their claims are otherwise valid, to receive pensions to the date of remarriage, if the deceased officer, soldier, or sailor on whose account they claim, left no legitimate child under sixteen years of age.

ACT OF JULY 27, 1868.

SECTION 1. DEPENDENT RELATIVES. — By this section, precedence is given to the dependent relatives hereinafter mentioned in the following order, to wit, First, mothers; second, fathers; third, orphan brothers and sisters under sixteen years of age, entitled jointly; and the title of each of the above classes of claimants accrues upon the death of the one preceding.

SECT. 2. DISABILITIES INCURRED SUBSEQUENT TO JULY 27, 1868. — This section provides for pensions by reason of disabilities incurred subsequent to the passage of this act, and specifies the circumstances under which said disabilities must have been contracted in order to effect a title.

SECT. 3. UNCLAIMED PENSIONS. — This section provides that pensions remaining unclaimed for fourteen months after the same have become due may be paid at the Pension Agency instead of at the offices of the Third and Fourth Auditors, as heretofore provided; that failure to claim such pension for *three* years shall be presumptive evidence that the same has legally terminated; and that on a new application, with evidence satisfactorily accounting for such failure, the pensioner may be restored to the rolls.

SECT. 4. INCREASE OF PENSIONS TO MINORS BY FORMER WIFE. — By this section the increase of two dollars per month for each minor child of a deceased soldier, provided for by Section 2, Act of July 25, 1866, is extended to include all the legitimate children of such soldier; and provides that the children of a former marriage (the soldier "leaving a widow, entitled to a pension") shall be "entitled to receive two dollars per month, to commence from the death of their father, and continue until they severally attain the age of sixteen years, to be paid to the guardian of such child or children for their use and benefit: *Provided, however*, That in all cases where such widow is charged with the care, custody, and maintenance of such child or children, the said sum of two dollars per month for each of said children shall be paid to her for and during the time she is, or may have been, so charged with the care, custody, and maintenance of such child or children, subject to the same conditions, provisions, and limitations as if they were her own children by her said deceased husband.

SECT. 5. MINOR CHILDREN IN CHARITABLE INSTITUTIONS. — This section provides that no widow or guardian, to whom an increase of pension has been or may be granted on account of minor children, shall be deprived thereof by reason of their being wholly, or in part, maintained or educated at the expense of the State or of the public.

SECT. 6. EXTENSION OF TIME FOR APPLICATION. — By this section, all pensions applied for within five years after the right thereto shall have accrued, and which have been or may be granted under the Act of July 14, 1862, or acts supplementary thereto, shall commence from the discharge or death of the person on whose account the pension has been or shall be granted; and in cases of insane persons and minors, who were without guardians or other legal representatives previous to said limitation, applications may be filed in their behalf after its expiration. This section applies only to cases in which title to pension has accrued subsequent to March 4, 1861. Allowance or arrears, under this section, is to be graded in amount according to the original certificate. A pensioner, under special act of Congress, is not entitled to arrears under this section.

SECT. 7. PAYMENT OF ARREARS. — This section provides for notification of title to arrears of pension under the preceding section, and that no person shall be entitled to compensation for making application for such arrears. In order to identify the claimant, the appropriate form should be followed by applicants under Section Six, and executed before a court of record, as in other cases.

SECT. 8. AMENDMENT OF SECTION 11, ACT OF JUNE 6, 1866. — This section dispenses with the requirement of the certificate of the court that satisfactory evidence has been adduced of the abandonment of the care of minor child or children of a deceased soldier by his widow, or of her unfitness to have custody of them; and that the presentation of satisfactory evidence thereof to the commissioner shall suffice for the suspension of said widow's pension.

SECT. 9. AMENDMENT OF SECTION 6, ACT OF JUNE 6, 1866, AND SECTION 4, ACT OF JULY 25, 1866. — By this section, the title to accrued pension of a person dying while application is pending is vested in the heirs, or legal representatives, provided that no widow or minor child survives the applicant, and the requirement of completion of proof before death is dispensed with.

SECT. 10. PENSION TO DATE OF REMARRIAGE. — This section provides for allowance of pension to widow (in case no children under sixteen years of age survive), or dependent mother, from death of soldier, to date of claimant's remarriage.

SECT. 11. EXTENSION OF LIMITATION OF UNENLISTED MEN OR THEIR DEPENDENTS. — By this section, the provisions of the Ninth Section of the Act of July 4, 1864, are continued in force until July 4, 1872.

SECT. 12. PENSION FOR LOSS OF ONE EYE. — This section provides for the allowance of a pension of twenty-five dollars for total loss of sight by reason of wounds or disease contracted in the service, though the pensioner had the sight of but one eye upon entering the service.

SECT. 13. AMENDMENT TO SECTION 3, ACT OF JULY 25, 1866. — This section places all persons pensioned on account of services rendered since the war of the Revolution, and prior to March 4, 1861, on the same footing with those pensioned under the Act of July 14, 1862, and acts subsequent thereto; and grants eight dollars per month to the widows of revolutionary soldiers now pensioned at less than that amount.

SECT. 14. ARTIFICIAL LIMBS TO OFFICERS. — This section entitles captains in the army and lieutenants in the navy, and officers of inferior rank, who have lost a leg or arm in the service, to receive an artificial limb upon the same terms as privates in the army.

SECT. 15. SPECIAL ACT PENSIONS. — This section provides that all pensions granted under special acts shall be graded in amount according to the provisions and limitations of the general pension laws.

SECT. 16. REPEALING CLAUSE. — This section comprises the customary repeal of inconsistent provisions of former acts.

Declarations in applications for pensions under this act should be made in accordance with the forms annexed to this chapter, and invariably before a court of record or pension notary.

A remark similar to that made at the close of the Chapter on Patents may be repeated here. The officers in Washington charged with the duty of attending to applications for pensions have every disposition to facilitate and not to hinder the obtaining pensions by those who ought to have them. But the strict provisions of law, as well as the necessity of guarding against deception or mistake, compel them to adhere rigidly to the rules above stated, which I have taken, substantially, from publications made by those officers, for the purpose of guiding and assisting applicants. The forms which follow are those prescribed by them. They would be sent to persons needing them, and are usually supplied by pension agents; and they are given here for the guidance of those who are so situated that they cannot conveniently apply to pension agents, or prefer not to do so.

(208.)

Declaration for an Invalid Pension.

STATE (DISTRICT OR TERRITORY) OF , } ss.
COUNTY OF }

On this day of , A.D. one thousand eight hundred and , personally appeared before me, (*here state the official character of the person administering the oath*) within and for the county and State aforesaid, , aged years, a resident of , in the State of , who, being duly sworn according to law, declares that he is the identical who enlisted in the service of the United States at , on the day of , in the year , as a in company , commanded by , in the regiment of , in the war of 1861, and was honorably discharged on the day of , in the year ; that while in the service aforesaid, and in the line of his duty, he received the following wound (*or other disability, as the case may be*), (*here give a particular and minute account of the wound or other injury, and state how, when, and where it occurred, where the applicant has resided since leaving the service, and what has been his occupation.*)

My post-office address is as follows:

(*Signature of claimant.*)

Also Personally Appeared and , residents of (*county, city, or town*) persons whom I certify to be respectable, and entitled to credit, and who, being by me duly sworn, say that they were present and saw sign his name (*or make his mark*) to the foregoing declaration; and they further swear that they have every reason to believe, from the appearance of the applicant and their acquaintance with him, that he is the identical person he represents himself to be; and they further swear that they have no interest in the prosecution of this claim.

(*Signatures of witnesses.*)

Sworn to and subscribed before me this day of A.D. 186 ; and I hereby certify that I have no interest, direct or indirect, in the prosecution of this claim.

(*Signature of judge or other officer.*)

(209.)

Declaration for obtaining a Widow's Army-Pension.

STATE (TERRITORY OR DISTRICT) OF , }
COUNTY OF } ss.

On this day of , A.D. , personally appeared before me, , of the , a resident of , in the County of , and State (*territory or district*) of , aged years, who being first duly sworn according to law, doth on her oath make the following declaration in order to obtain the benefit of the provisions made by the act of Congress approved July 14, 1862: That she is the widow of , who was a in company , commanded by in the Regiment of in the war of 1861, who (*here specify the time, place, and cause of death*). She further declares that she was married to the said on the day of in the year ; that her husband, the aforesaid , died on the day above mentioned, and that she has remained a widow ever since that period, as will more fully appear by reference to the proof hereto annexed. She also declares that she has not in any manner been engaged in, or aided or abetted, the Rebellion in the United States.

My post-office address is as follows:

(*Declarant's signature.*)

Also Personally Appeared and , residents of (*county, city, or town*) persons whom I certify to be respectable, and entitled to credit, and who, being by me duly sworn, say that they were present and saw sign her name (*or make her mark*) to the foregoing declaration; and they further swear that they have every reason to believe, from the appearance of the applicant and their acquaintance with her, that she is the identical person she represents herself to be, and that they have no interest in the prosecution of this claim.

(*Signatures of witnesses.*)

Sworn to and subscribed before me this day of A.D. 186 ; and I hereby certify that I have no interest, direct or indirect, in the prosecution of this claim.

(*Signature of judge or other officer.*)

(210.)

Declaration for Minor Children in order to obtain Army-Pensions.

STATE (TERRITORY OR DISTRICT) OF }
COUNTY OF } ss.

On this day of , A.D. , personally appeared before the of the , , a resident of , in the County of , and State (*territory or district*) of , aged years, who being first duly sworn according to law, doth on oath make the following declaration, as guardian of the minor child of , deceased, in order to obtain the benefits of the provisions made by the act of Congress approved July 14, 1862, granting pensions to minor children, under sixteen years of age, of deceased officers and soldiers; that he is the guardian of , (*naming the minor child or children, his ward or wards*) whose father was a in company , commanded by , in the Regiment of , in the war of 1861, and that the said died at on the day of , in the year (*here state the cause of death*); that the mother of the child aforesaid died (or again married, being now the wife of) on the day of , in the year ; and that the date of birth of his said ward as follows:

He further declares that the parents of his said ward were married at , on the day of , in the year by

My post-office address is as follows:

(*Guardian's signature.*)

Also Personally Appeared and , residents of (*county, city, or town*) persons whom I certify to be respectable, and entitled to credit, and who, being by me duly sworn, say that they were present and saw sign name (*or make his mark*) to the foregoing declaration; and they further swear that they have every reason to believe, from the appearance of the applicant and their acquaintance with him, that he is the identical person he represents himself to be, and that they have no interest in the prosecution of this claim.

(*Signatures of witnesses.*)

Sworn to and subscribed before me this day of A.D. 186 , and I hereby certify that I have no interest, direct or indirect, in the prosecution of this claim.

(*Signature of judge or other officer.*)

(211.)

Declaration for Mother's or Father's Application for Army-Pension.

STATE (TERRITORY OR DISTRICT) OF , } ss.
COUNTY OF }

On this day of , A.D , personally appeared before the of the , , a resident of in the County of , and State (*territory or district*) of , aged years, who, being first duly sworn according to law, doth on oath make the following declaration in order to obtain the benefits of the provisions made by the act of Congress approved July 14, 1862, and its amendments: That is the of , and of , who was a in company , commanded by , in the

Regiment of , in the war of 1861, who *(here state the time, place, and cause of death).*

further declares that said son, upon whom was wholly or in part dependent for support, having left no widow or minor child under sixteen years of age surviving, declarant makes this application for a pension under the above-mentioned act, and refers to the evidence filed herewith, and that in the proper department, to establish claim.

also declares that has not in any way been engaged in, or aided or abetted, the Rebellion in the United States; that is not in the receipt of a pension under the second section of the act above mentioned, or under any other act, nor has again married since the death of son, the said .

My post-office address is as follows:

(Declarant's signature.)

Also Personally Appeared and , residents of *(county, city, or town)* persons whom I certify to be respectable, and entitled to credit, and who, being by me duly sworn, say they were present and saw sign name *(or make mark)* to the foregoing declaration; and they further swear that they have every reason to believe, from the appearance of the applicant and their acquaintance with , that is the identical person represents to be, and that they have no interest in the prosecution of this claim.

(Signatures of witnesses.)

Sworn to and subscribed before me this day of , A.D. 186 ; and I hereby certify that I have no interest, direct or indirect, in the prosecution of this claim.

(Signature of judge or other officer.)

(212.)

Declaration of Orphan Brothers or Sisters for Army-Pension.

State (Territory or District) of , } ss.
County of }

On this day of , A.D. , personally appeared before the of the , a resident of in the County of , and State *(territory or district)* of , aged years, who, being first duly sworn according to law, doth on oath make the following declaration, in order to obtain a pension under the act of July 14, 1862, and its amendments: That he is the legally appointed guardian of *(here give the names and ages of his ward or wards*) who the only surviving child , under sixteen years of age, of and his wife, and of , who was a in company , commanded by , in the Regiment of , in the war of 1861, who (*here state the time, place, and cause of his death*). That the brother of his said ward , upon whom they are wholly or in part dependent for support, having left no widow, minor child or children, declarant as guardian, and on behalf of his ward , refers to the accompanying evidence, and such as may be found in the department, to establish claim under the law above named.

He further declares that his said ward is not in receipt of any pension under said act.

My post-office address is as follows:

(*Guardian's signature.*)

Also Personally Appeared and , residents of (*county, city, or town*) persons whom I certify to be respectable, and entitled to credit, and who, being by me duly sworn, say that they were present and saw sign name (*or make mark*) to the foregoing declaration; and they further swear that they have every reason to believe, from the appearance of the applicant and their acquaintance with that is the identical person represents to be, and that they have no interest in the prosecution of this claim.

(*Signatures of witnesses.*)

Sworn to and subscribed before me this day of A.D. 186 ; and I hereby certify that I have no interest, direct or indirect, in the prosecution of this claim.

(*Signature of judge or other officer.*)

(213.)

Declaration for the Increase of an Invalid Pension.

(*Under the First Section of the supplementary Pension Act of June* 6, 1866.)

STATE (TERRITORY OR DISTRICT) OF , } ss.
COUNTY OF , }

On this day of , A.D. 18 , personally appeared before me (*describing the official character of the person administering the oath*) , aged years, a resident of (*naming the town and post-office address*), in the County of , and State (*territory or district*) of , who, being duly sworn according to law, declares that he is a pensioner of the United States, duly enrolled at the pension agency, at the rate of $ per month, by reason of disability incurred in the military (*or naval*) service of the United States (*here state the company and regiment, if in the army, or the vessel and rank, if in the navy*), and that his present physical condition is such that he believes himself entitled to receive an increased pension of the (*first, second, or third*) grade provided for in the First Section of the supplementary Pension Act approved June 6, 1866. He further declares that he is disabled in the following manner, to wit (*here the declarant will particularly set forth the nature of his disability, and the extent to which he is incapacitated for manual labor, or dependent upon the personal aid and attendance of others*)

(*Signature of declarant.*)

Also Personally Appeared Before me, at the time and place aforesaid, of , and of , whom I certify to be credible persons, who, being duly sworn according to law, declare, each for himself, that they well know , who signed the foregoing declaration in their presence, and that he is the identical person he represents himself to be, and that he is disabled substantially in the manner alleged in said declaration. They further swear that they, or either of them, have no interest in this claim, either present or prospective, and that they are not concerned, directly or indirectly, in its prosecution.

(*Signatures of witnesses.*)

Sworn to and subscribed before me this day of A.D. 18 ; and I hereby certify that I have no interest, direct or indirect, in the prosecution of this claim.

(*Signature of judge or other officer.*)

(214.)

Declaration of the Guardian of a Minor Child.

(*Under the Eleventh Section of the Act of June* 6, 1866.)

STATE (TERRITORY OR DISTRICT) OF , } ss.
COUNTY OF , }

On this day of , A.D. , personally appeared before me (*describing the official character of the person administering the oath*) , aged years, a resident of (*naming town and post-office address*), in the County of , and State (*territory or district*) of , who, being duly sworn according to law, doth on oath make the following declaration, as guardian of the minor child (*or children*) of , deceased, in order to obtain the benefits of the provision made by the Eleventh Section of the Act of Congress, approved June 6, 1866, and its amendments, granting pensions to minor children under sixteen years of age, of deceased officers, soldiers, or seamen, who have left a widow still surviving, the latter having abandoned the care of said children, or having been declared an unsuitable person to have charge of them. He further declares that he is the guardian of (*naming the minor child or children, his ward or wards*), whose father was (*here describe the service of the deceased*), in the war of 1861, and that the said died at , on the day of , in the year (*here state the cause of death*), that the mother of the child (*or children*) aforesaid has abandoned the care, or is an unsuitable person, by reason of immoral conduct (*here state what specific conduct is referred to*), to have charge of the child (*or children*); and that the date of birth of his said ward (*or wards*) is as follows: —

He (*or she*) further declares that the parents of his (*or her*) said ward (*or wards*) were married at , on the day of , in the year , by .

(*Guardian's signature.*)

Also Personally Appeared and , residents of (*county, city, or town*), persons whom I certify to be respectable, and entitled to credit, and who, being by me duly sworn, say that they were present and saw sign name (*or make mark*) to the foregoing declaration; and they further swear that they have every reason to believe, from the appearance of the applicant, and their acquaintance with , that is the identical person represents to be, and that they have no interest in the prosecution of the claim.

(*Signatures of witnesses.*)

Sworn to and subscribed before me this day of A.D. 18 ; and I hereby certify that I have no ineretst, direct or indirect, in the prosecution of this claim.

(*Signature of judge or other officer.*)

(215.)

Widow's Declaration for an Increase of Pension.

(*Under the Second Section of the Act of July* 25, 1866.)

STATE (TERRITORY OR DISTRICT) OF , } ss.
COUNTY OF , }

On this day , A.D. , personally appeared before me, of the , a resident of , in the County of , and State (*territory or district*) of , aged years, who, being first duly sworn according to law, doth on her oath make the following declaration, in order to obtain the benefit of the provision made by the Second Section of the Act of Congress increasing the Pensions of Widows and Orphans, approved July 25, 1866: That she is the widow of , who was a in company , commanded by , in the Regiment of , in the war of 1861; and that by reason of his death in the service aforesaid, she has been granted a pension of eight dollars per month, in accordance with a certificate numbered , bearing date . She further swears that she has the following-named children of her deceased husband under sixteen years of age, who are now living, the dates of whose birth were as given below, to wit:

She further declares that she has not remarried since the death of her said husband, nor has she abandoned the support of any one of the children above named, nor permitted any one of the same to be adopted by any other person or persons as his, her, or their child.

My post-office address is as follows: .

(*Declarant's signature.*)

Also Personally Appeared and , residents of (*county, city, or town*), persons whom I certify to be respectable, and entitled to credit; and who, being by me duly sworn, say that they were present and saw sign her name (*or make her mark*) to the foregoing declaration; and they further swear that they have every reason to believe, from the appearance of the applicant, and their acquaintance with her, that she is the identical person she represents herself to be, and that they have no interest in the prosecution of this claim.

(*Signatures of witnesses.*)

Sworn to and subscribed before me, this day of A.D. 186 ; and I hereby certify that I have no interest, direct or indirect, in the prosecution of this claim.

(*Signature of judge or other officer.*)

(216.)

Guardian's Declaration for Increase of Pension.

(*Under the Second Section of the Act of July 25,* 1866.)

STATE (TERRITORY OR DISTRICT) OF , } ss.
COUNTY OF , }

On this day of , A.D. , personally appeared before me, of the , ; a resident of , and State (*territory or district*) of , aged years, who, being duly sworn according to law, doth on oath make the following declaration, in order to obtain the benefit of the provision made by the Second Section of the Act of Congress increasing the Pensions of Widows and Orphans, approved July 25, 1866: That (*he or she*) is the guardian of (*naming the minor child or children, ward or wards*), whose father was a in company , commanded by , in the Regiment of , in the war of 1861, and that the said (*naming the father*) died at , on the day of , in the year (*here state the cause of death*); that the mother of the child aforesaid died (or again married, being now the wife of), on the day of , in the year . ; and that the dates of birth of the said (*minor child or children, ward or wards*) were as follows, to wit:

He (*or she*) further declares that the parents of the said (*minor child or children, ward or wards*) were married at , on the day of , in the year , by , and that the maiden name of their mother was .

My post-office address is as follows:

(*Guardian's signature.*)

Also Personally Appeared and , residents of (*county, city, or town*), persons whom I certify to be respectable, and entitled to credit, and who, being by me duly sworn, say that they were present and saw sign (*his or her*) name (*or make his or her mark*) to the foregoing declaration; and they further swear that they have every reason to believe, from the appearance of the applicant, and their acquaintance with (*him or her,*) that (*he or she*) is the identical person (*he or she*) represents (*himself or herself*) to be, and that they have no interest the prosecution of this claim.

(*Signatures of witnesses.*)

Sworn to and subscribed before me, this day of , A.D. 186 ; and I hereby certify that I have no interest, direct or indirect, in the prosecution of this claim.

(*Signature of judge or other officer.*)

(217.)

Declaration for Widow's Pension and Increase.

(*Under the Act of July* 14, 1862, *and supplementary Act of July* 25, 1866.)

STATE OF , }
} SS.
COUNTY OF , }

On this day of , A.D. , personally appeared before me, a of a court of record in and for the county and State aforesaid, a resident of , in the County of , and State of , aged years, who, being duly sworn, makes the following declaration, in order to obtain the pension provided by the act of Congress, approved July 14, 1862: That she is the widow of , who was a in company , commanded by , in the Regiment of , in the war of 1861; that her maiden name was , and that she was married to said on or about the day of , A.D. , at , in the County of , and State of , by , and that there is record evidence of marriage.

She further declares that said , her husband, died in the service of the United States, as aforesaid, at , in the State of , on or about the day of , A.D. , of

She also declares that she has remained a widow ever since the death of said , and that she has the following-named children of her deceased husband, under sixteen years of age, who are now living, the dates of whose births are, as given below, to wit:

She further declares that she has not abandoned the support of any one of the children above named, nor permitted any one of the same to be adopted by any person or persons; that they are the only legitimate children of herself and the deceased, and that she has not in any manner been engaged in or aided or abetted the Rebellion in the United States.

My post-office address is .

(*Signature of claimant.*)

Also Personally Appeared , and , residents of , County and State of , to me well known as credible persons, who, being duly sworn, declare that they were present and saw said sign her name to the foregoing declaration, and that they have every reason to believe, from the appearance of said applicant, and their acquaintance with her, that she is the identical person she represents herself to be, and know that said deceased recognized the said applicant as his lawful wife, and that she was so recognized in the community in which they resided; and they further declare that they know the fact that she has not remarried, but is still a widow, and that she has not abandoned the support of any one of the said children, and that her statement in reference to the same is true to their personal knowledge, and that they have no interest, direct or indirect, in the prosecution of this claim.

(*Signatures of witnesses.*)

Sworn to and subscribed before me this day of , A.D. ; and I hereby certify that the contents of the above were made known and explained to the applicant and witnesses before signing, and that I have no interest, direct or indirect, in the prosecution of this claim.

(*Seal.*) (*Official signature.*)

(218.)

Declaration for Restoration to the Rolls.

(*Under Section* 3, *Act July* 27, 1868.)

STATE (TERRITORY OR DISTRICT) OF , } ss.
COUNTY OF ,

On this day of , A.D. one thousand eight hundred and , personally appeared before me (*here state the official character of the person administering the oath*), within and for the county and State aforesaid, , aged years, a resident of , in the State of , who, being duly sworn according to law, declares that is the identical to whom was granted pension certificate No. , payable at , dated the day of , in the year ; that having failed since the day of , 18 , by reason of (*here state the causes of such neglect*) , to apply for the payment due upon said certificate, and thereby been deprived of the same under the Third Section of the Act of July 27, 1868, makes this declaration in order to secure restoration to the pension-rolls and a new certificate, returning herewith the original.

post-office address is as follows:

(*Signature of claimant.*)

Also Personally Appeared and , residents of (*county, city, or town*), persons whom I certify to be respectable, and entitled to credit, and who, being by me duly sworn, say that they were present and saw sign name (*or make his or her mark*) to the foregoing declaration; and they further swear that they have every reason to believe, from the appearance of the applicant, and their acquaintance with , that is the identical person represents self to be; and they further swear that they have no interest in the prosecution of this claim.

(*Signatures of witnesses.*)

Sworn to and subscribed before me this day of , A.D. 186 ; and I hereby certify that I have no interest, direct or indirect, in the prosecution of this claim.

(*Signature of judge or other officer.*)

NOTE. — In cases of invalid pensioners, a certificate of a pension surgeon will be required that the disability still continues, except in cases of loss of limbs and of the eyes.

Widows and mothers should depose as to continuance of widowhood.

(219.)

Declaration for Arrears of Pensions.

(*Under Sections* 6 *and* 10, *Act of July* 27, 1868.)

STATE (TERRITORY OR DISTRICT) OF , }
COUNTY OF , } ss.

On this day of , A.D. one thousand eight hundred and , personally appeared before me (*here state the official character of the person administering the oath*), within and for the county and State aforesaid, , aged years, a resident of , in the State of , who, being duly sworn according to law, declares that is the identical to whom was granted pension certifiate No. , payable at the agency at and dated ; that under the limitations of the Act of was denied a pension from the date of the (*remarriage*), death, or discharge of ; and believing entitled to the same, under the Section of the Act of July 27, 1868, makes this declaration in order to secure the arrears accrued thereunder.

post-office address is as follows :

(*Signature of claimant.*)

Also Personally Appeared and residents of (*county, city, or town*) persons whom I certify to be respectable, and entitled to credit, and who, being by me duly sworn, say that they were present and saw sign name (*or make* *mark*) to the foregoing declaration; and they further swear that they have every reason to believe, from the appearance of the applicant and their acquaintance with that is the identical person represents self to be; and they further state that they have no interest in the prosecution of this claim.

(*Signatures of witnesses.*)

Sworn to and subscribed before me this day of A.D. 186 ; and I hereby certify that I have no interest, direct or indirect, in the prosecution of this claim.

(*Signature of judge or other officer.*)

Invalid applicants under Section Six should depose as to length of time they were employed in the civil service of the government between March 3, 1865, and June 6, 1866.

(220.)

Declaration for Increase of Pension.

(*Under Section Thirteen, Act of July* 27, 1868.)

STATE (TERRITORY OR DISTRICT) OF , } ss.
COUNTY OF , }

On this day of , A.D. one thousand eight hundred and personally appeared before me (*here state the official character of the person administering the oath*) within and for the County and State aforesaid, aged years, a resident of in the State of who, being duly sworn according to law, declares that is the identical to whom was granted pension certificate No. payable at at the rate of dollars per month, issued under the Act of 18 ; that makes this declaration in order to secure the increase of pension to which is entitled under the Thirteenth Section of the Act of July 27, 1868.

My post-office address is as follows:

(*Declarant's signature.*)

Also Personally Appeared and residents of (*county, city, or town*) persons whom I certify to be respectable, and entitled to credit, and who, being by me duly sworn, say that they were present and saw sign name (*or make mark*) to the foregoing declaration; and they further swear that they have every reason to believe, from the appearance of the applicant and their acquaintance with that is the identical person represents self to be, and that they have no interest in the prosecution of this claim.

(*Signatures of witnesses.*)

Sworn to and subscribed before me this day of A.D. 186 ; and I hereby certify that I have no interest, direct or indirect, in the prosecution of this claim.

(*Signature of judge or other officer.*)

Widows should depose that they have not remarried.

(221.)

Form of Surgeon's Affidavit. Navy Claims.

If the claimant for a pension has not been examined, and the degree of his disability certified, before his discharge, by a navy surgeon, and if the certificate of a navy surgeon or a board of survey is not obtainable, on satisfactory explanation of this fact, he may produce the affidavit of two surgeons reputable in their profession, and certified as such by the magistrate before whom their statement is sworn to, in accordance with the following form: —

(*Date.*)

It is hereby certified that who was a in the naval service of the United States (*here state the vessel or station on which applicant was engaged, and his particular service*) is suffering from (*here give a particular description of the wound, injury, or disease, and specify in what manner it has affected the applicant so as to produce disability in the degree stated*) and he is thereby not only incapacitated for naval duty, but, in the opinion of the undersigned, is ("*three-fourths,*" "*one-half,*" "*one-third,*" *&c., or* "*totally,*" *as the case may be*) disabled from obtaining his subsistence from manual labor. And we further certify that upon satisfactory evidence, and after accurate examination, we believe the said disability was incurred in the naval service of the United States, and in the line of duty.

(, *Surgeon.*)
(, *Surgeon.*)

Sworn to and subscribed before me this day of A.D. 186 ; and I hereby certify that the said and are known to me as surgeons in actual practice, reputable in their profession, and that I have no interest, direct or indirect, in the prosecution of this claim.

(*Magistrate's signature.*)

GUARDIAN'S CLAIMS UNDER SECTION 4, ACT OF JULY 27, 1868.

Guardians, in applying on account of minor children of a soldier whose widow is entitled to pension, may present their claim under the Fourth Section of the Act of July 27, 1868, in accordance with Form 210, with such obvious changes as the nature of the case may demand.

SPECIAL ACT CASES.

In cases authorized by special acts of Congress, formal declarations from the claimants thereunder are required, as in cases under the general law.

CHAPTER XXXVIII.

OF THE DISPOSAL OF PROPERTY BY WILL.

SECTION I.

OF WILLS.

FEW persons are aware how very difficult it is to make an unobjectionable will. There is nothing one can do, in reference to which it is more certain that he needs legal advice, and that of a trustworthy kind. Eminent lawyers, not practised in this peculiar branch of the law, have often failed in making their own wills, both in England and in this country. And there are seldom blank forms for wills printed and sold, as there are for deeds and leases. Nevertheless, it may happen that one is called upon to make his own will, or a will for his neighbor, under circumstances which do not admit of delay; or he may have some interest in the will of a deceased person, and questions may have arisen, which some knowledge of legal principles will answer. We shall try to state here what may be of use in such cases; and shall append a form for a will.

Any person of sound mind and proper age may make a will. A married woman cannot, unless in relation to trust property, whereof the trust or marriage settlement reserves to her this power; or the statute law of her State gives it, as is the case now in many States.

One must be of full age in order to devise real estate. But in most of our States minors may bequeath personal property; and a frequent limitation of the age for such bequest is eighteen years for males, and sixteen years for females.

The testator should say distinctly, in the beginning of the instrument, *that it is his last will.* If he has made other wills, it is usual and well to say, "hereby revoking all former wills;" but the law gives effect to a last will always.

It should close with the words of attestation: "In witness whereof, I have hereunto signed and sealed this instrument, and published and declared the same as and for my last will, at , on this day of ." Then should follow the signature and seal; for this latter, although not always required by law, is usually and properly affixed.

The witnessing part is very material. The requirements in the different States are not precisely alike; but they are all intended to secure such attestation as will leave the fact of the execution of the will, and its publication as such, beyond doubt. In a very few States, it is enough if the signature be proved by credible witnesses, although there be no witnesses who subscribed their names to the will. In many, two subscribing witnesses are enough. But in some it is necessary, *and in all I recommend*, that the testator should ask *three* disinterested persons to witness his will; and should then, in their presence, sign and seal it, and declare it to be his will; and they should then, each in the presence of the testator and of the other witnesses, sign his name as witness.

Each should see the execution which he says he witnesses; and the signing by the witnesses should all be seen by the testator; but the law is satisfied if the thing is done near the testator, and where he can see if he chooses to look. If the testator is too feeble to write his name, let him make his mark; and for this purpose any mark is enough, although a cross is commonly made. So, if a witness cannot write his name, he may make his mark; but this should be avoided if possible.

Over the witnesses' names should be written their attestation; and any alteration in the will should be noticed. If the attestation be in the following words, it will be safe in any part of this country: —

"At on this day of the above-named signed and sealed this instrument, and published and declared the same as and for his last will; and we, in his presence, and at his request, and in the presence of each other, have hereunto subscribed our names as witnesses."

Witnesses should be selected with care, where that is possible; for if any question arises about the testator's sanity, or any thing of the kind, their evidence is first to be taken, and is very important.

But any persons competent to do ordinary acts of business may be witnesses. Nor do the usual disqualifications for business apply. Thus, married women and minors may be witnesses of wills. But no person should be called upon to witness a will who is a legatee, or an executor, or otherwise interested in the will. If such a person were a witness, it might not avoid the will; but a legatee would lose or be obliged to renounce his legacy; and, generally, it might lead to unintended results. What was said in relation to deeds, of witnesses remembering, &c., or proof of handwriting in case of their death or absence, is true also of wills.

As to the body of the will, the testator must express his wishes as clearly and accurately as possible; and, unless he has good legal advice, he should make the disposition of his property as simple as possible.

The word "bequeath" applies, properly, to personal estate only; the word "devise," to real estate only. It is safe enough to begin, "I give, bequeath, and devise my estate and property, as follows: that is to say," — and then go on and tell what shall be done with this and that piece of property, or sum of money.

Words of inheritance should be added to any devise of land (if not intended for the life of the devisee only), as was said in reference to deeds; although they are not required in wills so peremptorily as in deeds. The words of inheritance are, — To A B "and his heirs."

If it is intended, as usually is the case, that the will should apply to all the real estate possessed by the testator at the time of his death, although purchased after the will is made, there should be a clause expressing this intention.

If children are not provided for in a will, the law presumes they were forgotten; and it gives to any such child the same share as if there were no will, unless the omission is explained and accounted for in the will, in such wise as to show that it was intentional. The same rule, applies, quite generally, to the issue of a deceased child. If the child were provided for in the lifetime of the father, the law, generally, might not presume that he was forgotten; it is best, however, to guard against any question of the kind, by naming the children, and giving them a small sum, or saying that the omission to give them any thing is intentional.

A testator should always name his executors; but the will is perfectly good without any executor being named, for the court of probate will appoint an "administrator with the will annexed."

SECTION II.

CODICILS.

A CODICIL is a little additional will. That is, it is a testamentary disposition, not revoking the former will, but varying it in some way, or making changes in it. There can be but one will, and that the last; but there may be any number of codicils, all valid. The changes made by a codicil in a will, or in former codicils, should be very distinctly stated; and some words like these should be used: "I hereby expressly confirm my former will, dated excepting so far as the disposition of my property is changed by this codicil." And the codicil should be called, at the beginning and end, a codicil, and executed and witnessed in the same manner as a will.

If a codicil gives one a legacy, who has already one by the will, the codicil should state whether it gives the second legacy instead of the first, or in addition to it. And if advances are made to a child during life, there should be an indorsement on the will (but a statement in the will or codicil would be better), stating whether these advances are to be charged to him, and in what way, whether with interest, &c.

SECTION III.

REVOCATION OF WILLS.

THE law concerning the revocation of a will is quite nice and technical. A codicil, we have seen, does not revoke, and a new will does. So might tearing off the name; but then the question might come, who tore it off. It is best to leave neither this nor any other question; and therefore to destroy a will which it is intended to revoke. If the will is out of the testator's reach and power, and so cannot be destroyed, it would be best to make a new will, revoking the old one; which any testator can always do.

A will is revoked by the operation of law, if the testator afterwards marry and have a child. If the testator, after this, intends that his will shall take effect, he should expressly confirm it; and the correct way to do this would be by making a new will. If he leaves any thing to his wife, and intends that she should have it instead of dower, or of the additional rights which recent statutes in some of the States have given her, he should say so. And then she will not have both, but may choose between the provision of the law and that of the will, taking whichever she prefers, and leaving the other.

For the rights of the wife or widow in the several States, I refer back to the abstract of the statutes of the several States, in Chapter V. from page 17 to 36.

It is impossible to do more than to give such forms and rules as will be applicable to all wills, and enable any person to draw a simple will with safety. No one can express accurately provisions for trust estates, remainders, executory devices, &c., without knowing the law on these subjects, — and this is an extensive and difficult department of the law. All that is necessary, and may be relied upon as generally sufficient, is as follows: —

(222.)

Form of a Will.

I,   of (*place and occupation*), make this my last will. I give, devise, and bequeath my estate and property, real and personal, as follows, that is to say: —

Then follow all the provisions and disposition of property which the testator intends, stated fully, plainly, and as accurately as possible, paying due regard to the rules and principles laid down in the chapter of this book on this subject. And if these provisions are carefully presented in distinct and intelligible language, the courts will generally supply whatever of technicality is wanting. Then follows, first, the appointment of an executor, and then the execution, and finally the declaration of the witnesses, thus: —

I appoint (*name, residence, and occupation*) executor (*or executors if more than one be desired*) of this my will.

In witness whereof, I have signed and sealed and published and declared this instrument as my will, at (*place*), on (*date*).

(*Signature.*) (*Seal.*)

The said at said (*place*), on said (*day*), signed and sealed this instrument, and published and declared the same as and for his last will. And we, at his request, and in his presence, and in the presence of each other, have hereunto written our names as subscribing witnesses.

(*Here follow the names of three witnesses.*)

A codicil should be written thus: —

I, of (*place and occupation*), do make this my codicil, hereby confirming my last will made on the (*date of the will*), and all my former codicils (*if there be any*), so far as this codicil is consistent therewith; and do hereby —

Then follows whatever disposition the testator chooses to make, stating and describing it as he would if it were a will, and executing it and having it attested in the same manner as if it were a will, excepting that, instead of calling it a will, wherever that word occurs, he says, "codicil" instead of "will."

CHAPTER XXXIX.

EXECUTORS AND ADMINISTRATORS.

An executor is a person named in the will of a deceased person, to settle his or her estate. There may be one or more; and they may be male or female. An administrator is one appointed by the court to settle the estate of a deceased person. If the deceased left a will, but did not appoint an executor, or the appointed executor refuses to act, or resigns or dies, or for any reason fails to act, an administrator is appointed by the court "with the will annexed." The husband of a deceased wife, or the wife of a deceased husband, has generally the right to be appointed administrator; after them the next of kin in the order of relationship. But the courts have some discretion in the matter.

They act as the personal representatives of the deceased, having in their hands his means, for the purpose of discharging his liabilities, or executing his contracts, and of carrying into effect his will, if he have left one; and, in general, they are liable only so far as these means (called *assets*), in their hands, are applicable to such a purpose. But they may become personally liable; and a clause in the statute of frauds refers to this subject, making them not liable to pay any debt out of their own means, unless they give a promise to that effect, in writing, signed by them.

In this country, the judicial officer, or judge who has the charge of the settlement of estates, of the proof of wills, and of proceedings under them, is generally called the Judge of Probate. But in some States he is called Surrogate, Register or Registrar of Wills or of Probate, Judge of the Orphan's Court, &c. His powers and duties are very similar all over the country. From his decrees or decisions an appeal may generally be taken, by a party who thinks himself aggrieved, to the Supreme Judicial Court. The Judge of Probate is usually a county officer, and his jurisdiction is limited to his county.

If an executor or administrator receives, as such, a promissory note or bill of the deceased, and indorses the same with his name, without adding "executor" or "administrator," he is liable upon it personally. If he makes a note or bill, signing it, "as executor," he is personally liable, unless he expressly limits his promise to pay, by the words, "out of the assets of my testator," or, "if the assets be sufficient," or in some equivalent way; but a note or bill so qualified would not be negotiable, because on condition. If an executor or administrator submits a disputed question to arbitration, in general terms, and without an express limitation of his liability, and the arbitrators award that he shall pay a certain sum, he is liable to pay it whether he has assets or not. But if the award be merely that a certain sum is due from the estate of the deceased, without saying that the executor or administrator is to pay it, he is not precluded from denying that he has assets.

Where the will of the deceased is of an executory nature, and the personal representative can fairly and sufficiently execute all that the deceased could have done, he may do so, and enforce the contract. But where an executory contract is of a strictly personal nature — as, for example, with an author for a specified work, or with an artist for a painting, the death of the writer before his book is completed, or of the artist before the painting is finished, absolutely determines the contract, unless what remains to be done — as, for example, in the case of a book, the preparing of an index, or table of contents, &c., can certainly be done as well and to the same purpose and effect by another.

If executors or administrators pay away money of the deceased by mistake, or enter into contracts for carrying on his business for the benefit of his personal estate, and to wind up his affairs, they may sue on such contracts either in their individual or their representative capacities; but they should sue in the latter capacity, in order to avoid a set off against them of their individual debts.

The title of an administrator does not exist until the grant of administration. Then it goes back to the death of the deceased; but only in order to protect the estate, and not for any other purpose. And if an agent sells goods of the deceased, after his death, and in ignorance of his decease, the administrator may adopt the contract, and sue upon it.

On the death of one of several executors, either before or after probate, the entire right of representation survives to the others. But if an administrator dies, or a sole executor dies, no interest and no right of representation is transmitted to his personal representatives.

An executor derives his authority from the will, and his duties begin at the death of the testator. They may be stated thus: —

1. He should cause the deceased to be buried in a suitable manner.

2. He should offer the will for probate as soon as he can with a reasonable regard to his convenience; and in proving the will, filing bonds, giving notice, making and returning an inventory, and the like, he must conform to the law of the State and the rules of the probate; and he will obtain at the office sufficient information on all these points.

3. He must collect the property, and, after paying the debts, he must distribute or dispose of the remainder as the will directs.

4. He must render his account from time to time, until a final settlement of the estate is made, and will be directed at the Probate Office when and how to file his accounts.

An administrator derives his authority from the court. But his duties are then substantially similar to those of an executor; excepting, that he must distribute and dispose of the estate as the law requires, as he has no will to direct him, unless he is an administrator with the will annexed. The debts must be paid in a certain order. This is not precisely the same in all the States; but it is very generally as follows:—

1. Funeral-expenses, charges of the last sickness, and probate charges.

2. Debts due to the United States.

3. Debts due to the State in which the deceased had his home.

4. Any liens attaching to the property by law.

5. To creditors generally.

If the estate is insufficient to pay all the debts due from it, as soon as the executor or administrator finds this to be the case, he should represent the estate as insolvent at the Probate Court, and thereafter follow the requirements of the law of the State and the rules of the Probate Office, in reference to insolvent estates of deceased persons.

In most of the States, all the necessary forms or instruments are given to applicants at the Probate Office. It may, however, be convenient to know how to frame some of the most necessary forms; and I give below those which, with such obvious changes as circumstances may require and indicate, may be found sufficient.

(223.)

Petition to be appointed Executor, without further Notice.

To the Honorable the Judge of the Probate Court in and for the County of

Respectfully Represents (*name of the executor*) of (*residence of executor*) that (*name of testator*) who last dwelt in (*residence of testator*) died on the day of in the year of our Lord one thousand eight hundred and possessed of goods and estate remaining to be administered, leaving a widow, whose name is (*name of the widow*) and as his only heirs-at-law and next of kin, the persons whose names, residences and relationship to the deceased are as follows, viz. (*here give all the names, stating the relationship of each person*). That said deceased left a will and a codicil herewith presented, wherein your petitioner is named executor.

Wherefore your petitioner prays that said will and codicil may be proved and allowed, and letters testamentary issued to him.

Dated this day of A.D. 186 .

(*Signature of executor.*)

The undersigned, being all the heirs-at-law and next of kin, and the only parties interested in the foregoing petition, request that the prayer thereof be granted without further notice.

(*Signatures of heirs.*).

[Minors must be so designated, and the names of their guardians given, if they have any. If any party is a married woman, her husband's name must be given.]

(224.)

Executor's Bond.

Know all Men by these Presents, That we (*name of the executor*) as principal, and (*names of his sureties*) as sureties, and all within the Commonwealth (*or State*) of are holden and stand firmly bound and obliged unto Judge of the Probate Court in and for the County of in the full and just sum of dollars, to be paid to said judge and his successors in said office; to the true payment whereof we bind ourselves and each of us, our and each of our heirs, executors, and administrators, jointly and severally, by these presents. Sealed with our seals. Dated the day of in the year of our Lord one thousand eight hundred and sixty-

The Condition of this Obligation is such, That if the above-bounden (*name of the executor*) executor of the last will and testament of (*name of the testator*) late of (*residence of testator*) deceased, testate, shall

First, make and return to the Probate Court for said County of within three months from his appointment, a true inventory of all the real estate and all the goods, chattels, rights and credits of said testator, which are by law to be administered, and which shall have come to his possession or knowledge;

Second, administer according to law and the will of said testator, all the goods, chattels, rights, and credits, and the proceeds of all the real estate that may be sold for the payment of debts or legacies, which shall come to the possession of said executor, or of any other person for him; and

Third, render upon oath a just and true account of his administration within one year, and at any other times when required by said court; then this obligation to be void; otherwise to remain in full force and virtue.

(Signature of executor.) *(Seal.)*
(Signature of surety.) *(Seal.)*
(Signature of surety.) *(Seal.)*

Signed, Sealed and Delivered in presence of

, ss. 18 . Examined and approved.
(name of judge)
Judge of Probate Court.

(225.)

Bond of Executor, who is also Residuary Legatee.

Know all Men by these Presents, That I *(name of the executor)* in the Commonwealth *(or State)* of * am holden and stand firmly bound and obliged unto Judge of the Probate Court in and for the County of in the full and just sum of dollars, to be paid to said judge and his successors in said office; to the true payment whereof I bind myself and my heirs, executors, and administrators, by these presents. Sealed with my seal. Dated the day of in the year of our Lord one thousand eight hundred and sixty-

The Condition of this Obligation is such, That, if the above-bounden *(name of executor)* executor of the last will and testament of *(name of testator)* late of *(residence of testator)* deceased, testate, being residuary legatee in said will, shall pay all debts and legacies of said testator, and such sums as may be allowed by said Probate Court for necessaries to the widow or minor children of said testator, then this obligation to be void, otherwise to remain in full force and virtue.

(Signature.) *(Seal.)*

Signed, Sealed and Delivered in the Presence of

, ss. 18 . Examined and approved.
(name of judge)
Judge of Probate Court.

(226.)

Administrator's Bond.

Know all Men by these Presents, That we *(name of administrator)* as principal, and *(name of sureties)* as sureties, and all within the State of are holden and stand firmly bound and obliged unto Judge of the Probate Court in and for the County of in the full and just sum of dollars, to be paid to said judge

* If sureties are required, they should be added here as in preceding Form.

and his successors in said office; to the true payment thereof we bind ourselves and each of us, our and each of our heirs, executors and administrators, jointly and severally, by these presents. Sealed with our seals. Dated the day of in the year of our Lord one thousand eight hundred and sixty

The Condition of this Obligation is such, That if the above-bounden (*name of administrator*) administrator of the estate of (*name of deceased*) late of (*residence of deceased*) deceased, intestate shall,

FIRST, make and return into said Probate Court, within three months after his appointment, a true inventory of all the real estate, and all the goods, chattels, rights and credits of said deceased, which have or shall come to his possession or knowledge;

SECOND, administer according to law all the goods, chattels, rights and credits of said deceased, and the proceeds of all his real estate that may be sold for the payment of his debts, which shall at any time come to the possession of said administrator, or of any other person for him;

THIRD, render upon oath a true account of his administration, within one year, and at any other times when required by said Court;

FOURTH, pay any balance remaining in his hands, upon the settlement of his accounts, to such persons as said Court shall direct; and

FIFTH, deliver the letters of administration into said Court, in case any will of said deceased is hereafter duly proved and allowed: Then this obligation to be void, otherwise to remain in full force and virtue.

(*Signature of administrator.*) (*Seal.*)
(*Signature of surety.*) (*Seal.*)
(*Signature of surety.*) (*Seal.*)

Signed, Sealed and Delivered in Presence of

ss. 186 . Examined and approved.
(*name of judge*)
Judge of Probate Court.

(227.)

Administrator's Petition for leave to sell a Part of the Real Estate.

TO THE HONORABLE THE JUDGE OF THE PROBATE COURT IN AND FOR THE COUNTY OF

Respectfully Represents (*name of the administrator*) as he is administrator of the estate of (*name of the deceased*) late of (*residence of the deceased*) in said County, deceased. That the debts due from the deceased, as nearly as they can now be ascertained, amount to . . . . $

And the charges on administration to . . . . $

Amounting in all to . . . . $

That the value of the personal estate in the hands of the petitioner (exclusive of the widow's allowance) is . . . . $

And that the personal estate is therefore insufficient to pay the debts of the deceased and the charges of administration, by the sum of $

Wherefore your petitioner prays that he may be licensed to sell so much of the real estate of said deceased as will raise the last mentioned sum, for the payment of said debts and charges of administration.

Dated the day of A.D. 186 .

(*Signature.*)

The undersigned, being all persons interested, hereby assent to the sale, as prayed for in the foregoing petition.

(*Here should follow the signatures of the widow and all the heirs.*)

[If the petitioner wishes the court for special reasons to direct what *specific part* of the real estate shall be sold, he must set forth the value, description, and condition of the estate, or of such part as he proposes to sell.]

(228.)

Administrator's Petition for leave to sell the Whole of the Real Estate.

To the Honorable the Judge of the Probate Court in and for the County of

Respectfully Represents (*name of administrator*) as he is administrator of the estate of (*name of deceased*) late of (*residence of the deceased*) in said County deceased That the debts due from the deceased, as nearly as they can now be ascertained, amount to . . . . $

And the charges of administration to . . . . $

Amounting in all to . . . . $

That the value of the personal estate in the hands of the petitioner (exclusive of the widow's allowance) is . . . . $

That the personal estate is therefore insufficient to pay the debts of the deceased, and the charges of administration, and it is necessary for that purpose to sell some part of the real estate to raise the sum of . . . . $

That the value of the real estate according to the appraisal is . . . $

And that by a partial sale, the residue of the estate would be greatly injured. Wherefore your petitioner prays that he may be licensed to sell the whole of the real estate of said deceased, for the payment of said debts and charges of administration, and for the reasons aforesaid.

Dated the day of A.D. 186 .

(*Signature.*)

The undersigned, being all persons interested, hereby assent to the sale, as prayed for in the foregoing petition.

(*Here should follow the signatures of the widow and all the heirs.*)

[If the petitioner wishes to sell only a *specific part* of the real estate, which is more than enough to pay debts and legacies, he must give a concise description thereof, sufficient to enable parties interested to identify it.]

(229.)

Bond of Administrator Licensed to sell Real Estate.

Know all Men by these Presents, That we (*name of person licensed*) as principal, and (*names of his sureties*) as sureties, and all within the State of are holden and stand firmly bound and obliged unto Esquire, Judge of the Probate Court in and for the county of in the full and just sum of dollars, to be paid to said judge, and his successors in said office; to the true payment whereof we bind ourselves, and each of us, our and each of our heirs, executors, and administrators, jointly and severally, by these presents. Sealed with our seals. Dated the day of in the year of our Lord one thousand eight hundred and sixty-

The Condition of this Obligation is such, That if the above-bounden (*name of the person licensed*) administrator of the estate of (*name of deceased*) late of (*residence of deceased*) deceased, who has been licensed by said court to sell real estate of said deceased, more than is necessary for the payment of debts, and charges of administration, shall account for and dispose of according to law, all proceeds of the sale remaining after payment of debts, and charges, — then this obligation to be void; otherwise to remain in full force and virtue.

(*Signature of administrator.*) (*Seal.*)
(*Signature of surety.*) (*Seal.*)
(*Signature of surety.*) (*Seal.*)

Signed, Sealed and Delivered in Presence of

SUFFOLK, *ss.* A.D. 186 . Examined and approved.

(*name of judge*)
Judge of Probate Court.

I, (*name of administrator*) do solemnly swear, that in disposing of the real estate of (*name of the deceased*) deceased, which I have been licensed by the

Probate Court to sell, I will use my best judgment in fixing on the time and place of sale, and will exert my utmost endeavors to dispose of the same in such manner as will be most for the advantage of all persons interested therein. So help me God.

(*Signature of administrator.*)

SUFFOLK, *ss.* 186 . Personally appeared the above-named and took and subscribed the above oath.

Before me,

Justice of the Peace.

(230.)

Account of Executor.

The first (*or second or other as the case may be*) account of (*name of executor*) executor of the last will and testament of (*name of the testator*) late of (*residence of the testator*) in the county of deceased.

Said accountant charges himself with the several amounts received as stated in Schedule A, herewith exhibited . . . . . $

And asks to be allowed for sundry payments and charges as stated in Schedule B, herewith exhibited . . . . $

Balance . . . . $

(*Signature.*) *Executor.*

The undersigned, being all the parties interested, having examined the foregoing account, request that the same may be allowed without further notice.

(*Signatures of the widow and all the heirs and legatees.*)

SCHEDULE A.

	Dolls.	Cts.
Amount of personal estate according to inventory		
Balance of former account		
Amount received from gain on sale of personal estate over appraised value, and from other property as follows: —		

SCHEDULE B.

Amount paid out and charges, as follows: —

1. For funeral-expenses and expenses of last sickness . .
2. For charges of administration . . . .
3. For debts of the deceased . . . .
4. For amounts paid to legatees or heirs . . . . .

CHAPTER XL.

GUARDIANS.

GUARDIANS of all descriptions are treated by courts as trustees; and in almost all cases they are required to give security for the faithful discharge of their duty, unless the guardian be appointed by will, and the testator has exercised the power given him by statute, of requiring that the guardian shall not be called upon to give bonds. But, even in this case, such testamentary provision is wholly personal; and if the individual dies, refuses the appointment, or resigns it, or is removed from it, and a substitute is appointed by court, this substitute must give bonds.

The guardian is held, in this country, to have only a naked authority, not coupled with an interest. His possession of the property of his ward is not such as gives him a personal interest, being only for the purpose of agency. But for the benefit of his ward he has a very general power over it. He manages and disposes of the personal property at his own discretion, although it is safer for him to obtain the power of the court for any important measure. He may lease the real estate, if appointed by will or court; he cannot, however, sell the real estate without leave of the proper court. Nor should he convert the personal estate into real, without such leave.

As trustee, a guardian is held to a strictly honest discharge of his duty, and cannot act in relation to the subject of his trust for his own personal benefit, in any contract whatever. And if a benefit arises thereby, as in the settlement of a debt due from the ward, this benefit belongs wholly to the ward. And it has been held that if a guardian makes use of his own money to erect buildings on the land of his ward, without having an order of the court therefor, he cannot charge the same in account with his ward, or recover the amount from the ward. But we doubt whether a rule so severe would be applied unless for special reasons. He must neither make nor suffer any waste of the inheritance, and is held very strictly to a careful management of all personal property. He is responsible not only for any misuse of the ward's money or stock, but for letting it lie idle; and if he does so without sufficient cause, he must allow the ward interest or compound interest in his account.

To secure the proper execution of his trust, he is not only liable to an action by the ward, after the guardianship terminates, but, during its pendency, the ward may call him to account by his next friend, or by a guardian appointed by the court for the action. The courts have gone so far as to set aside transactions which took place soon after the ward came of age, and which were beneficial only to the former guardian, on the presumption that undue influence was used, and on the ground of public utility and policy.

A guardian cannot, by his own contract, bind the person or estate of his ward; but if he promise, on a sufficient consideration, to pay the debt of his ward, he is personally bound by his promise, although he expressly promises as guardian. And it is a sufficient consideration if such promise discharge the debt of the ward. And a guardian who thus discharges the debt of his ward may lawfully indemnify himself out of the ward's estate, or if he be discharged from his guardianship, he may have an action against the ward for money paid for his use. An action will not lie against a guardian on a contract made by the ward, but must be brought against the ward, and be defended by the guardian.

The guardianship is a trust so strictly personal, or attached to the individual, that it cannot be transferred from him, either by his own assignment or devise, or by inheritance or succession.

A married woman cannot become a guardian without the consent of her husband; but with that she may. A single woman who is a guardian generally loses her guardianship by marriage; but she may be re-appointed. In some States, she loses it by statute; in others not.

CHAPTER XLI.

STAMP ACT.

SCHEDULE OF STAMPS REQUIRED FOR DIFFERENT INSTRUMENTS.

	Dolls. Cts.
Acknowledgment of deeds, exempt.	
Affidavit..	5
" in suits or legal proceedings, exempt.	
Agreement or appraisement (for each sheet or piece of paper on which the same is written)..	5
Assignment or transfer of mortgage, lease or policy of insurance, the same duty as the original instrument.	
" of patent right..	5
Bank Checks, drafts or orders, &c., at sight or on demand................	2
Bills of Exchange (Foreign), drawn in, but payable out of, the United States, each bill of set of three or more must be stamped.	
For every bill of each set, where the sum made payable does not exceed one hundred dollars, or the equivalent thereof in any foreign currency in which such bills may be expressed, according to the standard of value fixed by the United States....................................	2
For every additional hundred dollars, or fractional part thereof in excess of one hundred dollars..................................	2
(Foreign), drawn in, but payable out of, the United States (if drawn singly or in duplicate), pay the same duty as Inland Bills of Exchange.	
[The acceptor or acceptors of any bill of exchange, or order for the payment of any sum of money drawn, or purporting to be drawn, in any foreign country, but payable in the United States, must, before paying or accepting the same, place thereupon a stamp indicating the duty.]	
Bills of Exchange (Inland), draft or order, payable otherwise than at sight or on demand, and any promissory note, whether payable on demand or at a time designated (except bank-notes issued for circulation, and checks made and intended to be, and which shall be, forthwith presented for payment), for a sum not exceeding one hundred dollars	5
For every additional one hundred dollars, or fractional part thereof....	5
[The warrant of attorney to confess judgment on a note or bond is exempt from stamp-duty, if the note or bond is properly stamped.]	
Bills of Lading, of vessels for ports of the United States or British North America, exempt.	
" or receipt for goods to any foreign port............................	10

	Dolls. Cts.
Bill of Sale of any vessel, or part thereof, when the consideration does not exceed five hundred dollars....................................	50
" exceeding five hundred dollars, and not exceeding one thousand dollars.	1.00
" exceeding one thousand dollars, for each five hundred dollars, or fractional part thereof........................	50
" of personal property (other than ship or vessel)......................	5
Bond, personal for the payment of money. [See *Mortgage.*]	
" official	1.00
" for indemnifying any person for the payment of any sum of money, where the money ultimately recoverable thereupon is one thousand dollars, or less..	50
" where the money recoverable exceeds one thousand dollars, for every additional one thousand dollars, or fractional part thereof......... .	50
Bonds. — County, city, and town bonds, railroad and other corporation bonds and scrip, are subject to stamp-duty. [See *Mortgage.*]	
" of any description, other than such as are required in legal proceedings, and such as are not otherwise charged in this schedule	25
Certificates of deposit in bank, sum not exceeding one hundred dollars......	2
" of deposit in bank, sum exceeding one hundred dollars...............	5
" of stock in an incorporated company...............................	25
" general	5
" of record upon the instrument recorded, exempt.	
" of record upon the book, exempt.	
" of weight or measurement of animals, coal, wood, or other articles, except weigher's and measurer's returns, exempt.	
" of a qualification of a Justice of the Peace, Commissioner of Deeds, or Notary Public...	5
" of search of records...	5
" that certain papers are on file.....................................	5
" that certain papers cannot be found	5
" of redemption of land sold for taxes................................	5
" of birth, marriage, and death......................................	5
" of qualification of school-teachers................................	5
" of profits in an incorporated company for a sum not less than ten dollars, and not exceeding fifty dollars...........................	10
" exceeding fifty dollars, and not exceeding one thousand dollars........	25
" exceeding one thousand dollars, for every additional one thousand dollars, or fractional part thereof................................	25
" of damage, or otherwise, and all other certificates or documents issued by any port warden, marine surveyor, or other person acting as such.	25

	Dolls. Cts.
Certified Transcripts of judgments, satisfaction of judgments, and of all papers recorded or on file........	5
[N.B.—As a general rule, every certificate which has or may have a legal value in any court of law or equity will require a stamp-duty of five cents.]	
Charter Party, or letter, memorandum, or other writing between the captain, owner or agent of any ship, vessel, or steamer, and any other person, relating to the charter of the same, if the registered tonnage of said ship, vessel, or steamer does not exceed one hundred and fifty tons...	1.00
" exceeding one hundred and fifty tons, and not exceeding three hundred tons........	3.00
" exceeding three hundred tons, and not exceeding six hundred tons.....	5.00
" exceeding six hundred tons........	10.00
Check, draft or order for the payment of any sum of money exceeding ten dollars, drawn upon any person other than a bank, banker, or trust company, at sight or on demand........	2
Contract. [See *Agreement.*]	
" Broker's........	10
Conveyance, deed, instrument, or writing, whereby lands, tenements, or other realty sold, shall be conveyed, *the actual value* of which does not exceed five hundred dollars........	50
" exceeding five hundred dollars, and not exceeding one thousand dollars.	1.00
" for every additional five hundred dollars, or fractional part thereof in excess of one thousand dollars........	50
Entry of any goods, wares, or merchandise at any custom-house, either for consumption or warehousing, not exceeding one hundred dollars in value........	25
" exceeding one hundred dollars, and not exceeding five hundred dollars in value........	50
" exceeding five hundred dollars in value........	1.00
" for the withdrawal of any goods or merchandise from bonded warehouse.	50
Gauger's Returns, if for quantity not exceeding five hundred gallons gross.	10
" exceeding five hundred gallons........	25
Indorsement of any negotiable instrument, exempt.	
Insurance (Marine, Inland, and Fire) where the consideration paid for the insurance, in cash, premium notes, or both, does not exceed ten dollars.	10
" (Marine, Inland, and Fire) exceeding ten dollars, and not exceeding fifty dollars........	25
" (Marine, Inland, and Fire) exceeding fifty dollars........	50
Insurance (Life), when the amount insured does not exceed one thousand dollars........	25
" (Life) exceeding one thousand dollars, and not exceeding five thousand dollars........	50

	Dolls. Cts.
Insurance (Life) exceeding five thousand dollars	1.00
" (Life) limited to injury to persons while travelling, exempt.	
Lease of lands or tenements, where rent does not exceed three hundred dollars per annum	50
" exceeding three hundred dollars, for each additional two hundred dollars, or fractional part thereof in excess of three hundred dollars	50
" perpetual, subject to stamp-duty as a "conveyance," the stamp-duty to be measured by resolving the annual rental into a capital sum.	
" clause of guaranty of payment of rent, incorporated or indorsed, five cents additional.	
Manifest for custom-house entry or clearance of the cargo of any ship, vessel, or steamer for a foreign port, if the registered tonnage of such ship, vessel, or steamer, does not exceed three hundred tons	1.00
" exceeding three hundred tons, and not exceeding six hundred tons	3.00
" exceeding six hundred tons	5.00
Measurer's Returns, if for quantity not exceeding one thousand bushels	10
" exceeding one thousand bushels	25
Mortgage, trust deed, bill of sale, or personal bond for the payment of money exceeding one hundred dollars, and not exceeding five hundred dollars	50
" exceeding five hundred dollars, for every additional five hundred dollars, or fractional part thereof in excess of five hundred dollars	50
Pawner's Checks	5
Pension Papers. — Powers of attorney, and all other papers relating to applications for bounties, arrearages of pay, or pensions, or to receipt thereof, exempt.	
Passage Ticket from the United States to a foreign port, costing not more than thirty-five dollars	50
" from the United States to a foreign port, costing more than thirty-five dollars, and not exceeding fifty dollars	1.00
" for every additional fifty dollars, or fractional part thereof in excess of fifty dollars	1.00
Power of Attorney to sell or transfer stock, or collect dividends thereon	25
" to vote at election of incorporated company	10
" to receive or collect rents	25
" to sell, or convey, or rent, or lease real estate	1.00
" for any other purpose	50
Probate of Will, or letters of administration, where the value of both real and personal estate does not exceed two thousand dollars	1.00
" for every additional one thousand dollars, or fractional part thereof in excess of two thousand dollars	50
" bonds of executors, administrators, guardians, and trustees, are each subject to a stamp-duty of	1.00

	Dolls.	Cts.
Proprietary Medicines and Preparations. — For and upon every packet, box, bottle, pot, phial, or other enclosure, containing any pills, powders, tinctures, troches, lozenges, sirups, cordials, bitters, anodynes, tonics, plasters, liniments, salves, ointments, pastes, drops, waters, essences, spirits, oils, or other medicinal preparations or compositions whatsoever, sold, offered for sale, or removed for consumption and sale, by any person or persons whatever, where such packet, box, &c., with its contents, does not exceed at retail price or value the sum of twenty-five cents		1
Exceeding twenty-five, and not exceeding fifty cents		2
Exceeding fifty, and not exceeding seventy-five cents		3
Exceeding seventy-five cents, and not exceeding one dollar		4
Exceeding one dollar, for every additional fifty cents, or fractional part thereof in excess of one dollar		2
Officinal preparations and medicines mixed or compounded specially for any person according to the written recipe or prescription of any physician or surgeon, exempt.		
Perfumery and Cosmetics. — For and upon every packet, box, bottle, pot, phial, or other enclosure, containing any essence, extract, toilet-water, cosmetic, hair-oil, pomade, hair-dressing, hair-restorative, hair-dye, tooth-wash, dentifrice, tooth-paste, aromatic cachous, or any similar articles, by whatsoever name the same heretofore have been, now are, or may hereafter be, called, known, or distinguished, used or applied, or to be used or applied as perfumes or applications to the hair, mouth, or skin, sold, offered for sale, or removed for consumption and sale, the same rates per package, &c., as for medicines and preparations.		
Friction Matches. — For and upon every parcel or package of one hundred or less		1
More than one hundred, and not more than two hundred		2
For every additional one hundred, or fractional part thereof		1
Cigar Lights and Wax Tapers, double the rates for friction matches.		
Photographs, Ambrotypes, Daguerrotypes, or other sun pictures, except copies of engravings of works of art, and those used for the illustration of books, for and upon each picture, where the retail price does not exceed twenty-five cents		2
Exceeding twenty-five, and not exceeding fifty cents		3
Exceeding fifty cents, and not exceeding one dollar		5
Exceeding one dollar, for every additional dollar, or fractional part thereof		5
Playing Cards. — For and upon every pack, the retail price of which shall not exceed eighteen cents		2
Exceeding eighteen, and not exceeding twenty-five cents		4
Exceeding twenty-five, and not exceeding fifty cents		10
Exceeding fifty cents, and not exceeding one dollar		15
Exceeding one dollar, for every additional fifty cents, or fraction thereof.		5

	Dolls. Cts.
Probate of Will, certificate of appointment	5
Protest upon bill, note, check, or draft....................................	25
Promissory Note. — [See *Bills of Exchange*, Inland.]	
" deposit note to mutual insurance companies, when policy is subject to duty, exempt.	
" renewal of, subject to same duty as an original note.	
Quit Claim Deed, to be stamped as a conveyance, except when given as a release of a mortgage by the mortgagee to the mortgagor, in which case it is exempt.	
Receipt for the payment of any sum of money or debt due exceeding twenty dollars, or for the delivery of any property.........................	2
" for satisfaction of any mortgage or judgment, or decree of any court, exempt.	
Sheriff's return on writ, or other process, exempt.	
Trust Deed, made to secure a debt, to be stamped as a mortgage.	
" conveying estate to uses, to be stamped as a conveyance.	
Warehouse Receipt for any goods, wares, or merchandise, not otherwise provided for, deposited or stored in any public or private warehouse, not exceeding five hundred dollars in value	10
" exceeding five hundred dollars, and not exceeding one thousand dollars.	20
" exceeding one thousand dollars, for every additional one thousand dollars, or fractional part thereof, in excess of one thousand dollars.....	10
" for any goods, &c., not otherwise provided for, stored or deposited in any public or private warehouse or yard..............................	25

Remarks.

Revenue stamps may be used indiscriminately upon any of the matters or things enumerated in Schedule B, except proprietary and playing cards stamps, for which a special use has been provided.

Postage stamps cannot be used in payment of the duty chargeable on instruments.

It is the duty of the maker of an instrument to affix and cancel the stamp required thereon. If he neglects to do so, the party for whose use it is made may stamp it before it is used; but in no case can it be legally used without a stamp; if *used* without a stamp, it cannot be afterwards effectually stamped. Any failure upon the part of the maker of an instrument to appropriately stamp it renders him liable to a penalty of two hundred dollars.

Suits are commenced in many States by other process than writ, viz., summons warrant, publication, petition, &c., in which cases these, as the original processes, severally require stamps.

The jurat of an affidavit, taken before a justice of the peace, notary public, or other officer duly authorized to take affidavits, is held to be a certificate, and subject to a stamp duty of five cents, except when taken in suits or legal proceedings.

Certificates of loan, in which there shall appear any written or printed evidence of an amount of money to be paid on demand, or at a time designated, are subject to stamp duty as "promissory notes."

The assignment of a mortgage is subject to the same stamp duty as that imposed upon the original instrument; that is to say, for every sum of five hundred dollars, or any fractional part thereof of the amount secured by the mortgage at the time of its assignment, there must be affixed a stamp or stamps denoting a duty of fifty cents.

When two or more persons join in the execution of an instrument, the stamp to which the instrument is liable under the law may be affixed and cancelled by any one of the parties.

In conveyances of real estate, the law provides that the stamp affixed must answer to the *value* of the estate or interest conveyed.

No stamp is required on any warrant of attorney accompanying a bond or note, when such bond or note has affixed thereto the stamp or stamps denoting the duty required; and whenever any bond or note is secured by mortgage, but one stamp duty is required on such papers, and that stamp duty is the highest rate required for either of these instruments. In such case, a note or memorandum of the value or denomination of the stamp affixed should be made upon the margin or in the acknowledgment of the instrument which is not stamped.

INDEX.

A.

B.

C.

J.

K.

L.

M.

N.

O.

P.

R.

S.

T.

U.

INDEX OF FORMS.

WHOLE NUMBER OF PAGES, INCLUDING CONTENTS, 707.

LAWS OF BUSINESS

FOR

ALL THE STATES OF THE UNION;

WITH

Forms and Directions for all Transactions:

CONTAINING CHAPTERS ON

Commercial Law in General, on Infants or Minors, Married Women and their Rights, Sales, Guaranty, Payment, Notes and Bills of Exchange, Agency, Partnership, Arbitration, Carriage of Goods and Passengers by Railroads and other Carriers, Patents, Copyrights, Statute of Limitations, Interest and Usury, Bankruptcy, Shipping, Marine, Fire and Life Insurance, Deeds of Land, Mortgages of Land, Mortgages of Personal Property, Leases, Liens of Mechanics and Material Men, Pensions for Soldiers and Sailors, the Recovery of Debts, Wills, Executors and Administrators, Guardians, the Stamp Act, and other topics.

By THEOPHILUS PARSONS, LL. D.,

Professor of Law in Harvard University, Cambridge, and Author of Treatises on the Law of Contracts, on Mercantile Law, on the Law of Partnership, on the Laws of Promissory Notes and Bills of Exchange, on the Law of Insurance, and on the Law of Shipping and Admiralty.

The growing intelligence and mental activity of the American people, has created a demand, almost universal, for correct information concerning their social, civil, and business relations.

Books heretofore published for this end have, generally, been characterized by incompetent authorship, fatal errors and omissions. But the "LAWS OF BUSINESS," by Professor Parsons, embodying the results of continuous labor for many years in the study, practice, and teaching of the law, and the preparation of Law Books, fully meets this demand, and, as a reliable and correct authority, will never be superseded. Of its completeness and excellence, the name of the distinguished author is a sufficient guaranty.

It embodies and presents in the clearest, plainest, and most precise manner, all those rules and principles which regulate social intercourse, and govern every kind of business, with full directions for every transaction.

It explains the nature of every kind of contract, conveyance, and legal obligation.

It gives directions to Magistrates, to Administrators and Executors, to Landlords and Tenants, to Guardians and Wards, to Buyers and Sellers, Agents and Principals, Debtors and Creditors, to Trustees, Common Carriers, to Insolvents, to Insurers and Underwriters, to Inventors, Authors, Partners, Clerks, Corporations, and Shareholders, and all who have any business to transact.

It shows how to draw and perfect a Deed, to make an Agreement, an Assignment, a Lease, a Guaranty, a Note, a Check, an Order, a Due Bill, a Will, a Codicil, a Bill of Exchange, a Protest, an Indorsement, a Bill of Sale, an Indenture, a Mortgage, a Warranty, a Petition, an Affidavit, a Release, a Power of Attorney, Patent Forms, and every kind of Legal Instrument.

The Forms have been prepared from an extensive collection made by the author from those most approved in all parts of the country, and which have been tested in courts of law; and are so numerous as to meet almost every case that can arise.

IT IS ESSENTIAL TO

Every Farmer,
Every Manufacturer,
Every Contractor,
Every Landlord,
Every Executor,
Every Guardian,
Every Heir-at-Law,
Every Apprentice,
Every Partner,
Every Auctioneer,
Every Mechanic,
Every Public Officer,
Every Agent,
Every Tenant,
Every Administrator,
Every Minor,
Every Legatee,
Every Mariner,
Every Clerk,
Every Broker,
Every Notary,
Every Justice of Peace,
Every Constable,
Every Sheriff,
Every Assessor,
Every Grand Juror,
Every Married Woman,
Every Trader,
Every Employer,
Every Citizen,
Every Bank Officer,
Every Consignor,
Every Collector,
Every Deputy Sheriff,
Every Commissioner,
Every Treasurer,
Every Widow,
Every Market-Man,
Every Employee,
Every Property Holder.

In short, as a Compendium and Hand-Book, it is indispensable to all who desire to know their rights and duties, or to possess the means of transacting, unaided, and with correctness and safety, their own legal business.

It is for everybody, the safest and cheapest Counsellor and Legal Adviser, ready at hand at all times to be consulted, often superseding delays and costly consultations, and essentially enabling every man to be his own ready lawyer.

☞ The very many highly complimentary notices that this great work has received from eminent Lawyers, Jurists, and the Press, throughout the country, are sufficient to show the high esteem in which it is universally held by those most competent to judge of its merits.

Send for Circulars, Terms, and Testimonials. Address

NATIONAL PUBLISHING CO.,
Cincinnati, Ohio.

Or JONES, JUNKIN & CO.,
Chicago, Ills.

AGENTS WANTED.

WE are now publishing and will hereafter issue by subscription, as the public demand them, Standard Works of the highest literary and mechanical excellence, which will in all cases be books of permanent value, equal in all respects to the descriptions given in the Prospectus, and will be sold at such low prices as will place them within the reach of all classes.

It is and will be our aim to issue only such works as will, from their sterling worth, entitle them to a place in every library and in every household throughout the land, and will be a credit to the Canvasser who introduces them.

The advantage of long experience in the Subscription Book business, enables us to judge correctly of the wants of the public and of the works most readily sold, and to impart to Canvassers valuable practical information and assistance in their pursuits.

All who engage with us will receive not only verbal directions, but instructions in a printed form to guide them in every step of their progress. We shall also in all other suitable ways endeavor to render aid to our Agents, promptly attend to their wants, and make their employment as successful and satisfactory as possible.

School Teachers, Clergymen, Students, Farmers, Ladies, and all others who want pleasant and lucrative employment, are wanted to aid in introducing the following works which we are now publishing.

Circulars will be mailed promptly to any one desiring an agency.

For description of Books, see following pages.

Address

NATIONAL PUBLISHING CO.,

178 Elm Street, Cincinnati, Ohio.

Or JONES, JUNKIN & CO.,

167 South Clark Street, Chicago, Ills.

AN ILLUSTRATED

Dictionary of the Bible,

COMPRISING ITS

ANTIQUITIES, BIOGRAPHY, GEOGRAPHY,

AND

NATURAL HISTORY,

WITH NUMEROUS ILLUSTRATIONS AND MAPS, ALL ENGRAVED EXPRESSLY FOR THIS WORK.

EDITED BY WILLIAM SMITH, LL. D.

CLASSICAL EXAMINER OF THE UNIVERSITY OF LONDON

This work is universally admitted, by all who are competent to form an enlightened opinion, to be the best Book of its kind in the English language, and to have no rival in importance for the elucidation of the scenes and facts of Scripture, and is so full, accurate and comprehensive, as to leave little to be desired in the department of which it treats.

With the multiplication of Commentaries, and Treatises, and Discoveries illustrative of the Bible, in modern times, there has been an unsupplied and increasing demand for a work which should embrace the fruits of the ripest and best Biblical Scholarship. This has been done for the first time, in the present work, which is now offered to the million of Bible readers and students of our land.

The present work embraces the results of the most successful and approved Biblical labors and researches of scholars and travelers, including the latest of Layard, Rawlinson, and others, condensed for wide and common use, and constituting an indispensable aid to Teachers, Families, Sunday School Superintendents, and Bible Students, and Bible Readers generally.

It contains every name in the Bible and Apocrypha of which any thing can be said. It gives an accurate account of every place and every name in the Scriptures of which explanation or illustration is required. It describes every animal, bird, and insect and reptile, every plant and every mineral, every implement and domestic utensil mentioned or alluded to in the Bible. It gives an account of the manners and customs, costumes, habitations, laws, civil and ecclesiastical antiquities of the Jews and surrounding nations. It also embraces geographical descriptions of the Holy Land and other countries, according to the most recent and accurate surveys; and includes a history and analysis of each of the Books of the Bible; biographical sketches of the Writers and of all other Scripture Characters; while very many of the longer articles, being the results of the most finished scholarship, are complete treatises in themselves, and worthy of a separate publication.

A reference to the list of Contributors, whose labors are herein embodied, combining an unexampled array of the most eminent Scholars in America and Great Britain, is sufficient proof of the thoroughness and completeness of its articles.

All Dictionaries of the Bible, prepared before the recent great and important advances made in Biblical Science, and the numerous illustrations of the Sacred Volume brought to light by travelers and scholars in Bible lands, are necessarily incomplete and imperfect, and are many of them rendered comparatively useless.

This work is indispensable to every Clergyman, and necessary to every Christian family. All who use a Family Bible should possess this most valuable Dictionary.

The sale of *no two Books* ever published will furnish so *pleasant, useful* and *profitable* employment, to those possessing *intelligence, energy* and *perseverance*, as "The Devotional and Practical Family Bible" and "The Bible Dictionary." The Agent will find he can easily secure an order for the "Bible Dictionary" from those who already possess a Bible, and he will find the two are admirably adapted to go together.

Canvassing for the "Bible" and "Bible Dictionary" is comparatively a pleasant and satisfactory business.

Address

NATIONAL PUBLISHING CO.,

178 Elm St., Cincinnati, Ohio,

Or JONES, JUNKIN & CO.,

167 South Clark St., Chicago, Ills.

THE DEVOTIONAL AND PRACTICAL

POLYGLOTT FAMILY BIBLE,

CONTAINING THE

OLD AND NEW TESTAMENTS,

WITH THE MARGINAL READINGS, AND A FULL AND ORIGINAL SELECTION OF REFERENCES TO PARALLEL AND ILLUSTRATIVE PASSAGES, ARRANGED IN A MANNER HITHERTO UNATTEMPTED.

Together with a Concordance:—A Careful Index to the Bible, in which every Difficult Word is explained.

ALSO, A FAMILY RECORD, MANY USEFUL TABLES AND VALUABLE TREATISES, DESIGNED TO PROMOTE AND FACILITATE THE DEVOTIONAL STUDY OF THE HOLY SCRIPTURES.

It is the belief of the Publishers that the Devotional and Practical Family Bible embraces more valuable and practical helps to general readers and students of the Scriptures than any single volume yet issued from the press. Superintendents, Teachers, and Scholars in Sunday Schools, will find this work a most convenient and satisfactory aid to an intelligent and critical study of the Scriptures.

The text is accompanied by the most complete and simple system of references to marginal readings and parallel passages yet adopted. The numerous tables, treatises and explanatory writings which accompany it, and of which a list is found in the general contents, embody the results of the life-long labors of many eminent biblical students, and furnish almost an Encyclopedia of biblical knowledge.

The work is, moreover, very highly approved, and recommended by influential divines and pastors of churches, and is greatly prized by all who possess it. It embraces

I. The Preface.

II. Order of the Books of the Old and New Testaments.

III. A Critical Introduction to the Study of the Holy Scriptures, with General Observations on the Authority and History of the Books of the Pentateuch; by Rev. Joseph A. Warne.

IV. Treatises on the Correct Interpretation of the Writings in which the Revelations of God are contained; by James M'Knight, D. D.

V. Table showing at one view which of the Patriarchs were cotemporary with each other, and consequently how easy it was to hand down from Adam to Isaac (a period of 2,158 years) the particulars of the Creation and Fall of Man.

VI. A Chronological Harmony of the Scripture Histories, and of the Fulfillment of its Predictions.

VII. Tables of the Measures, Weights, Moneys, and Times, mentioned in Scripture, with an Appendix to the second table of Measures of Surface described by Moses.

VIII. The contents of the Old and New Testaments arranged in a manner by which the Books, Chapters, &c., may be read as one connected History.

IX. Chronological Tables of the Offices and Conditions of Men; Chronological Tables of the New Testament; of St. Paul's Apostolic Journeys; of the Evangelists, and exhibiting the Chronology of our Saviour's Life; of the Important Events of Profane History during the Life of Christ, and the Chronological Order of the Discourses, Parables, and Miracles of Christ.

X. Illustrations of Scripture with numerous Steel Engravings.

XI. The Books of the Old Testament.

XII. History of the Period included from the close of the Canon of the Old Testament, until the times of the New Testament.

XIII. Four Discourses on the Evidences of Christianity, and the Genuineness of the New Testament; by Philip Doddridge, D. D.

XIV. An Introduction to the Study of the New Testament, with a History of the several Books.

XV. The Books of the New Testament.

XVI. A new Geographical and Historical Table, exhibiting at one view all that is interesting in the Geography and History in the Holy Scriptures, and forming a complete Bible Gazetteer.

XVII. A new and complete General Index of the Bible, in which the various Places, Persons, and Subjects mentioned in it are accurately referred to, and every difficult word briefly explained.

XVIII. A Concordance of the Holy Scriptures of the Old and New Testaments, by which all of the principal texts of the Scriptures may be easily found out; by Rev. John Brown.

XIX. Table of Select Passages, arranged with a view to the Devotional Reading of the Bible, morning and evening, every day in the year.

It will be readily seen, that no single edition of the Holy Scriptures has ever been given to the public accompanied by so many and such valuable aids to their practical and profitable reading and study as this.

To Sabbath School Superintendents, Teachers and Scholars, this with the accompanying volume, is almost indispensable, and furnishes, in a convenient and practical form, nearly every requisite aid in *their* pursuits upon every subject and question which can arise.

This work has been very highly commended by influential Divines and Pastors of Churches, and should be found in every household in the land; while to aid in its sale will be both a useful and profitable work.

Agents write that this work is highly satisfactory and sells readily.

Descriptive Circulars will be forwarded to those desiring an agency. *Address,*

NATIONAL PUBLISHING CO. 178 Elm St. Cincinnati Ohio

PEOPLE'S EDITION.

THE LIFE AND EPISTLES

OF

SAINT PAUL,

EMBRACING

A Graphic and Eloquent Delineation of the Early Life, Education, Conversion, Teachings, Labors, Travels, Sufferings, Perils, Persecutions, and Missionary Career of St. Paul, thus constituting a Living Picture of the Great Apostle himself, and of the circumstances by which he was surrounded.

BY

Rev. W. J. CONYBEARE, M. A.,

LATE FELLOW OF TRINITY COLLEGE, CAMBRIDGE,

AND

Rev, J. S, HOWSON, D. D.

PRINCIPAL OF THE COLLEGIATE INSTITUTION, LIVERPOOL.

With a Preliminary Dissertation by

Rev. LEONARD BACON, D. D.,

PROFESSOR OF REVEALED THEOLOGY IN YALE COLLEGE.

This work delineates the early life, education, conversion, teachings and labors of a man, whose writings are now engaging more thought, calling forth more learned discussion, and more powerfully impressing the mind and heart of the age, than those of any other author, ancient or modern, inspired or uninspired. Jesus said of Paul, "He is a chosen vessel unto me," and the Scripture biography before us shows the wonderful care which God took in preparing that vessel before He filled it with his grace and set it apart for the Master's special use in His great house. Grand intellectual powers, united with a pure and loving heart, and a life filled with strange, heroic, and self-sacrificing adventures, made St. Paul the most wonderful man of all the ages. No better sub ject could be found for a biography, nor any better men selected to prepare it. The work faithfully portrays, in a very fresh and life-like manner, the character and doings of one of earth's noblest heroes.

This work contributes more to the correct understanding of St. Paul's Epistles, and to a thorough apprehension of his unparalleled character —of the communities upon which he labored,—of the countries through which he traveled,—of the chief characters whom he met, both friend and foe,—of his personal hopes and fears,—of his temporary failures and permanent triumphs,—than any other one volume. The scenes of his early youth; the character of the school in which he was educated; the habits of private life then prevalent; the principles which actuated him, and developed that intellectual character, and made him the foremost reasoner of the world, are all represented in a style which lends a charm to the work, at once pleasing and instructive, and makes it truly a "People's Edition." It embodies more information concerning ancient and Eastern life; carries the reader more agreeably and irresistably into the times and scenes of Paul's life; and illustrates better that large part of the New Testament which he wrote than any other book in biblical literature. It brings more learning, and the results of more biblical, geographical, and ethnological research than any other work, to bear in making interesting the life, and elucidating the writings of him who was, not only the great Apostle to the Gentiles, but also the great Theologian of the whole Bible,—whose name is second to no other human name in the history of the Church of God. It throws a flood of light on the character, travels, missionary labors and writings of the great Apostle, and throws open that wonderful period of the world's history as no other work has ever done. The reader is borne along by its clear and charming style, its picturesque and vivid descriptions of scenery, and its beautiful delineations of Apostolic characters and labors, and at every point is delighted and instructed. It is as fascinating as any story can be, and yet it is true to life and Bible History. The prodigious learning and power, and beauty of style, do not constitute its highest praise. This is found in its moral and religious spirit, in its pre-eminent Christian candor and impartiality, in its solemn earnestness for historic truth, and its manly and unvascillating faith in the doctrines proclaimed by the fearless subject of its biography. It is every way a masterly and unrivalled work, and so wholly worthy its subject in all the manner of its performance, that it is not saying too much to pronounce it a fitting tribute to the greatness of the Great Apostle.

The preliminary dissertation by Dr. Bacon, gives it additional value, and helps further to understand the character of the great Apostle, and the scenes of the early triumphs of the Gospel. His abilities, studies and travel, eminently fit him for the service he thus renders.

Send for our 16 page descriptive circular, giving full particulars, terms, and testimonials. Address

NATIONAL PUBLISHING CO.,

178 Elm St., Cincinnati, Ohio,

Or **JONES, JUNKIN & CO.,**

167 South Clark St., Chicago, Ills.

www.ingramcontent.com/pod-product-compliance
Lightning Source LLC
LaVergne TN
LVHW052205200926
848481LV00001B/32
* 9 7 8 1 4 2 5 5 6 9 0 2 0 *